Ties *of* Kinship

Cambridge, Massachusetts

Ties *of* Kinship

Genealogy and Dynastic Marriage in Kyivan Rus´

Distributed by Harvard University Press
for the Ukrainian Research Institute
Harvard University

The Harvard Ukrainian Research Institute was established in 1973 as an integral part of Harvard University. It supports research associates and visiting scholars who are engaged in projects concerned with all aspects of Ukrainian studies. The Institute also works in close cooperation with the Committee on Ukrainian Studies, which supervises and coordinates the teaching of Ukrainian history, language, and literature at Harvard University.

Publication of this book has been made possible in part by the generous support of Ukrainian studies at Harvard University by Dr. and Mrs. Wolynec.

Printed in the U.S. on acid-free paper

Library of Congress Cataloging-in-Publication Data

Names: Raffensperger, Christian.
Title: Ties of kinship : genealogy and dynastic marriage in Kyivan Rus' / Christian Raffensperger.
Description: Cambridge, Massachusetts : The Ukrainian Research Institute, Harvard University ; Distributed by Harvard University Press, 2016. | Series: Harvard series in Ukrainian studies | Includes bibliographical references and index.
Identifiers: LCCN 2015048253 | ISBN 9781932650136 (acid-free paper)
Subjects: LCSH: Vladimir, Grand Duke of Kiev, approximately 956-1015--Family.
| Kievan Rus--Genealogy. | Kievan Rus--Kings and rulers--History. | Kinship--Kievan Rus--History. | Royal houses--Kievan Rus--History. | Marriage--Kievan Rus--History.
Classification: LCC DK75 .R34 2016 | DDC 947/.02092--dc23
LC record available at http://lccn.loc.gov/2015048253

Cover illustration: Folio 1v of the *Izbornik Svjatoslava*, 1073. GIM 80370, Sinodal´noe sobranie no. 1043. Used with permission.
Cover by Wilcox Design

To Richard Hellie and Norman Ingham,
who helped to set my feet on the path

Contents

Acknowledgments

THE KERNEL THAT GREW into this project began with my dissertation at the University of Chicago. There, Richard Hellie not only allowed me to write more than six hundred pages, but encouraged me to. Part of that length was an appendix of more than one hundred fifty pages discussing dynastic marriages, which formed the basis for part 1 of this book. Chicago is also where I met Norman Ingham, who allowed me to audit his Slavic literature class and who shared my interest in genealogy. Norm invited me to present my first academic paper at a conference, and we coauthored an article together for *The American Genealogist*. I am sorry that neither of these fine, original, men will see this work.

This work would never have been created without the inspiration of David Birnbaum. I shared some of my initial ideas for this book with him and he helped me to refine it, encouraged me to run with it, and worked with me to develop an online version of this material accessible at genealogy.obdurodon.org.

I would also like to thank Wittenberg University for funding two excellent faculty aides, Adam Matthews and Kelsey Mazur, to assist me with crucial work on the project at various stages. The entire History Department at Wittenberg was a major source of emotional support and advice as well, specifically Tammy Proctor and Dar Brooks Hedstrom. Tammy mentored me and tirelessly answered questions about everything involved in scholarly writing, teaching, conferences, and anything else that occurred to me. Dar provided amazing friendship and encouragement that I could really complete this project while also teaching and working on other projects. Wittenberg also funded a sabbatical during which I was able to put the finishing touches on the book and see it go into production. That production took place at the Harvard Ukrainian Research Institute (HURI), whose Eugene and Daymel Shklar Fellowship supported my research in the 2013–2014 academic year. The Institute provided a comfortable environment for the year and allowed me to work with my editor, Marika Whaley, whose tolerance for my constant nudging has been enormous. From HURI I must also thank Michael Flier, whose suggestions improved the book immensely from its initial drafts, and Serhii Plokhy, who took an interest in the project and agreed to fund a digital humanities component of the book as part of the MAPA Project (gis.huri.harvard.edu).

A variety of other people all contributed their insights and critiques, such as Donald Ostrowski, Francis Butler, the participants in the Chicago Early Slavic Workshop, and Early Slavic Studies Association members generally. The mistakes that have survived, of course, are all my own.

Finally, I would like to thank my family, Cara, Iris, and Malcolm, for always supporting me and allowing me the time to work on something I love.

Introduction

> Izjaslav arrived in Volodymyr and sent to
> his brother-in-law, the king [of Hungary];
> to his in-laws in Poland, Bolesław, Mieszko,
> and Henry; and to his in-law Vladislav,
> the ruler of Bohemia, asking for help and
> military assistance to retake Kyiv.
> — Hypatian Chronicle, s. a. 1149[1]

In 1149, Izjaslav M´stislavič was removed as the ruler of Kyiv by his uncle Jurij Volodimerič, and Izjaslav's immediate recourse was to repair to the city of Volodymyr and call on his allies. The allies in question were not his plentiful Rusian relatives, but the rulers of Hungary, Poland, and Bohemia, all of whom he was related to. These familial relationships are important to note for their own sake, but the fact that the chronicler noted it as well, distinguishing each relationship with specific familial terminology (*zjat´* and *svat´*), reinforces the importance of genealogy in the construction of the medieval Rusian world. Genealogy is important to the study of history, and it was important to those making medieval history as well as chronicling it. Families and marriage ties were the warp and weft of the political fabric that made up medieval Europe, and the Volodimeroviči were a key strand. The quote above, and its implications, illustrate the importance of this book both specifically for those studying Rusian history, and more broadly to all of those studying medieval history.

Part 1 of the book deals with marriage, that essential component of genealogy; in particular, Volodimeroviči marriages made before 1146. Dynastic marriages were the glue that bound together medieval political relationships. Medieval kingdoms were, in many ways, indivisible from their ruling families, and thus when kingdoms made agreements with one another, familial ties were used to secure the arrangement. A treaty of peace and cooperation could be sealed with a marriage between the son of one ruler and the daughter of another. That new familial tie strengthened the political agreement and provided incentive to hold to its terms. Unfortunately, due to the vagaries of medieval chronicling and source preservation, such treaties are often lost or not recorded and historians are simply left with a record of marriage between the son of one ruler and the daughter of another. The details of what happened and why are questions that are left to the speculation of the modern historian. These marriages, though, are essential evidence for the interconnectivity of the Volodimeroviči with the other ruling families of Europe,[2] and as such deserve a place in a book related to those genealogical relationships.

The explication of those marriages and their purpose involves some level of speculation. As noted, there are very few recorded examples of the treaties made between these medieval kingdoms, and one must work backward from the political reality of the day and the marriage itself to attempt to formulate a reason that the marriage was arranged. Such speculation, carefully done and clearly noted, provides another avenue for scholars to investigate medieval events and people that may have been largely lost. Moreover these marriages help bring women back into the story of medieval Rus´. They were the major connective tissue for those dynastic and political relationships, yet they are often left out of the narration of medieval history. Twenty-one of the fifty-seven marriages discussed here focus on a Rusian woman and her role in the marriage process. These women were the main component of the dynastic marriage for Rus´ and a key factor in the success or failure of the policies dictated by the marriage. The analysis of Rusian dynastic marriage conducted here will help reinterpret the picture of Rusian women in medieval history, as well as display Rusian interconnectivity with the rest of Europe.

The twenty-two genealogical charts presented in part 2 serve as a tool for scholars to find their way through the often complex Volodimeroviči genealogy, and provide a reliable entry point for medievalists to access the Volodimeroviči relatives of their own ruling families. The first fourteen charts are arranged based upon the Volodimeroviči family, and follow the line of one patriarch of a particular section of the family, the first of which being Volodimer Svjatoslavič himself and the last, Jurij Dolgorukij Volodimerič. There are notations within these tables where one may proceed to the next table to find additional information on a particular person's children or grandchildren. The next eight tables are arranged based upon dynastic connections, such as those with the royal families of Poland, Hungary, or Scandinavia more broadly. These tables do not have all of the connective tissue of the kingdom married into, but focus solely on Rus´. For example, in table 17, "Polish Dynastic Marriages," there are three children of Mieszko II shown, but they are not connected to one another with a genealogical line and their father is not included at all. The guiding principle here is the Rusian marital connection with these other royal families. For all tables, subsequent to the visual depiction of the relationship are several pages of citations for all of the pieces of information shown on the chart. The order of people in those pages of citations follows a general left-to-right reading of the chart itself in an attempt to maintain consistency.

There are numerous place names mentioned throughout this volume, and many are likely unfamiliar to a modern audience. In partnership with the Harvard Ukrainian Research Institute's MAPA project, an online mapping tool for these genealogies has been developed. The data for all marriages discussed here are available in searchable format at http://gis.huri.harvard.edu/rusgen/.

Chronological Framework

The period covered in this book begins with the Christianization of Volodimer Svjatoslavič, and his marriage to Anna Porphyrogenita.[3] Volodimer is the patriarch of the Rusian royal family, and subsequent rulers will trace their descent back to him, creating the Volodimeroviči family, the subject of this book. The constraints I put on that family are conditioned by my interpretation of Rusian history and politics, as well as a desire to create a completed set of genealogical records that would be usable by scholars. The end date for this study is 1146, the date by which the various regions of Rus´ go their own way. This date is controversial, admittedly, but represents one potential endpoint for a unified kingdom of Rus´ centered in Kyiv and under a Volodimeroviči paterfamilias. This date is relevant primarily for part 1, where the dynastic marriages are examined in detail. In that section, I do not examine marriages that took place after 1146. The dating in part 2 is more complicated, as one cannot simply end at a particular date and not continue tracking the living Volodimeroviči past that point. To compensate, I chose to include five generations after Volodimer Svjatoslavič (his great-great-great-grandchildren) in the genealogical charts of part 2. Those generations comprise the vast majority of Volodimeroviči who were alive and politically active through the twelfth century. It was my goal that these restrictions of date and generations not limit the understanding of Rusian genealogy, but rather provide a framework for research.

Chronology also poses specific problems, since it is often difficult to determine precise dates for many of our Rusian individuals' lives. First, there is the matter of medieval East Slavic dating versus modern dating. The Rusian chronicles typically followed an *anno mundi* calendar beginning at the creation of the world, roughly 5508 BCE. However, there is the additional problem of when the year was considered to begin. The chronicles typically followed a March year, making January and February dates (if a month is listed within a year) problematic to determine in which year they fall. In addition to these and other dating problems, there is also the issue that different chronicles sometimes record different dates for the same event.[4] I have done my best here to follow best practices in determining in which year events occurred in part 2, but I have also provided my source base for making those determinations, so that anyone using this book may follow in my footsteps to come to their own conclusions. This method provides a resource for those who wish to find an easy answer to questions such as "When did Jurij Volodimerič die?" as well as for those who want to drill down into the sources to examine some of the differences between reported accounts.

Sources and Methodology

The classic reference tool for Rusian genealogy is the work of Nicolas de Baumgarten, who published extensively on Volodimeroviči genealogy, most famously in "Généalogies et mariages Occidentaux des Rurikides Russes du X-e au XIII-e siècle."[5] This work, published in 1927, is a collection of tables detailing Rusian genealogy and marriages for over two hundred years. The work is a tour de force of historical scholarship, but it is dated and contains a variety of flaws. Since its publication, the perception of the sources, how history is constructed, and many of the tools for analyzing primary sources have changed and evolved. Several attempts have been made to revisit and revise pieces of Baumgarten's work in different ways. For instance, Jukka Korpela compiled a prosopography of everyone listed in the *PVL* as a way of fleshing out the Rusian world,[6] while E. V. Pčelov has worked extensively on the genealogy of the Rusian rulers in works such as *Genealogija drevneruss-kix knjazej*, which discusses the Volodimeroviči through Volodimer's children.[7] Dariusz Dąbrowski has worked extensively with the family of M´stislav Volodimerič, doing an exhaustive survey of Mstislaviči through the fourteenth century.[8] His work includes biographical data for each of those individuals, utilizing a wide source base and elucidates this line of the Volodimeroviči in ways that simple genealogy cannot. These works and others have started this process of revising the ideas of Baumgarten, but have not superseded his work. That is the goal of this book, and the reason for the extensive tables that compose part 2. These tables provide the reader with reference material of the kind that made Baumgarten's work so enduring, with the major improvement of having all of the information on each chart sourced clearly in the annotations accompanying the chart. This book is also designed to be accessible to the greatest number of scholars working in not only Slavic, but medieval and Byzantine studies as well, and is thus in English. The excellent work done in Russian, Polish, Greek, etc., is accessible to parts of that larger audience, but not the entirety. The larger goal of my scholarship is to create a new portrait of medieval Europe that includes the Slavic and Byzantine worlds, and as such, the scholarship needs to be interoperable in ways that the current divisions do not encourage.

The changes from Baumgarten's period to the present come in many forms, most clearly perhaps with a change in the perception of Byzantium, as articulated in the tables of part 2. Under the Muscovite rulers, ties with Byzantium were lauded, such that the first Rusian dynastic marriage between Volodimer Svjatoslavič and Anna Porphyrogenita was connected to the marriage of Ivan III and Sofia Paleologina to create a continuum of Byzantine interest in Rus´ and subsequently in Muscovy.[9] The same principle held true in the writing and copying of the chronicles, which were the main source base for Baumgarten and this work as well. In those chronicles, Byzantine ties are elaborated beyond what is noted by other primary sources. In particular, marriages with members of the Byzantine imperial families are described in the Rusian sources that in many cases simply could not exist, and which are not corroborated by other primary sources. This element of source criticism was most fully developed by Alexander Każdan in his article, "Rus´-Byzantine Princely Marriages in the Eleventh and Twelfth Centuries,"[10] where he challenged the Rusian-Byzantine marriages listed in Baumgarten's genealogy by thoroughly investigating the primary sources for those marriages, and in the process decreased the number of confirmed unions from Baumgarten's seven to approximately three. This is an enormous reduction in the number of Byzantine marriages, and it also illustrates the amount of Byzantine inflation present in the sources. Każdan's article and other similar critiques inform the construction of this work and allows for a more accurate accounting of Rusian dynastic marriages.

In addition to these changes, this work incorporates numerous sources from throughout Europe, particularly those from the Latin-writing world and Scandinavia. Rus´, and Rusian women in particular, are mentioned much more commonly in those sources than has been widely recognized. The use of sources from France, the German Empire, Poland, Hungary, Anglo-Saxon England, Scotland, Denmark, and Norway not only expand the source base for the book, but also add valuable information that is left out of the Rusian chronicles.[11] Not used, however, are the various secondary sources which were often staples of earlier genealogies. Traditionally, the works of N. M. Karamzin and M. P. Pogodin have been cited as if they were primary source materials, often without question. Their works, however, accept much in the primary sources that has since been challenged, and also contain a healthy leavening of nineteenth-century nationalism, all of which should be excluded or heavily qualified in modern work. An attempt has been made, instead, to return to the primary sources, and flesh those out with recent secondary works that expand upon specific subject areas. For example, Martin Dimnik's work on Černihiv is unmatched, and deals with a region where the primary sources are not as rich or detailed as would be ideal.[12] The proliferation of scholarship over the last one hundred years, combined with modern research techniques, have made it possible to greatly improve upon the initial work that Baumgarten did. Even with all of the additional sources from the rest of Europe mentioned above, the main source for Rusian history of the tenth, eleventh, and even early twelfth century is still the *Pověst´ vremennyx lět* (*PVL*). To best utilize this source, I have relied upon the recent paradosis prepared by Donald Ostrowski, which brings together the best variant of the chronicle readings from a variety of different chronicle traditions.[13] For the period after the end of the *PVL*, the Rusian source base becomes more complex, though not necessarily more forthcoming with information. There are, for that period, a variety of regional chronicles that begin to tell their own narratives of events, such as the Kyivan Chronicle, the Suzdal Chronicle, and the Novgorod First and Fourth Chronicles.[14] The Kyivan Chronicle is preserved in the Hypatian redaction and published in the *Polnoe sobranie russkix letopisej* (*PSRL*) series as the "Hypatian Chronicle," and as this is the most widely available version of the chronicle, I have cited the Kyivan Chronicle as "Hypatian." The same is true of the Suzdal Chronicle, which is preserved in the slightly earlier Laurentian edition, and published in the *PSRL* as the "Laurentian Chronicle." Examining the citations for information presented in part 2, one can clearly see that the chronicles indeed shift to a regional focus, and begin to include more information about their own area and less information about wider Rusian affairs in this post-*PVL* period. However, there are a variety of other Rusian sources that also provide interesting information even though they may be composed later in time, and not just extant from later in time. For instance, the oft-maligned Nikon Chronicle contains interesting pieces of information in regard to Rusian relations with the rest of Europe. Serge Zenkovsky, in the introduction to his English translation of the chronicle, suggests that the chronicle's compilers used material from chronicles that have subsequently been lost, as well as information from the archives of the Rusian Church.[15] Though much of the text of the chronicle does appear to be simply expounding on the basic information provided by other sources, there are interesting nuggets of information preserved that seem to serve no, or little, purpose for the compiler; this suggests that there is a very real possibility that some additional sources were used in its composition.[16] Similarly, the Tver Chronicle contains information about a 1043 joint raid between

Casimir of Poland and Jaroslav of Rus´ against the Mazovians and their leader, Moislav.[17] Though that information is not present in the *PVL* for that year, it fits with the larger pattern of information presented there about raids on the Mazovians in 1041 and 1047, and even brings in the detail of the Mazovian ruler's name, which is mentioned later in the *PVL* in regard to the 1047 attack, as well as in the Polish *Gesta Principum Polonorum*.[18] This information is not being used alone, but is part of a larger case to be made for interaction between those parties at that time. On the other hand, the *Stepennaja kniga*, a fascinating source for a variety of historical, linguistic, and literary subjects, is more problematic when it comes to this period, as it contains fascinating information that is repeated nowhere else, especially about the family of the Polack rulers.[19] The lack of support from other sources, however, makes it difficult to accept such details wholeheartedly. In the current volume, information from this source is thus treated accordingly. Finally, the most problematic of sources when dealing with this period is the work of V. N. Tatiščev.[20] This has been made clear by the work of scholars, including Oleksij Toločko most recently, who have enumerated the problems of using him as a source.[21] That said, Tatiščev does occasionally provide some interesting and probable data which have been used here, properly qualified, when appropriate.

The difficulties of drawing information from the various sources described above point to the larger problems present in utilizing any of these sources for early Rusian history. All sources have problems—sometimes many problems—but they are our only window into the Rusian past. I have attempted to use this wide breadth of sources judiciously and in conjunction with one another and with a good dose of common sense. In some places this has resulted in the removal of figures who existed in Baumgarten's, or others', genealogies; less often, the inclusion of others. Where I have done so, I have included an explanation of the sources so that others can follow my footsteps and come to their own conclusions. For it is this breadth of both primary and secondary sources that provides modern scholars with the analytical tools they need to help build a larger picture of Rus´.

Genealogy and Women

In regard to women, there are several problems that become inherent when one attempts to assemble a genealogy. The most basic is that information about them is rarely recorded in Rusian sources, or if it is, what we have is simply phrases such as "daughter of...." Thus, the names given to these women are often creations of later chroniclers, or of nineteenth-century historians attempting to make sense of the past. Where one of these names is used commonly I will include it, though in quotation marks as a nickname, because this is a more accurate descriptor. If no name is known but just a kin relationship, I will use the genealogical standby of "N. N.," which simply means "no name." Though that means there will be several instances of "N. N." in the book, it is an unfortunate inevitability and I prefer not to guess at their names if I do not have to. It should be noted that this is different than a situation in which we have no information for a woman. For instance, if a known man has a known child, but we know absolutely nothing about the woman who must have been involved, I have listed her as "unknown" to indicate that fact. A similar lacuna exists in regard to birth dates for women, which are rarely recorded and as such we are left wondering how old the majority of women were when we do have dates for them, usually at their marriage or the birth of their children. Eve Levin notes that women in the Orthodox world were supposed to be no younger than twelve at marriage, though betrothals did happen earlier.[22] In Western Europe, the customs were slightly different and marriages were not made until the woman was roughly fifteen, with the rationale that the marriage was supposed to be consummated immediately, and the woman had to be of childbearing age. Carol Jean Diers and Darrell W. Amundsen in their study of menarche in medieval Europe found that women on average reached childbearing age in the medieval world at roughly fourteen years of age.[23] For the sake of this work, if a woman's birth date is missing, I will use the rough estimate that she is fourteen years of age at marriage. I concede that this is imprecise, but it is primarily used for the ordering of the tables in part 2, where I have attempted to arrange birth order from eldest (left) to youngest (right).

Names and Titles

A work of this sort has a plethora of titles and names that might be unfamiliar to the general reader, or for which the specialist has experience with a different translation or transliteration. For that reason, I have provided a brief description here of the rationale behind my choices.

The transliteration used throughout this work is that followed by the Harvard Ukrainian Research Institute. "Vladimir" in the English translation of the *Russian Primary Chronicle* of Samuel Hazzard Cross is here Volodimer, which is more faithful to the actual chronicle usage. The choice has been made to use scholarly—sometimes called linguistic—transliteration, so *-ja* rather than *-ya*, or *-ia* as may be seen elsewhere; similarly patronymics carry *-ič* endings rather than *-ich*. The majority of personal names here are Rusian, and have been transliterated into English following these guidelines.

The title of the Rusian rulers used here has been kept as *knjaz´* and there has been no attempt to translate it into English as anything other than "ruler." The exact translation of what a *knjaz´* was and when is no easy matter, and though I might prefer the title "king" rather than the more common translation of "prince," this is not the place to make what would require an extensive framework to make such a claim.[24] Similarly, to avoid confusion (and argument), I have not used the title *velikij knjaz´* even when it is attested in the sources. Who uses such a title, and when, has been discussed extensively in the literature, but the pattern and use is not clear enough, and I do not believe required, for the purposes of the material assembled here.[25] The biggest change has potentially already been noted by readers, and that is the use of Volodimeroviči instead of the more traditional Rjurikid designation for the ruling family of Rus´. The name or descriptor "Rjurikid" does not appear in the *PVL*, nor does it appear at all in the sources dealing with the early history of Rus´. The term seems to be a later appellation applied back throughout Rusian history, potentially as a way to create a continuum of familial descent from the eponymous mythological founder. The main figures of eleventh- and twelfth-century Rusian history dealt with here, when pressed for a familial history, or claiming the throne of Kyiv (for instance), traced their descent back to Volodimer Svjatoslavič. Though he was clearly not the first of the line, he was the first Christian male to rule Rus´, and the progenitor of all of the other, later Christian rulers of Rus´. Thus, a more accurate descriptor for the ruling family of Rus´ would be the Volodimeroviči, and as such that has been used here.[26]

In regard to Western European, Scandinavian, and Byzantine names and titles, traditional models have been followed, with an emphasis on standardization. The goal being that Knud is always Knud, and the various alternate spellings (Canute, Knute, etc.), although present in secondary literature, are eliminated. A similar circumlocution to that for *knjaz´* is used, though rarely, for the Scandinavian title *konungr* for the same reason. Depending upon the place and time within Scandinavia there were many individuals bearing such titles with complex relationships with one another. Only when the picture is relatively unclouded, as with Harald Hardraada in the mid-eleventh century is the title "king" applied. A similar problem arises with the title applied to the rulers of the various Polovcian tribes. In general I have simply titled them ruler; however, the tradition in the majority of the secondary literature, my own other work included, is to call them "khan."[27] The primary sources, however, lack such a title, and it is possible that it is a later appellation applied to the Polovcians, from knowledge of the Mongols due to their later interactions with Rus´. For instance, the only existence of the word "khan" in the *PVL* is as the second part of the name of Tugorkhan, a leader of the Polovcians whose daughter marries Svjatopolk Izjaslavič.[28] This leaves the historian with a lack of positive information upon which to draw to create a picture of Polovcian titulature. The goal of these various circumlocutions is not an intent to confuse the reader, but rather an attempt to be as accurate as is possible in regard to the correct English representation of titles and names.

A Note about Consanguinity

One of the keys to understanding medieval marriage, and marital politics, is a basic understanding of consanguinity. All marriage, but particularly elite marriage in the middle ages, was governed by an understanding of relationships and degrees of kinship that are collectively known as consanguinity, or shared blood relations. While these rules are based upon traditional principles that have been demonstrated in a variety of societies, for medieval Europe they were codified by the Christian Church, and largely based upon Roman models. Prior to roughly 800, the Christian Church in the West required that marriages be made outside of four degrees of kinship. That kinship was counted in the Roman method, where brothers and sisters were related in two degrees, and first cousins in four degrees. The method for counting was up to a common relative and back down to your intended partner. Between roughly 800 and the Fourth Lateran Council in 1215, the Christian Church in the West changed the method of calculating consanguinity and prohibited marriages of fewer than seven degrees. The increase in degrees was significant, but the change in method of calculation was more so. The new method involved counting not up and back down again as the Roman method, but simply counting back to a shared ancestor. Thus, siblings were now related in one degree, and cousins in two. Needless to say, the pool of consanguineous kin widened enormously.

The effect this had on marriage was greatest among royal marriages, where partners were chosen from a relatively limited pool of available and qualified applicants. It did not take long for this to become an enormous issue, and by the eleventh century there were significant problems with the system, such that royal families began constructing competing family trees to prove that they were, or were not, related, so that they could, or could not, marry each other. Wrapped up in all of this was the pope, who granted dispensations for marriages within the prohibited degrees. The pope was involved in two eleventh-century Rusian marriages in this regard. The first is the half-Rusian Philip I of France, son of Anna Jaroslavna and Henry I. Philip was engaged in multiple problematic marriages, and the pope called him to the council of Piacenza in 1095 to answer for his consanguineous relationships, but to no avail. The other is the one known papal dispensation for Rus´, which was to allow the marriage of Bolesław III of Poland and Sbyslava Svjatopolkovna.[29] The Constantinopolitan Church maintained consanguinity in the Roman pattern, but enforced between five and seven degrees over the course of the period covered here. There are no known patriarchal dispensations for marriages relating to Rus´, and the question of enforcement is an obvious one. In the West, the pope attempted to enforce consanguinity where and when he chose, but not uniformly. In Rus´, there is no record of enforcement, and in Byzantium, there are few cases. Further, the Byzantines' maintenance of the Roman method of counting allowed for a much smaller pool of consanguineous relations, perhaps minimizing the instances of the problem in the first place.

In the marriages discussed in this book there are several that are consanguineous by papal standards, though there is only the one dispensation mentioned above. Marriages with the Poles and the Danes were the most prone to such consanguinity violations because of the number of marriages, as well as their temporal proximity. Within Rus´, one of the main reasons for a lack of intra-Volodimeroviči marriages seems to have been observation of basic consanguinity laws, counting in the Roman method, to at least five degrees. Such marriages do not appear until roughly Volodimer Svjatoslavič's great-great-grandchildren, and largely only within the most distant of relations. That most distant line is that of Izjaslav Volodimerič of Polack. Theirs was the earliest house to separate from the larger group of Volodimeroviči, and by four generations after Volodimer, an enormous increase in intra-Volodimeroviči marriages begins to occur, largely between the Izjaslav Volodimerič line and that of Jaroslav Volodimerič.[30] The first of these marriages, between Glěb Vseslavič and a daughter of Jaropolk Izjaslavič, is exactly seven degrees of consanguinity. Whether the Volodimeroviči waited to intermarry because of a traditional prohibition, because of Christian law (Byzantine or otherwise), or because there was little need to do so before that time, is unknowable. But keeping in mind consanguinity practices and seeing that they were largely observed in Rus´ helps to explain the size and shape of the marital pool, both internally and externally.

One additional, perhaps obvious, factor needs to be mentioned: religion. After the conversion of Volodimer and Rus´, the only eligible marriage partners were Christians, or those willing to convert to Christianity. Though it is possible that Christian Rusians married into other, perhaps Muslim families and changed religion, there is no evidence for such. While the lack of evidence could be explained by the Christian bias of Rusian monastic chroniclers, there are also no sources from Muslim chroniclers, who do depict at least something of Rus´. Combining Christianity and consanguinity, the pool of eligible marital partners of appropriate rank in the eleventh century was largely outside of Rus´, and that was where the Volodimeroviči looked.[31] In Byzantium in the eleventh century, the frequent turnover in rulers opened the possibility for multiple non-consanguineous marriages, but there are very few that were recorded. The majority of the marriages, as noted elsewhere, are with families to the west and northwest of Rus´. Only the Slavs of the Balkans seem largely to be left out of this group. Whether this is for political, religious, or other reasons is unknown, though one might conjecture that there was simply no reason to marry into those families, or that Rusian political interests lay elsewhere. However, these factors of consanguinity and religion help to establish basic principles for the Rusian dynastic marriages that are discussed throughout this work, and thus clarification is necessary.

Genealogy as a discipline is often considered separate from history, but knowing who is related to whom is essential information in understanding the politics and interkingdom relations of the medieval world. Thus genealogy is an essential tool in the scholar's toolkit, no matter where one is working in the medieval world. This clear importance is highlighted during discussions of marriage, where families and politics are brought together in a concrete fashion to create new relationships. Examining marital relations can thus be a key to unlocking the political structure of medieval Europe and examining how rulers create ideas of kinship and use their kin groups to advance their regional interests. As such, this volume attempts to make sense of the Volodimeroviči dynasty of the eleventh and twelfth centuries, as well as the interconnectivity of Rus´ with the larger European world.

Part One

Marriages: Prelude

Volodimer Svjatoslavič
(tables 1, 20)

Volodimer Svjatoslavič is probably the most well known of the Rusian rulers. Though the majority of Slavists of all stripes (genealogists, historians, etc.) refer to the line of Rusian rulers as Rjurikids, after the legendary founder of the dynasty mentioned in the *PVL*, Volodimer was the historical ancestor from whom later members of the family worked to claim descent until the Time of Troubles. Volodimer had many children, as the chronicles record. These children had various mothers, the identities and statuses of whom are largely unknown. The *PVL* mentions one, Rogněda, by name, and the rest by ethnonym only. "From her [Rogněda] was born four sons Izjaslav, M´stislav, Jaroslav, Vsevolod, and two daughters. From the Greek woman Svjatopolk. From a Bohemian woman Vyšeslav, from another Svjatoslav and M´stislav. And from the Bulgarian woman Boris and Glěb."[1] The status of these women is unknown. The English translation of this passage of the *PVL* calls Rogněda "his [Volodimer's] lawful wife," though it appears that this should actually be a plural designation for the women that are about to be listed.[2] In many places these women are called "wives of Volodimer," perhaps because they are separated off from the "concubines" (*naložnici*) of which multiple hundreds are mentioned (though not by name or ethnonym) in the same *PVL* entry.[3] The status of marriage in a pagan society is hard to judge for modern scholars, because our sources have come down to us through a Christian filter, of whatever thickness, and our modern definition of marriage is largely a Christian one. Earlier in the chronicle it is stated that Volodimer wanted to take Rogněda for his wife—which would have gained him an alliance with a powerful ruler—but that she refused.[4] Volodimer reacted negatively to this, sacked her father's lands, and took Rogněda. According to Ostrowski's paradosis, Volodimer took her as his wife (*žene*).[5] As such, Rogněda is the only one of Volodimer's pagan wives

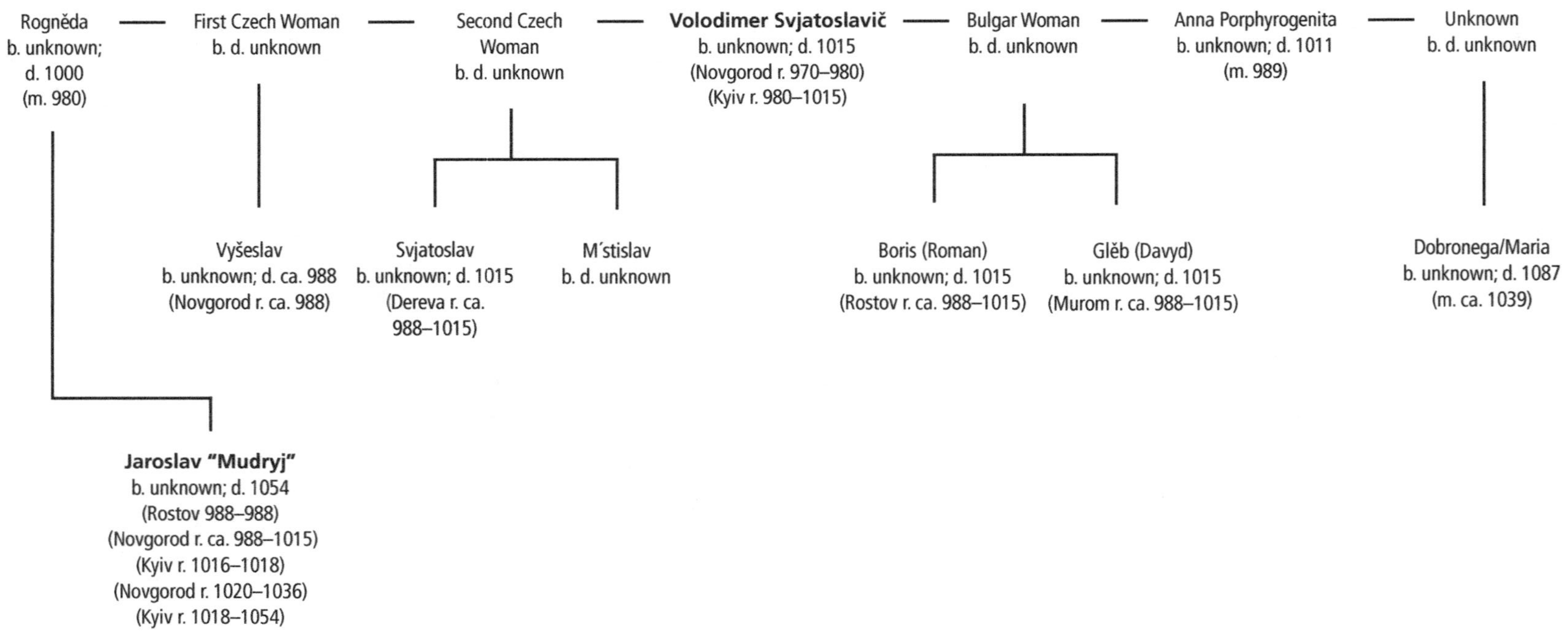

Rogněda
b. unknown;
d. 1000
(m. 980)
First Czech Woman
b. d. unknown
Second Czech
Woman
b. d. unknown
Volodimer Svjatoslavič
b. unknown; d. 1015
(Novgorod r. 970–980)
(Kyiv r. 980–1015)
Bulgar Woman
b. d. unknown
Anna Porphyrogenita
b. unknown; d. 1011
(m. 989)
Unknown
b. d. unknown
Vyšeslav
b. unknown; d. ca. 988
(Novgorod r. ca. 988)
Svjatoslav
b. unknown; d. 1015
(Dereva r. ca.
988–1015)
M′stislav
b. d. unknown
Boris (Roman)
b. unknown; d. 1015
(Rostov r. ca. 988–1015)
Glěb (Davyd)
b. unknown; d. 1015
(Murom r. ca. 988–1015)
Dobronega/Maria
b. unknown; d. 1087
(m. ca. 1039)
Jaroslav "Mudryj"
b. unknown; d. 1054
(Rostov 988–988)
(Novgorod r. ca. 988–1015)
(Kyiv r. 1016–1018)
(Novgorod r. 1020–1036)
(Kyiv r. 1018–1054)

to rate a separate story, including the title "wife" in the chronicles, and there is, most likely, a very simple reason for this—Rogněda was the mother of Jaroslav "Mudryj." It would be better in the worldview of the Christian chroniclers were Jaroslav to have been born of a wedded couple, rather than of Volodimer and one of his many concubines. Whether Volodimer actually took her as wife, mistress, or concubine, or if he would have even distinguished between the three, is impossible to know at this remove and with the documents available.

There is one marriage, by Christian standards, that is undisputed in all sources, and that is Volodimer's marriage to Anna Porphyrogenita. The marriage of Volodimer to Anna Porphyrogenita was the first foreign dynastic marriage in Rusian history and was responsible for bringing Rus´ into the Christian medieval world. The circumstances of the marriage are well known and are discussed in detail elsewhere.[6] Here, we will simply address the implications regarding the dynastic marriage itself.

Anna was the sister of the Byzantine emperors Basil II and Constantine VII and the daughter of the Byzantine emperor Romanus II. She was desired as a marital partner by both the Ottonian and Capetian royal houses, which sent embassies or wrote letters to her brothers to attempt to gain an alliance with the Byzantine Empire.[7] While both of those houses may have had greater prestige than the Volodimeroviči, only Rus´ offered what Basil II needed, when he needed it: troops, especially troops that would come and serve and then go home, with little, if any, chance of turning into an occupying force. The agreement made between Basil II and Volodimer was the prototypical dynastic marriage. Both sides had something the other wanted, and they made an agreement to exchange them. Binding the agreement was a part of what Volodimer wanted—a dynastic marriage with a Byzantine porphyrogenite princess, the most eligible marital partner in the medieval Christian world. A not insignificant additional benefit to this marriage was large-scale recognition of the entry of Volodimer, and Rus´, into the family of Christian kingdoms.[8] With the agreement made, Anna was able to come to Rus´ and marry Volodimer and provide Rus´ with a physical reminder—a porphyrogenite princess residing in Kyiv—of their new status.

This dynastic marriage, as most were, was part of an agreement between the two parties involved, but it was not the agreement that many later historians and scholars have characterized it as. It was not unification with Byzantium, but just one dynastic tie, albeit the best one that could be made in all of Christian Europe at that time. Setting aside the strong term "unification," it did not bring Rus´ into, more strongly into, or partly into, the orbit of Byzantium. Rather the marriage brought Rus´ into the family of Christian kingdoms in which

Byzantium played a major role as the last remnant of the Christian Roman Empire.[9] Because Rus´ had married so advantageously, they did not marry again with Byzantium for more than fifty years.

Byzantine princesses were trained as diplomats, and maintained a loyalty to their own families even when married in a foreign land,[10] so it seems likely that Anna exercised or attempted to exercise some influence on her own or Byzantium's behalf during her lifetime in Rus´. Unfortunately there is no evidence to indicate that influence or any evidence that she was active in any way. After the *PVL*'s description of her arrival, the only other mention of her is at her death in the year 1011.[11] There are two potential reasons for this. One is simply that women only rarely appear in the Rusian chronicles as actors in any way; while the other is the fact that the chronicle was not begun until nearly sixty years after her death. There is mention in the chronicle, however, of the retinue that Anna brought with her, which contained many dignitaries and priests from Byzantium.[12] This delegation has been assumed to have been part of the Byzantine Christianization of Rus´, but much of the Christianization seems to have been done by Chersonite priests. Most foreign princesses who participated in dynastic marriages took with them an entourage,[13] and this was Anna's. Conceptualizing these priests as part of Anna's entourage helps unravel them from the assumption that their purpose "must have been" to convert Rus´.

After Anna went to Rus´ she passed out of the purview of the Byzantine chronicles, but the Rusian sources have very little to say of her beyond the Christianization story.[14] Thus there is no record of her having any children. Some have thought that they might have had a daughter[15] or that Dobronega/Maria might have been her daughter,[16] but there is no conclusive evidence in these matters, and the majority of Volodimer's children were born before his marriage to Anna. As she did not have children, it made it harder for her legacy to endure in Rus´, and with no one with sufficient cause to uphold it she passed out of the focus of the chronicler.

The possibility has been raised that Volodimer remarried after Anna's death in 1011, four years before his own death in 1015. This idea originally comes from Thietmar of Merseburg who, in relating Bolesław I Chrobry's capture of Kyiv in 1018, mentions a stepmother of Jaroslav residing in Kyiv.[17] It seems clear from such a statement that a wife of Volodimer was alive in 1018, and the *PVL* clearly records Anna's death in 1011, so there is the possibility that he remarried. Baumgarten believed this woman was then the mother of Dobronega/Maria, but there is no positive evidence to support this view other than dating her life back from her marriage and guessing her age.[18] He also came to the conclusion, along with others, that the wife was a German princess and that this marriage created a tie between the Volodimeroviči and the German emperors.[19] Unfortunately, there is very little evidence to support the idea. The woman he suggests was the daughter of Cuno von Ennigen. She is mentioned in Thietmar's *Chronicon*, but disappears before reaching Rus´, and no marriage with Volodimer or connection to Rus´ is mentioned.[20] As it stands, it appears that Volodimer did remarry, but the identity of the woman remains a mystery.

As the progenitor of the dominant, and at the time sole, line of Rusian rulers, Volodimer set the tone for his children and grandchildren through his actions. Volodimer made the single best dynastic marriage possible in the Christian world, a Byzantine porphyrogenite princess, and entered into the world of Christian kingdoms. However, that marital tie with Byzantium was not reinforced for half a century, as Volodimer married all of his children to royalty from European kingdoms to his west. He thus tied Rus´ ever more firmly into the Christian European world, a trend that would be followed by his successors.

Svjatopolk Jaropolčič
(no tables)

Svjatopolk was adopted by Volodimer, and was thus the heir not only by dint of his being the son of Volodimer's older brother, but also because he was the eldest in Volodimer's own family. Because of his rank, his marriage would have been considered vitally important for the future of Rus´. It also seems logical that Volodimer would arrange a marriage for him, as he was his adopted father as well as the patriarch of the family. In 1009 Svjatopolk was married to a daughter of Bolesław I Chrobry, the ruler of Poland.[21] Poland[22] was the Rusians' closest neighbor and was one of their main foreign policy concerns. From a historical viewpoint it could have been an ideal marriage. Volodimer and Bolesław were the patriarchs of their respective clans, each a powerful ruler expanding his realm. A marriage between the children of the two, adopted or otherwise, could have been the stuff dynastic dreams are made of. Instead it became only the first example of Rusian-Polish dynastic marriages fueling dynastic strife.

Thietmar of Merseburg was an avid observer of the Poles, and he provides an interesting piece of evidence about this dynastic marriage and dynastic marriage in general. He records that the Boleslavna (that is, Bolesław's daughter) brought with her to Rus´ her personal confessor, Reinbern, bishop of Kolobrzeg (Kolberg).[23] This is a rare example, after Anna Porphyrogenita, of the foreign party in a Rusian dynastic marriage bringing with her an entourage of any kind. The presence of a bishop in a woman's entourage while traveling to marry and live with her husband in his home kingdom indicates that the woman had some prestige and influence—as she should as the daughter of the ruler of Poland—and although it is often assumed that women bring entourages,[24] it is encouraging to have evidence of a woman marrying into Rus´ bringing one.

Thietmar records that Volodimer began to suspect Svjatopolk was conspiring with Bolesław against him.[25] Though no reason for such suspicion is recorded, many could be suggested, the majority of which have to do with the influence of the dynastic marriage; whether it was the influence of his new wife, her entourage, or the bishop, the suspicion was present in Volodimer's mind that Svjatopolk's loyalties were shifting away from him and toward Poland. This was always a concern in dynastic marriage—a spouse brings her culture and influence and has a variable amount of power that may or may not be used to benefit the interests of her in-laws. In this case, Volodimer feared that encouraging the interests of the Boleslaviči was not in his interest and he threw Svjatopolk, the Boleslavna, and Bishop Reinbern into solitary cells.[26] The imprisonment of Reinbern alongside the others is the strongest hint that he was involved and that the reason for such imprisonment was related to increasing Polish influence on Svjatopolk.

The situation grew worse when Reinbern died,[27] followed shortly thereafter by Volodimer. Svjatopolk was able to escape from the prison, and his first destination was his father-in-law.[28] This shows the strength of the bond that was created by his marriage to Bolesław's daughter, and most likely shows that Volodimer had been correct in assuming that Svjatopolk was leaning toward Poland.[29] Acting on his own indignation at the death of Bishop Reinbern and on the strength of his marital ties with Svjatopolk, Bolesław mobilized an army, changed the foreign policy plans of his kingdom, and invaded Rus´ in order to place his son-in-law on the throne of Kyiv.[30] This is perhaps the most striking example of the effect a dynastic marriage can have. The chances are small that Bolesław, despite a wish to occupy more territory, would have stopped his war with Emperor Henry II and invaded Rus´ without a dynastic tie. Thus the dynastic marriage between Svjatopolk and the daughter of Bolesław created the situation in which Bolesław would stop his long-standing war with Henry II in order to invade Rus´ in support of his son-in-law and place him on the throne of Kyiv. The motive was not entirely altruistic, of course, as Bolesław received the Červen´ lands in return[31] as well as safety for his daughter, who was still held by anti-Svjatopolk forces.[32] But even with these considerations, it was the root dynastic marriage that made the whole situation possible.

The *PVL* does not record the existence of Svjatopolk's wife,[33] nor does the *Gesta principum Polonorum* (*Gesta*), which records a fanciful version of Bolesław's taking of Kyiv that does not even mention Svjatopolk by name.[34] Instead, historians are reliant on a German source for the knowledge of this marriage and the details surrounding it.[35] Nothing more is known of the Boleslavna, and no children are recorded to have been born to the couple, yet the impact of the dynastic marriage was felt by multiple kingdoms.

Marriages: Generation One

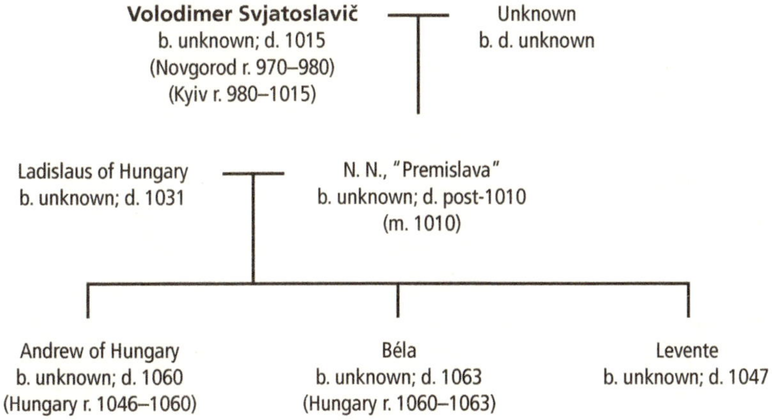

N. N. [Names Unknown] "Premislava" Volodimerovna
(tables 1, 17, 18)

Nothing is really known about this Volodimerovna. The name given to her by scholars studying the time period is Premislava, but that is most likely a creation of the modern period, as it does not exist in any primary sources.[1] What is recorded is that a Volodimerovna married Ladislaus of Hungary.[2] Ladislaus was the first cousin of King St. Stephen of Hungary, and a direct descendant of Árpád, the semi-legendary founder of the Hungarian royal house. The noble birth of both participants ensures that this was a dynastic marriage, even though no records exist to explain the circumstances or agreement. Volodimer did attempt to improve the foreign policy position of Rus´ by using dynastic marriage, so it seems likely that this marriage to a member of the Hungarian royal house would have furthered that goal. In fact, at the end of 996 the *PVL* records that Volodimer lived in peace with neighboring rulers, including Stephen of Hungary.[3] This record may be a remembrance of the tie made between Rus´ and Hungary by the marriage of this Volodimerovna and Ladislaus, a marriage that would have assured closer relations between the two kingdoms.[4]

Ladislaus and Volodimer's daughter were the historical heirs of the Árpád dynasty until its extinction. She bore three sons, Andrew, Béla, and Levente.[5] Andrew played on his familial relations and went to Rus´ in search of aid when he was in exile from Hungary. While there he found a bride for himself as well, increasing the closeness of ties between the Volodimeroviči and the Árpáds in the early eleventh century, even at the risk of infringing on Christian consanguinity rules.

N. N. Volodimerovna
(no tables)

Baumgarten records a marriage of an unnamed daughter of Volodimer to Bernhard, margrave of the Saxon Nordmark.[6] The sources for this marriage are particularly thin, and though it has been accepted by others, it is difficult to substantiate precisely who the Rusian woman was in this relationship. The Saxon World-Chronicle records that Bernhard II had four children (Wilhelm, Conrad, Oda, and Otto) with a woman from Rus´,[7] while Lambert of Hersefeld mentions that an Otto, brother of Wilhelm, had a Slavic mother.[8] Lambert is a relatively contemporary source for this information, while the Saxon World-Chronicle is a thirteenth-century source that mentions the Rusian mother while reconstructing the genealogy of the Saxon Nordmark. Whether its composer knew that the mother was from Rus´ could be debated, especially if Lambert refers to the woman (if it is the same woman, even) simply as a Slav. Thus an evidentiary problem is created, as neither source ever mentions Volodimer or contextualizes the marriage itself in any way.

More recently than Baumgarten, Nazarenko has accepted this evidence as meaning that Bernhard II was married to a daughter of Volodimer, a slight emendation of Baumgarten's assertion that it was Bernhard I.[9] He posits a very plausible theory that the marriage was arranged in the eleventh century to advance Rusian interests, a theory that fits well with the surrounding events of the time and place. That said, following E. V. Pčelov, I think the evidence is too thin to suggest that this is a daughter of Volodimer.[10] The one late source that reports that she was from Rus´ mentions nothing of her parentage, and in a source designed to validate the history of the Saxons such a dynastic marriage might have been worth mentioning. Morover, other contemporary sources that record Bernhard and Rus´, such as Thietmar of Merseburg and Adam of Bremen, do not mention this marriage at all, though both discuss Bernhard and his son Bernhard II.[11] In sum, though I am in favor of the ideas behind Nazarenko's theory of the marriage, I think the most that can be said is that Bernhard II married a Rusian, but who is unknown, and potentially unknowable.

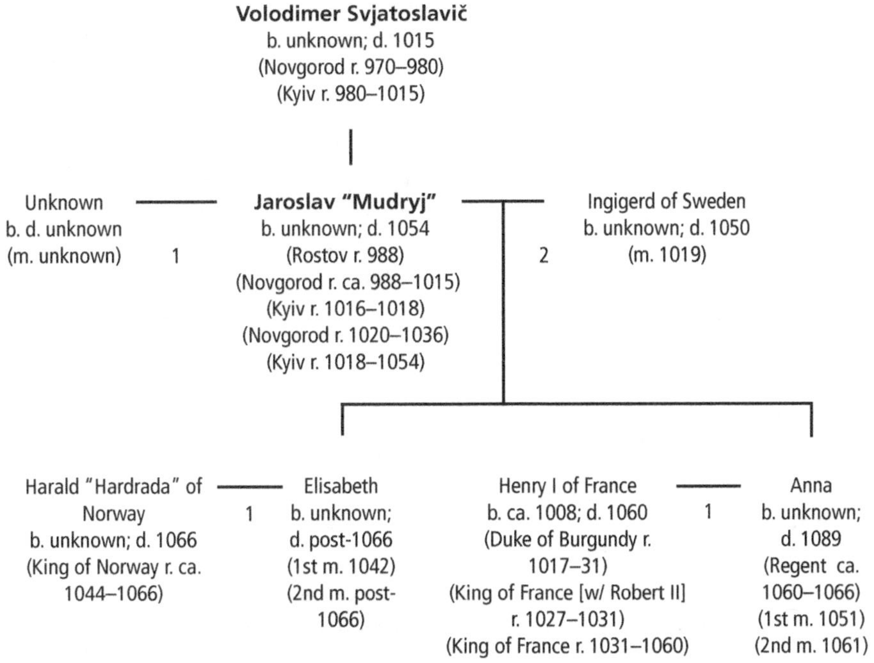

Jaroslav "Mudryj" Volodimerič
(tables 1, 3, 15, 16, 18, 19)

Jaroslav was ruler of Novgorod prior to his father's death in 1015, which gave him close connections with Scandinavia that would only be furthered through marriage. There is some confusion in the historical record over Jaroslav's marital history, chiefly in the timeline for Jaroslav's marriage to Ingigerd, daughter of Olof Skötkonnung, king of Sweden.[12] It is acknowledged that Jaroslav had a son, Ilja,[13] by a first wife or mistress who is unknown to historians.[14] Thietmar mentions that Jaroslav had a wife in Kyiv when Bolesław took the city in the summer of 1018,[15] and this only increases the confusion because the reference is most likely to the first wife/mistress and not Ingigerd, to whom he was married after this defeat.[16] The tale Snorre Sturluson recorded in *Heimskringla* bears this out. In the summer of 1018 messengers first reached Olof Skötkonnung on behalf of Jaroslav (who is recorded as being in Holmgard/Novgorod) asking to marry Olof's daughter Ingigerd.[17] Both the timing of these messengers and the recorded location of Jaroslav are important in this instance, for before the summer of 1018 Jaroslav was located in Kyiv. When he was driven out, he left there someone whom Thietmar later recorded was Jaroslav's wife. While resident in Novgorod in late 1018 or early 1019, the *PVL* records that Jaroslav, with the help of his cousin Kostjantin Dobrynič, was attempting to recruit Scandinavian soldiers to help him retake Kyiv.[18] This dovetails nicely with the marriage negotiations with king Olof.[19]

As has been discussed, dynastic marriages have many purposes, but the main one is securing an alliance. Jaroslav was in a tight spot after being evicted from Kyiv. The *PVL* records that he wanted to flee to Scandinavia and was stopped only by the heroics of his cousin, Kostjantin, and the generosity of the people of Novgorod.[20] This may be the case, but it is more likely that there was another element to Jaroslav's success, that while in Novgorod he sent men to Olof to negotiate a dynastic marriage that involved Olof supplying Jaroslav troops with which to regain Kyiv.[21] There is some circumstantial evidence for this in the *Heimskringla*'s description of the marriage contract. The impetus for these demands in *Heimskringla* comes from Ingigerd,[22] and while this is entirely possible, it may also be a later interpretation based upon the opinion in Scandinavian sagas that Ingigerd was a wise woman who became the power in Rus´.[23] Her first demand was for Ladoga "and the jarldom that goes with it" as her dowry, and she followed this up with a demand for Jarl Ragnvald Ulfson to accompany her and to be jarl in Ladoga.[24] The *Heimskringla* records that Ragnvald gathered his men and ships and accompanied her to Rus´.[25] There are multiple interesting things to discuss in regard to these demands, but the most immediate is that accompanying Ingigerd on her trip to Rus´ was a powerful Swedish jarl and his warriors, and he was to have a jarldom in Rus´. An alternate interpretation to that provided by Sturluson would be a request by Jaroslav, as part of the marriage agreement, for troops to reclaim Kyiv. In return for that aid, the jarl leading the troops would have the trading city of Ladoga and its demesne, with substantial revenues, as his own. This interpretation fits the facts and the model of medieval dynastic marriage quite well. The marriage was agreed upon in the summer of 1018 and in spring 1019 Jaroslav sent messengers to collect his bride and troops and lead them to Novgorod.[26] He then went on to make an attack on Svjatopolk, driving him out of Kyiv and reclaiming it for good,[27] making a success of his dynastic marriage alliance with Ingigerd.

The account in *Heimskringla* provides references to some practices involved in medieval dynastic marriages that are rarely recorded. The first is the consent of the woman to the marriage. Ingigerd is able to set conditions on the marriage agreement before it is ratified, thus playing a crucial role in the creation of the agreement itself, even to the point of choosing her retinue against her father's wishes.[28] As far as the medieval church was concerned, consent was the key to marriage, and women, or men, could not be forced by their parents or anyone else to marry.[29] Though this was countermanded often in practice, in theory it was an absolute, and many families may have honored it.[30] This is something that may have occurred in Rusian dynastic marriages, drawing as they did on Scandinavian traditions in other ways as well, and thus is important to know for the current study.

The process of how the marriage was arranged is also important to note. It seems logical when explained clearly, as in the *Heimskringla*, but it is rarely thought of by historians, nor are its implications considered. In 1018 Jaroslav sent messengers to arrange a marriage with King Olof's daughter, and again in 1019 he sent messengers to conclude the agreement and bring Ingigerd back to Rus´.[31] This was a typical part of the organizing of medieval dynastic marriages, and there are other Rusian examples. For instance, in 1043 Jaroslav sends messengers to the court of Henry III, and subsequently Henry I of France sends messengers to Jaroslav to negotiate for one of his daughters.[32] This information is not known for the majority of Rusian dynastic marriages, and so where it is mentioned one has to expand that to an understanding that this was commonplace for most dynastic marriages.[33] This exchange of messengers also addresses one of the problems some historians have found with dynastic marriage as a vehicle for cultural or political transmission. The effect is expanded now from one person and an entourage, to an exchange or multiple exchanges of messengers between kingdoms to arrange potential dynastic marriages. These trips would likely be in the way of embassies, perhaps high ranking individuals who would not travel the long distances of the Middle Ages for a night, but stay and discuss for some time, advertently or inadvertently sharing their culture with their hosts.

In this same vein is the helpful knowledge about the people Ingigerd brought with her. In *Heimskringla* it is she who requests the company of Ragnvald on her journey to Rus´.[34] Unmentioned in the account but surely present on the journey were the wives of Ragnvald and his men, especially Ragnvald's wife Ingebjörg, the sister of Olaf Tryggvason, who is connected to Ingigerd in other accounts.[35] Thus, the bride did not go into her marriage alone, but with an entourage from her own kingdom creating a pocket of people in the foreign kingdom, people who spoke the same language and had the same culture and customs. Overt examples of this are rare in Rusian marriages, though there is an example in the marriage of the daughter of Bolesław I Chrobry to Svjatopolk Jaropolčič,[36] and there is an implication of another in the marriage of Evpraksija Vsevolodovna.[37] Like the system of arranging dynastic marriages with messengers, entourages for these royal and noble women were the norm, despite the paucity of Rusian examples.

The last item of note regarding this alliance is that Ingigerd asks for the town of Ladoga and its jarldom as her dowry.[38] As mentioned, this was most likely not Olof's to give, and it came instead from Jaroslav to Ragnvald. But the existence of the request is what is important to note here. As in the examples above, this is a rare piece of evidence. Only one other marriage—that of Evpraksija Vsevolodovna—has evidence that she arrived for her marriage bearing property.[39] That these women brought not only entourages but property into their marriages and into their new kingdoms increases the effect the marriage would have on the new family and the culture of the new family. The most famous example of this is the marriage of the Byzantine princess Theophano to the German emperor Otto II. Multiple records exist of the goods she brought with her as well as the impact that they had on German society in the later tenth century.[40] This is just another important item to consider in a rich description of eleventh-century dynastic marriage.

Ingigerd played an important role in Rus´. As we have seen, her marriage to Jaroslav helped him regain the throne of Kyiv and made possible his reign. Her contacts with Scandinavia were also important in advancing the cause of Rusian foreign policy. Because of his ties to her, King Olaf of Norway fled to Rus´ with his son Magnus when he was beaten by Knud the Great in 1029, and even after he left Rus´ the next year Jaroslav and Ingigerd continued to foster his son Magnus, for five more years.[41] Theodoric, who wrote a Latin history of Norway in the twelfth century, records that it was her decision whether or not to send Magnus back with the Norwegian delegation who came to return him to the throne.[42] This visit of Olaf's set up the visit of his brother Harald Hardrada in 1031, and thus his eventual marriage to Ingigerd and Jaroslav's daughter Elisabeth. The impact of Jaroslav's dynastic marriage to Ingigerd went beyond obtaining a wife; it affected the immediate and long-term foreign policy of Rus´ and guaranteed both of them immortality in the Scandinavian sagas.[43]

Dobronega/Maria Volodimerovna
(tables 1, 17, 22)

The last of Volodimer's children to marry was his (most likely) last child Dobronega. As with the majority of royal daughters, Dobronega's birth was not recorded in the *PVL*, but there has been much discussion ever since, not only of her birth date, but also of her parentage.[44] Of more concern at present is the date of her marriage, which is discussed

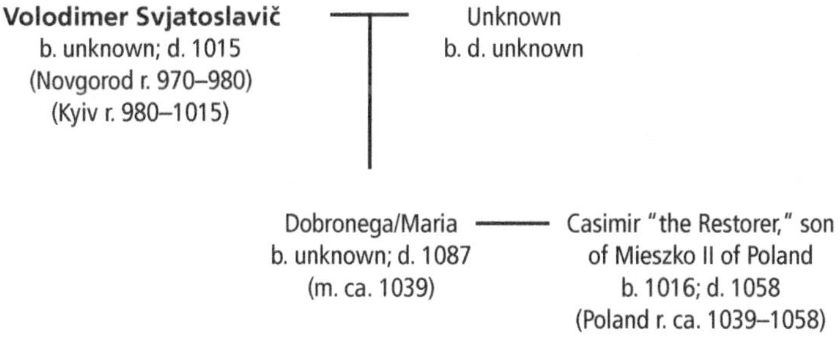

in regard to the circumstances surrounding this fascinating dynastic marriage.

Under the year 1030 the *PVL* records the death of Bolesław I Chrobry and a subsequent revolt and a period of chaos in Poland.[45] However, Bolesław Chrobry died in 1025, and this entry is actually referencing the death of his son and heir, Mieszko II, in 1034.[46] Despite getting the details wrong, or, rather, not quite right, this was an important event for Rus´ due to Poland's proximity, and it was recorded when the chronicle was created years later. The heir to the throne was Mieszko's son Casimir, who had fled to Saxony with his mother at Bolesław's death.[47] His mother was Richeza, the niece of the German emperor Otto III, and thus her family was quite powerful. In 1039, Casimir decided to reclaim his kingdom, which had in the meantime been taken over by rebellious nobles, and embarked on a plan to retake his grandfather's territory bit by bit from the groups that had divided it.[48]

It is likely that Rus´ preferred an indebted Piast ruler to chaos on its western border, and attempted to aid Casimir to this end. This is recorded in the Rusian chronicles in multiple instances over the course of the 1030s and 1040s. The first recorded instance of Rusian aid to Poland is in 1041, when Jaroslav attacked the Mazovians.[49] The Mazovians occupied a position on the northeastern corner of the Piast kingdom and had at one point been subjects of the Poles. They were also one of Casimir's most significant foes upon his return to Poland.[50] The *Gesta* records that Casimir was quickly able to bring the majority of Poland under his rule, and after doing so, married a Rusian noblewoman[51]—Jaroslav's sister Dobronega/Maria (her name is discussed below).[52] The *Chronica Poloniae Maioris* records that "to make peace in the Polish lands, he [Casimir] married a daughter of the Rusian ruler."[53] Only after that did Casimir go on to put down the other tribes, excepting only the Mazovians, who continued to rebel. The question of the relative reliability of the two chronicles is an open one; however the *Chronica Poloniae Maioris* has one mark in its favor on this issue, and that is its own surprise at the move. The quote from above begins, "in a surprising move,"[54] which suggests that the Polish chronicler, writing in the early thirteenth century from a time of more frequent Rusian-Polish warring, was surprised at Casimir's alliance with Rus′. This subtle note may lend enough credibility to the *Chronica Poloniae Maioris* for its interpretation that the marriage to Dobronega occurred before Casimir's reconquest of the Polish tribes, trumping the *Gesta*'s assertions.

All of this discussion sets up the issue of the date for this marriage. Both the *Gesta* and the *Chronica Poloniae Maioris* are largely undated, especially in these early sections, and thus cannot be of much assistance in attributing an actual calendar date to these events. The date for the *PVL* entry in which Jaroslav sends his sister to marry Casimir of Poland is 1043, listed after the Rusian attack on Constantinople,[55] but this is after Jaroslav has made his first attack on the Mazovians in 1041.[56] A generally reliable source from the German Empire, *Annalista Saxo*, records the marriage as taking place in 1039, immediately after Casimir returns to Poland.[57] Lambert of Hersefeld uses this date of 1039 to record the marriage of Dobronega and Casimir, and moves forward from this date to record the birth of their children.[58] Thus, the date of the marriage is in dispute in the primary sources, and this has only been complicated by the secondary sources.[59] The issue is made more confusing by the fact that the modern editors of the *Gesta* went so far as to include in a footnote a marriage date of 1041 and birth dates of 1039 for Bolesław and 1040 for Władysław.[60] The confusion of the primary sources does not permit certainty, but the evidence of two Latin chronicles for the 1039 date, the 1041 attack on the Mazovians recorded in the *PVL*, and the evidence of the *Chronica Poloniae Maioris* lead me to support the 1039 date for the marriage, prior to Casimir's reconquest of Poland, and certainly prior to the joint attacks on the Mazovians.

This is supported by the likelihood that Jaroslav would not have made the 1041 raid on the Mazovians "by boat"[61]—most likely up the Bug River—without either Mazovian provocation or an agreement with the Poles. Mazovian provocation is possible, but unlikely, as Casimir was at that time firmly in Poland and attempting to consolidate his power, which meant diminishing Mazovian power. It is rather more plausible that Jaroslav, in fulfillment of the agreement sealed by the dynastic marriage of his sister to Casimir, could have attacked the Mazovians on their rear front, in support of an assault of Casimir's. Though the *Gesta* is undated, the next listing after Casimir's marriage is an attack he made on the Mazovians.[62] After a brief listing of the defeat of the Mazovians and their leader "Miecław" at the hands of Casimir, the *Gesta* moves on to discuss the Pomeranians.[63] This is, however, where the Rusian chronicles are able to fill in some gaps. Various Rusian chronicles list Rusian attacks on the Mazovians in 1041, 1043, and 1047.[64] While the *PVL* has only the 1041 and 1047 attacks, the Nikon and Tver chronicles both include a 1043 attack, in which Jaroslav and Casimir fought jointly against the Mazovians and their leader "Moislav,"[65] clearly the same leader described in the *Gesta*. Moislav is mentioned later in the *PVL*, when he is defeated by Jaroslav in 1047 and subjected to Casimir.[66] The 1047 attack on Moislav and the Mazovians is the only instance in the *PVL* in which a Rusian ruler defeats someone and then subjects the loser to another ruler. In general this is unique, and betokens some relationship between the two parties. If we accept the possibility that the Nikon and Tver chronicles provide unique information, then their portrayal of the joint 1043 attacks, also against Moislav, demonstrates a further link between Jaroslav and Casimir in their attacks on the Mazovians. Which link derives directly from the dynastic marriage of Jaroslav's sister to Casimir of Poland, and leads to the subjection of the Mazovians to Casimir's rule. As such, a date for the marriage of Dobronega and Casimir must come before the first of Jaroslav's attacks on the Mazovians in order to give the attack a purpose.

The marriage of Dobronega and Casimir is the first time that the *PVL* records some of the terms of a dynastic marriage, in this case an exchange of property in which Casimir hands over eight hundred people who were taken when Bolesław invaded Rus′ on Svjatopolk's behalf.[67] Though at this point it would be twenty years after Bolesław's attack, some of the people may have been alive or could have had children.[68] More likely, the villages in which the people lived were handed back to Rus′. The other side of this exchange could be twofold. The first aspect is the already discussed alliance against the Mazovians and the agreement to subject them to Casimir's rule, rather than Jaroslav's, which was especially advantageous for Casimir. The second factor derives from the *Gesta*'s description of Dobronega as a wealthy woman when she comes into the marriage,[69] implying perhaps that she brought a large dowry with her, though there are no specifics.[70] Either way, this is an interesting dynastic marriage in regard to its treatment in the Rusian chronicles, as so many of the marriage's repercussions are recorded there, where Rusian women are so rarely mentioned.

The last detail to mention in regard to Dobronega is her name. The first recorded instance of her carrying the name Maria is in a letter from Pope Benedict IX to Casimir and his wife.[71] E. V. Pčelov suggested that Maria was likely the name given to her in Poland and Dobronega was her Rusian name.[72] However, I do not believe that we have to reach as far as that for an explanation. Rusian elites often had multiple names, as demonstrated through numerous examples (her father Volodimer was also named Basil and her brother Jaroslav was also named George), typically a Christian baptismal name and a traditional Slavic name. Some even had more names, such as Volodimer Monomax, or his son, M′stislav Harald.[73] There is no need then to suggest alternative origins for the name such as conversion to Latin Christianity, as has been done.[74]

The marriage of Casimir and Dobronega set the tone for Rusian-Polish relations for the next hundred years. Over that time, two of their children ruled Poland, Casimir's sister married a Rusian, and several of their grandchildren married other Volodimeroviči. Close ties between the two kingdoms, especially between certain branches of the Volodimeroviči, began with this marriage, and the future Piast rulers of Poland had one Rusian foremother, if not many, to look back on.

Marriages: Generation Two

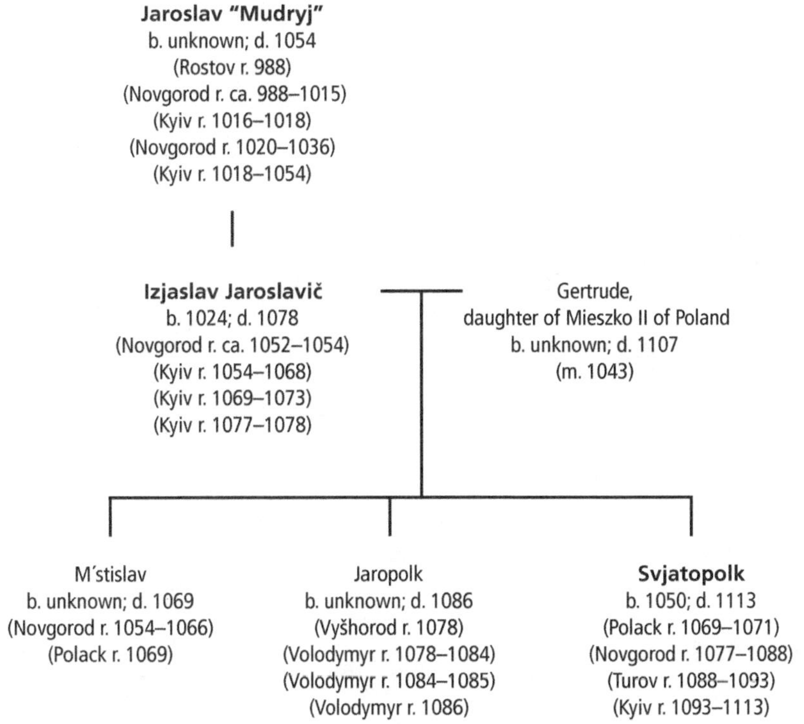

Izjaslav Jaroslavič
(tables 3, 5, 17)

Izjaslav was not the oldest of Jaroslav's living sons when he made his dynastic marriage, and though it is an extraordinarily important tie later, Izjaslav's marriage to a Piast princess was a simple dynastic marriage when it was concluded.[1] Izjaslav's marriage is, in fact, not recorded in the *PVL*, though it is one of the more well known dynastic marriages in eleventh-century Rusian history. Izjaslav married Gertrude, the daughter of Mieszko II of Poland and sister of Casimir. Though the *PVL* does not record the event in either the Laurentian or Hypatian redactions, it is recorded in both the Nikon and Tver chronicles under the year 1043 in conjunction with the marriage of Dobronega/Maria and Casimir and Jaroslav's attack on Moislav and the Mazovians.[2] Its placement alongside the other marriage and the attack sets it in time as well as in relation to those events; moreover it is possible to conclude that the reason for this marriage was the same as for Dobronega's, and in fact the two marriages strengthened the bond between Jaroslav and Casimir and their joint resolve to deal with the Mazovians. As for a date, the marriage of Dobronega can be reliably placed in 1039 due to the Latin sources, and a marriage date of 1043 for Izjaslav makes sense as part of reinforcing the existing Rusian-Polish alliance at that time.[3] We can accept, provisionally then, the dating of the marriage to 1043, and its purpose, which is indicated by its placement in the chronicles, as strengthening the alliance between Casimir and Jaroslav to deal with the Mazovians.

The implications of this marriage and its proximate cause are largely addressed in the implications and causes of the marriage of Casimir and Dobronega, which preceded Izjaslav's marriage in forming this Rusian-Polish alliance. However, this marriage would have far-reaching consequences for the history of Rus´ beyond that short-term alliance against the Mazovians. The first time this was evident was in 1068, when Izjaslav was forced to flee from Kyiv due to an insurrection, and chose to go to Poland. This is recorded in the *PVL* along with the simple statement that "Izjaslav fled to the Liakhs [Poles]."[4] We know that Izjaslav's wife was a Piast princess and that he could probably find allies there, especially in light of the situation with Svjatopolk Jaropolčič, who also fled to the Poles for support.[5] Bolesław II, Casimir's son, was now ruling Poland and was the most likely source for aid for Izjaslav, who believed that he could rely on Bolesław because of the familial relation confirmed by Izjaslav's marriage to Bolesław's aunt, as well as the familial connections between Bolesław's mother and Izjaslav.[6] As it turned out, Izjaslav was correct and by relying on the connections made by dynastic marriage, both his and his aunt's, he received aid from Bolesław to reclaim the throne of Kyiv.[7]

Izjaslav was again removed from power in 1073 and forced to rely on his wife's relations.[8] Izjaslav, taking a good part of the Rusian treasury, fled to Poland with his wife and his son Jaropolk. In Poland he attempted to procure aid from Bolesław again, but instead was robbed by Bolesław's men and turned out of the country[9] in what was most likely a clever dynastic-political move by Svjatoslav.[10] Polish sources do not recall this visit of Izjaslav, but the theft of the money is referenced later in a letter from Pope Gregory VII to Bolesław II.[11] Izjaslav and his family still needed a place to go, and if possible a place to find aid to return to power in Kyiv. Again the solution was to draw on the resources brought about by his dynastic marriage, his wife's family. Gertrude was the daughter of Mieszko II and his wife Richeza, the niece of German Emperor Otto III, and so she had kinship connections with many German families. Izjaslav was able to trade on her name and connections and find a place with Dedi, margrave of the Saxon Nordmark. Not incidentally, this connection was solidified with another dynastic marriage between Izjaslav's son Jaropolk and a stepdaughter of Dedi's, Cunigunda, to seal their alliance. This connection enabled Izjaslav to meet Emperor Henry IV and enlist his aid (unsuccessful) and also provided a base of operations from which he could reach out to the pope (more successful). With the pope's backing Izjaslav was able to return to Poland, and his cousin/nephew Bolesław II, and again request aid, which was granted after Svjatoslav's death in late 1076, when Polish forces assisted Izjaslav in regaining the throne of Kyiv.[12] This whole exhausting ordeal, related here in brief, was made possible only because of Izjaslav's dynastic marriage to Gertrude and his (or potentially their) utilization of her extensive familial ties in the interest of his political career.[13] Their marriage not only fulfilled these goals, but bound the Poles and the Izjaslaviči together for the next fifty years and helped to dictate Rusian foreign policy aims, as the Izjaslaviči strengthened these ties and other families reacted against them.

Izjaslav had three sons who are known in the historical record: M´stislav, Jaropolk, and Svjatopolk; at issue is whether or not Gertrude was the mother of all of them. This has been discussed by various scholars and hinges on two key pieces of evidence. The first is from Gertrude's Psalter, known as the *Codex Gertrudianus*, which contains an illustration of Jaropolk/Peter, the caption of which reads "my only son."[14] The second piece of evidence is a graffito on the wall of St. Sophia in Kyiv that says "Lord help your servant Olisava, mother of Svjatopolk, Rusian princess."[15] The reference in the graffito is unspecific in regard to which Svjatopolk is referred to, though V. L. Janin, one of the main investigators of this controversy, believes it to be Svjatopolk Izjaslavič due to the phrasing of the inscription. The obvious inference then would be that Svjatopolk and Jaropolk had the same father but different mothers. However, Janin then goes to great lengths to disprove this conclusion and show that Olisava might instead have been another name for Gertrude. While I cannot accept his reliance on a conversion-related name change, his argument is widely accepted.[16] This still leaves the reference to "my only son" from Gertrude's Psalter, which Janin cleverly deduces was composed during Jaropolk's trip to Rome, as part of Izjaslav and Gertrude's exile from Rus´, and thus the artists would have known only one son of Gertrude's to include. Neither explanation is entirely convincing to my mind, but the graffito is too slim as evidence upon which to base an entirely separate marriage of Izjaslav's. This is not the case for A. V. Nazarenko, however, who has come up with a theory for who this woman was and why the marriage was created, as part of a larger system of political-dynastic ties in eleventh century Europe.[17] Despite the incredible creativity of Nazarenko's suggestion, I do not think it is correct, or at least it is entirely too tenuous. Thus, I have left all the children as sons of Gertrude, noting additionally that there is this controversy that others may pursue in the sources.

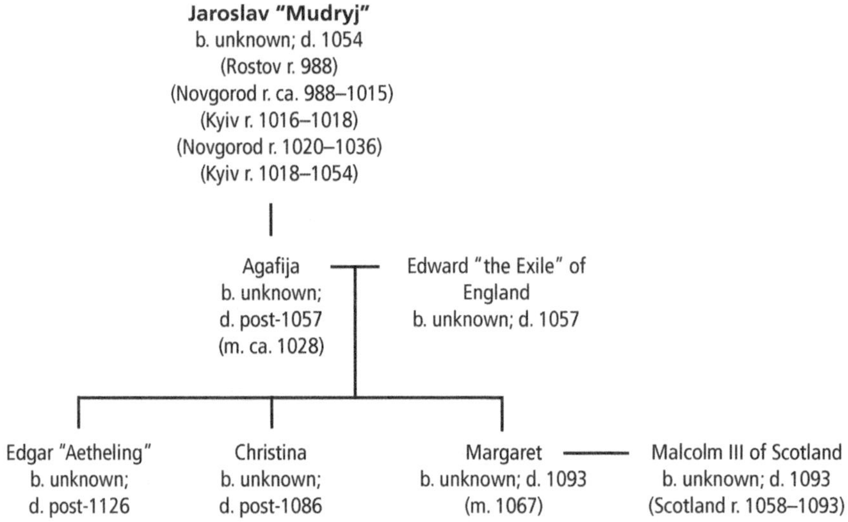

Agafija Jaroslavna
(tables 3, 16)

For years scholars have debated the identity of Agatha, wife of Prince Edward the Exile of England, who was son of Edmund II Ironside, king of England. This mystery has reached a conclusion, I believe, in recent years with the arguments of René Jetté and Norman Ingham.[18] These two scholars make the convincing argument, following the primary sources, that Agatha (perhaps Agafija in Rus´) was another daughter of Jaroslav Mudryj and that she was married to Edward during his exile in Rus´. This was clearly a dynastic marriage of the sort made by Jaroslav with exiled royalty in the middle third of the eleventh century, and thus deserves to be discussed here.

In late 1016 Edmund "Ironside" was poisoned and Knud, who came to control nearly the entire Baltic and North Sea region, became king of England. Adam of Bremen records that Edmund's young sons, Edmund and Edward, were sent into exile in Rus´.[19] Their path there was actually more circuitous than Adam describes; they first went to Olof Skötkonnung in Sweden, only moving on to Rus´ after Knud deposed Olof in 1028.[20] An exiled prince in Rus´ was not an uncommon occurrence; coming through Rus´ in this time period were exiles from Sweden, including Olof Skötkonnung; from Norway, St. Olaf, and his son Magnus, and Olaf's brother Harald Hardrada; and from Hungary, Andrew and his brother Levente. Jaroslav took advantage of the majority of these opportunities to build relations with these exiles and expand the reach of Rus´. These exiles might someday again rule the lands of their birth, at which time a Volodimeroviči princess would be in place as an influential figure in their kingdom. To that end, he married his daughter Agafija to Edmund's son, Edward "the Exile." This was a gamble on Jaroslav's part. The goal of dynastic marriages was to advance the political policy of the kingdom or of the family (though these were often coterminous) and a marriage with an exile was not immediately advantageous. However, the marriage would become advantageous for Jaroslav should Edward succeed to the English throne, at which time Jaroslav would become the king of England's father-in-law and his daughter would be the queen.

Edward and Agafija went to Hungary with or in the wake of Agafija's sister Anastasija, and her husband Andrew (a similar situation in which Jaroslav married one of his daughters to an exiled royal; see the next entry for more information).[21] Edward and Agafija had three children, Edgar, Christina, and Margaret, the significance of whose names is discussed elsewhere.[22] Some twelfth-century chronicles record Edward and Agafija living in Hungary[23] because this is where they were found by Edward "the Confessor" in 1054 when he asked Edward the Exile to return to England and become his heir.[24] The couple and their children then returned to England, arriving in 1057 only to have Edward the Exile die mysteriously before he could be confirmed as heir by Edward the Confessor.[25] Agafija then took charge of the family and moved them to Scotland, where her daughter Margaret was married to Malcolm III, king of Scotland. There has been much interest in Margaret in recent scholarship because she was such an active queen and clearly an influential woman in the Middle Ages.[26] Agafija lived with her daughter until her death, potentially continuing to be an influential part of her life. Agafija's heritage is recorded in the *Leges Edwarde Confessoris*, which states that she was the daughter of the Rusian king Jaroslav.[27] The purpose of the work is even more interesting than its plain statement of Agatha's origin. The document was created to codify Margaret's royal heritage so that she might rule for her daughter Mathilda,[28] which was also required for Mathilda's marriage to Henry I, king of England, in 1100.[29]

Agafija's marriage to Edward the Exile was a gamble on Jaroslav's part, but it was a calculated one. It was also one that nearly paid off perfectly, since Edward was recalled to England to be heir to Edward the Confessor. What did happen was beneficial for Rus´ as well, though not immediately for Jaroslav. The prestige of Margaret, a half-Rusian princess, ruling in Scotland may have increased the renown of Rus´ in western Europe. Additionally, Rusian blood was considered good European royal blood for the purposes of Agafija's granddaughter's marriage to the king of England according to the *Leges*.

In an interesting postscript to this particular dynastic marriage, there is evidence that Rusian cousins in western Europe were involved with one another. Edgar "Aetheling," son of Agafija and Edward the Exile, and Philip, king of France, corresponded in the fourth quarter of the eleventh century. The Anglo-Saxon chronicle records that in 1074 Philip sent Edgar a letter in Scotland where he was staying with his sister Margaret, the queen, and "ordered him to come to him, and he would give him the castle at Montreuil so that afterwards he could daily do ill-turns to those not his friends."[30] The relationship between the two has puzzled historians.[31] Edgar was the last or one of the last of the Saxon royal blood in Norman-occupied England, and perhaps that alone would have made him an ally of the French king should he wage war against the Normans. But as they were first cousins their relationship was not just a bond of mutual interest, but also a familial relationship. Thus, the dynastic marriage of Agafija Jaroslavna sheds light on multiple historical mysteries in medieval England.

Anastasija Jaroslavna
(tables 1, 3, 18, 19, 22)

In the 1030s Rus´ was home to another group of exiled royalty, the Hungarian princes Andrew and Levente.[32] They had fled Hungary after King Stephen told them that their lives were in danger upon his death.[33] Their other brother, Béla, had originally fled with them, but stayed at their first stop in Poland where he had married the daughter of Mieszko II, the ruler of Poland.[34] Jaroslav and his court took in these exiles, as they had others, with their own interests in mind. Interestingly, Dimitri Obolensky states that Jaroslav even had Andrew baptized while he was in Kyiv,[35] though there is no primary source attesting to it. Levente is known in the Hungarian chronicles as lapsing back

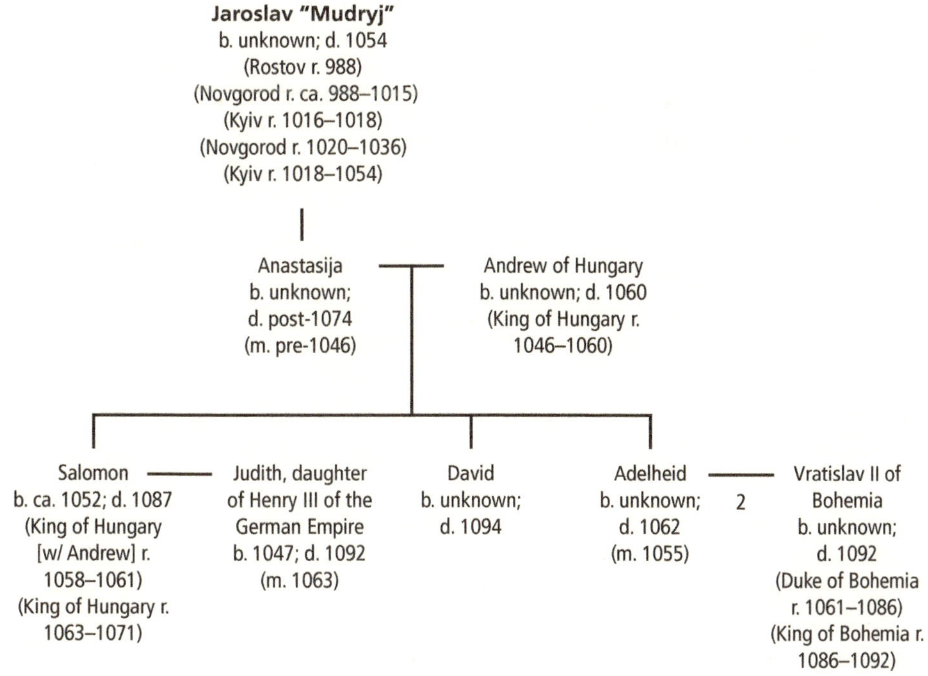

into paganism and leading a pagan revolt in Hungary.[36] However, it is difficult to imagine that their parents would not have raised them as Christian, as their mother was a Rusian princess, as noted above.[37] Regardless of whether or not Jaroslav had Andrew baptized, Jaroslav did marry one of his daughters to Andrew.[38]

As with many of the dynastic marriages Jaroslav arranged in this period, the marriage of Andrew and Anastasija was a gamble. It was unsure whether or not Andrew would return to rule his country, thus the safer situation for Jaroslav would be to wait and arrange a marriage with a sitting ruler, rather than an exile. These were the kinds of chances that Jaroslav seemed to take with dynastic marriage, however, and there were many foreign policy gains to be made. The first and most basic was that it would benefit Rus´ to have a friendly ruler in a neighboring kingdom, especially in one that neighbored the steppe as well. Perhaps just as important was that Andrew's next youngest brother was married to the daughter of the ruler of the Poles, and should he succeed to the throne the Poles would be in a stronger position than the Rusians vis-à-vis Hungary. Despite increasing ties with Poland, this was probably an unacceptable outcome for Jaroslav. Because of these factors it is possible to imagine that Rusian forces might have been used to assist Andrew in claiming the Hungarian throne for himself, though this is not recorded in the primary sources.[39]

Andrew returned to Hungary in 1046 with his wife Anastasija. Not much is recorded of their rule there, though it is known that Anastasija had an influential role in the kingdom. They had three children, Salomon, David, and Adelheid, and as is discussed elsewhere,[40] Anastasija was instrumental in naming these children. János Bak, in his work on Hungarian queens, has stated that foreign queens were vital for the cultural life of medieval Hungary,[41] and there are indeed multiple examples of the influence she had on her eldest son's career as king and also as exile.

Salomon was betrothed to Judith, the daughter of the late German Emperor Henry III and sister to Emperor Henry IV, in 1058.[42] Like many dynastic marriages, it sealed a peace between the two countries after a period of war. Later that same year, Andrew took ill and had his five-year-old son, Salomon, crowned king alongside him.[43] This was clearly an attempt to create a lineal succession pattern, which, while becoming more common throughout Europe in the eleventh century, was not the norm in Hungary or in many other places (including Rus´).[44] The combination of Salomon's connection with the hated Germans and the crowning of a child when Andrew had a perfectly healthy brother alienated the Hungarian nobility, and after Andrew's death in 1060, Salomon and Anastasija were forced to flee to the court of German Emperor Henry IV.[45] As Henry IV was still a minor, his regency was managed by his mother and Judith's mother Agnes, who assisted Anastasija and her son-in-law Salomon. Agnes gave Anastasija one of her estates in Austria for herself and kept Salomon and Judith with her at the imperial court.[46] This did not stop Anastasija from maneuvering on behalf of her son. Lambert of Hersfeld records that in 1063 Anastasija gave a Hungarian royal relic, the Sword of Attila, to Otto of Nordheim, duke of Bavaria, with the express intention of convincing him to aid her son in the reconquest of the kingdom that she viewed as rightfully his.[47] Otto was at that time a member of Henry IV's regency and thus had some power over imperial policy. Later that same year imperial troops accompanied by Salomon, and some of his loyal Hungarian troops who had come with him and his mother to the German Empire, returned to Hungary and took over.[48]

Anastasija is irregularly mentioned as advising her son during his tumultuous reign in (and out of) Hungary, in which he battled with his cousin Géza. She usually counseled peace between the cousins and urged Salomon to be content with his role as king and accept his cousin as a duke.[49] This advice was disregarded, and Salomon preferred to attempt to drive his cousin out of the kingdom. It is recorded that she, as well as his wife Judith,[50] traveled with Salomon through Hungary,[51] presumably with the intention of advising him.

A short aside on the strength of the Rusian-Hungarian ties ensured by Anastasija's marriage is the story of Ladislaus, brother of Géza and cousin to Salomon, who came to Rus´ for aid. In the early 1070s Géza needed assistance in his war against Salomon, and to that end he sent his brother Ladislaus to Rus´ to petition for aid.[52] Géza and Ladislaus were the grandchildren of N. N. Volodimerovna and the first Ladislaus, but that could not compete with the ties Salomon had through both the Volodimerovna and his mother Anastasija Jaroslavna, so Ladislaus was turned away.[53] As in many cases, we do not have the details from either the Hungarian or Rusian chronicles, but the evident marital ties make backing anyone against Salomon, nephew of the Rusian ruler, unlikely.[54]

Anastasija died sometime after 1074, the last year for which we have information on her whereabouts, and the same year that her son Salomon was expelled for the last time from Hungary.[55] She was laid to rest at Admont Abbey in Austria, where she had stayed at times while Salomon was warring.[56] Her life was, unfortunately, not very well documented by contemporary historians, but her actions still come through nevertheless. She was able to influence the selection of names for her children, something rare in the Middle Ages, and she was a counselor to her husband and to her son, helping the latter to regain and hold Hungary. This was quite a life for a woman whose name or very existence is not recorded by the chroniclers in the land of her birth. But the dynastic marriage did seem to ally Hungary with Rus´. Salomon was able to count on Rusian aid, or the lack thereof for a rival, at least twice in his lifetime that we know of from Hungarian accounts. This shows that the Rusians must also have been receiving something in return for them to continue to support the embattled Hungarian ruler.

Elisabeth Jaroslavna
(tables 3, 15)

One of the most famous characters of the Middle Ages was the Viking, and few Vikings are better known today than the itinerant Harald Hardrada, who became ruler of Norway and later died at Stamford Bridge fighting Harold Godwinsson of England. Harald was the brother of Olaf, king of Norway (later St. Olaf),[57] who himself was brother-in-law to Jaroslav Mudryj.[58] Harald's first recorded visit to Rus´ came in 1031, the year after the battle of Stiklestad in which Olaf and his forces were defeated by armies of King Knud the Great.[59] Rus´ would have been an easy option for him, not only for its proximity, but also because there were close ties between his family and the Volodimeroviči. In addition to marital ties, at this time Jaroslav and Ingigerd were raising Magnus, St. Olaf's son and Harald's nephew.[60] The Scandinavian sources record that Harald, upon his arrival in Rus´, became the head of Jaroslav's bodyguard.[61] This seems unlikely due to

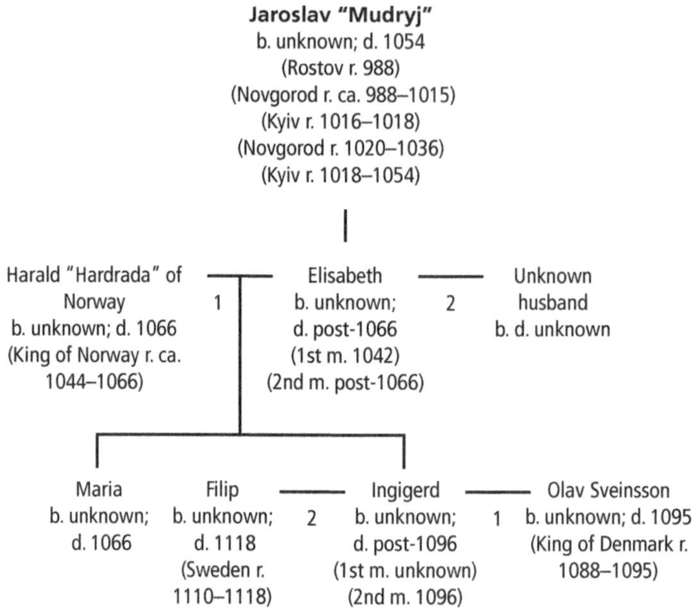

his young age, and probable inexperience, at the time. However, after some time in Rus´ he traveled to Byzantium to serve as a mercenary, finding success, and sending his booty to Novgorod for Jaroslav to keep safe, perhaps as a way to prove his growing worth to his potential father-in-law.[62] In 1042 Harald heard that his nephew Magnus was ruling Norway and left Byzantium to reclaim his family lands. On the way home he stopped in Rus´ to reclaim the wealth that he had stored with Jaroslav.[63] While there he married Jaroslav's daughter Elisabeth.[64] Sturluson quotes one stanza of a poem that Harald composed on the way home from Greece, the refrain of which says "Yet the gold-ring-Gerth from / Garthar lets me dangle.[65] The refrain references a woman from Rus´, "Garthar," (Garðar) and can be used to indicate that there was an existing relationship between Harald and such a woman, most likely Elisabeth, despite Sturluson's talk of Harald's interest in marrying a royal Byzantine woman named Maria or the Empress Zoe's interest in marrying Harald herself.[66] It is unclear if this marriage was prearranged or even if it was just a preexisting relationship. The *Flateyjarbók* records that Harald in fact asked for Elisabeth's hand while he was living in Kyiv as captain of Jaroslav's bodyguard.[67] Jaroslav turned him down saying that he was well-born, but had not yet achieved the necessary wealth or fame for Jaroslav to contemplate the marriage. This was likely the impetus for him to go to Byzantium, and it provides a nice explanation for why he sent his riches to Jaroslav to store for him, as evidence of his growing wealth. The story is convenient in the *Flateyjarbók*, but it also fits the known details. Harald was in Rus´, knew Jaroslav, was at the age when he would be looking to marry, probably knew Jaroslav's daughters, did send his riches to Jaroslav to hold for him, and the poem he composed on the way home indicates a previous association with a Rusian woman.

The marriage between Harald Hardrada and Elisabeth Jaroslavna was certainly a dynastic marriage. Jaroslav was following his policy of wedding his daughters to exiled princes on the chance that they would return home and become kings and his daughters, queens. With Harald he had an excellent chance of Harald's returning home to at least a share of the kingship, as it was Harald's nephew, also foster-son (of a sort) to Ingigerd and Jaroslav, who ruled Norway and who had been raised partly in Rus´. The marriage was also a continuation of a relationship with the Norwegian royal family that had been begun by Jaroslav and Ingigerd with Harald's brother St. Olaf over a decade earlier. Unsurprisingly, the marriage is not recorded in the *PVL*, which does not once mention either Harald or Elisabeth. But it is well recorded in Sturluson's *Heimskringla*, which even records Elisabeth's name, a pleasant change for medievalists who are used to dealing with unnamed women identified only by their patronymic. Interestingly enough, she is recorded with two names: "her name was Elizabeth, whom Northmen call Ellisif."[68] This is an interesting note because it indicates that Elisabeth was the name she was given in Rus´ and not a Scandinavian adoption.

The kinship of this event was of enormous importance to the Scandinavians, and Sturluson records multiple examples of that. The first is a poem by Stuf the Blind on the occasion of the marriage between Harald and Elisabeth. "Kinship won the keen-eyed / king which he had wished / gold a-plenty as guerdon / gained he, and eke the princess."[69] Harald got the king's daughter, Elisabeth, but he also received kinship, and in fact it was the kinship that was more prized in the eyes of the poet. The next example comes when Harald went to Sigtuna, where he met Svein Estridsson with whom he was almost instantly close, largely because of the kinship relations between them, traced through Harald's new wife.[70] All this helps to explain the importance of kinship, as related the poem quoted above, to Harald's campaign to gain the Norwegian throne. The importance of kinship relations in such matters is stated again in that same meeting between Harald and Svein, when Svein's power is explained because of his numerous kin relations.[71] Kinship in this period, especially in Scandinavia, was the key to power, and Harald's marriage to Elisabeth ensured him a proper start on that path.

Not much is known of Elisabeth's life in Scandinavia. We do know that she is always called "queen" in the *Heimskringla*, even after Harald takes another wife.[72] The existence of the second wife is surprising, but immediately after Sturluson makes note of the marriage he states that Thora, the second wife, bore him two sons, while "Queen Ellisif" bore him two daughters.[73] This may show the ultimate reason for the marriage—the creation of an heir for Harald's kingdom. The relationship could also have been something less than a marriage. Since the issue of Harald's bigamy is not addressed by Sturluson or by Adam of Bremen,[74] she might simply have been a mistress for the purpose of bearing sons or, as she was Scandinavian, cementing internal relations.

Elisabeth does seem to have been the closer wife, apart from the fact that she is always called "queen." Harald takes her with him when he goes to England in 1066,[75] as well as their daughters and his younger son by Thora, Olaf. Maybe because of Harald's attachment to Elisabeth, they named their younger daughter Ingigerd, a Scandinavian name, but also an obvious reference to Elisabeth's mother. As is discussed elsewhere,[76] the names of children generally come from the paternal family, so this may suggest Elisabeth's influence with her husband.

Elisabeth passes out of Sturluson's purview after Harald's death. She is noted as returning with her daughter Ingigerd and her stepson Olaf to Norway after Harald's death in England, but that is his last mention of her in the *Heimskringla*.[77] She is believed to have remarried after his death, though to whom is a matter of contention. Adam of Bremen notes that "He [Haakon the Red of Sweden] married the young Olaf's mother."[78] Olaf is identified by Francis J. Tschan, the editor and translator of Adam of Bremen, as Olaf Kyrre of Norway, son of Harald Hardrada.[79] However, Olaf's mother was not Elisabeth, but Thora. Nonetheless, the assumption has been made that Adam was speaking of Elisabeth. There is also a school of thought that Elisabeth's second marriage was to Svein Estridsson, king of Denmark. This is propagated by Baumgarten, where he cites *Heimskringla* and a secondary genealogy as his sources for both marriages of Elisabeth.[80] However, Nazarenko believes that this interpretation comes from a misreading of Adam of Bremen's scholium, quoted above.[81] The marital history shows that this marriage would have been unlikely, as Svein Estridsson's son Olav marries Elisabeth's daughter Ingigerd, something that would have never been allowed if Svein and Elisabeth had been married themselves.[82] Though it seems more than unlikely that her second husband was Svein, it cannot be conclusively shown that it was Haakon the Red, as records for early Swedish history are sparse and his family did not live on past the period. Elisabeth's life after the death of Harald Hardrada may be a mystery currently unsolvable.

The marriage of Elisabeth Jaroslavna was a foreign policy victory for Jaroslav as it solidified friendship ties and marital ties with a

Scandinavian dynasty that was steadily increasing its power. The tie also kept the Volodimeroviči in connection with their Scandinavian roots and paved the way for connections in the next two generations of Volodimeroviči rulers and their families.

Svjatoslav Jaroslavič
(tables 3, 6, 19)

There is, perhaps, more mystery and controversy about the marriages of Svjatoslav Jaroslavič than any other figure in Rusian medieval history. Even the preceding statement would engender controversy because of the use of the word "marriages," as some believe there was only one marriage.[83] This is not the place to get into the specifics of any of these arguments, though reference to them will be made in the text with further information or citations in the notes. Instead, this section will merely focus on the available data.

There are two women who are connected to Svjatoslav, or at the very least two different names, the first of which is Kilikia. The name Kilikia for the wife of Svjatoslav is recorded in the *Ljubeč Sinodik*, a very late, and often contested, source for information on the Svjatoslaviči.[84] Martin Dimnik, whose work has concentrated on the restoration of the Svjatoslaviči to the pages of Rusian history, has theorized that the

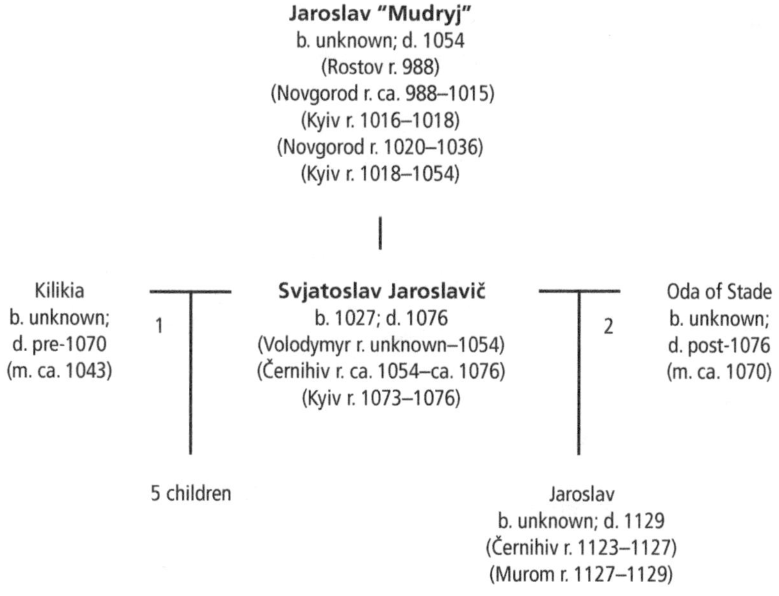

marriage to Kilikia took place between the marriages of his older and younger brothers, Izjaslav and Vsevolod, which Dimnik dates to 1043 and 1046 respectively.[85] This is merely a supposition, however, as no actual information exists about the marriage or about Kilikia herself, but for the sake of argument the logical supposition that the brothers would marry in order of seniority has been accepted as a starting point for discussion. As mentioned, there is no record of Kilikia's identity. Dimnik, among others, has advanced the idea that the name indicates that she is Byzantine, from the province of Cilicia, which is rendered in Greek as Kilikia.[86] This seems possible simply based on the onomastic evidence of the name, but in the window created by Dimnik, there does not seem to be a reason for a marriage between Rus´ and Byzantium. In 1043 Rus´ attacked Constantinople, and in 1046 there was the marriage of a Monomaxina to Vsevolod Jaroslavič.[87] A marriage with a Byzantine woman not from the royal house (which at the time was that of Constantine IX Monomachus), would seem an odd choice to make. The only explanation that makes sense from the perspective of the Byzantines would be if perhaps Svjatoslav was allying himself or being allied with a rival faction, but such a faction from Cilicia in this time period is not known, and no such marriage is recorded in contemporary Byzantine sources. With the overwhelming lack of evidence, it is impossible to confirm that this was a Byzantine marriage. Alternately, V. M. Mošin has suggested that the woman may have been of Norman origin, though this is just as speculative.[88] The identity of Kilikia will have to wait for the discovery of more evidence.

Following the theory of multiple marriages, Kilikia was the mother of all of Svjatoslav's children with the exception only of his youngest son, Jaroslav. The mother of Jaroslav Svjatoslavič was a German woman by the name of Oda of Stade. Oda of Stade was the daughter of Ida of Elsdorf and Lippold, count of Ditmarschen. Ida was herself the niece of Emperor Henry III and Pope Leo IX, and thus a woman of some importance in the German Empire.[89] This marriage can be dated to the early 1070s. A continuer of Herman of Reichenau recorded under the year 1072 that the "king of Rus´" married the daughter of "Count Lippold and Ita of Oterisburg"[90] with the mediation of Henry IV.[91] Potentially corroborating this account is a story from Bruno's Saxon chronicle that Henry IV sent an embassy to Rus´, though the story is undated and serves only to advance the idea of Henry IV as a crafty ruler.[92] Nazarenko suggests that the embassy was sent in 1069/70 to discuss the marriage between Svjatoslav and Henry IV's cousin.[93] Though this is not concrete corroboration, it is acceptable as a basis to build the theory that Henry IV was involved in Oda of Stade's marriage. He was Ida's cousin as well as the ruler of the German Empire, and thus would have had the ability to marry off his cousin's daughter, should he so choose. Nazarenko has suggested that the reason behind such a marriage would be an anti-Polish alliance between the Svjatoslaviči and the Salian dynasty.[94] If the marriage negotiations began in 1069/70, it was after the Poles had restored Izjaslav to the throne, and Bolesław II was beginning to war against the Bohemians (who had attacked Poland while Bolesław was in Rus´), staunch allies of the German Empire. This reasoning makes sense on the surface, as the Svjatoslaviči and Izjslaviči are often contrasted in their stance toward Poland, but it is difficult to reconcile with the earlier marriage of Vyšeslava Svjatoslavna to Bolesław II of Poland.[95] The marriage may have just been another form of insurance against Polish interference in the internal Rusian struggle with Vseslav Brjačeslavič, or as part of the future planning of Svjatoslav, who was already preparing a campaign against Izjaslav and wanted to take extra measures to be sure that the Poles were both unwilling (because of Bolesław's marriage to Svjatoslav's daughter) and unable (because of the threat of attack) to aid Izjaslav's return to Kyiv.

Svjatoslav and Oda had only one known child. The *Izbornik Svjatoslava* of 1073 carries a picture of Svjatoslav and his family in which his children are grown except for a baby held by his wife. This baby was most likely Jaroslav, and the wife, Oda of Stade.[96] After Svjatoslav's death, Oda returned to the German Empire with Jaroslav, and he was not seen again in Rus´ until 1096,[97] after which he began to rule various Svjatoslaviči towns.[98]

Svjatoslav's marriage to Oda is best known for the assistance it gave him when Henry IV sent an embassy to Rus´ in 1075 ostensibly on behalf of Izjaslav. The head of Henry's delegation was Burchard, the dean of Trier, specifically chosen because he was the brother of Oda of Stade, and thus the brother-in-law of Svjatoslav.[99] Burchard was sent to Rus´ to negotiate a peaceful settlement to the struggles between Izjaslav and Svjatopolk. Burchard returned from his brother-in-law's court with riches for both himself and Henry IV, most likely as further inducement not to intervene in the struggle.[100] The marriage, then, had served its purpose of allowing Svjatoslav an entrée to Henry IV that allowed him to maintain his seat in Kyiv and frustrate his brother's chances to return to Rus´.

This marriage, for all of the convoluted struggles in the historiography, was a very important one for Rus´. It fulfilled its goal of an alliance with Henry IV, as well as preventing Polish aid to Izjaslav while Svjatoslav ruled in Kyiv. But perhaps more importantly, it brought imperial Salian blood into the Volodimeroviči line (in the person of Jaroslav Svjatoslavič), an important symbol that the Rusians were eligible partners throughout Europe and potentially leading the way for Henry IV himself to marry a Rusian princess.

Jaroslav "Mudryj"
b. unknown; d. 1054
(Rostov r. 988)
(Novgorod r. ca. 988–1015)
(Kyiv r. 1016–1018)
(Novgorod r. 1020–1036)
(Kyiv r. 1018–1054)

Henry I of France
b. ca. 1008; d. 1060
(Duke of Burgundy r. 1017–31)
(King of France [w/ Robert II] r. 1027–1031)
(King of France r. 1031–1060)

1 — Anna
b. unknown;
d. 1089
(Regent ca. 1060–1066)
(1st m. 1051)
(2nd m. 1061)

— 2 Raoul de Crépy
b. unknown; d. 1074

Philip I of France
b. 1052; d. 1108
(King of France r. 1059–1108)

Robert
b. ca. 1053;
d. ca. 1053

Hugh
b. ca. 1053; d. 1101
(Count of Vermandois r. 1085–1101)

Anna Jaroslavna
(tables 3, 16)

In 1043 Jaroslav Mudryj sent an embassy to the German ruler Henry III to discuss a marriage between Henry and one of Jaroslav's daughters.[101] This would have been the best dynastic marriage Jaroslav could have made with the resources available to him. From the beginning of his reign, he had attempted to make an alliance with the German Empire, and now in 1043 he believed he had that chance. The marriage would have bolstered the pan-European prestige of Rus´ and created a situation in which Rusian women were the queens of much of Europe, ruling the German Empire, Hungary, Norway, and Poland in the mid-eleventh century. Unfortunately for Jaroslav, the proposition was turned down, and the alliance with the German emperor would not happen in his lifetime. The reasons the marriage was turned down are not recorded and it has been left to historians to hypothesize. It seems likely that Henry was more interested in securing his western frontier than allying with Rus´, and thus arranged a marriage with Agnes of Poitou, the daughter of the duke of Aquitaine. As there was already a considerable struggle between the various territories of France and the German Empire, this was a more immediate necessity than an alliance with Rus´.

However, Jaroslav's embassy was noticed in Europe, and in 1049 when Henry I of France was again on the market for a bride, it was remembered. As Andrew Lewis has said, "Henry I married deliberately and well."[102] His first engagement was to a young daughter of Emperor Conrad II to seal an alliance against Count Odo II of Blois, though she died within a year of the 1033 engagement. Henry continued the alliance by marrying the German princess Mathilda, the niece of Henry III. Mathilda lived long enough to consummate her marriage with Henry (like Conrad II's daughter she had been underage at the time of the initial engagement). She bore him one daughter, who died in infancy before herself dying in 1044.[103] Henry, however, was still in need of an heir, and thus a bride.

In mid-eleventh-century western Europe the church's consanguinity laws were still being enforced and honored by the majority of nobles, and so after many years of intermarrying there were few eligible partners for royalty. This was especially true in the case of France. Henry I wanted to marry a woman who had suitably royal blood but to whom he was not related.[104] According to some, like Constance Bouchard, this was the only or main reason for Henry's marriage to Anna Jaroslavna—she was royal and they were not related.[105] However, other options have been advanced as well. Two French scholars, R. H. Bautier and André Poulet, have both advanced the notion that this was a dynastic marriage to seal an alliance, as so many were, and not just for the procreation of heirs.[106] The reasoning put forth by both of these authors relies on the established dynastic history of Rus´. Earlier in the eleventh century, Anna's aunt Dobronega/Maria Volodimerovna married Casimir, the king of Poland, and her brother, Izjaslav Jaroslavič, married Casimir's sister Gertrude.[107] Casimir had spent his early life at the Abbey of Cluny in France[108] and so was knowledgeable about France, even as the ruler of Poland. It is thought that he brokered the marriage between Rus´ and France with the aim of consolidating an anti–German Empire alliance so that should the empire falter, the two kingdoms on either border might be able to move in and snap up some new territory. While the rule of Emperor Henry III seemed strong, the empire was actually quite fragile, as became apparent when Henry III died in 1056 and his young son Henry IV became king under a regency.[109] Jean Dunbabin also points out that power was a personal commodity in the medieval world and thus such a collapse might have been expected by a savvy ruler such as Henry I.[110] The gains for both the Poles and the French are easy to see in this agreement; both would have the potential to capitalize on a possible opportunity in the German Empire. There also would have been a tangible gain for

Rus´. Obviously there was the prestige of having a Rusian princess as queen of France, the farthest kingdom from Kyiv a Rusian had yet ruled, but this would also have been a deliberate public relations measure for Rus´ to get its name and people out into the courts of Western Europe and familiarize the people with their neighbors to the east.[111] Perhaps more politically important in the immediate present was that Jaroslav was helping his brother-in-law Casimir to focus Poland's attention west—that is, away from Rus´. Though the two were allies in this period, the historical interactions between Rus´ and Poland had always included raiding across the border and trading possession of the Červen´ towns. Keeping Poland focused west was a worthy political, and thus marital, goal. Despite all of this, it must be acknowledged that such a pan-European, anti-German alliance mediated by Casimir is supposition, as plausible as it may be.

Regardless of the reasoning behind the marriage, the process of the marriage is very interesting. In 1049 Henry I sent Gauthier of Meaux and Gauzlin of Chauny, two French bishops, to Kyiv as the leaders of an embassy.[112] As with many medieval records, though only the two are recorded, the embassy of two high-ranking bishops representing the king of France would have contained many other people as well, most likely a sizeable delegation. The purpose of the embassy was, of course, the negotiation of a marriage between the king of France and one of the daughters of Jaroslav Mudryj (Anna is specifically named in one record).[113] Unfortunately for the modern historian, no record of the negotiations has been preserved; thus the meetings between the bishops and Jaroslav and his representatives or advisors is left to the imagination. They must have been concluded successfully, because one record states that they returned with her from Rus´ with many gifts[114]—if only the occasion had been described slightly more elaborately, as was the arrival of Evpraksija Vsevolodovna in the German Empire approximately thirty years later. The modern historian can only wonder what the gifts were, and to whom they were presented. Many of them may have been Anna's to give as she would, or to use to support herself in her new land.[115] Nevertheless, Anna and the French bishops and their entourage returned to France most likely in 1050, and the couple was married in 1051.[116]

In February of 1052 Anna gave birth to her first son, to whom she gave the name Philip.[117] This was the first time such a name had appeared in the French royal line, and is discussed in detail elsewhere.[118] As Philip was Henry's firstborn son, he was also the heir and was crowned alongside his father in 1059 to so designate him.[119] Anna gave birth to two more of Henry's sons, Robert and Hugh. Robert died in childhood, but Hugh lived and went on to marry a well-off widow and become a leader of the First Crusade.[120]

Despite all of this negotiation and prelude, Anna's marriage to Henry was not to last long, as he was already an older man when they married. He became sick and died on 4 August 1060.[121] André Poulet suggests that before he died he left specific instructions that Baldwin V, count of Flanders, was to head the regency for Philip.[122] There was a medieval tradition in the Capetian royal house specifically, and in medieval royalty in general, that the queen, the mother of the heir, would act as the heir's regent until his age of majority.[123] Some historians believe that Anna was excluded from the regency because her command of both politics and the French language were "suspect."[124] However this does not appear to have been the case. Baldwin did take control of the regency, as "procurator," but Anna as queen mother was also part of the regency and served as an advisor to her young son.[125] Illustrative of Anna's influence on the regency of Philip are the numerous documents they signed jointly, especially during the first year or so after Henry's death.[126] One extreme example is in a charter of Bishop Agobert of Chartres in which Philip and Anna are jointly called "king."[127] These documents were possible because Anna accompanied Philip on the rounds he made of the kingdom in the years after his father's death.[128] Her presence, as well as her influence on Philip, illustrates the familial nature of government in the medieval world. As Poulet has expressed it, "the Capetian trinity [was] a dynastic machine formed by the king, the queen, and the designated heir, who shared sovereign authority."[129] This machine was transformed in 1061, and the nature of its transformation also elucidates Anna's influence on the ruling of France and on her son the king.

In the summer of 1061 Anna married again, this time to Raoul de Crépy, count of Valois, one of the most powerful lords of France.[130] Raoul had originally been an opponent of Henry during his reign, but after being defeated by Henry in 1041, Raoul became an ardent supporter of first Henry and then Philip.[131] Part of Anna's dowry was the abbey of Notre Dame at Laon, which was quite a valuable piece of property.[132] It was most likely given to her by Henry as part of their original marriage agreement. Most royal women were given land by their husbands so that they would have their own funds to maintain themselves and their households.[133] Also accompanying Anna into the marriage with Raoul was her substantial influence with Philip. After her marriage Raoul begins to appear as part of the regency council, and his name begins to appear on royal documents.[134] Concomitant with the increase in Raoul's appearance in royal diplomas was the decrease in Anna's appearance in the same.[135] This has led some to a misunderstanding of Anna's importance to the regency. Because Anna's name began to disappear from charters after 1061 and her marriage to Raoul, it has been thought that Philip was unhappy about her remarriage or that she had been ousted from the inner circle. An alternate reading of the events would show that Philip accepted this outsider, Raoul, as one of his closest advisors (indeed there is a debate over whether he was the most powerful advisor after this time or the second-most powerful)[136] only because of Raoul's marriage to Anna and Anna's endorsement of him. Anna had transferred her influence, in a manner of speaking, to Raoul. Though it is impossible to say for sure, it seems likely that as Raoul traveled with Philip throughout France, Anna may have continued to as well, lending her advice if not her name to royal decisions.

Philip's regency ended in 1066,[137] and along with it the record of Anna's activities in France. It is recorded that Anna had an influence on her second family by introducing the name Philip into the de Crépy line as well, spreading the name beyond the royal family.[138] What is missing from this account of Anna's life and influence is the Rusian record. Anna was well known in western Europe and included in many Latin chronicles (a Russian historian even suggests that she received a personal letter from Pope Nicholas II),[139] she endorsed French royal documents with her own name, "Anna regina,"[140] and served an important foreign policy purpose for her homeland of Rus´, not to mention being the daughter of Jaroslav Mudryj and the sister to three other rulers of Kyiv. Yet, with all of these considerations she does not receive even one mention in the Rusian chronicles. This illustrates the difficulty of studying Rusian women's history. If we look only at Rusian sources, apart from Ol´ga Rusian women played little or no part in their history, even as powerful a woman as Anna Jaroslavna.[141] Many Rusian women were known throughout Europe, and surely in their homeland, but not recorded in Rus´, whether due to a misogynistic bias, a parochial interest in internal events, or for another, unknown reason. Anna Jaroslavna was a powerful Rusian woman whose marriage advanced the foreign policy of Rus´. In France she was an influential advisor to both her husband and her son, inscribing many royal documents with her own name, and introducing the name Philip into the royal line.

Vsevolod Jaroslavič
(tables 3, 7, 19, 20)

The youngest of Jaroslav's sons, and some say the favorite, Vsevolod was the last of the Jaroslaviči to marry. His first marriage was to a "cěsarica gr´kyna,"[142] a Greek princess, who has no name in the *PVL*. Because of the typical lack of a name, historians have felt at some liberty to assign her one, as well as a familial line. The most common ascription is that she was the daughter of Constantine IX Monomachus, the third husband of Empress Zoe.[143] Like so much else in regard to these marriages, this is conjectural, as Byzantine sources do not record her

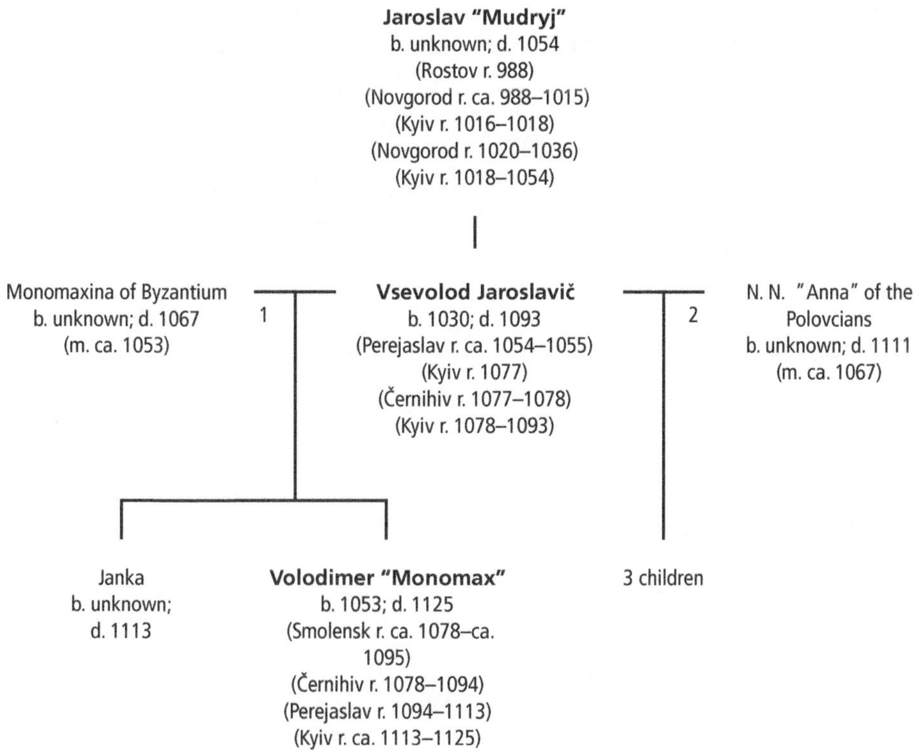

marriage or many details of Constantine IX's family.[144] The ascription to the house of Monomachus comes from the famous appellation of her firstborn son, Volodimer Monomax. While this leads an observer to the conclusion that Volodimer had a connection to the house of Monomachus,[145] it does not necessarily require his mother to have been the daughter of the most famous member of that house. Perhaps a safer assertion would be simply that she was a Monomaxina, and to stipulate that her exact parentage is unknown.[146] Even were she not the daughter of Constantine IX, there would have been no question that he could have, had he wished, arranged marriages for all of the members of his extended family. Thus, for the purposes of her participation in the world of dynastic marriage it is not necessary that she be the daughter of Constantine IX, just a Monomaxina.

The date of the marriage between Vsevolod and the unknown Monomaxina is unknown, as is the proximate cause of the marriage. Both Baumgarten and Bernard Leib date the marriage to 1046.[147] Leib's opinion, shared by others, is that the marriage was intended to seal the rift caused by the Rusian attack on Constantinople in 1043 and that it is because of this attack that the marriage is dated as it is. However, the first notation anywhere of the marriage is the record in the *PVL* under the year 1053 of the birth to Vsevolod and a Greek princess of a son, Volodimer.[148] Because of this late date, some scholars have chosen a later date, such as 1050, for the marriage.[149] From the outstanding records it is odd to find a couple who marry and do not have their first child for years unless one of the parties to the marriage is prepubescent. This piece of evidence alone leads one to the conclusion that the 1046 date, apart from being entirely speculative, is incorrect. That being said, the reason behind the marriage advanced by Leib and others may still be correct.

The 1043 attack on Constantinople was the first such attack since Rus´ was Christianized, and has always been a surprising note in history.[150] There is nothing in the historical record, either on the Byzantine or Rusian side, to indicate that relations had been souring during the long conversion of the Rus´ to Christianity. In fact, there is little evidence at all of communication between the two sides. But after the 1043 attack, the reparations paid by the Byzantines to the Rusians for property damaged in retribution,[151] and the 1051 appointment of Ilarion as the first Rusian metropolitan of Kyiv,[152] it is only logical to believe that a new accord between the Byzantines and Rusians might be required. Such an accord would have been reached between Jaroslav and Constantine IX, and as has been shown would likely have been sealed with a dynastic marriage. As Vsevolod was then at a ripe age for marriage (twenty in 1050), and was the last unmarried son of Jaroslav, he would have been a likely candidate.[153] It is unfortunate that this marriage cannot be confirmed by any of the primary sources. Michael Psellus, the well-known Byzantine scholar who was writing at this time, took pains to record the attack on Constantinople by the Rusians, but did not mention the ensuing peace or marriage.[154] But the existence of the marriage can be inferred from the clear reference to a "cěsarica gr´kyna" in the *PVL*[155] and Volodimer Vsevolodovič's later surname of "Monomax," something he could only have received through association with the house of Monomachus.[156]

V. N. Tatiščev records that Vsevolod's Greek princess died in 1067[157] and that he married a Polovcian woman this same year. This information, however, is not contained in any other source, and thus must be used and examined carefully. There were Rusian-steppe marriages beginning in this period as a means of helping to ensure the agreements between both sides, and these marriages always involved a Rusian ruler and a daughter of a Polovcian ruler.[158] They were typically concluded after a military engagement between the two sides, and usually after a Rusian victory, such as the one by Svjatoslav Izjaslavič in 1068, which included the capture of a Polovcian ruler.[159] Thus, the situation may have been ripe for a marriage between the two sides. The death and burial of a "knjagina Vsevoložaja" is recorded under the year 1111.[160] Baumgarten has taken this to be the death of the second wife,[161] sometimes referred to as Anna because of a notation in the Xlebnikov codex.[162] With the notation that the evidence for the Polovcian identity of, and existence of, a second wife comes only from Tatiščev, I have included both marriages in the relevant tables of part 2.[163] However, such a decision must be considered provisional due to the lack of supporting information. It is unfortunate that the wife or wives of Vsevolod cannot be identified with more certainty, as the line he spawned, specifically Volodimer Monomax and his children, rose to such prominence and became key sponsors for the chronicles that record early Rusian history.[164]

Marriages: Generation Three

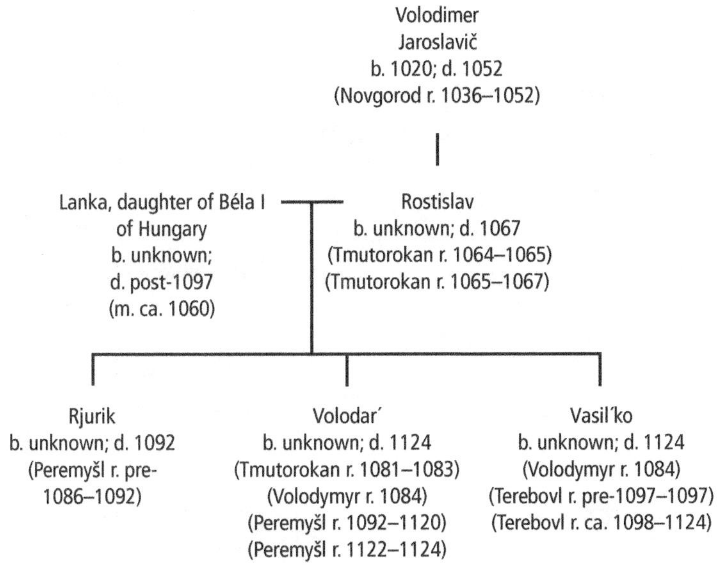

Rostislav Volodimerič
(tables 4, 18)

Rostislav Volodimerič was the eldest son of Volodimer, ruler of Novgorod, himself the eldest son of Jaroslav Mudryj, and so it seemed he would be destined for great things as the eldest son of the heir to the Kyivan throne. The actual result was that Rostislav was marginalized in the power politics of Rus′, as Volodimer predeceased Jaroslav by two years and thus Rostislav could not hope to rule Kyiv, or Rus′, through legitimate political measures. Despite this setback, Rostislav was still a grandson of Jaroslav Mudryj, a great-grandson of the first Volodimer, and, some have suggested, a ruler of Novgorod upon his father's death. Martin Dimnik, for instance, suggests that Izjaslav sent Ostromir as *posadnik* to Novgorod in 1055 to be his regent,[1] as Rostislav is nowhere listed as ruler of Novgorod, not even in the *NPL* listing of rulers of Novgorod that goes from the death of Volodimer to Izjaslav's placement of his son M´stislav.[2] Acknowledging the problems involved with this conclusion, it is certainly possible that he was ruler of Novgorod, even if only nominally as a minor after his father's death. However, without a clear primary source indicating such, I have not included him as a knjaz´ of Novgorod in part 2.

As an orphaned Volodimeroviči, and possibly a minor,[3] Rostislav's marital fate was determined by the head of his family, in this case Izjaslav, ruler of Kyiv. In 1060 the need for a new dynastic marriage arose, and as Izjaslav did not have a son of age, he turned to Rostislav to conclude this marriage.[4] As discussed in regard to Anastasija Jaroslavna, in 1060 Andrew of Hungary died, and Anastasija and her son Salomon were expelled to the German Empire, with Andrew's brother Béla taking over the throne.[5] Béla was closely tied to the Poles, as he had been living in Poland for many years and was married to a daughter of Mieszko II.[6] Though this made him Izjaslav's brother-in-law (Izjaslav and Béla's wives were sisters), as well as cousin (Izjaslav's aunt was Béla's mother), there was no direct marital connection between Béla and Rus´. More importantly, there was a strong connection between Béla's rival Salomon and Rus´. To this end, Izjaslav arranged the marriage of Béla's daughter Lanka and Rostislav of Novgorod, most likely early in 1060.[7] This marriage provided a direct tie between Rus´ and the new leadership in Hungary.

The marriage was only a few years old when Béla died in 1063 and Salomon regained the throne in Hungary. At the time it was made it was a necessary tie between the Volodimeroviči and a different branch of the Árpáds, and would potentially be important when Lanka's brothers Géza and Ladislaus took the throne as kings of Hungary. Rostislav died of poisoning after capturing Tmutorokan in 1066, but he left behind three sons, Rjurik,[8] Volodar´, and Vasil´ko.[9] Tatiščev records that after Rostislav's death, Lanka wanted to return with her children to Hungary, but Izjaslav would not allow her to go.[10] Because of the source, the information has to be taken with a grain of salt, but it seems a likely possibility. After the death of Svjatoslav Jaroslavič, his second wife, Oda of Stade, returned to her homeland with their son,[11] as did Jaropolk Izjaslavič's wife, Cunigunda, after his death.[12] Byzantine women often returned home after their dynastic marriages ended as well.[13] So it may be a possibility that Lanka wanted to do so, but that Izjaslav preferred to have her Rusian children stay in Rus´, and they were granted territories to hold in Galicia-Volyn´ when they came of age.

The two youngest sons, Volodar´ and Vasil´ko, would become famous when Svjatopolk Izjaslavič, as ruler of Kyiv, attempted to displace them from their territories at the end of the eleventh century. To do this, Svjatopolk called on his dynastic connections with the Hungarian ruler Koloman, the one point at which Lanka makes an appearance in the historical record by name. The *Chronica de gestis Hungarorum* records that Lanka, widow of a Rusian ruler, begged Koloman for mercy for her people.[14] This entry makes more sense when it is explained that Lanka was begging her nephew for the lives of her sons. Her attempt to play on familial ties was unsuccessful as "the King [Koloman] kicked and pushed her away, saying: 'It is not fitting that royal majesty should be defiled by the weeping of a woman.'"[15] She had the last laugh though—she prayed for help for her people and the Polovcians came and destroyed the Hungarians,[16] though cause and effect are hard to establish.

As with many women who married into Rus´, there are hardly any records of Lanka, and thus there is an incomplete picture of her in the historical record, but what can be determined has been shown here, including the reasons for her dynastic marriage to Rostislav and her role in her children's lives.

Vyšeslava Svjatoslavna
(tables 1, 6, 17)

The marriage of Vyšeslava to Bolesław II of Poland is recorded in the book of Jan Długosz,[17] as well as by Tatiščev,[18] both sources whose credibility has been questioned at one time or another. However, the marriage has largely been accepted in the secondary sources and will be considered here as plausible.[19]

Events in Rus´ were disordered in 1067 as Vseslav, ruler of Polack, captured Novgorod and some towns in the north and had to be driven out by the combined forces of Izjaslav, Svjatoslav, and Vsevolod. The situation was resolved in midsummer when Vseslav was captured and imprisoned in Kyiv.[20] Despite the relatively speedy solution to the problem recounted in the *PVL*, this internal chaos was probably the prime motivator for the marriage of Vyšeslava to Bolesław II. In order to join forces and march against Vseslav, the Jaroslaviči would have needed to secure their western border against threats. This same tactic had been used by both Bolesław I Chrobry, who made peace with the Germans to invade Rus´, and Koloman of Hungary, who made peace with the Poles to invade Rus´. As usual, an effective way of securing the agreement was a dynastic marriage. Unfortunately, Izjaslav did not have any daughters that he could use for this marriage agreement,

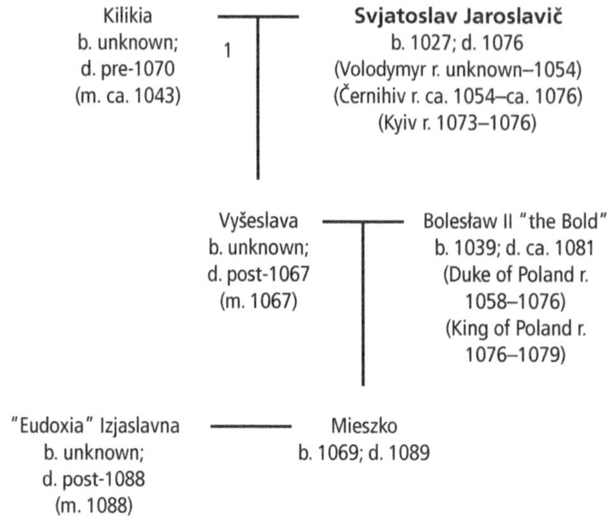

but his brother Svjatoslav did, and because it had to happen quickly, Vyšeslava was sent to Poland to marry Bolesław II.[21]

This was unfortunate for Izjaslav not in the short term, as the Jaroslaviči achieved their goal of a peaceful western border while they dealt with their internal troubles, but in the long term, as it would affect his political aspirations. In 1073 when Izjaslav was expelled by his brothers Svjatoslav and Vsevolod he went to Poland to his cousin/nephew Bolesław II, who promptly took his money and expelled him from the country. Why Bolesław would help Izjaslav in 1069 but not in 1073 has always been something of a mystery. But in 1069 Bolesław and Izjaslav were fighting against Vseslav as usurper. In 1073, the usurper was Svjatoslav, Bolesław's father-in-law. It is understandable that he would not want to fight against his own father-in-law, and that Svjatoslav was able to use this marital connection to his advantage and prevent the Poles from aiding the ousted Izjaslav. It was only after Svjatoslav's death at the end of 1076 that Bolesław aided Izjaslav in returning to the throne of Kyiv, once the conflict of interest, brought on by marital connections, was no more.[22]

The initial purpose of the marriage of Vyšeslava and Bolesław as a dynastic marriage for Rus´ was fulfilled in keeping the western border safe during a chaotic time. The familial context of the marriage, as a marriage with Svjatoslav's family, was also successful, as Svjatoslav was able to maintain control of Kyiv by denying Polish aid, via his son-in-law, to his enemy, something exiled Rusian rulers had often counted on.

Monomaxina of Byzantium
b. unknown; d. 1067
(m. ca. 1053)

1

Vsevolod Jaroslavič
b. 1030; d. 1093
(Perejaslav r. ca. 1054–1055)
(Kyiv r. 1077)
(Černihiv r. 1077–1078)
(Kyiv r. 1078–1093)

Gyða Haroldsdottir
b. unknown; d. 1107
(m. ca. 1074)

1

Volodimer "Monomax" Vsevolodič
b. 1053; d. 1125
(Smolensk r. ca. 1078–ca. 1095)
(Černihiv r. 1078–1094)
(Perejaslav r. 1094–1113)
(Kyiv r. ca. 1113–1125)

2

N. N.
b. unknown;
d. 1126
(m. 1108)

M′stislav "Harald"
b. 1076; d. 1132
(Novgorod r. 1095–1117)
(Bilhorod r. 1117–1125)
(Kyiv r. 1125–1132)

11 other children

Volodimer "Monomax" Vsevolodič
(tables 7, 12, 15, 16, 19, 20, 21)

Volodimer Monomax is one of the most well known rulers of Rus′, and there is good reason for this. Apart from his relatively peaceful reign and his victories against the Polovcians, he was an early sponsor of the chronicle tradition in Rus′, and was glorified by its authors.[23] Despite prominent mentions of him in the *PVL*, his wives are rarely mentioned at all. In fact, the Rusian chronicles only mention the deaths of two wives of Monomax, the first in 1107 and the second in 1126.[24] Neither entry includes a name, so it is unclear who each was when only the Rusian sources are considered.[25] This has resulted in confusion in some secondary sources, including Baumgarten's article, which lists wives for Volodimer as Gyða, an unknown woman, and a daughter of Aepa of the Polovcians.[26] The identity of the third wife results most likely from a misreading of the 1107 entry in the *PVL*, which states, "i poja Volodimer′ za Jurgja Aepinu d″ščer′" ("and Volodimer took the daughter of Aepa for Jurij [his son]"),[27] clearly indicating that it was Jurij who was to marry the daughter of Aepa. Instead, Baumgarten has both Volodimer and Jurij marrying daughters of Aepa, Volodimer before 1107 and Jurij in 1108,[28] despite the fact that it seems highly unlikely that father and son would both marry daughters of the same ruler to secure a relationship.[29]

The situation regarding Volodimer's marriages is extremely unclear in the *PVL*, and apart from Gyða, unmentioned in foreign sources. It is clear from the *PVL* that a wife of Volodimer died in 1107 and as the only recorded marriage thus far for Volodimer is to Gyða, it makes sense that this was she.[30] The next mention of a wife of Volodimer is at the death of one in 1126, whose identity is a mystery. Because of the complete lack of sources for Volodimer's second marriage and the unreliable nature of Baumgarten's report of a third marriage to a daughter of Aepa, ruler of a group of Polovcians, only the marriage of Gyða, for which there is substantial evidence, will be discussed in this section.

Thus the one marriage of Volodimer's that can be positively identified is his first marriage to Gyða, the daughter of Harold Godwinsson, the last Anglo-Saxon king of England. As we have seen, this marriage is not recorded in Rusian sources, but it is recorded in multiple Scandinavian sources. Saxo Grammaticus records that a daughter of Harold fled to Denmark with two of her brothers, and that Sven Estridsson took them in and at some point married Harold's daughter to Volodimer.[31] Sven and Harold were first cousins, and Gyða was in fact named after her grandmother, who was Sven's aunt.[32] The marriage of Volodimer to Harold's daughter is also included in the *Heimskringla*, where the genealogies of both parties are traced.[33] Though the marriage is established in primary sources, the date of the marriage is almost pure guesswork. Baumgarten, for an unknown reason, attributes it to 1070,[34] but the more commonly accepted date is 1074/5.[35] This date is based on the recorded birth of Volodimer's firstborn son, M´stislav, in 1076.[36] Normally scholars only suppose one year of marriage before the birth of a child, but as Saxo stipulated that it was Sven Estridsson who arranged the marriage and he died in 1074, the date has often been pushed back.

This date occurs at a very interesting time in Rusian history, and this has caused a number of theories to come to the fore in regard to the political motivations behind the marriage. Presumably working from independent angles, both Eric Christiansen in his 1980 edited translation of Saxo Grammaticus and A. V. Nazarenko in his 2001 book come to the conclusion that the purpose of the marriage was a political alliance between Denmark and Rus´, with the aim of consolidating Vsevolod and Svjatoslav's position with the German Empire and further buttressing the Rusian position against the Poles.[37] This was possible because of the close ties between Henry IV and Sven Estridsson, as well as the continuing conflict between the Piasts and the Danes at this time. Christiansen even goes so far as to advance the idea that perhaps Gyða went to Rus´ with Burchard's embassy in 1075,[38] which would represent an incredible coordination of an anti-Piast campaign across Europe. The only fault with this theory is the lack of positive evidence to support it. One would suspect that such a campaign, and the marriage, would have been included in the large number of stories told by Sven to Adam of Bremen, the prolific chronicler who was writing at this time. Adam's archbishop, Liemar, was also a close ally of Henry IV, even going so far as to be excommunicated by Pope Gregory VII because of his loyalty to Henry IV, and Sven was one of Adam's chief informants.[39] But nowhere does Adam record such planning, though there is mention of collaboration with the Danes against the Saxons in the 1070s. Nor does he record the marriage, though many other marriages are recorded. This, of course, does not invalidate any of the evidence provided elsewhere about the marriage, but it is important to note that it is not included in a major source on Scandinavian interkingdom relations of the time.

Gyða's influence in Rus´ can be seen in two particulars that lived on past her time. The first relates to her firstborn son, who in Rus´ was called M´stislav, but in Scandinavian sources he is known as Harold or Harald.[40] In this particular case the name's probable origin was Gyða's father, Harold Godwinsson.[41] While this could refer back to the early medieval policy of naming a child after the more dominant line of his parentage, it seems unlikely, as the Normans were firmly in control of England by the time of M´stislav's birth. Nevertheless, it is a clear reference to Gyða's natal family preserved in her marital family. The name Harold may also have given M´stislav more familiarity to the Scandinavians with whom he became related during his reign, as he married several daughters into Scandinavian royal houses.[42]

Gyða's influence was also felt in her husband's *Poučenie*, a common type of testament in Anglo-Saxon England, but heretofore unheard-of in Rus´.[43] It has been theorized that its very existence at this particular time is no coincidence, and represents the influence that Gyða and the Anglo-Saxon traditions she brought to Rus´ had on Volodimer Monomax. Whether or not this is true, it is nonetheless a fascinating document, and the only one of its kind for medieval Rus´.

The influence of foreign princesses in Rus´ is generally difficult to discern because of the lack of contemporaneous Rusian sources that mention them. This has left modern historians with the impression that foreign brides were swallowed up by Rus´ never to be heard from again, though the opposite is clearly true of Rusian brides going west. Fortunately, Gyða represents a particularly striking deviation from this example—her influence on Rus´ and on her husband left documentable traces.

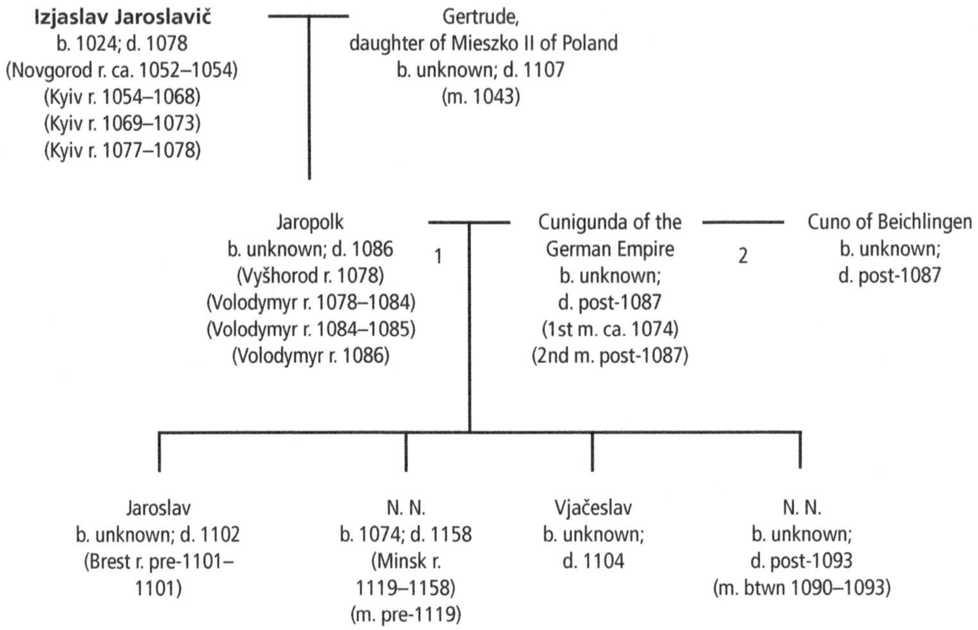

Jaropolk Izjaslavič
(tables 5, 19)

As was mentioned in the discussion of his father's, Izjaslav Jaroslavič's, dynastic marriage, Jaropolk fled Rus´ in 1073 with his father and mother and ended up at the court of Dedi, margrave of the Saxon Nordmark. The traditional wisdom is that while there, Izjaslav arranged a marriage between his son Jaropolk and one of Dedi's stepdaughters, Cunigunda, to seal an agreement in which Dedi would present Izjaslav and his case to Henry IV and use his influence to help Izjaslav. Recently, however, Nazarenko has suggested that this narrative may not be accurate. Instead, he suggests that the reason for going to Dedi's after fleeing Poland was because Jaropolk was already married to Cunigunda.[44] In this scenario, the marriage was made in 1073 as a counter to Svjatoslav's marriage to Oda of Stade, daughter of a rival of Dedi's, implying that the politics of the German Empire and Rus´ were intertwined and playing off one another.[45] This argument is persuasive, but contains problematic elements. The main, substantive, piece of evidence for this theory is the notice of the death of Jaropolk's daughter in the Hypatian Chronicle. It says that she died in 1158 and that she had lived for eighty-four years, placing her birth sometime in the year 1074.[46] With only this evidence it is possible to revise the estimate of Jaropolk and

Cunigunda's marriage to 1073 (or early 1074 at the latest). Izjaslav and his family did not leave Bolesław II's court until Easter 1074, making the timeline for the marriage and consummation quite quick if the daughter was born in 1074.[47] However, the idea that Jaropolk traveled to the German Empire in 1073, at the time of his father's expulsion, or slightly before, is entirely unsourced. Not to mention that it would be an amazing amount of good planning on Izjaslav's part, something that is difficult to accept, even though Izjaslav was a clever political actor in his foreign relations.[48] Despite these complications, the reason Nazarenko gives for the marriage can still be valid. Not only would an alliance with Dedi help Izjaslav to gain access to and potentially influence Henry IV, but it would also ally the Izjaslaviči with the enemies of Svjatoslav's marital kin. Thus the date for their marriage can be slightly altered, and the reasons for the dynastic marriage can be reconciled. Like many dynastic marriages, there turn out to be multiple reasons behind it.

Not much is recorded of the marriage of Jaropolk and Cunigunda. Saxo records the fact of their marriage in a listing of the history of Dedi's family, under the year 1062.[49] The Rusian chronicles do not record the marriage, but they note three of the children of the marriage, two sons who lived into the twelfth century, and the aforementioned daughter. Another daughter of the marriage returned with Cunigunda to the German Empire after Jaropolk's death in 1086, and was later married to Count Gunther of Keffenburg.[50]

The political success of the dynastic marriage depends on the interpretation of the cause of the marriage. Izjaslav was introduced to Henry IV by Dedi, and Henry IV did send an embassy to Svjatoslav at least to attempt a negotiation,[51] though the embassy may have been doomed to failure from the start because of the presence at its head of Svjatoslav's brother-in-law, Burchard, dean of Trier. However, Jaropolk's marriage with Cunigunda may also have been useful to him on his mission to Pope Gregory VII,[52] establishing the Izjaslaviči as tied to Latin Christians, and thus, potentially, loyal to the pope. It does not seem that there were further political considerations of their marriage after the successful return of the Izjaslaviči to Rus´ in 1077, though Cunigunda's influence may have been influential in Jaropolk's construction of the first Church of St. Peter to be built in Kyiv, which in turn led to the start of the cult of St. Peter in Rus´.[53] Whether or not there were long-term consequences to their dynastic marriage, it seems to have fulfilled its goal in the short term of helping Izjaslav regain the Kyivan throne. A secondary consequence was that Rusian children ended up with positions of prominence in both Rus´ and the German Empire.

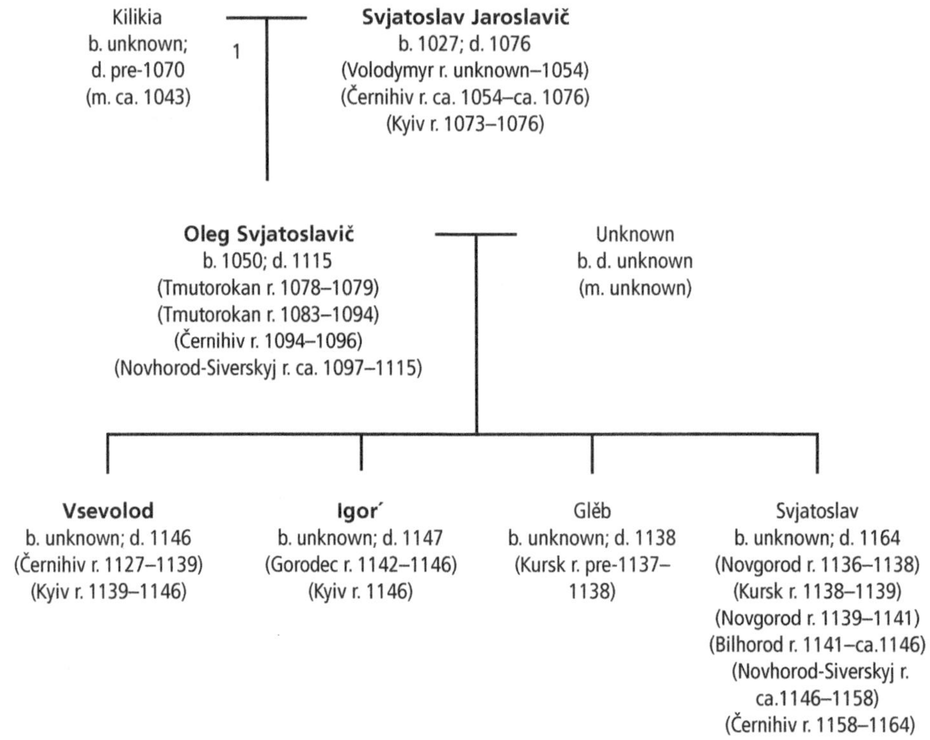

Oleg Svjatoslavič
(tables 6, 10)

In 1079 Oleg Svjatoslavič was ruler of Tmutorokan and a single man, as far as is known, when he was captured by the Khazars and shipped to Constantinople.[54] Abbot Daniil, on his trip to the Holy Land early in the twelfth century, noted that Oleg had lived on the island of Rhodes for two years.[55] Oleg appears in the *PVL* again four years later, when he makes his successful return to Tmutorokan in 1083 and does away with his enemies.[56] After his return from exile, most likely, he had a child who was named Vsevolod, indicating that there was a woman involved in his life, but who she was exactly is unknown.

There are theories that postulate a wife for Oleg, particularly a Byzantine one named Theophano Mouzalonissa, based upon a few pieces of evidence.[57] A copy of the *Ljubeč Sinodik* records a Michael (Oleg's Christian name)[58] of Černihiv married to a Theophano, and a seal bearing the inscription, "Theofano Muzalonissa, archontissa of Rus´" have provided the basis for the identities of those involved in this marriage.[59] Alexander Każdan, whose analysis of Rus´-Byzantine marriages is an important corrective to Baumgarten's Byzantine inflation, disagrees with the very existence of this marriage, however.[60] In his analysis of the marriage Každan admits that he once accepted the marriage, but that he ultimately could not maintain that opinion due to three main factors. One was the character and quality of Loparev's scholarship. The second was problems with the *Sinodik* itself, including the late date of the version of the *Sinodik* in which the name "Michael" was found, its accompanying absence in earlier versions of the *Sinodik*, and the identification in another *Sinodik* of Theophano and a Michael being married in the thirteenth century. Third is the Byzantine evidence, or lack thereof; for instance, the marriage itself is absent in any Byzantine source; the fact that the Mouzalon family was prominent in the thirteenth century, not the eleventh; and that the seal actual reads "Rosia" which has been identified both with Rus´ and with a "settlement near Matracha."[61] For all of these reasons, persuasively stated and argued, Každan was unable to accept the existence of this marriage.

In sum, I accept Každan's analysis of the problems inherent in this marriage, despite Dimnik's own fascinating arguments about this marriage, especially in regard to the dynastic importance of Oleg and the Svjatoslaviči line.[62] Due to the widespread acceptance of this marriage, I have included a note about it here to explain its absence from the genealogical tables of part 2.

Evpraksija Vsevolodovna
(tables 7, 19)

One of the most interesting marital alliances made in the eleventh century was between Rus´ and the German Empire. This marriage is a showpiece in the history of Rusian dynastic marriage, as there are numerous sources that discuss Evpraksija as well as the incredible fame of her second husband and the accord she received in Rus´. This entry is thus longer than the majority to account for both the importance of this marriage as well as the fact that there is so much information available.

The alliance between Rus´ and the German Empire was made through the union of three people, not the usual two. On the Rusian side was the daughter of Vsevolod Jaroslavič of Kyiv, Evpraksija, and on the side of the German Empire was the emperor himself, Henry IV. The first marriage arranged was brokered by Henry IV, but as he was married at the time, Evpraksija was married to the young Henry III "the Long" of Stade, margrave of the Saxon Nordmark.[63] Upon the death of both Margrave Henry of Stade and Henry IV's wife, Henry IV renewed his alliance with Rus´ by marrying Evpraksija himself.[64] Many reasons have been put forward for the strategy behind such a marriage. German historians, focusing on internal concerns, concluded that the marriage of Henry IV to Evpraksija was meant to placate the Saxon

Vsevolod Jaroslavič
b. 1030; d. 1093
(Perejaslav r. ca. 1054–1055)
(Kyiv r. 1077)
(Černihiv r. 1077–1078)
(Kyiv r. 1078–1093)

— 2 —

N. N. "Anna" of the Polovcians
b. unknown; d. 1111
(m. ca. 1067)

Henry III "the Long" of Stade b. unknown; d. 1087 (Margrave of Saxon Nordmark r. ca. 1082–1087)	1	Evpraksija b. 1071; d. 1109 (1st m. ca. 1082) (2nd m. 1089)	2	Henry IV of the German Empire b. ca. 1050; d. 1106 (King of the German Empire r. 1056–1106) (Emperor 1084–1106)

nobles, who, as was often the case, were nearing revolt.[65] However, despite the fact that she was the widow of a Saxon margrave, because of her foreign origins and childless marriage to Margrave Henry it is highly doubtful that the Saxons would have looked upon her as one of their own. To understand this marriage, one must look outside of the boundaries of the German Empire and examine the world of interkingdom politics that spawned most of these marriages. The most convincing rationale for the marriage alliance has been proposed by Nazarenko,[66] who posits a complex theory in which Henry IV's goal was to increase the power of his newly elected antipope, Clement III, as well as to cause trouble for the Poles (a consistent interest for the German emperors). For Vsevolod the alliance was important not only for prestige, but also to combat domestic problems. The Izjaslaviči had closely allied themselves with the Poles, both through marriage and through their territorial associations on the western fringes of Rus´.[67] Throughout Vsevolod's reign, various Izjaslaviči attempted to take back their father's throne and received Polish assistance. An alliance between the German Empire and Rus´, specifically with Vsevolod, who was ruling Kyiv at the time, would put Poland between allies, and allow those allies to put pressure on both Poland's eastern and western borders. This alliance would limit the support that the Poles could give to any Rusian usurpers—chiefly the Izjaslaviči. The alliance would also allow Clement III a chance to draw Rus´ into his fold, thus increasing his own political and ecclesiastical power.[68]

In the early 1080s Henry IV was still married and thus could not conclude a marriage for himself. Instead, he married the Rusian princess to the young margrave, Henry of Stade. The rank and prestige of the margrave of the Saxon Nordmark would have shown Vsevolod that Henry IV was serious about the alliance, and this match may have been kind to both parties, as Henry of Stade was not much older than Evpraksija. However, when Henry of Stade died, the bond holding the alliance together was in danger, and it was only with the death of Empress Bertha that Henry IV saw the way to reaffirm the alliance—he would marry Evpraksija himself. This theory seems the most reasonable for this discussion, as it places the marriages in the context of the European political scheme as a whole and reflects the importance and even necessity of dynastic marriages as a key component of politics.

Evpraksija's life in Rus´ before her marriage is a mystery. When her marriage to Henry of Stade took place is not known, but it is believed that she was still quite young. The first mention of it is in *Annalista Saxo* under the year 1082.[69] This is the year that Henry of Stade inherited the Nordmark after the death of his father, and his wife is listed as "Evpraksija, daughter of the king of Rus´,[70] who in our language is called Adelheid,"[71] though the chronicle was written later and may possibly backdate the marriage to Henry of Stade's inheritance of the mark. The dating is further complicated by issues of the proper age of marriage, whether or not this was observed, and many other details that are specific to the era of the marriage and not generally relevant here for the purposes of discussing the marriage as a whole.[72]

Though the exact date of the marriage is not recorded, Evpraksija's arrival in the German Empire is; she "arrived in this country with much pomp, with camels burdened with precious clothes and stones, and also with countless riches."[73] This brief account of her arrival gives the historian an invaluable piece of evidence regarding the manner of travel, not just of Rusian princesses but generally of princesses in the medieval world.[74] The Rusian princess did not arrive alone and unheralded, but rather with ceremony and a rich entourage emphasizing her royal position and the honor that the Rusians expected would be paid to her. With her came also many riches, some surely as dowry, but some also perhaps to maintain Evpraksija in her marriage. It was a tradition in the Ottonian and Salian royal houses to gift their wives with land (often the same land generation after generation) so that they could use that income for their own purposes.[75] Women in the middle ages often had their own means. This money would allow her to maintain her own household staff, who were undoubtedly part of the entourage she brought with her from Rus´.[76]

The marriage did not last long, as Henry of Stade died in 1087.[77] Upon his death, Evpraksija was left an approximately sixteen-year-old widow with no children. Key to her well-being, or lack thereof, was her childless state. With a son, Evpraksija would have inherited the mark on his behalf and been his regent or part of the regency in general.[78]

However, with no children, Henry of Stade's brother inherited the mark and forced Evpraksija to leave.[79]

Evpraksija took refuge in the Abbey of Quedlinburg,[80] where the abbess was Adelheid, sister to Emperor Henry IV. Evpraksija is mentioned as being there in the summer of 1088, at which time she was already engaged to the emperor.[81] At this point, it had been a year since the death of Henry of Stade and six months since the death of Henry IV's wife, Empress Bertha. Evpraksija's reasons for remarrying are clear-cut: although women in this period exercised their influence and held power, it was more accepted that they would do this through men or through a lack of men as nuns in nunneries. Thus, without a son and with no monastic desire as yet, she was virtually obligated to remarry.[82] The reasons for her family to encourage, or force, such a remarriage are discussed elsewhere.[83]

Widely discussed in relation to this marriage is the *Canonical Responses of Metropolitan Ioann II*, written in the second half of the 1080s. In article 13, Ioann II scolds the Rusian rulers for marrying their daughters outside of the faith.[84] Though he does not explicitly name the Latins, it is the most common inference.[85] Volodimeroviči men themselves married either Latins, or more rarely Polovcians (presumably Christianized), and they married their daughters chiefly to Latin nobles.[86] Ioann II certainly had knowledge of the German marriages of Evpraksija, as antipope Clement III contacted him at Henry IV's behest about a union of the churches under the auspices of Clement III. Ioann II, however, rebuked him in a letter that is extant, and directed Clement III to discuss the matter with the patriarch of Constantinople.[87] Though the initiative failed, the contact served as one of the reasons behind Henry IV's desired alliance with Rus´. The attempt itself shows Rus´ as a viable player in the European political situation of the eleventh century, and that the dynastic marriage connection did breed further connections, or at least attempts at them.

Henry IV and Evpraksija were married in the summer of 1089 in Cologne by Archbishop Hartwig of Magdeburg. As the chronicler Ekkehard records, "The Emperor celebrated, in Cologne, his wedding, taking to wife the widow of Margrave Udo [Henry III][88] the daughter of the king of the Rusians."[89] After the marriage ceremony, Evpraksija Vsevolodovna was crowned empress of the German Empire under the name Adelheid.[90] This was momentous for Rus´ as well as for Evpraksija. In the generation before her, Rusian women had been the queens of France, Poland, Hungary, and Norway.[91] However, by the time of her coronation Evpraksija was the only Rusian queen in Europe outside of Rus´, and she was not only queen, but empress. This made her the most visible Rusian, male or female, for the majority of Europe. It is impossible to say from this remove whether or not this was how she thought of herself, but it can be safely assumed that this was how she was seen by many of the nobility of Europe. In nearly every chronicle entry in which she appears, she is listed as the daughter of the king of the Rusians. Thus, irrespective of their familiarity with Evpraksija, the chroniclers, and perhaps the nobles, constantly remembered Evpraksija's kingdom of origin. This made Evpraksija the chief ambassador for Rus′ in the West in the late eleventh century.

Due to lingering frustration with Henry IV and Archbishop Hartwig, some of the German nobles evinced discontent with Evpraksija. This discontent was more directed at Henry IV and his style of rule, but when considered along with their later marital discord, has led some historians to conclude that Henry IV and Evpraksija's marriage was rocky from the start.[92] There is no evidence to make this claim, but it is clear that within a few years the marriage effectively dissolved. The reasons for this dissolution are also unclear despite the fact that extant are Evpraksia's stated reasons for ending the marriage with Henry IV. It is unlikely that these stories are true, however, as they were crafted by pro-papacy (anti–Henry IV) polemicists in the pay of Duke Welf of Swabia and Countess Mathilda of Tuscany, with whom Evpraksija would later ally herself.[93]

These stories describe Henry IV, with references to the book of Revelation, as a Nicoletian,[94] a member of a sect that practiced sexually "deviant" acts and held orgies. This was not the first time such charges had been brought against Henry IV; in the 1070s he briefly separated from his first wife, Bertha, and she, also in the company of pro-papacy forces, brought such charges against him.[95] In Evpraksija's version, she at first participated in such rites out of naïveté and love for her husband. However, once she found herself pregnant and unable to determine who was the father of the baby, she was filled with disgust and a resolve to do something.[96] This resolve translated into leaving her husband and joining the propapacy side of Mathilda of Tuscany.[97]

The pregnancy aspect of the story may have been true and may thus account for the estrangement between Henry IV and Evpraksija. In Mathilda's *Vita*, it is recorded that in 1092 the son of Henry IV died during the siege of the castle of Montebelle.[98] As the deaths of Henry IV's children by Bertha are all reliably attested elsewhere and generally occurred much later, this could only be a child by Evpraksija (or by a mistress). But as the only reference to the child exists in Mathilda's *Vita*, it is unsure whether this was corroborating evidence added for the polemical attack on Henry IV, or the truth.

Evpraksija's tale of victimization at the hands of her emperor-husband is a sad story of the mistreatment of a young woman by a powerful man. Even though it is widely regarded as false now,[99] the story sold wonderfully to the bishops of Europe, whom the pope was attempting to woo to his side in his ongoing struggles with Henry IV. The first venue for this story was at a council of bishops in Swabia in 1094. After hearing Evpraksija's story (whether Evpraksija read it herself or it was read on her behalf is unknown)[100] the attendant bishops found Henry IV guilty, and placed themselves firmly on the pope's side.[101] It is also on this occasion that Evpraksija first met Pope Urban II. Urban II then asked her to speak at his first papal synod, which he was convening in Piacenza the following year. 1095 found Evpraksija in Piacenza personally telling her story to the assembled bishops.[102] This was a major coup for the pope—he had garnered Henry IV's own wife to testify against him at the first papal synod of Urban II's pontificate.

Modern historians, those of Rus´ in particular, must share the pope's excitement, though for different reasons. In the modern era, the common picture of Rus´ is still one of a northern province of Byzantium, generally cut off from the rest of Europe. However, in 1095, a Rusian princess was the main event at a papal synod held in Italy, at which she addressed a crowd of Latin bishops from France, the German Empire, Italy, and Burgundy.[103] Moreover, she was not even the only Rusian on the synod's agenda. During their week of meetings, they also dealt with Evpraksija's first cousin, King Philip I of France, and his marital foibles.[104] This occurrence must add more than a footnote to our understanding of Rusian and European history of this period. Like other events in the life of Evpraksija, it demonstrates the continuing presence of Rusians throughout Europe.

After the synod, the papal side was momentarily victorious in their battle with Henry IV and they felt that they had no more need for Evpraksija. She managed to stay another two years in Italy, living with her stepson King Conrad of Lombardy,[105] who had himself joined the papal side soon after Evpraksija.[106] But in approximately 1097, she decided to return to Rus´.[107]

At this point, Evpraksija generally drops out of the chronicles for a few years as she journeys back to Rus´ and gets settled there. Gerhoha, who had chronicled Evpraksija's anti-Henry polemics, states that she went first to Hungary to stay with relatives.[108] She would have found family in Hungary had she gone there, first cousins who she had most likely never met and also possibly her aunt, Anastasija Jaroslavna (if she were still living). But Rusian-Hungarian ties were well developed at the end of the eleventh century, and it made sense for her to pass that way on her route back to Rus´.

Two particular assumptions need to be made and stated about this trip. The first is that Evpraksija was not alone. Evpraksija was born a Rusian princess and had most recently been the German empress. She most assuredly had attendants with whom she would travel. Therefore, despite the fact that she is spoken of in the singular, she represents her entire party, as would be the case with other European nobility of the time. The second assumption is that Evpraksija had money. To travel one requires it, and she had a long way to travel to return to Kyiv. Thus, our picture is not of a destitute woman traveling alone through Europe, but of an empress returning to her homeland.

S. P. Rozanov peppers his account of Evpraksija's return to Rus´ with interesting anecdotes and theories about her reception and a possible foray into political life, none of which is recorded in the sources.[109] The first mention of Evpraksija in the *PVL* is under the year 1106, where on "6 December, Evpraksija, daughter of Vsevolod, took monastic vows."[110] As this was approximately four months after her husband Emperor Henry IV died (7 August), it seems clear that Evpraksija was awaiting the death of her husband to take her next step in life and join a nunnery. This may show Evpraksija's devotion to her marital vows. She never married again and waited to enter into monastic life until after the death of her husband. Despite her entry into a nunnery in Rus´, she did not pass out of the purview of the Latin chroniclers who recorded her entrance into the nunnery.[111] Interestingly enough, they also recorded that she became the abbess there, but as the Rusian sources do not record which abbey she joined, it is impossible to say whether she was the abbess or not.[112]

Evpraksija served in the nunnery for three years until her death in 1109. Her death was recorded in the *PVL*, and she was buried in the Caves Monastery.[113] At her death, multiple honors were bestowed upon Evpraksija. The first is historical. Few women are mentioned by name in the Rusian chronicles of this period. For instance, neither Evpraksija's birth nor her marriages were recorded. Yet her taking monastic vows and her death merited a place for her in the chronicle under her own name.[114] This is a singular honor, as the majority of women who do get mentioned in the Rusian chronicles are identified only as "daughter of" or "sister of." The other honor was contemporary. Both Evpraksija's mother and her sister Janka were buried in the Andreevskij nunnery,[115] while Evpraksija was awarded a burial and the erection of her own chapel in the premier monastery in Rus´—the Caves Monastery. The few records extant from this time do not record numerous burials in the Caves Monastery and very few of those are women. Thus, the honor bestowed upon Evpraksija was significant.

To what, or whom, should these honors be attributed? The easiest assumption is that it was the doing of her brother Volodimer Monomax, but there are multiple problems with this association. The first is that he was not ruler in Kyiv until four years after Evpraksija's death, thus he may not have had the political might to arrange Evpraksija's burial. If he did have that kind of power, why did he not use it for the burial of his other sister Janka, or for his stepmother?[116] He may have been responsible for the chronicle entries, as his chronicle writing had begun by this period, but it seems unlikely that he was responsible for Evpraksija's chapel. Another suspect is the ruler of Kyiv, Svjatopolk Izjaslavič. He was, however, no friend to the line of Vsevolod, and Evpraksija's whole sojourn in the West might have been arranged to thwart his plans to achieve the throne of Kyiv. The final candidates for motivating force are the monks of the Caves Monastery. The Caves Monastery was the most venerated monastery in Rus´ in this period, which allowed the monks to occasionally flout the will of the Volodimeroviči knjazja and the Byzantine Church.[117] That they would choose to honor Evpraksija in such a manner shows that she was honored in Rus´ and received a fitting burial for an empress. This honorable burial, and her monastic commitment, would also indicate that the monks had no problem with her stay in Latin lands, her two marriages to Latin men, or her participation in a papal synod.

The story of Evpraksija's life highlights many of the problems inherent with examining the stories of Rusian women in this period. As far as the Rusian sources show, she only appears in 1106, three years before her death as a princess taking monastic vows, and then in 1109 as a dead nun who receives an honorable burial in the Caves Monastery.[118] There is no context for understanding anything about her life as the empress of the German Empire, or any other aspect of her life, for that matter. It is only by combining the Latin sources with the Rusian that the historian achieves a more complete understanding of her life. She arrived in the German Empire with pomp and circumstance[119] and she left the world in the same way.[120] But only by looking at a variety of sources from across Europe can one begin to get a true picture of her life. That picture is then fleshed out with the help of contemporary portraits of European princesses, brides, widows, and nuns to understand more of what Evpraksija experienced. Her life and marriages are not typical of the dynastic marriage tradition, but they are well illustrated and very relevant to our picture of what was going on in Rusian interkingdom relations in the later eleventh century.

Eudoxia Izjaslavna
(tables 5, 6)

The name of the daughter of Izjaslav Jaroslavič is not properly known, but she is called Eudoxia because of a brief reference to that name in a version of Długosz's chronicle, one of the only sources for her marriage.[121] As with many other Rusian royal daughters, she is not mentioned at all in the *PVL*. However, due to her marriage to a Polish prince, her existence, and I would argue her identity, are known and the knowledge of her dynastic marriage has survived.[122]

Izjaslav Jaroslavič
b. 1024; d. 1078
(Novgorod r. ca. 1052–1054)
(Kyiv r. 1054–1068)
(Kyiv r. 1069–1073)
(Kyiv r. 1077–1078)

Gertrude,
daughter of Mieszko II of Poland
b. unknown; d. 1107
(m. 1043)

"Eudoxia"
b. unknown;
d. post-1088
(m. 1088)

Mieszko, son of
Bolesław II of Poland
b. 1069; d. 1089

In 1088 both Władysław Herman, duke of Poland, and his nephew Mieszko, son of Bolesław II of Poland, took brides. This was the third marriage for Władysław, but only the first for Mieszko, who was nineteen and was called back from Hungary expressly for the purpose. He had been living in Hungary, raised by King Ladislaus, since his father Bolesław II's death in exile there between 1079 and 1081.[123] Władysław called his nephew back from Hungary because the Rusians wanted to make a dynastic marriage with the Poles,[124] and he was already set to marry Judith, the widow of Salomon of Hungary and the daughter of Emperor Henry III. Długosz, in his chronicle, expressly refers to the fact that Svjatopolk Izjaslavič had long held an interest in dynastic marriage, one of the few such overt references on the subject.[125] While her name is not known, Gallus Anonymous refers to Mieszko's bride as "a girl from Ruthenia,"[126] while Długosz is more explicit: "the sister of Duke Svjatopolk of Kyiv."[127] Unfortunately, nothing more is known of this Izjaslavna, as Mieszko died (possibly poisoned) the next year in 1089,[128] and his line passed out of the Polish chronicles. It is possible to assume that Eudoxia returned home to Kyiv to live or potentially joined a nunnery,[129] but the Rusian chronicles maintained their silence in regard to women and her fate is unknown.

The most notable feature of this marriage is the fact that one chronicler records explicitly the purpose of the wedding as the creation of ties with the neighboring kingdom of Rus´. However, the question remains, who arranged the marriage and why? In 1088 Vsevolod Jaroslavič, not Svjatopolk, was ruling in Kyiv, and only a few years before, Svjatopolk's brother Jaropolk had fled to Poland after rising up against Vsevolod. Jaropolk may have even attempted to press Władysław Herman for assistance in claiming the throne of Kyiv, and only returned to make peace when that failed. Vsevolod then may have wanted to make an agreement with Władysław to prevent such things from happening in the future, but if so, an Izjaslaviči would not have been the instrument he would have chosen. Which leads us to the other occurrence of 1088: following his brother's death in 1087, Svjatopolk moved from Novgorod, a premier spot in the realm, to Turov, perhaps the family seat but still less prestigious than Novgorod, though much closer to Kyiv.[130] The speculation of historians on this move has generally led to the consensus that he wanted to solidify his familial power base at Turov and be near to Kyiv should old age finally claim Vsevolod. A marriage tie with Władysław Herman would enhance Svjatopolk's position by reinforcing his Izjaslaviči relations with their most powerful ally, as well as perhaps keeping his back safe should he attempt to move on Kyiv. This reasoning is admittedly speculative, but the marriage of an Izjaslavna and a Polish prince at this time fits the political situation within Rus´ in such a manner that it seems to be a logical conclusion.

Svjatopolk Izjaslavič

(tables 5, 9, 17, 18, 21)

Unrelated to the disputed parentage of Svjatopolk are his own marital questions. Baumgarten lists three marriages for Svjatopolk, or at least three women whom he was with at some time.[131] The first was a concubine, the second was a daughter of Tugorkhan, and the third was a woman identified as "Barbe Comnène," presumably the daughter of a Comneni emperor of Byzantium.[132] This idea of a Comnena marrying a Rusian ruler stems from a twelfth-century German chronicle, the *Ortliebi Zwifaltensis Chronicon*, in which it says that a Byzantine emperor gave his daughter in marriage to a king of the Rusians.[133] An editor's note identifies the king as Svjatopolk, but here there is no mention of which Byzantine emperor it was. Alexander Každan addresses this marriage briefly in his work on Rus´-Byzantine marriages, and finds that the assumption among historians was that the emperor was Alexius Comnenus, and that in fact he had no daughter named Barbara.[134] The attribution of the name Barbara first appears only in the seventeenth century, connected with the relics of the Christian martyr Barbara.[135] It seems unlikely that such a marriage would have occurred at this time without any corresponding record in either Byzantium or Rus´, and so it must be dismissed.

The evidence for Svjatopolk's concubine is also thin, but seems much more reasonable, though Baumgarten's assertion that all of the children were born from an "ancienne concubine" is unacceptable.[136] Baumgarten has this concubine dying in 1094 or earlier, and then has Svjatopolk going on to have two more marriages and live another nearly twenty years. Jan Długosz wrote explicitly that M´stislav Svjatopolčič was the son of Svjatopolk and a concubine and that Jaroslav was his brother,[137] while M´stislav is placed by Baumgarten outside

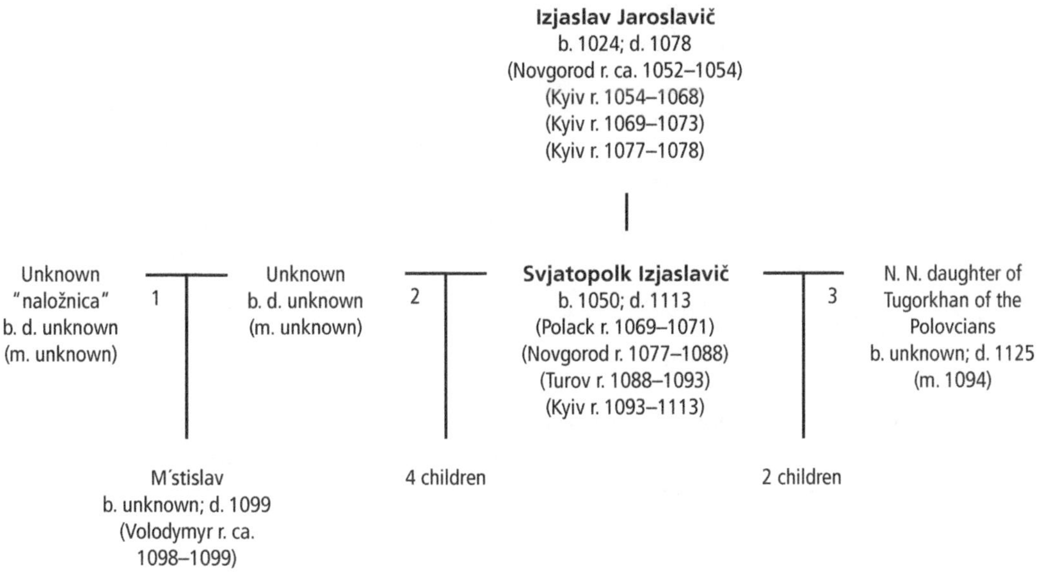

of the rest of the children and thus presumably prior to the arrival of the "ancienne concubine."[138] Both of these writings probably draw, in their own way, on the account of the "Blinding of Vasil′ko" in the *PVL*, where M′stislav is referred to as the son of a concubine (*naložnica*) and Jaroslav a few sentences later is simply the "son of Svjatopolk."[139] Adding fuel to this fire is Długosz's confusion of dates, where he places the union of Tugorkhan's daughter and Svjatopolk in 1086,[140] thus giving Svjatopolk eight fewer years with his concubine. As there is so little evidence here, the best course seems to be to acknowledge that Svjatopolk had at least one concubine that bore him a child or children, specifically M′stislav. Concubinage was well known in Rus′ and medieval Europe in general, if not always accepted. The identity of the mother of Svjatopolk's other children is unknown, but using tentative birth dates for the women based upon their marital dates, we can postulate that Marija and Brjačeslav were born of the daughter of Tugorkhan, while the other children came from a previous relationship. What that relationship was, or who it was with, are still unknown. The situation is complicated further by the *PVL* referring to Jaroslav simply as the "son of Svjatopolk," after the reference to M′stislav as the son of a concubine. Sadly, our sources do not provide us with an answer, or even enough material to conjecture.

Svjatopolk's first known marriage was with a daughter of Tugorkhan, which the *PVL* dates to 1094 as part of a peace arrangement with the Polovcians.[141] As the *PVL* was already a living document at this date, it seems more likely to be correct than Długosz's 1086 date, which is from a much later source.[142] This dynastic marriage sealed the agreement with the Polovcians in ways that a simple handshake deal could not; such marriages were beginning to be used more often for Rusian agreements with the steppe peoples at this time, as they had been with Christian kingdoms for over a century. This system, and the peace, broke down only two years later when Tugorkhan, identified in the *PVL* as Svjatopolk's "test′" (wife's father, father-in-law), attacked Perejaslav.[143] He was killed in the fighting and Svjatopolk brought his body back to Kyiv for burial because of his familial connections to him.[144] This shows that despite Tugorkhan's disregard for this particular agreement, Svjatopolk acknowledged his kin obligations, and perhaps would have honored the agreement he had made, as he treated his father-in-law's body with respect. As has been shown with reference to Každan, the marriage to Barbe Comnène most likely did not occur, thus the listing for the death of "knjagyni Svjatopolčaja" in 1125[145] seems to be for this steppe princess, barring another marriage about which nothing is known. The question of which children belong to which woman is a question that is impossible to answer with the available evidence. The *PVL* occasionally mentions parentage, such as in the case of Volodimer's children, but we have not been so fortunate for information on the parentage of Svjatopolk's many children.

The question of what constitutes marriage occurs in regard to this union between Svjatopolk and the daughter of Tugorkhan as well. The Hypatian Chronicle says that Svjatopolk "poja sobě ženu" (took as wife) the daughter of Tugorkhan, and that has been the accepted state of affairs.[146] However, Długosz says that Svjatopolk took her "in consortem,"[147] not in uxorem, or in matrimonium as a wife, but as a "sharer" or "partner," a consort. The existence of the two statements in regard to the union presents an interesting question, but unfortunately one that cannot be definitively answered. Długosz, though writing from many sources, wrote much later than these events, and he may have interpreted them through his own cultural lens in which a Christian Rusian could take a pagan steppe princess as a consort but not as a wife, but we have no way of knowing. However, the question is one that should be open for consideration since so little is known about marriages between pagans or of pagans with Christians, except the Church's prohibition on the latter.

Marriages: Generation Four

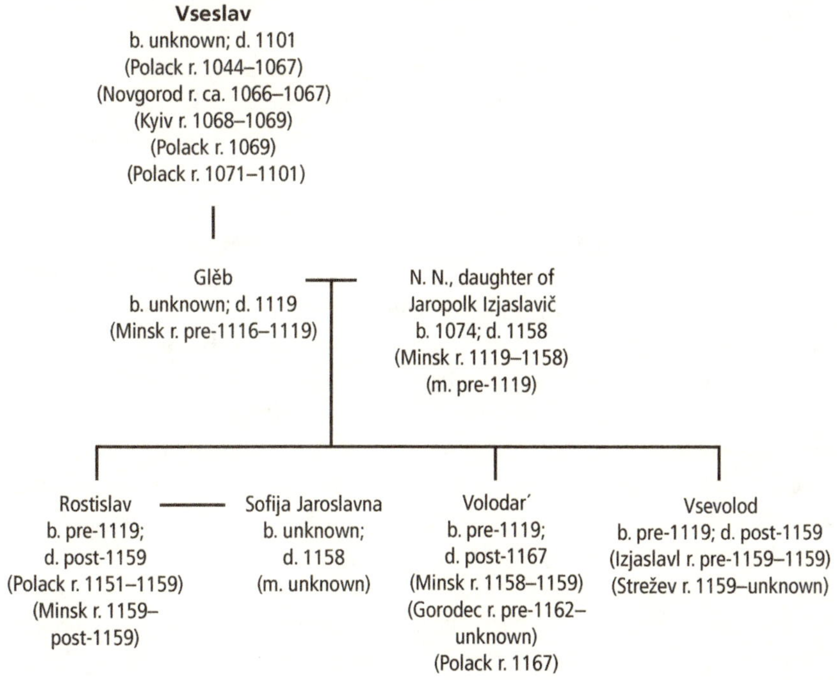

Glĕb Vseslavič
(tables 2, 5)

The marriage of Glĕb Vseslavič and a daughter of Jaropolk Izjaslavič exemplifies the lacunae that exist in studying Rusian history. The marriage is recorded only upon the death of the Jaropolkovna in 1158, approximately forty years after her husband's death.[1] The Hypatian Chronicle provides a glowing recollection of her, including the donations that she and her husband made to various monasteries and her burial in the Caves Monastery in Kyiv. It also notes that after Glĕb's death she donated additional money, as well as leaving money in her will, all incredibly rare details about women in Rus´, even royal women. The rarest and most interesting detail only increases our curiousity about the marriage, that upon Glěb's death, the Jaropolkovna took over as ruler of Minsk and ruled for forty years until her own death.[2] Apart from Ol´ga in the tenth century there are very few other examples of female rulers in Rus´, and none for long.[3]

All of this interesting detail aside, however, there is very little information to allow for a discussion of the marriage itself. The Jaropolkovna was born in approximately 1074,[4] and given typical practices would have been married by 1094 at the latest. Her father Jaropolk Izjaslavič died in 1086,[5] potentially before arranging her marriage, which would have left the arrangement in the hands of her uncle Svjatopolk. Glěb enters the chronicle record only a couple of times: his rule in Minsk is noted in 1116 in relation to raiding of the Smolensk lands, and his death is recorded in 1119, following his defeat and capture by Volodimer Monomax.[6] The politics of that period are understood in relation to Kyiv and the seekers for its throne, the Vsevolodoviči, Izjaslaviči, and Svjatoslaviči, but the Polack rulers, of which Glěb was one, are absent from the chronicle records of those struggles. As such, there is little basis for discussion, beyond noting two items. First, Turov, ruled by her uncle Svjatopolk, Volodymyr, which had been ruled by her father, and Polack are all territories that border one another, which is often enough cause to build relationships. This might especially be true to overcome any legacy of bitterness between the heirs of Izjaslav Jaroslavič, and Vseslav Brjačeslavič, Izjaslav's usurper.[7] Second, both the Vseslaviči and the Izjaslaviči were opposed to the Vsevolodiči, the patriarch of which family ruled in Kyiv until 1093, as indicated by Jaropolk's many fights with Vsevolod and his son Volodimer, and Glěb Vseslavič's later conflicts with Volodimer. These two reasons may be enough to explain the marriage, but it should be acknowledged that there are many lacunae in our sources, and though we might want to know the history of this marriage and especially the remarkable Jaropolkovna, there is very little information to go on.

The last item to note about this marriage is that it is the first intra-Volodimeroviči dynastic marriage. The line of Izjaslav Volodimerič was the most distant from the main Jaroslaviči lines that dominate the story of Kyivan Rus´.[8] That genealogical separation allowed for a rebuilding of ties in the seventh generation, counting in the traditional Roman model of consanguinity that was followed in both Constantinople and the West (though the Roman Church changed the model in this period and it was only returned the Roman model in 1215).[9] Though at the outer limits of consanguinity, this was the first time the Volodimeroviči had been plentiful, and divided, enough to make dynastic marriages with their own kin. Following this, the house of Polack would often be a source for such internal Rusian dynastic marriages as the descendants of Jaroslav Volodimerič vied with one another for supremacy in Rus´.

Lanka, daughter of Béla I of Hungary
b. unknown;
d. post-1097
(m. ca. 1060)

Rostislav
b. unknown; d. 1067
(Tmutorokan r. 1064–1065)
(Tmutorokan r. 1065–1067)

Volodar´
b. unknown; d. 1124
(Tmutorokan r. 1081–1083)
(Volodymyr r. 1084)
(Peremyšl r. 1092–1120)
(Peremyšl r. 1122–1124)

Unknown
b. d. unknown
(m. unknown)

4 children

Volodar´ Rostislavič
(tables 4, 18, 20)

This marriage exists in Baumgarten's genealogy,[10] but his only citation is to an older article of his own. In that article, Baumgarten says explicitly that Volodar's wife's identity is unknown, though some have suggested the name Laura.[11] I have been able to find no other evidence of a marriage between Volodar´ and a princess of Pomerania, so at this time this marriage cannot be accepted, though it must be noted that he does have children, and as such there must have been a partner of some sort.[12]

Jaroslav Svjatopolčič
(tables 9, 13, 17, 18)

Jaroslav was the second son of Svjatopolk Izjaslavič, as far as is known. This assumption is made based on the passage in the *PVL* story of the "Blinding of Vasil´ko" where M´stislav is listed first as a son of Svjatopolk and assigned to rule Volodymyr, while Jaroslav is listed second and sent on a mission to Hungary.[13] Jaroslav's mother is unknown and he is referred to simply as the "son of Svjatopolk," with no reference to his

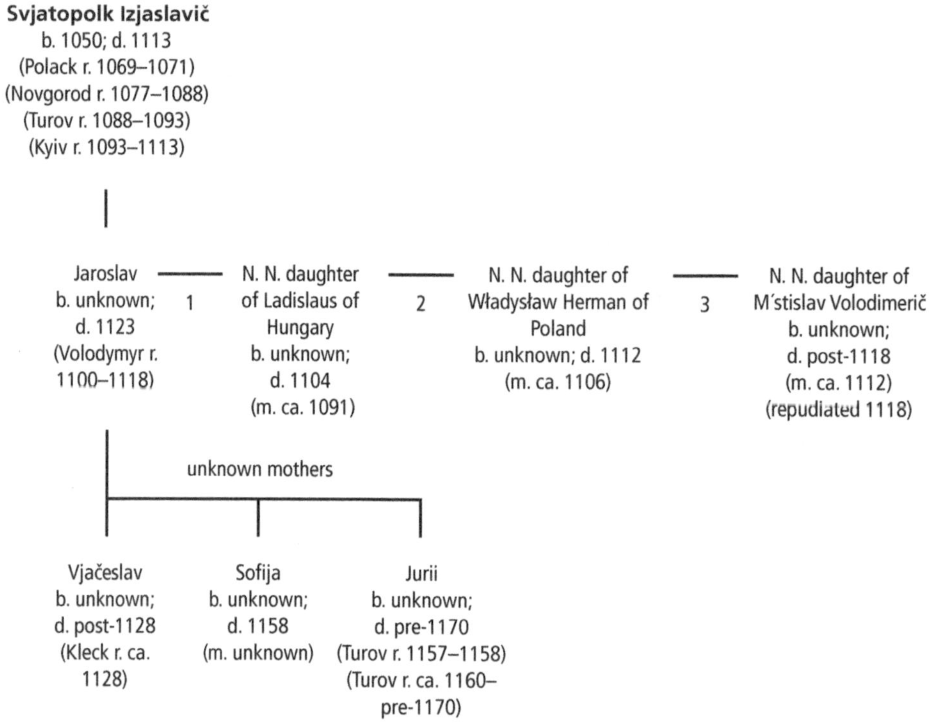

mother as there was for M´stislav. Perhaps, because Jaroslav made the majority of dynastic marriages among the Svjatopolčiči, he was born of a "wife" rather than a "concubine," however as noted above (under the entry for Svjatopolk Izjaslavič), there is insufficient information on the women from which a reasonable conjecture could be formed.

Jaroslav's first dynastic marriage was arranged sometime before 1091. In that year there is an entry in a Hungarian chronicle referring to Jaroslav as the "gener" (son-in-law) of King Ladislaus.[14] So, by this point, as the later chronicler understood it, Jaroslav was already married to the daughter of Ladislaus. This was an important marriage for the Izjaslaviči to maintain their foreign connections. The Izjaslaviči had always had a power base in the west of Rus´, and so creating a powerful tie with the Hungarians was an important part of keeping the peace there so that they could focus on internal Rusian politics. This was tested soon after, when the Polovcians invaded Hungary, either in 1091 or 1092.[15] After routing the Polovcians in his country, Ladislaus attacked Rus´, so the Hungarian chronicle informs us, "for it was by their advice that the Comans [Pechenegs][16] had come into Hungary."[17] Nazarenko, I believe correctly, interprets this to mean that certain Rusian parties, namely either Vsevolod Jaroslavič or Davyd Igorič, were attempting to create strife with an ally of the Izjaslaviči.[18] This may also have provided additional impetus for Svjatopolk to make peace with the Polovcians, as he did in 1094.[19] We are not told whether it affected the relationship between Jaroslav and his wife or father-in-law, but it seems unlikely in light of later events. After Svjatopolk's ascension to the throne this alliance becomes very important, as during the Blinding of Vasil′ko Svjatopolk sends Jaroslav to the Hungarians to seek help.[20] This is recorded in multiple places, including the *Chronica de Gestis Hungarorum*,[21] and Tatiščev's *Istorija Rossijskaja*.[22] Tatiščev adds to the story saying that Jaroslav was sent to his "zjat′" for help. "Zjat′" traditionally meant "brother-in-law," but here it can be interpreted more broadly for his cousin-in-law whom he brought back, King Koloman.[23] Though their army was defeated, spectacularly according to the *Chronica de gestis Hungarorum*,[24] the dynastic marriage did allow Svjatopolk to call on a foreign army for domestic political assistance. It probably also allowed him the freedom to do so without worrying about a permanent Hungarian presence in Rus′.

The date of the death of Jaroslav's first wife is unknown, but it is believed that he remarried around 1106/7. Interestingly, there may have been a breakdown in relations between Svjatopolk and the Hungarians as in 1104, Svjatopolk's daughter Peredslava married a Hungarian prince, most likely Almos, Koloman's brother.[25] The reason this might suggest a breakdown in relations is because Almos and Koloman spent most of Koloman's reign fighting over who should rule.[26] This is supported by the marriage in 1112 between Koloman and a daughter of Volodimer Monomax, Evfimija.[27] However, there is not enough evidence to prove such a breakdown, and in 1123 there were reportedly Hungarians fighting on the side of Jaroslav against Monomax.[28] This example illustrates the enormous complexities in understanding and untangling the dynastic marriage situation nearly a millennium after the fact.

Jaroslav's next marriage was reputedly to a Polish princess, the daughter of Władysław Herman. Unfortunately, there is no solid evidence for this marriage, but it does seem plausible. One of the daughters of Władysław Herman is said to have "married a husband in Rus′."[29] This entry comes in the form of a biographical note and is thus undated, but it is clear that Jaroslav has a very close relationship later with Bolesław III, his putative wife's brother, though this could also be explained by the marriage of Bolesław III to Jaroslav's sister Sbyslava.[30] Oswald Balzer, historically the definitive genealogist of the Piasts, used as evidence for the marriage the 1106/7 mediation of Jaroslav between the feuding brothers Bolesław III and Zbigniew.[31] Gallus Anonymous writes that Jaroslav and Bishop Baldwin of Cracow were able to bring Zbigniew peacefully before Bolesław III to pledge obedience.[32] Jaroslav's part in this mediation seems to be major, but the question remains, why is he doing it? The Rusian sources add to the picture by telling us that in 1106 Zbigniew took refuge with Svjatopolk in Rus´.[33] Gallus Anonymous does not mention this at all, but does say that Bolesław III called on the king of the Rusians to assist him in his war with his brother, and that his armies arrived just before Jaroslav acted as mediator.[34] Thus it stands to reason that Jaroslav may have led the army to Poland and yet supported a peaceful solution to the conflict. Whether or not this was because of his kinship with Bolesław III, and to what degree that kinship existed, is unknown.

Despite the fact that this marriage lacks solid evidence, it is quite plausible. The purpose of the marriage would have been to tie Jaroslav, now *knjaz´* of Volodymyr-Volyn´, more closely to his Polish neighbor. In this it was similar to the purpose of the marriage with the Hungarians, though more urgent, as Jaroslav now personally possessed the borderland between Rus´ and Poland. He also may have been looking forward to the future, when he would need protection at his back as well as support in the upcoming contest to succeed his father. This marriage has been conjecturally accepted in the tables of part 2, though the nature of the evidence has been made clear here.

Again we do not know the death date for Jaroslav's second wife, but it is generally dated to before 1112. In that year, Jaroslav sent to M´stislav Volodimerič of Novgorod to marry his daughter.[35] This dynastic marriage was meant to connect the Izjaslaviči and Monomaxoviči, perhaps in an attempt to end the struggles between the two. Unfortunately it did not work as planned. In 1118, Volodimer and M´stislav launched a campaign against Jaroslav, forcing him to flee Rus´,[36] because of his poor treatment of Volodimer's granddaughter (Jaroslav's M´stislavna wife).[37] The same entries record that the next year, Jaroslav repudiated the M´stislavna. It appears that the gulf between the Izjaslaviči and the Vsevolodoviči had grown too wide to be bridged by a dynastic marriage. However, there are two particularly instructive points about this marriage, the first quite simply that dynastic marriage was chosen as the tool that the Volodimeroviči attempted to use to bridge the divide. Of all the alliances that could have been made between the Izjaslaviči and Monomaxoviči, it was a marital one that attempted to cease the internecine warfare, a typical purpose for dynastic marriages externally, but not always internally.[38] Second, that this was one of the first non-Polack, intra-Rusian dynastic marriages. This is a trend that will only continue over the course of the twelfth century as the Volodimeroviči grow in numbers.

Jaroslav's life seems to have been structured around the importance of dynastic marriage. He married three times, each time for political reasons. The importance of dynastic marriage is illustrated at the end of his life when he was thrown out of Volodymyr-Volyn´ because of his close ties with Hungary and Poland.[39] In exile he is able to use both his Hungarian and Polish connections to attempt to regain his throne. The Hypatian Chronicle records that in his final attempt, in 1123, he brought with him soldiers from Hungary, Poland, and Bohemia to fight for him.[40] Though he lost his throne and eventually his life, he was always able to call on connections created through his and his family's dynastic marriages.

M´stislav "Harald" Volodimerič
(tables 12, 13, 15, 18, 20)

M´stislav was the son of Volodimer Monomax, and over the course of his life occupied the two premier spots in the Rusian hierarchy as ruler of Novgorod and of Kyiv. M´stislav also married twice, once a dynastic marriage with a foreign princess, and a second time with a Rusian woman.

The date for M´stislav's first marriage is not known precisely, though Baumgarten following Tatiščev chooses to date it to the year 1095,[41] the year of M´stislav's inception as ruler of Novgorod.[42] At approximately this time M´stislav married Kristín, the daughter of King Inge Steinkelsson of Sweden.[43] Typically, the Rusian chronicles record none of these details, though the *NPL* does record her name as "Xristina."[44] Even the Scandinavian sources that record the marriage do not record the context. Sturluson simply mentions it as part of the

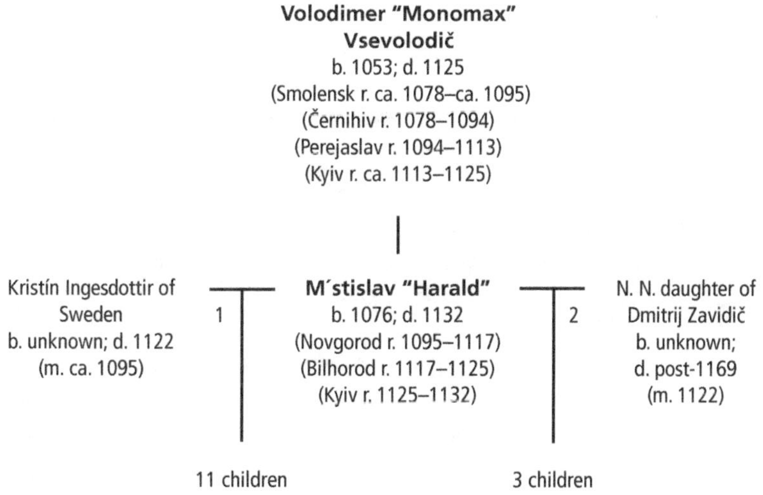

genealogy of the marriage of Malfrid and King Sigurd of Norway,[45] and Abbot Wilhelm uses it as background for the marriage of Malfrid's sister Ingeborg to Knud Lavard.[46] To search for a reason, we must stretch the sources a bit further.

Inge of Sweden was the son of King Steinkel. Steinkel died around the year 1066, and was followed by a series of other rulers, including two Erics and possibly Inge's brother, Alstan, before Haakon took the throne.[47] During that time, Inge was forced to flee, most likely in the years 1075–80,[48] because one of the current rulers was attempting to eliminate all possible rivals. Inge found refuge in that paradise for Scandinavian refugees, Rus´, where he probably lived in Kyiv, or possibly Novgorod, though the latter may have been too close to home for safety. During that time in Rus´, it is quite possible that he became friendly with the Volodimeroviči and was grateful for their assistance. When the Swedes were again in need of a king, they called him home from Rus´ to rule.[49] The possible reasons for a marriage between Inge and the then ruling Vsevolodoviči are numerous, but there are two probable ones. The first is that it was an alliance made because of the friendship created during Inge's exile. An outgrowth of this idea is that the marriage was pledged during Inge's time in Rus´, and only occurred when both M´stislav and Inge's daughter Kristín were old enough. Prearranged marriages of this sort were relatively common; see the marriage of Sbyslava Svjatopolkovna and Bolesław III of Poland as just one example.[50] The other potential reason for the alliance was that it was part of Inge's attempt to forge peace with his neighbors. In the 1090s, he was warring with King Magnus Barefoot of Norway over disputed lands,[51] and it would have been prudent for him to ensure that he was at peace with his other neighbors. Indeed that conflict was finally resolved with a marriage between Magnus and Inge's other daughter, Margaret, who was called the "Frithkolla" (Peace Woman).[52] Unfortunately there is not enough evidence to report a definite reason for the marriage, but it would seem logical for a marriage agreement to have been concluded while Inge was in Rus´, despite the fact that M´stislav was then only a boy. This would fit with the Rusian policy of marrying exiles in the hopes that they would return to power.

Kristín's death is recorded in 1122 and there is an interesting question of property that becomes important at her death.[53] In Scandinavian tradition a daughter inherits part of her father's patrimony, though not the core lands.[54] In Denmark in the early twelfth century, we see Kristín's sister, Margaret, pass on her patrimony to various people, including her niece Ingeborg.[55] Kristín would have had the same potential to pass on land she had inherited from her father King Inge, and the question is, where did that land go? Because of the dearth of Rusian sources, and their profound ignorance of the activities of women, we have no idea, but the fact that she had such land and that something must have happened to it is important to remember in attempting to understand this period of Rusian history. This land would have created or added to Kristín's power and influence in Rus´, and it could have been a gift she passed on to her children to increase their power and influence.

The 1122 chronicle entry in the *NPL* that announces the death of Kristín also announces the second marriage of M´stislav, this time to a daughter of Posadnik Dmitrij Zavidič of Novgorod.[56] This was also a politically advantageous marriage, but an internal one, attempting to strengthen the ties between Kyiv and Novgorod by having a Volodimeroviči marry one of the daughters of the Novgorodian nobility. Though there are certainly caveats, such as the simple lack of information on non-Volodimeroviči Novgorod politics at that time (despite the rich Novgorod chronicle tradition), this is an acceptable conclusion when put in such broad terms. A familial relationship between M´stislav and Dmitrij Zavidič is unlikely, as Dmitrij died in 1118,[57] and his son (a potential arranger of the marriage) did not hold the position of posadnik until 1128.[58] However, the idea of a sense of corporate loyalty is possible in which M´stislav would be creating a familial relationship with the Novgorod nobility, as an entity rather than one single family. This would be especially important, as M´stislav had left Novgorod in 1117 to assist his father in Kyiv.[59] If this interpretation is correct, the marriage can then be seen to serve the purpose of uniting the two poles of Rus´, Kyiv and Novgorod, and ideally bringing the Novgorodian nobility onto the side of M´stislav in an assumed succession battle after his ailing father's death. This conclusion, while speculative, offers a reasonable suggestion for a marriage between a Volodimeroviči and non-Volodimeroviči Rusian, the first of its kind. It also seemed to correctly anticipate the succession struggles that followed and perhaps helped to cement M´stislav's position on the throne of Kyiv.

Sbyslava Svjatopolkovna
(tables 9, 17)

As with the marriage of her brother Jaroslav, Sbyslava's dynastic marriage is illustrated in the tale of the Blinding of Vasil´ko as told under the year 1097 in the *PVL*. The *PVL* records Svjatopolk's attempt to oust Davyd Igorevič from his home in Volodymyr-Volyn´, which led Svjatopolk to make a deal with Władysław Herman of Poland ensuring that Władysław would not support Davyd.[60] Tatiščev then adds to this account a meeting between Władysław and Svjatopolk at which they formally agreed upon these actions and engaged their minor children, Bolesław (later Bolesław III) and Sbyslava, to be married when they

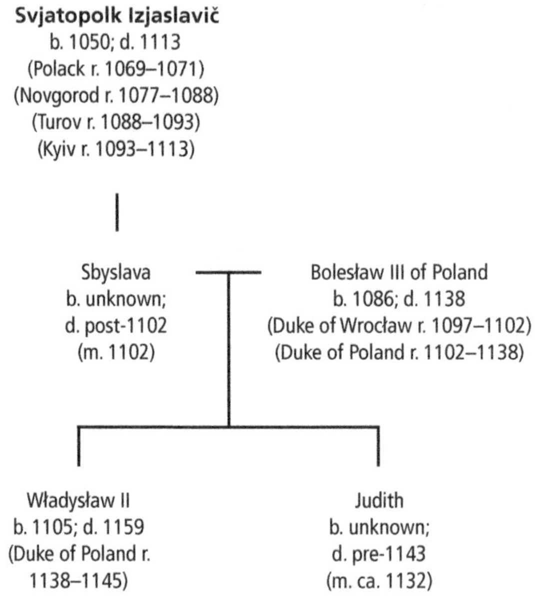

came of age.[61] While Tatiščev's evidence is often suspect,[62] in this case it fits the expected pattern of dynastic marriage being used to seal an agreement, an agreement that can be read between the lines in the *PVL*. The marriage itself is recorded a few years later in 1102, when Sbyslava is sent to Poland to marry Bolesław.[63] This is a rare occurrence in the *PVL* where both the name of the bride and the name of the groom are noted. However, this was not the only thing distinctive about Sbyslava's marriage.

Sbyslava Svjatopolkovna has an incredible distinction in the history of Rusian dynastic marriage. After all the consanguineous marriages made in the eleventh and early twelfth centuries, only Sbyslava's consanguineous marriage to Bolesław III received a papal dispensation.[64] Sbyslava's grandfather Izjaslav Jaroslavič had married the sister of Casimir of Poland, and Casimir was the grandfather of Bolesław III, thus in terms of medieval consanguinity, the two were related in the third degree.[65] This, in and of itself, was not strange, as dynastic marriages had a tendency to be consanguineous at this time due to the expanded interpretation of consanguinity by the Latin Church, but it is remarkable that no other Rusians received a dispensation from either the papacy or the patriarchate. The same might be said of the Poles, judging by the lack of evidence we have for other dispensations or dispensation requests. However, in this instance a papal dispensation was important for Bolesław. The reason for this seems to be his desire to be given the title *rex* by the Roman Church, possibly because of his struggles with his older half-brother Zbigniew, who held part of the Polish kingdom.[66] All in all, this is an interesting example of politics again motivating religious action.

Sbyslava and Bolesław had two children, Władysław (later Władysław II) and a daughter known as Judith.[67] At some point, perhaps in the first decade of the twelfth century, Sbyslava died, though an exact date is unknown. Following her death, Bolesław remarried, this time to Salomea, a member of the Salian dynasty of the German Empire, and the two of them had four sons and an unknown number of daughters before his death in 1138.[68] This division in the families, reminiscent of Louis the Pious centuries earlier, would divide the Piasts against themselves and fracture Poland.

Peredslava Svjatopolkovna
(tables 9, 18, 22)

Very little is known of Peredslava Svjatopolkovna, though she shares with only a few Rusian women the distinction of having her name written in the *PVL*. Peredslava was the daughter of Svjatopolk Izjaslavič and became part of his dynastic marriage plan when she was sent to Hungary in 1104 to marry a Hungarian prince.[69] The identity of the Hungarian prince is unknown, but theories have been advanced. The editor of the *PSRL* volume of the Hypatian chronicle lists Peredslava in the index as the wife of King Ladislaus.[70] This is implausible, as of the two king Ladislauses in this period one died before her recorded

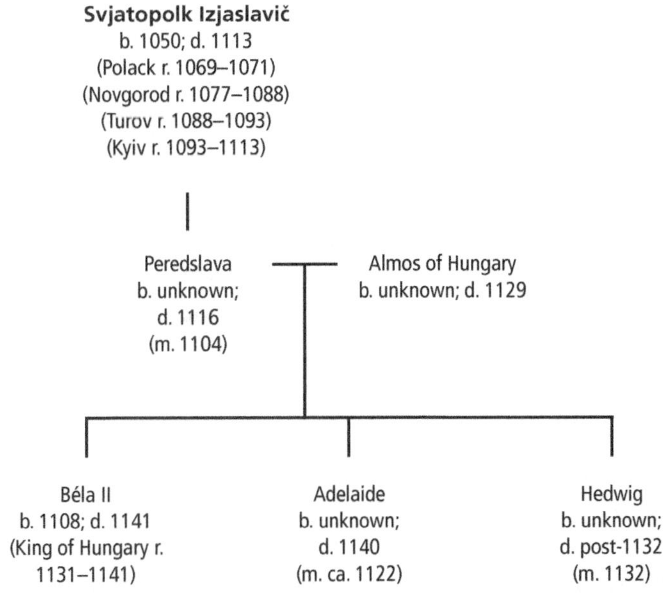

marriage date and one was born after.[71] The more plausible identity for the husband is Almos, son to King Géza and brother to King Koloman.[72] He is known to have had interaction with Rus´ in this period, as he was feuding with his brother Koloman over a share of the kingdom, and he is one of the very few eligible Hungarian princes that is known at this time.

The purpose behind this marriage is unclear. Ladislaus and Svjatopolk had a relationship because of the marriage of Ladislaus's daughter to Jaroslav, Svjatopolk's son. This relationship was strong enough to allow Svjatopolk, via Jaroslav, to call on Hungarian assistance against Volodar´ and Vasil´ko Rostislavič even after Ladislaus's death.[73] However, Jaroslav's wife may have died by this time, as he soon after married a Polish princess. Thus there may have been a need for another bond between the Svjatopolčiči and the Árpáds. In one scenario, Koloman and Svjatopolk may have arranged the marriage jointly. Theoretically this would have been a peaceful time between the brothers, and thus Almos might have been trusted.[74] But such trust is rare in dynastic marriages in which inheritance is on the line. Brothers are more often rivals, and enriching their political connections is not a smart or safe thing to do. Another scenario would posit that there was a falling out of some sort between Koloman and Svjatopolk, perhaps after the devastating defeat of the Hungarians in 1097 when they answered Svjatopolk's call.[75] Almos may then have played on that disaffection to create a tie with Svjatopolk, perhaps in an attempt to unseat Koloman.[76] This idea is buttressed by the later marriage of Koloman with a daughter of Volodimer Monomax, a clear rival of Svjatopolk, while Svjatopolk still ruled in Kyiv.[77] However, again complicating the picture is the marriage in the same year between Jaroslav Svjatopolčič and a daughter of M´stislav Volodimerič, a granddaughter of Monomax.[78] This would seem to indicate a rapprochement between the two sides. Though each of these scenarios is interesting, neither is entirely convincing, as there are too many complicating factors and too little solid information. Suffice it to say that Peredslava Svjatopolkovna married a Hungarian prince, probably Almos, in 1104, and this created, at the least, a relationship between that prince and the Svjatopolčiči, at least for the duration of the marriage.

Svjatoslav "Svjatoša" Davydič
(table 11)

Svjatoslav, called Svjatoša, Davydič is most famous for his assumption of monastic orders in 1106, an uncommon act for a Rusian ruler not on his deathbed.[79] There is no record of his marriage, apart from Zotov's reference to the Ljubeč *Sinodik*, where he has a wife named Anna.[80]

Davyd Svjatoslavič
b. 1051; d. 1123
(Novgorod r. post-1088–1095)
(Smolensk r. 1095–1096)
(Černihiv r. 1096–1123)

|

Svjatoša
(Nicola)
b. unknown; d. 1143
(Luck r. pre-1097–
1097)
(monastic vows: 1106)

There is no other information in either source for her, and it is only in Baumgarten where she is given a patronymic, Svjatopolkovna.[81] Dimnik, in the first volume of his *Dynasty of Chernigov* duology, uses Baumgarten's identification of "Anna" as a reason for Svjatoša's assistance of Svjatopolk Izjaslavič's military campaigns of the late eleventh century, but unfortunately there is no primary source evidence for this marriage, nor is Dimnik's rationale entirely convincing.[82] His identification rests on Baumgarten's, and his explanation, while plausible, could also be explained by Svjatoša's desire to increase his own wealth, or a distancing himself from his own family in a bid for power, an event seen later as well.[83] For these reasons, I cannot accept the identification of a wife of Svjatoša as a Svjatopolkovna, even if one stipulates that there was a wife at all.

Svjatoslav Ol´govič
(tables 10, 21)

Svjatoslav Ol´govič was one of the handful of Volodimeroviči whose marriages were made with the steppe peoples and were reported in the sources. This trend began near the end of the eleventh century as the rulers of Rus´ attempted to apply the foreign policy tactic that was working for their other relations to the problem of the Polovcians.

In 1107 there were many battles between the Polovcians and the Rusians.[84] Various Volodimeroviči united to battle the Polovcians until finally Volodimer Monomax, Davyd Svjatoslavič, and Oleg Svjatoslavič went to make peace with two of the leaders of the Polovcian clans, both named Aepa.[85] As part of this peace agreement, Volodimer and Oleg committed their sons in marriage, and Oleg's son married the daughter of Aepa, son of Girgen.[86] The identity of this son is not

Oleg Svjatoslavič
b. 1050; d. 1115
(Tmutorokan r. 1078–1079)
(Tmutorokan r. 1083–1094)
(Černihiv r. 1094–1096)
(Novhorod-Siverskyj r. ca. 1097–1115)

N. N., daughter of Khan Aepa, son of Girgen b. unknown; d. pre-1136 (m. 1107)	1	Svjatoslav b. unknown; d. 1164 (Novgorod r. 1136–1138) (Kursk r. 1138–1139) (Novgorod r. 1139–1141) (Bilhorod r. 1141–ca.1146) (Novhorod-Siverskyj r. ca.1146–1158) (Černihiv r. 1158–1164)	2	N. N. b. unknown; d. 1166 (m. 1136) (Černihiv r. 1164)

5 children

mentioned in the text, and it is only through later historians' work that is has been assumed to be Oleg's youngest son Svjatoslav.[87] This identification cannot be confirmed, as much information is missing for all of Oleg's children and their spouses, but the identification of this son as Svjatoslav has gained widespread acceptance, including by Martin Dimnik.[88] Unfortunately, nothing more is known of this steppe princess, as she does not again appear in any extant records.

This marriage was designed to keep the peace for Rus´ in general, and like other dynastic marriages, to provide an advantage to the family making it, by making an alliance between the Volodimeroviči (or factions thereof) and one or more Polovcian clans. The primary goal of peace was not accomplished, as the Polovcians still raided Rus´ in general, but the marriage of an Ol´govič to the family of a Polovcian ruler created or cemented a relationship between the two that allowed Svjatoslav and other Ol´goviči to call on Polovcian aid in their future campaigns.[89]

It should also be noted that Svjatoslav married a second time in 1136, this time as ruler of Novgorod. The marriage, though not the name of the bride, is mentioned in multiple chronicles.[90] The bride may have been a daughter of a Novgorodian posadnik, a member of the Mikul´čič family of Novgorod, multiple members of which held the position at this time.[91] However, while this is possible, it is unlikely. The majority of the chronicles that record this marriage, *NPL*, *NČL*, and the Voskresenskij Chronicle all record that the marriage was conducted without the approval or services of Vladyka Nifont, and even the one outlying chronicle, Tver, records that Svjatoslav was forced to use his own priests to perform the marriage.[92] Though largely in communion with one another in the twelfth century, the Latin and Orthodox Churches (broadly construed) often had ecclesiastical conflicts that extended into the political world.[93] It was not unheard of for rulers to use their own, loyal, clergy to officiate because of those occasional conflicts. In this case, the Novgorodian ecclesiastical hierarchy would have supported a lawful marriage of their chosen ruler and the daughter of one of the local noble, posadnik, families, as was the case with M´stislav Volodimerič before, and others after this time. The refusal of Nifont to adjudicate or allow his priests to attend may indicate that the marriage was unlawful in some way, perhaps even suggesting that Svjatoslav's first wife was still alive. Despite our ignorance of the identity of the bride, the marriage was made, and it seems that it did not ingratiate Svjatoslav with the Novgorodians, as they evicted him a few short years later.[94] Though, of course, this may have simply been the typical Novgorodian response to the changing political situation in Rus´ as a whole. In sum, it can be safely stated that Svjatoslav married a second time, though with whom is not known.

Jurij "Dolgorukij" Volodimerič
(tables 12, 14, 21)

Jurij Dolgorukij was the second-youngest son of Volodimer Monomax, and though he is more well known today than the majority of figures in these pages, in the early twelfth century he was still a young man in the shadow of his oldest brother M´stislav. While M´stislav had an arranged dynastic marriage with a Swedish princess, Jurij was married to the daughter of a Polovcian ruler. On the Rusian scale of dynastic marriages, it was a much less grand achievement.

Jurij's marriage took place at the same time as the marriage of Svjatoslav Ol´govič discussed above. Their fathers, Volodimer Monomax and Oleg Svjatoslavič, had ridden forth, along with Oleg's brother Davyd, to make peace with the Polovcians, who had been causing havoc in the Rusian lands.[95] To arrange a peace agreement, Volodimer married his son Jurij to the daughter of Aepa, son of Osen.[96] The primary purpose of the marriages seems to have been to make peace between these groups of Volodimeriči and Polovcians, but it does not seem to have had lasting success. Because of the complete absence of Polovcian sources and the Rusian choniclers' preference for leaving out women, nothing is known of Jurij's bride. In fact, it is only because of the Monomaxoviči emphasis of the extant chronicles that we know

Volodimer "Monomax" Vsevolodič
b. 1053; d. 1125
(Smolensk r. ca. 1078–ca. 1095)
(Černihiv r. 1078–1094)
(Perejaslav r. 1094–1113)
(Kyiv r. ca. 1113–1125)

N. N. daughter of Khan Aepa, son of Osen
b. unknown; d. pre-1162
(m. 1107)

1

Jurij "Dolgorukij" Volodimerič
b. unknown; d. 1157
(Suzdal r. pre-1138–1157)
(Perejaslav r. 1132)
(Perejaslav r. 1135)
(Kyiv r. 1149–1150)
(Perejaslav r. 1151)
(Kyiv r. 1155–1157)

2

N. N.
b. unknown; d. post-1162
(m. unknown)

9 children

4 children

the name of Monomax's son, Jurij, who married the steppe princess. The same sentence describes the marriage to another steppe princess of a son of Oleg, who is not mentioned by name.[97]

Baumgarten mentions a possible second wife for Jurij, a woman "vraisemblement Byzantine d'origine," citing Karamzin.[98] While it is possible to explain this simply as another attempt to add to the Byzantine connections of venerable Rusians, it is likely that there was another wife, whoever she might have been. The evidence comes to us from several sources, including four different chronicles—Hypatian, Tver, Nikon, and Voskresenskij—which all record Andrej Bogoliubskij Jurevič's exile of his brothers M´stislav, Vasil´ko, and Vsevolod with their mother and their respective children to Byzantium.[99] A Byzantine source, John Kinnamos, also records that land was given along the Danube to Vasil´ko Jurevič, after he was exiled from Rus´.[100] While it is likely that this combination of sources is where Karamzin and Baumgarten each derived their origin for the second wife, there is no positive evidence to substantiate this, and it seems quite likely that had Jurij married a Byzantine woman, the union would have been recorded by at least one of the preserved sources. Apart from her origin, however, the fact that Andrej Jurevič was attempting to remove a certain subset of his brothers from Rus´, along with their mother, indicates that this was probably not Andrej's mother as well, and thus a second marriage, or at least relationship, for Jurij must be postulated, though there is almost no other information about it, or her.

Evfimija Volodimerovna
(tables 12, 18)

The marriage of Evfimija Volodimerovna to Koloman, king of Hungary, has been a subject of intense scrutiny because of its outcome.[101] The marriage seems to have taken place in 1112, when Evfimija, who is identified by name in the Hypatian Chronicle, is sent to Hungary to marry the king.[102] Though the king is not identified by name, the king at the time was Koloman and the marriage is recognized in numerous other sources.[103] The purpose of the marriage seems clear: with the death of Koloman's first wife earlier that year,[104] Koloman was free to create a new alliance, and Volodimer Monomax felt himself in need of a connection with Hungary. At this time Svjatopolk Izjaslavič still ruled in Kyiv, and the Izjaslaviči held the upper hand in terms of foreign dynastic connections, especially with Poland and Hungary, two dangerous border areas that could shelter them and provide troops as necessary. To remedy that, and counter the marriage of Svjatopolk's daughter Peredslava with Koloman's brother Almos, Volodimer sent his daughter Evfimija to marry Koloman.[105] As in all of these cases, there must be reciprocal advantage, and for Koloman it may have been connected to the death of his eldest son Ladislaus that same year.[106] Though he may already have been unwell at the time, perhaps he hoped to sire more sons to protect his lineage from his brother, with whom he often warred.

The marriage lasted less than a year before Koloman repudiated Evfimija and sent her home to Kyiv.[107] At the time, Evfimija was preg-

Volodimer "Monomax" Vsevolodič
b. 1053; d. 1125
(Smolensk r. ca. 1078–ca. 1095)
(Černihiv r. 1078–1094)
(Perejaslav r. 1094–1113)
(Kyiv r. ca. 1113–1125)

Koloman of Hungary
b. unknown; d. 1116
(King of Hungary r. 1095–1116)

Evfimija
b. unknown;
d. 1138 (m. 1112)
(repudiated ca. 1112)

Boris
b. 1114; d. 1156

nant, and the assumption has been that she was pregnant with someone else's child. However, multiple contemporary sources identify the son she bore in Kyiv, Boris, as the son of Koloman.[108] Interestingly, both Cosmas and Otto would have had better reason to disprove Boris's lineage, as they were each allied with Boris's foes in Hungary.[109] Thus their testimony in favor of his legitimacy means a great deal. Unfortunately, we are then left with an unanswerable conundrum. Evfimija, who went to Hungary to seal an alliance and produce sons for the king, became pregnant with a son (seemingly by the king), but was repudiated and sent home. The cause of the repudiation is unknown. It is clear from future events that the marriage did not secure its purpose, as would seem obvious from its abrupt end. Indeed, after Koloman's death in 1116 his son Stephen II supported Jaroslav Svjatopolčič against Volodimer Monomax in Jaroslav's attempts to stay independent.[110]

The fate of Boris was constant warfare to reclaim his birthright. He was raised in Rus´ and over the course of his life allied with Bolesław III of Poland and the Comneni emperors of Byzantium to attempt to take the throne of Hungary after the death of his half-brother Stephen II.[111] As for Evfimija, some maintain that she entered a monastery in Rus´.[112] This would certainly have been a common option for a princess in her position, but no reliable primary source records such an event as it was recorded for Evpraksija Vsevolodovna.[113] Her death is recorded in 1138 and she was laid to rest in the Holy Savior's Church.[114] Her burial in a high-status location indicates that the family felt no shame over her failed marriage, but the lack of a response to her curt dismissal from Hungary and the absence of sources on her activities in the intervening years leave a mystery surrounding the dissolution of her marriage.

Roman Volodimerič
(tables 4, 12)

The first mention of Roman, son of Volodimer "Monomax" Vsevolodič, in the Rusian chronicles comes with his dynastic marriage to a daughter of Volodar´ Rostislavič in 1113.[115] Though not the first intra-Rusian dynastic marriage, it is part of the same complex of alliances as the marriage between Jaroslav Svjatopolčič and a daughter of M´stislav Volodimerič.[116] In 1113, Volodimer Monomax was newly installed in Kyiv and his largest internal problem was the growing split between his family and that of the Izjaslaviči, represented at the time by Jaroslav Svjatopolčič. This was especially true as Volodimer may have already been envisioning a transition to lineal, rather than lateral, succession and the installation of his son M´stislav in Bilhorod,[117] a move which would have removed the remaining Izjaslaviči from the succession to Kyiv completely. The marriage of Roman Volodimerič seems designed

Volodimer "Monomax" Vsevolodič
b. 1053; d. 1125
(Smolensk r. ca. 1078–ca. 1095)
(Černihiv r. 1078–1094)
(Perejaslav r. 1094–1113)
(Kyiv r. ca. 1113–1125)

N. N. daughter of Volodar´ Rostislavič
b. unknown;
d. post-1113
(m. 1113)

Roman
b. unknown;
d. 1119
(Volodymyr r. 1118–1119)

to assist in managing this fraught relationship. Volodar´ Rostislavič was the longtime ruler of Peremyšl in Halyč, and a neighbor of Jaroslav Svjatopolčič who was ruling in Volodymyr. Though Volodar´ and his brother Vasil´ko were treated poorly by Jaroslav's father, Svjatopolk Izjaslavič, they were on good terms with Jaroslav.[118] Thus the marriage would have served the purpose of strengthening Monomaxoviči ties with a particularly troublesome area for the family. Unfortunately for Rus´, these marriages did not serve to keep the peace, and Jaroslav and Volodimer were at war only a few years after the conclusion of this marriage. Whether or not this marriage, like Jaroslav's, would have ended in repudiation is unknown, as Roman died in 1119 after only six years of marriage, and after holding Jaroslav's territory of Volodymyr for just a year.[119]

Marija Volodimerovna
(tables 12, 20)

The marriage of Marija Volodimerovna is almost completely speculative but has been included here because it is widely commented on, if not always recognized, in the scholarship. Marija was the daughter of Volodimer Monomax, and it is believed that she married Leo Diogenes. The only reference to Leo in the Rusian chronicles is under the year 1116, when "Leon Diogenevič´" attacked Alexius Comnenus and was killed.[120] In the Hypatian Chronicle his surname is left out and he is referred to only as "Leon carevič."[121] As is mentioned in other examples, however, the chroniclers' attribution of the title *carevič* may not always refer exactly to the son of a tsar. The important fact for these purposes is that in that entry he is explicitly identified as Volodimer Monomax's

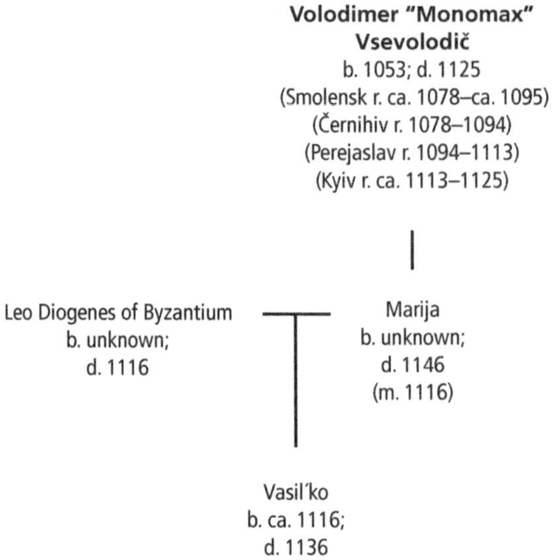

"zjat´."[122] "Zjat´," like the Greek "gambros," can mean either brother-in-law or son-in-law, but in this case it has been taken to be son-in-law.[123] Baumgarten advanced the idea that Leo was the son of Romanus IV Diogenes, the Byzantine emperor,[124] which is most likely not true given his complete absence in Byzantine sources. There is some corroboration for the existence of this marriage, though, in multiple chronicles in the year 1136. In that year, a "Vasilko Maričič´" dies; he is further identified in the Hypatian Chronicle as Vasilko "Leonovič´."[125] This person, otherwise completely unknown in the chronicles, combines the two names of Marija and Leo in different patronymics, or one patro- and one matronymic, as the case may be. This is the best evidence of the identity of Marija, and the existence of the marriage. Litvina and Uspenskij further discuss the onomastic evidence for the marriage in this child, and show that he was named after the Christian name of his grandfather, Volodimer-Vasilij Monomax.[126] This is certainly plausible, adding to the evidence for the marriage, as well as of the naming power of Rusian women.

However, Leo as the son of Romanus IV Diogenes seems unacceptable, as shown by Każdan in his analysis of Rus´-Byzantine marriages, where he illustrates the fate of all the known children of Romanus IV.[127] Thus we are left with a Leo Diogenes ("Leon Diogenevič´"), who was almost assuredly a Byzantine and married to a daughter of Volodimer Monomax. Leo may have been another royal refugee who went to Rus´, perhaps even a member of the extended Diogenes family, but he was certainly not the son of Romanus IV. If he was a Diogenes, of whatever rank, it would have been in keeping with Rusian policy for Volodimer to marry a relative to him, in case his fortunes changed and he was able to return home with some measure of power, as had worked so effectively for Volodimer's aunts. But no more can be made of his identity than this.

Jaropolk Volodimerič
(tables 12, 20)

The marriage of Jaropolk Volodimerič was not a typical dynastic marriage, and perhaps does not belong in this listing, but it has been included because it involves an important medieval custom that is not discussed in any of the other marriages—a wife as hostage. In 1116 Volodimer Monomax sent his son Jaropolk to the Polovcian lands along the Don to attack the Polovcians and to capture people and cities.[128] Jaropolk did this and while there he also captured many "Jasy," including one whom he took as a wife.[129] This woman is believed to be the same woman who is mentioned as the wife of Jaropolk in 1145 in regard to her reburial of Jaropolk next to his aunt Janka, and is called there Elena.[130] The Hypatian Chronicle identifies Elena at her capture as the daughter of the ruler of the Jasy.[131] This was clearly not an arranged marriage, since capture is a clear part of the entry, but it may have been a case where Jaropolk took her to ensure the cooperation or lack of retaliation from her family. Alternately, she could also have been taken for her great beauty ("Jaropolk privede sobě ženu krasnu velmi"), which is explicitly mentioned.[132]

If we can assume that this is the same woman who was listed in 1145 as Jaropolk's wife, which is a safe assumption based upon her iden-

Volodimer "Monomax" Vsevolodič
b. 1053; d. 1125
(Smolensk r. ca. 1078–ca. 1095)
(Černihiv r. 1078–1094)
(Perejaslav r. 1094–1113)
(Kyiv r. ca. 1113–1125)

Elena of Ossetia
b. unknown;
d. post-1145
(m. 1116)

Jaropolk
b. unknown; d. 1139
(Minsk r. 1115–1116)
(Perejaslav r.1114–1132)
(Kyiv r. 1132–1139)
(Perejaslav r. 1134–1135)

tification there as a "Jaska,"[133] the question of her religious affiliation arises. When she was captured this was unknown, and might depend on a correct identification of the Jasy. The most common interpretation is that they were Ossetians or Alans,[134] and thus a Turkic people living in the Caucasus and the lower steppe, leaving their religion a mystery as they could have been pagan or Muslim. However, they could also have been a group of Volga Bulgars, as a recent study suggests,[135] in which case a safer assumption would be that they were Muslim. Elena, which was most likely her Christian name, was referred to in the Nikon chronicle as "Christ-loving," a clear indication of her faith to that chronicler at least.[136] While the conversion of non-Christian wives has been assumed, there is not much evidence for the practice, which makes this case important. The marriage of Jaropolk Volodimerič and Elena of the Jasy was not a dynastic marriage in the traditional sense, but it was a marriage between two kingdoms that had a political purpose and thus deserves inclusion in this area and consideration when discussing Rusian foreign politics of this period.

Vsevolodko Davydič
(tables 8, 12, 21)

Vsevolodko Davydič was the great grandson of Jaroslav Mudryj, and the grandson of Jaroslav's youngest son, Igor´. His father, Davyd Igorič, led quite an eventful life, but Vsevolodko appears just a few times in the primary sources as the ruler of the small city of Hrodna.[137] His marriage was arranged after his father's death at the behest of Volodi-

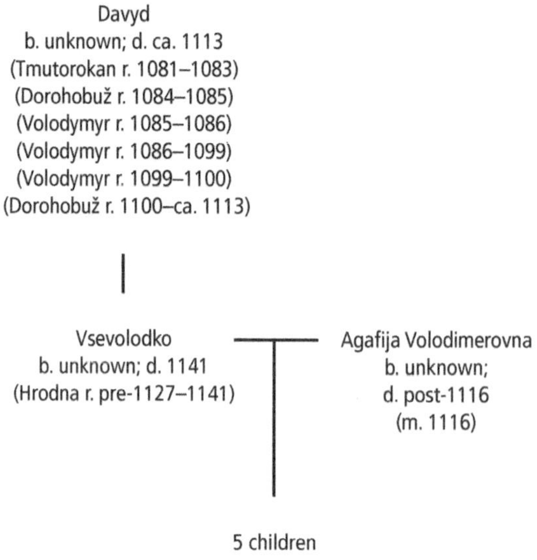

mer Monomax, then ruling in Kyiv, who married his daughter Agafija to Vsevolodko.[138] There is no reason for the marriage apparent in the Hypatian Chronicle entry for 1116, but it seems clear that Volodimer was attempting to tie this collateral branch of the Volodimeroviči to his own, thereby reinforcing his and his son's rule. In fact, Vsevolodko is portrayed, after this time, as "brother" to M´stislav Volodimerič, and at his beck and call for military operations along with his natal brothers.[139] Thus, it appears that the marriage served that purpose at the least, and demonstrated the ability of the ruler of Kyiv to arrange marriages both for his own advantage and to tie the larger Volodimeroviči family together.

Marija Svjatopolkovna
(tables 9, 17)

This marriage remains something of a mystery for multiple reasons. The first is the fact that the very identity of Marija is in dispute. Baumgarten identifies her as the daughter of Svjatopolk Izjaslavič,[140] while others, including V. T. Pašuto and the editor of Długosz's *Annales*, identify her as the daughter of Oleg Svjatoslavič.[141] No primary source, whether Latin or Rusian describes her parentage, leaving us further in the dark. However, two different Polish sources describe her as a consanguineous relation of Bolesław III's wife Sbyslava Svjatopolkovna.[142] The editor of Długosz dismisses this as false, but we cannot take it so lightly.[143] With all the work that has been done on consanguinity in the Middle Ages, it can be safely said that medieval peoples were well aware of

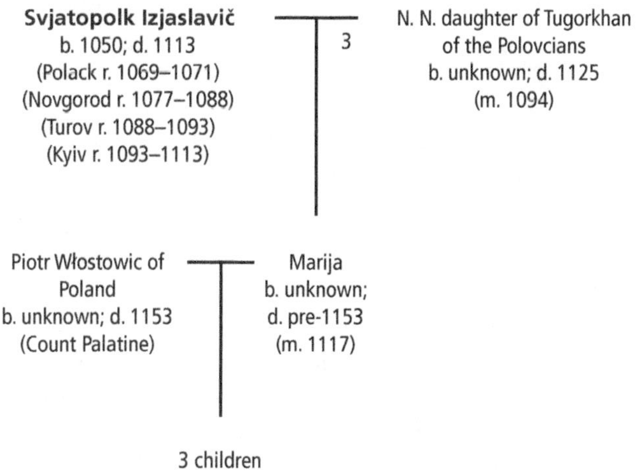

their blood relations and those of their spouses. A chronicler who was writing down the marriage of a popular count would certainly not neglect to mention such a fact. I do not believe that we can dismiss two statements that the wives of Bolesław III and Piotr Włostowic were blood relatives, and thus Marija is listed here as a Svjatopolkovna. This makes more sense for the political context of the marriage, as we will see momentarily.

The popularity of Marija's marriage partner leads to the second half of the complication for this marriage. Piotr Włostowic was a very famous figure in Poland at the time.[144] He was a favorite of Bolesław III and the founder of one of the major clans of late medieval Poland. Because Piotr was such a well-known figure much of his life has been mythologized, and thus it is hard for us to discern some of the true details of his early life.

In 1113 when Volodimer Monomax became ruler of Kyiv, he began a series of moves against Jaroslav Svjatopolčič, ruler of Volodymyr-Volyn, whom he viewed as one of his major rivals. One of the reasons that he viewed Jaroslav in this way was because of Jaroslav's close ties with Poland and Hungary, ties that Monomax did not have.[145] Monomax's campaign was steadily successful, and in 1117 Jaroslav attempted to buttress his position by again connecting his family to that of Bolesław III, to whom his sister was already married.[146] To that end, he arranged the marriage of his sister Marija to one of Bolesław's new favorites, Piotr Włostowic. The *Chronica Poloniae Maioris* records that Piotr married the Rusian princess at the directive of Bolesław.[147] Because of the bindings of consanguinity, which Bolesław III and Sbyslava barely avoided themselves, there could not be another marriage between the Piasts and any Izjaslaviči; however a marriage with one of his most powerful liegemen was easily arranged. This marriage would ideally strengthen the relationship between Poland and the Izjaslaviči at a time when Jaroslav Svjatopolčič was in need of assistance.

This interpretation of events differs from that offered by Pašuto, who posits a marriage between Marija, as daughter of Oleg Svjatoslavič, and Skarbimir, another of Bolesław's counts. The purpose of the marriage was to connect Skarbimir into a Rusian coalition including the Svjatoslaviči, Volodimer Monomax, and Volodar´ Rostislavič, ruler of Peremyšl, so that he would have Rusian backing to rebel against Bolesław III. Unfortunately for him, his rebellion was a failure, and Pašuto believes that his lands, titles, and wife were all given to Piotr Włostowic.[148] Since there is no clear attribution of Marija as an Olegovna and since she may be a blood relative of Sbyslava Svjatopolkovna, this seems a more unlikely hypothesis.

While in Poland Marija founded the church of the Blessed Virgin Mary in Arena, outside the walls of Wrocław.[149] This is the only known church explicitly known to have been founded by a Rusian woman in her new country, and it might also be the only known church at this time (mid-twelfth century) to have been founded by a Volodimeroviči woman anywhere in Europe. Marija may have also had a hand in the foundation of the Monastery of St. Vincent built at the same site,[150] which was where she and Piotr were buried in an elaborate stone coffin, drawings of which have survived to this day.[151] Unfortunately, much of Marija's identity is conjecture, but it has been included here, and in the tables in part 2, as a reasonable conjecture.

Andrej Volodimerič
(tables 12, 21)

The youngest son of Volodimer Monomax was given, like his brother Jurij, in marriage to a steppe princess by his father. However, while the marriage of Jurij is presented with context in the chronicles, the marriage of Andrej contains almost none. The Hypatian Chronicle records that in 1117 "poja Volodimer za Andrěja vnuku Tug″rt″kanovu" (Volodimer took for Andrej a granddaughter of Tugorkhan).[152] Before and after are completely unrelated events each with their own "in that year" preface. The brief entry itself provides little information about who Andrej was marrying. Later chronicles such as the Tver Chronicle provide a fuller sentence, but still no context, saying that, "togo že lěta

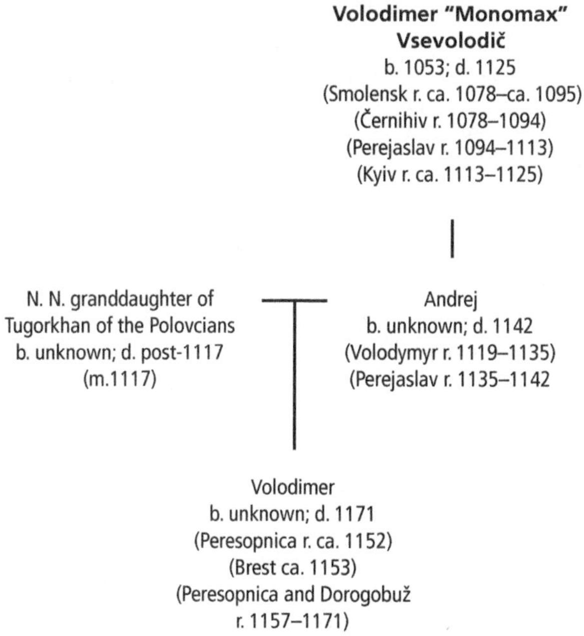

knjaz´ velikij ženi syna svoego Andrea, poa za nego vnuku Tugurkanja, knjazja Poloveckago" (That same year, the *velikij knjaz´* took for his son Andrej the granddaughter of Tugorkhan, *knjaz´* of the Polovcians).[153] There is slightly more clarification here, in particular the position of the grandfather of Andrej's bride. With such little information only hesitant guesses can be made as to the purpose of the marriage. The traditional purpose of the steppe marriage, as was seen with Andrej's brother Jurij, was to make peace between the two parties. Though entries indicate warring with the Polovcians around this time, there is no indication that Tugorkhan's son or grandson was in charge or that he was the person to make peace with. The last time Tugorkhan was seen in the Rusian chronicles was as the father-in-law of Svjatopolk Izjaslavič, receiving honorable burial after attacking Rus´.[154] Thus, because of the lack of information on the descendants of Tugorkhan and the lack of context in the notation concerning the marriage, few conclusions can be drawn.

One additional chronicle muddies, rather than clears, the picture. The Voskresenskij Chronicle carries the same statement read above, but with a slight difference. It identifies the woman not as a granddaughter of Tugorkhan, but of Tmutorokan, "vnuku Tmutorokanju Poloveč´skago knjazja."[155] This raises the specter of Tmutorokan and adds to the list of possibilities. Instead of making a rash judgment, it is better to believe that the chronicler or a later copyist merely attempted to make sense of an unfamiliar Turkic personal name by making a minor emendation. Thus it seems as with so many other marriages with the steppe, a hesitant guess as to the purpose of the marriage, peace between Volodimer and this particular clan of the Polovcians, is the best that can be accomplished.

Vsevolod Davydič
(tables 11, 17)

Not much is known about the marriage of the second son of Davyd Svjatoslavič. There is only one enigmatic line recorded in a couple of chronicles that says that "Tom že lětě vedoša Ljaxovicju Mjuromu za Davydoviča Vsevoloda" (In that year, a Polish woman arrived in Murom for Vsevolod Davydič).[156] The traditional assumption made by everyone from Baumgarten to Dimnik is that this Polish woman was the daughter of Bolesław III and thus was most likely the daughter of Sbyslava Svjatopolkovna.[157]

Despite the widespread acceptance of this conclusion, there are two problems that exist. The first and most pressing for the historian is that there is no evidence that gives her identity as a Boleslavna. The reign

Davyd Svjatoslavič
b. 1051; d. 1123
(Novgorod r. post-1088–1095)
(Smolensk r. 1095–1096)
(Černihiv r. 1096–1123)

|

Vsevolod b. unknown; d. post-1124 (Murom r. ca. 1124)	———	N. N., Polish woman b. unknown; d. post-1124 (m. 1124)

of Bolesław III is generally well recorded in Polish chronicles, but no daughter is mentioned as having married a Davydič.[158] Even Długosz, whose work contains many later additions from foreign sources, does not ever mention Vsevolod Davydič.[159] The second problem is that such a marriage is improbable considering the political situation of the time. Even Dimnik, who stretches to explain foreign connections of the Svjatoslaviči, does not offer an explanation as to why a Polish princess would marry a Svjatoslavič prince of Murom.[160]

Bolesław III and his entire family had a longer association with the Izjaslaviči, often working against the Svjatoslaviči. In the year before this marriage, 1123, there was a concerted effort by various Rusian rulers, including the Svjatoslaviči, to kill Jaroslav Svjatopolčič,[161] who had strong ties to Poland through his family heritage, as well as through his second wife, the sister of Bolesław III.[162] It seems highly improbable that the next year Bolesław III would ally himself with a minor ruler whose powerful father Davyd of Černihiv had already died and whose power had passed to his younger brother Jaroslav.[163] The only marginally acceptable explanation is offered by N. I. Ščaveleva, who suggests that Bolesław III may have arranged the marriage to keep up an anti-Monomaxovič alliance.[164] This seems to be a misinterpretation of his earlier policies, which could better be characterized as pro-Izjaslaviči, and thus is doubtful as a solution.

Though it can be claimed without a doubt that the woman Vsevolod married was a Pole, her actual identity remains unknown, and it is doubtful that she was a daughter of Bolesław III. The possibilities for marriageable Polish women were increasing in the twelfth century, as Polish noble families began to develop their own connections abroad. This may have been an attempt by such a family, or by the Svjatoslaviči, to establish a connection between two groups of powerful but not royal[165] families.

Oleg Svjatoslavič
b. 1050; d. 1115
(Tmutorokan r. 1078–1079)
(Tmutorokan r. 1083–1094)
(Černihiv r. 1094–1096)
(Novhorod-Siverskyj r. ca. 1097–1115)

Vsevolod
b. unknown; d. 1146
(Černihiv r. 1127–1139)
(Kyiv r. 1139–1146)

— Marija,
daughter of M´stislav Volodimerič
b. unknown; d. 1178
(m. ca. 1127)

Svjatoslav
b. unknown; d. 1194
(Turov r. 1142)
(Volodymyr r. 1142–1146)
(Busk r. 1146–ca. 1154)
(Turov r. 1154–1155)
(Novhorod-Siverskyj r. 1158–1164)
(Černihiv r. 1164–1177)
(Kyiv r. 1174)
(Kyiv r. 1177–1180)
(Novgorod r. 1180–1181)
(Kyiv r. 1180–1194)

— N. N., daughter of Vasil'ko Svjatoslavič
b. unknown;
d. post-1143
(m. 1143)

Zvenislava
b. unknown;
d. post-1142
(m. 1142)

— Bolesław the Tall
b. unknown;
d. 1201

Jaroslav
b. 1140; d. 1198
(Cernihiv r. 1177–1198)

Vsevolod Ol´govič
(tables 10, 13, 17)

The only known marriage of the last ruler of Kyiv during the period of a united Rus´ is difficult to find information about, despite its importance. His bride is typically identified as Marija M´stislavna, daughter of M´stislav Volodimerič,[166] mostly because of a passage in the Hypatian Chronicle under the year 1141 where the M´stislaviči obliquely reference a sister with Vsevolod Ol´govič.[167] The date of the marriage is entirely unknown, though Dimnik speculates that it took place after the Ljubeč conference in 1097.[168] In part, I imagine that he dates the marriage to this time because of the estimation of Vsevolod's birthdate circa 1083.[169] While that does make Vsevolod a maritally eligible fourteen-year old in 1097, any potential daughter of M´stislav could only be two years of age in 1097.[170] Zotov uses a more viable date of 1116, following Pogodin, but that too is unsubstantiated by primary source material, or convincing analysis.[171] The reporting of birth dates are uncommon in the early twelfth century, but marriage dates are more reliable, and M´stislav has daughters who marry in 1111 (Malfrid M´stislavna), 1112 (N. N. M´stislavna to Jaroslav Sviatopolčič), and 1115 (Ingeborg M´stislavna). Marital age in the Rusian world was typically in the teens, with children being born within the first year, or so, of marriage.[172] Thus, M´stislav's daughter who married in 1111 would have been, at a minimum, approximately fourteen years of age upon her marriage—thus her birth year would be 1097. Similarly, the children of Vsevolod Ol´govič can be used to determine the approximate date of his marriage. He has children who marry in 1141 (Zvenislava Vsevolodovna), and 1143 (Svjatoslav Vsevolodič). Assuming a minimum age of fourteen for the marriage of a woman in Rus´,[173] Zvenislava would have been born in 1127 at the latest, and certainly no earlier than 1121, based upon prevailing marital customs. It would be extremely unlikely to have a gap of twenty or more years between marriage and the birth of a first child, especially in such a society focused upon familial place, and especially for a ruler in such high office. Thus, we must date this marriage to the 1120s broadly. Further, I will offer a suggestion for a specific date and reason for the marriage below.

Vsevolod Ol´govič appeared upon the Rusian political scene for the first time in 1127/28 when he usurped his uncle's throne and took Černihiv for himself.[174] The Hypatian Chronicle in particular records that M´stislav Volodimerič, then ruling in Kyiv, mobilized against this usurpation, but there was no result to that campaign other than Jaroslav Svjatoslavič settling into Murom, his prior place of rule.[175] Invariably such military campaigns were settled with peace agreements and the two parties kissing the cross to one another, and often the peace agreement was sealed by a marriage between the two main families involved. Though it is not explicitly noted in this case, this is what I would suggest occurred as part of the peace agreement between Vsevolod Ol´govič and M´stislav Volodimerič in 1127.[176] A marriage between the new ruler of Černihiv, one of the major cities of Rus´, and the daughter of the new ruler of Kyiv would cement Vsevolod into place as part of the political hierarchy of Rus´, despite the past problems of the Ol´goviči. This marriage would also reinforce Vsevolod's place in the familial hierarchy of Rus´, making Vsevolod not only one of the Volodimeroviči, but also a son-in-law of M´stislav, and thus (theoretically) bound to his authority. This marriage date makes sense in the context of the political relationships, as well as the dates of the marriages of Vsevolod's children.[177] This marriage bound together two of the most powerful families in Rus´, and laid the foundation, perhaps, for Vsevolod's own succession to Kyiv, as well as reinforcing the peace of M´stislav's reign.

Davyd Svjatoslavič
b. 1051; d. 1123
(Novgorod r. post-1088–1095)
(Smolensk r. 1095–1096)
(Černihiv r. 1096–1123)

Volodimer
b. unknown;
d. 1151
(Černihiv r. 1139– 1151)

1

N. N., daughter of
Vsevolodko Davydič
b. unknown;
d. post-1159
(1st m. 1144)
(2nd m. between
1151–1159)

2

Baškord of the
Polovcians
b. unknown;
d. post-1159
(Polovcian tribe
r. ca. 1159)

2 children

Volodimer Davydič
(tables 8, 11)

Vsevolod Ol´govič arranged two marriages for daughters of Vsevolodko Davydič in 1144. Due to the structure of this chapter, which is based upon generations from Volodimer and focused on Rusian males as a guiding principle, the second daughter, who was married to Vsevolod's own cousin Volodimer Davydič, will be dealt with first.[178] This is another example of the Kyivan ruler's ability to arrange marriages for the Volodimeroviči family at large, but it also bears very specifically on his own larger family, the Svjatoslaviči. Volodimer Davydič, in 1144, was already the ruler of Černihiv, having succeeded Vsevolod himself when Vsevolod took control of Kyiv.[179] Thus, his marriage would have been important to the larger Svjatoslaviči interests, but perhaps not to the interests of Vsevolod's own burgeoning ambitions. One possible reason to arrange this marriage was to provide his cousin with a wife, an outwardly good gesture, for the sake of the larger family, but a wife who brought with her almost no political power whatsoever. Vsevolodko Davydič had died in 1141, his sons were largely nonexistent in the power plays within Rus´, and the family as a whole would not have brought territory, influence, or connections of any sort to Volodimer.[180] It also would have stopped Volodimer from making a more advantageous marriage on his own. Though speculation, it is possible that this was an attempt by Vsevolod to manage Volodimeroviči marital relations broadly, and Svjatoslaviči relations specifically, to the advantage of his branch of the family. Of course, the fact must also be considered that there were few options among the Svjatoslaviči for a partner for the

Vsevolodkovna, as the majority were married, dead, or too young, with only Igor´ Ol´govič as a notable exception.[181] For Volodimer Davydič, then, the purpose of the marriage was largely focused on procreation, and the couple had one son, Svjatoslav, before Volodimer's death in 1151.[182] It is unlikely that it was due to Vsevolod's manipulation, but Volodimer Davydič's line never challenged his own.

Volodimer's death was not the last heard of the Vsevolodkovna. In a rarely seen event, she remarried following Volodimer's death, moreover she married a Polovcian ruler, something completely unprecedented in Rusian dynastic marriage until this time. Marriages between the Volodimeroviči and the Polovcians had been occurring since the end of the eleventh century,[183] but always between Volodimeroviči men and daughters of the Polovcian rulers, most likely because of religious issues regarding Christianization. However, in the Tver Chronicle under the year 1159, there is reference made to Svjatoslav Volodimerič's stepfather, Baškord of the Polovcians.[184] Beyond a simple mention, Baškord assists Svjatoslav Volodimerič, most likely because of those familial ties which are explicitly mentioned by the chronicler. Though she never appears in a chronicle after her marriage in 1144, this unknown Vsevolodkovna is the first Volodimeroviči woman to marry a Polovcian ruler, and she even extends her familial connections among the Polovcians to help her son by her first husband. Who arranged this marriage and the purpose of the marriage are unknown, but that it was beneficial to her family was made clear in 1159, even if all that existed of her family at that time was her son.

Marriages: Generation Five

Volodar´ b. unknown; d. 1124 (Tmutorokan r. 1081–1083) (Volodymyr r. 1084) (Peremyšl r. 1092–1120) (Peremyšl r. 1122–1124)		
N. N. b. unknown; d. post-1104 (m. 1104)	——	N. N., "Carevič" Comnenus of Byzantium b. unknown; d. post-1104

N. N. Volodarovna
(tables 4, 20)

The *PVL* records that in 1104 a daughter of Volodar´ Rostislavič was sent to Constantinople to marry a *carevič*, the son of Emperor Alexius Comnenus.[1] Baumgarten identifies this *carevič* as Sebastocrator Isaac.[2] However, Isaac would have been only eleven years old at this time, and thus this seems unlikely. Każdan, in reviewing the scholarship and sources on this marriage, cannot find any support for the identification of the *carevič* as Isaac or as any son of Alexius.[3] The only Byzantine source that offers the hope of identification is the *Typikon* of the Nunnery of the Theotokos founded by Alexius's wife Irene, which mentions two daughters-in-law, both of whom were also named Irene.[4] This source, however, does not identify the women any further, with place of origin or their name before it was changed to Irene, leaving the situation unresolved. The *PVL* identifies the daughter of Volodar´ Rostislavič as marrying a Comnenian *carevič*, but this cannot be verified by other sources. Rusian chroniclers may also have used the title *carevič* indiscriminately, which leads to modern problems of identification. As far as an explanation for such a marriage, the Rostislaviči were still holding on to their positions in the west of Rus´. As such, they were the closest to the Byzantine-held lands of Bulgaria and to the more Byzantine-influenced land of Hungary, so there might have been an interest in maintaining such ties. Some decades later there was a great deal of interaction between a Rostislavič ruler, Jaroslav Osmomysl (who was the nephew of this Volodarovna), and the Comneni, as described by Ioannes Kinnamos.[5] Though the *PVL* mentions this marriage, there is nothing to substantiate that reference, so it retains an air of mystery. It may be accepted that a Volodarovna married a Byzantine, but exactly who he was and what his position was is as yet unknown.

Kristín Ingesdottir of Sweden b. unknown; d. 1122 (m. ca. 1095)	1	**M´stislav "Harald" Volodimerič** b. 1076; d. 1132 (Novgorod r. 1095–1117) (Bilhorod r. 1117–1125) (Kyiv r. 1125–1132)

Sigurd "the Crusader" Magnusson of Norway b. unknown; d. 1130 (Norway r. 1103–1130)	1	Malfrid b. unknown; d. post-1135 (1st m. 1111) (2nd m. 1132)	2	Eric "Emune" Ericsson of Denmark b. unknown; d. 1137 (Denmark r. 1134–1137)

Malfrid M´stislavna
(tables 13, 15)

Being ruler of Novgorod allowed one to make a wide array of foreign connections. This was no different for M´stislav Volodimerič, especially since his wife was Kristín, daughter of King Inge Steinkelsson of Sweden. M´stislav made use of his wife's, as well as his own, Scandinavian connections to arrange the marriages of two of his daughters.[6]

Malfrid M´stislavna is an enigma in the Rusian sources, where she does not appear. We know, however, from Latin and Old Norse sources that she married King Sigurd "the Crusader" of Norway.[7] V. T. Pašuto has dated this marriage to 1111, and added that she was in Schleswig at the time as a guest of Duke Welf.[8] Those details cannot be confirmed, but the approximate time of the marriage is correct. Sigurd was on crusade in the eastern Mediterranean from 1107–1110,[9] and at the time of his return was only twenty years old, thus it was reasonable that he would not have married before leaving. Why the marriage was arranged remains a mystery, though perhaps there is a simple explanation, such as increasing preexisting family ties[10] or tying together Baltic powers such as Rus´ and Norway.[11] A. F. Litvina and F. B. Uspenskij, however, have noted Orderic Vitalis's conclusion that Sigurd returned from the crusades via Rus´, and met and married Malfrid while there.[12] Though this is not widely accepted,[13] it provides an interesting possibility, and another example of the many Scandinavian royal visitors to Rus´. Snorre Sturluson in his *Heimskringla* narrates the history of the Norse kings, but Sigurd's marriage to Malfrid, or "Malmfrid" as she is referred to in the text, receives very little description, though her genealogy is extensively traced, especially her Scandinavian connections.[14] This may be because the marriage to Malfrid was slightly fraught, as is apparent from Sigurd's demand that he be allowed to marry his mistress Cecilia, though the author prefaces this with such statements as "his mind wandered."[15] Malfrid is not mentioned at all in the episode, only Sigurd and multiple bishops who unsuccessfully attempted to dissuade the king from his goal. But even if he did marry Cecilia, who left him in 1130 when he was on his deathbed, he never set aside Malfrid, and may in fact have been married to both at the same time. The *Heimskringla* presents this as the whim of an older king, and no other reason is available to us, though the story may also be a set piece designed to portray the negative foreign influence of German ecclesiastics in Scandinavia, which would make the whole episode suspect. The issue of inheritance, which might have motivated such a decision, was not in doubt as Malfrid had borne him a daughter, Christina,[16] and a previous mistress, Borghild, had given him a son, Magnus,[17] so he had a living male heir. Although Magnus was illegitimate, this was not a problem in early twelfth-century Scandinavia. Sigurd died in 1130, leaving Malfrid a widow.[18] But unlike many women in dynastic marriages, she did not return home upon her husband's death;[19] instead she stayed in the Norwegian royal court as stepmother to the new king, Magnus, which placed her in an effective position to aid her sister the next year.

In 1131, Knud Lavard, duke of Schleswig, king of the Abodrites, and not insignificantly husband of Malfrid's sister Ingeborg, was murdered by his cousin Magnus Nielsson.[20] After a failed bid at retaliation by Lothar, king of the German Empire, Knud's brother Eric took up his cause and began to battle Magnus Nielsson and Magnus's father.[21] According to Saxo Grammaticus, Magnus of Norway approached Eric, who was acting as guardian for his sister-in-law Ingeborg and her children, about a marriage alliance between Magnus of Norway and Ingeborg and Knud's eldest daughter Kristín.[22] As part of that alliance, Eric proposed that he also marry Malfrid, Magnus' stepmother, to strengthen the ties between them. The main purpose of the alliance was that Magnus, who had inherited the vast majority of his father's fleet and arms, would assist Eric in his battle against Magnus Nielsson. As it stands, this is already a fascinating tale of a double dynastic marriage designed to advance the cause of two realms. Eric needed weapons and ships, and Magnus needed a measure of support in terms of manpower and legitimacy as he waged a semi–cold war with his uncle Harald.[23] But if one takes into account the Rusian factor, and reads Saxo's account with that purpose and with a better opinion of the importance of women than a medieval writer would have had, the story becomes even better. After Knud Lavard was murdered, the German king attempted to avenge him, but was bought off. Eric, his brother, attempted to avenge him, but was beaten. It took the intervention of Malfrid to push Magnus to make the overture to Eric to aid his cause, which was, in fact, the cause of Malfrid's sister, and eventually of Malfrid's infant nephew Valdemar, who was named after their grandfather, Volodimer Monomax. The marriage for her may simply have been a way of causing the alliance to take immediate effect, as Kristín, Knud's daughter, was yet too young to be married.[24] Considering the web of family relations involved it is easy to see how Malfrid could have been a driving force to aid her sister's family.

The alliance came in handy quite quickly, since Eric, Malfrid, and Eric's son Svein had to flee the next year (1132) after losing a battle to Magnus Nielsson and his father. They were able to seek refuge in Norway with King Magnus Sigurdsson, who sheltered them for a time.[25] Unfortunately these marital ties were not as strong as money; that winter Eric, Malfrid, and Svein were forced to flee in the night after having been warned by Magnus's wife Kristín (Ingeborg's daughter and Malfrid's niece) that Magnus Sigurdsson had been bought off by King Niels of Denmark.[26] Kristín valued her natal ties more than her marital ties and destroyed her marriage (she was repudiated afterwards)[27] to save her aunt and uncle.

It would be wonderful to have more details of the life of Malfrid, as she seems to have led an interesting one. She was married at a relatively young age, had to deal with a succession of mistresses sharing her husband, was queen of both Norway and Denmark, and may have arranged an international alliance to aid her sister and her family.

Ingeborg M′stislavna
(tables 13, 15)

After assuming the Kyivan throne in 1113, one of the main goals of Volodimer Monomax seems to have been to counter the foreign ties of the Izjaslaviči and thus prevent them from seizing power. One of the ways in which he did this was by arranging a marriage between his granddaughter Ingeborg and Knud Lavard. Knud was a son of the Danish king Eric Ejegod, but he had been displaced by his uncle Niels

Kristín Ingesdottir of Sweden
b. unknown; d. 1122
(m. ca. 1095)

1

M´stislav "Harald" Volodimerič
b. 1076; d. 1132
(Novgorod r. 1095–1117)
(Bilhorod r. 1117–1125)
(Kyiv r. 1125–1132)

Ingeborg
b. unknown;
d. post-1137
(m. ca. 1115)

Knud "Lavard" Ericsson of Denmark
b. unknown; d. 1131
(Duke of Schleswig r. 1115–1131)
(King of the Abodrite Slavs r. ca. 1128–1131)

after his father's death on crusade.[28] After he came of age he went to the court of Lothar, duke of Saxony,[29] who appointed him to the vacant post of duke of Schleswig in 1115.[30] The date of the marriage was not recorded, but it most likely occurred at this time.[31] Lothar was a major power in central Europe and a foe of the Poles, and Knud was one of his favorites. This alliance meant that, as was the case with Evpraksija, the ruling power in Kyiv had protection against the Izjaslaviči because the Poles were threatened from multiple sides.[32] This was all part of Monomax's overall plan to isolate Jaropolk Svjatopolčič in Volodymyr-Volyn and eventually drive him from power.

Saxo Grammaticus offers a different explanation for the marriage, one grounded in Scandinavian familial connections. He asserts that the marriage was arranged by Queen Margaret of Denmark, daughter of Inge Steinkelsson of Sweden and sister to M´stislav Volodimerič's wife, Kristín. Margaret was married to Niels Sveinsson, the king of Denmark, who had succeeded Knud's father, Eric Ejegod. According to Saxo, in an attempt to draw the family closer together and build support for her son Magnus, she arranged a marriage between her niece Ingeborg and her nephew by marriage, Knud (and also arranged another marriage between kinsmen).[33] This is an important acknowledgment of medieval kinship ties and the power of marital ties, both of which are generally assumed and illustrated, but rarely stated outright in the sources. That said, this may be a rationalization of the marriage based on too little information and the author's reliance on genealogical explanations for causation, as is evident in other places in Saxo. The marriage of Ingeborg and Knud was made in the large-scale arena of interkingdom politics, and while Saxo's explanation is reasonable, the larger picture of European politics should also be considered when looking at this marriage.

In Saxo's portrayal, Margaret seemed truly interested in building loyalty for Magnus, and once the two marriages she arranged had occurred, she divided her patrimony into three, keeping one piece for herself, and giving one piece each to her two nieces.[34] Although we are forced to guess at the material means that other Rusian queens had, we know in the case of Ingeborg that she owned land in Sweden that was deeded to her from her aunt. Eric Christiansen in his commentary on Saxo notes that Scandinavian royal women regularly inherited property, though usually patrimonial, not royal, lands.[35] This suggests that Kristín, wife of M´stislav, would also have inherited patrimonial land in Sweden, which she could have kept to maintain herself in Novgorod or later deeded to her children.[36] This is a fascinating insight into the maintenance of medieval women abroad in general, and specifically the maintenance of Rusian women and women in Rus´.

The *Knýtlinga Saga* offers up a third version of the marriage to contrast with the two already given. This later saga states that Knud Lavard knew of Ingeborg and her family and that he dispatched a friendly Baltic trader whom he had converted to Christianity, Vidgaut, as his emissary to "Harald" (M´stislav Volodimerovič) to negotiate a marriage agreement. Harald is clearly identified via his, his mother's, and his wife's genealogies. In the saga Vidgaut successfully impresses Harald with tales of Knud, about whom Harald has already heard, and with Ingeborg's consent the marriage is arranged. Vidgaut then returns to inform Knud, who prepares for the festivities while Ingeborg is dispatched from Rus´ "with a splendid retinue."[37] This version of the story is particularly interesting, as it contains many details that are not seen elsewhere that develop the ideas behind the importance of dynastic marriages—that is, an emissary is sent to arrange the marriage, the consent of the woman involved is received, and the bride brings a retinue with her to her new kingdom.[38] The details are very important in the dynastic marriage process, and the account in *Knýtlinga Saga* becomes more convincing because of their inclusion. Whether Knud arranged the marriage himself via the embassy of Vidgaut, or whether it was arranged through the auspices of Queen Margaret, is impossible to say with any certainty. Even if Margaret had arranged the marriage, an emissary to her sister Kristín and her brother-in-law M´stislav would have been required, as would an accompanying retinue for the returning bride. While not always mentioned, these parts of the dynastic marriage tradition were still necessary, and thus the stories might contain complementary pieces of information.

Knud's relationship with his uncle and cousin was a complex one. Niels was, most likely, the rightful heir to Knud's father Eric Ejegod, as the Danes practiced a system of lateral succession from brother to brother (similar to Rus´).[39] Thus, Knud's loyalty to Lothar of Saxony and Knud's subsequent naming as king of the Abodrites[40] are viewed as evidence of animus between Knud and Niels, especially in light of later actions. This situation is made more complicated by evidence from the chronicle of Helmold, who notes a collegial relationship between Niels as king of Denmark and Knud as a powerful neighbor.[41] This relationship, while not necessarily friendly, was in Helmold's portrayal worrisome to Margaret, who was interested in the succession of her own son to the throne (a concern also made evident in Saxo). Her worries were, in all likelihood, well founded, as following a system of lateral succession, Knud would have precedence over her son Magnus, which is likely why she incited Magnus to kill Knud. Margaret's actions, while plausible, also fit into the medieval topos of the manipulative queen, and thus must be read with caution.[42] Magnus's plotting roused Ingeborg to warn her husband about Magnus, about whom she had misgivings because of a premonition in a dream.[43] A dream foreshadowing the future is a tool of the narration of saint's lives (Knud is later sainted), as well as other medieval writings, but it does serve as another mention of Ingeborg, and notice of her agency. Knud disregarded his wife's advice, and in 1131 Magnus arranged for an ambush, killing Knud after giving him the kiss of peace.[44] Eight days after the death of her husband, Ingeborg gave birth to their fourth child, their first son.[45] The boy was named Valdemar, in honor of Ingeborg's grandfather and the patriarch of her family, Volodimer Monomax.[46] The *Knýtlinga Saga* records that Ingeborg was in Rus´ at the time and thus gave the baby a Rusian name.[47] This was probably an attempt to explain the foreign name of Valdemar, which could more easily be explained by maternal influence, as has been shown in other Rusian cases,[48] particularly the case of the firstborn daughter of Ingeborg, Kristín.[49] Further, if one accepts some truth in her premonition and warning, that would require her to be in some proximity to Knud soon before his death.

As we have seen in the case of the dynastic marriage of her sister Malfrid, Ingeborg was aided by her brother-in-law Eric, who looked after her and her children and fought to avenge her husband, his brother. Ingeborg also received assistance from her sister, who was able to arrange the aid of her stepson King Magnus of Norway, and even married Eric Emune, who after avenging his brother Knud became king of Denmark.[50] While waging his war against Magnus, Eric operated from land in Scania in Sweden, using the people and resources of that territory as his own. Where he came by this land is unknown, but it can be suggested that this was part of the territory given to Ingeborg or Malfrid by their mother Kristín, who had gotten the land from her father Inge Steinkelsson, king of Sweden.[51] This land may have been granted permanently or temporarily to Eric to aid him in his campaign against the murderer of Ingeborg's husband.

Ingeborg's last known appearance in the primary sources is at the death of King Eric Emune, when the people of Denmark ask for her son Valdemar to be made king. However, because of his age (only eight years old), Ingeborg and other counselors advised that Eric Lamb be made king until Valdemar reached his age of majority.[52] Adviser was a typical role for a mother to play, but it is atypical for it to be recorded, so this an important instance to keep in mind. Unfortunately it is the last instance in which she is mentioned. It is known that one of her three daughters, Katrina, "was married in the east," which in the language of the *Knýtlinga Saga* almost always refers to Rus´.[53] Ingeborg would have likely had a hand in the marriage, but her actual involvement is uncorroborated. Nevertheless, the sources that we do have of her, and her role in these events, creates the picture of a remarkable life for the Rusian princess, including several items that show her loyalty, or consideration for, her natal family.

Davyd
b. unknown;
d. post-1129
(Polack r. 1101–1128)
(Polack r. 1129)

M´stislav "Harald" Volodimerič
b. 1076; d. 1132
(Novgorod r. 1095–1117)
(Bilhorod r. 1117–1125)
(Kyiv r. 1125–1132)

Brjačeslav
b. unknown;
d. post-1128
(Izjaslavl r. ca. 1128)

N. N.
b. unknown;
d. post-1127
(m. pre-1127)

Brjačeslav Davydič
(tables 2, 13)

There is no easily assignable date for the marriage of Brjačeslav Davydič and a daughter of M´stislav Volodimerič. The chronicles note the marriage simply through a familial relationship between Brjačeslav and the M´stislaviči, when Izjaslav M´stislavič helps his "zjat´" Brjačeslav during M´stislav's campaign against Polack in 1127.[54] However, put into the context of the wider Rusian political world of the early twelfth century, it is perhaps inevitable that a marriage between the M´stislaviči, or Volodimeriči more broadly, would have been made with someone of the Polack clan. The only prior dynastic marriage made by the Polack branch of the Volodimeroviči was with a daughter of Jaropolk Izjaslavič, a member of the rival Izjaslaviči branch of the family. In an effort to broaden his base of support, Volodimer, or more likely his son, might have arranged the marriage with the ruler of Polack, Davyd Vseslavič, for their children to marry. The effects of the marriage are seen in Izjaslav's intervention on behalf of his brother-in-law, and the subsequent protection of his sister's interests in Izjaslavl, Brjačeslav and his wife's home, during the Volodimeriči campaign against Polack.[55] Despite these efforts, however, Davyd of Polack and M´stislav were unable to come to a lasting accord, and in 1129 M´stislav banished Davyd and his kin to Constantinople.[56] In question is whether or not Brjačeslav and his wife were part of the banished. It would seem unlikely for M´stislav to banish his own daughter, a woman that he put in that position in the first place, but it is certainly not impossible. The two chronicles that specifically mention the banished by name do not list Brjačeslav or his wife,[57] while the chronicles that are more general in their statement include the children of Davyd, which would be Brjačeslav. Baumgarten has chosen to include Davyd and his wife among the banished, and has gone so far as to list a name for the M´stislavna, Xenia.[58] He does this based upon the "Itinerary of St. Antony of Novgorod," which describes Antony viewing a tomb of Xenia, daughter of Brjačeslav, during his stay in Constantinople.[59] In this context it is possible to acknowledge that Brjačeslav may have been banished and lived out the remainder of his life in Constantinople, most likely (in that case) with his wife.[60]

Rostislav Glěbovič
(tables 2, 5, 9)

Five of the thirteen internal Rusian dynastic marriages involve rulers from the Polack family, originating from Izjaslav Volodimerič. In large part this is because Polack went its own separate way much of this time, however the simple fact that the vast majority of Volodimeroviči were descended from Jaroslav created a separation that allowed for acceptable—that is, non-consanguineous—marriages sooner than with other branches of the larger family. The marriage of Rostislav Glěbovič and Sofija Jaroslavna, daughter of Jaroslav Svjatopolčič, was one of those marriages between Polack and the more populous Jaroslav Volodimerič line of Volodimeroviči, but by strict standards it was, in fact, consanguineous. The couple shared a great-grandfather, Izjaslav Jaroslavič, and were thus related in six degrees, one shy of the minimum requirement for marriage, though potentially acceptable in the Constantinopolitan Church.[61] This is a rare thing for Rusian internal marriages and bears mentioning because of that fact. When Rusians marry outside of Rus´, one common explanation has been that they are serving to broaden the

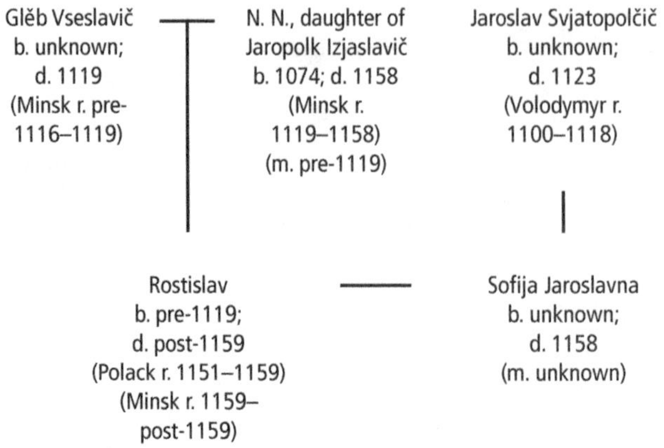

pool of consanguineous marriage partners.[62] This has not always been the case, as there are consanguineous marriages between Rusian and Polish couples, as well as Rusian and Hungarian couples. Whether the Rusians cared about consanguinity laws is unclear, and whether they cared or not may have been trumped by politics, as was often the case in the rest of Europe, but the observance or lack thereof of religious rules and norms presents an interesting case study, and one must ask why the rule or norm was broken.

This marriage seems to be part of a larger web of alliances that was being created as Polack was drawn back into larger Rusian, or Volodimeroviči, politics. The marriages of Glěb Vseslavič and Brjačeslav Davydič that preceded this[63] set the tone of Polack being drawn either into the Izjaslaviči, children of Izjaslav Jaroslavič, or M´stislaviči, children of M´stislav Volodimerič, camps (broadly construed). Glěb's son Rostislav continued his own alliance with the Izjaslaviči, marrying a daughter of Jaroslav Svjatopolčič, who had such trouble himself with the M´stislaviči, including his own failed marriage to a M´stislavna. The date of the marriage is difficult, if not impossible, to determine based on existing evidence. Jaroslav Svjatopolčič died in 1123,[64] and there is little information on Rostislav Glěbovič before his assumption of rule in 1151.[65] But an earlier date of marriage, perhaps in the 1120s, is probably correct. It is likely that Rostislav's mother arranged the marriage, or at least participated heavily, after his father's death in 1119.[66] She was the ruler of Minsk following Glěb's death, and was a member of the Izjaslaviči, thus putting her in a perfect position to arrange such a marriage to bolster her natal and marital families. There is, unfortunately, a potential problem with this theory of alliances that needs to be enumerated. In the Hypatian Chronicle entry for 1158, Izjaslav M´stislavič makes war on Jurij Jaroslavič in Turov.[67] This is, in a larger context, a continuation of the M´stislaviči versus Izjaslaviči battles of the early century. To do so, Izjaslav M´stislavič gathers a broad coalition including the people of Polack, a city which was ruled by Jurij's brother-in-law Rostislav Glěbovič. However, the chronicle entry further states that the Polack people support the war because of proximity and no ruler is ever mentioned for Polack, unlike all of the other forces assembled, and when defeated Jurij flees to Izjaslavl, which was ruled by his other brother-in-law, Vsevolod Glěbovič.[68] Thus, the single entry presents a conundrum. Why would the people of Polack support a war against their ruler's brother, and could they even do so without his favor? Further, why would Jurij flee to his brother-in-law after forces from another brother-in-law had just attacked him? Perhaps the entry for 1159 in which the people of Polack throw Rostislav out in favor of Rogvolod Borisič (perhaps not coincidentally married to a daughter of Izjaslav M´stislavič) helps explain the situation.[69] The boyars of Polack may have acted semi-independently in making war on Jurij Jaroslavič in 1158 and then worked to expel Rostislav Glěbovič in 1159 in favor of a ruler who was better connected in the current political climate. Such would be a move worthy of the people of Novgorod, who replaced their rulers with great frequency based on the strength of the ruler in Kyiv, or lack thereof. Though this does not provide us with concrete answers, it does weave Polack into the larger fabric of Rus´ through dynastic marriage.

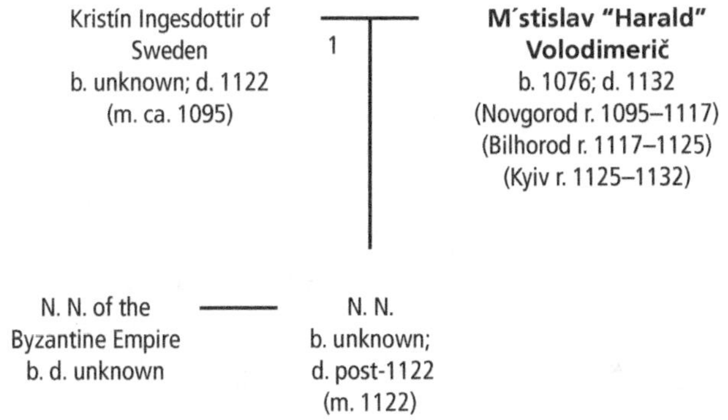

N. N. M´stislavna
(tables 13, 20)

As with the unknown Volodarovna, this M´stislavna presents a controversy in the historical scholarship. The Hypatian Chronicle records that in 1122 she went to Constantinople to marry the emperor.[70] The emperor at this time was John II, who was very well known and whose spouse was the Hungarian princess, Irene-Piroska. So it seems rather unlikely that he was the intended spouse of the M´stislavna. Historians have since tried out various theories, including having her marry the sons of John II.[71] There are no extant Byzantine records that record her existence, so one is left with only gray areas and suppositions. She is included in Każdan's study of Rus´-Byzantine marriages, although he cannot find evidence either to confirm or deny the existence of a marriage between a M´stislavna and a Byzantine.[72] Though a union is mentioned in the Hypatian Chronicle, it does not appear in the Laurentian or elsewhere,[73] and neither the marriage nor the M´stislavna are present in any Byzantine records. Also in the Hypatian account for 1122 is the notation that Metropolitan Nikita arrived from Constantinople.[74] This part of the entry is propagated throughout multiple chronicles, demonstrating that there was a consistent knowledge of Byzantine ties, as well as a penchant for duplication of Byzantine information in the chronicles.[75] This may seem irrelevant, but is in fact important to note. The Rusian chroniclers were good at excising, or simply not including, information that was not of interest to them, but ties with Byzantium were almost never excised; rather, they were generally inflated.[76] That such an important entry as the marriage of a M´stislavna with a Byzantine emperor was left out indicates that such an event was not commonly known or believed to have occurred.

The Rusian political situation at the time would have allowed for an alliance between Rus´ and Byzantium. Such an alliance, however, would have been more high profile than this seems to have been, and one can assume it would have been recorded in more than one chronicle, especially as the M´stislaviči were so successful in propagating themselves and their version of events. As mentioned above, the best conclusion that can be reached is that a M´stislavna may have married a Byzantine, though his name and rank are unknown. The claim that he was tsar or *carevič* seems unlikely, and combined with the lack of multiple sources of information, makes the marriage implausible. It has been included in the tables of part 2, but the extensive description here should indicate the extremely thin source base for the identity of the husband.

Vsevolod M´stislavič
(table 13)

It is clear from multiple chronicle sources that Vsevolod M´stislavič married in 1123, but whom he married is just as unclear.[77] The *NPL*, *NČL*, and Nikon chronicles all record Vsevolod's marriage in Novgorod, where he was ruling in that year. Similarly, there are records for the birth of a son, Ioann, a few years later, and then that son's death in 1128.[78] The name of a wife or even the hint of a wife's name never appears in any of the chronicles. However, Baumgarten, following Zotov, lists

Kristín Ingesdottir of Sweden
b. unknown; d. 1122
(m. ca. 1095)

1

M´stislav "Harald" Volodimerič
b. 1076; d. 1132
(Novgorod r. 1095–1117)
(Bilhorod r. 1117–1125)
(Kyiv r. 1125–1132)

Vsevolod
b. unknown; d. 1137
(Novgorod r. 1117–1132)
(Perejaslav r. 1132)
(Novgorod r. 1132–1136)
(Vyšehorod r. 1136–1137)
(Pskov r. 1137)

N. N.
b. unknown;
d. post-1136
(m. 1123)

her as a daughter of Svjatoslav Davydič of Černihiv.[79] This is purely conjectural, as far as I can determine, based upon a close reading of the progress of names in the chronicle entry. As such, I simply do not believe that it can be substantiated, as there is no primary source evidence for her identity. It is clear that there was a woman involved, but her identity is simply unknown.[80]

Volodar´
b. unknown; d. 1124
(Tmutorokan r. 1081–1083)
(Volodymyr r. 1084)
(Peremyšl r. 1092–1120)
(Peremyšl r. 1122–1124)

Volodimerko
b. unknown; d. 1152
(Zvenigorod r. 1126–pre-1140)
(Halyč [w/ Ivan Vasilkovič] r. pre-1140–1141)
(Halyč r. 1141–1152)

N. N., daughter of Koloman of Hungary
b. unknown;
d. post-1126
(m. pre-1126)

Volodimerko Volodarič
(tables 4, 18)

Volodimerko Volodarič was another in the line of rulers of Volodymyr-Volyn and Halyč, following in the footsteps of his father and uncles Volodar´ and Vasil´ko. The question here is who Volodimerko's wife was and thus who was the mother of Jaroslav Osmomysl, one of the most famous members of this line of rulers. The Rusian chronicles contain no mention of such a woman, though Tatiščev's work does. Tatiščev records a fascinating encounter, one that is recorded nowhere else that I have seen, under the year 1126, in which Volodimerko and his brother Rostislav went to war for control of their father's territory.[81] The battle is important because during it, as during many battles we have seen, the two sides expanded the conflict by seeking aid. Rostislav Volodarič called on his cousins the Vasilkoviči for assistance, while Volodimerko sent to the Hungarians. Moreover, when things turned against Volodimerko, he took his wife and children and fled to his "test´" in Hungary.[82] Ruling at the time in Hungary was Stephen II, the son of Koloman. Stephen II had just married in 1121, and so it is impossible that he had a daughter who would have already been married to Volodimerko and produced children.[83] In this instance "test´" is used beyond its modern meaning of "father-in-law" to mean "brother-in-law."[84] Wertner, in his history of the Árpáds and their genealogy, discusses a potential daughter of Koloman.[85] Though he does not link such a child to this marriage, it seems the most likely solution. Further it seems unlikely that Tatiščev would make such information up out of whole cloth without providing more information and embellishment. Instead of a full account of their marriage, which he has provided for others, he merely mentions her in passing as she is gathered up with the children to flee to Hungary. Moreover, the whole account of the strife over the territory of Volodar´ Rostislavič has the ring of truth, and the Hungarian component is only an element of the whole story, a place for Volodimerko to call for aid, find refuge, and get troops—the obvious purpose of the marriage for a western Rusian ruler. Potentially providing some measure of corroboration is an account from the Hypatian Chronicle from 1144, in which Volodimerko is captured and made to swear to Vsevolod but is helped by Hungarians.[86] Though it is thin, perhaps this is a continuance of Volodimerko's reliance on Hungarian troops because of his marriage, even though the regime had changed in Hungary.

All of this leads me to the conclusion that despite the dubious nature of the sole source, there does seem to have been a marriage between Volodimerko and a Hungarian princess, and a daughter of Koloman seems a likely candidate to fit the available facts.

Pribyslava Jaroslavna
(no tables)

This marriage exists in Baumgarten's genealogy,[87] but in no primary sources. It is documented in Pomeranian sources that Ratibor of Pomerania was married to a Pribyslava, but the identity of the Pribyslava is not confirmed anywhere.[88] Baumgarten, in a separate article, draws a fascinating picture of the identity of this Pribyslava in which he connects her to a daughter of Jaroslav Svjatopolčič and N. N. M´stislavna (daughter of M´stislav Volodimerič).[89] The article, and any chance at Pribyslava's identification, hinges on an identification by Saxo Grammaticus of Margaret, daughter of Pribyslava and Ratibor, as a relation of Valdemar I of Denmark.[90] Baumgarten draws this path through Valdemar's mother Ingeborg, and through Margaret's grandmother, who would be a daughter of M´stislav Volodimerič and thus a sister of Ingeborg.[91] Baumgarten's argument is convincing, as is an analysis of the political situation, which suggests that M´stislav was the supposed author of the marriage. Jaroslav Svjatopolčič had repudiated his M´stislavna wife in 1118 and subsequently died in 1123,[92] and M´stislav was attempting to shore up as much support in the north as he could. This marriage may have played a key part in keeping peace in the Baltic region, as well as playing an interesting role in the conversion of Pomerania. Ratibor converted in 1128, and Baumgarten dates the marriage to around 1130. Though Ratibor's conversion was through Otto of Bamberg,[93] some of the earliest priests in Pomerania around the ruler may have been from the Rusian micro-Christendom, the confessor of Pribyslava, and her entourage.

Despite all of this, however, there are no primary sources that substantiate the identity of Pribyslava as a daughter of Jaroslav Svjatopolčič, and thus it is difficult to list these participants on a genealogical chart. I find Baumgarten's argument highly plausible given the particular political situation in Europe, and have listed this marriage, derived largely from his suppositions, here, but have not included it on the genealogical tables.

N. N. Vasilkovna
(no tables)

The marriage of the daughter of Vasil´ko Rostislavič remains largely a mystery, even to the question of whether it was the daughter of Vasil´ko who was married at all. Baumgarten records the marriage, but no primary source evidence exists for the identity of the Rusian woman.[94] The identity of her suitor, on the other hand, is well established as the Moravian duke Vratislav.[95] In the continuation of the chronicle of Cosmas of Prague under the year 1132 there is a listing that Vratislav, duke of Brno, took a wife from Rus´.[96] Other than a lengthy account of her beauty and comparisons to Helen of Troy (which resulted in the name Helena being ascribed to her),[97] neither the identity of this woman nor of her father (most common in Latin chronicles) is established. That being said, I cannot support Baumgarten's opinion that the woman is the daughter of Vasil´ko without further evidence.

The political situation at the time also raises questions as to the cause of the marriage. At the time of the marriage in 1132, Vasil´ko had been dead for some time, and it is unclear who would have been handling his daughter's marriage. Her eldest brother Igor´ was ruler of Halyč, and married to a daughter of Vsevolod Ol´govič, and thus may have had some power in the west of Rus´ and could have contracted his sister's marriage.[98] Vratislav was in exile from roughly 1129–30, potentially in Rus´, as his cousin Otto III was contemporaneously.[99] This opens up the possibility of a meeting in Rus´, or in an area of Rus´ such as Halyč, which could have led to an arranged marriage. Further, in 1132 he took his position as Duke of Brno,[100] a city in Moravia that was, most likely, on the east-west land route between Kyiv and Prague, and would have played a major trading role for both Moravia and Halyč. The gain for both sides may have been economic, while also creating a new tie between Rus´ and Moravia, though all of this is pure conjecture, since the identity of the bride rests solely on Baumgarten's identification. Due to this, I have not listed this marriage in any of the tables.

Vasil´ko
b. unknown; d. 1124
(Volodymyr r. 1084)
(Terebovl r. pre-1097–1097)
(Terebovl r. ca. 1098–1124)

|

Ivan
b. unknown; d. 1141
(Halyč [w/ Vladimirko
Volodarič] r. pre-1140–1141)

Ivan Vasilkovič
(table 4)

Ivan Vasilkovič appears only in the Hypatian Chronicle, and only in two entries under the years 1140 and 1141, where in 1140 he is seen ruling part of Halyč with his cousin Volodimerko Volodarič and then in 1141 his death is recorded.[101] There is no marriage or a hint of a marriage in the primary sources as far as can be determined. However, Baumgarten lists a marriage of Ivan Vasilkovič, whom he refers to as Igor´, with a daughter of Vsevolod Ol´govič, Anna.[102] As I have been unable to find this "Anna" or evidence of a marriage of Ivan's in the primary sources, I would suggest that this marriage does not, in fact, exist, and I have only listed it here (not in the tables of part 2) in deference to Baumgarten's inclusion of the marriage in his tables.

Vsevolod
b. unknown; d. 1146
(Černihiv r. 1127–1139)
(Kyiv r. 1139–1146)

Marija,
daughter of M′stislav
Volodimerič
b. unknown; d. 1178
(m. ca. 1127)

Zvenislava
b. unknown;
d. post-1142
(m. 1142)

Bolesław the Tall
b. unknown;
d. 1201

Zvenislava Vsevolodovna
(tables 10, 17)

In both 1141 and 1142 the Hypatian Chronicle records Vsevolod as sending a daughter to the Poles.[103] However, in 1142 the entry is more extensive, saying that Vsevolod's daughter Zvenislava was sent to the Poles for Bolesław.[104] It is a rare example in the Rusian chronicles for the bride's name, her father's name, and the groom's name to be recorded. The Vsevolod is Vsevolod Ol′govič, at that time ruler of Kyiv, and the Bolesław is Bolesław the Tall, the son of Władysław II, ruler of Silesia and contestant for the throne of Poland against his younger brother Bolesław IV. This marriage thus can be shown clearly through primary sources.

The marriage between Vsevolod's daughter and Władysław's son was designed to seal an agreement between the two factions so that Vsevolod could aid Władysław in his struggle with Bolesław IV, who, not coincidentally, was allied with the M′stislaviči, perennial enemies of the Ol′goviči.[105] Thus, the dueling alliances pitted one Piast and one Volodimeroviči against a different Piast and a different Volodimeroviči. This purpose for the marriage was confirmed during the same year when Vsevolod sent forces under the command of his son Svjatoslav to help his *zjat′* Władysław against Władysław's younger brother.[106] This marriage represents some of the clearest evidence that dynastic marriage in the medieval world was often used as a tool to seal alliances, very often specifically military alliances. Władysław called upon other marital alliances as well, and in 1146 his brother-in-law Conrad III led an expedition to help him against Bolesław IV.[107] Though the marriage between Zvenislava and Bolesław did not solve Władysław's problem or give Vsevolod an ally on the Piast throne, it serves as a clear example of medieval dynastic marriage practice.

Vsevolod
b. unknown; d. 1146
(Černihiv r. 1127–1139)
(Kyiv r. 1139–1146)

— Marija,
daughter of M'stislav
Volodimerič
b. unknown; d. 1178
(m. ca. 1127)

Svjatoslav
b. unknown; d. 1194
(Turov r. 1142)
(Volodymyr r. 1142–1146)
(Busk r. 1146–ca. 1154)
(Turov r. 1154–1155)
(Novhorod-Siverskyj r. 1158–1164)
(Černihiv r. 1164–1177)
(Kyiv r. 1174)
(Kyiv r. 1177–1180)
(Novgorod r. 1180–1181)
(Kyiv r. 1180–1194)

— N. N., daughter of
Vasil'ko Svjatoslavič
b. unknown;
d. post-1143
(m. 1143)

Svjatoslav Vsevolodič
(table 10)

Two marriages with the family of Polack rulers occurred in, or around, the year 1143.[108] The second, discussed below, was between Rogvolod Borisič and a daughter of Izjaslav M'stislavič. The first was between the son of the reigning ruler of Kyiv, Vsevolod Ol'govič, and the daughter of the ruler of Polack, Vasil'ko Svjatoslavič. This marriage, like the other Polack marriages discussed, was in part about reintegrating the Polack family back into the larger Volodimeroviči clan after an absence of several generations. The three main branches of Jaroslav Volodimerič's family (Izjaslaviči, Svjatoslaviči, and Vsevolodiči) were all vying for connections with the Polack rulers, and as such, made connections with three different children of Vseslav Brjačeslavič and their respective families. The Polack family of rulers was the largest branch outside of the main line of Jaroslaviči descent and represented a powerful and hitherto untapped marital connection, as well as occupying an increasingly politically important territory. This marriage seems to have been an attempt by Vsevolod Ol'govič to make a connection to reinforce both his family's and Vasil'ko Svjatoslavič's family's hold on their respective thrones. His own usurpation of the Kyivan throne was bound to be unstable after being passed on, but he was connected by marriage already to his main rivals, the M'stislaviči, through his own marriage. An alliance with the ruler of Polack, one heretofore unallied might have been not only advisable for his eldest son's dynastic position, but one of the few internal marriages that was possible within the bounds of consanguinity.[109]

The marriage may have also given the people of Polack the reinforcement needed to change rulers in the next decade. In 1151, Rogvolod Borisič was evicted from Polack and he was sent to Minsk. He was replaced with Rostislav Glěbovič, and the Hypatian Chronicle notes that the people then sent to Svjatoslav Ol´govič, asking Svjatoslav to be as their father.[110] Perhaps this is simply recognition of Svjatoslav's growing power in Rus´, but more likely marital politics and the growing web of Polack connections played a large role. Rogvolod Borisič was the son-in-law of Izjaslav M´stislavič, co-ruler of Kyiv with his uncle Vjačeslav Volodimerič, and as such it was likely that Izjaslav might have had an interest in his son-in-law retaining the Polack throne.[111] Rostislav Glěbovič was the in-law of the Izjaslaviči, who ruled in no cities at the time, and would not until Jurij Jaroslavič's (Rostislav's brother-in-law) rule in Turov, slightly later in the decade. That left the Svjatoslaviči (broadly construed). Svjatoslav Ol´govič was the uncle of Svjatoslav Vsevolodič and, at times, his friend and protector. As such, he may have been an ideal person to turn to because of his family's prior connection to Polack, and antipathy for Izjaslav M´stislavič and his growing power in Rus´. Thus, the marriage, though most likely for larger dynastic reasons, may also have had concrete applications as well, allowing the people of Polack to change rulers without repercussions.

Rogvolod Borisič
(table 2)

The marriage of Rogvolod Borisič of Polack and a daughter of Izjaslav M´stislavič of Perejaslavl is one of the first for which a wedding is noted in the chronicles. Multiple chronicles record a gala affair in Perejaslavl attended by both families as well as the ruler of Kyiv, Vsevolod Ol´govič, and all of his boyars.[112] This was the second wedding of the year with the broader family of Polack rulers, but arranged with different lines of the broader Jaroslav Volodimerič clan. The specific purpose of the marriage, if any, is unknown, but the marriage does continue the effort of tying the Polack rulers into the larger web of Rusian politics. In this particular case, the line of Rogvolod Borisič, son of Boris Vseslavič, is being tied to the M´stislaviči, while both Glěb Vseslavič and his son Rostislav Glěbovič were tied into the Izjaslaviči, and Vasil´ko Svjatoslavič, son of Svjatoslav Vseslavič, the then current ruler of Polack was himself tied into the line of Svjatoslaviči. The three main feuding branches of Jaroslaviči were each allying themselves with a different son of Vseslav Brjačeslavič and their respective lines.

This marriage worked out well for the parties involved, since a

Boris
b. unknown; d. 1129
(Strežev r. pre-1127–1129)
(Polack r. 1129)

|

Rogvolod b. unknown; d. post-1162 (Polack r. ca. 1143–1151) (Druck r. 1159–post-1162) (Polack r. 1159–1162)	——	N. N., daughter of Izjaslav M´stislavič b. unknown; d. post-1144 (m. 1144)

decade later Izjaslav M´stislavič would make sure that his son-in-law was put on the throne of Polack.[113] Moreover, once he was ruler of Kyiv, he acted against the Izjaslaviči-allied line of Polack rulers, helping to remove Rostislav Glěbovič that same year, and moved against Rostislav's brother-in-law Jurij Jaroslavič of Turov.[114] Though the situation would once again change and Rogvolod would be removed from power after internal struggles,[115] the marriage clearly had a purpose and the familial ties were subsequently acted upon to the benefit of all involved parties, reinforcing the idea and execution of the dynastic marriage.

Svjatopolk M´stislavič
(table 22)

Svjatopolk M´stislavič, son of M´stislav Volodimerič, was married between Christmas 1143 and Epiphany 1144 to a woman from Moravia.[116] The *NČL* incorrectly records that the ruler who was married was Svjatopolk Vsevolodovič.[117] However, it is clear from the records that at that time Svjatopolk M´stislavič was ruler of Novgorod,[118] and thus the only Volodimeroviči likely to be married in the city. The confusion may stem from the fact that in the same year, 1143, Vsevolod Ol´govič married off his son Svjatoslav.[119]

The identity of the groom, therefore, is relatively straightforward, but not that of the bride. All of the chronicle records clearly state that Svjatopolk's bride came from Moravia.[120] Moravia was mentioned in the *PVL* due to its importance as the first home for the Slavonic Liturgy and for hosting Constantine and Methodius, but apart from that it does not often make an appearance.[121] Baumgarten, in pursuing his research on dynastic marriages, even went so far as to track down the potential royal brides from Bohemia for this union with Svjatopolk. He

Svjatopolk M´stislavič b. unknown; d. 1154 (Polack r. 1132) (Pskov r. 1137–1140) (Brest r. 1140–1142) (Novgorod r.1142–1148) (Volodymyr r. 1148–1149) (Luck r. 1149–1150) (Volodymyr r. 1150–1154)	——	N. N., of Moravia b. unknown; d. post-1143 (m. 1143)

did this through a process of elimination, finding which daughters had been born, died, and married to determine who was available, similar to Nazarenko's search, also involving Bohemia, for the mother of Svjatopolk Izjaslavič.[122] The end result for Baumgarten was the conclusion that the bride could only have been Ephrosina, daughter of Otto II.[123] Otto II was duke or vice-duke of Olomouc, one of the main centers of Moravia, and was beholden to the Duke of Bohemia.[124] Adding to the credibility of Baumgarten's identification of the bride is the fact that Otto III, Otto II's son and Ephrosina's brother, was in exile in Rus´ from roughly 1126 until 1140.[125] Where he was and what he was doing are unknown, however, and in fact no Rusian chronicle mentions his existence whatsoever. If one might speculate, however, it seems likely that such an exile would go to Kyiv, as had happened many times in the past. M´stislav Volodimerič was ruling in Kyiv at that time, and for the first half of Otto's exile in Rus´. To speculate further, M´stislav and Otto may have gotten on well, and he may have come to know M´stislav's sons, including Svjatopolk, who had not yet assumed rule of a city and was thus most likely with his father in Kyiv.[126] Though this is just speculation, it fits a record of Rusian rulers building alliances with exiled royalty and tying them together through marriage. It also fits later events, in which Bohemian forces march to the aid of Svjatopolk's brother Izjaslav.[127] It is not the only possibility however, as trading ties are always a possibility, especially with Svjatopolk ruling the important trading cities of Pskov and Novgorod from roughly 1137–48, or simply acknowledging the fact that the M´stislaviči largely controlled the territory of Volodymyr, which occupied territory on the east-west trade route that goes through Bohemia as well.

These questions and the lack of source material add to the mystery surrounding some of the Rusian dynastic marriages, their participants, and their purposes, even in the more well-documented twelfth century. And though the conjecture regarding Ephrosina is fascinating, it is not supported by enough evidence to list her as such in the tables of part 2.

Jaroslav
b. unknown;
d. 1123
(Volodymyr r.
1100–1118)

Vsevolodko
b. unknown; d. 1141
(Hrodna r. pre-1127–1141)

Agafija Volodimerovna
b. unknown;
d. post-1116
(m. 1116)

Jurii
b. unknown;
d. pre-1170
(Turov r. 1157–1158)
(Turov r. ca. 1160–
pre-1170)

N. N. Vsevolodkovna
b. unknown;
d. post-1144
(m. 1144)

Jurij Jaroslavič
(tables 8, 9, 12)

Vsevolod Ol´govič, ruling in Kyiv, arranged two marriages in 1144 with daughters of the recently deceased ruler of Hrodna, Vsevolodko Davydič, and his wife Agafija Volodimerovna.[128] The Vsevolodkovni married Jurij Jaroslavič and Volodimer Davydič, and Vsevolod's arrangement of the marriages demonstrates the power that the ruler of Kyiv wielded among the Volodimeroviči family in this period. Though the Hypatian Chronicle unequivocally records that it was he who arranged the marriages, it is difficult to assess how the marriages benefited his personal or familial politics.

Though the brides were sisters, their respective grooms were from different generations of Volodimeroviči and thus the two marriages are in separate generations here in part 1. The first of these marriages, that with Volodimer Davydič, was discussed above in Generation Four, while the other marriage, with Jurij Jaroslavič,[129] is placed in Generation Five , though both marriages took place at the same time. Jurij was the son of Jaroslav Svjatopolčič and the last remaining male member of the once-powerful Izjaslaviči family. Despite this, he does not appear in the chronicle record from 1144 until 1158, when he is expelled from Turov, though he regains it two years later.[130] In 1144, there is no record of where he is or what he is doing. Thus there is virtually no information to allow us to suggest a possible reason for the arrangement of this marriage, perhaps apart from an attempt by Vsevolod Ol´govič to mend fences with the last of the Izjaslaviči with whom the Svjatoslaviči broadly, and Ol´goviči specifically, were once at such odds.

Despite this inability to discuss motive, the existence of the marriage is clearly stated in the Hypatian Chronicle, and Vsevolod's arrangement of the marriage provides interesting information about the ruler of Kyiv's ability to arrange marriages for the broader Volodimeroviči family, of which he was the titular head.

M´stislav "Harald" Volodimerič
b. 1076; d. 1132
(Novgorod r. 1095–1117)
(Bilhorod r. 1117–1125)
(Kyiv r. 1125–1132)

2

N. N. daughter of Dmitrij Zavidič
b. unknown; d. post-1169
(m. 1122)

Evfrosinija
b. unknown;
d. ca. 1193
(m. 1144)

Géza II of Hungary
b. 1130; d. 1162
(King of Hungary r. 1141–1162)

Evfrosinija M´stislavna
(table 13)

Evfrosinija M´stislavna was the youngest of the daughters of M´stislav Volodimerič of Kyiv, born near the end of his reign to his second wife, the daughter of Dmitrij Zavidič of Novgorod.[131] Evfrosinija's marriage is not explicitly recorded in any sources that I have been able to find, but there is plentiful ancillary evidence to identify her, her husband, and even her name. The best source on the marriage itself is Abbot Wilhelm's genealogy of the Danish kings, which mentions that Ingeborg M´stislavna's sister was married to a Hungarian king and was the mother of Béla, the then current Hungarian king.[132] From the date of composition of the genealogy, it is easy to see that the current Hungarian king was Béla III, whose father was Géza II, and thus Ingeborg's sister was married to Géza II. The name of Ingeborg's sister was not recorded by Abbot Wilhelm or by any Rusian chronicle, but another child of hers did record her mother's name. Wertner cites a Latin document of Elisabeth, daughter of Géza II, in which she refers to her mother as "Eurosine," from whence we get the Rusian Evfrosinija.[133] This type of name also confirms the Slavic ancestry of Elisabeth's mother and Géza II's wife, adding to the identification provided by Abbot Wilhelm. Though the Rusian sources do not mention Evfrosinija explicitly, there are multiple mentions of her husband. Izjaslav M´stislavič, Evfrosinija's brother, had become ruler of Kyiv in 1146,[134] and in at least one of his many battles to retain his power he called on his *zjat´*, the king of Hungary.[135] Furthermore, there is a fascinating note in the Hypatian Chronicle under the year 1155, when

Volodimer M´stislavič, the youngest of the M´stislaviči, sent his mother to Hungary to his *zjat´* the king, essentially because she is the Hungarian king's mother-in-law (*teščia*).[136] These small pieces of evidence built around Abbot Wilhelm's identification of the marriage show a complete picture in which Evfrosinija M´stislavna married Géza II of Hungary.

The purpose of the marriage also becomes clear from the evidence that has been presented here. Izjaslav M´stislavič needed to maintain his throne against a variety of claimants, and he needed allies to do that. In 1149 he not only called on his *zjat´* from Hungary, but various *svat´*(s) from Poland, for military assistance.[137] Géza II intervened multiple times to help his brother-in-law remain in Kyiv, and thus the marriage was well arranged by Izjaslav to advance his and the M´stislaviči's position in Rus´. This dynastic marriage also had an interesting additional angle, part of which was the role of Boris, son of Koloman of Hungary and grandson of Volodimer Monomax. Boris, as mentioned above under his mother Evfimija's entry, fought for most of his life to attempt to gain the Hungarian throne, which he considered his birthright. In those battles, he allied with the Byzantine emperors, the Comneni, and fought against Géza II.[138] For Izjaslav, this was probably not even part of his consideration, as he was also fighting off Monomaxoviči uncles, such as Jurij of Suzdal, to maintain his throne.[139] The marriage of Evfrosinija and Géza II was part of a much larger struggle for power in which Jurij of Suzdal, Volodimerko of Halyč, and the Comneni emperors were allied against the M´stislaviči, Géza II of Hungary, and the Boleslaviči of Poland. This enormous struggle was played out for control over the kingdoms of Hungary, Rus´, and Poland, with only the Byzantine Empire safe. Understanding the place of one small dynastic marriage in such a morass of politics, infighting, and war is essential to understanding the place of Rus´ in Europe as a whole.

Marriages: Postscript

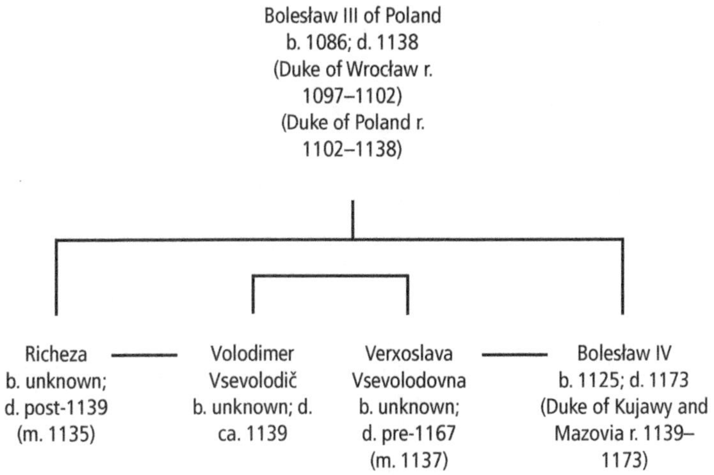

Volodimer Vsevolodič
(table 17)

Volodimer Vsevolodič, son of Vsevolod M′stislavič, provides another example of siblings marrying siblings. The next entry details the marriage of his sister Verxoslava to Bolesław IV of Poland, but Volodimer was himself to marry Bolesław's elder sister Richeza ("Ryksa" in Polish). Richeza had previously been married to Magnus Nielsson of Denmark,[1] but after Magnus's death in 1134[2] she remarried. In 1135, Richeza married Volodimer Vsevolodič, presumably as part of her father, Bolesław III's, attempt to increase his ties with the M′stislaviči. Volodimer died not long after their marriage, in 1139, and Richeza remarried again, this time to Swerker I, king of Sweden.[3]

While there is much to say about Richeza, her marriages, and her children that is substantiated by quite a few primary sources, the identity of Volodimer Vsevolodič is mostly an educated guess. This hypothesis of identification is subscribed to by many, including Baumgarten,

Balzer, and more recently Nazarenko.[4] There is a rival school of thought, however—the two biggest proponents of which seem to be J. Gallén and E. A. Rydzevskaja,[5] though I first came across it in the work of Litvina and Uspenskij, as well as that of N. I. Ščaveleva[6]—that the proper identification for Richeza's Rusian husband is Volodar´ Glěbovič, ruler of Minsk. The argument, as put forward by Ščaveleva for the identification of Valadar (the name from the Scandinavian sources) as Volodar´ Glěbovič, is that during the later twelfth century there was a battle between Volodimerko Volodarič (son of Volodar´ Glěbovič of Minsk) and Vasil´ko Jaropolčič (grandson of Izjaslav M´stislavič of Kyiv) over Bereste, and the Volodariči (Volodimerko's brother, also named Vasil´ko) got involved as they were able to utilize Polish connections to stymie their opponents.[7] However, the argument is not entirely convincing, only in part because Tatiščev is the main source for the battle and the terminology for the Polish kinship ties.[8] Tatiščev's kinship ties are occasionally dubious and thus not always reliable, but moreover the argument for the relationship between the families is confused and confusing and once again has no solid basis in primary sources. The final nail in the coffin is that Volodar´ Glěbovič did not die until 1159, thus giving Richeza no reason to leave Rus´ and marry Swerker of Sweden in 1139.[9]

This debate between the two sides effectively illustrates the problem that exists when there is little or no primary source information. The only primary sources to mention the name Volodimer Vsevolodič are a few Rusian chronicles that briefly mention his role in freeing his father from Novgorod in 1136.[10] The source for Richeza's Rusian husband comes in two Scandinavian sources, *Knýtlinga Saga* and *Fagrskinna*, which record the same basic information. Richeza was married to a Valadar, king of so-called Polinalande, which is often translated as Poland.[11] However, following Peter Sawyer, we can make the assumption that Poland is not meant, but rather the land of the Poljanians, especially since a similar remark is made in Adam of Bremen for Rus´, and thus bring the problem back to one of which Rusian it was she married.[12] The identity of Richeza's second husband is mentioned in these sagas because her daughter with Valadar, Sofija,[13] married Valdemar of Denmark at the instigation of Richeza's son in Denmark, King Knud. Of additional interest, as Nazarenko points out, if Valadar is Volodimer Vsevolodovič, then the marriage is consanguineous, though that may not have been a burning concern for them, as it was neither the first nor the last consanguineous marriage in Rusian history.[14] The problem of the identity of Valadar of Polinalande remains, and is relatively insoluble due to the lack of adequate primary sources.

Having stipulated this, the identification of Valadar as Volodimer Vsevolodič is tentatively accepted because the marriage of Richeza and a M´stislaviči makes good political sense, which seems to be the underlying motivation for many if not all of these dynastic marriages. A marriage between the two would have strengthened the ties between Bolesław III, who was ruling at the time, and the Monomaxoviči, who were ruling in Kyiv. Such a marriage between a Polack ruler of Minsk, such as Volodar´ Glěbovič, makes much less sense in terms of the large-scale politics in which Bolesław III participated.

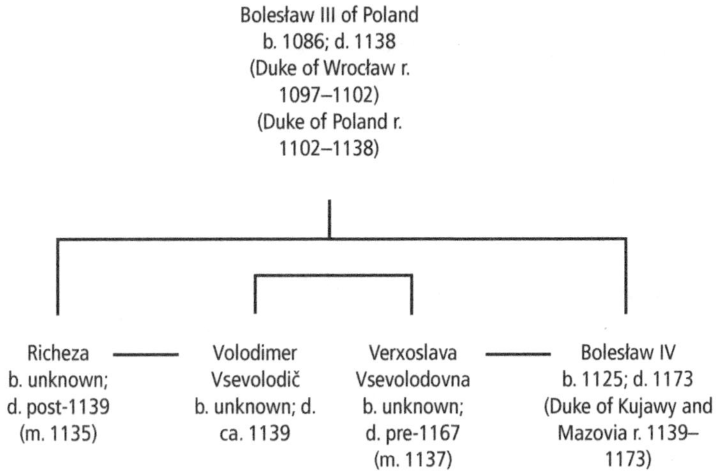

Verxoslava Vsevolodovna
(table 17)

The daughter of Vsevolod M´stislavič and great-granddaughter of Monomax, Verxoslava is mentioned by name as having been sent to Poland in 1137.[15] Though no reason for the trip is mentioned, such trips were almost exclusively for the purpose of marriage. Unfortunately, no source that I have found records the person she married, but Baumgarten lists him as Bolesław IV of Poland, as does Balzer.[16] However, Stanisław Smolka, whom Balzer cites in other instances, identifies Bolesław IV's wife as a daughter of either M´stislav or Jaropolk Volodimerič, and thus a granddaughter of Monomax.[17] Smolka's identification, which he characterizes as tenuous, becomes even more problematic with his identification of her name as "Anastazya." It thus seems that Smolka is incorrect, and though we have no primary source evidence to support the identification of Verxoslava's spouse as Bolesław IV, he seems the most likely match under the circumstances, especially considering the marriages that followed.

The marriage of a M´stislavna and a Piast was an important step in binding the two ruling families closer together, but it was actually much more than that. For years the Piasts had been allies of the Izjaslaviči, but after the destruction of Izjaslavič power, and the death of Sbyslava Svjatopolkovna in the early twelfth century, it was time for new alliances to be made. The death of Sbyslava is particularly relevant, as she was wife to Bolesław III and mother to Władysław II. After her death, Bolesław III remarried and had more children, including Bolesław IV. The stepbrothers (Władysław II on one side versus Bolesław IV, Mieszko, and Henryk on the other) would war for control of the Piast territories through the mid-twelfth century. As was seen above in the marriage of Zvenislava Vsevolodovna, each side of this Piast struggle made Volodimeroviči connections. Bolesław IV married into the M´stislaviči, while Władysław II married into the Ol´goviči (through his son Bolesław the Tall). The division in Piasts then mirrored the division among the Volodimeroviči, and the basis for mutual assistance in the coming wars was created.[18] As the M´stislaviči would win in Rus´, the side of Bolesław IV would win in Poland, though neither victory was lasting.

Notes

Introduction

1. *Ipat´evskaja letopis´*, vol. 2 of *Polnoe sobranie russkix letopisej* (Moscow: Jazyki slavjanskoj kul´tury, 2001) [hereafter: Hypatian Chronicle], s.a. 1149.
2. For more information on this topic see my *Reimagining Europe: Kievan Rus´ in the Medieval World, 988–1146* (Cambridge, Mass.: Harvard University Press, 2012).
3. Andrzej Poppe has discussed this timeline at some length, and concludes that this marriage occurred in 989. Andrzej Poppe, "The Political Background to the Baptism of Rus´: Byzantine-Russian Relations between 986–989," *Dumbarton Oaks Papers* 30 (1976): 195–244.
4. The classic reference volume on this work is N. G. Berežkov, *Xronologija russkogo letopisanija* (Moscow: Izdatel´stvo Akademija nauk SSSR, 1963). I have only scratched the surface of the complexity here in my explanation, and probably elided too much for some. The study of the chronicles is an enormous field, especially in Russian. Those with an interest may begin with the introduction to Donald Ostrowski's volume of the *PVL*, where some of these issues are discussed. *The "Pověst´ vremennykh lět": An Interlinear Collation and Paradosis*, comp. and ed. Donald Ostrowski, with David Birnbaum and Horace G. Lunt, Harvard Library of Early Ukrainian Literature: Texts 10 (Cambridge, Mass.: Harvard Ukrainian Research Institute, 2003) [henceforth *PVL*], introduction.
5. N. de Baumgarten, "Généalogies et mariages Occidentaux des Rurikides Russes du X-e au XIII-e siècle," *Orientalia Christiana* 9, no. 25 (1927): 5–95.
6. Jukka Korpela, *Beiträge zur Bevölkerungsgeschichte und Prosopographie der Kiever Rus´ bis zum Tode von Vladimir Monomakh* (Jyväskylä: University of Jyväskylä, 1995).
7. E. V. Pčelov, *Genealogija drevnerusskix knjazej* (Moscow: Rossijskij gosudarstvennyj gumanitarnyj universitet, 2001).
8. Dariusz Dąbrowski, *Genealogia Mścisławowiczów: Pierwsze pokolenia (do początku XIV wieku)* (Cracow: Avalon, 2008). I am incredibly grateful to Professor Dąbrowski for sending me a copy of this book. Though we do

not always reach the same conclusions, I have been stimulated by his ideas and I have attempted to demonstrate in the text of this book where I do and do not agree with him.

9. John Meyendorff, "From Byzantium to Russia: Religious and Cultural Legacy," in *Studies on the Slavo-Byzantine and West European Middle Ages: In Memoriam Ivan Dujčev*, ed. Petăr Dinekov, Aksinija Džurova, et al. (Sofija: Centr dlja slavjano-vizantijskix issledovanij imeni Ivana Dujčeva, 1988), 1:105–7, exemplifies this kind of relationship between Rus´ and Byzantium.
10. A. P. Každan [Kazhdan], "Rus´-Byzantine Princely Marriages in the Eleventh and Twelfth Centuries," *Harvard Ukrainian Studies* 12/13 (1988/89): 414–29.
11. Labels such as "Poland" and "Hungary" can often be misleading when dealing with the Middle Ages, as they are typically used to refer to modern states and then simply applied to past eras. While I would like to avoid that practice, I will use the terms here for the sake of convenience, with one caveat: When I am referring to Poland, I mean the realm governed by the Piast family; when Hungary, the territory ruled by the Árpáds. It is these royal families that defined medieval politics and shaped kingdoms, not borders drawn on a map.
12. Martin Dimnik, *Dynasty of Chernigov, 1054–1146* (Toronto: Pontifical Institute of Mediaeval Studies, 1994); Dimnik, *Dynasty of Chernigov, 1146–1246* (Cambridge: Cambridge University Press, 2003).
13. *PVL* (full citation in n. 5, above). For additional specificity, Ostrowski says that he "used five manuscript copies (and the typeset version of the Trinity Chronicle) of the PVL and three copies of the Novgorod I Chronicle," Personal correspondence, 3 December 2012. In an attempt to create consistency, I have cited the *PVL* by year, rather than by page and line as is common. The "s.a." citation method is used across sources from a variety of areas.
14. The edition of the Hypatian Chronicle used is cited in n. 1, above; *Lavrent´evskaja letopis´*, vol. 1 of *Polnoe sobranie russkix letopisej* (Moscow: Jazyki slavjanskoj kul´tury, 2001) [hereafter: Laurentian Chronicle]; *Novgorodskaja pervaja letopis´ staršego i mladšego izvodov*, vol. 3 of *Polnoe sobranie russkix letopisej* (Moscow: Jazyki slavjanskoj kul´tury, 2000) [hereafter: *NPL*]; *Novgorodskaja četvertaja letopis´*, vol. 4, pt. 1 of *Polnoe sobranie russkix letopisej* (Moscow: Jazyki slavjanskoj kul´tury, 2000) [hereafter: *NČL*]. There is an English translation of the Kyivan Chronicle as well, but it may only be purchased online to my knowledge. Lisa Heinrich, "The Kievan Chronicle: A Translation and Commentary" (PhD dissertation, Vanderbilt University, 1977). There is also an English translation of one redaction of the Novgorod Chronicle, *The Chronicle of Novgorod, 1016–1471*, trans. Robert Michell and Nevill Forbes, Camden Third Series 25 (London: Offices of the Society, 1914).
15. *The Nikonian Chronicle: From the Beginning to the Year 1132 (Volume One)*, trans. Serge A. and Betty Jean Zenkovsky, ed. Serge A. Zenkovsky (Princeton, N.J.: Kingston Press, 1984), xxxvi–xxxvii.
16. For example, the delivery of relics to Volodimer at Cherson in 988 is

recorded in the Nikon Chronicle. *Letopisnyj sbornik, imenuemyj: Patriaršej ili Nikonovskoj letopis´ju*, vol. 9 of *Polnoe sobranie russkix letopisej* (Moscow: Jazyki russkoj kul´tury, 2000) [hereafter: Nikon Chronicle], s.a. 988. There is no evidence corroborating this from the side of the papacy, but that is unsurprising, as papal records do not become well preserved until the reign of Pope Gregory VII, nearly one hundred years later. However, it must be noted that Andrzej Poppe has challenged this idea, asserting that the compilers of the Nikon Chronicle deliberately created papal contacts to emphasize Volodimer's adoption of the Orthodox Church. Poppe, "Political Background to the Baptism of Rus´," 200.

Further, I would suggest that this is dissimilar to the specific anti-Tatar insertions of the Nikon chronicle noted by Donald Ostrowski. *Muscovy and the Mongols: Cross-cultural Influences on the Steppe Frontier, 1304–1589* (Cambridge: Cambridge University Press, 1998), 148–55.

17. Nikon Chronicle, s.a. 1043; *Rogožskij letopisets / Tverskoj sbornik*, vol. 15 of *Polnoe sobranie russkix letopisej* (Moscow: Jazyki slavjanskoj kul´tury, 2000) [hereafter: Tver Chronicle], s.a. 1143.
18. *PVL*, s.a. 1047; Gallus Anonymous, *Gesta principum Polonorum / The Deeds of the Princes of the Poles*, trans. Paul W. Knoll and Frank Schaer (Budapest: Central European University Press, 2003), 81.
19. See table 2 in part 2, for example.
20. V. N. Tatiščev, *Istorija Rossijskaja*, vol. 2 of 7 (Moscow: Akademija nauk SSSR, 1963).
21. Oleksij [Aleksej] Toločko, *"Istorija Rossijskaja" Vasilija Tatiščeva: istočniki i izvestija* (Kyiv: Kritika, 2005).
22. Eve Levin, *Sex and Society in the World of the Orthodox Slavs, 900–1700* (Ithaca, N.Y.: Cornell University Press, 1989), 96; but also ch. 2 in general.
23. Carol Jean Diers and Darrell W. Amundsen, "The Age of Menarche in Medieval Europe," *Human Biology* 45 (1973): 363–69.
24. For such an argument, see C. Raffensperger, *The Kingdom of Rus´* (forthcoming).
25. There is a great deal of discussion on the matter. The three modern participants in this discussion are Martin Dimnik, "The Title 'Grand Prince' in Kievan Rus´," *Mediaeval Studies* 66 (2004): 253–312; A. P. Toločko, *Knjaz´ v drevnej Rusi: Vlast´, sobstvennost´, ideologija* (Kyiv: Naukova dumka, 1992), 127–35; Andrzej Poppe, "Words that Serve the Authority: On the Title of 'Grand Prince' in Kievan Rus´," in *Christian Russia in the Making*, 159–91 (Aldershot: Ashgate, 2007).
26. Donald Ostrowski, "Systems of Succession in Rus´ and Steppe Societies," *Ruthenica* 11 (2012): 29–58.
27. Raffensperger, *Reimagining Europe*, 77–79.
28. *PVL*, s.a. 1094.
29. The dispensation from Pope Paschal II is noted by the chronicler Gallus Anonymous. Gallus Anonymous, *Gesta principum Polonorum*, 158–61.
30. These are largely depicted in part 2, table 2.
31. Contrast this with Muscovy, for example, where marital partners for the ruling Rjurikid line were found among the lower-ranked boyar families. For more information, see Russell E. Martin, *A Bride for the Tsar:*

Bride-Shows and Marriage Politics in Early Modern Russia (DeKalb, Ill.: Northern Illinois University Press, 2012).

Marriages: Prelude

1. *PVL*, s.a. 980.
2. Samuel Hazzard Cross and Oleg P. Sherbowitz-Wetzor, ed., *The Russian Primary Chronicle: Laurentian Text* (Cambridge, Mass.: The Mediaeval Academy of America, 1953), s.a. 980.
3. *PVL*, s.a. 980.
4. Ibid.
5. Ibid.
6. Raffensperger, *Reimagining Europe*, 160–63; Poppe, "Political Background to the Baptism of Rus´."
7. For Otto I's attempts, see *Ottonian Germany: The "Chronicon" of Thietmar of Merseburg*, trans. David A. Warner (Manchester: Manchester University Press, 2001) (hereafter cited as Thietmar of Merseburg), bk. 7, chap. 72. For Robert of France's attempt, see Adalbert Davids, "Marriage Negotiations between Byzantium and the West and the Name of Theophano in Byzantium (Eighth to Tenth Centuries)," in *The Empress Theophano: Byzantium and the West at the Turn of the Millennium*, ed. Adalbert Davids (Cambridge: Cambridge University Press, 1995), 109.
8. By my use of "family" here I do not reference the Byzantine imperial concept of a family of rulers with the emperor at its head. I am simply referring to the kingdoms that have been converted to Christianity, a larger world that some have referred to as "Christendom."
9. For more on the place of Byzantium in medieval Europe, see my *Reimagining Europe*, ch. 1, "The Byzantine Ideal."
10. There has been a little written about this in recent years. See Judith Herrin, "Theophano: Considerations on the Education of a Byzantine Princess," in *Empress Theophano*, ed. Adalbert Davids, 64–85 (Cambridge: Cambridge University Press, 1995); and Cecily Hilsdale, "Diplomacy by Design: Rhetorical Strategies of the Byzantine Gift," PhD diss., University of Chicago, 2003, for examples.
11. *PVL*, s.a. 1011.
12. *PVL*, s.a. 988.
13. This is discussed in detail elsewhere. See, for example, Raffensperger, *Reimagining Europe*, ch. 2.
14. John Scylitzes mentions that Anna and Volodimer are married and that Volodimer and Basil II are thus related. John Scylitzes, *Ioannis Scylitzae Synopsis historiarum*, ed. Hans Thurn, Corpus fontium historiae Byzantinae 5 (Berlin: De Gruyter, 1973), 336, 354, 367.
15. Poppe believes that he has found a daughter of Volodimer and Anna married to a *posadnik* of Novgorod. A. Poppe, "Feofano Novgorodskaja," *Novgorodskij istoričeskij sbornik* 6, no. 16 (1997): 102–20.
16. Pčelov states that the Hustynja Chronicle and Jan Długosz both make the statement that Dobronega is Anna's daughter. Pčelov, *Genealogija drevnerusskix knjazej*, 207. However, I have been unable to find any men-

tion of this in Długosz. Jan Długosz, *Annales seu cronicae incliti regni Poloniae*, vols. 1–4 (Warsaw: Państwowe Wydawnictwo Naukowe, 1964–70).

17. Thietmar of Merseburg, bk. 8, chap. 32.
18. Baumgarten, "Généalogies," 7–8, table 1.
19. Most recently, E. V. Pčelov, "Pol´skaja knjagina — Marija Dobronega Vladimirovna," in *Vostočnaja Evropa v drevnosti i srednevekov´e: Drevnjaja Rus´ v sisteme ètnopolitičeskix i kul´turnyx svjazej: čtenija pamjati členakorrespondenta AN SSSR Vladimira Terent´eviča Pašuto, Moskva, 18-20 aprelja 1994 g.: tezisy dokladov*, ed. V. T. Pašuto, A. P. Novosel´cev, et al., 31–33 (Moscow: RAN, 1994), 32.
20. Thietmar of Merseburg, bk. 7.
21. Thietmar records a marriage between a daughter of Bolesław by his third wife and a "son of King Vladimir." Thietmar of Merseburg, bk. 4, chap. 58; bk. 7, chap. 72.
22. Though I will use the term "Poland" throughout this work, the Rusian chronicles generally refer to the people of that land as the Ljaxs, and their ruler as ruler of the Ljaxs. This is similar to the Latin usage of "dux Polonorum," traditionally rendered as "duke of the Poles." Though it might be a fine point, it should be acknowledged that what is being discussed is the political entity ruled by the Piast dynasty, and largely coterminous with that dynasty. The same is true for Hungary, Denmark, etc. discussed throughout this work.
23. Thietmar of Merseburg, bk. 7, chap. 72.
24. This assumption is usually made based on more well-documented cases from western Europe. The various marriages of women into pagan Anglo-Saxon households serve as one example.
25. Thietmar of Merseburg, bk. 7, chap. 72.
26. Ibid.
27. Ibid.
28. Ibid., bk. 7, chap. 73.
29. Of course, the opposite might be true as well; Volodimer's false imprisonment of Svjatopolk and his wife may have driven Svjatopolk to the Poles.
30. Thietmar of Merseburg, bk. 7, chap. 65, where he incorrectly identifies Svjatopolk as brother-in-law, not son-in-law.
31. *PVL*, s.a. 1018.
32. Thietmar of Merseburg, bk. 8, chap. 33.
33. Though it does record Svjatopolk's flight "to the Ljaxs" as well as his return with Bolesław. *PVL*, s.a. 1016, 1018.
34. Gallus Anonymous, *Gesta principum Polonorum*, 41–47.
35. As has been shown, Thietmar mentions the marriage and many other details in multiple places. Thietmar of Merseburg.

Marriages: Generation One

1. Baumgarten, "Généalogies," 7, table 1; and Mór Wertner, *Az Árpádok családi története* (Zrenjanin [Nagybecskerek]: Pleitz Fer. Pál könyvnyomdája, 1892), 112–13. Both record the name.

2. Dezso Dercsényi, ed., *The Hungarian Illuminated Chronicle / Chronica de gestis Hungarorum* (Budapest: Corvina Press, 1969), 113. Though there is dispute in the historiography over whether she married him or his brother Vazul, most scholars believe it was Ladislaus, as the chronicle records state. See note 171 of the *Chronica* for an alternate opinion.
3. *PVL*, s.a. 996, where Stephen is lumped in with other "knjazja." The marriage is never dated, but it most likely occurred in the 1010s before Volodimer's death, due to the probable birth dates of their children.
4. O. M. Rapov also theorizes that relations between Rus´ and Hungary were close beginning in the late tenth and early eleventh century. O. M. Rapov, "Vnešnjaja politika Vladimira Velikogo posle oficial´nogo prinjatija Rus´ju xristianstva," in *Vostočnaja Evropa v drevnosti i srednevekov´e: Drevnjaja Rus´ v sisteme ètnopolitičeskix i kul´turnyx svjazej: čtenija pamjati člena-korrespondenta AN SSSR Vladimira Terent´eviča Pašuto, Moskva, 18-20 aprelja 1994 g.: tezisy dokladov*, ed. V. T. Pašuto, A. P. Novosel´cev, et al., 33–36 (Moscow: RAN, 1994), 35.
5. Dercsényi, *Chronica de gestis Hungarorum*, 100, 113.
6. Baumgarten, "Généalogies," 7, table 1.
7. *Sächsische Weltchronik*, ed. Ludwig Weiland, in [untitled volume of] Monumenta Germaniae Historica: Deutsche Chroniken und andere Geschichtsbücher des Mittelalters 2 (Hannover: Hahnsche Buchhandlung, 1877), 199.
8. *Lamberti Hersfeldensis Annales*, publ. V. Cl. Lud. Frid. Hesse, in *Annales et chronica aevi Salici*, 134–263, Monumenta Germaniae Historica: Scriptores 5 (Hanover: Impensis Bibliopolii Hahniani, 1843), s. a. 1057.
9. A. V. Nazarenko, "Rus´ i germanija v IX–X vv," *Materialy i issledovanija 1991 god*, issue of *Drevnejšie gosudarstva Vostočnoj Evropy*, 1994, 134.
10. Pčelov, *Genealogija drevnerusskix knjazej*, 180–81.
11. Adam of Bremen, *History of the Archbishops of Hamburg-Bremen*, trans. Francis J. Tschan (New York: Columbia University Press, 2002; hereafter Adam of Bremen), xxv; bk. 2, ch. xxiv, 21. Thietmar of Merseburg discusses him several times in his narrative.
12. Nazarenko briefly reviews the controversy and the positions of various Russian authors. A. V. Nazarenko, *Drevnjaja Rus´ na meždunarodnyx putjax: Meždisciplinarnye očerki kul´turnyx, torgovyx, politčeskix svjazej IX–XII vekov* (Moscow: Jazyki russkoj kul´tury, 2001), 492–93. Additionally, Olof was technically king of the Svear, as there was not a kingdom of Sweden at this time.
13. Ilja is listed in the *NPL*'s list of rulers of Novgorod as Jaroslav's son, who ruled in Novgorod after Jaroslav had gone to Kyiv, and later died. *NPL*, s.a. 989.
14. Though Nazarenko has an elaborate theory that her name was Anna, based upon a convoluted chain of reasoning that begins with Volodimer Jaroslavič's mother being misnamed by a fifteenth-century chronicler or copyist. Nazarenko, *Drevnjaja Rus´ na meždunarodnyx putjax*, 490–91.
15. Thietmar of Merseburg, bk. 8, ch. 32.
16. Simon Franklin and Jonathan Shepard, *The Emergence of Rus, 750–1200*, Longman History of Russia (New York: Longman, 1996), 202.

17. Snorri Sturluson, *Heimskringla: History of the Kings of Norway*, trans. with an introduction by Lee M. Hollander (Austin, Tx.: University of Texas Press, 1964; hereafter *Heimskringla*), 340.
18. *PVL*, s.a. 1018.
19. Further buttressing the 1019 marriage date is the 1020 date, recorded in multiple copies of the Rusian chronicles, of the birth of Jaroslav's son Volodimer, who is elsewhere described as the oldest of his children, presumably with reference to the oldest of his children by Ingigerd or from his Christian marriage. *PVL*, s.a. 1020 (the birth); s.a. 1052 (death of eldest son of Jaroslav); Nikon Chronicle, s.a. 1020, 1052.
20. *PVL*, s.a. 1018.
21. Other scholars have advanced this assertion before. V. T. Pašuto, *Vnešnjaja politika Drevnej Rusi* (Moscow: Nauka, 1968), 27; Nazarenko, *Drevnjaja Rus′ na meždunarodnyx putjax*, 492–97. Nazarenko posits a much grander theory of a Rusian-Danish-Swedish coalition against Poland formed by dynastic marriage. Vernadsky, on the other hand, mentions Scandinavian reinforcements, but does not mention the marriage at all here, contextualizing this as a Novgorod versus Kyiv conflict. George Vernadsky, *Kievan Russia*, vol. 2 of *A History of Russia* (New Haven, Conn.: Yale University Press, 1948), 75–76.
22. Sturluson, *Heimskringla*, 342–43.
23. Cross has listed multiple examples of this from a wide range of Scandinavian saga sources. Samuel Hazzard Cross, "Yaroslav the Wise in Norse Tradition," *Speculum* 4, no. 2 (1929): 192.
24. Sturluson, *Heimskringla*, 342–43.
25. Ibid.
26. Ibid.
27. *PVL*, s.a. 1018, 1019.
28. Sturluson, *Heimskringla*, 342.
29. Michael M. Sheehan, "Choice of Marriage Partner in the Middle Ages: Development and Mode of Application of a Theory of Marriage," in *Marriage, Family, and Law in Medieval Europe: Collected Studies*, ed. James K. Farge (Toronto: University of Toronto Press, 1997), 91.
30. This is especially true in the Scandinavian sagas, where daughters are usually given the choice with their father's endorsement of one candidate. Saxo Grammaticus gives multiple examples of consent as an issue as well, in both mythical and historical times. Saxo Grammaticus, *Gesta Danorum: The History of the Danes*, ed. Hilda Ellis Davidson, trans. Peter Fisher (Totowa, N.J.: Rowman and Littlefield, 1979).
31. Sturluson, *Heimskringla*, 340, 342.
32. Both of these situations are discussed in more detail below in regard to Anna Jaroslavna.
33. And it was commonplace. Examples range from tenth-century expeditions from the German Empire to Byzantium to negotiate for a bride for Otto II, and later for Otto III, to twelfth-century embassies from Denmark to Portugal, and beyond.
34. Sturluson, *Heimskringla*, 342–43.
35. Ibid.

36. It is explicitly stated that Reinbern the priest came with her. Thietmar of Merseburg, bk. 7, ch. 72.
37. J. Vogt, *Monumenta inedita rerum Germanicarum praecipue Bremensium* (Bremen 1740), 1. bd. 125, cited in S. P. Rozanov, "Evpraksija-Adel′geida Vsevolodovna (1071–1109)," *Izvestija Akademii nauk SSSR VII Serija: Otdelenie gumanitarnyx nauk* 8 (1929): 623.
38. Sturluson, *Heimskringla*, 342.
39. J. Vogt, *Monumenta inedita rerum Germanicarum praecipue Bremensium*, 1. bd. 125, cited in Rozanov, "Evpraksija-Adel′geida Vsevolodovna (1071–1109)," 623.
40. Saint Bernward talks about the contemporary artifacts and influence of Theophano. Francis J. Tschan, ed., *His Works of Art*, vol. 2 of *Saint Bernward of Hildesheim* (South Bend, Ind.: University of Notre Dame, 1951). More recently, there has been an entire conference dedicated to Theophano. Adalbert Davids, ed., *The Empress Theophano: Byzantium and the West at the Turn of the First Millennium* (Cambridge: Cambridge University Press, 1995).
41. Sturluson, *Heimskringla*, 474, 486.
42. Theodoricus Monachus, "Theodrici monachi historia de antiquitate regum Norwagiensium," in *Monumenta Historica Norvegiae*, ed. Gustav Storm, 1–68 (Oslo [Kristiania]: A. W. Brøgger, 1880), 45.
43. As an interesting sidenote on this, in the sagas Ingigerd is mentioned alone or when with her husband as "King Jarisleif and Queen Ingigerd." Jaroslav is rarely mentioned on his own. It is her presence that lends him the literary immortality.
44. This is dealt with briefly in the section on Volodimer Svjatoslavič. For more information, see the works of E. V. Pčelov. At stake is whether she was the daughter of Anna Porphyrogenita or of another wife of Volodimer, perhaps a German princess. Pčelov, *Genealogija drevnerusskix knjazej*, 207–8.
45. *PVL*, s.a. 1030.
46. Cross and Sherbowitz-Wetzor, eds., *Russian Primary Chronicle*, n. 158. The turbulent period may have begun earlier than 1034, because Mieszko initially had to abdicate in 1031 to his brother Otto, but regained the throne at Otto's death in 1032, only to die insane in 1034.
47. Gallus Anonymous, *Gesta principum Polonorum*, 81. Casimir did not stay the whole time in Saxony, but traveled to Paris, joined the Benedictine order, enrolled at the monastery of Cluny in France, and only returned to Saxony after receiving a papal dispensation to marry. "Boguphali II episcopi Posnaniensis Chronicon Poloniae, cum continuatione Basconis custodis Posnaniensis," ed. August Bielowski, in *Monumenta Poloniae Historica*, 2:467–600 (Lviv: Nakładem Własnym, 1872; hereafter *Chronica Poloniae Maioris*), ch. 12.
48. Gallus Anonymous, *Gesta principum Polonorum*, 81.
49. *PVL*, s.a. 1041.
50. Gallus Anonymous, *Gesta principum Polonorum*, 83–85.
51. Ibid., 80–81. When the *Gesta* records that he brought the majority of Poland under his rule, it excludes the Mazovians and Pomeranians, who

were still in revolt and were dealt with in separate expeditions sometime after the initial conquering and after Casimir's marriage.

52. *PVL*, s.a. 1043.
53. *Chronica Poloniae Maioris*, ch. 12. The description of Dobronega as "daughter" of the Rusian prince is an interesting feature of this text. Some modern historians have wondered if she was indeed a daughter of Jaroslav, rather than his sister. This view gains endorsement from this text, but is generally considered incorrect.
54. Ibid., ch. 12.
55. *PVL*, s.a. 1043.
56. *PVL*, s.a. 1041.
57. *Annalista Saxo*, publ. D. G. Waitz and P. Killon, in *Chronica et annales aevi Salici*, 542–777, Monumenta Germaniae Historica: Scriptores 6 (Hannover: Impensis Bibliopolii Avlici Hahniani, 1844), s.a. 1039.
58. *Lamberti Hersfeldensis Annales*, s.a. 1039.
59. For instance, Baumgarten complicates the issue and adds a hypothetical 1038 marriage date based on the 1039 birth of Bolesław. Baumgarten, "Généalogies," table 1.
60. Gallus Anonymous, *Gesta principum Polonorum*, 82n1.
61. *PVL*, s.a. 1041.
62. Gallus Anonymous, *Gesta principum Polonorum*, 83.
63. The *Chronica Poloniae Maioris* is equally unhelpful here as it devotes only a small part of a passage to the campaign against the Mazovians. It also says that the Mazovians were aided by many groups, including Rusians, though the editor correctly contradicts the statement. *Chronica Poloniae Maioris*, 70n13.
64. *PVL*, s.a. 1041, 1047, which contains only the 1041 and 1047 raids; Nikon Chronicle, s.a. 1041, 1043, 1047; Tver Chronicle, s.a. 1041, 1043, 1046, both of which contain all three.
65. Nikon Chronicle, s.a. 1043; Tver Chronicle, s.a. 1143.
66. *PVL*, s.a. 1047. The Tver Chronicle also calls Casimir Jaroslav's *zjat´*. Tver Chronicle, s.a. 1046.
67. *PVL*, s.a. 1043.
68. Children are specifically mentioned in the Tver Chronicle, s.a. 1043.
69. Gallus Anonymous, *Gesta principum Polonorum*, 81.
70. Pčelov also reads this as recognition of a large dowry brought into the marriage. Pčelov, "Pol´skaja knjagina — Marija Dobronega Vladimirovna," 32.
71. Ibid., 33. Ščaveleva, in the commentary to the *Chronica Poloniae Maioris*, also notes this origin, but there is no citation to the source, and I have not been able to find it among Benedict IX's extant letters. *Velikaia Khronika*, 70n10. Both names, however, are noted in the *Chronica Poloniae Maioris* itself, both in the original and Ščaveleva's translation. "Boguphali II Episcopi Posnaniensis Chronicon Poloniae," 485; N. I. Ščaveleva, ed., *"Velikaja xronika" o Pol´še, Rusi i ix sosedjax XI–XIII vv.* (Moscow: Izdatel´stvo Moskovskogo universiteta, 1987). For more information about this name, see A. F. Litvina and F. B. Uspenskij, *Vybor imeni u russkix knjazej v X–XVI vv.* (Moscow: Indrik, 2006), 541.

72. Pčelov, "Pol′skaja knjagina — Marija Dobronega Vladimirovna," 33.
73. Litvina and Uspenskij cover this topic at some length in *Vybor imeni u russkix knjazej*; alternately one can look at their copious appendix of Rusians and their names in the same volume.
74. See the information in Litvina and Uspenskij, *Vybor imeni u russkix knjazej*, 541.

Marriages: Generation Two

1. Jaroslav's eldest son with Ingigerd was Volodimer, who died in 1052, only two years before his father. *PVL*, s.a. 1052.
2. Nikon Chronicle, s.a. 1043; Tver Chronicle, s.a. 1043.
3. *Annalista Saxo*, s.a. 1039; *Lamberti Hersfeldensis Annales*, s.a. 1039.
4. *PVL*, s.a. 1068.
5. See Svjatopolk Jaropolčič's entry above for details of this affair.
6. Izjaslav and Bolesław were related by blood as first cousins, as well as by marriage.
7. See *Gesta principum Polonorum*, 88–89, for the Polish perspective. The *PVL* also records the attack under 1069, and Bolesław's critical role. *PVL*, s.a. 1069.
8. *PVL*, s.a. 1073.
9. Ibid.
10. See the marriage of Vyšeslava Svjatoslavna for more on these events.
11. Gregory VII, Pope, *The Register of Pope Gregory VII 1073–1085*, trans. H. E. J. Cowdrey (Oxford: Oxford University Press, 2002), letter 2.73.
12. *PVL*, s.a. 1077.
13. For a longer version of this story focused on these ties see my "Iziaslav Iaroslavich's Excellent Adventure: Constructing Kinship to Gain and Regain Power in Eleventh-Century Europe," *Medieval Prosopography* 30 (2015; forthcoming).
14. "*Unicus filius meus.*" Nazarenko, *Drevnjaja Rus′ na meždunarodnyx putjax*, 567. However, upon my examination of a copy of the plate in the Regenstein Library collection (U. Chicago), I was not able to see such an inscription. H. U. Sauerland and A. Haselhoff, eds., *Der Psalter Ezbischof Egberts von Trier: Codex Gertrudianus, in cividale* (Trier: Selbstverlag der Gesellschaft für nützliche forschungen, 1901), table 42.
15. V. L. Janin, "Russkaja knjaginja Olisava-Gertruda i ee syn Jaropolk," *Numizmatika i epigrafika* 4 (1963): 142.
16. Ibid., 158. See my *Reimagining Europe*, ch. 5, for more discussion on the religious position of Rus′ vis-à-vis the rest of Europe in the eleventh century.
17. Nazarenko, *Drevnjaja Rus′ na meždunarodnyx putjax*, 559–84. In his version, Olisava turns out to be a Bohemian princess.
18. René Jetté, "Is the Mystery of the Origin of Agatha, Wife of Edward the Exile, Finally Solved?" *The New England Historical and Genealogical Register* 150, no. 600 (1996): 417–32; and Norman W. Ingham, "Has a Missing Daughter of Iaroslav Mudry Been Found?" *Russian History* 25, no. 3 (1998): 231–70. Nazarenko also addresses this issue, coming to the conclusion that Edward was initially in Rus′, but married someone else.

Nazarenko, *Drevnjaja Rus´ na meždunarodnyx putjax*, 499–501. For a thorough survey of the many theories regarding Agafija's possible marital partners see the online article "Agatha" by Stewart Baldwin, http://sbaldw.home.mindspring.com/hproject/prov/agath000.htm, 20 June 2010. Baldwin comes to the conclusion that "pending further discoveries, Agatha's parentage remains unknown."

19. Adam of Bremen, bk. 2, ch. liii, 51.
20. Jetté, "Is the Mystery of the Origin of Agatha, Wife of Edward the Exile, Finally Solved?" 418.
21. Ingham, "Has a Missing Daughter of Iaroslav Mudry Been Found?" 234–35.
22. See the discussion on onomastics in Christian Raffensperger, "Rusian Influence on European Onomastic Traditions," in *Imenoslov: Istoričeskaja semantika imeni*, ed. F. B. Uspenskij (Moscow: Indrik, 2007), 116–34.
23. Ingham, "Has a Missing Daughter of Iaroslav Mudry Been Found?" 234–35.
24. Jetté, "Is the Mystery of the Origin of Agatha, Wife of Edward the Exile, Finally Solved?" 418.
25. Ibid., 419.
26. See Pauline Stafford, "The Portrayal of Royal Women in England, Mid-Tenth to Mid-Twelfth Centuries," in *Medieval Queenship*, ed. John Carmi Parsons (Gloucestershire: Sutton Publishing, 1994), 153–54, for example.
27. Ingham, "Has a Missing Daughter of Iaroslav Mudry Been Found?" 252–54.
28. Ibid.
29. Jetté, "Is the Mystery of the Origin of Agatha, Wife of Edward the Exile, Finally Solved?" 419.
30. *The Anglo-Saxon Chronicle*, trans. M. J. Swanton (London: J. M. Dent Publishers, 1996), s. a. 1074.
31. Ingham, "Has a Missing Daughter of Iaroslav Mudry Been Found?" 269n99.
32. *Chronica de gestis Hungarorum*, 111.
33. Ibid., 107.
34. Ibid., 110–11.
35. Dimitri Obolensky, *The Byzantine Commonwealth: Eastern Europe 500–1453* (London: Weidenfeld and Nicolson, 1971), 159.
36. *Chronica de gestis Hungarorum*, 113.
37. Though there was a pagan resurgence in Hungary around the time of King Stephen's death and this may have affected the brothers' religious beliefs. Ibid.
38. Ibid. Adam of Bremen explicitly mentions the marriage as well. Adam of Bremen, bk. 3, ch. xiii.12; schol. 62 (63).
39. As some historians have claimed before, including Z. J. Kosztolynik, *Hungary under the Early Árpáds, 890s to 1063* (Boulder, Co.: East European Monographs, 2002), 398.
40. Raffensperger, "Rusian Influence on European Onomastic Traditions."
41. János M. Bak, "Roles and Functions of Queens in Árpádian and Angevin Hungary (1000–1386 A.D.)," in *Medieval Queenship*, ed. John Carmi Parsons (Gloucestershire: Sutton Publishing, 1994), 14.

42. *Chronica de gestis Hungarorum*, 115.
43. Ibid.
44. Rus′ practiced collateral succession, while Hungary, Denmark, and others may have followed a similar practice, or instead utilized a system of tanistry, in which the ruler is chosen from among a pool of eligible members of the family. This is a matter of debate, and difficult to determine as the succession was never as smooth in practice as it can appear on paper.
45. Pál Engel, *The Realm of St. Stephen: A History of Medieval Hungary, 895–1526* (London and New York: I. B. Tauris, 2005), 31.
46. Kosztolynik, *Hungary under the Early Árpáds, 890s to 1063*, 376.
47. *Lamberti Hersfeldensis Annales*, s.a. 1071.
48. *Chronica de gestis Hungarorum*, 117, where his arrival is recorded after the death of Béla in 1063. Note 331 makes it clear that the arrival of the army happened before Béla's death, though an easier victory may have come because of it.
49. Ibid., 125.
50. After Salomon's death, Judith was married to Władysław Herman of Poland, securing an alliance between the Poles and the German Empire. *Chronica Poloniae Maioris*, ch. 15; *Gesta principum Polonorum*, bk. 2, ch. 1.
51. *Chronica de gestis Hungarorum*, 125.
52. Ibid., 121. See also "Chronici Hungarici compositio saeculi XIV," ed. Alexander Domanovszky, in *Scriptores Rerum Hungaricarum*, ed. Imre Szentpétery, 1:217–505 (Budapest: Academia Litter. Hungarica atque Societate Histor. Hungarica, 1937), 377.
53. *Chronica de gestis Hungarorum*, 122.
54. Whoever was prince of Kyiv at the time of Ladislaus's arrival in the early 1070s, all the Jaroslaviči were uncles of Salomon.
55. Wertner places her death in 1074. Wertner, *Az Árpádok családi története*, chart. However, this is simply the last year that we have information about her. In that year Salomon left her at Admont Abbey when he was expelled from Hungary and went to fight further with his cousins. *Chronica de gestis Hungarorum*, 124.
56. *Chronica de gestis Hungarorum*, 129; and "Chronici Hungarici," 411.
57. Adam of Bremen, bk. 3, ch. xiii.12; Sturluson, *Heimskringla*, 577.
58. Both Jaroslav and Olaf married daughters of Olof Skötkonnung, king of Sweden. In fact, Olaf was betrothed to Ingigerd before Jaroslav took her away. Sturluson, *Heimskringla*, 342.
59. Ibid., 578.
60. Ibid., 486.
61. Ibid., 578.
62. Ibid., 581.
63. Ibid., 587, 589–90.
64. Ibid., 590; and Adam of Bremen, bk. 3, ch. xiii.12, schol. 62 (63).
65. Sturluson, *Heimskringla*, 589.
66. Ibid., 587–89.
67. *Flateyjarbók*, ed. C. R. Unger, vol. 3 (Oslo [Christiania]: P. T. Mallings, 1868), 290.
68. Sturluson, *Heimskringla*, 590.
69. Ibid.

70. Ibid., 591. "Óláf Soenski, King of Sweden, was the grandfather of Ellisif, Harald's wife; and Ástríth, Svein's mother, was the sister of King Saint Óláf."
71. Ibid.
72. Ibid., 602.
73. Ibid.
74. Though Adam does castigate Harald for other ecclesiastical sins, chiefly not recognizing the primacy of the Archbishop of Hamburg-Bremen. Adam of Bremen, bk. 3, ch. xvii.16.
75. Sturluson, *Heimskringla*, 647.
76. Raffensperger, "Rusian Influence on European Onomastic Traditions."
77. Sturluson, *Heimskringla*, 660.
78. Adam of Bremen, bk. 3, ch. liii, 52, schol. 84 (85, 86).
79. Ibid., note to bk. 3, ch. liii, 52, schol. 84 (85, 86).
80. Baumgarten, "Généalogies," 7, 9, table 1.
81. Nazarenko, *Drevnjaja Rus´ na meždunarodnyx putjax*, 523.
82. Sturluson, *Heimskringla*, 666.
83. S. M. Kaštanov might be such a one. S. M. Kaštanov, "Byla li Oda Štadenskaja ženoj velikogo knjazja Svjatoslava Jaroslaviča?" in *Vostočnaja Evropa v drevnosti i srednevekov´e: Drevnjaja Rus´ v sisteme ètnopolitičeskix i kul´turnyx svjazej: čtenija pamjati člena-korrespondenta AN SSSR Vladimira Terent´eviča Pašuto, Moskva, 18–20 aprelja 1994 g.: tezisy dokladov*, ed. V. T. Pašuto, A. P. Novosel´cev, et al. (Moscow: RAN, 1994), 18; as would Baumgarten, whose involved theory of the marriage of Svjatoslav will be discussed briefly later. Baumgarten, "Généalogies," 7, table 1.
84. R. V. Zotov, *O černigovskix knjazjax po Ljubeckomu sinodiku v tatarskoe vremja* (St. Petersburg: Tipografija brat´ev Panteleevyx, 1892), 24, 33.
85. Dimnik, *The Dynasty of Chernigov, 1054–1146*, 37.
86. Ibid.; A. V. Nazarenko, "Kievskaja knjagina — vnuka papy Lv´a IX (1049–1054): Imperatora Genrixa III (1039–1056): Novye dannye o vnešnej politike Rusi v 70-kh gg. XI v.," in *Vostočnaja Evropa v drevnosti i srednevekov´e: Drevnjaja Rus´ v sisteme ètnopolitičeskix i kul´turnyx svjazej: čtenija pamjati člena-korrespondenta AN SSSR Vladimira Terent´eviča Pašuto, Moskva, 18-20 aprelja 1994 g.: tezisy dokladov*, ed. V. T. Pašuto, A. P. Novosel´cev, et al. (Moscow: RAN, 1994), 28.
87. More on which can be found in the marriage of Vsevolod Jaroslavič.
88. V. V. Mošin, "Russkie na Afone i russko-vizantijskie otnošenija v XI–XII vv.," *Byzantinoslavica* 9 (1947–48): 773.
89. There are multiple sources for the genealogy of Ida. The best is Albert of Stade: *Annales Stadenses auctore M. Alberto*, publ. I. M. Lappenberg, in *Annales aevi Suevici*, 271–379, Monumenta Germaniae Historica: Scriptores 16 (Hannover: Impensis Bibliopolii Avlici Hahniani, 1859), s.a. 1112; Nazarenko provides a Russian translation as well. Nazarenko, *Drevnjaja Rus´ na meždunarodnyx putjax*, 506–10.
90. Oterisburg is very near to Elsdorf, and she may have held both properties.
91. I was unable to find the primary source that Nazarenko cites, and have as a result simply cited Nazarenko himself. Nazarenko, *Drevnjaja Rus´ na meždunarodnyx putjax*, 515.
92. *Bruno de Bello Saxonico*, publ. George Pertz, in *Annales et chronica aevi*

Salici, 327–84, Monumenta Germaniae Historica: Scriptores 5 (Hannover: Impensis Bibliopolii Avlici Hahniani, 1844), 333, chap. 13.

93. Nazarenko, *Drevnjaja Rus´ na meždunarodnyx putjax*, 519–20.
94. Ibid., 520–21.
95. Unfortunately due to the structure of this section, the marriages of Svjatoslav are dealt with before the marriage of his daughter Vyšeslava, which occurred after his marriage to Kilikia, but before his marriage to Oda of Stade. See "Marriages: Generation Three" in this volume for the marriage of Vyšeslava Svjatoslavna.
96. T. S. Morozov, ed., *Izbornik velikago knjazja Svjatoslava Jaroslaviča 1073 goda*, Monumenta Linguae Slavicae Dialecti Veteris 3 (Wiesbaden: Otto Harrassowitz, 1965), 1.
97. *PVL*, s.a. 1096.
98. See Dimnik for more details of his life and rule. *Dynasty of Chernigov, 1054–1146.*
99. *Lamberti Hersfeldensis Annales*, s.a. 1075.
100. Ibid. Also recorded obliquely in the *PVL*. *PVL*, s.a. 1075.
101. *Lamberti Hersfeldensis Annales*, s.a. 1043.
102. Andrew W. Lewis, *Royal Succession in Capetian France: Studies on Familial Order and the State* (Cambridge, Mass.: Harvard University Press, 1981), 45.
103. Ibid.
104. Constance B. Bouchard, "Consanguinity and Noble Marriages in the Tenth and Eleventh Centuries," *Speculum* 56, no. 2 (1981): 277.
105. Ibid.
106. Robert-Henri Bautier, "Anne de Kiev, reine de France, et la politique royale au XI-e siècle, étude critique de la documentation," *Revue des études Slaves* 57, no. 4 (1985): 545; and André Poulet, "Capetian Women and the Regency: The Genesis of a Vocation," in *Medieval Queenship*, ed. John Carmi Parsons (Gloucestershire: Sutton Publishing, 1994), 100.
107. See the above entries for Dobronega/Marija Volodimerovna and Izjaslav Jaroslavič for further details.
108. Jean Dunbabin, "What's in a Name? Phillip, King of France," *Speculum* 68, no. 4 (1993): 956, wherein she claims Casimir was a monk.
109. I. S. Robinson, *Henry IV of Germany, 1056–1106* (Cambridge: Cambridge University Press, 1999), 21–25.
110. Dunbabin, "What's in a Name?" 956.
111. Though public relations is certainly an anachronistic term for the middle ages, I think that medieval rulers of all kinds would have understood the concept. The sponsorship of chronicles, the endowment of monastaries, and various other public activities were conducted by rulers and others to create a positive impression of themselves and their rule on others.
112. "Chronicon Sancti-Petri-Vivi Senonensis: Auctore Clario," in *Bibliothèque Historique de'Lyonne*, vol. 2 (Auxerre: Perriquet et Rouillé, Imprimeurs de la Société, 1863), s.a. 1046. There is some confusion over the date of the arrival of the embassy that is discussed here, as well as the participants.
113. Maurice Prou, ed., *Recueil des actes de Philippe I-er, roi de France (1059–1108)* (Paris: Imprimerie Nationale, 1908); n. 1 on p. xvii is to the *Psalter of*

Odalric, with the relevant section excerpted in Latin. It relates the arrival of Bishop Roger ("episcopum R.") in Rus´ to negotiate for the "daughter of the king, named Anna."

114. Clarius records that "Quos ille cum pluribus donis et cum filia remisit in Francia." "Chronicon Sancti-Petri-Vivi Senonensis: Auctore Clario," s.a. 1046.
115. As will be discussed when examining the slightly more elaborate description of Evpraksija's entourage in "Marriages: Generation Three" of this volume.
116. "Chronicon: Vindocinense seu de Aquaria," in *Chroniques des églises D'Anjou*, ed. Paul Marchegay and Émile Mabille (Paris: Libraire de la société de l'histoire de France, 1869), s.a. 1051: "MLI. Heinricus, Francorum rex, uxorem duxit Scithicam et Rufam." The marriage, though not the date, is also recorded by Adam of Bremen. Adam of Bremen, bk. 3, ch. xiii.12, schol. 62 (63).
117. Prou, *Recueil des actes de Philippe I-er, roi de France (1059–1108)*, xxiii.
118. Raffensperger, "Rusian Influence on European Onomastic Traditions"; Dunbabin, "What's in a Name?"
119. Lewis, *Royal Succession in Capetian France*, 46.
120. Steven Runciman, *A History of the Crusades*, vol. 1 (New York: Penguin, 1951), 111–12.
121. "Chronicon Sancti-Petri-Vivi Senonensis: Auctore Clario," s.a. 1060; *Bertholdi Annales*, publ. George Pertz, in *Annales et chronica aevi Salici*, 264–326, Monumenta Germaniae Historica: Scriptores 5 (Hannover: Impensis Bibliopolii Avlici Hahniani, 1844; hereafter Berthold of Reichenau), s.a. 1060.
122. Poulet, "Capetian Women and the Regency: The Genesis of a Vocation," 106.
123. Ibid. This was also true in an example from the German Empire, when Theophano was regent, or part of a regency team, for her young son Otto III, as well as Agnes for her young son Henry IV.
124. Ibid.
125. Berthold of Reichenau, s.a. 1060, Lewis, *Royal Succession in Capetian France*, 46.
126. Berthold of Reichenau, s.a. 1060.
127. Prou, *Recueil des actes de Philippe Ier, roi de France (1059–1108)*, no. 6.
128. Poulet, "Capetian Women and the Regency: The Genesis of a Vocation," 107.
129. Ibid.
130. "Chronicon Sancti-Petri-Vivi Senonensis: Auctore Clario," s.a. 1060; *Hugo Floriacensis opera historica: accedunt aliae Francorum historiae*, ed. Georgio Waitz, in *Chronica et annales aevi Salici*, 337–406, Monumenta Germaniae Historica: Scriptores 9 (Hannover: Impensis Bibliopolii Avlici Hahniani, 1851), 389; Frédéric Soehnée, ed. and trans., *Catalogue des Actes d'Henri Ier Roi de France (1031–1060)* (Paris: Librairie Honoré Champion, 1907), no. 102.
131. Jean Dunbabin, *France in the Making, 843–1180* (Oxford: Oxford University Press, 1985), 215.

132. Ibid., 216.
133. In the Ottonian example, the land was often the same from generation to generation.
134. Prou, *Recueil des actes de Philippe Ier, roi de France (1059–1108)*, nos. 18, 21, 23, 27.
135. Ibid., no. 18, notes her last diploma.
136. Poulet, "Capetian Women and the Regency: The Genesis of a Vocation," 107, says he was the highest royal counselor. Dunbabin, *France in the Making, 843–1180*, 215, says he was second to Baldwin.
137. Poulet, "Capetian Women and the Regency: The Genesis of a Vocation," 107.
138. Dunbabin, "What's in a Name?" 954.
139. Natalia Pushkareva, *Women in Russian History: From the Tenth to the Twentieth Century*, trans. Eve Levin (Armonk, N.Y.: M. E. Sharpe, 1997), 13.
140. For a comprehensive study of her signatures, see A. N. Xolodilin, "Avtografy Anny Jaroslavny – koroleva Francii," *Russkaja reč'*, no. 2 (1985): 109–13.
141. For a slightly longer discussion of the problem of the record of Rusian women in the chronicles and where they can, in fact, be found, see my "The Missing Rusian Women: The Case of Evpraksia Vsevolodovna."
142. *PVL*, s.a. 1053.
143. Michael Angold, *The Byzantine Empire, 1025–1204* (New York: Longman, 1997), 36.
144. Leib, citing Karamzin, says that Constantine IX had three daughters: Eudoxia, Theodora, and Zoe. However, these are the three daughters of Constantine VIII, and it seems unlikely Constantine IX would have three with the same names. Bernard Leib, *Rome, Kiev et Byzance à la fin du XIe siècle* (Paris: Auguste Picard, 1924), 169n3.
145. Hypatian Chronicle, s.a. 1115.
146. Sherbowitz-Wetzor advances the same conclusion in his notes to the English translation of the *PVL*. Cross and Sherbowitz-Wetzor, *Russian Primary Chronicle*, n. 192.
147. Baumgarten, "Généalogies," 22–23, table 5; and Leib, *Rome, Kiev et Byzance*, 169.
148. *PVL*, s.a. 1053.
149. Cross and Sherbowitz-Wetzor, *Russian Primary Chronicle*, n. 192.
150. Jonathan Shepard sorts through the various theories to present an extremely interesting and well-researched account of both the history and historiography of the attack. Jonathan Shepard, "Why Did the Russians Attack Byzantium in 1043," *Byzantinische-neugriechische Jahrbücher* 22 (1985): 147–212.
151. Angold, *Byzantine Empire, 1025–1204*, 36.
152. *PVL*, s.a. 1051. Obolensky thinks that the appointment of Ilarion was included in the new Byzantino-Rusian agreement negotiated with the marriage. Obolensky, *Byzantine Commonwealth: Eastern Europe 500–1453*, 227.
153. Vsevolod's age is probably one of the reasons that some date the marriage

to 1046, the year in which Vsevolod turned 16, generally considered to be one of the earliest ages for men to marry.

154. Michael Psellus, *Fourteen Byzantine Rulers: The Chronographia of Michael Psellus*, trans. E. R. A. Sewter (New York: Penguin Books, 1966), 199–203.
155. *PVL*, s.a. 1053.
156. Constantine IX was the only member of the house of Monomachus to occupy the imperial throne. After his death in 1055, imperial power returned to Theodora, the last living member of the Macedonian dynasty. This makes it unlikely that Volodimer Jaroslavič could have had a connection during his life with the Monomachus family, as he was only two years old at Constantine IX's death.
157. Tatiščev, *Istorija Rossijskaja*, 2:85.
158. There is a growing debate about the use of the term "khan" in reference to the leaders of the Polovcians, so I have chosen to default in this work to the title "ruler." In all of the Rusian sources their leaders are referred to as *knjazja*, and apart from their inclusion in the personal name of Tugorkhan, we do not see the use of the title "khan." This title, and variants, were used by the Khazars and the Mongols, and it has been applied to the Polovcians potentially because of those groups' usage of the title and their relations with Rus´. But because the title does not appear in our sources and it lends a certain pejorative aspect to the Polovcians, I have chosen not to use it here. I would like to thank Don Ostrowski for several spirited exchanges about this topic.
159. *PVL*, s.a. 1068. The Polovcian ruler is referred to there as *knjaz´*.
160. Hypatian Chronicle, s.a. 1111.
161. Baumgarten, "Généalogies," 7, 9, table 1.
162. *The Old Rus´ Kyivan and Galician-Volhynian Chronicles: The Ostroz´kyj (Xlebnikov) and Četvertyns´kyj (Pogodin) Codices*, Harvard Library of Early Ukrainian Literature: Texts 8 (Cambridge, Mass.: Harvard Ukrainian Research Institute, 1990), 126.
163. In searching for corroboration, the death of Janka Vsevolodovna records her link to her father and her brother, Volodimer, but there is no notation of a mother. Hypatian Chronicle, s.a. 1112: "daughter of Vsevolod, sister of Volodimer." None of the other children of Vsevolod elicit as much information as that in their death notices. As a further note, in part 2 I separate out the children between the two wives based upon the death date of the Monomaxina from Tatiščev, and provide speculative birth dates for the children, generally based upon their marriage dates.
164. Omeljan Pritsak discusses the impact of both Monomax and his son M´stislav on the chronicle tradition in *Old Rus´ Kyivan and Galician-Volhynian Chronicles*, xx–xxi.

Marriages: Generation Three

1. Dimnik, *Dynasty of Chernigov, 1054–1146*, 46.
2. *NPL*, s.a. 989. This particular listing of rulers is found only in the *Komissionnyj spisok* of the *NPL*, not in the *Sinodal´nyj*.

3. Baumgarten places his birth at approximately 1045, though it is not recorded in the Rusian chronicles, and I have accepted this approximate date as a starting point for discussion. Baumgarten, "Généalogies," 15, table 3. The general age of marriage was fifteen or sixteen for men, though some did occur younger, and Rostislav may have begun to rule Novgorod on his own behalf at fourteen, as his father did. See Tver Chronicle, s.a. 1052, for the length of Volodimer's rule.
4. Though there are no exact dates for the births of his sons, they are believed to have been born just on either side of 1050, making them too young for a marriage in 1060 that needed to happen immediately. Baumgarten, "Généalogies," 10, table 2.
5. See above in the entry for Anastasija Jaroslavna.
6. *Chronica de gestis Hungarorum*, 110–11.
7. Whether or not Rostislav was the ruler of Novgorod, he was still of Novgorod, as his flight from there indicates in the 1060s, as well as his company at the time, identified as other Novgorodians. *PVL*, s.a. 1064.
8. As a very interesting sidenote, this is the first time in the recorded history of Rus´ that the name Rjurik appeared in the Volodimeroviči line.
9. Rostislav's only appearance in the *PVL* comes when he leaves Novgorod with friends and takes over the southern city of Tmutorokan. He leaves in 1064 and is poisoned by Byzantines in 1066. *PVL*, s.a. 1064.
10. Tatiščev, *Istorija Rossijskaja*, 2:83–84.
11. Dimnik, *Dynasty of Chernigov, 1054–1146*, 129.
12. *Annalista Saxo*, s.a. 1062, 1103.
13. Cecily Hilsdale, "The Social Life of the Byzantine Gift: The Royal Crown of Hungary Re-Invented," *Art History* 31, no. 5 (2008): 621, but see also n. 64.
14. *Chronica de gestis Hungarorum*, 131.
15. Ibid.
16. Ibid., 131; and *PVL*, s.a. 1097.
17. Długosz, *Annales*, 95.
18. Tatiščev, *Istorija Rossijskaja*, 2:123.
19. Both Baumgarten and Dimnik accept the marriage. Baumgarten, "Généalogies," 18–20, table 5; and Dimnik, *Dynasty of Chernigov, 1054–1146*, 41. Balzer, however, is not as accepting of the identity of the bride. Balzer, *Genealogia Piastów*, 98–99.
20. *PVL*, s.a. 1067.
21. This interpretation is in contrast with Martin Dimnik's, who believes that the marriage was not at all for wider political reasons, but only for the advancement of the Svjatoslaviči. Dimnik, *Dynasty of Chernigov, 1054–1146*, 57.
22. It is debatable whether or not Bolesław would have aided Izjaslav the next spring had Svjatoslav not died. Izjaslav did bring with him to Poland two papal legates, who, most likely, crowned Bolesław II as king, with the purpose of getting his aid for Izjaslav.
23. *Old Rus´ Kyivan and Galician-Volhynian Chronicles*, xxi.
24. *PVL*, s.a. 1107; Laurentian Chronicle, s.a. 1126; Hypatian Chronicle, s.a. 1127; Voskresenskij Chronicle, s.a. 1126; Nikon Chronicle, s.a. 1126.

25. Tatiščev records the name of the princess who died in 1126 as Anna, but this is also the name he gives to Volodimer's stepmother, and could be simply an error. Tatiščev, *Istorija Rossijskaja*, 2:128 (stepmother's death), 138.
26. Baumgarten, "Généalogies," 22–23, table 5.
27. *PVL*, s.a. 1107.
28. Baumgarten, "Généalogies," 22–23, table 5.
29. My interpretation is corroborated by the translation of the *PVL* by Horace G. Lunt, which is being prepared for publication by the Harvard Ukrainian Research Institute.
30. As do others, beginning with Cross and Sherbowitz-Wetzor, *Russian Primary Chronicle*, 203n373.
31. Saxo Grammaticus, *Danorum Regum heroumque historia: Books X–XVI*, trans. Eric Christiansen, 3 vols., vol. 1, bks. 10–13 (Oxford: B.A.R., 1980), 58, bk. 11, 6.
32. Sven's father was Duke Ulf, whose sister Gyða married Duke Godwin and bore his sons, including King Harold.
33. Sturluson, *Heimskringla*, 702. The reference is to Harold Valdemarsson [M´stislav Volodimerovič], and his parents are listed as Volodimer and Gyða, daughter of Harold Godwinsson.
34. Baumgarten, "Généalogies," 22–23, table 5.
35. Nazarenko, *Drevnjaja Rus´ na meždunarodnyx putjax*, 522.
36. *PVL*, s.a. 1076.
37. Saxo Grammaticus, *Danorum Regum heroumque historia*, 228–29; Nazarenko, *Drevnjaja Rus´ na meždunarodnyx putjax*, 522–24.
38. Saxo Grammaticus, *Danorum Regum heroumque historia*, 229. Her participation or presence in the embassy is not mentioned in the account of it provided by Lambert of Hersefeld, or elsewhere. *Lamberti Hersfeldensis Annales*, s.a. 1075.
39. Adam of Bremen, bk. 4, xxi (21).
40. Sturluson, *Heimskringla*, 702. There is also extensive discussion in Nazarenko of a central European source referring to M´stislav as Harald. Nazarenko, *Drevnjaja Rus´ na meždunarodnyx putjax*, 585–616.
41. Raffensperger, "Rusian Influence on European Onomastic Traditions."
42. These marriages are discussed more in the sections on the dynastic marriages of M´stislav (in "Marriages: Generation Four") and his daughters (in "Marriages: Generation Five").
43. M. P. Alekseev, "Anglo-saksonskaja parallel´ k *Poučeniju* Vladimira Monomaxa," *Trudy otdela drevnorusskoj literatury* 2 (1935).
44. Nazarenko, *Drevnjaja Rus´ na meždunarodnyx putjax*, 527–28.
45. Ibid.
46. Hypatian Chronicle, s.a. 1158.
47. Laurentian Chronicle, p. 247. This information comes from Volodimer Monomax's "Testament."
48. I think quite highly of Izjaslav's conduct of foreign relations, which can be seen in my "Iziaslav Iaroslavich's Excellent Adventure."
49. *Annalista Saxo*, s.a. 1062.
50. Ibid., s.a. 1062, 1103. This marriage has not been included in the list of

Rusian dynastic marriages presented here because it appears that the marriage was arranged by Cunigunda's new husband and did not concern Rus´.

51. *Lamberti Hersfeldensis Annales*, s.a. 1075.
52. H. E. J. Cowdrey, *Pope Gregory VII, 1073–1085* (Oxford: Clarendon Press, 1998), 452–53. For Gregory's letter to Jaropolk and Izjaslav, see Gregory VII, *Register of Pope Gregory VII 1073–1085*, 2.74.
53. *PVL*, s.a. 1086, for his construction of the church. Ščaveleva discusses it and its implications in more depth. N. I. Ščaveleva, "Knjaz´ Jaropolk Izjaslavič i xristianskaja cerkov´ XI v.," in *Vostočnaja Evropa v drevnosti i srednevekov´e: X čtenija k 80-letiju člena-korrespondenta AN SSSR Vladimira Terent´eviča Pašuto*, ed. V. T. Pašuto, E. A. Mel´nikova (Moscow: RAN, 1998), 135.
54. *PVL*, s.a. 1079.
55. "Xoženie Daniila, igumena Russkoj zemli," in *Kniga xoženij: zapiski russkix puteŝestvennikov XI–XV vv.* (Moscow: Sovetskaja Rossija, 1984), 30.
56. *PVL*, s.a. 1083.
57. This marriage has been reconstructed in multiple secondary sources. Chiefly, X. Loparev, "Vizantijskaija pečat´ s imenem russkoj knjagini," *Vizantijskij vremennik* 1, no. 1 (1894): 159–66; Janin, "Pečati Feofano Muzalon," *Numizmatika i sfragistika* 2 (1965): 76–90; and more recently, Dimnik, *Dynasty of Chernigov, 1054–1146*, 160–61.
58. Janin, "Pečati Feofano Muzalon," 80.
59. Loparev, "Vizantijskaija pečat´ s imenem russkoj knjagini," 160–61. See also Zotov, *O černigovskix knjazjax*, 24.
60. Každan notes that he accepted the idea in his early scholarship, but later developed major doubts about the authenticity of the marriage. A. P. Každan, "Vizantijskij podatnoj sborščik na beregax kimmerijskogo bospora v konce XII v.," in *Problemy obščestvenno-političeskoj istorij Rossii i slavjanskix stran; Sbornik statej k 70–letiju akademika M. N. Tixomirova*, ed. V. I. Šunkov (Moscow: Izdatel´stvo vostočnoj literatury, 1963), 93; Každan, "Rus´-Byzantine Princely Marriages in the Eleventh and Twelfth Centuries," 417–18.
61. Každan, "Rus´-Byzantine Princely Marriages in the Eleventh and Twelfth Centuries," 417–18.
62. Dimnik, *Dynasty of Chernigov, 1054–1146*, 163–64. Dimnik here also cites multiple authors who subscribe to this view. Franklin and Shepard also note Alexius's ascension as a motive for Oleg's return. Franklin and Shepard, *Emergence of Rus 750–1200*, 262.
63. *Annalista Saxo*, s.a. 1082.
64. Ibid., s.a. 1089.
65. See Robinson, *Henry IV of Germany, 1056–1106*, 269.
66. Nazarenko, *Drevnjaja Rus´ na meždunarodnyx putjax*, 540–46, 553. See also O. B. Holovko, *Drevnjaja Rus´ i Pol´ša v političeskix vzaimo-otnošenijax X–pervoj treti XIII vv.* (Kyiv: Naukova dumka, 1988), 58, who discusses a similar theory.
67. Even non-Izjaslaviči occupants of the western principalities were more closely tied to the Poles than other Rusians, as shown by Davyd Igorič,

who made an alliance with Władysław Hermann after he inherited Volhynia upon the death of Jaropolk Izjaslavič. Holovko, *Drevnjaja Rus´ i Pol'ša*, 59.

68. For more on this idea, see Raffensperger, *Reimagining Europe*, ch. 5.
69. *Annalista Saxo*, s.a. 1082.
70. Rusian rulers are generally referred to as *rex* in the Latin chronicles.
71. *Annalista Saxo*, s.a. 1082.
72. These issues are discussed briefly, with references, in the introduction.
73. J. Vogt, *Monumenta inedita rerum Germanicarum praecipue Bremensium* (Bremen 1740), 1. bd. 125, cited in Rozanov, "Evpraksija-Adel´geida Vsevolodovna (1071–1109)," 623.
74. Another such record is the book created for a French queen who was coming to Byzantium. The book depicts her arrival. For details, see Hilsdale, "Constructing a Byzantine 'Augusta.'"
75. Carolyn Edwards, "Dynastic Sanctity in Two Early Medieval Women's *Lives*," in *Medieval Family Roles: A Book of Essays*, ed. Cathy Jorgensen Itnyre (New York: Garland Publishing, 1996), 13–14.
76. For more discussion of these entourages, see Raffensperger, *Reimagining Europe*, ch. 2.
77. *Annales Stadenses auctore M. Alberto*, s.a. 1144, in listing of history of the family dates Henry of Stade's death to 1087.
78. As had occurred with her aunts Anna in France and Anastasija in Hungary some years before. See their respective entries in this section for more information.
79. This expulsion also shows that the Saxons would not have accepted her as one of their own in a marriage to Henry IV, as has been posited by some historians.
80. S. P. Rozanov suggested that Quedlinburg had been Evpraksija's initial home upon her arrival in Germany. Rozanov, "Evpraksija-Adel´geida Vsevolodovna (1071–1109)." She would have lived there learning the local languages, German and Latin, and customs, and waiting to come of age for a legal marriage.
81. Walram, Bishop of Naumburg, *Liber de unitate ecclesiae conservanda*, ed. Wilhelm Schwenkenbecher, Monumenta Germaniae Historica: Scriptores rerum Germanicarum in usum scholarum separatim editi 39 (Hannover: Impensis Bibliopolii Hahniani, 1883), bk. 2, ch. 35, 114.
82. Levin, *Sex and Society in the World of the Orthodox Slavs, 900–1700*, 132–35.
83. Christian Raffensperger. "Evpraksia Vsevolodovna between East and West," *Russian History/Histoire Russe* 30, no. 1–2 (2003): 23–34.
84. "Kanoničeskie otvety mitropolita Ioanna II," *Russkaja istoričeskaja biblioteka* 6 (1908): art. 13, p. 7.
85. Many historians make this claim, beginning with N. M. Karamzin, *Istorija gosudarstva Rossijskogo*, vol. 2 (Moscow: Kniga, 1988), 60. The only other explanation would be marriages to Jews or Muslims, both of which would have been extraordinary enough to preserve mention of it elsewhere.
86. The only exception to this policy that I have found in this period is the second marriage of the daughter of Vsevolodko Davydič to Baškord of the Polovcians, discussed below under Volodimer Davydič (her first husband).

87. D. S. Lixačev and N. V. Ponyrko, eds., *Epistoljarnoe nasledie Drevnej Rusi XI–XIII: issledovanija, teksty, perevody* (Saint Petersburg: Nauka, 1992), 30–35.
88. The chronicler makes the mistake of confusing son and father, a common mistake in medieval chronicles that modern editors correct automatically.
89. *Ekkehardi Chronicon*, publ. D. G. Waitz and P. Killon, in *Chronica et annales aevi Salici*, 1–267, Monumenta Germaniae Historica: Scriptores 6 (Hannover: Impensis Bibliopolii Avlici Hahniani, 1844), s.a. 1089; also listed in *Annalista Saxo*, s.a. 1089; and Frutolf of Michelsburg, *Chronica*, ed. F.-J. Schmale and I. Schmale-Ott (Darmstadt: Ausgewählte Quellen zur deutschen Geschiste des Mittelalters, 1972), s.a. 1089.
90. Walram, *Liber de unitate ecclesiae conservanda*, bk. 2, ch. 26, 100. Her enthronement is also recorded in one of Henry's diplomata from 1089. *Heinrici IV: Diplomata*, ed. Dietrich von Gladiss and Alfred Gawlik, Monumenta Germaniae Historica: Die Urkunden der deutschen Könige und Kaiser (Diplomatum regum et imperatorum Germaniae) 6, vol. 2 of 3 (Weimar: Hermann Bohlaus Nachfolger, 1953), 407.
91. Anna Jaroslavna, Dobronega Volodimerovna, Anastasija Jaroslavna, and Elisabeth Jaroslavna.
92. Rozanov, "Evpraksija-Adel´geida Vsevolodovna (1071–1109)," 627, among others.
93. Robinson, *Henry IV of Germany, 1056–1106*, 289–90.
94. Revelation 2:6, 2:15.
95. Helmold, *The Chronicle of the Slavs by Helmold, Priest of Bosau*, trans. Francis J. Tschan (New York: Columbia University Press, 1935), 108.
96. Gerhoh of Reichersburg, "De investigatione Antichristi liber I," ed. E. Sackur, in *Gerhohi praepositi Reichersbergensis libelli selecti*, 304–95, Monumenta Germaniae Historica: Libelli de lite imperatorum et pontificum 3 (Hannover: Impensis Bibliopolii Avlici Hahniani, 1897), 324.
97. As it is recorded in Mathilda's *Vita*, Evpraksija arranged to send a message to Mathilda from where Henry had her imprisoned in Verona. Mathilda then led some soldiers to free her in 1092/3. *Donizonis vita Mathildis*, publ. L. Bethmann, in *Historiae aevi Salici*, Monumenta Germaniae Historica: Scriptores 12 (Hannover: Impensis Bibliopolii Avlici Hahniani, 1861), 394.
98. Ibid., 392.
99. Though it was accepted as fact in George Vernadsky, *Kievan Russia* (New Haven, Conn: Yale University Press, 1948), 340–42.
100. Robinson, *Henry IV of Germany, 1056–1106*, 290. Robinson suggests that Welf may have written the deposition, and there is an implication that he read it, though Robinson also says that Evpraksija made a public appearance there.
101. Gerhoh of Reichersburg, "De investigatione Antichristi liber I," 324.
102. *Bernoldi Chronicon*, publ. George Pertz, in *Annales et chronica aevi Salici*, 385–467, Monumenta Germaniae Historica: Scriptores 5 (Hannover: Impensis Bibliopolii Avlici Hahniani, 1844), s.a. 1095.
103. Ibid.
104. Ibid.
105. The Pope had crowned Conrad of Lombardy emperor soon after the papal

synod at Piacenza, though it was never widely recognized. Robinson, *Henry IV of Germany, 1056–1106*, 292.

106. Or just before Evpraksija did; the accounts are varied. Rozanov, "Evpraksija-Adel´geida Vsevolodovna (1071–1109)," 642; Robinson, *Henry IV of Germany, 1056–1106*, 289.
107. Though it is recorded under the year 1093, with other statements including that she joined a nunnery and became abbess. *Annales Stadenses auctore M. Alberto*, s.a. 1093.
108. Gerhoh of Reichersburg, "De investigatione Antichristi liber I," 324.
109. Rozanov, "Evpraksija-Adel´geida Vsevolodovna (1071–1109)."
110. *PVL*, s.a. 1106.
111. *Annales Sancti Disibodi*, publ. G. Waitz, in *Annales aevi Suevici*, 4–30, Monumenta Germaniae Historica: Scriptores 17 (Hannover: Impensis Bibliopolii Avlici Hahniani, 1861), 14; *Annales Stadenses auctore M. Alberto*, s.a. 1093; Cesare Baronio, *Annales ecclesiastici Caesaris Baronii* (Barri-Ducis: Guerin, 1864), 17:606. It should be noted that it is likely that this last source is reliant upon at least one of the earlier sources.
112. Rozanov theorizes that she joined the Andreevskij nunnery, where her half sister Janka was the abbess, though there is no evidence for or against this theory. Rozanov, "Evpraksija-Adel´geida Vsevolodovna (1071–1109)," 645. The Church of St. Andrew was founded in 1086 by Vsevolod, as was the convent next door for Janka. Hypatian Chronicle, s.a. 1086.
113. *PVL*, s.a. 1109.
114. *PVL*, s.a. 1106, 1109.
115. Hypatian Chronicle, s.a. 1111; Laurentian Chronicle, s.a. 1113. Janka's death is recorded here, also by name as with other of her entries.
116. Keeping in mind the supposition that Vsevolod had two wives and that Volodimer and Janka may have been from one mother, while Evpraksija was from another. See Vsevolod Izjaslavič for more information on this topic.
117. The creation of the cult of Boris and Glěb, for instance, may have been done in opposition to the will of the Byzantine Church, or its officers in Rus´. Ja. N. Ščapov, *Gosudarstvo i cerkov´: Drevnej Rusi X–XIII vv.* (Moscow: Nauka, 1989), 177–78. Admittedly, others have differing opinions: Jonathan Shepard, "Byzantium and Russia in the Eleventh Century: A Study in Political and Ecclesiastical Relations" (PhD dissertation, Oxford, 1973), chap. 3; and *The Hagiography of Kievan Rus´*, trans. and introd. Paul Hollingsworth, Harvard Library of Early Ukrainian Literature: Translations 2 (Cambridge, Mass.: Harvard Ukrainian Research Institute, 1992), introduction. Also of note would be possible Byzantine opposition to the translation of the relics of Theodosius. *PVL*, s.a. 1091; and for the idea of Byzantine opposition, Cross and Sherbowitz-Wetzor, *Russian Primary Chronicle*, 274–75, n273. Dissent with the rulers of Rus´ is more unambiguous, as the abbot of the monastery refused to eat with the usurpers Svjatoslav and Vsevolod and condemned their usurpation. *The Paterik of the Kievan Caves Monastery*, trans. Muriel Heppell, Harvard Library of Early Ukrainian Literature: Translations 1 (Cambridge, Mass.: Harvard Ukrainian Research Institute, 1989), 74–75.
118. Raffensperger, "Missing Rusian Woman."

119. J. Vogt, *Monumenta inedita rerum Germanicarum praecipue Bremensium* (Bremen 1740), 1. bd. 125, cited in Rozanov, "Evpraksija-Adel′geida Vsevolodovna (1071–1109)," 623.
120. *PVL*, s.a. 1109.
121. Długosz, *Annales*, 4:161, see especially n. 5.
122. Balzer working from the same primary sources acknowledged these various pieces but believed the best that could be said was that she was a Rusian princess, not specifically an Izjaslavna. Oswald Balzer, *Genealogia Piastów* (Cracow: Nakładem Akademij Umiejętności, 1895), 113.
123. Gallus Anonymous, *Gesta principum Polonorum*, 101.
124. Długosz, *Annales*, 4:161.
125. Ibid. "Quatenos Russie regiones a patre suo subacte hac *affinitate* magis sinceres et devote in fide persisterent" (emphasis added).
126. Gallus Anonymous, *Gesta principum Polonorum*, 101.
127. Długosz, *Annales*, 4:161.
128. Gallus Anonymous, *Gesta principum Polonorum*, 101–3.
129. Długosz records a belief that Mieszko and Eudoxia joined a monastery together in Poland. Długosz, *Annales*, 4:214.
130. *PVL*, s.a. 1088.
131. Baumgarten, "Généalogies," 10–11, table 2.
132. Ibid., 10, table 2, person no. 3.
133. *Ortliebi de fundatione monasterii Zwivildensis*, publ. Ottone Abel, in *Annales et chronica aevi Salici: Vitae aevi Carolini et Saxonici*, 64–92, Monumenta Germaniae Historica: Scriptores 10 (Hannover: Impensis Bibliopolii Avlici Hahniani, 1852), 90–92.
134. Každan, "Rus′-Byzantine Princely Marriages in the Eleventh and Twelfth Centuries," 419.
135. Ibid.
136. Baumgarten, "Généalogies," 10, persons no. 11–17.
137. Długosz, *Annales*, 183.
138. Baumgarten, "Généalogies," 10, person no. 10.
139. *PVL*, s.a. 1097.
140. Długosz, *Annales*, 4:157.
141. *PVL*, s.a. 1094.
142. Though I fully recognize that the *PVL* is extant only from later versions, by the end of the eleventh century the style of composition has changed such that more detail is paid to contemporary events, as well as celestial observations, suggesting that the chronicler was writing or compiling it at that time. Donald Ostrowski notes that there are nineteen such celestial observations between 1063 and 1114, whereas none before 1054. Donald Ostrowski, "Pagan Past and Christian Identity in the *Primary Chronicle*," in *Historical Narratives and Christian Identity on a European Periphery: Early History Writing in Northern, East-Central, and Eastern Europe (c. 1070–1200)*, ed. Ildar H. Garipzanov (Turnhout: Brepols, 2011), 252.
143. *PVL*, s.a. 1096.
144. Ibid.
145. Hypatian Chronicle, s.a. 1125; Laurentian Chronicle, s.a. 1124.

146. *PVL*, s.a. 1094.
147. Długosz, *Annales*, 4:157.

Marriages: Generation Four

1. Hypatian Chronicle, s.a. 1158.
2. Ibid. See the article by Inés García de la Puente, "Anastasia of Minsk: Neglected Evidence on the Rule of a Woman in Rus' History?" *Russian History* 39 (2012): 347–78, which discusses this woman's remarkable forty-year rule in more detail.
3. The wife of Svjatoslav Ol´govič ruled briefly in Černihiv after her husband's death. However, the Greek bishop sent to Svjatoslav Vsevolodič, her nephew, informing him of Svjatoslav Ol´govič's death and his wife's mismanagement of the territory. Once Svjatoslav Vsevolodič and his cousin Oleg Svjatoslavič arrived in Černihiv, she was displaced as ruler. Hypatian Chronicle, s.a. 1164.
4. Hypatian Chronicle, s.a. 1158. Upon her death her age, eighty-four, is recorded, thus placing her birth in approximately 1074.
5. *PVL*, s.a. 1086.
6. Hypatian Chronicle, s.a. 1116, 1119.
7. *PVL*, s.a. 1068.
8. See part 2, table 2.
9. For more on consanguinity, see the introduction.
10. Baumgarten, "Généalogies," table 3.
11. N. de Baumgarten, "Pervaja vetv´ knjazej Galickix," *Letopis´ istoriko-rodoslovnago obščestva v Moskve* 4 (1907): 6.
12. See part 2, table 4. Alternately, the child is cited in Hypatian Chronicle, s.a. 1140, for one example.
13. *PVL*, s.a. 1097.
14. Georgii Fejér, ed., *Codex diplomaticus Hungariae, ecclesiasticus ac civilis*, vol. 1 (Buda: Regiae Universitatis Ungaricae, 1829), 469. Wertner discusses this in more depth, including explaining the connection between "Gerazclauus" and Jaroslav. Wertner, *Az Árpádok családi története*, 205.
15. *Chronica de gestis Hungarorum*, 129.
16. The chronicler rather than the editor is correct here. It was most likely the Cumans/Polovcians/Qipchaks who invaded, not the Pechenegs.
17. *Chronica de gestis Hungarorum*, 129.
18. Nazarenko, *Drevnjaja Rus´ na meždunarodnyx putjax*, 555–56.
19. *PVL*, s.a. 1094.
20. *PVL*, s.a. 1097.
21. *Chronica de gestis Hungarorum*, 131.
22. Tatiščev, *Istorija Rossijskaja*, 2:119.
23. *PVL*, s.a. 1097. Terminology for brothers and first cousins is often interchangeable in the medieval period in chronicles of various languages.
24. "Rarely did Hungarians suffer such slaughter as in this battle." *Chronica de gestis Hungarorum*, 132.
25. *PVL*, s.a. 1104. The identification of the groom is supported by Wertner.

Wertner, *Az Árpádok családi története*, 242–56, see also his comprehensive genealogical chart. For more information on this marriage, see the entry for Peredslava Svjatopolkovna below.

26. For example, *Chronica de gestis Hungarorum*, 132. Interestingly, one chronicle records that they inherited the throne jointly, and this may provide a less Koloman-centric view than the *Chronica de gestis Hungarorum*. "Annales Posonienses," ed. Emericus Madszar, in *Scriptores Rerum Hungaricarum*, ed. Imre Szentpétery (Budapest: Academia Litter. Hungarica atque Societate Histor. Hungarica, 1937), 1:126.
27. *Chronica de gestis Hungarorum*, 132. There is an interesting story that Koloman had a Rusian bodyguard who protected him in Hungary; the truth of the story is unknown, though Kotliar tells it dismissively. M. [N.] F. Kotljar, *Diplomatija južnoj Rusi* (St. Petersburg: Aleteija, 2003), 63.
28. Hypatian Chronicle, s.a. 1123.
29. Gallus Anonymous, *Gesta principum Polonorum*, 117.
30. For more information on this marriage, see the entry for Sbyslava Svjatopolkovna below.
31. Balzer, *Genealogia Piastów*, 124. The mediation can be found in Gallus Anonymous, *Gesta principum Polonorum*, 189.
32. Gallus Anonymous, *Gesta principum Polonorum*, 189.
33. *PVL*, s.a. 1106.
34. Gallus Anonymous, *Gesta principum Polonorum*, 187–89.
35. *NPL*, s.a. 1113; Hypatian Chronicle, s.a. 1112.
36. Hypatian Chronicle, s.a. 1118; *NPL*, s.a. 1118.
37. Nikon Chronicle, s.a. 1119. See also Voskresenskij Chronicle, s.a. 1118; Tver Chronicle, s.a. 1118.
38. For examples of such peacemaking marriages in Rus´, see Raffensperger, *Reimagining Europe*, ch. 3.
39. Pašuto, *Vnešnjaja politika Drevnej Rusi*, 151.
40. Hypatian Chronicle, s.a. 1123. Długosz even records that it was Bolesław III and Koloman themselves that led their armies to aid Jaroslav. The action during the battles, as he records it, was primarily motivated by them. However, Koloman had been dead since 1114, so it was unlikely that he participated in person. Długosz, *Annales*, 297–98.
41. Baumgarten, "Généalogies," 22–23, table 5.
42. *PVL*, s.a. 1095.
43. Wilhelm, "Wilhelmi abbatis genealogia regum Danorum," in *Scriptores minores historiae Danicae medii aevi*, ed. M. Cl. Getz (Copenhagen: I Kommission hos G. E. C. Gad, 1917), 182.
44. *NPL*, s.a. 1122.
45. Sturluson, *Heimskringla*, 702.
46. Wilhelm, "Wilhelmi abbatis genealogia regum Danorum," 182.
47. Adam of Bremen, bk. 3, ch. liii.52, schol. 84 (85, 86). See also Sturluson, *Heimskringla*, 678.
48. Adam of Bremen, note to bk. 3, ch. liii.52, schol. 84 (85, 86).
49. Ibid., bk. 3, ch. liii.52, schol. 84 (85, 86).
50. See the entry for Sbyslava Svjatopolkovna below.
51. Sturluson, *Heimskringla*, 678–80.

52. Ibid., 680.
53. Laurentian Chronicle, s.a. 1122; *NPL*, s.a. 1122.
54. Saxo Grammaticus, *Danorum Regum heroumque historia*, bk. 13, p. 110, n. 8. There is a similar, though not identical, tradition of female inheritance in Rus′, which is described in the *Russkaja Pravda. Medieval Russian Laws*, trans. George Vernadsky (New York: Oxford University Press, 1947), 51–53.
55. Saxo Grammaticus, *Danorum Regum heroumque historia*, bk. 13, 110.
56. *NPL*, s.a. 1122. This is replicated in several other chronicles as well. Hypatian Chronicle, s.a. 1122; *NČL*, s.a. 1122; Nikon Chronicle, s.a. 1122.
57. *NČL*, s.a. 1118.
58. *NPL*, s.a. 1128; *NČL*, s.a. 1128. This is also the year of Zavid Dmitreevič's death after his having been in office as posadnik for only a few months.
59. *NPL*, s.a. 1117.
60. *PVL*, s.a. 1097.
61. Tatiščev, *Istorija Rossijskaja*, 2:117.
62. For the latest and best refutation of Tatiščev as a source, see Toločko, *"Istorija Rossijskaja" Vasilija Tatiščeva*.
63. *PVL*, s.a. 1102. The marriage is also recorded in more detail in Długosz. Długosz, *Annales*, 210–11. Długosz actually mentions Sbyslava numerous times in his chronicle.
64. The dispensation from Pope Paschal II is noted by the chronicler Gallus Anonymous, *Gesta principum Polonorum*, 158–61.
65. For an excellent overview of medieval consanguinity see Bouchard, "Consanguinity and Noble Marriages in the Tenth and Eleventh Centuries."
66. For more on their struggle, including an attack by Zbigniew at Bolesław's wedding, see Gallus Anonymous, *Gesta principum Polonorum*.
67. *Chronica Poloniae Maioris*, ch. 27.
68. *Chronica Poloniae Maioris*, ch. 27, 30.
69. *PVL*, s.a. 1104. The word used for prince is *korolevič*, a rare use of the word in the Rusian chronicles.
70. Hypatian Chronicle, xxv.
71. See Wertner, *Az Árpádok családi története*, for information on both of these individuals, as well as the other, later, rulers named Ladislaus (László).
72. Ibid., 251.
73. For more information about this episode, see the section in this volume on Jaroslav Svjatopolčič.
74. *Chronica de gestis Hungarorum*, 132.
75. For a Hungarian record of the defeat see ibid., 132. For Rusian accounts, see *PVL*, s.a. 1097.
76. Almos would make many such attempts over the years, enlisting aid in Poland and Germany as well. *Chronica de gestis Hungarorum*, 132.
77. Hypatian Chronicle, s.a. 1112.
78. Ibid. See also the section in this volume on Jaroslav Svjatopolčič, in "Marriages: Generation Four," above.
79. *NPL*, s.a. 1106; *NČL*, s.a. 1106.
80. Zotov, *O černigovskix knjazjax*, 38, 261.
81. Baumgarten, "Généalogies," table 4.

82. Dimnik, *Dynasty of Chernigov, 1046–1146*, 231. Though admittedly I did find it so at one time and followed Dimnik's argument in other work; see my *Reimagining Europe*, 56. In part I was convinced otherwise by A. V. Nazarenko, *Drevnjaja Rus´ i slavjane: istoriko-filologičeskie issledovanija* (Moscow: Russkij fond sodejstvija obrazovaniju i nauke, 2009), 152–53.
83. Rostislav Jurevič flees his father to Izjaslav Mstislavič in 1148 in an attempt to receive land and recognition that he did not receive at home in Vladimir-Suzdal. Hypatian Chronicle, s.a. 1148.
84. *PVL*, s.a. 1107.
85. Ibid. The Voskresenskij Chronicle records one as Aepa and one as Kaepa, though it seems more than likely that this is a later misprint that has been interpolated into the text. Voskresenskij Chronicle, s.a. 1107.
86. *PVL*, s.a. 1107.
87. Baumgarten, "Généalogies," 18–19, table 4.
88. Dimnik, *Dynasty of Chernigov, 1054–1146*, 240.
89. There are many examples of this in the various Rusian chronicles. See also Martin Dimnik's *Dynasty of Chernigov* books for a refutation of the negative characterization of Oleg and the Ol´goviči because of this behavior. One of the best-known examples of Rusian-Polovcian interaction is contained in the twelfth-century Igor´ Tale. *Slovo o polku Igoreve: Perevod, predislovie i pojasnenija Ivana Novikova*, ed. N. K. Gudzija (Moscow: Xudožestvennaja literatura, 1938).
90. *NPL*, s.a. 1136; *NČL*, s.a. 1136; Voskresenskij Chronicle, s.a. 1136; Tver Chronicle, s.a. 1136.
91. Dimnik, *Dynasty of Chernigov, 1054–1146*, 337–40; Baumgarten, "Généalogies," table 4.
92. *NPL*, s.a. 1136; *NČL*, s.a. 1136; Voskresenskij Chronicle, s.a. 1136; Tver Chronicle, s.a. 1136. "Vladyka" is the title that the Novgorodian, and some other chronicles, used for the head of the Novgorodian Church. It is often translated as "archbishop," though the hierarchical issues implied by that are difficult to apply to the Rusian Church.
93. In *Reimagining Europe*, I discuss Peter Brown's idea of "micro-Christendoms" at some length. That discussion highlights some of the internal divides in Christian Europe. Raffensperger, *Reimagining Europe*, ch. 5.
94. *NPL*, s.a. 1138; Laurentian Chronicle, s.a. 1138; Hypatian Chronicle, s.a. 1139; *NČL*, s.a. 1138; Voskresenskij Chronicle, s.a. 1138; Tver Chronicle, s.a. 1138; Nikon Chronicle, s.a. 1138.
95. *PVL*, s.a. 1107.
96. Ibid.
97. Ibid.; also see the discussion above in regard to Svjatoslav Ol´govič.
98. Baumgarten, "Généalogies," 23–24, table 5. Každan also does not accept this identification. Každan, "Rus´-Byzantine Princely Marriages in the Eleventh and Twelfth Centuries," 423–24.
99. Hypatian Chronicle, s.a 1162; Tver Chronicle, s.a. 1162; Voskresenskij Chronicle, s.a. 1162; Nikon Chronicle, s.a. 1160.
100. Joannes Kinnamos, *Deeds of John and Manuel Comnenus*, trans. Charles M. Brand (New York: Columbia University Press, 1976), bk. 5, ch. 12. I have cited the English here and throughout for convenience, but there

is also the Greek text, *Ioannis Cinnami Epitome rerum ab Ioanne et Alexio Comnenis gestarum*, ed. Augustus Meineke, vol. 26 of *Corpus Scriptorum Historiae Byzantinae* (Bonn: Weberi, 1836), 236.

101. For two examples, see S. P. Rozanov, "Evfimija Vladimirovna i Boris Kolomanovič: Iz evropejskoj politiki XII v.," *Izvestija Akademij Nauk SSSR VII Serija: Otdelenie gumanitarnyx nauk* 8 (1930): 585–99, and my "Identity in Flux: Finding Boris Kolomanovich in the Interstices of Medieval Europe," *Medieval Globe* 2, no. 2 (2015): forthcoming.
102. Hypatian Chronicle, s.a. 1112.
103. Rozanov and my articles cited above have contrasting views of the marriage, but also the relevant sources listed. Rozanov, "Evfimija Vladimirovna i Boris Kolomanovič: Iz evropejskoj politiki XII v."; Raffensperger, "Identity in Flux."
104. *Chronica de gestis Hungarorum*, n. 436; Wertner, *Az Árpádok családi története*, 222.
105. See above for the political context of Peredslava Svjatopolkovna's marriage.
106. *Chronica de gestis Hungarorum*, 132; Rozanov, "Evfimija Vladimirovna i Boris Kolomanovič," 591.
107. *Chronica de gestis Hungarorum*, 132.
108. "Cosmae chronicon Boemorum cum continuatoribus," in *Fontes rerum Bohemicarum*, ed. Jos. Emler, vol. 2 (Prague: Nákladem Musea Království Českého, 1874), 215–16; and Otto, Bishop of Freising, *The Two Cities: A Chronicle of Universal History to the Year 1146 A.D.*, trans. Charles Christopher Mierow (New York: Octagon Books, 1966), bk. 7, sec. 21.
109. Though admittedly, Otto's position is slightly more complex given that part of his family supported Boris's attempts at usurpation. See Raffensperger, "Identity in Flux."
110. There are multiple examples of Hungarian support for Jaroslav in the various chronicles. See Hypatian Chronicle, s.a. 1118, 1123, for two examples.
111. Kinnamos, *Deeds of John and Manuel Comnenus*, bk. 3, ch. 11; *Chronica Poloniae Maioris*, ch. 29.
112. Tatiščev, for instance, records her original name as Sofija and her monastic name as Evfimija. Tatiščev, *Istorija Rossijskaja*, 2:128, 149.
113. *PVL*, s.a. 1106.
114. Laurentian Chronicle, s.a. 1138; Hypatian Chronicle, s.a. 1139; Nikon Chronicle, s.a. 1138.
115. Hypatian Chronicle, s.a. 1113.
116. See above.
117. *NPL*, s.a. 1117; Laurentian Chronicle, s.a. 1117; Hypatian Chronicle, s.a. 1117; *NČL*, s.a. 1117; Voskresenskij Chronicle, s.a. 1117; Tver Chronicle, s.a. 1117; Nikon Chronicle, s.a. 1117.
118. This may be seen in their support for Jaroslav in his rebellion against Volodimer Monomax later in the decade. Hypatian Chronicle, s.a. 1117.
119. Laurentian Chronicle, s.a. 1119; Voskresenskij Chronicle, s.a. 1118; Tver Chronicle, s.a. 1118; Nikon Chronicle, s.a. 1119.
120. Laurentian Chronicle, s.a. 1116.
121. Hypatian Chronicle, s.a. 1116.
122. Laurentian Chronicle, s.a. 1116; Hypatian Chronicle, s.a. 1116.

123. See Každan, "Rus′-Byzantine Princely Marriages in the Eleventh and Twelfth Centuries," 420.
124. Baumgarten, "Généalogies," 22–23, table 5.
125. Hypatian Chronicle, s.a. 1136; Laurentian Chronicle, s.a. 1136; *NČL*, s.a. 1136; Voskresenskij Chronicle, s.a. 1136; Nikon Chronicle, s.a. 1136.
126. Litvina and Uspenskij, *Vybor imeni u russkix knjazej v X–XVI vv.*, 140–41.
127. Každan, "Rus′-Byzantine Princely Marriages in the Eleventh and Twelfth Centuries," 420–22.
128. Laurentian Chronicle, s.a. 1116; Hypatian Chronicle, s.a. 1116; Voskresenskij Chronicle, s.a. 1116; Nikon Chronicle, s.a. 1117.
129. Ibid.
130. Laurentian Chronicle, s.a. 1145; Hypatian Chronicle, s.a. 1145.
131. Hypatian Chronicle, s.a. 1117.
132. Ibid.
133. Hypatian Chronicle, s.a. 1145.
134. Hypatian Chronicle, xiv.
135. Riza Bariev, *Volžskie bulgary: Istorija i kul′tura* (Saint Petersburg, 1999), accessed online at http://www.balkaria.info/library/b/bariev/2/bariev.htm.
136. Nikon Chronicle, s.a. 1145.
137. Where he first appears in 1127/28. Laurentian Chronicle, s.a. 1127; Hypatian Chronicle, s.a. 1128.
138. Hypatian Chronicle, s.a. 1116. Davyd Igorič's death is recorded in multiple sources: Hypatian Chronicle, s.a. 1112; *NPL*, s.a. 1113; Laurentian Chronicle, s.a. 1113; Voskresenskij Chronicle, s.a. 1112; Tver Chronicle, s.a. 1112; Nikon Chronicle, s.a. 1113.
139. Laurentian Chronicle, s.a. 1127; Hypatian Chronicle, s.a. 1128.
140. Baumgarten, "Généalogies," 10–11, table 2.
141. Długosz, *Annales*, 447; and Pašuto, *Vnešnjaja politika Drevnej Rusi*, 151.
142. Długosz, *Annales*, 299; and *Chronica Poloniae Maioris*, ch. 27.
143. Długosz, *Annales*, 447.
144. The Ortliebi Zwifaltensis Chronicon refers to Piotr as "princeps," while elsewhere he is referred to as "comes." *Ortliebi de fundatione monasterii Zwivildensis*, 91. For "comes," see Długosz, *Annales*.
145. Pašuto, *Vnešnjaja politika Drevnej Rusi*, 151.
146. The 1117 is listed in Gerard Labuda and Zdzisław Stieber, eds., *Słownik starożytności słowiańskich: encyklopedyczny zarys kultury słowian od czasów najdawniejszych*, vol. 4 (Wrocław: Zakład Narodowy imienia Ossolińskich, 1970), 113.
147. *Chronica Poloniae Maioris*, ch. 27.
148. Pašuto, *Vnešnjaja politika Drevnej Rusi*, 151.
149. "Chronica Petri comitis Poloniae" [Kronika o Piotrze Właście], ed. Alexander Semkowicz, in *Monumenta Poloniae Historica*, 3:745–84 (Lviv: W Komisie Księgarni Gubrynowicza i Schmidta, 1878), 766.
150. "Chronica Polono-Silesiaci: loci ad Petrum spectantes," in *Monumenta Poloniae Historica: Series Nova*, ed. Marian Plezia, 31–33 (Cracow: Subsidio Ministerii Scholarum Superiorum et Studiorum, 1951), 32.
151. "Chronica Petri comitis Poloniae," 783–84.
152. The quote is from the Hypatian Chronicle, but other chronicles also list

the same or similar information. Hypatian Chronicle, s.a. 1117 (location of the quote); Voskresenskij Chronicle, s.a. 1117; Tver Chronicle, s.a. 1117; Nikon Chronicle, s.a. 1118.

153. Tver Chronicle, s.a. 1117.
154. *PVL*, s.a. 1096; and above under Svjatopolk Izjaslavič's dynastic marriage.
155. Voskresenskij Chronicle, s.a. 1117.
156. Hypatian Chronicle, s.a. 1124; Voskresenskij Chronicle, s.a. 1124.
157. Baumgarten, "Généalogies," 18–19, table 4; and Dimnik, *Dynasty of Chernigov, 1054–1146*, 304.
158. The *Chronica Poloniae Maioris* and Gallus Anonymous, *Gesta principum Polonorum*, are the two main sources for his reign.
159. Długosz, *Annales*.
160. Dimnik, *Dynasty of Chernigov, 1054–1146*, 304.
161. Multiple chronicles, Rusian as well as Polish, record this account. Hypatian Chronicle, s.a. 1123; and Długosz, *Annales*, 297–98.
162. For Jaroslav Svjatopolčič's foreign marriages, including one with a Polish princess, see above under his entry.
163. Balzer in his understanding of this marriage explains that Vsevolod should have inherited Černihiv and thus been more of a power in Rus´. Balzer, *Genealogia Piastów*, 137.
164. N. I. Ščaveleva, "Pol´ki—ženy russkix knjazej (XI–seredina XIII v.)," *Drevnejšie gosudarstva na territorii SSSR 1987* (1989), 55.
165. The Piast family were the royal family of Poland, even after its fragmentation into three or more territories.
166. Dimnik, *Dynasty of Chernigov, 1054–1146*, 254, 313; Baumgarten, "Généalogies," table 4.
167. Hypatian Chronicle, s.a. 1141. Additionally, there seem to be seals with her name on them found, but they do little to advance our understanding of the marriage. V. L. Janin, ed., *Aktovye pečati drevnej Rusi X–XV vv.* (Moscow: Nauka, 1970), 1:71.
168. Dimnik, *Dynasty of Chernigov, 1054–1146*, 313.
169. Ibid., 165.
170. See the entry for M´stislav Volodimerič for the dating of his marriage.
171. Zotov, *O černigovskix knjaz´jax po Ljubeckomu sinodiku*, 262.
172. For more on age of marriage see the introduction, or Levin, *Sex and Society in the World of the Orthodox Slavs, 900–1700*, ch. 2; as well as Diers and Amundsen, "The Age of Menarche in Medieval Europe."
173. It appears that menarche began about the age of fourteen in the medieval world. Diers and Amundsen, "Age of Menarche in Medieval Europe," 363. See the introduction for more information.
174. Hypatian Chronicle, s.a. 1128; Voskresenskij Chronicle, s.a. 1127; Tver Chronicle, s.a. 1127; Nikon Chronicle, s.a. 1127.
175. Hypatian Chronicle, s.a. 1128.
176. Dąbrowski comes to a similar conclusion (though we arrived at them quite separately). See his entry for Marija M´stislavna in Dąbrowski, *Genealogia Mścisławowiczów*, 148–55.
177. As well as their death dates. His eldest son Svjatoslav dies in 1194, making his birth in the late 1120s entirely likely. Hypatian Chronicle, s.a. 1194.

178. Following the marriage between a Vsevolodkovna and Jurij Jaroslavič discussed below.
179. Volodimer assumes the throne in 1138. Laurentian Chronicle, s.a. 1138; Voskresenskij Chronicle, s.a. 1138; Nikon Chronicle, s.a. 1138.
180. Vsevolodko's death is recorded in multiple chronicles: Laurentian Chronicle, s.a. 1141; Hypatian Chronicle, s.a. 1141; Voskresenskij Chronicle, s.a. 1141; Nikon Chronicle, s.a. 1141. Only two of Vsevolodko's sons, Boris and Glěb, appear in the chronicles, both during an 1144 attack on Volodimerko of Halyč.
181. Tables 10 and 11 in part 2 of this volume serve to illustrate this point.
182. Hypatian Chronicle, s.a. 1151.
183. See part 2, table 21 for an illustration of these marriages.
184. Tver Chronicle, s.a. 1159.

Marriages: Generation Five

1. *PVL*, s.a. 1104.
2. Baumgarten, "Généalogies," 15, table 3.
3. Každan, "Rus´-Byzantine Princely Marriages in the Eleventh and Twelfth Centuries," 419–20.
4. P. Gautier, "Le typikon de la Théotokos Kécharitôménè," *Revue des études Byzantines* 43 (1985): p. 123, lines 1837–41.
5. Kinnamos, *Deeds of John and Manuel Comnenus*, bk. 5, chs. 10, 11, 12.
6. For additional detail and discussion of Malfrid and Ingeborg M´stislavna's marriages, see Christian Raffensperger, "Dynastic Marriage in Action: How Two Rusian Princesses Changed Scandinavia," in *Imenoslov: Istorija jazyka, istorija kul´tury*, ed. F. B. Uspenskij (Moscow: Aleteja, 2010), 187–99.
7. For example, Saxo Grammaticus, *Danorum Regum heroumque historia*; and Sturluson, *Heimskringla*, 702.
8. Pašuto, *Vnešnjaja politika Drevnej Rusi*, 146.
9. Sturluson, *Heimskringla*, 699.
10. Ibid., 716.
11. Witness the refounding of Lübeck slightly later, where both Norway and Rus´ are mentioned as major Baltic traders. Helmold, *Chronicle of the Slavs*, ch. 86 (85).
12. Litvina and Uspenskij, *Vybor imeni u russkix knjazej*, 246n26; Orderic Vitalis, *The Ecclesiastical History of Orderic Vitalis*, vol. 5 (bks. 9 and 10), ed. and trans. by Marjorie Chibnall (Oxford: Clarendon Press, 1975), bk. 10, ch. 6.
13. Orderic Vitalis, *Ecclesiastical History*, bk. 10, ch. 6n3.
14. Sturluson, *Heimskringla*, 702.
15. Snorre Sturluson, *Heimskringla or The Lives of the Norse Kings*, ed. Erling Monsen, trans. A. H. Smith (New York: Dover Publications, 1990), 630–32, 641–42. This episode does not appear in the Hollander translation of the *Heimskringla*. It is from a variant of the earliest *Kringla* manuscript, but does appear in the Morkinskinna. *Morkinskinna: The Earliest*

Icelandic Chronicle of the Norwegian Kings (1030–1157), trans. Theodore M. Andersson and Kari Ellen Gade (Ithaca: Cornell University Press, 2000), ch. 80.

16. Sturluson, *Heimskringla*, 751.
17. Ibid., 701.
18. Ibid., 714.
19. Oda of Stade, wife of Svjatoslav Jaroslavič, returned to the German empire after Svjatoslav's death. Dimnik, *Dynasty of Chernigov, 1054–1146*, 129n292 (citing an unnamed German annalist); additionally, the Byzantine princess who married Géza of Hungary returns home after his death. Hilsdale, "Social Life of the Byzantine Gift," 621.
20. See Helmold, *Chronicle of the Slavs*, 155, for the murder. See also Saxo Grammaticus, bk. 13, 126–28. Incidentally, Magnus was also a cousin, as his father Niels was married to Margaret, daughter of Inge Steinkelsson. Margaret and Kristín, Malfrid's mother, were therefore sisters.
21. Helmold, *Chronicle of the Slavs*, 156.
22. Saxo Grammaticus, *Danorum Regum heroumque historia*, bk. 13, 134.
23. Magnus and Harald had split the country between them, with Magnus inheriting all of his father's weapons and treasury. Harald had a slight advantage in land. Sturluson, *Heimskringla*, 715.
24. Saxo Grammaticus, *Danorum Regum heroumque historia*, bk. 13, 134.
25. Ibid., bk. 13, 138.
26. Ibid., bk. 13, 140.
27. Ibid., bk. 13, 142.
28. Helmold, *Chronicle of the Slavs*, 152.
29. Lothar would become king of Germany in 1125 and German emperor in 1133.
30. Helmold, *Chronicle of the Slavs*, 152. Knut later became king of the Abodrite Slavs, a position he also received from Lothar, probably in approximately 1128. Ibid., 153.
31. Wilhelm, "Wilhelmi abbatis genealogia regum Danorum," 180.
32. Pašuto, *Vnešnjaja politika Drevnej Rusi*, 147.
33. With the stated purpose that she "wanted to create a stronger family feeling towards him [her son Magnus] among his kin by means of marriage alliances." Saxo Grammaticus, *Danorum Regum heroumque historia*, bk. 13, 110.
34. Ibid., bk. 13, 110.
35. Ibid., bk. 13, 110n8.
36. Ibid., The land did pass down through multiple generations. Magnus Nielsson inherited his mother's land after her death and used it to declare himself king of Sweden.
37. *Knýtlinga Saga: The History of the Kings of Denmark*, trans. Hermann Pálsson and Paul Edwards (Odense: Odense University Press, 1986), 128–30.
38. These ideas are developed in recent works, but I have specifically dealt with the Rusian situation in Raffensperger, *Reimagining Europe*, ch. 2.
39. I know of no definitive study on the topic of Danish succession, but at least in the second half of the eleventh century and into the twelfth it

appears that the succession is lateral. It is also possible, as Don Ostrowski has suggested in personal correspondence, that it was more akin to tanistry, in which a king was chosen from a pool of eligible successors.

40. Helmold, *Chronicle of the Slavs*, 153.
41. Ibid., 154.
42. For more on the complex view of Margaret in the many sources on Knud's death, see Thomas A. Dubois and Niels Ingwersen, "St. Knud Lavard: A Saint for Denmark," in *Sanctity in the North: Saints, Lives, and Cults in Medieval Scandinavia*, ed. Thomas A. Dubois (Toronto: University of Toronto Press, 2008), 162–63.
43. Helmold, *Chronicle of the Slavs*, 155.
44. Ibid.; Saxo Grammaticus, *Danorum Regum heroumque historia*, bk. 13, 126–28. The kiss is an obvious biblical allusion and is repeated in most variants.
45. Saxo Grammaticus, *Danorum Regum heroumque historia*, bk. 13, 130.
46. Valdemar is the common Latin version of Volodimer. It appears in Latin chronicles in reference to both Volodimer Svjatoslavič and Volodimer Vsevolodovič.
47. *Knýtlinga Saga*, 135–36.
48. Raffensperger, "Rusian Influence on European Onomastic Traditions," 116–34.
49. There is also no need to call such a name "outlandish," as Eric Christiansen does in his notes to Saxo Grammaticus. Saxo Grammaticus, *Danorum Regum heroumque historia*, bk. 13, 130n66. For Kristín's name, see Sturluson, *Heimskringla*, 716.
50. Helmold, *Chronicle of the Slavs*, 158.
51. As discussed above in reference to land given to Ingeborg by Kristín's sister Queen Margaret. Saxo Grammaticus, *Danorum Regum heroumque historia*, bk. 13, 110.
52. *Knýtlinga Saga*, 145.
53. Ibid., 135.
54. Laurentian Chronicle, s.a. 1127; Voskresenskij Chronicle, s.a. 1127; Hypatian Chronicle, s.a. 1128; Nikon Chronicle, s.a. 1127.
55. Specifically the Hypatian Chronicle, s.a. 1128, which refers to Vjačeslav Volodimerič protecting M′stislav's daughter's possessions during the sack of the city.
56. They are listed by name in Voskresenskij Chronicle, s.a. 1129; Tver Chronicle, s.a. 1129; the banishment is mentioned more generally in Hypatian Chronicle, s.a. 1130; Laurentian Chronicle, s.a. 1129.
57. Voskresenskij Chronicle, s.a. 1129; Tver Chronicle, s.a. 1129.
58. Baumgarten, "Généalogies," table 8.
59. Antoine, Archevêque de Novgorod, "Description des Lieux-Saints de Constantinople," in *Itinéraires Russes en Orient*, ed. B. de Khitrowo (Geneva: Imprimerie Jules-Guillaume Fick, 1889), 109.
60. This is made more likely by the later banishment of several Jureviči and their families, who made a life for themselves in Byzantium, including holding territory from the emperor. Hypatian Chronicle, s.a. 1162.
61. See the introduction for more discussion of consanguinity.

62. Bouchard, "Consanguinity and Noble Marriages in the Tenth and Eleventh Centuries."
63. Both marriages are discussed above; Glěb Vseslavič in "Marriages: Generation Four"; and Brjačeslav Davydič in the current section.
64. Laurentian Chronicle, s.a. 1123; Hypatian Chronicle, s.a. 1123; Voskresenskij Chronicle, s.a. 1123; Nikon Chronicle, s.a. 1123.
65. Hypatian Chronicle, s.a. 1151.
66. Laurentian Chronicle, s.a. 1119; Hypatian Chronicle, s.a. 1119; Voskresenskij Chronicle, s.a. 1119; Nikon Chronicle, s.a. 1119.
67. Hypatian Chronicle, s.a. 1158. I think it is coincidence, but should note that this is also the year that Sofija Jaroslavna, Rostislav's wife, dies.
68. Hypatian Chronicle, s.a. 1158. For Vsevolod's rule in Izjaslavl, see Hypatian Chronicle, s.a. 1159.
69. Hypatian Chronicle, s.a. 1159.
70. Hypatian Chronicle, s.a. 1122: "Vedena M´stislavna v Greky za car´" (the Mstislavna was sent to the Greeks for the tsar).
71. Baumgarten refers to her as Irene-Dobrodeja. Baumgarten, "Généalogies," table 5. Dąbrowski identifies Alexius, son of John II, and has developed a considerable analysis of the marriage. Dąbrowski, *Genealogia Mścisławowiczów*, 134–41.
72. Każdan, "Rus´-Byzantine Princely Marriages in the Eleventh and Twelfth Centuries," 422–23.
73. The Voskresenskij, Nikon, Rogožskij, and Tver chronicles all do not mention her marriage under 1122.
74. Hypatian Chronicle, s.a. 1122.
75. Tver Chronicle, s.a. 1122; Rogožskij Chronicle, s.a. 1122; Nikon Chronicle, s.a. 1122; and Voskresenskij Chronicle, s.a. 1122.
76. This is discussed in more depth in the section on "Byzantine Inflation" in chapter 2 of Raffensperger, *Reimagining Europe*.
77. *NPL*, s.a. 1123; *NČL*, s.a. 1123; Nikon Chronicle, s.a. 1123.
78. For the birth, see *NPL*, s.a. 1127; anecdotally noted in *NČL*, s.a. 1127. For the death, see *NPL*, s.a. 1128; *NČL*, s.a. 1128; Tver Chronicle, s.a. 1128; Nikon Chronicle, s.a. 1128.
79. Baumgarten, "Généalogies," table 4; Zotov, *O černigovskix knjaz´jax po Ljubeckomu sinodiku*, 266.
80. Dąbrowski, who follows Baumgarten in the identity of the woman as a Svjatoslavna, discusses the problems with the source base and other identities as well before reaching his conclusion. Dąbrowski, *Genealogia Mścisławowiczów*, 111–14.
81. Tatiščev, *Istorija Rossijskaja*, 2:138.
82. Ibid.
83. For Stephen's marriage, see Wertner, *Az Árpádok családi története*, 233.
84. Numerous examples of this are present in all of the Rusian chronicles.
85. Wertner, *Az Árpádok családi története*, 218.
86. Hypatian Chronicle, s.a. 1144.
87. Baumgarten, "Généalogies," table 2.
88. Klaus Conrad, ed., *Pommersches Urkundenbuch*, vol. 1 (Cologne: Böhlau, 1970), 51–53.

89. Baumgarten, "Pribyslava de Russie," *Orientalia Christiana* 20, no. 3 (1930): 156–61.
90. Saxo Grammaticus, *Danorum Regum heroumque historia*, bk. 14. See Christiansen's note for his critique of the genealogical connections here, which he believes make no sense because he identifies the Pribyslava as a daughter of Bolesław III. Making Pribyslava a Rusian, following Baumgarten, rather than a Pole, makes the relationships expressed by Saxo correct. Ibid., 456, n320.
91. Baumgarten, "Pribyslava de Russie," 158–59.
92. See his entry in "Marriages: Generation Four" for more information.
93. Baumgarten, "Pribyslava de Russie," 159, 157.
94. Baumgarten, "Généalogies," 15–16, table 3.
95. "Cosmae chronicon Boemorum cum continuatoribus," 215.
96. Ibid.
97. Lisa Wolverton, *Hastening toward Prague: Power and Society in the Medieval Czech Lands* (Philadelphia: University of Pennsylvania Press, 2001), 94. Wolverton also identifies Vratislav as Duke of Brno.
98. Vsevolod Ol´govič at the time was on the eve of his ascent to the throne of Kyiv, and thus his link to Igor´ Vasilkovič would have been an important political move for the Vasilkoviči.
99. Wolverton, *Hastening toward Prague*, 214–15.
100. Ibid., 216n161.
101. Hypatian Chronicle, s.a. 1140, 1141.
102. Baumgarten, "Généalogies," table 3.
103. Hypatian Chronicle, s.a. 1141, 1142.
104. Hypatian Chronicle, s.a. 1142.
105. For this marriage alliance, see Verxoslava Vsevolodovna.
106. Hypatian Chronicle, s.a. 1142.
107. Norman Davies, *The Origins to 1795*, vol. 1 of *God's Playground: A History of Poland in Two Volumes* (Oxford: Oxford University Press, 2005), 68.
108. Hypatian Chronicle, s.a. 1143. The second marriage is listed in 1144 in the Laurentian Chronicle, s.a. 1144.
109. For a discussion of consanguinity in general, as well as in regard to Rus´, see the introduction.
110. Hypatian Chronicle, s.a. 1151.
111. Rogvolod would, in fact, receive such help a few years later from Roman Mstislavič, Izjaslav's brother. Hypatian Chronicle, s.a. 1159.
112. Laurentian Chronicle, s.a. 1144; Hypatian Chronicle, s.a. 1143; Voskresenskij Chronicle, s.a. 1144; Nikon Chronicle, s.a. 1144.
113. Hypatian Chronicle, s.a. 1159.
114. Hypatian Chronicle, s.a. 1159, 1158.
115. Hypatian Chronicle, s.a. 1162.
116. *NPL*, s.a. 1143.
117. *NČL*, s.a. 1143.
118. *NPL*, s.a. 1142; Laurentian Chronicle, s.a. 1141; Hypatian Chronicle, s.a. 1142; Voskresenskij Chronicle, s.a. 1141; Tver Chronicle, s.a. 1142.
119. See above for Svjatoslav Vsevolodič.
120. Though Vernadsky assumed this meant Bohemia, or Czechia, it is possible

to accept the specificity of the chronicler that she was in fact from Moravia, a territory governed by the Slavniks until the end of the tenth century, and then controlled by the Přemyslids, who also controlled Bohemia. Vernadsky, *Kievan Russia*, 330.

121. *PVL*, s.a. 898.
122. Nazarenko, *Drevnjaja Rus´ na meždunarodnyx putjax*, 566ff.
123. Baumgarten, "Généalogies," 25, table 5.
124. Wolverton, *Hastening toward Prague*, 104–5, 215.
125. Ibid., 214–15.
126. Svjatopolk does not appear as a ruler of a city until ruling Polack briefly in 1132. Laurentian Chronicle, s.a. 1132; Tver Chronicle, s.a. 1132; Nikon Chronicle, s.a. 1132.
127. Hypatian Chronicle, s.a. 1149.
128. Hypatian Chronicle, s.a. 1144. Vsevolodko's death is recorded in multiple chronicles under the year 1141. Laurentian Chronicle, s.a. 1141; Hypatian Chronicle, s.a. 1141; Voskresenskij Chronicle, s.a. 1141; Nikon Chronicle, s.a. 1141.
129. Hypatian Chronicle, s.a. 1144.
130. Hypatian Chronicle, s.a. 1158, 1160.
131. See above in "Marriages: Generation Four" for M´stislav Volodimerič's marriages.
132. Wilhelm, "Wilhelmi abbatis genealogia regum Danorum," 182.
133. Wertner, *Az Árpádok családi története*, 314.
134. *NPL*, s.a. 1146; Hypatian Chronicle, s.a. 1146; Laurentian Chronicle, s.a. 1146; *NČL*, s.a. 1146; Voskresenskij Chronicle, s.a. 1146; Rogožskij Chronicle, s.a. 1146; Tver Chronicle, s.a. 1146; Nikon Chronicle, s.a. 1146.
135. Hypatian Chronicle, s.a. 1149.
136. Ibid., s.a. 1155.
137. Ibid., s.a. 1149.
138. Kinnamos, *Deeds of John and Manuel Comnenus*, bk. 3, ch. 11.
139. Hypatian Chronicle, s.a. 1146, for example. Franklin and Shepard discuss the situation as well. Franklin and Shepard, *Emergence of Rus, 750–1200*, 330.

Marriages: Postscript

1. *Knýtlinga Saga*, 130. The *Knýtlinga Saga* records that they had two children, Knud and Nicholas, but whether they followed their mother or stayed in Denmark is unknown. Knud, however, is there years later and becomes king. Incidentally Magnus was the cousin and murderer of Knud Lavard (ibid., 134–35), husband of Ingeborg M´stislavna. See above for Ingeborg M´stislavna.
2. Magnus was killed by Eric Emune, brother of Knud Lavard, and husband of Malfrid discussed above. Ibid., 139.
3. Ibid., 151.
4. Baumgarten, "Généalogies," table 5; Balzer, *Genealogia Piastów*, 150–51; Nazarenko, *Drevnjaja Rus´ na meždunarodnyx putjax*, 582.
5. J. Gallén, "Vem var Valdemar den stores drottning Sofia?" *Historisk Tid-*

skrift för Finland 61 (1976): 273–88; and E. A. Rydzevskaja, "Drevnjaja Rus′ i Skandinavija v IX–XIV vv.: Materialy i issledovanija," *Drevnejšie gosudarstva na territorii SSSR 1978* (1978): 8–236.

6. A. F. Litvina and F. B. Uspenskij, "Var′irovanie rodovogo imeni na russkoj počve: Ob odnom iz sposobov imjanarečenija v dinastij Rjurikovičej," *Imenoslov* (2003): 164; and N. I. Ščaveleva, *Drevnjaja Rus′ v "Pol′skoj istorii" Jana Dlugoša, knigi I–VI: Tekst, perevod, kommentarij*, ed. A. V. Nazarenko (Moscow: Pamjatniki istoričeskoj mysli, 2004), 435. Dąbrowski does not subscribe to this view in *Genealogia Mścisławowiczów*, but he also does not believe that Richeza's husband was Volodimer Vsevolodič (210–11).
7. Ščaveleva, *Drevnjaja Rus′ v "Pol′skoj istorii" Jana Dlugoša*, 435.
8. Tatiščev, *Istorija Rossijskaja*, vol. 2, s.a. 1077.
9. Ščaveleva, "Pol′ki—ženy russkix knjazej (XI–seredina XIII v.)," 56n42.
10. *NPL*, s.a. 1136, for example.
11. *Knýtlinga Saga*, 242; and Finnur Jónsson, ed., *Fagrskinna, Nóregs kononga tal* (Copenhagen: S. L. Møllers Bogtrykkeri, 1902–1903), 300. For translation as Poland, see *Knýtlinga Saga*, 150.
12. Peter Sawyer, *Kings and Vikings: Scandinavia and Europe, AD 700–1100* (London and New York: Methuen, 1982), 141; for the remark in Adam of Bremen, see *Adami gesta Hammaburgensis ecclesiae pontificum*, ed. J. M. Lappenberg, Scriptores rerum germanicarum in usum scholarum ex Monumentis Germaniae historicis recusi (Hannover: Impensis Biblipolii Hahniani, 1876), bk. 3, ch. xv.14.
13. For more on Sofija, see N. de Baumgarten, "Sofija russkaja, koroleva datskaja, a zatem landgrafinja tjuringenskaja," *Seminarium Kondakovianum* 4 (1931): 95–104.
14. Nazarenko, *Drevnjaja Rus′ na meždunarodnyx putjax*, 582.
15. Hypatian Chronicle, s.a. 1137.
16. Baumgarten, "Généalogies," table 5; and Balzer, *Genealogia Piastów*, 158–60.
17. Stanisław Smolka, *Mieszko Stary i jego wiek* (Warsaw: Geberthner i Wolff, 1881), 213, genealogical table.
18. This starts immediately upon the marriage of Zvenislava Vsevolodovna (discussed above) in 1142, when Vsevolod Olgovič sends troops to assist his *zjat′* Władysław II. Hypatian Chronicle, s.a. 1142. While in 1149, Izjaslav M′stislavič was able to call on his brothers-in-law Bolesław IV, Mieszko, and Henryk to aid him in his own internal Rusian struggles. Hypatian Chronicle, s.a. 1149. This is a particularly interesting event in regards to dynastic marriage as Izjaslav called upon Polish, Hungarian, and Bohemian help, all through familial connections, and received help from all of them.

Part Two

Table 1: Volodimer Svjatoslavič

Rogněda
Birth date: unknown
Death date: *PVL*, s.a. 1000
Marriage to Volodimer Svjatoslavič: *PVL*, s.a. 980.

First Czech Woman
Birth date: unknown
Death date: unknown
Relationship with Volodimer Svjatoslavič: *PVL*, s.a. 980.

Second Czech Woman
Birth date: unknown
Death date: unknown
Relationship with Volodimer Svjatoslavič: *PVL*, s.a. 980.

Volodimer Svjatoslavič
Birth date: unknown
Death date: *PVL*, s.a. 1015
Knjaz´ of Novgorod start: *PVL*, s.a. 970; knjaz´ of Novgorod end: *PVL*, s.a. 980
Knjaz´ of Kyiv start: *PVL*, s.a. 980; knjaz´ of Kyiv end: *PVL*, s.a. 1015
Marriage to Rogněda: *PVL*, s.a. 980
Relationships with the other women listed: *PVL*, s.a. 980
Marriage to Anna Porphyrogenita: *PVL*, s.a. 988; John Scylitzes, *Ioannis Scylitzae Synopsis historiarum*, ed. Hans Thurn, Corpus fontium historiae Byzantinae 5 (Berlin: De Gruyter, 1973), 336, 354, 367; Andrzej Poppe, "The Political Background to the Baptism of Rus´: Byzantine-Russian Relations between 986–989," *Dumbarton Oaks Papers* 30 (1976): 195–244 (extensively redates the marriage). For more on this marriage see part 1, "Marriages: Prelude," "Volodimer Svjatoslavič."

Table 1: Volodimer Svjatoslavič

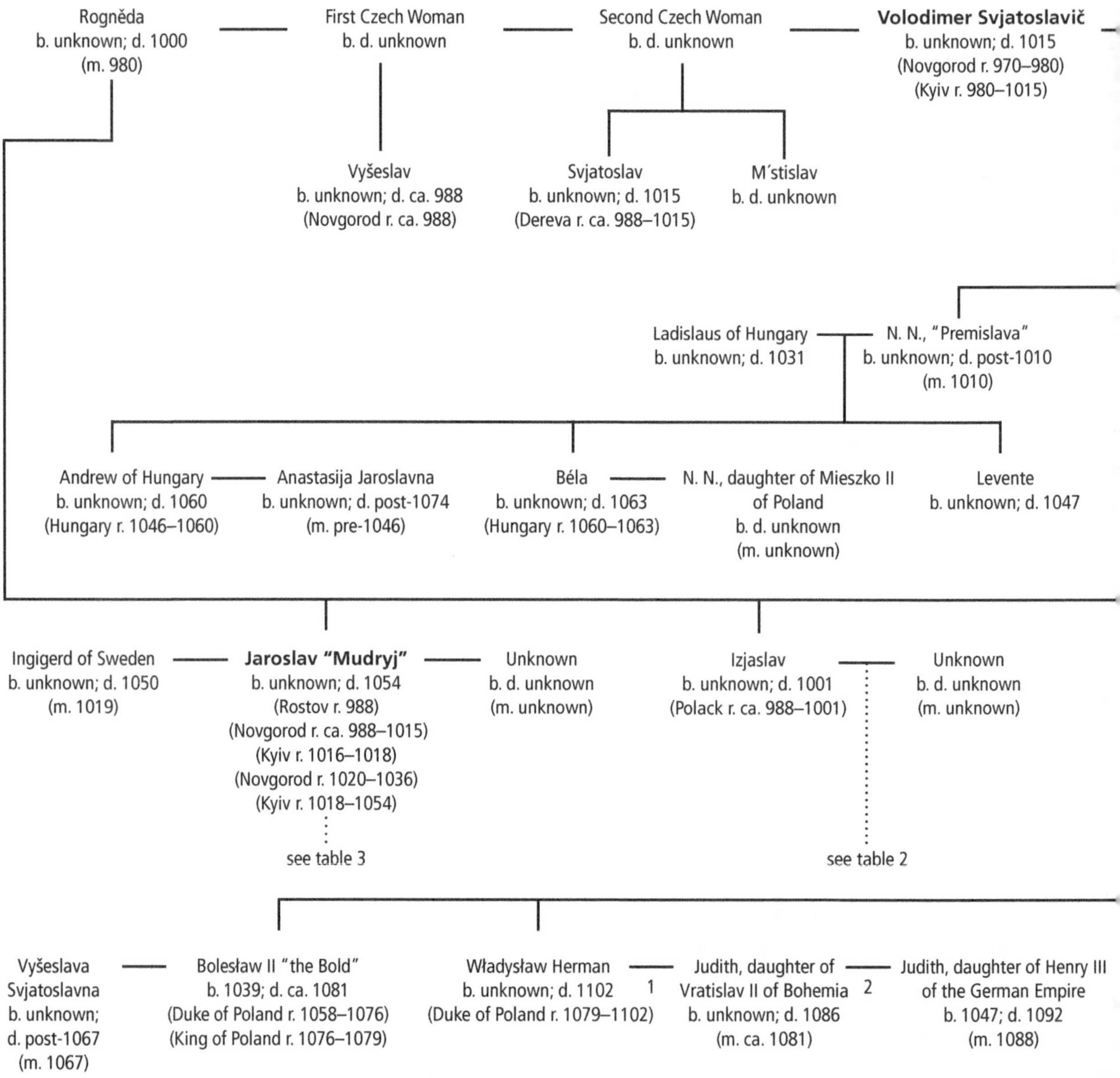

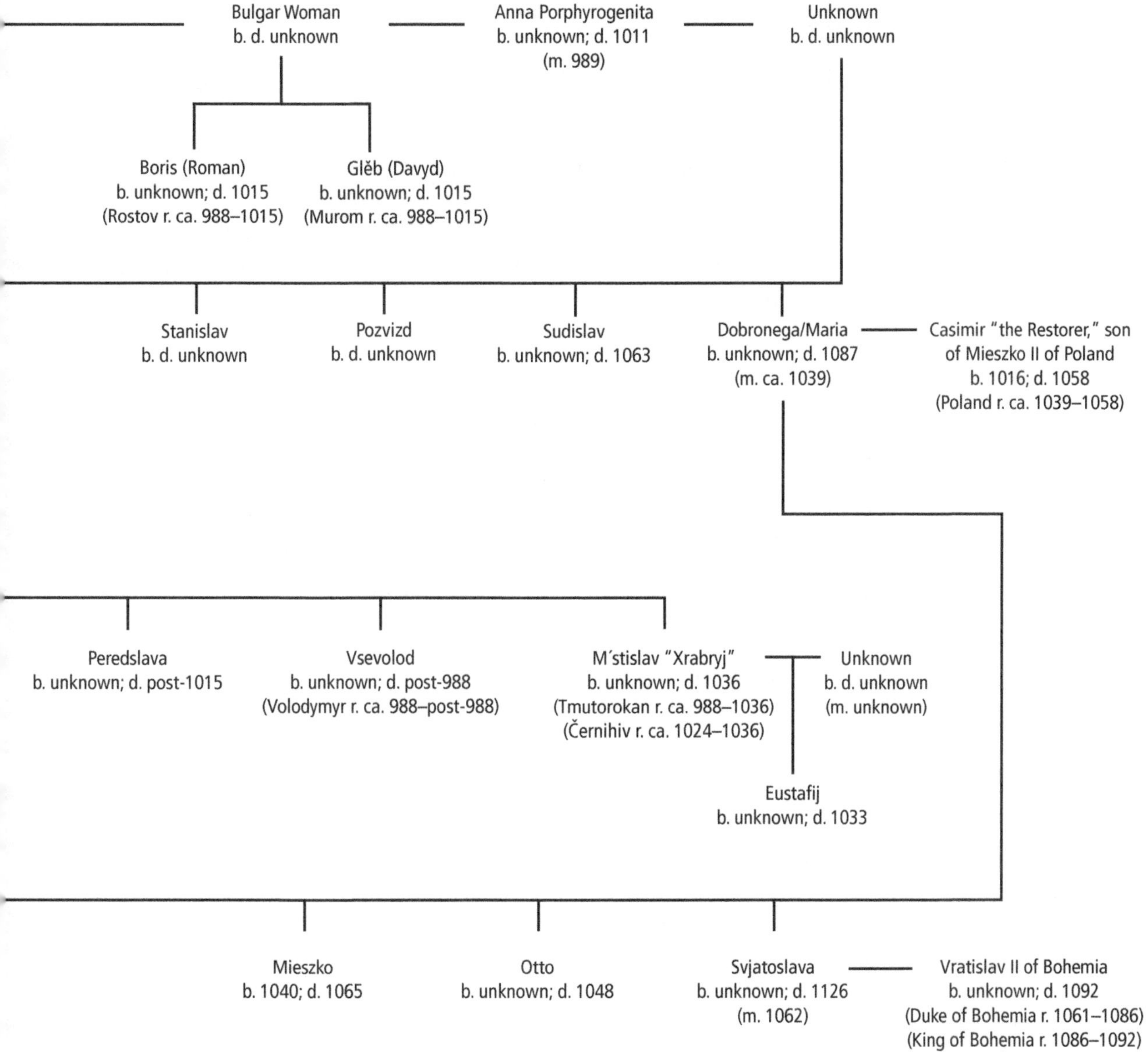
Bulgar Woman
b. d. unknown
Anna Porphyrogenita
b. unknown; d. 1011
(m. 989)
Unknown
b. d. unknown
Boris (Roman)
b. unknown; d. 1015
(Rostov r. ca. 988–1015)
Glěb (Davyd)
b. unknown; d. 1015
(Murom r. ca. 988–1015)
Stanislav
b. d. unknown
Pozvizd
b. d. unknown
Sudislav
b. unknown; d. 1063
Dobronega/Maria
b. unknown; d. 1087
(m. ca. 1039)
Casimir "the Restorer," son
of Mieszko II of Poland
b. 1016; d. 1058
(Poland r. ca. 1039–1058)
Peredslava
b. unknown; d. post-1015
Vsevolod
b. unknown; d. post-988
(Volodymyr r. ca. 988–post-988)
M′stislav "Xrabryj"
b. unknown; d. 1036
(Tmutorokan r. ca. 988–1036)
(Černihiv r. ca. 1024–1036)
Unknown
b. d. unknown
(m. unknown)
Eustafij
b. unknown; d. 1033
Mieszko
b. 1040; d. 1065
Otto
b. unknown; d. 1048
Svjatoslava
b. unknown; d. 1126
(m. 1062)
Vratislav II of Bohemia
b. unknown; d. 1092
(Duke of Bohemia r. 1061–1086)
(King of Bohemia r. 1086–1092)

Bulgar Woman
Birth date: unknown
Death date: unknown
Relationship with Volodimer Svjatoslavič: *PVL*, s.a. 980.

Anna Porphyrogenita
Birth date: unknown
Death date: *PVL*, s.a. 1011
Marriage to Volodimer Svjatoslavič: *PVL*, s.a. 988; Scylitzes, *Ioannis Scylitzae Synopsis historiarum*, 336, 354, 367; Poppe, "Political Background to the Baptism of Rus´" (extensively redates the marriage). For more on this marriage see part 1, "Marriages: Prelude," "Volodimer Svjatoslavič."

Unknown
The mothers of several of Volodimer Svjatoslavič's children are not specified in the primary sources, so they have been listed under an unknown mother, though it may be likely that they are children of more than one woman, and in fact, children of some of the women listed individually.

Vyšeslav Volodimerič
Birth date: unknown
Death date: *PVL*, s.a. 988
Knjaz´ of Novgorod start: *PVL*, s.a. 988; knjaz´ of Novgorod end: *PVL*, s.a. 988.

Svjatoslav Volodimerič
Birth date: unknown
Death date: *PVL*, s.a. 1015
Knjaz´ of Dereva start: *PVL*, s.a. 988; knjaz´ of Dereva end: *PVL*, s.a 1015.

M´stislav Volodimerič
Birth date: unknown
Death date: unknown.

Boris (Roman) Volodimerič
Birth date: unknown
Death date: *PVL*, s.a. 1015
Knjaz´ of Rostov start: *PVL*, s.a. 988; knjaz´ of Rostov end: *PVL*, s.a. 1015.

Glěb (Davyd) Volodimerič
Birth date: unknown
Death date: *PVL*, s.a. 1015
Knjaz′ of Murom start: *PVL*, s.a. 988; knjaz′ of Murom end: *PVL*, s.a. 1015.

Ladislaus of Hungary
Birth date: unknown
Death date: Mór Wertner, *Az Árpádok családi története* (Zrenjanin [Nagybecskerek]: Pleitz Fer. Pál könyvnyomdája, 1892), 111
Marriage to "Premislava" Volodimerovna: Dezso Dercsényi, ed., *The Hungarian Illuminated Chronicle / Chronica de Gestis Hungarorum* (Budapest: Corvina Press, 1969), 100, 107, 113; the date is conjectural based upon her father's death, and the approximate birth dates of the children. For more on this marriage see part 1, "Marriages: Generation One," "Premislava Volodimerovna."

N. N., "Premislava" Volodimerovna
Birth date: unknown
Death date: Her death date can reasonably be assumed to have occurred after her marriage, though when is unknown.
Marriage to Ladislaus of Hungary: Dercsényi, *Chronica de Gestis Hungarorum*, 100, 107, 113; the date is conjectural based upon her father's death, and the approximate birth dates of the children. For more on this marriage see part 1, "Marriages: Generation One," "Premislava Volodimerovna."

Stanislav Volodimerič
Birth date: unknown
Death date: unknown; existence noted in *PVL*, s.a. 988.

Pozvizd Volodimerič
Birth date: unknown
Death date: unknown; existence noted in *PVL*, s.a. 988.

Sudislav Volodimerič
Birth date: unknown
Death date: *PVL*, s.a. 1063.

Dobronega/Maria Volodimerovna
Birth date: unknown
Death date: "Rocznik Kapitulny Krakowski," in *Monumenta Poloniae Historica*, vol. 2, ed. August Bielowski (Lviv: Nakładem Własnym, 1872), s.a. 1087

Marriage to Casimir "the Restorer": *Annalista Saxo*, publ. D. G. Waitz and P. Killon, Monumenta Germaniae Historica: Scriptores 6 (Hannover: Impensis Bibliopolii Avlici Hahniani, 1844), s.a. 1039; *Lamberti Hersfeldensis Annales*, publ. V. Cl. Lud. Frid. Hesse, Monumenta Germaniae Historica: Scriptores 5 (Hanover: Impensis Bibliopolii Hahniani, 1843); s.a. 1039, *PVL*, s.a. 1043; Gallus Anonymous, *Gesta principum Polonorum: The Deeds of the Princes of the Poles*, trans. Paul W. Knoll and Frank Schaer (Budapest: Central European University Press, 2003), 80–81; *Chronica Poloniae Maioris* (there are several useful editions of this; in Latin see "Boguphali II episcopi Posnaniensis Chronicon Poloniae, cum continuatione Basconis custodis Posnaniensis," ed. August Bielowski, in *Monumenta Poloniae Historica* [Lviv: Nakładem Własnym, 1872], 2:467–600; in Russian, N. I. Ščaveleva, ed., *"Velikaja Xronika" o Pol'še, Rusi i ix sosedjax XI–XIII vv.* [Moscow: Izdatel'stvo Moskovskogo universiteta, 1987]), ch. 12. For more on this marriage see part 1, "Marriages: Generation One," "Dobronega/Maria Volodimerovna."

Casimir "the Restorer," son of Mieszko II of Poland

Birth date: Oswald Balzer, *Genealogia Piastów* (Cracow: Nakładem Akademij Umiejętności, 1895), table 2

Death date: *Chronica Poloniae Maioris*, ch. 12

King of Poland start: Gallus Anonymous, *Gesta principum Polonorum*, 81; king of Poland end: *Chronica Poloniae Maioris*, ch. 12

Marriage to Dobronega/Maria Volodimerovna: Annalista Saxo, s.a. 1039; Lambert of Hersefeld, s.a. 1039; *PVL*, s.a. 1043; Gallus Anonymous, *Gesta Principum Polonorum*, 80–81; *Chronica Poloniae Maioris*, ch. 12. For more on this marriage see part 1, "Marriages: Generation One," "Dobronega/Maria Volodimerovna."

Andrew of Hungary

Birth date: unknown

Death date: *Bertholdi Annales*, publ. George Pertz, in *Annales et chronica aevi Salici*, Monumenta Germaniae Historica: Scriptores 5 (Hannover: Impensis Bibliopolii Avlici Hahniani, 1844) [hereafter Berthold of Reichenau], s.a. 1060; *Lamberti Hersfeldensis Annales*, s.a. 1061 (referencing his brother's succession)

King of Hungary start: Berthold of Reichenau, s.a. 1046; Wertner, *Az Árpádok családi története*, 114–15; king of Hungary end: *Lamberti Hersfeldensis Annales*, s.a. 1061

Marriage to Anastasija Jaroslavna: Dercsényi, *Chronica de Gestis Hungarorum*, 113; Adam of Bremen, *History of the Archbishops of Hamburg-Bremen*, trans. Francis J. Tschan (New York: Columbia University Press, 2002), bk. 3, ch. xiii.12, schol. 62 (63). For more on this marriage see part 1, "Marriages: Generation Two," "Anastasija Jaroslavna."

Anastasija Jaroslavna

Birth date: unknown

Death date: Wertner places her death in 1074; see *Az Árpádok családi története*, chart. However, this is simply the last year that we have information about her. In that year Salomon left her at Admont Abbey when he was expelled from Hungary and went to fight further with his cousins. Dercsényi, *Chronica de gestis Hungarorum*, 124

Marriage to Andrew of Hungary: Dercsényi, *Chronica de Gestis Hungarorum*, 113; Adam of Bremen, *History of the Archbishops of Hamburg-Bremen*, bk. 3, ch. xiii.12, schol. 62 (63). For more on this marriage see part 1, "Marriages: Generation Two," "Anastasija Jaroslavna."

Béla I of Hungary

Birth date: unknown

Death date: *Lamberti Hersfeldensis Annales*, s.a. 1063

King of Hungary start: *Lamberti Hersfeldensis Annales*, s.a. 1061; king of Hungary end: *Lamberti Hersfeldensis Annales*, s.a. 1063

Marriage to daughter of Mieszko II of Poland: Dercsényi, *Chronica de Gestis Hungarorum*, 110–11, 121.

N. N., daughter of Mieszko II of Poland

Birth date: unknown

Death date: unknown

Marriage to Béla I of Hungary: Dercsényi, *Chronica de Gestis Hungarorum*, 110–11, 121.

Levente

Birth date: unknown

Death date: Wertner places his death in 1047; see *Az Árpádok családi története*, chart.

Ingigerd of Sweden

Birth date: unknown

Death date: *PVL*, s.a. 1050

Marriage to Jaroslav Volodimerič: Snorri Sturluson, *Heimskringla: History of the Kings of Norway*, trans. Lee M. Hollander (Austin, Tx.: University of Texas Press, 1964), 342–43; *Morkinskinna: The Earliest Icelandic Chronicle of the Norwegian Kings (1030-1157)*, trans. Theodore M. Andersson and Kari Ellen Gade (Ithaca: Cornell

University Press, 2000), ch. 1. For more on this marriage see part 1, "Marriages: Generation One," "Jaroslav Volodimerič."

Jaroslav "Mudryj" Volodimerič
Birth date: unknown
Death date: *PVL*, s.a. 1054
Knjaz′ of Rostov: *PVL*, s.a. 988
Knjaz′ of Novgorod start (1): *PVL*, s.a. 988; knjaz′ of Novgorod end (1): *PVL*, s.a. 1015
Knjaz′ of Kyiv (1) start: *PVL*, s.a. 1016; knjaz′ of Kyiv (1) end: *PVL*, s.a. 1018
Knjaz′ of Kyiv (2) start: *PVL*, s.a. 1018; knjaz′ of Kyiv (2) end: *PVL*, s.a. 1054
Knjaz′ of Novgorod (2) start: *PVL*, s.a. 1020; knjaz′ of Novgorod (2) end: *PVL*, s.a. 1036
Marriage to Ingigerd: Sturluson, *Heimskringla*, 342–43; *Morkinskinna*, ch. 1
Relationship with unknown: conjectural based upon a son cited in *NPL*, s.a. 989. For more on these marriages see part 1, "Marriages: Generation One," "Jaroslav Volodimerič."

Unknown partner of Jaroslav "Mudryj"
Birth date: unknown
Death date: unknown
Relationship with Jaroslav "Mudryj": conjectural based upon a son cited in *NPL*, s.a. 989. For more on these marriages see part 1, "Marriages: Generation One," "Jaroslav Volodimerič."

Peredslava Volodimerovna
Birth date: unknown
Death date: Peredslava is listed as notifying Jaroslav of the death of Volodimer in 1015, thus she must have died after that time, but when is unknown. *PVL*, s.a. 1015.

Izjaslav Volodimerič
Birth date: unknown
Death date: *PVL*, s.a. 1001
Knjaz′ of Polack start: *PVL*, s.a. 988; knjaz′ of Polack end: *PVL*, s.a. 1001
Relationship with unknown woman: conjectural based upon children cited in *PVL*, s.a. 1001, 1003.

Unknown partner of Izjaslav Volodimerič
Birth date: unknown
Death date: unknown

Relationship with Izjaslav Volodimerič: conjectural based upon children cited in *PVL*, s.a. 1001, 1003.

Vsevolod Volodimerič
Birth date: unknown
Death date: As he is listed as the ruler of Volodymyr in 988, it is likely he died after that time, though when is unknown; *PVL*, s.a. 988.
Knjaz´ of Volodymyr start: *PVL*, s.a. 988; knjaz´ of Volodymyr end: unknown, as Vsevolod is not listed again in any primary sources.

M´stislav "Xrabryj" Volodimerič
Birth date: unknown
Death date: *PVL*, s.a 1036
Knjaz´ of Tmutorokan start: *PVL*, s.a. 988; knjaz´ of Tmutorokan end: *PVL*, s.a. 1036
Knjaz´ of Černihiv start: *PVL*, s.a. 1024; knjaz´ of Černihiv end: *PVL*, s.a. 1036
Relationship with unknown partner: conjectural based upon a child cited in *PVL*, s.a. 1033.

Unknown partner of M´stislav "Xrabryj"
Birth date: unknown
Death date: unknown
Relationship with M´stislav "Xrabryj": conjectural based upon a child cited in *PVL*, s.a. 1033.

Eustafij M´stislavič
Birth date: unknown
Death date: *PVL*, s.a .1033.

Vyšeslava Svjatoslavna
Birth date: unknown
Death date: Her death date can reasonably be assumed to have occurred after her marriage, though when is unknown.
Marriage to Bolesław II of Poland: Jan Długosz, *Annales seu cronicae incliti regni Poloniae* (Warsaw: Państwowe Wydawnictwo Naukowe, 1970), bk. 3, p. 95; V. N. Tatiščev, *Istorija Rossijskaja* (Moscow: Akademija Nauk SSSR, 1963), 2:123; Baumgarten, "Généalogies," 18–20, table 5; Dimnik, *Dynasty of Chernigov, 1054–1146*, 41. For more on this marriage see part 1, "Marriages: Generation Three," "Vyšeslava Svjatoslavna."

Bolesław II "the Bold"
Birth date: Balzer, *Genealogia Piastów*, table 2

Death date: Balzer, *Genealogia Piastów*, table 2; Gallus Anonymous, *Gesta Principum Polonorum*, bk. 1, ch. 28

Duke of Poland start: *Chronica Poloniae Maioris*, ch. 12; Gallus Anonymous, *Gesta Principum Polonorum*, bk. 1, ch. 22; duke of Poland end: *Lamberti Hersfeldensis Annales*, s.a. 1077

King of Poland start: *Lamberti Hersfeldensis Annales*, s.a. 1077, Bernold of St. Blasien, "Chronicle," In *Eleventh-Century Germany: The Swabian Chronicles*, ed. and trans. I. S. Robinson (Manchester: Manchester University Press, 2008), s.a. 1077; king of Poland end: Gallus Anonymous, *Gesta Principum Polonorum*, bk. 1, ch. 27

Marriage to Vyšeslava Svjatoslavna: Długosz, *Annales*, bk. 3, p. 95, Tatiščev, *Istorija Rossijskaja*, 2:123; Baumgarten, "Généalogies," 18–20, table 5; and Dimnik, *Dynasty of Chernigov, 1054–1146*, 41. For more on this marriage see part 1, "Marriages: Generation Three," "Vyšeslava Svjatoslavna."

Władysław Herman

Birth date: unknown

Death date: *PVL*, s.a. 1102, *Chronica Poloniae Maioris*, ch. 16; Cosmas of Prague, *The Chronicle of the Czechs by Cosmas of Prague*, trans. Lisa Wolverton (Washington, D.C.: The Catholic University of America Press, 2009), bk. 3, ch. 16; Gallus Anonymous, *Gesta Principum Polonorum*, bk. 2, ch. 21

Duke of Poland start: conjectural based upon Gallus Anonymous, *Gesta Principum Polonorum*, bk. 1, chs. 27, 30; duke of Poland end: *PVL*, s.a. 1102, *Chronica Poloniae Maioris*, ch. 16; Cosmas of Prague, *Chronicle of the Czechs*, bk. 3, ch. 16; Gallus Anonymous, *Gesta Principum Polonorum*, bk. 2, ch. 21

Marriage to Judith, daughter of Vratislav II of Bohemia: Cosmas of Prague, *Chronicle of the Czechs*, bk. 2, ch. 36; Gallus Anonymous, *Gesta Principum Polonorum*, bk. 1, ch. 30

Marriage to Judith, daughter of Henry III of the German Empire: *Chronica Poloniae Maioris*, ch. 15; Gallus Anonymous, *Gesta Principum Polonorum*, bk. 2, ch. 1.

Judith, daughter of Vratislav II of Bohemia

Birth date: unknown

Death date: Cosmas of Prague, *Chronicle of the Czechs*, bk. 2, ch. 36; Gallus Anonymous, *Gesta Principum Polonorum*, bk. 2, ch. 1

Marriage to Władysław Herman: Cosmas of Prague, *Chronicle of the Czechs*, bk. 2, ch. 36; Gallus Anonymous, *Gesta Principum Polonorum*, bk. 1, ch. 30.

Judith, daughter of Henry III of the German Empire

Birth date: Balzer, *Genealogia Piastów*, 105; "Annales Altahenses maiores," publ. Wilhelm de Giesebrecht et Edmundi L. B. ab Oefele, in *Supplementum Tomi V*, Monumenta Germaniae Historica: Scriptores 20 (Hannover: Impensis Bibliopolii Avlici Hahniani, 1868), s.a. 1047 (where the birth of a child to Henry III is recorded); I am following Balzer in his identification of this child as Judith.

Death date: Balzer, *Genealogia Piastów*, 106

Marriage to Władysław Herman: *Chronica Poloniae Maioris*, ch. 15; see also A. V. Nazarenko, *Drevnjaja Rus´ na meždunarodnyx putjax: Meždisciplinarnye očerki kul´turnyx, torgovyx, politčeskix svjazej IX–XII vekov.* (Moscow: Jazyki russkoj kul´tury, 2001), 551.

Mieszko

Birth date: Balzer, *Genealogia Piastów*, table 2

Death date: Balzer, *Genealogia Piastów*, table 2; Gallus Anonymous, *Gesta Principum Polonorum*, bk. 1, ch. 30.

Otto

Birth date: unknown

Death date: Balzer, *Genealogia Piastów*, table 2; Gallus Anonymous, *Gesta Principum Polonorum*, bk. 1, ch. 30.

Svjatoslava

Birth date: unknown

Death date: Balzer, *Genealogia Piastów*, table 2

Marriage to Vratislav II: Cosmas of Prague, *Chronicle of the Czechs*, bk. 2, ch. 20.

Vratislav II of Bohemia

Birth date: unknown

Death date: Cosmas of Prague, *Chronicle of the Czechs*, bk. 2, ch. 50

Duke of Bohemia start: Cosmas of Prague, *Chronicle of the Czechs*, bk. 2, ch. 18; duke of Bohemia end: Cosmas of Prague, *Chronicle of the Czechs*, bk. 2, ch. 37

King of Bohemia start: Cosmas of Prague, *Chronicle of the Czechs*, bk. 2, ch. 37; king of Bohemia end: Cosmas of Prague, *Chronicle of the Czechs*, bk. 2, ch. 50

Marriage to Svjatoslava: Cosmas of Prague, *Chronicle of the Czechs*, bk. 2, ch. 20.

Table 2: Izjaslav Volodimerič

Izjaslav Volodimerič
Birth date: unknown
Death date: *PVL*, s.a. 1001
Knjaz´ of Polack start: *PVL*, s.a. 988; knjaz´ of Polack end: *PVL*, s.a. 1001
Relationship with unknown woman: conjectural based upon children cited in *PVL*, s.a. 1001, 1003.

Unknown partner of Izjaslav Volodimerič
Birth date: unknown
Death date: unknown
Relationship with Izjaslav Volodimerič: conjectural based upon children cited in *PVL*, s.a. 1001, 1003.

Unknown partner of Brjačeslav Izjaslavič
Birth date: unknown
Death date: unknown
Relationship with Brjačeslav Izjaslavič: conjectural based upon children cited in *PVL*, s.a. 1044.

Brjačeslav Izjaslavič
Birth date: unknown
Death date: *PVL*, s.a. 1044
Knjaz´ of Polack start: *PVL*, s.a. 1001; knjaz´ of Polack end: *PVL*, s.a. 1044
Knjaz´ of Novgorod start: *PVL*, s.a. 1021; knjaz´ of Novgorod end: *PVL*, s.a. 1021
Relationship with unknown woman: conjectural based upon children cited in *PVL*, s.a. 1044.

Vseslav Izjaslavič
Birth date: unknown
Death date: *PVL*, s.a. 1003.

Table 2: Izjaslav Volodimerič

Izjaslav Volodimerič
b. unknown; d. 1001
(Polack r. ca. 988–1001)

Unknown
b. d. unknown
(m. unknown)

Unknown
b. d. unknown
(m. unknown)

Brjačeslav
b. unknown; d. 1044
(Polack r. ca. 1001–1044)
(Novgorod r. 1021)

Vseslav
b. unknown; d. 1101
(Polack r. 1044–1067)
(Novgorod r. ca. 1066–1067)
(Kyiv r. 1068–1069)
(Polack r. 1069)
(Polack r. 1071–1101)

Unknown
b. d. unknown
(m. unknown)

Unknown
b. d. unknown
(m. unknown)

Davyd
b. unknown;
d. post-1129
(Polack r. 1101–1128)
(Polack r. 1129)

Roman
b. unknown;
d. 1116

Unknown
b. d. unknown
(m. unknown)

Boris
b. unknown; d. 1129
(Strežev r. pre-1127–1129)
(Polack r. 1129)

Glěb
b. unknown;
d. 1119
(Minsk r. pre-1116–1119)

N. N., daughter of
Jaropolk Izjaslavič
b. 1074; d. 1158
(Minsk r.
1119–1158)
(m. pre-1119)

Brjačeslav
b. unknown;
d. post-1128
(Izjaslavl r. ca. 1128)

N. N., daughter of
M'stislav Volodimerič
b. unknown;
d. post-1127
(m. pre-1127)

Rogvolod
b. unknown;
d. post-1162
(Polack r. ca. 1143–1151)
(Druck r. 1159–post-1162)
(Polack r. 1159–1162)

N. N., daughter of
Izjaslav M'stislavič
b. unknown;
d. post-1144
(m. 1144)

Zvenislava
(Evpraksija)
b. d. unknown

Rostislav
b. pre-1119;
d. post-1159
(Polack r. 1151–1159)
(Minsk r. 1159–post-1159)

Sofija Jaroslavna
b. unknown;
d. 1158
(m. unknown)

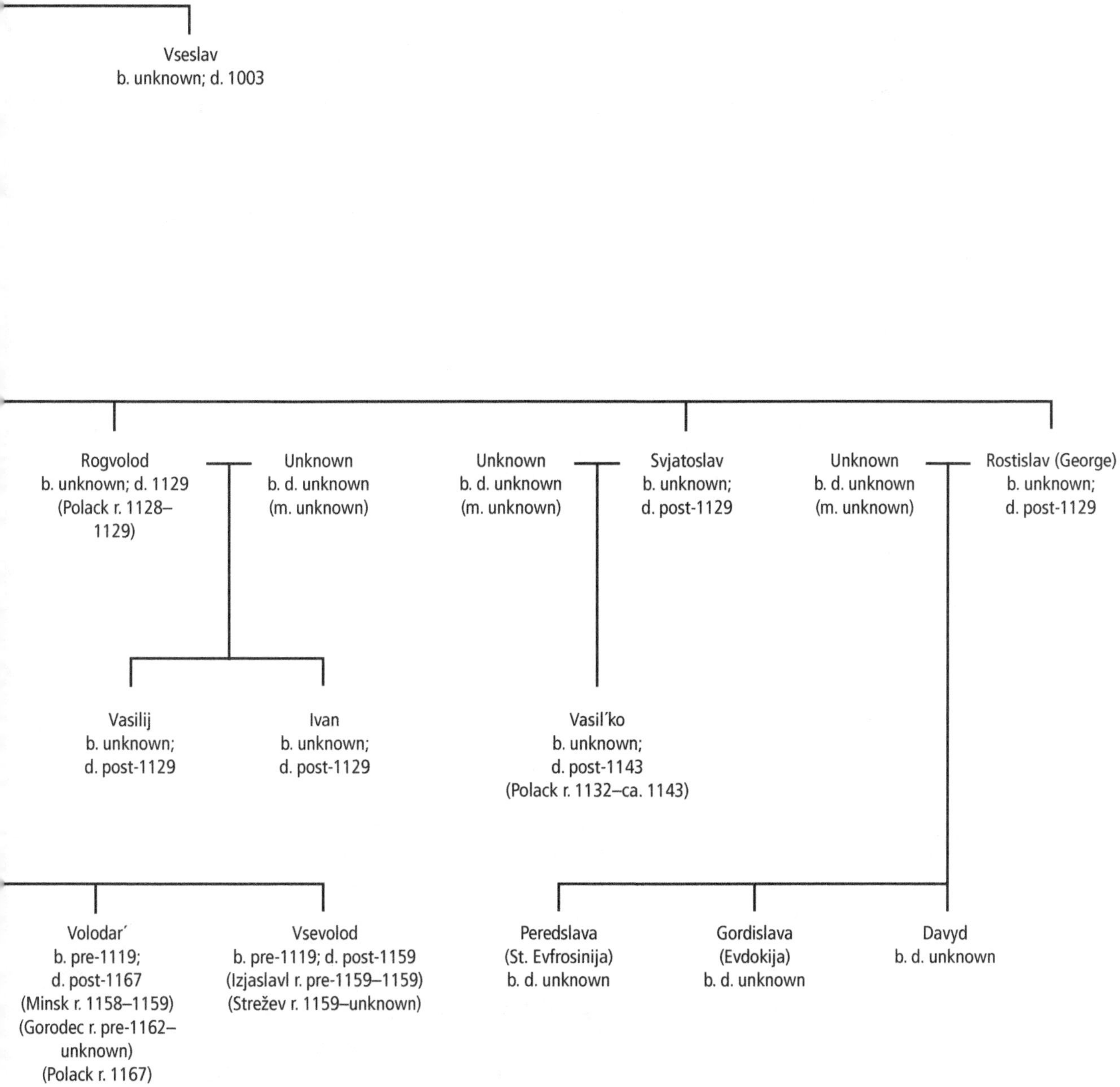
Vseslav
b. unknown; d. 1003
Rogvolod
b. unknown; d. 1129
(Polack r. 1128–1129)
Unknown
b. d. unknown
(m. unknown)
Unknown
b. d. unknown
(m. unknown)
Svjatoslav
b. unknown;
d. post-1129
Unknown
b. d. unknown
(m. unknown)
Rostislav (George)
b. unknown;
d. post-1129
Vasilij
b. unknown;
d. post-1129
Ivan
b. unknown;
d. post-1129
Vasil′ko
b. unknown;
d. post-1143
(Polack r. 1132–ca. 1143)
Volodar′
b. pre-1119;
d. post-1167
(Minsk r. 1158–1159)
(Gorodec r. pre-1162–unknown)
(Polack r. 1167)
Vsevolod
b. pre-1119; d. post-1159
(Izjaslavl r. pre-1159–1159)
(Strežev r. 1159–unknown)
Peredslava
(St. Evfrosinija)
b. d. unknown
Gordislava
(Evdokija)
b. d. unknown
Davyd
b. d. unknown

Vseslav Brjačeslavič
Birth date: unknown
Death date: *PVL*, s.a. 1101
Knjaz´ of Polack (1) start: *PVL*, s.a. 1044; knjaz´ of Polack (1) end: *PVL*, s.a. 1067
Knjaz´ of Novgorod start: *PVL*, s.a. 1067; *NPL*, s.a. 1066; knjaz´ of Novgorod end: *PVL*, s.a. 1067
Knjaz´ of Kyiv start: *PVL*, s.a. 1068; knjaz´ of Kyiv end: *PVL*, s.a. 1069
Knjaz´ of Polack (2) start: *PVL*, s.a. 1069; knjaz´ of Polack (2) end: *PVL*, s.a. 1069
Knjaz´ of Polack (3) start: *PVL*, s.a. 1071; knjaz´ of Polack (3) end: *PVL*, s.a. 1101
Relationship with unknown woman/women: conjectural based upon children cited elsewhere, including *NPL*, s.a. 1128.

Unknown partner(s) of Vseslav Brjačeslavič
Birth date: unknown
Death date: unknown
Relationship with Vseslav Brjačeslavič: conjectural based upon children cited elsewhere, including *NPL*, s.a. 1128.

Unknown partner(s) of Davyd Vseslavič
Birth date: unknown
Death date: unknown
Relationship with Davyd Vseslavič: conjectural based upon a child cited in Laurentian Chronicle, s.a. 1127.

Davyd Vseslavič
Birth date: unknown
Death date: exiled to Constantinople in 1129, Voskresenskij Chronicle, s.a. 1129; Tver Chronicle, s.a. 1129
Knjaz´ of Polack (1) start: conjectural based upon father's death. In 1103, he leads forces against the Polovcians, possibly from Polack, and in 1104 against his brother Glěb in Minsk; see *PVL*, s.a. 1103, 1104; knjaz´ of Polack (1) end: Laurentian Chronicle, s.a. 1127; Hypatian Chronicle, s.a. 1128; Voskresenskij Chronicle, s.a. 1127
Knjaz´ of Polack (2) start: *NPL*, s.a. 1128; Laurentian Chronicle, s.a. 1128; Hypatian Chronicle, s.a. 1129; *NČL*, s.a. 1128; Voskresenskij Chronicle, s.a. 1128; Tver Chronicle, s.a. 1128; Nikon Chronicle, s.a. 1128; all state Boris's death as ruler of Polack, conjectural that Davyd might step back in, thus violating an oath to M´stislav and resulting in his exile; knjaz´ of Polack (2) end: Voskresenskij Chronicle, s.a. 1129; Tver Chronicle, s.a. 1129.

Relationship with unknown partner(s): conjectural based upon a child cited in Laurentian Chronicle, s.a. 1127.

Roman Vseslavič
Birth date: unknown
Death date: Hypatian Chronicle, s.a. 1116; Voskresenskij Chronicle, s.a. 1114; Tver Chronicle, s.a. 1114; Nikon Chronicle, s.a. 1114.

Unknown partner(s) of Boris Vseslavič
Birth date: unknown
Death date: unknown
Relationship with Boris Vseslavič: conjectural based upon children cited elsewhere, including Laurentian Chronicle, s.a. 1144.

Boris Vseslavič
Birth date: unknown
Death date: *NPL*, s.a. 1128; Laurentian Chronicle, s.a. 1128; Hypatian Chronicle, s.a. 1129; *NČL*, s.a. 1128; Voskresenskij Chronicle, s.a. 1128; Tver Chronicle, s.a. 1128; Nikon Chronicle, s.a. 1128
Knjaz´ of Strežev start: Hypatian Chronicle, s.a. 1128; knjaz´ of Strežev end: conjectural at his death; *NPL*, s.a. 1128; Laurentian Chronicle, s.a. 1128; Hypatian Chronicle, s.a. 1129; *NČL*, s.a. 1128; Voskresenskij Chronicle, s.a. 1128; Tver Chronicle, s.a. 1128; Nikon Chronicle, s.a. 1128
Knjaz´ of Polack start: Hypatian Chronicle, s.a. 1128; Laurentian Chronicle, s.a. 1127; knjaz´ of Polack end: *NPL*, s.a. 1128; Laurentian Chronicle, s.a. 1128; Hypatian Chronicle, s.a. 1129; *NČL*, s.a. 1128; Voskresenskij Chronicle, s.a. 1128; Tver Chronicle, s.a. 1128; Nikon Chronicle, s.a. 1128
Relationship with unknown partner(s): conjectural based upon children cited elsewhere, including Laurentian Chronicle, s.a. 1144.

Glěb Vseslavič
Birth date: unknown
Death date: Laurentian Chronicle, s.a. 1119; Hypatian Chronicle, s.a. 1119; Voskresenskij Chronicle, s.a. 1119; Nikon Chronicle, s.a. 1119
Knjaz´ of Minsk start: It is possible that Glěb was in Minsk already in 1104 when Minsk was ordered to be attacked by Svjatopolk Izjaslavič, and Gleb was personally attacked by his brother Davyd; see *PVL* s.a. 1104; Hypatian Chronicle, s.a. 1116, records his rule there; knjaz´ of Minsk end: Laurentian Chronicle, s.a. 1119; Hypatian Chronicle, s.a. 1119; Voskresenskij Chronicle, s.a. 1119; Nikon Chronicle, s.a. 1119
Marriage to N. N., daughter of Jaropolk Izjaslavič: Hypatian Chronicle,

s.a. 1158; Voskresenskij Chronicle, s.a. 1158; Nikon Chronicle, s.a. 1158. For more information on this marriage see part 1, "Marriages: Generation Four," "Glěb Vseslavič."

N. N., daughter of Jaropolk Izjaslavič
Birth date: Hypatian Chronicle, s.a. 1158; Voskresenskij Chronicle, s.a. 1158; Nikon Chronicle, s.a. 1158 (all note that she is eighty-four at her death)
Death date: Hypatian Chronicle, s.a. 1158; Voskresenskij Chronicle, s.a. 1158; Nikon Chronicle, s.a. 1158
Knjaginja of Minsk start: conjectural upon her husband's death; knjaginja of Minsk end: Hypatian Chronicle, s.a. 1158; Voskresenskij Chronicle, s.a. 1158; Nikon Chronicle, s.a. 1158 (all note that she ruled for forty years)
Marriage to Glěb Vseslavič: Hypatian Chronicle, s.a. 1158; Voskresenskij Chronicle, s.a. 1158; Nikon Chronicle, s.a. 1158. For more information on this marriage see part 1, "Marriages: Generation Four," "Glěb Vseslavič."

Rogvolod Vseslavič
Birth date: unknown
Death date: Hypatian Chronicle, s.a. 1129 (notes Boris's assumption of power in Polack, and presumes Rogvolod's death)
Knjaz´ of Polack start: Voskresenskij Chronicle, s.a. 1127; Laurentian Chronicle, s.a. 1127; knjaz´ of Polack end: Hypatian Chronicle, s.a. 1129 (notes Boris's assumption of power in Polack, and presumes Rogvolod's death)
Relationship with unknown partner(s): conjectural based upon children cited in Voskresenskij Chronicle, s.a. 1129.

Unknown partner(s) of Rogvolod Vseslavič
Birth date: unknown
Death date: unknown
Relationship with Rogvolod Vseslavič: conjectural based upon children cited in Voskresenskij Chronicle, s.a. 1129.

Unknown partner of Svjatoslav Vseslavič
Birth date: unknown
Death date: unknown
Relationship with Svjatoslav Vseslavič: conjectural based upon a child cited in Laurentian Chronicle, s.a. 1132.

Svjatoslav Vseslavič
Birth date: unknown

Death date: exiled to Constantinople in 1129: Voskresenskij Chronicle, s.a. 1129; Tver Chronicle, s.a. 1129.

Unknown partner of Rostislav Vseslavič

Birth date: unknown

Death date: unknown

Relationship with Rostislav Vseslavič: conjectural based upon children cited in "Kniga stepennaja tsarskogo rodoslovija," vol. 21 of *Polnoe sobranie russkix letopisej*, pt. 1 (St. Petersburg: Tipografija M. A. Aleksandrova, 1908), 207, 211, 216.

Rostislav Vseslavič

Birth date: unknown

Death date: exiled to Constantinople in 1129; see Voskresenskij Chronicle, s.a. 1129; Tver Chronicle, s.a. 1129.

Brjačeslav Davydič

Birth date: unknown

Death date: the last known date for Brjačeslav is his rule in Izjaslavl; see Hypatian Chronicle, s.a. 1128

Knjaz´ of Izjaslavl´ start: Hypatian Chronicle, s.a. 1128 (the people of Izjaslavl refer to him as their knjaz´); knjaz´ of Izjaslavl end: Hypatian Chronicle, s.a. 1128

Marriage to N. N., daughter of M´stislav Volodimerič: Laurentian Chronicle, s.a. 1127; Voskresenskij Chronicle, s.a. 1127 (refers to him as the *zjat´* of M´stislav's son Izjaslav); Hypatian Chronicle, s.a. 1128; Nikon s.a. 1127 (refers to the M´stislaviči as his *zjatja*). For more information on this marriage see part 1, "Marriages: Generation Five," "Brjačeslav Davydič."

N. N., daughter of M´stislav Volodimerič

Birth date: unknown

Death date: the last mention of her is in 1127, in regard to her relationship with Brjačeslav; see Laurentian Chronicle, s.a. 1127; Voskresenskij Chronicle, s.a. 1127 (these chronicles refer to him as the *zjat´* of M´stislav's son Izjaslav); Hypatian Chronicle, s.a. 1128; Nikon Chronicle, s.a. 1127 (these refer to the M´stislaviči as his *zjatja*)

Marriage to Brjačeslav Davydič: Laurentian Chronicle, s.a. 1127; Voskresenskij Chronicle, s.a. 1127 (which refer to him as the *zjat´* of M´stislav's son Izjaslav); Hypatian Chronicle, s.a. 1128; Nikon Chronicle, s.a. 1127 (refers to the M´stislaviči as his *zjatja*). For more information on this marriage see part 1, "Marriages: Generation Five," "Brjačeslav Davydič."

Rogvolod Borisič
Birth date: unknown
Death date: The last known mention of him is in 1162 and he presumably dies after that time
Knjaz´ of Polack (1) start: Hypatian Chronicle, s.a. 1151; Voskresenskij Chronicle, s.a. 1151 (both list him already ruling); knjaz´ of Polack (1) end: Hypatian Chronicle, s.a. 1151; Voskresenskij Chronicle, s.a. 1151
Knjaz´ of Druck start: Hypatian Chronicle, s.a. 1159; Voskresenskij Chronicle, s.a. 1159; Nikon Chronicle, s.a. 1158; knjaz´ of Druck end: unknown
Knjaz´ of Polack (2) start: Hypatian Chronicle, s.a. 1159; Voskresenskij Chronicle, s.a. 1159; Nikon Chronicle, s.a. 1158; knjaz´ of Polack (2) end: Hypatian Chronicle, s.a. 1162; Voskresenskij Chronicle, s.a. 1161
Marriage to N. N., daughter of Izjaslav M´stislavič: Laurentian Chronicle, s.a. 1144; Hypatian Chronicle, s.a. 1143; Voskresenskij Chronicle, s.a. 1144; Nikon Chronicle, s.a. 1144. For more on this marriage, see part 1, "Marriages: Generation Five," "Rogvolod Borisič."

N. N., daughter of Izjaslav M´stislavič
Birth date: unknown
Death date: Her death date can reasonably be assumed to have occurred after her marriage, though when is unknown.
Marriage to Rogvolod Borisič: Laurentian Chronicle, s.a. 1144; Hypatian Chronicle, s.a. 1143; Voskresenskij Chronicle, s.a. 1144; Nikon Chronicle, s.a. 1144. For more on this marriage see part 1, "Marriages: Generation Five," "Rogvolod Borisič."

Zvenislava "Evpraksija" Borisovna
Birth date: unknown
Death date: unknown; reference to her is from "Kniga stepennaja tsarskogo rodoslovija," 212.

Rostislav Glěbovič
Birth date: conjectural based upon father's death
Death date: The last known mention of him is in 1159, and he presumably dies after that time
Knjaz´ of Polack start: Hypatian Chronicle, s.a. 1151; Voskresenskij Chronicle, s.a. 1151; knjaz´ of Polack end: Hypatian Chronicle, s.a. 1159; Voskresenskij Chronicle, s.a. 1159; Nikon Chronicle, s.a. 1158
Knjaz´ of Minsk start: Hypatian Chronicle, s.a. 1159; Voskresenskij Chronicle, s.a. 1159; Nikon Chronicle, s.a. 1158 (all with the implication that he takes over from his brother when he flees there); knjaz´ of Minsk end: unknown

Marriage to Sofija Jaroslavna: Hypatian Chronicle, s.a. 1158 (at her death). For more on this marriage see part 1, "Marriages: Generation Five," "Rostislav Glěbovič."

Sofija Jaroslavna
Birth date: unknown
Death date: Hypatian Chronicle, s.a. 1158
Marriage to Rostislav Glěbovič: Hypatian Chronicle, s.a. 1158 (at her death). For more on this marriage see part 1, "Marriages: Generation Five," "Rostislav Glěbovič."

Volodar′ Glěbovič
Birth date: conjectural based upon father's death
Death date: The last known mention of him is in 1167 and he presumably dies after that time
Knjaz′ of Minsk start: conjectural based upon his mother's death date; see Hypatian Chronicle, s.a. 1158; knjaz′ of Minsk end: Hypatian Chronicle, s.a. 1159
Knjaz′ of Gorodec start: conjectural based upon expulsion from Minsk; see Hypatian Chronicle, s.a. 1162; Voskresenskij Chronicle, s.a. 1161; knjaz′ of Gorodec end: unknown
Knjaz′ of Polack start: Hypatian Chronicle, s.a. 1167; Voskresenskij Chronicle, s.a. 1166; knjaz′ of Polack end: Hypatian Chronicle, s.a. 1167; Voskresenskij Chronicle, s.a. 1166.

Vsevolod Glěbovič
Birth date: conjectural based upon father's death
Death date: The last known mention of him is in 1159, and he presumably dies after that time
Knjaz′ of Izjaslavl start: Hypatian Chronicle, s.a. 1159 (already as ruler); knjaz′ of Izjaslavl end: Hypatian Chronicle, s.a. 1159
Knjaz′ of Strežev start: Hypatian Chronicle, s.a. 1159; knjaz′ of Strežev end: unknown.

Vasilij Rogvolodič
Birth date: unknown
Death date: exiled to Constantinople in 1129; see Voskresenskij Chronicle, s.a. 1129; Tver Chronicle, s.a. 1129.

Ivan Rogvolodič
Birth date: unknown
Death date: exiled to Constantinople in 1129; see Voskresenskij Chronicle, s.a. 1129; Tver Chronicle, s.a. 1129.

Vasil′ko Svjatoslavič
Birth date: unknown
Death date: conjectural based upon the marriage of his daughter ca. 1143
Knjaz′ of Polack start: Laurentian Chronicle, s.a. 1132; Voskresenskij Chronicle, s.a. 1131; Tver Chronicle, s.a. 1132; Nikon Chronicle, s.a. 1132; knjaz′ of Polack end: conjectural based upon the marriage of his daughter ca. 1143; see Pskov Chronicle, s.a. 1138 (still ruling in Polack).

Peredslava "St. Evfrosinija" Rostislavna
Birth date: unknown
Death date: unknown; reference to her is from "Kniga stepennaja tsarskogo rodoslovija," 207.

Gordislava "Evdokija" Rostislavna
Birth date: unknown
Death date: unknown; reference to her is from "Kniga stepennaja tsarskogo rodoslovija," 211.

Davyd Rostislavič
Birth date: unknown
Death date: unknown; reference to him is from "Kniga stepennaja tsarskogo rodoslovija," 216.

Table 3: Jaroslav "Mudryj" Volodimerič

Unknown partner of Jaroslav "Mudryj"
Birth date: unknown
Death date: unknown
Relationship with Jaroslav "Mudryj": conjectural based upon a son cited in *NPL*, s.a. 989. For more on these marriages see part 1, "Marriages: Generation One," "Jaroslav Volodimerič."

Jaroslav "Mudryj" Volodimerič
Birth date: unknown
Death date: *PVL*, s.a. 1054
Knjaz´ of Rostov start: *PVL*, s.a. 988; knjaz´ of Rostov end: *PVL*, s.a. 988
Knjaz´ of Novgorod start (1): *PVL*, s.a. 988; knjaz´ of Novgorod end (1): *PVL*, s.a. 1015
Knjaz´ of Kyiv (1) start: *PVL*, s.a. 1016; knjaz´ of Kyiv (1) end: *PVL*, s.a. 1018
Knjaz´ of Kyiv (2) start: *PVL*, s.a 1018; knjaz´ of Kyiv (2) end: *PVL*, s.a. 1054
Knjaz´ of Novgorod (2) start: *PVL*, s.a. 1020; knjaz´ of Novgorod (2) end: *PVL*, s.a. 1036
Marriage to Ingigerd: Sturluson, *Heimskringla*, 342–43; *Morkinskinna*, ch. 1
Relationship with unknown woman: conjectural based upon a son cited in *NPL*, s.a. 989. For more on these marriages see part 1, "Marriages: Generation One," "Jaroslav Volodimerič."

Ingigerd of Sweden
Birth date: unknown
Death date: *PVL*, s.a. 1050
Marriage to Jaroslav Volodimerič: Sturluson, *Heimskringla*, 342–43;

Table 3: Jaroslav "Mudryj" Volodimerič

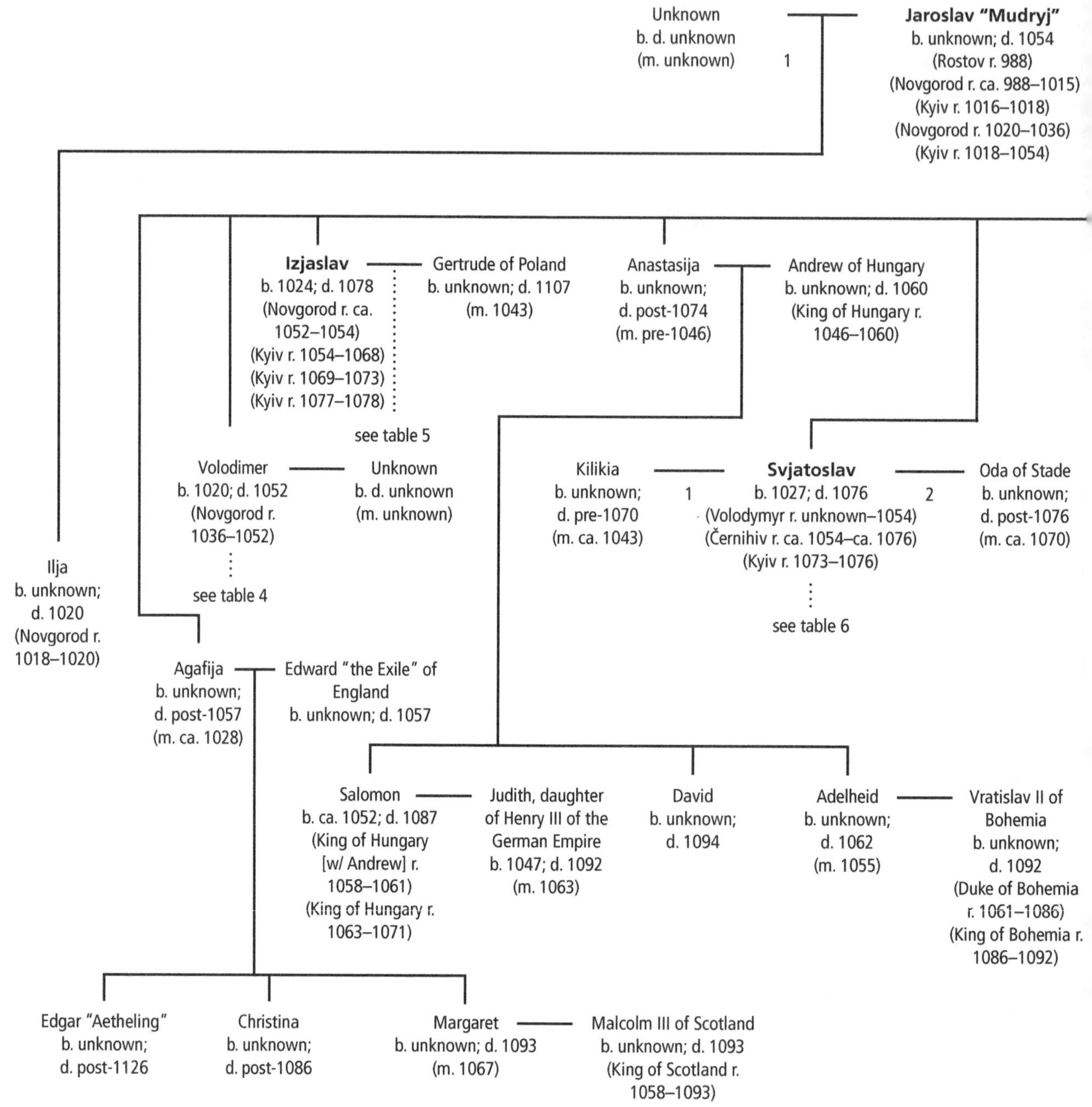

Ingigerd of Sweden
b. unknown; d. 1050
(m. 1019)
2

Harald "Hardrada" of Norway
b. unknown; d. 1066
(King of Norway r. ca. 1044–1066)
1

Elisabeth
b. unknown;
d. post-1066
(1st m. 1042)
(2nd m. post-1066)

2

Unknown husband
b. d. unknown

Unknown
b. d. unknown
(m. unknown)

Vjačeslav
b. 1036; d. 1057
(Smolensk r. 1054–1057)

Boris
b. unknown; d. 1078
(Černihiv r. 1077)

Henry I of France
b. ca. 1008; d. 1060
(Duke of Burgundy r. 1017–31)
(King of France [w/ Robert II] r. 1027–1031)
(King of France r. 1031–1060)
1

Anna
b. unknown;
d. 1089
(Regent ca. 1060–1066)
(1st m. 1051)
(2nd m. 1061)

2

Raoul de Crépy
b. unknown; d. 1074

Igor´
b. unknown; d. 1060
(Volodymyr r. ca. 1054–1057)
(Smolensk r. 1057–1060)

see table 8

Unknown
b. d. unknown
(m. unknown)

N. N., "Anna"
b. unknown; d. 1111
(m. ca. 1067)

Vsevolod
b. 1030; d. 1093
(Perejaslav r. 1054–1055)
(Kyiv r. 1077)
(Černihiv r. 1077–1078)
(Kyiv r. 1078–1093)

see table 7

"Monomaxina" of Byzantium
b. unknown; d. 1067
(m. ca. 1053)

Maria
b. unknown;
d. 1066

Olav Sveinsson
b. unknown; d. 1095
(King of Denmark r. 1088–1095)
1

Ingigerd
b. unknown;
d. post-1096
(1st m. pre-1095)
(2nd m. 1096)

2

Filip
b. unknown;
d. 1118
(Sweden r. 1110–1118)

Bertha of Holland
b. d. unknown
(m. pre-1075)
(repudiated 1092 with multiple reconciliations)
1

Philip I of France
b. 1052; d. 1108
(King of France r. 1059–1108)

2

Bertrada of Anjou
b. unknown;
d. post-1108
(m. 1092)
(repudiated multiple times)

Robert
b. ca. 1053;
d. ca. 1053

Hugh
b. ca. 1053; d. 1101
(Count of Vermandois r. 1085–1101)

Adele of Vermandois
b. unknown;
d. post-1101
(m. ca. 1080)

Morkinskinna, ch. 1. For more on this marriage see part 1, "Marriages: Generation One," "Jaroslav Volodimerič."

Ilja Jaroslavič

Birth date: unknown

Death date: conjectural based upon Brjačeslav Izjaslavič's assumption of power in Novgorod in 1021

Knjaz′ of Novgorod start: conjectural based upon Jaroslav's assumption of power in Kyiv, as well as Ilja's place in the *NPL*'s list of rulers; see *NPL*, s.a. 989; knjaz′ of Novgorod end: conjectural based upon Brjačeslav Izjaslavič's assumption of power in Novgorod in 1021; *PVL* s.a. 1021, as well as Brjaceslav Izjaslavic's subsequent position on the *NPL*'s list of rulers.

Agafija Jaroslavna

Birth date: unknown

Death date: Agafija arrived in England in 1057 with her husband Edward, and died only after that time; see René Jetté, "Is the Mystery of the Origin of Agatha, Wife of Edward the Exile, Finally Solved?" *The New England Historical and Genealogical Register* 150, no. 600 (1996): 419

Marriage to Edward "the Exile" of England: Norman W. Ingham, "Has a Missing Daughter of Iaroslav Mudry Been Found?" *Russian History* 25, no. 3 (1998): 231–70; Jetté, "Is the Mystery of the Origin of Agatha, Wife of Edward the Exile, Finally Solved?" For more on this marriage see part 1, "Marriages: Generation Two," "Agafija Jaroslavna."

Edward "the Exile"

Birth date: unknown

Death date: *The Anglo-Saxon Chronicle*, trans. M. J. Swanton (London: J. M. Dent Publishers, 1996), s.a. 1057; John of Fordun, *Chronicle of the Scottish Nation*, ed. William F. Skene and trans. Feliz J. H. Skene (Edinburgh: Edmonston and Douglas, 1872), bk. 5, chs. 9, 11

Marriage to Agafija Jaroslavna: Ingham, "Has a Missing Daughter of Iaroslav Mudry Been Found?"; Jetté, "Is the Mystery of the Origin of Agatha, Wife of Edward the Exile, Finally Solved?" For more on this marriage see part 1, "Marriages: Generation Two," "Agafija Jaroslavna."

Volodimer Jaroslavič

Birth date: *PVL*, s.a. 1020

Death date: *PVL*, s.a. 1052

Knjaz´ of Novgorod start: *PVL*, s.a. 1036; knjaz´ of Novgorod end: *PVL*, s.a. 1052

Relationship with unknown woman: conjectural based upon a child cited in *PVL*, s.a. 1064.

Unknown partner of Volodimer Jaroslavič

Birth date: unknown

Death date: unknown

Relationship with Volodimer Jaroslavič: conjectural based upon a child cited in *PVL*, s.a. 1064.

Izjaslav Jaroslavič

Birth date: *PVL*, s.a. 1024

Death date: *PVL*, s.a. 1078; *NPL*, s.a. 1078

Knjaz´ of Novgorod start: conjectural based upon the death of Volodimer Jaroslavič; see *PVL*, s.a. 1052; as well as Izjaslav's place in Novgorod at the death of Jaroslav in 1054; see *PVL* s.a. 1054. This is buttressed by the *NPL*'s listing of Novgorod along with Kyiv as his possessions after he assumed power in Kyiv; see *NPL*, s.a. 989; knjaz´ of Novgorod end: conjectural based upon his assumption of power in Kyiv; see *PVL*, s.a. 1054. This is also the time when his son M´stislav may have been assigned to rule Novgorod, according to the regnal list in *NPL*, s.a. 989.

Knjaz´ of Kyiv (1) start: *PVL*, s.a. 1054; knjaz´ of Kyiv (1) end: *PVL*, s.a. 1068

Knjaz´ of Kyiv (2) start: *PVL*, s.a. 1069; knjaz´ of Kyiv (2) end: *PVL*, s.a. 1073

Knjaz´ of Kyiv (3) start: *PVL*, s.a. 1077; knjaz´ of Kyiv (3) end: *PVL*, s.a. 1078

Marriage to Gertrude: Tver Chronicle, s.a. 1043; Nikon Chronicle, s.a. 1043. For more on this marriage see part 1, "Marriages: Generation Two," "Izjaslav Jaroslavič."

Gertrude of Poland

Birth date: unknown

Death date: Nikon Chronicle, s.a. 1107

Marriage to Izjaslav Jaroslavič: Tver Chronicle, s.a. 1043; Nikon Chronicle, s.a. 1043. For more on this marriage see part 1, "Marriages: Generation Two," "Izjaslav Jaroslavič."

Anastasija Jaroslavna

Birth date: unknown

Death date: Wertner places her death in 1074; see his *Az Árpádok családi története*, chart. However, this is simply the last year that we have information about her. In that year Salomon left her at Admont Abbey when he was expelled from Hungary and went to fight further with his cousins; Dercsényi, *Chronica de gestis Hungarorum*, 124.

Marriage to Andrew of Hungary: Dercsényi, *Chronica de Gestis Hungarorum*, 113; Adam of Bremen, *History of the Archbishops of Hamburg-Bremen*, bk. 3, ch. xiii.12, schol. 62 (63). For more on this marriage see part 1, "Marriages: Generation Two," "Anastasija Jaroslavna."

Andrew of Hungary

Birth date: unknown

Death date: Berthold of Reichenau, s.a. 1060, *Lamberti Hersfeldensis Annales*, s.a. 1061 (referencing his brother's succession)

King of Hungary start: Berthold of Reichenau, s.a. 1046; Wertner, *Az Árpádok családi története*, 114–15; king of Hungary end: *Lamberti Hersfeldensis Annales*, s.a. 1061

Marriage to Anastasija Jaroslavna: Dercsényi, *Chronica de Gestis Hungarorum*, 113; Adam of Bremen, *History of the Archbishops of Hamburg-Bremen*, bk. 3, ch. xiii.12, schol. 62 (63). for more on this marriage see part 1, "Marriages: Generation Two," "Anastasija Jaroslavna."

Kilikia

Birth date: unknown

Death date: It can be safely assumed that she died sometime prior to Svjatoslav's second marriage, though when is unknown.

Marriage to Svjatoslav Jaroslavič: R. V. Zotov, *O černihivskix knjaz´jax po Ljubeckomu Sinodiku v tatarskoe vremja* (St. Petersburg: Tipografija brat´ev Panteleevyx, 1892), 24, 256; Dimnik, *Dynasty of Chernigov, 1054–1146*, 37; A. V. Nazarenko, "Kievskaja knjagina: vnuka papy L´va IX (1049–1054): Imperatora Genrixa III (1039–1056): Novye dannye o vnešnej politike Rusi v 70–x gg. XI v.," in *Vostočnaja Evropa v drevnosti i srednevekov´e: Drevnjaja Rus´ v sisteme etnopolitičeskix i kul´turnyx svjazej: čtenija pamjati člena-korrespondenta AN SSSR Vladimira Terent´eviča Pašuto, Moskva, 18–20 aprelja 1994 g.: tezisy dokladov*, ed. V. T. Pašuto, A. P. Novosel´cev, et al. (Moscow: RAN, 1994), 28; V. V. Mošin, "Russkie na Afone i russko-vizantijskie otnošenija v XI–XII vv.," *Byzantinoslavica* 9 (1947–48): 73. For more on this marriage see part 1, "Marriages: Generation Two," "Svjatoslav Jaroslavič."

Svjatoslav Jaroslavič

Birth date: *PVL*, s.a. 1027

Death date: *PVL*, s.a. 1076

Knjaz´ of Volodymyr start: unknown; knjaz´ of Volodymyr end: *PVL*, s.a. 1054

Knjaz´ of Černihiv start: *PVL*, s.a. 1054; knjaz´ of Černihiv end: *PVL*, s.a. 1076

Knjaz´ of Kyiv start: *PVL*, s.a. 1073; knjaz´ of Kyiv end: *PVL*, s.a. 1076

Marriage to Kilikia: Zotov, *O černihivskix knjaz´jax*, 24, 256; Dimnik, *Dynasty of Chernigov, 1054–1146*, 37; Nazarenko, "Kievskaja knjagina," 28; Mošin, "Russkie na Afone i russko-vizantijskie otnošenija v XI–XII vv.," 73

Marriage to Oda of Stade: Nazarenko, *Drevnjaja Rus´ na meždunarodnyx putjax*, 515; *Bruno de Bello Saxonico*, publ. George Pertz, in *Annales et chronica aevi Salici*, 327–84, Monumenta Germaniae Historica: Scriptores 5 (Hannover: Impensis Bibliopolii Avlici Hahniani, 1844), 333, ch. 13. For more on these marriages see part 1, "Marriages: Generation Two," "Svjatoslav Jaroslavič."

Oda of Stade

Birth date: unknown

Death date: Oda returned to the German Empire after Svjatoslav's death, and died only after that time; see part 1, "Marriages: Generation Two," "Svjatoslav Jaroslavič," for more information

Marriage to Svjatoslav Jaroslavič: Nazarenko, *Drevnjaja Rus´ na meždunarodnyx putjax*, 515; *Bruno de Bello Saxonico*, 333, ch. 13. For more on this marriage see part 1, "Marriages: Generation Two," "Svjatoslav Jaroslavič."

Harald "Hardrada"

Birth date: unknown

Death date: Sturluson, *Heimskringla*, 655; *Morkinskinna*, ch. 14

King of Norway start: Sturluson, *Heimskringla*, 593; *Morkinskinna*, ch. 14; king of Norway end: Sturluson, *Heimskringla*, 655; *Morkinskinna*, ch. 14

Marriage to Elisabeth Jaroslavna: Sturluson, *Heimskringla*, 590; *Morkinskinna*, ch. 13; Adam of Bremen, *History of the Archbishops of Hamburg-Bremen*, bk. 3, xiii.12, schol. 62 (63); *Flateyjarbók*, ed. C. R. Unger, vol. 3 (Oslo [Christiania]: P. T. Mallings, 1868), 290. For more on this marriage see part 1, "Marriages: Generation Two," "Elisabeth Jaroslavna."

Elisabeth Jaroslavna

Birth date: unknown

Death date: Elisabeth's last mention is in 1066 after the death of Harald in England; see Sturluson, *Heimskringla*, 660

Marriage to Harald "Hardrada": Sturluson, *Heimskringla*, 590; *Mor-*

kinskinna, ch. 13; Adam of Bremen, *History of the Archbishops of Hamburg-Bremen*, bk. 3, xiii.12, schol. 62 (63); *Flateyjarbók*, 290

Marriage to unknown husband: see the discussion in part 1 for a full explanation. For more on these marriages see part 1, "Marriages: Generation Two," "Elisabeth Jaroslavna."

Unknown husband of Elisabeth Jaroslavna

For the details of this unknown husband, see part 1, "Marriages: Generation Two," "Elisabeth Jaroslavna."

Henry I of France

Birth date: Detlev Schwennicke, *Die ausserdeutschen Staaten*, vol. 2 of *Europäische Stammtafeln: Stammtafeln zur Geschichte der Europäischen Staaten, Neue Folge* (Marburg: J. A. Stargardt, 1984), table 187.

Death date: "Chronicon Sancti-Petri-Vivi Senonensis: Auctore Clario," in *Bibliothèque Historique de'Lyonne*, vol. 2 (Auxerre: Perriquet et Rouillé, Imprimeurs de la Société, 1863), s.a. 1060; Berthold of Reichenau, s.a. 1060; *Anglo-Saxon Chronicle*, s.a. 1060

Duke of Burgundy start: Rodulfus Glaber, *The Five Books of the Histories*, ed. and trans. John France (Oxford: Clarendon Press, 1989), bk. 3, ch. 34; Frédéric Soehnée, ed. and trans., *Catalogue des Actes d'Henri Ier Roi de France (1031–1060)* (Paris: Librairie Honoré Champion, 1907), no. 1; duke of Burgundy end: Glaber, *Five Books of the Histories*, bk. 3, ch. 37

King of France (joint rule with Robert II) start: Glaber, *Five Books of the Histories*, bk. 3, ch. 34; king of France (joint rule with Robert II) end: Glaber, *Five Books of the Histories*, bk. 3, ch. 36

King of France start: Glaber, *Five Books of the Histories*, bk. 3, ch. 36; king of France end: "Chronicon Sancti-Petri-Vivi Senonensis: Auctore Clario," s.a. 1060; Berthold of Reichenau, s.a. 1060; *Anglo-Saxon Chronicle*, s.a. 1060

Marriage to Anna Jaroslavna: "Chronicon: Vindocinense seu de Aquaria," in *Chroniques des églises D'Anjou*, ed. Paul Marchegay and Émile Mabille (Paris: Libraire de la société de l'histoire de France, 1869), s.a. 1051; Adam of Bremen, *History of the Archbishops of Hamburg-Bremen*, bk. 3, ch. xiii.12, schol. 62 (63); "Chronicon Sancti-Petri-Vivi Senonensis: Auctore Clario," s.a. 1046; *Hugo Floriacensis opera historica: accedunt aliae Francorum historiae*, ed. Georgio Waitz, in *Chronica et annales aevi Salici*, 337–406, Monumenta Germaniae Historica: Scriptores 9 (Hannover: Impensis Bibliopolii Avlici Hahniani, 1851), 388–89; *Psalterium Partitum*, s.a. 1049, cited in "Roger II, XLIVe eveque de Chalons, sa vieet sa mission en Russie," in *La Chronique de Champagne* (Reims: Impr.

de L. Jacquet, 1837), 2:89–99. For more information on this marriage see part 1, "Marriages: Generation Two," "Anna Jaroslavna."

Anna Jaroslavna

Birth date: unknown

Death date: Jean Dhondt, "Sept femmes et un trio de rois," *Contributions à l'histoire économique et sociale* 3 (1964–65): 60

Regency start: Maurice Prou, ed., *Recueil des actes de Philippe Ier, roi de France (1059–1108)* (Paris: Imprimerie Nationale, 1908), no. 6; Berthold of Reichenau, s.a. 1060; regency end: Prou, *Recueil des actes de Philippe Ier*, no. 18

Marriage to Henry I of France: «Chronicon: Vindocinense seu de Aquaria,» s.a. 1051; Adam of Bremen, *History of the Archbishops of Hamburg-Bremen*, bk. 3, ch. xiii.12, schol. 62 (63); "Chronicon Sancti-Petri-Vivi Senonensis: Auctore Clario," s.a. 1046; *Hugo Floriacensis opera historica*, 388–89, *Psalterium Partitum*, s.a. 1049

Marriage to Raoul de Crépy: "Chronicon Sancti-Petri-Vivi Senonensis: Auctore Clario," s.a. 1060; *Hugo Floriacensis opera historica*, 389; Soehnée, *Catalogue des Actes d'Henri Ier Roi de France*, no. 102. For more information on these marriages see part 1, "Marriages: Generation Two," "Anna Jaroslavna."

Raoul de Crépy

Birth date: unknown

Death date: Dhondt, "Sept femmes et un trio de rois," 58, Prou, *Recueil des actes de Philippe Ier*, no. 88

Marriage to Anna Jaroslavna: "Chronicon Sancti-Petri-Vivi Senonensis: Auctore Clario," s.a. 1060; *Hugo Floriacensis opera historica*, 389. For more information on this marriage see part 1, "Marriages: Generation Two," "Anna Jaroslavna."

N. N., "Anna"

Birth date: unknown

Death date: Hypatian Chronicle, s.a. 1111

Marriage to Vsevolod Jaroslavič: Tatiščev, *Istorija Rossijskaja*, 2:85. For more on this marriage see part 1, "Marriages: Generation Two," "Vsevolod Jaroslavič."

Vsevolod Jaroslavič

Birth date: *PVL*, s.a. 1030

Death date: *PVL*, s.a. 1093

Knjaz′ of Perejaslav start: *PVL*, s.a. 1054; knjaz′ of Perejaslav end: *PVL*, s.a. 1093

Knjaz´ of Kyiv (1) start: *PVL*, s.a. 1076; knjaz´ of Kyiv (1) end: *PVL*, s.a. 1077

Knjaz´ of Černihiv start: *PVL*, s.a. 1077; knjaz´ of Černihiv end: *PVL*, s.a. 1078

Knjaz´ of Kyiv (2) start: *PVL*, s.a. 1078; knjaz´ of Kyiv (2) end: *PVL*, s.a. 1093, *NPL*, s.a. 1093

Marriage to Monomaxina: *PVL*, s.a. 1053

Marriage to N. N., "Anna": Tatiščev, *Istorija Rossijskaja*, 2:85. For more on these marriages see part 1, "Marriages: Generation Two," "Vsevolod Jaroslavič."

Monomaxina

Birth date: unknown

Death date: Tatiščev, *Istorija Rossijskaja*, 2:85

Marriage to Vsevolod Jaroslavič: *PVL*, s.a. 1053. For more on this marriage see part 1, "Marriages: Generation Two," "Vsevolod Jaroslavič."

Igor´ Jaroslavič

Birth date: unknown

Death date: *PVL*, s.a. 1060

Knjaz´ of Volodymyr start: *PVL*, s.a. 1054; knjaz´ of Volodymyr end: *PVL*, s.a. 1057

Knjaz´ of Smolensk: *PVL*, s.a. 1057; knjaz´ of Smolensk end: *PVL*, s.a. 1060

Relationship with unknown woman: conjectural based upon a son cited in *PVL*, s.a. 1097.

Unknown partner of Igor´ Jaroslavič

Birth date: unknown

Death date: unknown

Relationship with Igor´ Jaroslavič: conjectural based upon a son cited in *PVL*, s.a. 1097.

Unknown partner of Vjačeslav Jaroslavič

Birth date: unknown

Death date: unknown

Relationship with Vjačeslav Jaroslavič: conjectural based upon a son cited in *PVL*, s.a. 1078.

Vjačeslav Jaroslavič

Birth date: *PVL*, s.a. 1036

Death date: *PVL*, s.a. 1057

Knjaz´ of Smolensk start: *PVL*, s.a. 1054; knjaz´ of Smolensk end: *PVL*, s.a. 1057

Relationship with unknown woman: conjectural based upon a son cited in *PVL*, s.a. 1078.

Edgar "Aetheling"
Birth date: unknown
Death date: Jetté, "Is the Mystery of the Origin of Agatha, wife of Edward the Exile, finally solved?" 419.

Christina
Birth date: unknown
Death date: *Anglo-Saxon Chronicle*, s.a. 1086, records that she became a nun in this year; John of Fordun, *Chronicle of the Scottish Nation*, bk. 5, chs. 9, 16.

Margaret
Birth date: unknown
Death date: *Anglo-Saxon Chronicle*, s.a. 1093 (referenced obliquely); *Annals of Ulster*, accessed online at http://www.ucc.ie/celt/published/T100001A/index.html, s.a. 1093; John of Fordun, *Chronicle of the Scottish Nation*, bk. 5, ch. 21
Marriage to Malcolm III of Scotland: *Anglo-Saxon Chronicle*, s.a. 1067; John of Fordun, *Chronicle of the Scottish Nation*, bk. 5, chs. 15, 16.

Malcolm III of Scotland
Birth date: unknown
Death date: *Anglo-Saxon Chronicle*, s.a. 1093; *Annals of Ulster*, s.a. 1093; John of Fordun, *Chronicle of the Scottish Nation*, bk. 5, ch. 20
King of Scotland start: *Annals of Ulster*, s.a. 1058; John of Fordun, *Chronicle of the Scottish Nation*, bk. 5, ch. 9; king of Scotland end: *Anglo-Saxon Chronicle*, s.a. 1093; *Annals of Ulster*, s.a. 1093; John of Fordun, *Chronicle of the Scottish Nation*, bk. 5, ch. 20
Marriage to Margaret: *Anglo-Saxon Chronicle*, s.a. 1067; John of Fordun, *Chronicle of the Scottish Nation*, bk. 5, chs. 15, 16.

Salomon
Birth date: conjectural; see Wertner, *Az Árpádok családi története*, 128
Death date: Dercsényi, *Chronica de Gestis Hungarorum*, 129; Bernold of St. Blasien, "Chronicle," s.a. 1087
King of Hungary with Andrew start: Dercsényi, *Chronica de Gestis Hungarorum*, 115; king of Hungary with Andrew end: Berthold of Reichenau, s.a. 1060
King of Hungary start: *Lamberti Hersfeldensis Annales*, s.a. 1063; Dercsényi, *Chronica de Gestis Hungarorum*, 115 (listed under 1058: coruler with father); Bernold of St. Blasien, "Chronicle," s.a. 1063;

king of Hungary end: Gallus Anonymous, *Gesta Principum Polonorum*, bk. 1, ch. 27; *Lamberti Hersfeldensis Annales*, s.a. 1071; Berthold of Reichenau, s.a. 1074

Marriage to Judith, daughter of Henry III: Dercsényi, *Chronica de Gestis Hungarorum*, 115; Gallus Anonymous, *Gesta Principum Polonorum*, bk. 2, ch. 1; *Lamberti Hersfeldensis Annales*, s.a. 1063; Berthold of Reichenau, s.a. 1059; Długosz, *Annales*, 161.

Judith, daughter of Henry III

Birth date: Balzer, *Genealogia Piastów*, 105; "Annales Altahenses maiores," s.a. 1047 (where the birth of a child to Henry III is recorded); I am following Balzer in his identification of this child as Judith.

Death date: Balzer, *Genealogia Piastów*, 106

Marriage to Salomon: Dercsényi, *Chronica de Gestis Hungarorum*, 115; Gallus Anonymous, *Gesta Principum Polonorum*, bk. 2, ch. 1; *Lamberti Hersfeldensis Annales*, s.a. 1063; Berthold of Reichenau, s.a. 1059; Długosz, *Annales*, 161. For Judith's marriage to Władysław Herman see table 1, above.

David

Birth date: unknown

Death date: Wertner, *Az Árpádok családi története*, 135–36.

Adelheid, daughter of Andrew of Hungary

Birth date: unknown

Death date: Cosmas of Prague, *Chronicle of the Czechs*, bk. 2, ch. 20

Marriage to Vratislav II of Bohemia: Cosmas of Prague, *Chronicle of the Czechs*, bk. 2, ch. 16.

Vratislav II of Bohemia

Birth date: unknown

Death date: Cosmas of Prague, *Chronicle of the Czechs*, bk. 2, ch. 50

Duke of Bohemia start: Cosmas of Prague, *Chronicle of the Czechs*, bk. 2, ch. 18; duke of Bohemia end: Cosmas of Prague, *Chronicle of the Czechs*, bk. 2, ch. 37

King of Bohemia start: Cosmas of Prague, *Chronicle of the Czechs*, bk. 2, ch. 37; king of Bohemia end: Cosmas of Prague, *Chronicle of the Czechs*, bk. 2, ch. 50

Marriage to Adelheid, daughter of Andrew of Hungary: Cosmas of Prague, *Chronicle of the Czechs*, bk. 2, ch. 16.

Maria Haraldsdottir

Birth date: unknown

Death date: *Morkinskinna*, ch. 51.

Filip
Birth date: unknown
Death date: Lars O. Lagerqvist, *Sverige och dess regenter under 1000 år* (Stockholm: Alb. Bonniers boktryckeri, 1976), 45
Marriage to Ingigerd Haraldsdottir: Lagerqvist, *Sverige och dess regenter under 1000 år*, 45.

Ingigerd Haraldsdottir
Birth date: unknown
Death date: Her death date can reasonably be assumed to have occurred after her second marriage, though when is unknown.
Marriage to Olav Sveinsson: Sturluson, *Heimskringla*, 666; *Morkinskinna*, ch. 53
Marriage to Filip: Lagerqvist, *Sverige och dess regenter under 1000 år*, 45.

Olav Sveinsson
Birth date: unknown
Death date: conjectural based upon the end date of his rule cited in Sturluson, *Heimskringla*, 666
King of Denmark start: Sturluson, *Heimskringla*, 666; king of Denmark end: Sturluson, *Heimskringla*, 666
Marriage to Ingigerd Haraldsdottir: Sturluson, *Heimskringla*, 666; *Morkinskinna*, ch. 53.

Bertha of Holland
Birth date: unknown
Death date: unknown
Marriage to Philip I: Dhondt, "Sept femmes et un trio de rois," 61n72; Prou, *Recueil des actes de Philippe Ier*, no. 78; Bernold of St. Blasien, s.a. 1095, 1096 (mentioned in regard to his excommunication); Orderic Vitalis, *The Ecclesiastical History of Orderic Vitalis*, vol. 5 (books 9 and 10), ed. and trans. Marjorie Chibnall (Oxford: Clarendon Press, 1975), bk. 9, ch. 2.

Philip I
Birth date: Prou, *Recueil des actes de Philippe Ier*, xxiii
Death date: *Anglo-Saxon Chronicle*, s.a. 1108; "Chronicon Sancti-Petri-Vivi Senonensis: Auctore Clario," s.a. 1108
King of France start: *Hugo Floriacensis opera historica*, 389; Prou, *Recueil des actes de Philippe Ier*, no. 6; Berthold of Reichenau, s.a. 1060; king of France end: *Anglo-Saxon Chronicle*, s.a. 1108; "Chronicon Sancti-Petri-Vivi Senonensis: Auctore Clario," s.a. 1108
Marriage to Bertha of Holland: Dhondt, "Sept femmes et un trio de rois," 61–69; Prou, *Recueil des actes de Philippe Ier*, no. 78, Ber-

nold of St. Blasien, s.a. 1095, 1096 (mentioned in regard to his excommunication)

Marriage to Bertrada of Anjou: Dhondt, "Sept femmes et un trio de rois," 61–69; Bernold of St. Blasien, s.a. 1095, 1096 (mentioned in regard to his excommunication); Orderic Vitalis, *Ecclesiastical History*, bk. 9, ch. 2.

Bertrada of Anjou

Birth date: unknown

Death date: conjectural based upon mentions of her after the death of Philip

Marriage to Philip I: Dhondt, "Sept femmes et un trio de rois," 61–69; Bernold of St. Blasien, s.a. 1095, 1096 (mentioned in regard to his excommunication); Orderic Vitalis, *Ecclesiastical History*, bk. 9, ch. 2.

Robert

Birth date: conjectural based upon Philip's birth date

Death date: Dhondt, "Sept femmes et un trio de rois," 58.

Hugh

Birth date: conjectural based upon the date of Henry I's death

Death date: Fulcher of Chartres, *Historia Hierosolymitana*, ed. Heinrich Hagenmeyer (Heidelberg: Carl Winters Universitätbuchhandlung, 1913), bk. 2, ch. 16

Count of Vermandois start: Jean Dunbabin, *France in the Making, 843–1180*, 2nd ed. (Oxford: Oxford University Press, 2000), 218; count of Vermandois end: Fulcher of Chartres, *Historia Hierosolymitana*, bk. 2, ch. 16

Marriage to Adele of Vermandois: Augustin Fliche, *Le Règne de Philippe 1er, Roi de France (1060–1108)* (Genève: Slatkine-Megariotis Reprints, 1975), 98; "Albrici Monachi triumfontium chronicon," publ. P. Scheffer-Boichorst, in *Chronica aevi Suevici*, 631–950, Monumenta Germaniae Historica: Scriptores 23 (Leipzig: Karl W. Hiersemann, 1925), s.a. 1061; Guibert of Nogent, *De Vita Sua: De electione domini Bartholomaei episcopi; et nobilitate ejusdem*, in *Patrologia Latina*, ed. J. Migne, vol. 156 (Paris: J. P. Migne, 1853), 966–67.

Adele of Vermandois

Birth date: unknown

Death date: Guibert of Nogent, *De Vita Sua*, 966–67

Marriage to Hugh: Fliche, *Règne de Philippe 1er*, 98; "Albrici Monachi triumfontium chronicon," s.a. 1061; Guibert of Nogent, *De Vita Sua*, 966–67.

Boris Vjačeslavič
Birth date: unknown
Death date: *PVL*, s.a. 1078; *NPL*, s.a. 1078
Knjaz´ of Černihiv start: *PVL*, s.a. 1077; knjaz´ of Černihiv end: *PVL*, s.a. 1077.

Table 4: Volodimer Jaroslavič

Volodimer Jaroslavič
Birth date: *PVL*, s.a. 1020
Death date: *PVL*, s.a. 1052; knjaz´ of Novgorod start: *PVL*, s.a. 1036; knjaz´ of Novgorod end: *PVL*, s.a. 1052
Relationship with unknown woman: conjectural based upon a child cited in *PVL*, s.a. 1064.

Unknown partner of Volodimer Jaroslavič
Birth date: unknown
Death date: unknown
Relationship with Volodimer Jaroslavič: conjectural based upon a child cited in *PVL*, s.a. 1064.

Lanka, daughter of Béla I of Hungary
Birth date: unknown
Death date: Her last mention is begging Koloman to spare her children during their conflict at the end of the eleventh century; see *PVL*, s.a. 1097, for the conflict; and Dercsényi, *Chronica de Gestis Hungarorum*, 131, for her supplication
Marriage to Rostislav Volodimerič: Tatiščev, *Istorija Rossijskaja*, 2:83–84; Dercsényi, *Chronica de Gestis Hungarorum*, 131. For more on this marriage see part 1, "Marriages: Generation Three," "Rostislav Volodimerič."

Rostislav Volodimerič
Birth date: unknown
Death date: *PVL*, s.a. 1066
Knjaz´ of Tmutorokan (1) start: *PVL*, s.a. 1064; knjaz´ of Tmutorokan (1) end: *PVL*, s.a. 1065
Knjaz´ of Tmutorokan (2) start: *PVL*, s.a. 1065; knjaz´ of Tmurotokan (2) end: *PVL*, s.a. 1066
Marriage to Lanka, daughter of Béla I of Hungary: Tatiščev, *Istorija*

Table 4: Volodimer Jaroslavič

Volodimer Jaroslavič
b. 1020; d. 1052
(Novgorod r. 1036–1052)
⚭ Unknown
b. d. unknown
(m. unknown)

- Rostislav
  b. unknown; d. 1067
  (Tmutorokan r. 1064–1065)
  (Tmutorokan r. 1065–1067)
  ⚭ Lanka, daughter of Béla I of Hungary
  b. unknown;
  d. post-1097
  (m. ca. 1060)

  - Rjurik
    b. unknown; d. 1092
    (Peremyšl r. pre-1086–1092)
  - Volodar′
    b. unknown; d. 1124
    (Tmutorokan r. 1081–1083)
    (Volodymyr r. 1084)
    (Peremyšl r. 1092–1120)
    (Peremyšl r. 1122–1124)
    ⚭ Unknown
    b. d. unknown
    (m. unknown)
    - Rostislav
      b. unknown;
      d. post-1126
      (Zvenyhorod r. 1126)
    - N. N.
      b. unknown;
      d. post-1104
      (m. 1104)
      ⚭ N. N., "Carevič" Comnenus of Byzantium
      b. unknown;
      d. post-1104
    - N. N.
      b. unknown;
      d. post-1113
      (m. 1113)
      ⚭ Roman Volodimerič
      b. unknown;
      d. 1119
      (Volodymyr r. 1118–1119)
    - Volodimerko
      b. unknown; d. 1152
      (Zvenyhorod r. 1126–pre-1140)
      (Halyč [w/ Ivan Vasilkovič] r. pre-1140–1141)
      (Halyč r. 1141–1152)
      ⚭ N. N., daughter of Koloman of Hungary
      b. unknown;
      d. post-1126
      (m. pre-1126)
  - Vasil′ko
    b. unknown; d. 1124
    (Volodymyr r. 1084)
    (Terebovl r. pre-1097–1097)
    (Terebovl r. ca. 1098–1124)
    ⚭ Unknown
    b. d. unknown
    (m. unknown)
    - Ivan
      b. unknown; d. 1141
      (Halyč [w/ Vladimirko Volodarič] r. pre-1140–1141)

Rossijskaja, 2:83–84; Dercsényi, *Chronica de Gestis Hungarorum*, 131. For more on this marriage see part 1, "Marriages: Generation Three," "Rostislav Volodimerič."

Rjurik Rostislavič
Birth date: unknown
Death date: *PVL*, s.a. 1092
Knjaz´ of Peremyšl start: *PVL*, s.a. 1086 (records him already ruling there); knjaz´ of Peremyšl end: *PVL*, s.a. 1092.

Volodar´ Rostislavič
Birth date: unknown
Death date: Laurentian Chronicle, s.a. 1124; Hypatian Chronicle, s.a. 1124
Knjaz´ of Tmutorokan start: *PVL*, s.a. 1081; knjaz´ of Tmutorokan end: *PVL*, s.a. 1083
Knjaz´ of Volodymyr start: *PVL*, s.a. 1084; knjaz´ of Volodymyr end: *PVL*, s.a. 1084
Knjaz´ of Peremyšl (1) start: *PVL*, s.a. 1097 (records his rule there, but conjectural that it began at his brother's death); knjaz´ of Peremyšl (1) end: *Chronica Poloniae Maioris*, ch. 28
Knjaz´ of Peremyšl (2) start: Hypatian Chronicle, s.a. 1122; knjaz´ of Peremyšl´ (2) end: Laurentian Chronicle, s.a. 1124; Hypatian Chronicle, s.a. 1124
Relationship with unknown partner(s): conjectural based upon children cited elsewhere; see Hypatian Chronicle, s.a. 1140, for example.

Unknown partner of Volodar´ Rostislavič
Birth date: unknown
Death date: unknown
Relationship with Volodar´ Rostislavič: conjectural based upon children cited elsewhere; see Hypatian Chronicle, s.a. 1140, for example.

Vasil´ko Rostislavič
Birth date: unknown
Death date: Laurentian Chronicle, s.a. 1124; Hypatian Chronicle, s.a. 1124
Knjaz´ of Volodymyr start: *PVL*, s.a. 1084; knjaz´ of Volodymyr end: *PVL*, s.a. 1084
Knjaz´ of Terebovl (1) start: *PVL*, s.a. 1097 (records him ruling there, but it is likely that he began before that time); knjaz´ of Terebovl (1) end: *PVL*, s.a. 1097 (his capture and blinding mark a definitive break in his rule)

Knjaz′ of Terebovl (2) start: *PVL*, s.a. 1097, 1098; knjaz′ of Terebovl (2) end: Laurentian Chronicle, s.a. 1124; Hypatian Chronicle, s.a. 1124
Relationship with unknown partner: conjectural based upon children cited elsewhere; see Hypatian Chronicle, s.a. 1140, for example.

Unknown partner of Vasil′ko Rostislavič
Birth date: unknown
Death date: unknown
Relationship with Vasil′ko Rostislavič: conjectural based upon children cited elsewhere; see Hypatian Chronicle, s.a. 1140, for example.

Rostislav Volodarič
Birth date: unknown
Death date: conjectural based upon mention of his battle with Volodimerko in this year, recorded in Tatiščev, *Istorija Rossijskaja*, 2:138
Knjaz′ of Zvenyhorod: Tatiščev, *Istorija Rossijskaja*, 2:138.

N. N. Volodarovna
Birth date: unknown
Death date: Her death date can reasonably be assumed to have occurred after her marriage, though when is unknown
Marriage to N. N., "Carevič" Comnenus: *PVL*, s.a. 1104; for clarification see Každan, "Rus′-Byzantine Princely Marriages in the Eleventh and Twelfth Centuries," 419–20. For more information on this marriage see part 1, "Marriages: Generation Five," "N. N. Volodarovna."

N. N., "Carevič" Comnenus
Birth date: unknown
Death date: His death date can reasonably be assumed to have occurred after his marriage, though when is unknown
Marriage to N. N. Volodarovna: *PVL*, s.a. 1104; for clarification see Každan, "Rus′-Byzantine Princely Marriages in the Eleventh and Twelfth Centuries," 419–20. For more information on this marriage see part 1, "Marriages: Generation Five," "N. N. Volodarovna."

N. N. Volodarovna
Birth date: unknown
Death date: Her death date can reasonably be assumed to have occurred after her marriage, though when is unknown
Marriage to Roman Volodimerič: Hypatian Chronicle, s.a. 1113; Voskresenskij Chronicle, s.a. 1113; Tver Chronicle, s.a. 1113. For more on this marriage see part 1, "Marriages: Generation Four," "Roman Volodimerič."

Roman Volodimerič

Birth date: unknown

Death date: Laurentian Chronicle, s.a. 1119; Voskresenskij Chronicle, s.a. 1118; Tver Chronicle, s.a. 1118; Nikon Chronicle, s.a. 1119

Knjaz′ of Volodymyr start: Laurentian Chronicle, s.a. 1119; Hypatian Chronicle, s.a. 1117; Voskresenskij Chronicle, s.a. 1118; Tver Chronicle, s.a. 1118; Nikon Chronicle, s.a. 1119; knjaz′ of Volodymyr end: Laurentian Chronicle, s.a. 1119; Voskresenskij Chronicle, s.a. 1118; Tver Chronicle, s.a. 1118; Nikon Chronicle, s.a. 1119

Marriage to N. N. Volodarovna: Hypatian Chronicle, s.a. 1113; Voskresenskij Chronicle, s.a. 1113; Tver Chronicle, s.a. 1113. For more on this marriage see part 1, "Marriages: Generation Four," "Roman Volodimerič."

Volodimerko Volodarič

Birth date: unknown

Death date: Hypatian Chronicle, s.a. 1152; Tver Chronicle, s.a. 1153; Laurentian Chronicle, s.a. 1152; Voskresenskij Chronicle, s.a. 1152; Nikon Chronicle, s.a. 1152

Knjaz′ of Zvenyhorod start: Tatiščev, *Istorija Rossijskaja*, 2:138; knjaz′ of Zvenyhorod end: conjectural based upon presence as co-ruler of Halyč mentioned in Hypatian Chronicle, s.a. 1140

Knjaz′ of Halyč [with Ivan Vasilkovič] start: Hypatian Chronicle, s.a. 1140 (already in place); knjaz′ of Halyč [with Ivan Vasilkovič] end: Hypatian Chronicle, s.a. 1141

Knjaz′ of Halyč start: Hypatian Chronicle, s.a. 1141; knjaz′ of Halyč end: Hypatian Chronicle, s.a. 1152; Tver Chronicle, s.a. 1153; Laurentian Chronicle, s.a. 1152; Voskresenskij Chronicle, s.a. 1152; Nikon Chronicle, s.a. 1152

Marriage to N. N., daughter of Koloman of Hungary: Tatiščev, *Istorija Rossijskaja*, 2:138. For more on this marriage see part 1, "Marriages: Generation Five," "Volodimerko Volodarič."

N. N., daughter of Koloman of Hungary

Birth date: unknown

Death date: Her death date can reasonably be assumed to have occurred after her marriage, though when is unknown.

Marriage to Volodimerko Volodarič: Tatiščev, *Istorija Rossijskaja*, 2:138. For more on this marriage see part 1, "Marriages: Generation Five," "Volodimerko Volodarič."

Ivan Vasilkovič

Birth date: unknown

Death date: Hypatian Chronicle, s.a. 1141

Knjazʹ of Halyč [with Volodimerko Volodarič] start: Hypatian Chronicle, s.a. 1140; knjazʹ of Halyč [with Volodimerko Volodarič] end: Hypatian Chronicle, s.a. 1141.

Table 5: Izjaslav Jaroslavič

Izjaslav Jaroslavič
Birth date: *PVL*, s.a. 1024
Death date: *PVL*, s.a. 1078; *NPL*, s.a. 1078
Knjaz´ of Novgorod start: conjectural based upon the death of Volodimer Jaroslavič; see *PVL*, s.a. 1052, as well as Izjaslav's place in Novgorod at the death of Jaroslav in 1054; see *PVL*, s.a. 1054. This is buttressed by the *NPL*'s listing of Novgorod along with Kyiv as his possessions after he assumed power in Kyiv; see *NPL*, s.a. 989.
Knjaz´ of Novgorod end: conjectural based upon his assumption of power in Kyiv; see *PVL*, s.a. 1054. This is also the time when his son M´stislav may have been assigned to rule Novgorod, according to the regnal list in *NPL*, s.a. 989.
Knjaz´ of Kyiv (1) start: *PVL*, s.a. 1054; knjaz´ of Kyiv (1) end: *PVL*, s.a. 1068
Knjaz´ of Kyiv (2) start: *PVL*, s.a. 1069; knjaz´ of Kyiv (2) end: *PVL*, s.a. 1073
Knjaz´ of Kyiv (3) start: *PVL*, s.a. 1077; knjaz´ of Kyiv (3) end: *PVL*, s.a. 1078
Marriage to Gertrude: Tver Chronicle, s.a. 1043; Nikon Chronicle, s.a. 1043. For more on this marriage see part 1, "Marriages: Generation Two," "Izjaslav Jaroslavič."

Gertrude of Poland
Birth date: unknown
Death date: Nikon Chronicle, s.a. 1107
Marriage to Izjaslav Jaroslavič: Tver Chronicle, s.a. 1043; Nikon Chronicle, s.a. 1043. For more on this marriage see part 1, "Marriages: Generation Two," "Izjaslav Jaroslavič."

M´stislav Izjaslavič
Birth date: unknown
Death date: *PVL*, s.a. 1069

Table 5: Izjaslav Jaroslavič

Izjaslav Jaroslavič
b. 1024; d. 1078
(Novgorod r. ca. 1052–1054)
(Kyiv r. 1054–1068)
(Kyiv r. 1069–1073)
(Kyiv r. 1077–1078)

Gertrude,
daughter of Mieszko II of Poland
b. unknown; d. 1107
(m. 1043)

M′stislav
b. unknown; d. 1069
(Novgorod r. 1054–1066)
(Polack r. 1069)

Unknown
b. d. unknown
(m. unknown)

Jaropolk
b. unknown; d. 1086
(Vyšhorod r. 1078)
(Volodymyr r. 1078–1084)
(Volodymyr r. 1084–1085)
(Volodymyr r. 1086)

1

Cunigunda of the
German Empire
b. unknown;
d. post-1087
(1st m. ca. 1074)
(2nd m. post-1087)

2

Cuno of Beichlingen
b. unknown;
d. post-1087

Rostislav
b. unknown;
d. 1093

Jaroslav
b. unknown; d. 1102
(Brest r. pre-1101–
1101)

N. N.
b. 1074; d. 1158
(Minsk r.
1119–1158)
(m. pre-1119)

Glěb Vseslavič
b. unknown; d. 1119
(Minsk r. pre-1116–
1119)

Rostislav
b. pre-1119; d. post-1159
(Polack r. 1151–1159)
(Minsk r. 1159– unknown)

Sofija Jaroslavna
b. unknown; d. 1158
(m. unknown)

Volodar′
b. pre-1119; d. post-1167
(Minsk r. 1158–1159)
(Gorodec r. pre-1162– unknown)
(Polack r. 1167)

Vsevolod
b. pre-1119; d. post-1159
(Izjaslavl r. unknown–1159)
(Streževo r. 1159–unknown)

N. N., daughter of
Tugorkhan of the
Polovcians
b. unknown; d. 1125
(m. 1094)

Svjatopolk
b. 1050; d. 1113
(Polack r. 1069–1071)
(Novgorod r. 1077–1088)
(Turov r. 1088–1093)
(Kyiv r. 1093–1113)

see table 9

Unknown
b. d. unknown
(m. unknown)

"Eudoxia"
b. unknown;
d. post-1088
(m. 1088)

Mieszko, son of
Bolesław II of Poland
b. 1069; d. 1089

Vjačeslav
b. unknown;
d. 1104

Gunther
b. unknown;
d. post-1093
(Count of Keffenburg)

N. N.
b. unknown;
d. post-1093
(m. btwn 1090–1093)

Knjaz´ of Novgorod start: *NPL*, s.a. 989 (the list of rulers of Novgorod included under the year 989 in the *NPL* has M´stislav following Volodimer Jaroslavič, and ruling until he flees from the city. However, as Izjaslav Jaroslavič is found in Novgorod at the death of Jaroslav Volodimerič [*PVL* s.a. 1054], and his territory after he inherited his rule in Kyiv includes Novgorod [*NPL*, s.a. 989], it seems likely Izjaslav ruled there initially, following Volodimer's death. Thus M´stislav only began his rule in Novgorod after Izjaslav's assumption of power in Kyiv); knjaz´ of Novgorod end: *NPL*, s.a. 989 (the *NPL* list of rulers of Novgorod includes his flight from the city, presumably caused by Vseslav Brjačeslavič), 1066; *PVL*, s.a. 1066 (notes Vseslav Brjačeslavič taking the city)

Knjaz´ of Polack start: *PVL*, s.a. 1069; knjaz´ of Polack end: *PVL*, s.a. 1069

Marriage: conjectural based upon a son cited in *PVL*, s.a. 1093.

Unknown wife of M´stislav Izjaslavič

Birth date: unknown

Death date: unknown

Marriage to M´stislav Izjaslavič: conjectural based upon a son cited in *PVL*, s.a. 1093.

Jaropolk Izjaslavič

Birth date: unknown

Death date: *PVL*, s.a. 1086

Knjaz´ of Vyšhorod start and end: *PVL*, s.a. 1078

Knjaz´ of Volodymyr (1) start: *PVL*, s.a. 1078; knjaz´ of Volodymyr (1) end: *PVL*, s.a. 1084

Knjaz´ of Volodymyr (2) start: *PVL*, s.a. 1084; knjaz´ of Volodymyr (2) end: *PVL*, s.a. 1085

Knjaz´ of Volodymyr (3) start and end: *PVL*, s.a. 1086

Marriage to Cunigunda: *Annalista Saxo*, s.a. 1062. For more on this marriage see part 1, "Marriages: Generation Three," "Jaropolk Izjaslavič."

Cunigunda of the German Empire

Birth date: unknown

Death date: Her death date can reasonably be assumed to have occurred after her second marriage, though when is unknown

Marriage to Jaropolk Izjaslavič: *Annalista Saxo*, s.a. 1062. For more on this marriage see part 1, "Marriages: Generation Three," "Jaropolk Izjaslavič."

Marriage to Cuno of Beichlingen: *Annalista Saxo*, s.a. 1062.

Cuno of Beichlingen
Birth date: unknown
Death date: His death date can reasonably be assumed to have occurred after his marriage, though when is unknown.
Marriage to Cunigunda: *Annalista Saxo*, s.a. 1062.

N. N., daughter of Tugorkhan
Birth date: unknown
Death date: Laurentian Chronicle, s.a. 1124, Hypatian Chronicle, s.a. 1125
Marriage to Svjatopolk Izjaslavič: Hypatian Chronicle, s.a. 1094. For more on this marriage see part 1, "Marriages: Generation Three," "Svjatopolk Izjaslavič."

Svjatopolk Izjaslavič
Birth date: *NPL*, s.a. 1050 (though patronymic is not specified and identification is conjectural)
Death date: Laurentian Chronicle, s.a. 1114; Hypatian Chronicle, s.a. 1113; *NPL*, s.a. 1113; *NČL*, s.a. 1114; Rogožskij Chronicle, s.a. 1114; Tver Chronicle, s.a. 1113; Nikon Chronicle, s.a. 1114
Knjaz′ of Polack start: *PVL*, s.a. 1069; knjaz′ of Polack end: *PVL*, s.a. 1071
Knjaz′ of Novgorod start: conjectural based upon surrounding rulers; knjaz′ of Novgorod end: *PVL*, s.a. 1088
Knjaz′ of Turov start: *PVL*, s.a. 1088; knjaz′ of Turov end: *PVL*, s.a. 1093
Knjaz′ of Kyiv start: *PVL*, s.a. 1093, *NPL*, s.a. 1093; knjaz′ of Kyiv end: Laurentian Chronicle, s.a. 1114; Hypatian Chronicle, s.a. 1113; *NPL*, s.a. 1113, *NČL*, s.a. 1114; Rogožskij Chronicle, s.a. 1114; Tver Chronicle, s.a. 1113; Nikon Chronicle, s.a. 1114
Marriage to daughter of Tugorkhan: Hypatian Chronicle, s.a. 1094
Relationship with unknown partners: *PVL*, s.a. 1097. For more on these marriages see part 1, "Marriages: Generation Three," "Svjatopolk Izjaslavič."

Unknown partner of Svjatopolk Izjaslavič
Birth date: unknown
Death date: unknown
Relationship with Svjatopolk Izjaslavič: Additional children are born to Svjatopolk before his marriage to the daughter of Tugorkhan, such as a son cited in *PVL*, s.a. 1097; thus one can posit one or more unknown partners of Svjatopolk.

N. N., "Eudoxia" Izjaslavna
Birth date: unknown

Death date: Her death date can reasonably be assumed to have occurred after her marriage, though when is unknown.
Marriage to Mieszko of Poland: Gallus Anonymous, *Gesta Principum Polonorum*, bk. 1, ch. 29; Długosz, *Annales*, 161. For more on this marriage see part 1, "Marriages: Generation Three," "Eudoxia Izjaslavna."

Mieszko of Poland
Birth date: Balzer, *Genealogia Piastów*, table 2
Death date: Gallus Anonymous, *Gesta Principum Polonorum*, bk. 1, ch. 29
Marriage to "Eudoxia" Izjaslavna: Gallus Anonymous, *Gesta Principum Polonorum*, bk. 1, ch. 29; Długosz, *Annales*, 161. For more on this marriage see part 1, "Marriages: Generation Three," "Eudoxia Izjaslavna."

Rostislav M′stislavič
Birth date: unknown
Death date: *PVL*, s.a. 1093.

Jaroslav Jaropolčič
Birth date: unknown
Death date: *PVL*, s.a. 1102
Knjaz′ of Brest start: The *PVL* mentions that he is preparing for war there, and it is possible that he ruled there as well; knjaz′ of Brest end: *PVL*, s.a. 1101.

N. N. Jaropolkovna
Birth date: Hypatian Chronicle, s.a. 1158; Voskresenskij Chronicle, s.a. 1158; Nikon Chronicle, s.a. 1158 (all note that she is eighty-four at her death)
Death date: Hypatian Chronicle, s.a. 1158; Voskresenskij Chronicle, s.a. 1158; Nikon Chronicle, s.a. 1158
Knjaginja of Minsk start: conjectural upon her husband's death; knjaginja of Minsk end: Hypatian Chronicle, s.a. 1158; Voskresenskij Chronicle, s.a. 1158; Nikon Chronicle, s.a. 1158 (all note that she ruled for forty years)
Marriage to Glěb Vseslavič: Hypatian Chronicle, s.a. 1158; Voskresenskij Chronicle, s.a. 1158; Nikon Chronicle, s.a. 1158. For more information on this marriage see part 1, "Marriages: Generation Four," "Glěb Vseslavič."

Glěb Vseslavič
Birth date: unknown

Death date: Laurentian Chronicle, s.a. 1119; Hypatian Chronicle, s.a. 1119; Voskresenskij Chronicle, s.a. 1119; Nikon Chronicle, s.a. 1119

Knjaz´ of Minsk start: Hypatian Chronicle, s.a. 1116; knjaz´ of Minsk end: Laurentian Chronicle, s.a. 1119; Hypatian Chronicle, s.a. 1119; Voskresenskij Chronicle, s.a. 1119; Nikon Chronicle, s.a. 1119

Marriage to N. N., daughter of Jaropolk Izjaslavič: Hypatian Chronicle, s.a. 1158; Voskresenskij Chronicle, s.a. 1158; Nikon Chronicle, s.a. 1158. For more information on this marriage see part 1, "Marriages: Generation Four," "Glěb Vseslavič."

Vjačeslav Jaropolčič

Birth date: unknown

Death date: *PVL*, s.a. 1104.

Gunther

Birth date: unknown

Death date: His death date can reasonably be assumed to have occurred after his marriage, though when is unknown.

Marriage: *Annalista Saxo*, s.a. 1062, 1103; Raisa Bloch, "Verwandtschaftliche Beziehungen des sächsischen Adels zum russischen Fürstenhause im XI. Jahrhundert," in *Festschrift: Albert Brackmann, Dargebracht von Freunden, Kollegen und Schülern*, ed. Leo Santifaller (Weimar: Hermann Böhlaus Nachf. G.M.B.H., 1931), 201.

N. N. Jaropolkovna

Birth date: unknown

Death date: Her death date can reasonably be assumed to have occurred after her marriage, though when is unknown.

Marriage: *Annalista Saxo*, s.a. 1062, 1103; Bloch, "Verwandtschaftliche Beziehungen des sächsischen Adels zum russischen Fürstenhause im XI. Jahrhundert," 201.

Rostislav Glěbovič

Birth date: conjectural based upon his father's death

Death date: conjectural based upon the last mention of him in the sources

Knjaz´ of Polack start: Hypatian Chronicle, s.a. 1151; Voskresenskij Chronicle, s.a. 1151; knjaz´ of Polack end: Hypatian Chronicle, s.a. 1159; Voskresenskij Chronicle, s.a. 1159; Nikon Chronicle, s.a. 1158

Knjaz´ of Minsk start: Hypatian Chronicle, s.a. 1159; Voskresenskij Chronicle, s.a. 1159; Nikon Chronicle, s.a. 1158 (all with the implication that he takes over from his brother when he flees there); knjaz´ of Minsk end: unknown

Marriage to Sofija Jaroslavna: Hypatian Chronicle, s.a. 1158 (the marriage is noted at her death).

Sofija Jaroslavna
Birth date: unknown
Death date: Hypatian Chronicle, s.a. 1158
Marriage to Rostislav Glěbovič: Hypatian Chronicle, s.a. 1158 (the marriage is noted at her death).

Volodar′ Glěbovič
Birth date: conjectural based upon his father's death
Death date: conjectural based upon the last mentions of him in the sources; see Hypatian Chronicle, s.a. 1167; Voskresenskij Chronicle, s.a. 1166
Knjaz′ of Minsk start: conjectural based upon his mother's death date; see Hypatian Chronicle, s.a. 1158; knjaz′ of Minsk end: Hypatian Chronicle, s.a. 1159
Knjaz′ of Gorodec start: conjectural based upon expulsion from Minsk; see Hypatian Chronicle, s.a. 1162; Voskresenskij Chronicle, s.a. 1161; knjaz′ of Gorodec end: unknown
Knjaz′ of Polack start: Hypatian Chronicle, s.a. 1167; Voskresenskij Chronicle, s.a. 1166; knjaz′ of Polack end: Hypatian Chronicle, s.a. 1167; Voskresenskij Chronicle, s.a. 1166.

Vsevolod Glěbovič
Birth date: conjectural based upon his father's death
Death date: conjectural based upon the last mention of him in the sources
Knjaz′ of Iziaslavl start: Hypatian Chronicle, s.a. 1159 (already as ruler); knjaz′ of Iziaslavl end: Hypatian Chronicle, s.a. 1159
Knjaz′ of Strežev start: Hypatian Chronicle, s.a. 1159; knjaz′ of Strežev end: unknown.

Table 6: Svjatoslav Jaroslavič

Kilikia

Birth date: unknown

Death date: It can be safely assumed that she died sometime prior to Svjatoslav's second marriage, though when is unknown.

Marriage to Svjatoslav Jaroslavič: Zotov, *O černihivskix knjaz´jax*, 24, 256; Dimnik, *Dynasty of Chernigov, 1054–1146*, 37; Nazarenko, "Kievskaja knjagina," 28; Moshin, "Russkie na Afone i russko-vizantijskie otnošenija v XI–XII vv.," 73. For more on this marriage see part 1, "Marriages:Generation Two," "Svjatoslav Jaroslavič."

Svjatoslav Jaroslavič

Birth date: *PVL*, s.a. 1027

Death date: *PVL*, s.a. 1076

Knjaz´ of Volodymyr start: unknown; knjaz´ of Volodymyr end: *PVL*, s.a. 1054

Knjaz´ of Černihiv start: *PVL*, s.a. 1054; knjaz´ of Černihiv end: *PVL*, s.a. 1076

Knjaz´ of Kyiv start: *PVL*, s.a. 1073; knjaz´ of Kyiv end: *PVL*, s.a. 1076

Marriage to Kilikia: Zotov, *O černihivskix knjaz´jax*, 24, 256; Dimnik, *Dynasty of Chernigov, 1054–1146*, 37; Nazarenko, "Kievskaja knjagina," 28; Mošin, "Russkie na Afone i russko-vizantijskie otnošenija v XI–XII vv.," 73

Marriage to Oda of Stade: Nazarenko, *Drevnjaja Rus´ na meždunarodnyx putjax*, 515; *Bruno de Bello Saxonico*, 333, ch. 13. For more on these marriages see part 1, "Marriages:Generation Two," "Svjatoslav Jaroslavič."

Oda of Stade

Birth date: unknown

Death date: Oda returned to the German Empire after Svjatoslav's death, and died only after that time; see part 1, "Marriages: Generation Two," "Svjatoslav Jaroslavič," for more information.

Table 6: Svjatoslav Jaroslavič

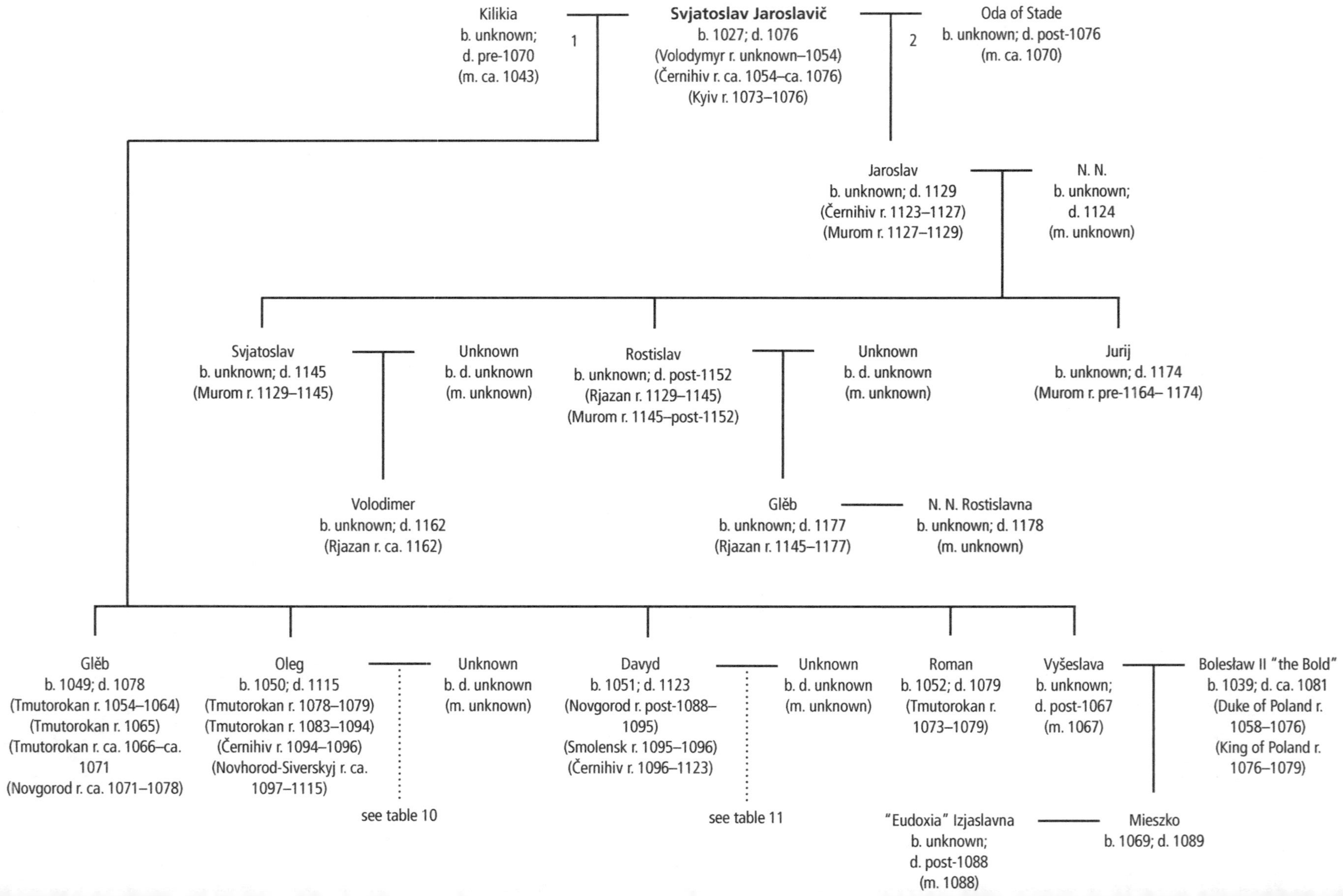

Marriage to Svjatoslav Jaroslavič: Nazarenko, *Drevnjaja Rus′ na meždunarodnyx putjax*, 515; *Bruno de Bello Saxonico*, 333, ch. 13. For more on this marriage see part 1, "Marriages: Generation Two," "Svjatoslav Jaroslavič."

Glĕb Svjatoslavič

Birth date: Dimnik, *Dynasty of Chernigov, 1054–1146*, 31

Death date: *PVL*, s.a. 1078; *NPL*, s.a. 1079

Knjaz′ of Tmutorokan (1) start: conjectural based upon Jaroslav's death and Glĕb's presence there in 1064; knjaz′ of Tmutorokan (1) end: *PVL*, s.a. 1064

Knjaz′ of Tmutorokan (2) start: *PVL*, s.a. 1065; knjaz′ of Tmutorokan (2) end: *PVL*, s.a. 1065

Knjaz′ of Tmutorokan (3) start: *The Paterik of the Kievan Caves Monastery*, trans. Muriel Heppell, Harvard Library of Early Ukrainian Literature: Translations 1 (Cambridge, Mass.: Harvard Ukrainian Research Institute, 1989), 51–52; knjaz′ of Tmutorokan (3) end: conjectural based upon his assumption of power in Novgorod; see *PVL*, s.a. 1071

Knjaz′ of Novgorod start: *PVL*, s.a. 1071; knjaz′ of Novgorod end: *PVL*, s.a. 1078; *NPL*, s.a. 1079, *Paterik of the Kievan Caves Monastery*, 144.

Oleg Svjatoslavič

Birth date: Dimnik, *Dynasty of Chernigov, 1054–1146*, 39

Death date: *NPL*, s.a. 1115; Laurentian Chronicle, s.a. 1115; Hypatian Chronicle, s.a. 1115; Tver Chronicle, s.a. 1115; Nikon Chronicle, s.a. 1115 (also listed s.a. 1117)

Knjaz′ of Tmutorokan (1) start: *PVL*, s.a. 1078; knjaz′ of Tmutorokan (1) end: *PVL*, s.a. 1079

Knjaz′ of Tmutorokan (2) start: *PVL*, s.a. 1083; knjaz′ of Tmutorokan (2) end: *PVL*, s.a. 1094

Knjaz′ of Černihiv start: *PVL*, s.a. 1094; knjaz′ of Černihiv end: *PVL*, s.a. 1096

Knjaz′ of Novhorod-Siverskyj start: slightly conjectural based upon a division of Svjatoslav's territory in *PVL*, s.a. 1097—it is, however, clear that his descendants rule there; knjaz′ of Novhorod-Siverskyj end: *NPL*, s.a. 1115; Laurentian Chronicle, s.a. 1115; Hypatian Chronicle, s.a. 1115; Tver Chronicle, s.a. 1115; Nikon Chronicle, s.a. 1115 (also listed s.a. 1117)

Relationship with unknown partner: This relationship has a complicated history; for a discussion of the issues, see part 1, "Marriages: Generation Three," "Oleg Svjatoslavič."

Unknown partner of Oleg Svjatoslavič
Birth date: unknown
Death date: unknown
Marriage to Oleg Svjatoslavič: This relationship has a complicated history; for a discussion of the issues, see part 1, "Marriages: Generation Three," "Oleg Svjatoslavič."

Davyd Svjatoslavič
Birth date: Dimnik, *Dynasty of Chernigov, 1054–1146*, 39–40
Death date: Laurentian Chronicle, s.a. 1123; Hypatian Chronicle, s.a. 1123; Voskresenskij Chronicle, s.a. 1123; Tver Chronicle, s.a. 1123; Nikon Chronicle, s.a. 1123
Knjaz´ of Novgorod start: unknown; knjaz´ of Novgorod end: *PVL*, s.a. 1095
Knjaz´ of Smolensk start: *PVL*, s.a. 1095; knjaz´ of Smolensk end: conjectural based upon his possession of the inheritance of Svjatoslav mentioned in *PVL*, s.a. 1097
Knjaz´ of Černihiv start: conjectural based upon his possession of the inheritance of Svjatoslav mentioned in *PVL*, s.a. 1097; knjaz´ of Černihiv end: Laurentian Chronicle, s.a. 1123; Hypatian Chronicle, s.a. 1123; Voskresenskij Chronicle, s.a. 1123; Tver Chronicle, s.a. 1123; Nikon Chronicle, s.a. 1123
Relationship with unknown partner: based on a child cited in Hypatian Chronicle, s.a. 1124, and elsewhere.

Unknown partner of Davyd Svjatoslavič
Birth date: unknown
Death date: unknown
Relationship with Davyd Svjatoslavič: based on a child cited in Hypatian Chronicle, s.a. 1124, and elsewhere.

Roman Svjatoslavič
Birth date: Dimnik, *Dynasty of Chernigov, 1054–1146*, 39–40
Death date: *PVL*, s.a. 1079
Knjaz´ of Tmutorokan start: conjectural based upon his father's assumption of power in Kyiv, already present there as ruler in 1077; see *PVL*, s.a. 1077; knjaz´ of Tmutorokan end: *PVL*, s.a. 1079; conjectural that he and Oleg were able to share power during Oleg's stay in Tmutorokan.

Vyšeslava Svjatoslavna
Birth date: unknown
Death date: Her death date can reasonably be assumed to have occurred after her marriage, though when is unknown

Marriage to Bolesław II of Poland: Długosz, *Annales*, bk. 3, p. 95; Tatiščev, *Istorija Rossijskaja*, 2:123, Baumgarten, "Généalogies," 18–20, table 5; and Dimnik, *Dynasty of Chernigov, 1054–1146*, 41. For more on this marriage see part 1, "Marriages: Generation Three," "Vyšeslava Svjatoslavna."

Bolesław II "the Bold"

Birth date: Balzer, *Genealogia Piastów*, table 2

Death date: Balzer, *Genealogia Piastów*, table 2; Gallus Anonymous, *Gesta Principum Polonorum*, bk. 1, ch. 28

Duke of Poland start: *Chronica Poloniae Maioris*, ch. 12; Gallus Anonymous, *Gesta Principum Polonorum*, bk. 1, ch. 22; duke of Poland end: *Lamberti Hersfeldensis Annales*, s.a. 1077

King of Poland start: *Lamberti Hersfeldensis Annales*, s.a. 1077; Bernold of St. Blasien, "Chronicle," s.a. 1077; king of Poland end: Gallus Anonymous, *Gesta Principum Polonorum*, bk. 1, ch. 27

Marriage to Vyšeslava Svjatoslavna: Długosz, *Annales*, bk. 3, p. 95; Tatiščev, *Istorija Rossijskaja*, 2:123; Baumgarten, "Généalogies," 18–20, table 5; Dimnik, *Dynasty of Chernigov, 1054–1146*, 41. For more on this marriage see part 1, "Marriages: Generation Three," "Vyšeslava Svjatoslavna."

Jaroslav Svjatoslavič

Birth date: unknown

Death date: Laurentian Chronicle, s.a. 1129; Hypatian Chronicle, s.a. 1130; Voskresenskij Chronicle, s.a. 1129; Tver Chronicle, s.a. 1129; Nikon Chronicle, s.a. 1129

Knjaz´ of Černihiv start: Hypatian Chronicle, s.a. 1123; Voskresenskij Chronicle, s.a. 1123; Tver Chronicle, s.a. 1123; Nikon Chronicle, s.a. 1123; knjaz´ of Černihiv end: Laurentian Chronicle, s.a. 1127; Hypatian Chronicle, s.a. 1128; Voskresenskij Chronicle, s.a. 1127; Tver Chronicle, s.a. 1127; Nikon Chronicle, s.a. 1127

Knjaz´ of Murom start: Laurentian Chronicle, s.a. 1127; Hypatian Chronicle, s.a. 1128; Voskresenskij Chronicle, s.a. 1127; Nikon Chronicle, s.a. 1127; knjaz´ of Murom end: Laurentian Chronicle, s.a. 1129; Hypatian Chronicle, s.a. 1130; Voskresenskij Chronicle, s.a. 1129; Tver Chronicle, s.a. 1129; Nikon Chronicle, s.a. 1129

Relationship with unknown partner: Hypatian Chronicle, s.a. 1124 (records her death).

Unknown partner of Jaroslav Svjatoslavič

Birth date: unknown

Death date: Hypatian Chronicle, s.a. 1124

Relationship with Jaroslav Svjatoslavič: Hypatian Chronicle, s.a. 1124 (records her death).

Svjatoslav Jaroslavič
Birth date: unknown
Death date: Hypatian Chronicle, s.a. 1145
Knjaz′ of Murom start: conjectural based upon his father's death; knjaz′ of Murom end: Hypatian Chronicle, s.a. 1145
Relationship with unknown partner: conjectural based upon a child cited in Hypatian Chronicle, s.a. 1162.

Unknown partner of Svjatoslav Jaroslavič
Birth date: unknown
Death date: unknown
Relationship with Svjatoslav Jaroslavič: conjectural based upon a child cited in Hypatian Chronicle, s.a. 1162.

Rostislav Jaroslavič
Birth date: unknown
Death date: Hypatian Chronicle, s.a. 1152; Tver Chronicle, s.a. 1152; Nikon Chronicle, s.a. 1152 (last mention of him in the sources)
Knjaz′ of Rjazan start: conjectural based upon his father's death; knjaz′ of Rjazan end: Voskresenskij Chronicle, s.a. 1146; Hypatian Chronicle, s.a. 1145 (though it is possible that he keeps control of Rjazan through his son, as multiple chronicles refer to him as ruler of Rjazan even after this time)
Knjaz′ of Murom start: Hypatian Chronicle, s.a. 1145; knjaz′ of Murom end: Hypatian Chronicle, s.a. 1152; Tver Chronicle, s.a. 1152; Nikon Chronicle, s.a. 1152 (last mention of him in the sources)
Relationship with unknown partner: conjectural based upon children cited in the sources; see Hypatian Chronicle, s.a. 1145, for example.

Unknown partner of Rostislav Jaroslavič
Birth date: unknown
Death date: unknown
Relationship with Rostislav Jaroslavič: conjectural based upon children cited in the sources; see Hypatian Chronicle, s.a. 1145, for example.

Jurij Jaroslavič
Birth date: unknown
Death date: Hypatian Chronicle, s.a. 1174; Tver Chronicle, s.a. 1174; Laurentian Chronicle, s.a. 1174; Voskresenskij Chronicle, s.a. 1174; Nikon Chronicle, s.a. 1174
Knjaz′ of Murom start: Tver Chronicle, s.a. 1164; Laurentian Chronicle,

s.a. 1164 (both have him already ruling there); knjaz´ of Murom end: Hypatian Chronicle, s.a. 1174; Tver Chronicle, s.a. 1174; Laurentian Chronicle, s.a. 1174; Voskresenskij Chronicle, s.a. 1174; Nikon Chronicle, s.a. 1174.

Volodimer Svjatoslavič
Birth date: unknown
Death date: Hypatian Chronicle, s.a. 1162; Voskresenskij Chronicle, s.a. 1161; Nikon Chronicle, s.a. 1160
Knjaz´ of Rjazan: Hypatian Chronicle, s.a. 1162; Voskresenskij Chronicle, s.a. 1161; Nikon Chronicle, s.a. 1160 (all record his title as knjaz´ of Rjazan, though there is no other specific information about his rule. It is conjectural that he ruled Rjazan after the death of Rostislav Jaroslavič, replacing Glěb Rostislavič, during the time when Jurij Jaroslavič was ruling Murom).

Glěb Rostislavič
Birth date: unknown
Death date: *NPL*, s.a. 1177; Hypatian Chronicle, s.a. 1177; Tver Chronicle, s.a. 1177; Voskresenskij Chronicle, s.a. 1177; Nikon Chronicle, s.a. 1177
Knjaz´ of Rjazan start: Hypatian Chronicle, s.a. 1145; knjaz´ of Rjazan end: *NPL*, s.a. 1177; Hypatian Chronicle, s.a. 1177; Tver Chronicle, s.a. 1177; Voskresenskij Chronicle, s.a. 1177; Nikon Chronicle, s.a. 1177 (conjectural that there might have been a break in his reign, as Volodimer Svjatoslavič [see above] is listed as ruling Rjazan as well. This may have occurred after the death of Rostislav Jaroslavič, during Jurij Jaroslavič's rule of Murom.)
Marriage to N. N. Rostislavna: *NPL*, s.a. 1176; Voskresenskij Chronicle, s.a. 1175 (both reference Glěb Rostislav as *zjat´* to M´stislav Rostislavič).

N. N. Rostislavna
Birth date: unknown
Death date: Hypatian Chronicle, s.a. 1178
Marriage to Glěb Rostislavič: *NPL*, s.a. 1176; Voskresenskij Chronicle, s.a. 1175 (both reference Glěb Rostislav as *zjat´* to M´stislav Rostislavič).

N. N., "Eudoxia" Izjaslavna
Birth date: unknown
Death date: Her death date can reasonably be assumed to have occurred after her marriage, though when is unknown.
Marriage to Mieszko of Poland: Gallus Anonymous, *Gesta Principum*

Polonorum, bk. 1, ch. 29; Długosz, *Annales*, 161. For more on this marriage see part 1, "Marriages: Generation Three," "Eudoxia Izjaslavna."

Mieszko of Poland

Birth date: Balzer, *Genealogia Piastóow*, table 2

Death date: Gallus Anonymous, *Gesta Principum Polonorum*, bk. 1, ch. 29

Marriage to "Eudoxia" Izjaslavna: Gallus Anonymous, *Gesta Principum Polonorum*, bk. 1, ch. 29; Długosz, *Annales*, 161. For more on this marriage see part 1, "Marriages: Generation Three," "Eudoxia Izjaslavna."

Table 7: Vsevolod Jaroslavič

Monomaxina
Birth date: unknown
Death date: Tatiščev, *Istorija Rossijskaja*, 2:85
Marriage to Vsevolod Jaroslavič: *PVL*, s.a. 1053. For more on this marriage see part 1, "Marriages: Generation Two," "Vsevolod Jaroslavič."

Vsevolod Jaroslavič
Birth date: *PVL*, s.a. 1030
Death date: *PVL*, s.a. 1093
Knjaz´ of Perejaslav start: *PVL*, s.a. 1054; knjaz´ of Perejaslav end: *PVL*, s.a. 1093
Knjaz´ of Kyiv (1) start: *PVL*, s.a. 1076; knjaz´ of Kyiv (1) end: *PVL*, s.a. 1077
Knjaz´ of Černihiv start: *PVL*, s.a. 1077; knjaz´ of Černihiv end: *PVL*, s.a. 1078
Knjaz´ of Kyiv (2) start: *PVL*, s.a. 1078; knjaz´ of Kyiv (2) end: *PVL*, s.a. 1093; *NPL*, s.a. 1093
Marriage to Monomaxina: *PVL*, s.a. 1053
Marriage to N. N., "Anna": Tatiščev, *Istorija Rossijskaja*, 2:85. For more on these marriages see part 1, "Marriages: Generation Two," "Vsevolod Jaroslavič."

N. N., "Anna"
Birth date: unknown
Death date: Hypatian Chronicle, s.a. 1111
Marriage to Vsevolod Jaroslavič: Tatiščev, *Istorija Rossijskaja*, 2:85. For more on this marriage see part 1, "Marriages: Generation Two," "Vsevolod Jaroslavič."

Janka Vsevolodovna
Birth date: unknown

Table 7: Vsevolod Jaroslavič

Monomaxina of Byzantium
b. unknown; d. 1067
(m. ca. 1053)

— 1 —

Vsevolod Jaroslavič
b. 1030; d. 1093
(Perejaslav r. ca. 1054–1055)
(Kyiv r. 1077)
(Černihiv r. 1077–1078)
(Kyiv r. 1078–1093)

— 2 —

N. N. "Anna" of the Polovcians
b. unknown; d. 1111
(m. ca. 1067)

Children of marriage 1:

Janka
b. unknown;
d. 1113

Volodimer "Monomax"
b. 1053; d. 1125
(Smolensk r. ca. 1078–ca. 1095)
(Černihiv r. 1078–1094)
(Perejaslav r. 1094–1113)
(Kyiv r. ca. 1113–1125)

Volodimer's wives:

Gyða Haroldsdottir (wife 1)
b. unknown;
d. 1107
(m. ca. 1074)

N. N. (wife 2)
b. unknown;
d. 1126
(m. 1108)

see table 12

Children of marriage 2:

Rostislav
b. 1070; d. 1093
(Perejaslav r. ca. 1078–1093)

Evpraksija
b. 1071; d. 1109
(1st m. ca. 1082)
(2nd m. 1089)

Katerina
b. unknown;
d. 1108

Evpraksija's husbands:

Henry III "the Long" of Stade (husband 1)
b. unknown; d. 1087
(Margrave of Saxon Nordmark r. ca. 1082–1087)

Henry IV of the German Empire (husband 2)
b. ca. 1050; d. 1106
(King of the German Empire r. 1056–1106)
(Emperor 1084–1106)

Death date: Laurentian Chronicle, s.a. 1113; Hypatian Chronicle, s.a. 1112; Nikon Chronicle, s.a. 1113.

Gyða Haroldsdottir
Birth date: unknown
Death date: *PVL*, s.a. 1107; marriage to Volodimer "Monomax" Vsevolodič: Saxo Grammaticus, *Danorum Regum heroumque historia: Books X–XVI*, trans. Eric Christiansen, vol. 1: bks. 10, 11, 12, and 13 (Oxford: B.A.R., 1980), bk. 11, ch. 6, 58; Sturluson, *Heimskringla*, 702. For more on this marriage see part 1, "Marriages: Generation Three," "Volodimer 'Monomax' Vsevolodič."

Volodimer "Monomax" Vsevolodič
Birth date: *PVL*, s.a. 1053
Death date: Laurentian Chronicle, s.a. 1125; *NPL*, s.a. 1125; Rogožskij Chronicle, s.a. 1125; Tver Chronicle, s.a. 1125; Nikon Chronicle, s.a. 1125
Knjaz′ of Smolensk start: *PVL*, s.a. 1078; knjaz′ of Smolensk end: *PVL*, s.a. 1095 (based on the assumption that Davyd Svjatoslavič takes power in Smolensk in that year)
Knjaz′ of Černihiv start: *PVL*, s.a. 1078; knjaz′ of Černihiv end: *PVL*, s.a. 1094
Knjaz′ of Perejaslav start: *PVL*, s.a. 1094; knjaz′ of Perejaslav end: *PVL*, s.a. 1113 (conjectural based upon his assumption of power in Kyiv)
Knjaz′ of Kyiv start: Laurentian Chronicle, s.a. 1114; Hypatian Chronicle, s.a. 1113; *NPL*, s.a. 1113; Rogožskij Chronicle, s.a. 1114; Tver Chronicle, s.a. 1113; Nikon Chronicle, s.a. 1114; knjaz′ of Kyiv end: Laurentian Chronicle, s.a. 1125; *NPL*, s.a. 1125; Rogožskij Chronicle, s.a. 1125; Tver Chronicle, s.a. 1125; Nikon Chronicle, s.a. 1125
Marriage to Gyða Haroldsdottir: Saxo Grammaticus, *Danorum Regum heroumque historia*, bk. 11, ch. 6, 58; Sturluson, *Heimskringla*, 702
Marriage to N. N.: Laurentian Chronicle, s.a. 1126; Hypatian Chronicle, s.a. 1127; Voskresenskij Chronicle, s.a. 1126; Nikon Chronicle, s.a. 1126. For more on these marriages see part 1, "Marriages: Generation Three," "Volodimer 'Monomax' Vsevolodič."

N. N., wife of Volodimer "Monomax" Vsevolodič
Birth date: unknown
Death date: Laurentian Chronicle, s.a. 1126; Hypatian Chronicle, s.a. 1127; Voskresenskij Chronicle, s.a. 1126; Nikon Chronicle, s.a. 1126
Marriage to Volodimer "Monomax" Vsevolodič: Laurentian Chronicle, s.a. 1126; Hypatian Chronicle, s.a. 1127; Voskresenskij Chronicle, s.a. 1126; Nikon Chronicle, s.a. 1126. For more on these marriages

see part 1, "Marriages: Generation Three," "Volodimer 'Monomax' Vsevolodič."

Rostislav Vsevolodič

Birth date: *PVL*, s.a. 1070; *NPL*, s.a. 1070

Death date: *PVL*, s.a. 1093

Knjaz´ of Perejaslav start: conjectural based upon his father's assumption of power in Kyiv; knjaz´ of Perejaslav end: *PVL*, s.a. 1093.

Henry III "the Long" of Stade

Birth date: unknown

Death date: *Annales Stadenses auctore M. Alberto*, publ. I. M. Lappenberg, in *Annales aevi Suevici*, 271–379, Monumenta Germaniae Historica: Scriptores 16 (Hannover: Impensis Bibliopolii Avlici Hahniani, 1859), s.a. 1144 (in listing of history of the family dates Henry of Stade's death to 1087)

Margrave of the Saxon Nordmark start: *Annalista Saxo*, s.a. 1082; margrave of the Saxon Nordmark end: *Annales Stadenses*, s.a. 1144 (in listing of history of the family dates Henry of Stade's death to 1087)

Marriage to Evpraksija Vsevolodovna: *Annalista Saxo*, s.a. 1082; *Annales Stadenses*, s.a. 1144. For more on this marriage see part 1, "Marriages: Generation Three," "Evpraksija Vsevolodovna."

Evpraksija Vsevolodovna

Birth date: conjectural based upon age at date of marriage; for more details see Christian Raffensperger, "Evpraksia Vsevolodovna: Between East and West," *Russian History/Histoire Russe* 30, no. 1–2 (2003): 23–34

Death date: *PVL*, s.a. 1109

Marriage to Henry III "the Long" of Stade: *Annalista Saxo*, s.a. 1082; *Annales Stadenses*, s.a. 1144

Marriage to Henry IV: Walram, Bishop of Naumburg, *Liber de unitate ecclesiae conservanda*, ed. Wilhelm Schwenkenbecher, Monumenta Germaniae Historica: Scriptores rerum Germanicarum in usum scholarum separatim editi 39 (Hannover: Impensis Bibliopolii Hahniani, 1883), bk. 2.26, 100; *Heinrici IV: Diplomata*, ed. Dietrich von Gladiss and Alfred Gawlik, Monumenta Germaniae Historica: Die Urkunden der deutschen Könige und Kaiser (Diplomatum regum et imperatorum Germaniae) 6, vol. 2 of 3 (Weimar: Hermann Bohlaus Nachfolger, 1953), 407; *Annalista Saxo*, s.a. 1082, 1089; *Annales Augustani*, publ. George Pertz, in *Annales, chronica et historiae aevi Saxonici*, 123–36, Monumenta Germaniae Historica: Scriptores 3 (Hannover: Impensis Bibliopolii Avlici Hahniani,

1839), s.a. 1089. For more on this marriage see part 1, "Marriages: Generation Three," "Evpraksija Vsevolodovna."

Henry IV of the German Empire

Birth date: Herman of Reichenau, "Chronicle," in *Eleventh-Century Germany: The Swabian Chronicles*, ed. and trans. I. S. Robinson (Manchester: Manchester University Press, 2008), s.a. 1051 (for baptism); Berthold of Reichenau, s.a. 1056 (references Henry's age as seven)

Death date: *Annalista Saxo*, s.a. 1106; Cosmas of Prague, *Chronicle of the Czechs*, bk. 3, ch. 18; Orderic Vitalis, *Ecclesiastical History*, bk. 10, ch. 1

King of the German Empire start: Bernold of St. Blasien, "Chronicle," s.a. 1057; Berthold of Reichenau, s.a. 1056; *Annalista Saxo*, s.a. 1056

Emperor of the German Empire start: Bernold of St. Blasien, "Chronicle," s.a. 1084; *Annalista Saxo*, s.a. 1084; I. S. Robinson, *Henry IV of Germany, 1056–1106* (Cambridge: Cambridge University Press, 1999), 230–31; king and emperor of the German Empire end: *Annalista Saxo*, s.a. 1106; Cosmas of Prague, *Chronicle of the Czechs*, bk. 3, ch. 18, Orderic Vitalis, *Ecclesiastical History*, bk. 10, ch. 1

Marriage to Evpraksija Vsevolodovna: Walram, *Liber de unitate ecclesiae conservanda*, bk. 2.26, 100; *Heinrici IV: Diplomata*, 407; *Annalista Saxo*, s.a. 1082, 1089; *Annales Augustani*, s.a. 1089. For more on this marriage see part 1, "Marriages: Generation Three," "Evpraksija Vsevolodovna."

Katerina Vsevolodovna

Birth date: unknown

Death date: *PVL*, s.a. 1108.

Table 8: Igor´ Jaroslavič

Igor´ Jaroslavič
Birth date: unknown
Death date: *PVL*, s.a. 1060
Knjaz´ of Volodymyr start: *PVL*, s.a. 1054; knjaz´ of Volodymyr end: *PVL*, s.a. 1057
Knjaz´ of Smolensk: *PVL*, s.a. 1057; knjaz´ of Smolensk end: *PVL*, s.a. 1060
Relationship with unknown partner: conjectural based upon a son cited in *PVL*, s.a. 1097.

Unknown partner of Igor´ Jaroslavič
Birth date: unknown
Death date: unknown
Relationship with Igor´ Jaroslavič: conjectural based upon a son cited in *PVL*, s.a. 1097.

Unknown partner of Davyd Igorič
Birth date: unknown
Death date: unknown
Relationship with Davyd Igorič: conjectural based upon a child cited in Laurentian Chronicle, s.a. 1127, and elsewhere.

Davyd Igorič
Birth date: unknown
Death date: Hypatian Chronicle, s.a. 1112; *NPL*, s.a. 1113; Laurentian Chronicle, s.a. 1113; Voskresenskij Chronicle, s.a. 1112; Tver Chronicle, s.a. 1112; Nikon Chronicle, s.a. 1113
Knjaz´ of Tmutorokan start: *PVL*, s.a. 1081; knjaz´ of Tmutorokan end: *PVL*, s.a. 1083
Knjaz´ of Dorogobuž (1) start: *PVL*, s.a. 1084; knjaz´ of Dorogobuž (1) end: *PVL*, s.a. 1085

Table 8: Igor´ Jaroslavič

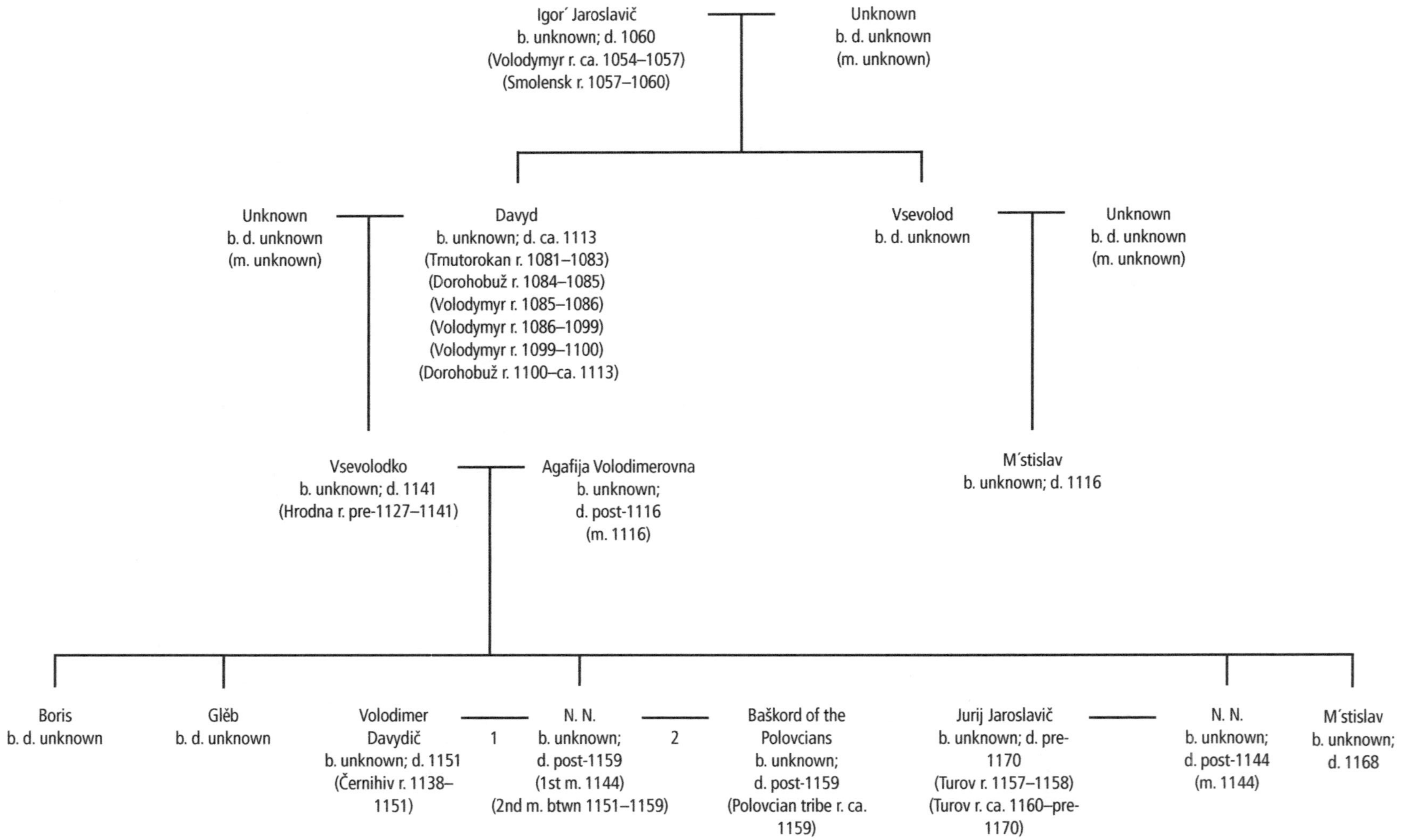

Knjaz´ of Volodymyr (1) start: *PVL*, s.a. 1085; knjaz´ of Volodymyr (1) end: *PVL*, s.a. 1086

Knjaz´ of Volodymyr (2) start: *PVL*, s.a. 1086; knjaz´ of Volodymyr (2) end: *PVL*, s.a. 1099

Knjaz´ of Volodymyr (3) start: *PVL*, s.a. 1097; knjaz´ of Volodymyr (3) end: *PVL*, s.a. 1097, 1100

Knjaz´ of Dorogobuž (2) start: *PVL*, s.a. 1097, 1100; knjaz´ of Dorogobuž (2) end: Hypatian Chronicle, s.a. 1112; *NPL*, s.a. 1113; Laurentian Chronicle, s.a. 1113; Voskresenskij Chronicle, s.a. 1112; Tver Chronicle, s.a. 1112; Nikon Chronicle, s.a. 1113

Relationship with unknown partner: conjectural based upon a child cited in Laurentian Chronicle, s.a. 1127, and elsewhere.

Vsevolod Igorič

Birth date: unknown

Death date: unknown; existence based upon child cited in *PVL*, s.a. 1103, and elsewhere

Relationship with unknown partner: conjectural based upon a child cited in *PVL*, s.a. 1103, and elsewhere.

Unknown partner of Vsevolod Igorič

Birth date: unknown

Death date: unknown

Relationship with Vsevolod Igorič: conjectural based upon a child cited in *PVL*, s.a. 1103, and elsewhere.

Vsevolodko Davydič

Birth date: unknown

Death date: Laurentian Chronicle, s.a. 1141; Hypatian Chronicle, s.a. 1141; Voskresenskij Chronicle, s.a. 1141; Nikon Chronicle, s.a. 1141

Knjaz´ of Hrodna start: Laurentian Chronicle, s.a. 1127; Hypatian Chronicle, s.a. 1128 (first mention of his rule there); knjaz´ of Hrodna end: Laurentian Chronicle, s.a. 1141; Hypatian Chronicle, s.a. 1141; Voskresenskij Chronicle, s.a. 1141; Nikon Chronicle, s.a. 1141

Marriage to Agafija Volodimerovna: Hypatian Chronicle, s.a. 1116. For more on this marriage see part 1, "Marriages: Generation Four," "Vsevolodko Davydič."

Agafija Volodimerovna

Birth date: unknown

Death date: Her death date can reasonably be assumed to have occurred after her marriage, though when is unknown.

Marriage to Vsevolodko Davydič: Hypatian Chronicle, s.a. 1116. For more on this marriage see part 1, "Marriages: Generation Four," "Vsevolodko Davydič."

M´stislav Vsevolodič
Birth date: unknown
Death date: Hypatian Chronicle, s.a. 1116; Voskresenskij Chronicle, s.a. 1114; Tver Chronicle, s.a. 1114; Nikon Chronicle, s.a. 1114.

Boris Vsevolodkovič
Birth date: unknown
Death date: unknown; existence cited in Hypatian Chronicle, s.a. 1144, but not in any other primary source.

Glěb Vsevolodkovič
Birth date: unknown
Death date: unknown; existence cited in Hypatian Chronicle, s.a. 1144, but not in any other primary source.

Volodimer Davydič
Birth date: unknown
Death date: Hypatian Chronicle, s.a. 1151; Laurentian Chronicle, s.a. 1151; Voskresenskij Chronicle, s.a. 1151; Nikon Chronicle, s.a. 1151
Knjaz´ of Černihiv start: Laurentian Chronicle, s.a. 1138; Voskresenskij Chronicle, s.a. 1138; Nikon Chronicle, s.a. 1138; knjaz´ of Černihiv end: Hypatian Chronicle, s.a. 1151; Laurentian Chronicle, s.a. 1151; Voskresenskij Chronicle, s.a. 1151; Nikon Chronicle, s.a. 1151
Marriage to N. N. Vsevolodkovna: Hypatian Chronicle, s.a. 1144. For more information on this marriage see part 1, "Marriages: Generation Four," "Volodimer Davydič."

N. N. Vsevolodkovna
Birth date: unknown
Death date: Her death date can reasonably be assumed to have occurred after her second marriage, though when is unknown
Marriage to Volodimer Davydič: Hypatian Chronicle, s.a. 1144
Marriage to Baškord of the Polovcians: Tver Chronicle, s.a. 1159; Nikon Chronicle, s.a. 1158; for more information on this marriage see part 1, "Marriages: Generation Four," "Volodimer Davydič."

Baškord of the Polovcians
Birth date: unknown
Death date: his death presumably occurred only after he is mentioned in various sources as a knjaz´ of the Polovcians; see Tver Chronicle, s.a. 1159; Nikon Chronicle, s.a. 1158

Knjaz´ of the Polovcians: Tver Chronicle, s.a. 1159; Nikon Chronicle, s.a. 1158 (only mentions as ruler)
Marriage to N. N. Vsevolodkovna: Tver Chronicle, s.a. 1159; Nikon Chronicle, s.a. 1158. For more on this marriage see part 1, "Marriages: Generation Four," "Volodimer Davydič."

Jurij Jaroslavič
Birth date: unknown
Death date: Hypatian Chronicle, s.a. 1170 (has his son ruling in Turov)
Knjaz´ of Turov (1) start: Nikon Chronicle, s.a. 1157; knjaz´ of Turov (1) end: Hypatian Chronicle, s.a. 1158; Voskresenskij Chronicle, s.a. 1157; Nikon Chronicle, s.a. 1157
Knjaz´ of Turov (2) start: Hypatian Chronicle, s.a. 1160; Voskresenskij Chronicle, s.a. 1162 (his son leads forces from Turov); knjaz´ of Turov (2) end: Hypatian Chronicle, s.a. 1170 (has his son ruling in Turov)
Marriage to N. N. Vsevolodkovna: Hypatian Chronicle, s.a. 1144. For more on this marriage see part 1, "Marriages: Generation Five," "Jurij Jaroslavič."

N. N. Vsevolodkovna
Birth date: unknown
Death date: Her death date can reasonably be assumed to have occurred after her marriage, though when is unknown.
Marriage to Jurij Jaroslavič: Hypatian Chronicle, s.a. 1144. For more on this marriage see part 1, "Marriages: Generation Five," "Jurij Jaroslavič."

M´stislav Vsevolodkovič
Birth date: unknown
Death date: Nikon Chronicle, s.a. 1168 (though he is identified as M´stislav Vsevolodkovič, grandson of M´stislav, I believe that is an incorrect attribution).

Table 9: Svjatopolk Izjaslavič

Unknown "naložnica" of Svjatopolk Izjaslavič
Birth date: unknown
Death date: unknown
Relationship with Svjatopolk Izjaslavič: conjectural based upon a son cited in *PVL*, s.a. 1097. For more on this relationship see part 1, "Marriages: Generation Three," "Svjatopolk Izjaslavič."

Unknown partner of Svjatopolk Izjaslavič
Birth date: unknown
Death date: unknown
Relationship with Svjatopolk Izjaslavič: conjectural based upon the birth dates of Svjatopolk's children, which predate his marriage to the daughter of Tugorkhan. Similarly, his son, Jaroslav, is listed in *PVL*, s.a. 1097, as son of Svjatopolk, separate from the entry for M´stislav, son from Svjatopolk's "naložnica," who may or may not be the same person. For more on this relationship see part 1, "Marriages: Generation Three," "Svjatopolk Izjaslavič."

Svjatopolk Izjaslavič
Birth date: *NPL*, s.a. 1050 (though patronymic is not specified and identification is conjectural)
Death date: Laurentian Chronicle, s.a. 1114; Hypatian Chronicle, s.a. 1113; *NPL*, s.a. 1113, *NČL*, s.a. 1114; Rogožskij Chronicle, s.a. 1114; Tver Chronicle, s.a. 1113; Nikon Chronicle, s.a. 1114
Knjaz´ of Polack start: *PVL*, s.a. 1069; knjaz´ of Polack end: *PVL*, s.a. 1071
Knjaz´ of Novgorod start: conjectural based upon surrounding rulers; knjaz´ of Novgorod end: *PVL*, s.a. 1088
Knjaz´ of Turov start: *PVL*, s.a. 1088; knjaz´ of Turov end: *PVL*, s.a. 1093
Knjaz´ of Kyiv start: *PVL*, s.a. 1093, *NPL*, s.a. 1093; knjaz´ of Kyiv end: Laurentian Chronicle, s.a. 1114; Hypatian Chronicle, s.a. 1113;

Table 9: Svjatopolk Izjaslavič

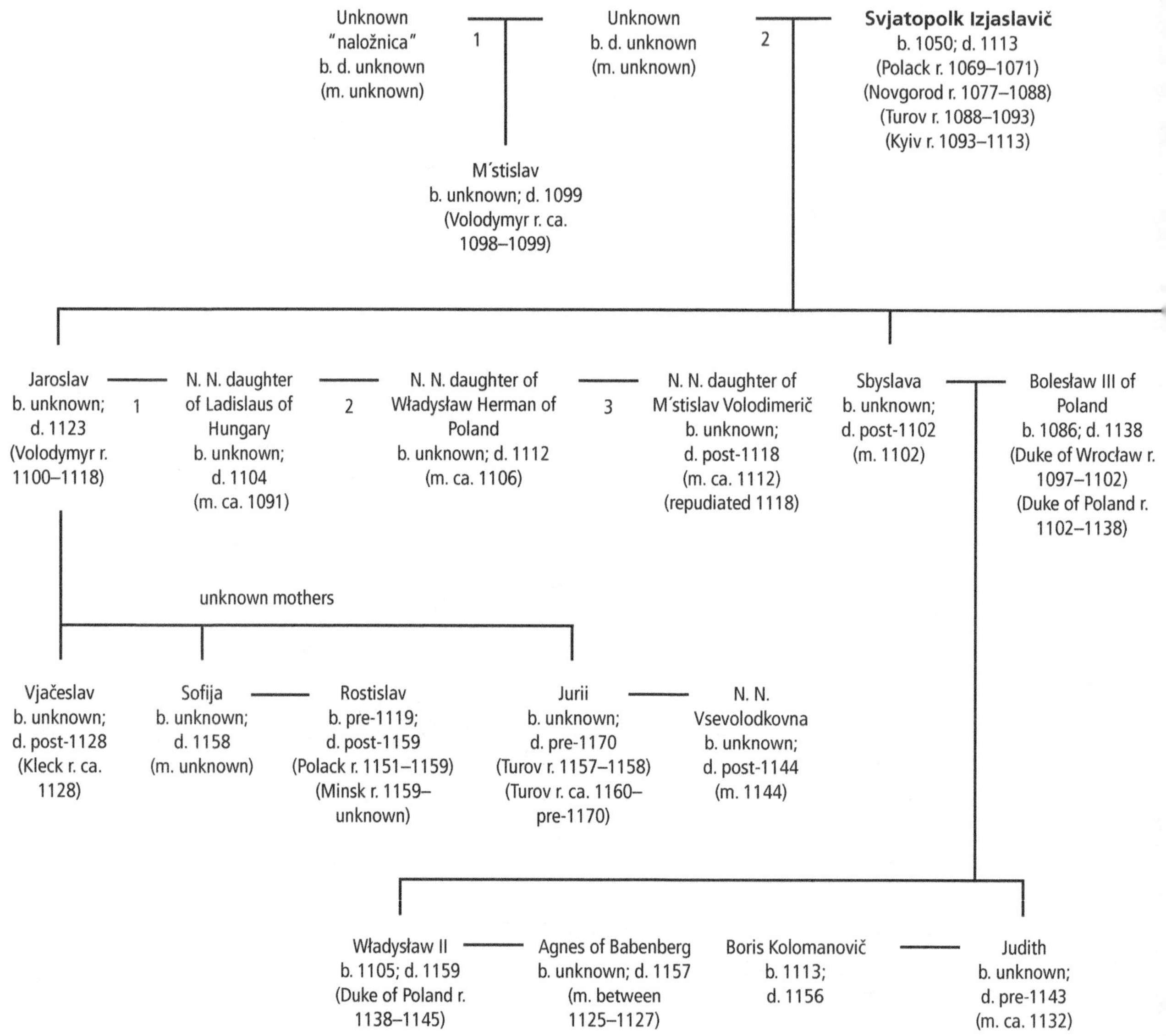

3

N. N. daughter of Tugorkhan
of the Polovcians
b. unknown; d. 1125
(m. 1094)

Izjaslav
b. unknown;
d. 1127

Peredslava
b. unknown;
d. 1116
(m. 1104)

Almos of Hungary
b. unknown; d. 1129

Piotr Włostowic of
Poland
b. unknown; d. 1153
(Count Palatine)

Marija
b. unknown;
d. pre-1153
(m. 1117)

Brjačeslav
b. 1104; d. 1127

Béla II
b. 1108; d. 1141
(King of Hungary r.
1131–1141)

Jelena, daughter of
Uroš I of Serbia
b. unknown;
d. 1146
(m. 1129)

Adelaide
b. unknown;
d. 1140
(m. ca. 1122)

Soběslav of
Bohemia
b. ca. 1090; d. 1140
(Duke of Bohemia r.
1125–1140)

Hedwig
b. unknown;
d. post-1132
(m. 1132)

Adalbert of
Babenberg
b. unknown;
d. 1137

Konstantin
b. d. unknown
(Ruler of Skrzynno)

Svjatoslav
b. d. unknown

Jaksa of Miechów
b. d. unknown
(Prince of Miechów)

N. N.
b. d. unknown
(m. unknown)

NPL, s.a. 1113, *NČL*, s.a. 1114; Rogožskij Chronicle, s.a. 1114; Tver Chronicle, s.a. 1113; Nikon Chronicle, s.a. 1114
Marriage to daughter of Tugorkhan: Hypatian Chronicle, s.a. 1094
Relationship with unknown partners: *PVL*, s.a. 1097. For more on these marriages see part 1, "Marriages: Generation Three," "Svjatopolk Izjaslavič."

N. N., daughter of Tugorkhan
Birth date: unknown
Death date: Laurentian Chronicle, s.a. 1124; Hypatian Chronicle, s.a. 1125
Marriage to Svjatopolk Izjaslavič: Hypatian Chronicle, s.a. 1094. For more on this marriage see part 1, "Marriages: Generation Three," "Svjatopolk Izjaslavič."

M´stislav Svjatopolčič
Birth date: unknown
Death date: *PVL*, s.a. 1099
Knjaz´ of Volodymyr start: *PVL*, s.a. 1097; knjaz´ of Volodymyr end: *PVL*, s.a. 1099.

Jaroslav Svjatopolčič
Birth date: unknown
Death date: Laurentian Chronicle, s.a. 1123; Hypatian Chronicle, s.a. 1123; Voskresenskij Chronicle, s.a. 1123; Nikon Chronicle, s.a. 1123
Knjaz´ of Volodymyr start: *PVL*, s.a. 1097; *PVL*, s.a. 1100; knjaz´ of Volodymyr end: Hypatian Chronicle, s.a. 1118; Laurentian Chronicle, s.a. 1119; Voskresenskij Chronicle, s.a. 1118; Tver Chronicle, s.a. 1118; Nikon Chronicle, s.a. 1119
Marriage to unknown daughter of Ladislaus of Hungary: Georgii Fejér, ed., *Codex diplomaticus Hungariae, ecclesiasticus ac civilis*, vol. 1 (Buda: Regiae Universitatis Ungaricae, 1829), 469; Wertner, *Az Árpádok családi története*, 205
Marriage to unknown daughter of Władysław Herman: Gallus Anonymous, *Gesta Principum Polonorum*, 117
Marriage to N. N. M´stislavna: *NPL*, s.a. 1113; Hypatian Chronicle, s.a. 1112; Voskresenskij Chronicle, s.a. 1112; Tver Chronicle, s.a. 1113; repudiated N. N. M´stislavna: Voskresenskij Chronicle, s.a. 1118; Tver Chronicle, s.a. 1118; Nikon Chronicle, s.a. 1119. For more on these marriages see part 1, "Marriages: Generation Four," "Jaroslav Svjatopolčič."

N. N., daughter of Ladislaus of Hungary
Birth date: unknown
Death date: conjectural based upon the date of Jaroslav's remarriage

Marriage to Jaroslav Svjatopolčič: Fejér, *Codex diplomaticus Hungariae*, 469; Wertner, *Az Árpádok családi története*, 205. For more on this marriage see part 1, "Marriages: Generation Four," "Jaroslav Svjatopolčič."

N. N., daughter of Władysław Herman of Poland

Birth date: unknown

Death date: conjectural based upon the date of Jaroslav's remarriage

Marriage to Jaroslav Svjatopolčič: Gallus Anonymous, *Gesta Principum Polonorum*, 117. For more on this marriage see part 1, "Marriages: Generation Four," "Jaroslav Svjatopolčič."

N. N. M'stislavna

Birth date: unknown

Death date: The last mention of her is at her repudiation, or mistreatment followed by repudiation; see Voskresenskij Chronicle, s.a. 1118; Tver Chronicle, s.a. 1118; Nikon Chronicle, s.a. 1119.

Marriage to Jaroslav Svjatopolčič: *NPL*, s.a. 1113; Hypatian Chronicle, s.a. 1112; Voskresenskij Chronicle, s.a. 1112; Tver Chronicle, s.a. 1113; repudiated by Jaroslav Svjatopolčič: Voskresenskij Chronicle, s.a. 1118; Tver Chronicle, s.a. 1118; Nikon Chronicle, s.a. 1119. For more on this marriage see part 1, "Marriages: Generation Four," "Jaroslav Svjatopolčič."

Sbyslava Svjatopolkovna

Birth date: unknown

Death date: Her death date can reasonably be assumed to have occurred after her marriage, though when is unknown.

Marriage to Bolesław III: Laurentian Chronicle, s.a. 1102; Długosz, *Annales*, 210–11. For more on this marriage see part 1, "Marriages: Generation Four," "Sbyslava Svjatopolkovna."

Bolesław III of Poland

Birth date: *Chronica Poloniae Maioris*, ch. 30 (records that he was 56 when he died), Cosmas of Prague, *Chronicle of the Czechs*, bk. 2, ch. 36; Gallus Anonymous, *Gesta Principum Polonorum*, bk. 2, ch. 1

Death date: "Chronica Petri comitis Poloniae" [Kronika o Piotrze Właście], ed. Alexander Semkowicz, in *Monumenta Poloniae Historica*, 3:745–84 (Lviv: W Komisie księgarni gubrynowicza I schmidta, 1878), 766; *Chronica Poloniae Maioris*, ch. 30

Duke of Wrocław start: Gallus Anonymous, *Gesta Principum Polonorum*, bk. 2, chs. 7, 8, 13; duke of Wrocław end: "Chronica Petri comitis Poloniae," 766; *Chronica Poloniae Maioris*, ch. 30

Duke of Poland start: *Chronica Poloniae Maioris*, ch. 16; Cosmas of Prague, *Chronicle of the Czechs*, bk. 3, ch. 16; duke of Poland end:

"Chronica Petri comitis Poloniae," 766; *Chronica Poloniae Maioris*, ch. 30

Marriage to Sbyslava Svjatopolkovna: Laurentian Chronicle, s.a. 1102; Długosz, *Annales*, 210–11. For more on this marriage see part 1, "Marriages: Generation Four," "Sbyslava Svjatopolkovna."

Izjaslav Svjatopolčič
Birth date: unknown
Death date: Laurentian Chronicle, s.a. 1127; Hypatian Chronicle, s.a. 1128; Voskresenskij Chronicle, s.a. 1127; Nikon Chronicle, s.a. 1127.

Peredslava Svjatopolkovna
Birth date: unknown
Death date: Hypatian Chronicle, s.a. 1116, where she is listed as Peredslava Svjatoslavna
Marriage to Almos of Hungary: Laurentian Chronicle, s.a. 1104; Hypatian Chronicle, s.a. 1104. For more on this marriage see part 1, "Marriages: Generation Four," "Peredslava Svjatopolkovna."

Almos of Hungary
Birth date: unknown
Death date: Wertner, *Az Árpádok családi története*, table
Marriage to Peredslava Svjatopolkovna: Laurentian Chronicle, s.a. 1104; Hypatian Chronicle, s.a. 1104. For more on this marriage see part 1, "Marriages: Generation Four," "Peredslava Svjatopolkovna."

Piotr Włostowic
Birth date: unknown
Death date: "Chronica Petri comitis Poloniae," 783
Marriage to Marija Svjatopolkovna: *Chronica Poloniae Maioris*, ch. 27. For more on this marriage see part 1, "Marriages: Generation Four," "Marija Svjatopolkovna."

Marija Svjatopolkovna
Birth date: unknown
Death date: "Chronica Petri comitis Poloniae," 783 (records Piotr's death, and notes that she predeceased him)
Marriage to Piotr Włostowic: *Chronica Poloniae Maioris*, ch. 27. For more on this marriage see part 1, "Marriages: Generation Four," "Marija Svjatopolkovna."

Brjačeslav Svjatopolčič
Birth date: *PVL*, s.a. 1104

Death date: Laurentian Chronicle, s.a. 1127; Voskresenskij Chronicle, s.a. 1127; Nikon Chronicle, s.a. 1127.

Vjačeslav Jaroslavič
Birth date: unknown
Death date: conjectural based upon his mention in the sources as ruler of Kleck
Knjaz´ of Kleck: Laurentian Chronicle, s.a. 1127; Hypatian Chronicle, s.a. 1128 (only mention of him in the primary sources).

Sofija Jaroslavna
Birth date: unknown
Death date: Hypatian Chronicle, s.a. 1158
Marriage to Rostislav Glěbovič: Hypatian Chronicle, s.a. 1158 (at her death). For more on this marriage see part 1, "Marriages: Generation Five," "Rostislav Glěbovič."

Rostislav Glěbovič
Birth date: conjectural based upon father's death
Death date: conjectural based upon his last mention in the sources
Knjaz´ of Polack start: Hypatian Chronicle, s.a. 1151; Voskresenskij Chronicle, s.a. 1151; knjaz´ of Polack end: Hypatian Chronicle, s.a. 1159; Voskresenskij Chronicle, s.a. 1159; Nikon Chronicle, s.a. 1158
Knjaz´ of Minsk start: Hypatian Chronicle, s.a. 1159; Voskresenskij Chronicle, s.a. 1159; Nikon Chronicle, s.a. 1158 (all with the implication that he takes over from his brother when he flees there); knjaz´ of Minsk end: unknown
Marriage to Sofija Jaroslavna: Hypatian Chronicle, s.a. 1158 (at her death). For more on this marriage see part 1, "Marriages: Generation Five," "Rostislav Glěbovič."

Jurij Jaroslavič
Birth date: unknown
Death date: Hypatian Chronicle, s.a. 1170 (has his son ruling in Turov)
Knjaz´ of Turov (1) start: Nikon Chronicle, s.a. 1157; knjaz´ of Turov (1) end: Hypatian Chronicle, s.a. 1158; Voskresenskij Chronicle, s.a. 1157; Nikon Chronicle, s.a. 1157
Knjaz´ of Turov (2) start: Hypatian Chronicle, s.a. 1160; Voskresenskij Chronicle, s.a. 1162 (his son leads forces from Turov); knjaz´ of Turov (2) end: Hypatian Chronicle, s.a. 1170 (has his son ruling in Turov)
Marriage to N. N. Vsevolodkovna: Hypatian Chronicle, s.a. 1144. For more on this marriage see part 1, "Marriages: Generation Five," "Jurij Jaroslavič."

N. N. Vsevolodkovna
Birth date: unknown
Death date: Her death date can reasonably be assumed to have occurred after her marriage, though when is unknown
Marriage to Jurij Jaroslavič: Hypatian Chronicle, s.a. 1144. For more on this marriage see part 1, "Marriages: Generation Five," "Jurij Jaroslavič."

Władysław II
Birth date: Balzer, *Genealogia Piastów*, table 3; Długosz, *Annales*, 293
Death date: *Chronica Poloniae Maioris*, ch. 33
Duke of Poland start: "Chronica Petri comitis Poloniae," 766, "Kronika polska (Chronica Polonorum)," ed. Ludwik Ćwikliński, in *Monumenta Poloniae Historica*, 3:578–656 (Lviv: W Komisie Księgarni Gubrynowicza i Schmidta, 1878), 629; *Chronica Poloniae Maioris*, ch. 31; duke of Poland end: *Chronica Poloniae Maioris*, ch. 32
Marriage to Agnes of Babenberg: Otto of Friesing and his continuator, Rahewin, *The Deeds of Frederick Barbarossa*, trans. Charles Christopher Mierow, with Richard Emery (New York: Norton and Co., 1953), bk. 3, ch. 2 (see n. 16); "Chronica Petri comitis Poloniae," 766; Długosz, *Annales*, 293 (the date given here is 1121; it also says her name was Christina, which the editor corrects to "daughter of Henry V"; however, Agnes was, in fact, the granddaughter of Henry IV, her mother was Agnes, daughter of Henry IV, and her father was Margrave Leopold III. The date I have used comes from Balzer, who has an analysis of possible dates from the sources); Balzer, *Genealogia Piastów*, 129–30.

Agnes of Babenberg
Birth date: unknown
Death date: Balzer, *Genealogia Piastów*, 131
Marriage to Władysław II: Otto of Friesing, *Deeds of Frederick Barbarossa*, bk. 3, ch. 2 (see n. 16); "Chronica Petri comitis Poloniae," 766; Długosz, *Annales*, 293 (the date given here is 1121; it also says her name was Christina, which the editor corrects to "daughter of Henry V"; however, Agnes was, in fact, the granddaughter of Henry IV, her mother was Agnes, daughter of Henry IV, and her father was Margrave Leopold III. The date I have used comes from Balzer, who has an analysis of possible dates from the sources); Balzer, *Genealogia Piastów*, 129–30.

Judith Boleslavna
Birth date: unknown
Death date: conjectural based upon Boris's remarriage
Marriage to Boris Kolomanovič: *Chronica Poloniae Maioris*, ch. 27

(listed simply as son of Koloman); Przemysław Wiszewski, *Domus Bolezlai: Values and Social Identity in Dynastic Traditions of Medieval Poland (c. 966–1138)* (Leiden and Boston: Brill, 2010), 110 (source for the name as well).

Boris Kolomanovič:

Birth date: *Cosmae Chronicon Boemorum*, published by Rudolf Köpke, in *Chronica et annales aevi Salici*, Monumenta Germaniae Historica: Scriptores 9 (Hannover: Impensis Bibliopolii Avlici Hahniani, 1851), 215–16; Otto, Bishop of Freising, *The Two Cities: A Chronicle of Universal History to the Year 1146 A.D.*, trans. Charles Christopher Mierow (New York: Octagon Books, 1966), bk. 7, sec. 21; Dercsényi, *Chronica de Gestis Hungarorum*, 131 (all roughly refer to his birth, parentage, and mother's repudiation)

Death date: Otto of Freising, *Deeds of Frederick Barbarossa*, bk. 2, ch. 53

Marriage to Judith Boleslavna: *Chronica Poloniae Maioris*, ch. 27 (listed simply as son of Koloman); Wiszewski, *Domus Bolezlai*, 110.

Béla II of Hungary

Birth date: Wertner, *Az Árpádok családi története*, 295

Death date: Wertner, *Az Árpádok családi története*, 296–97

King of Hungary start: Wertner, *Az Árpádok családi története*, 295; king of Hungary end: Wertner, *Az Árpádok családi története*, 296–97

Marriage to Jelena of Serbia: Wertner, *Az Árpádok családi története*, 298.

Jelena of Serbia

Birth date: unknown

Death date: Wertner, *Az Árpádok családi története*, 300–301

Marriage to Béla II of Hungary: Wertner, *Az Árpádok családi története*, 298.

Adelaide

Birth date: unknown

Death date: Wertner, *Az Árpádok családi története*, 286–87

Marriage to Soběslav: Wertner, *Az Árpádok családi története*, 286–87; *Annalista Saxo*, s.a. 1116 (references peace made between Hungary and Bohemia, which may have provided a proximate cause for the marriage); Cosmas of Prague, *Chronicle of the Czechs*, bk. 3, ch. 52.

Soběslav

Birth date: *Annalista Saxo*, s.a. 1061 (references his father, mother, and brothers together, but no specifics); Cosmas of Prague, *Chronicle of the Czechs*, bk. 3, ch. 20 (records his flight to Poland as a young man); conjectural based upon his father's death in 1192

Death date: Wolverton, *Hastening Toward Prague*, 11–12

Duke of Bohemia start: Cosmas of Prague, *Chronicle of the Czechs*, bk. 3, ch. 60; duke of Bohemia end: Wolverton, *Hastening Toward Prague*, 11–12
Marriage to Adelaide: Wertner, *Az Árpádok családi története*, 286–87; *Annalista Saxo*, s.a. 1116 (references peace made between Hungary and Bohemia, which may have provided a proximate cause for the marriage); Cosmas of Prague, *Chronicle of the Czechs*, bk. 3, ch. 52.

Hedwig
Birth date: unknown
Death date: Her death date can reasonably be assumed to have occurred after her marriage, though when is unknown.
Marriage to Adalbert of Babenberg: Otto, Bishop of Freising, *Two Cities*, bk. 7, sec. 21.

Adalbert of Babenberg
Birth date: unknown
Death date: Wertner, *Az Árpádok családi története*, 293–95
Marriage to daughter of Almos II of Hungary: Otto, Bishop of Freising, *Two Cities*, bk. 7, sec. 21.

Konstantin Petrovič
Birth date: unknown
Death date: unknown
Ruler of Skrzynno: *Chronica Poloniae Maioris*, ch. 32.

Svjatoslav Petrovič
Birth date: unknown
Death date: unknown; existence cited in "Spominki Wrocławskie," in *Monumenta Poloniae Historica*, ed. Aleksander Semkowicz, 3:732–34 (Lviv: W Komisie księgarni gubrynowicza I schmidta, 1878), 732.

Jaksa of Miechów
Birth date: unknown
Death date: unknown
Prince of Miechów: *Chronica Poloniae Maioris*, ch. 32 (text reads prince of Sorabia, editor corrects to Miechów)
Marriage to N. N. Petrovna: *Chronica Poloniae Maioris*, ch. 32.

N. N. Petrovna
Birth date: unknown
Death date: unknown
Marriage to Jaksa of Miechów: *Chronica Poloniae Maioris*, ch. 32.

Table 10: Oleg Svjatoslavič

Oleg Svjatoslavič
Birth date: Dimnik, *Dynasty of Chernigov, 1054–1146*, 39
Death date: *NPL*, s.a. 1115; Laurentian Chronicle, s.a. 1115; Hypatian Chronicle, s.a. 1115; Tver Chronicle, s.a. 1115; Nikon Chronicle, s.a. 1115 (also listed s.a. 1117)
Knjaz´ of Tmutorokan (1) start: *PVL*, s.a. 1078; knjaz´ of Tmutorokan (1) end: *PVL*, s.a. 1079
Knjaz´ of Tmutorokan (2) start: *PVL*, s.a. 1083; knjaz´ of Tmutorokan (2) end: *PVL*, s.a. 1094
Knjaz´ of Černihiv start: *PVL*, s.a. 1094; knjaz´ of Černihiv end: *PVL*, s.a. 1096
Knjaz´ of Novhorod-Siverskyj start: slightly conjectural based upon a division of Svjatoslav's territory in *PVL*, s.a. 1097; clear that his descendants rule there; knjaz´ of Novhorod-Siverskyj end: *NPL*, s.a. 1115; Laurentian Chronicle, s.a. 1115; Hypatian Chronicle, s.a. 1115; Tver Chronicle, s.a. 1115; Nikon Chronicle, s.a. 1115 (also listed s.a. 1117)
Marriage to unknown partner: this relationship has a complicated history. For a discussion of the issues, see part 1, "Marriages: Generation Three," "Oleg Svjatoslavič."

Unknown partner of Oleg Svjatoslavič
Birth date: unknown
Death date: unknown
Marriage to Oleg Svjatoslavič: This relationship has a complicated history; for a discussion of the issues, see part 1, "Marriages: Generation Three," "Oleg Svjatoslavič."

Vsevolod Ol´govič
Birth date: unknown
Death date: *NPL*, s.a. 1146; Hypatian Chronicle, s.a. 1146; *NČL*, s.a.

Table 10: Oleg Svjatoslavič

Oleg Svjatoslavič
b. 1050; d. 1115
(Tmutorokan r. 1078–1079)
(Tmutorokan r. 1083–1094)
(Černihiv r. 1094–1096)
(Novhorod-Siverskyj r. ca. 1097–1115)

Unknown
b. d. unknown
(m. unknown)

Vsevolod
b. unknown; d. 1146
(Černihiv r. 1127–1139)
(Kyiv r. 1139–1146)

Marija,
daughter of M′stislav
Volodimerič
b. unknown; d. 1178
(m. ca. 1127)

Igor′
b. unknown; d. 1147
(Gorodec r. 1142–1146)
(Kyiv r. 1146)

N. N.,
daughter of Jurij
Volodimerič
b. unknown;
d. ca. 1165
(m. 1150)

1

Oleg
b. unknown; d. 1178
(Novhorod-Siverskyj
r. 1164–1178)

2

Agafija,
daughter of Rostislav
M′stislavič
b. unknown;
d. post-1165
(m. 1165)

N. N.
b. unknown;
d. post-1148
(m. 1148)

Roman Rostislavič
b. unknown; d. 1180
(Novgorod r. 1155)
(Smolensk r. 1160–1174)
(Kyiv r. 1174)
(Smolensk r. 1174–1175)
(Kyiv r. 1175–1177)
(Smolensk r. 1177–1180)
(Novgorod r. 1178–1179)

Svjatoslav
b. unknown; d. 1194
(Turov r. 1142)
(Volodymyr r. 1142–1146)
(Busk r. 1146–ca. 1154)
(Turov r. 1154–1155)
(Novhorod-Siverskyj r. 1158–1164)
(Černihiv r. 1164–1177)
(Kyiv r. 1174)
(Kyiv r. 1177–1180)
(Novgorod r. 1180–1181)
(Kyiv r. 1180–1194)

N. N., daughter of
Vasil′ko Svjatoslavič
b. unknown;
d. post-1143
(m. 1143)

Zvenislava
b. unknown;
d. post-1142
(m. 1142)

Bolesław the Tall
b. unknown;
d. 1201

Jaroslav
b. 1140; d. 1198
(Cernihiv r. 1177–1198)

Glěb
b. unknown; d. 1138
(Kursk r. pre-1137–1138)

Unknown
b. d. unknown
(m. unknown)

Izjaslav
b. unknown; d. 1134

N. N., daughter of Khan Aepa, son of Girgen
b. unknown; d. pre-1136
(m. 1107)

1

Svjatoslav
b. unknown; d. 1164
(Novgorod r. 1136–1138)
(Kursk r. 1138–1139)
(Novgorod r. 1139–1141)
(Bilhorod r. 1141–ca.1146)
(Novhorod-Siverskyj r. ca.1146– 1158)
(Černihiv r. 1158–1164)

2

N. N.
b. unknown; d. 1166
(m. 1136)
(Černihiv r. 1164)

unknown mothers

Igor´
b. unknown; d. 1202
(Novhorod-Siverskyj r. 1178–1198)
(Černihiv r. 1198–1202)

Evfrosinija, daughter of Jaroslav Volodimerkovič
b. unknown;
d. post-1169
(m. after 1169)

Vsevolod
b. unknown;
d. 1196
(Trubeck r. pre-1185–1196)

N. N., daughter of Glěb Jurevič
b. d. unknown
(m. unknown)

Marija
b. 1149;
d. post-1166
(m. 1166)

Jaropolk Izjaslavič
b. unknown;
d. 1170
(Busk r. pre-1168–1170)

1146; Voskresenskij Chronicle, s.a. 1146; Rogožskij Chronicle, s.a. 1146; Tver Chronicle, s.a. 1146; Nikon Chronicle, s.a. 1146

Knjaz′ of Černihiv start: Hypatian Chronicle, s.a. 1128; Voskresenskij Chronicle, s.a. 1127; Tver Chronicle, s.a. 1127; Nikon Chronicle, s.a. 1127; knjaz′ of Černihiv end: Laurentian Chronicle, s.a. 1138; *NČL*, s.a. 1138; Voskresenskij Chronicle, s.a. 1138; Nikon Chronicle, s.a. 1138

Knjaz′ of Kyiv start: *NPL*, s.a. 1139; Laurentian Chronicle, s.a. 1138; Hypatian Chronicle, s.a. 1140; *NČL*, s.a. 1138; Voskresenskij Chronicle, s.a. 1138; Rogožskij Chronicle, s.a. 1138; Tver Chronicle, s.a. 1138; Nikon Chronicle, s.a. 1138; knjaz′ of Kyiv end: *NPL*, s.a. 1146; Hypatian Chronicle, s.a. 1146; *NČL*, s.a. 1146; Voskresenskij Chronicle, s.a. 1146; Rogožskij Chronicle, s.a. 1146; Tver Chronicle, s.a. 1146; Nikon Chronicle, s.a. 1146

Marriage to Marija M′stislavna: Hypatian Chronicle, s.a. 1141 (obliquely); Dimnik, *Dynasty of Chernigov, 1054–1146*, 254–55; date conjectural based upon my analysis; Dąbrowski comes to a similar conclusion; see Dąbrowski, *Genealogia Mścisławowiczów*, 148–55 (for the whole entry on Marija). For more information on this marriage see part 1, "Marriages: Generation Four," "Vsevolod Ol′govič."

Marija M′stislavna

Birth date: unknown

Death date: Hypatian Chronicle, s.a. 1178

Marriage to Vsevolod Ol′govič: Hypatian Chronicle, s.a. 1141 (obliquely); Dimnik, *Dynasty of Chernigov, 1054–1146*, 254–55; date conjectural based upon my analysis; Dąbrowski comes to a similar conclusion; see Dąbrowski, *Genealogia Mścisławowiczów*, 148–55 (for the whole entry on Marija). For more information on this marriage see part 1, "Marriages: Generation Four," "Vsevolod Ol′govič."

Igor′ Ol′govič

Birth date: unknown

Death date: Laurentian Chronicle, s.a. 1147; *NPL*, s.a. 1147; *NČL*, s.a. 1147; Hypatian Chronicle, s.a. 1147; Tver Chronicle, s.a. 1147; Voskresenskij Chronicle, s.a. 1147; Nikon Chronicle, s.a. 1147

Knjaz′ of Gorodec start: Hypatian Chronicle, s.a. 1142; knjaz′ of Gorodec end: conjectural based upon his forced entrance into a monastery

Knjaz′ of Kyiv start and end: *NPL*, s.a. 1146; Laurentian Chronicle, s.a. 1146; Hypatian Chronicle, s.a. 1146; *NČL*, s.a. 1146; Tver Chronicle, s.a. 1146; Nikon Chronicle, s.a. 1146.

Glěb Ol′govič
Birth date: unknown
Death date: Laurentian Chronicle, s.a. 1138
Knjaz′ of Kursk start: *NPL*, s.a. 1137; *NČL*, s.a. 1137; Voskresenskij Chronicle, s.a. 1137 (first mention); knjaz′ of Kursk end: Laurentian Chronicle, s.a. 1138
Marriage to unknown woman: conjectural based upon the existence of their son, cited in Hypatian Chronicle, s.a. 1134.

Unknown partner of Glěb Ol′govič
Birth date: unknown
Death date: unknown
Marriage to Glěb Ol′govič: conjectural based upon the existence of their son, cited in Hypatian Chronicle, s.a. 1134.

N. N., daughter of Khan Aepa, son of Girgen
Birth date: unknown
Death date: conjectural based upon Svjatoslav's second marriage
Marriage to Svjatoslav Ol′govič: Laurentian Chronicle, s.a. 1107; Hypatian Chronicle, s.a. 1107; Nikon Chronicle, s.a. 1107. For more on this marriage see part 1, "Marriages: Generation Four," "Svjatoslav Ol′govič."

Svjatoslav Ol′govič
Birth date: unknown
Death date: Hypatian Chronicle, s.a. 1164; Tver Chronicle, s.a. 1164; Voskresenskij Chronicle, s.a. 1164; Nikon Chronicle, s.a. 1165
Knjaz′ of Novgorod (1) start: *NPL*, s.a. 1136; Hypatian Chronicle, s.a. 1138; Laurentian Chronicle, s.a. 1138; *NČL*, s.a. 1136; Pskov Chronicle, s.a. 1138; Voskresenskij Chronicle, s.a. 1136; Tver Chronicle, s.a. 1136; Nikon Chronicle, s.a. 1135; knjaz′ of Novgorod (1) end: *NPL*, s.a. 1138; Laurentian Chronicle, s.a. 1138; Hypatian Chronicle, s.a. 1139; *NČL*, s.a. 1138; Voskresenskij Chronicle, s.a. 1138; Tver Chronicle, s.a. 1138; Nikon Chronicle, s.a. 1138
Knjaz′ of Kursk start: conjectural based upon death of Glěb, and expulsion from Novgorod; knjaz′ of Kursk end: Nikon Chronicle, s.a. 1139 (has him summoned from Kursk)
Knjaz′ of Novgorod (2) start: *NPL*, s.a. 1139; Laurentian Chronicle, s.a. 1139; Hypatian Chronicle, s.a. 1140; *NČL*, s.a. 1139; Voskresenskij Chronicle, s.a. 1139; Tver Chronicle, s.a 1139; Nikon Chronicle, s.a. 1139; knjaz′ of Novgorod (2) end: *NPL*, s.a. 1141; Hypatian Chronicle, s.a. 1140; Voskresenskij Chronicle, s.a. 1140; Tver Chronicle, s.a. 1141; Nikon Chronicle, s.a. 1140
Knjaz′ of Bilhorod start: Hypatian Chronicle, s.a. 1141; knjaz′ of Bil-

horod end: conjectural based upon the death of Vsevolod and the assumption of power in Novhorod-Siverskyj

Knjaz´ of Novhorod-Siverskyj start: Hypatian Chronicle, s.a. 1146 (has him fighting for these lands versus his cousins, the Davydoviči); Hypatian Chronicle, s.a. 1148 (has his daughter sent from here in marriage), Nikon Chronicle, s.a. 1152 (has him ruling here outright); knjaz´ of Novhorod-Siverskyj end: Hypatian Chronicle, s.a. 1158; Nikon Chronicle, s.a. 1157

Knjaz´ of Černihiv start: Hypatian Chronicle, s.a. 1158; Tver Chronicle, s.a. 1157; Voskresenskij Chronicle, s.a. 1157; Nikon Chronicle, s.a. 1157; knjaz´ of Černihiv end: Hypatian Chronicle, s.a. 1164; Tver Chronicle, s.a. 1164; Voskresenskij Chronicle, s.a. 1164; Nikon Chronicle, s.a. 1165

Marriage to N. N., daughter of Khan Aepa, son of Girgen: Laurentian Chronicle, s.a. 1107; Hypatian Chronicle, s.a. 1107; Nikon Chronicle, s.a. 1107

Marriage to N. N., wife of Svjatoslav Ol´govič: *NPL*, s.a. 1136; *NČL*, s.a. 1136; Voskresenskij Chronicle, s.a. 1136; Tver Chronicle, s.a. 1136; for a possible identification see Dimnik, *Dynasty of Chernigov, 1054–1146*, 337–40. For more information on these marriages see part 1, "Marriages: Generation Four," "Svjatoslav Ol´govič."

N. N., wife of Svjatoslav Ol´govič

Birth date: unknown

Death date: Hypatian Chronicle, s.a. 1166; knjaginja of Černihiv: Hypatian Chronicle, s.a. 1164

Marriage to Svjatoslav Ol´govič: *NPL*, s.a. 1136; *NČL*, s.a. 1136; Voskresenskij Chronicle, s.a. 1136; Tver Chronicle, s.a. 1136; for a possible identification see Dimnik, *Dynasty of Chernigov, 1054–1146*, 337–40. For more information on this marriage see part 1, "Marriages: Generation Four," "Svjatoslav Ol´govič."

Svjatoslav Vsevolodič

Birth date: unknown

Death date: Hypatian Chronicle, s.a. 1194; Laurentian Chronicle, s.a. 1195; Voskresenskij Chronicle, s.a. 1194; Nikon Chronicle, s.a. 1194

Knjaz´ of Turov (1): Laurentian Chronicle, s.a. 1142; Voskresenskij Chronicle, s.a. 1142; Tver Chronicle, s.a. 1142; Nikon Chronicle, s.a. 1142

Knjaz´ of Volodymyr start: Laurentian Chronicle, s.a. 1142; Hypatian Chronicle, s.a. 1142; Voskresenskij Chronicle, s.a. 1142; Tver Chronicle, s.a. 1142; Nikon Chronicle, s.a. 1142; knjaz´ of Volodymyr end: Hypatian Chronicle, s.a. 1146

Knjaz´ of Busk start: Hypatian Chronicle, s.a. 1146; Voskresenskij

Chronicle, s.a. 1147 (he also rules four other towns near Kyiv); knjaz′ of Busk end: conjectural based upon his assumption of power in Turov and Pinsk

Knjaz′ of Turov (2) start: Hypatian Chronicle, s.a. 1154; Voskresenskij Chronicle, s.a. 1154; knjaz′ of Turov (2) end: Hypatian Chronicle, s.a. 1155

Knjaz′ of Novhorod-Siverskyj start: Hypatian Chronicle, s.a. 1158; Tver Chronicle, s.a. 1157; Voskresenskij Chronicle, s.a. 1157; Nikon Chronicle, s.a. 1157; knjaz′ of Novhorod-Siverskyj end: Hypatian Chronicle, s.a. 1164; Tver Chronicle, s.a. 1164; Voskresenskij Chronicle, s.a. 1164; Nikon Chronicle, s.a. 1165

Knjaz′ of Černihiv start: Hypatian Chronicle, s.a. 1164; Tver Chronicle, s.a. 1164; Laurentian Chronicle, s.a. 1175 (references him there); Voskresenskij Chronicle, s.a. 1164; Nikon Chronicle, s.a. 1165; knjaz′ of Černihiv end: Hypatian Chronicle, s.a. 1177 (has him assume power in Kyiv); Hypatian Chronicle, s.a. 1178 (has his brother ruling in Černihiv)

Knjaz′ of Kyiv (1): Hypatian Chronicle, s.a. 1174; Tver Chronicle, s.a. 1175; Laurentian Chronicle, s.a. 1175; Voskresenskij Chronicle, s.a. 1174; Nikon Chronicle, s.a. 1175 (rules there for no more than fifteen days)

Knjaz′ of Kyiv (2) start: Hypatian Chronicle, s.a. 1177; knjaz′ of Kyiv (2) end: Hypatian Chronicle, s.a. 1180

Knjaz′ of Kyiv (3) start: Hypatian Chronicle, s.a. 1180; Laurentian Chronicle, s.a. 1185 (notes him as ruler in Kyiv); Voskresenskij Chronicle, s.a. 1181; Nikon Chronicle, s.a. 1185 (already ruling there); knjaz′ of Kyiv (3) end: Hypatian Chronicle, s.a. 1194; Laurentian Chronicle, s.a. 1195; Voskresenskij Chronicle, s.a. 1194; Nikon Chronicle, s.a. 1194

Knjaz′ of Novgorod: *NPL*, s.a. 1180, 1181 (record a brief reign as ruler of Novgorod that is recorded in no other source)

Marriage to N. N., daughter of Vasil′ko Svjatoslavič: Laurentian Chronicle, s.a. 1143; Hypatian Chronicle, s.a. 1143; Voskresenskij Chronicle, s.a. 1143; Rogožskij Chronicle, s.a. 1143; Nikon Chronicle, s.a. 1143. For more information on this marriage see part 1, "Marriages: Generation Five," "Svjatoslav Vsevolodič."

N. N., daughter of Vasil′ko Svjatoslavič

Birth date: unknown

Death date: Her death date can reasonably be assumed to have occurred after her marriage, though when is unknown.

Marriage to Svjatoslav Vsevolodič: Laurentian Chronicle, s.a. 1143; Hypatian Chronicle, s.a. 1143; Voskresenskij Chronicle, s.a. 1143; Rogožskij Chronicle, s.a. 1143; Nikon Chronicle, s.a. 1143. For more information on this marriage see part 1, "Marriages: Generation Five," "Svjatoslav Vsevolodič."

Zvenislava Vsevolodovna
Birth date: unknown
Death date: Her death date can reasonably be assumed to have occurred after her marriage, though when is unknown.
Marriage to Bolesław "the Tall": Hypatian Chronicle, s.a. 1141, 1142. For more information on this marriage see part 1, "Marriages: Generation Five," "Zvenislava Vsevolodovna."

Bolesław "the Tall"
Birth date: unknown
Death date: H. Grotefend, *Stammtafeln der schlesischen Fürstenbis zum jahre 1740* (Breslau: Josef Max and Comp., 1889), table 1
Marriage to Zvenislava Vsevolodovna: Hypatian Chronicle, s.a. 1141, 1142. For more information on this marriage see part 1, "Marriages: Generation Five," "Zvenislava Vsevolodovna."

Jaroslav Vsevolodič
Birth date: Hypatian Chronicle, s.a. 1140
Death date: Hypatian Chronicle, s.a. 1198; Tver Chronicle, s.a. 1200; Laurentian Chronicle, s.a. 1200; Voskresenskij Chronicle, s.a. 1200; Nikon Chronicle, s.a. 1200
Knjaz´ of Černihiv start: Hypatian Chronicle, s.a. 1178; *NPL*, s.a. 1195; Nikon Chronicle, s.a. 1195 (both *NPL* and Nikon Chronicle reference him ruling there); knjaz´ of Černihiv end: Hypatian Chronicle, s.a. 1198; Tver Chronicle, s.a. 1200; Laurentian Chronicle, s.a. 1200; Voskresenskij Chronicle, s.a. 1200; Nikon Chronicle, s.a. 1200.

Izjaslav Glěbovič
Birth date: unknown
Death date: Hypatian Chronicle, s.a. 1134.

N. N., daughter of Jurij Volodimerič
Birth date: unknown
Death date: Voskresenskij Chronicle, s.a. 1166 (where she is referred to mistakenly as Andreevna, but it is made explicit that after her death, Oleg marries the daughter of Rostislav); Hypatian Chronicle, s.a. 1167 (where she is referred to mistakenly as Andreevna)
Marriage to Oleg Svjatoslavič: Hypatian Chronicle, s.a. 1150.

Oleg Svjatoslavič
Birth date: unknown

Death date: Hypatian Chronicle, s.a. 1178; Zotov, *O černigovskix knjazjax*, 269, notes an 1180 date for his death
Knjaz´ of Novhorod-Siverskyj start: Hypatian Chronicle, s.a. 1164; Tver Chronicle, s.a. 1164; Voskresenskij Chronicle, s.a. 1164; Nikon Chronicle, s.a. 1165; knjaz´ of Novhorod-Siverskyj end: Hypatian Chronicle, s.a. 1178
Marriage to N. N., daughter of Jurij Volodimerič: Hypatian Chronicle, s.a. 1150
Marriage to Agafija Rostislavna: Hypatian Chronicle, s.a. 1165; Voskresenskij Chronicle, s.a. 1166.

Agafija Rostislavna
Birth date: unknown
Death date: Her death date can reasonably be assumed to have occurred after her marriage, though when is unknown.
Marriage to Oleg Svjatoslavič: Hypatian Chronicle, s.a. 1165; Voskresenskij Chronicle, s.a. 1166.

N. N. Svjatoslavna
Birth date: unknown
Death date: Her death date can reasonably be assumed to have occurred after her marriage, though when is unknown.
Marriage to Roman Rostislavič: Hypatian Chronicle, s.a. 1148; Tver Chronicle, s.a. 1149; Voskresenskij Chronicle, s.a. 1149; Nikon Chronicle, s.a. 1149.

Roman Rostislavič
Birth date: unknown
Death date: Hypatian Chronicle, s.a. 1180
Knjaz´ of Novgorod (1): Tver Chronicle, s.a. 1155; Laurentian Chronicle, s.a. 1154; Voskresenskij Chronicle, s.a. 1154; Nikon Chronicle, s.a. 1154
Knjaz´ of Smolensk (1) start: Hypatian Chronicle, s.a. 1160; Laurentian Chronicle, s.a. 1168; Nikon Chronicle, s.a. 1170 (both Laurentian and Nikon are first mentions of his rule there); knjaz´ of Smolensk (1) end: Hypatian Chronicle, s.a. 1174; Voskresenskij Chronicle, s.a. 1172; Nikon Chronicle, s.a. 1172
Knjaz´ of Kyiv (1) start: *NPL*, s.a. 1171; Hypatian Chronicle, s.a. 1174; Rogožskij Chronicle, s.a. 1172; Tver Chronicle, s.a. 1172; Laurentian Chronicle, s.a. 1172; Voskresenskij Chronicle, s.a. 1172; Nikon Chronicle, s.a. 1172; knjaz´ of Kyiv (1) end: *NPL*, s.a. 1172; Hypatian Chronicle, s.a. 1174; Tver Chronicle, s.a. 1173; Voskresenskij Chronicle, s.a. 1174; Nikon Chronicle, s.a. 1172

Knjaz´ of Smolensk (2) start: Hypatian Chronicle, s.a. 1174; knjaz´ of Smolensk (2) end: Hypatian Chronicle, s.a. 1175
Knjaz´ of Kyiv (2) start: *NPL*, s.a. 1174; Hypatian Chronicle, s.a. 1175; Tver Chronicle, s.a. 1176; knjaz´ of Kyiv (2) end: Hypatian Chronicle, s.a. 1177
Knjaz´ of Smolensk (3) start: Hypatian Chronicle, s.a. 1177; Voskresenskij Chronicle, s.a. 1179 (notes him in Smolensk); knjaz´ of Smolensk (3) end: Hypatian Chronicle, s.a. 1180
Knjaz´ of Novgorod (2) start: *NPL*, s.a. 1178; Tver Chronicle, s.a. 1178; Nikon Chronicle, s.a. 1180; knjaz´ of Novgorod (2) end: *NPL*, s.a. 1179; Tver Chronicle, s.a. 1179; Nikon Chronicle, s.a. 1180
Marriage to N. N. Svjatoslavna: Hypatian Chronicle, s.a. 1148; Tver Chronicle, s.a. 1149; Voskresenskij Chronicle, s.a. 1149; Nikon Chronicle, s.a. 1149.

Igor´ Svjatoslavič
Birth date: unknown
Death date: Tver Chronicle, s.a. 1202; Laurentian Chronicle, s.a. 1202; Voskresenskij Chronicle, s.a. 1202; Nikon Chronicle, s.a. 1202
Knjaz´ of Novhorod-Siverskyj start: Hypatian Chronicle, s.a. 1178; knjaz´ of Novhorod-Siverskyj end: conjectural upon his assumption of power in Černihiv
Knjaz´ of Černihiv start: Hypatian Chronicle, s.a. 1198; knjaz´ of Černihiv end: Tver Chronicle, s.a. 1202; Laurentian Chronicle, s.a. 1202; Voskresenskij Chronicle, s.a. 1202; Nikon Chronicle, s.a. 1202
Marriage to Evfrosinija Jaroslavna: Zotov, *O černigovskix knjazjax*, 270.

Evfrosinija Jaroslavna
Birth date: unknown
Death date: Her death date can reasonably be assumed to have occurred after her marriage, though when is unknown.
Marriage to Igor´ Svjatoslavič: Zotov, *O černigovskix knjazjax*, 270.

Vsevolod Svjatoslavič
Birth date: unknown
Death date: Hypatian Chronicle, s.a. 1196
Knjaz´ of Trubeck: Hypatian Chronicle, s.a. 1185; Tver Chronicle, s.a. 1186 (first mention as ruler there); knjaz´ of Trubeck end: Hypatian Chronicle, s.a. 1196
Marriage to N. N. Glěbovna: Zotov, *O černigovskix knjazjax*, 271.

N. N., daughter of Glěb Jurevič
Birth date: unknown

Death date: unknown
Marriage to Vsevolod Svjatoslavič: Zotov, *O černigovskix knjazjax*, 271.

Marija Svjatoslavna
Birth date: Hypatian Chronicle, s.a. 1149
Death date: Her death date can reasonably be assumed to have occurred after her marriage, though when is unknown.
Marriage to Jaropolk Izjaslavič: Hypatian Chronicle, s.a. 1166; Voskresenskij Chronicle, s.a. 1166.

Jaropolk Izjaslavič
Birth date: unknown
Death date: Hypatian Chronicle, s.a. 1170
Knjaz´ of Busk start: Hypatian Chronicle, s.a. 1168; Voskresenskij Chronicle, s.a. 1167 (first mention as ruler there); knjaz´ of Busk end: Hypatian Chronicle, s.a. 1170
Marriage to Marija Svjatoslavna: Hypatian Chronicle, s.a. 1166; Voskresenskij Chronicle, s.a. 1166.

Table 11: Davyd Svjatoslavič

Davyd Svjatoslavič

Birth date: Dimnik, *Dynasty of Chernigov, 1054–1146*, 39–40

Death date: Laurentian Chronicle, s.a. 1123; Hypatian Chronicle, s.a. 1123; Voskresenskij Chronicle, s.a. 1123; Tver Chronicle, s.a. 1123; Nikon Chronicle, s.a. 1123

Knjaz´ of Novgorod start: conjectural based upon the end date of Svjatopolk Izjaslavič's rule in Novgorod; knjaz´ of Novgorod end: *PVL*, s.a. 1095

Knjaz´ of Smolensk start: *PVL*, s.a. 1095; knjaz´ of Smolensk end: conjectural based upon his possession of the inheritance of Svjatoslav mentioned in *PVL*, s.a. 1097

Knjaz´ of Černihiv: conjectural based upon his possession of the inheritance of Svjatoslav mentioned in *PVL*, s.a. 1097; knjaz´ of Černihiv end: Laurentian Chronicle, s.a. 1123; Hypatian Chronicle, s.a. 1123; Voskresenskij Chronicle, s.a. 1123; Tver Chronicle, s.a. 1123; Nikon Chronicle, s.a. 1123

Relationship with unknown partner: based on a child cited in Hypatian Chronicle, s.a. 1124; and elsewhere.

Unknown partner of Davyd Svjatoslavič

Birth date: unknown

Death date: unknown

Relationship with Davyd Svjatoslavič: based on a child cited in Hypatian Chronicle, s.a. 1124; and elsewhere.

Svjatoša (Nicola) Davydič

Birth date: unknown

Death date: Dimnik, *Dynasty of Chernigov, 1054–1146*, 398

Knjaz´ of Luck start: *PVL*, s.a. 1097 (already ruling there); knjaz´ of Luck end: *PVL*, s.a. 1097; takes monastic vows: *PVL*, s.a. 1106.

Table 11: Davyd Svjatoslavič

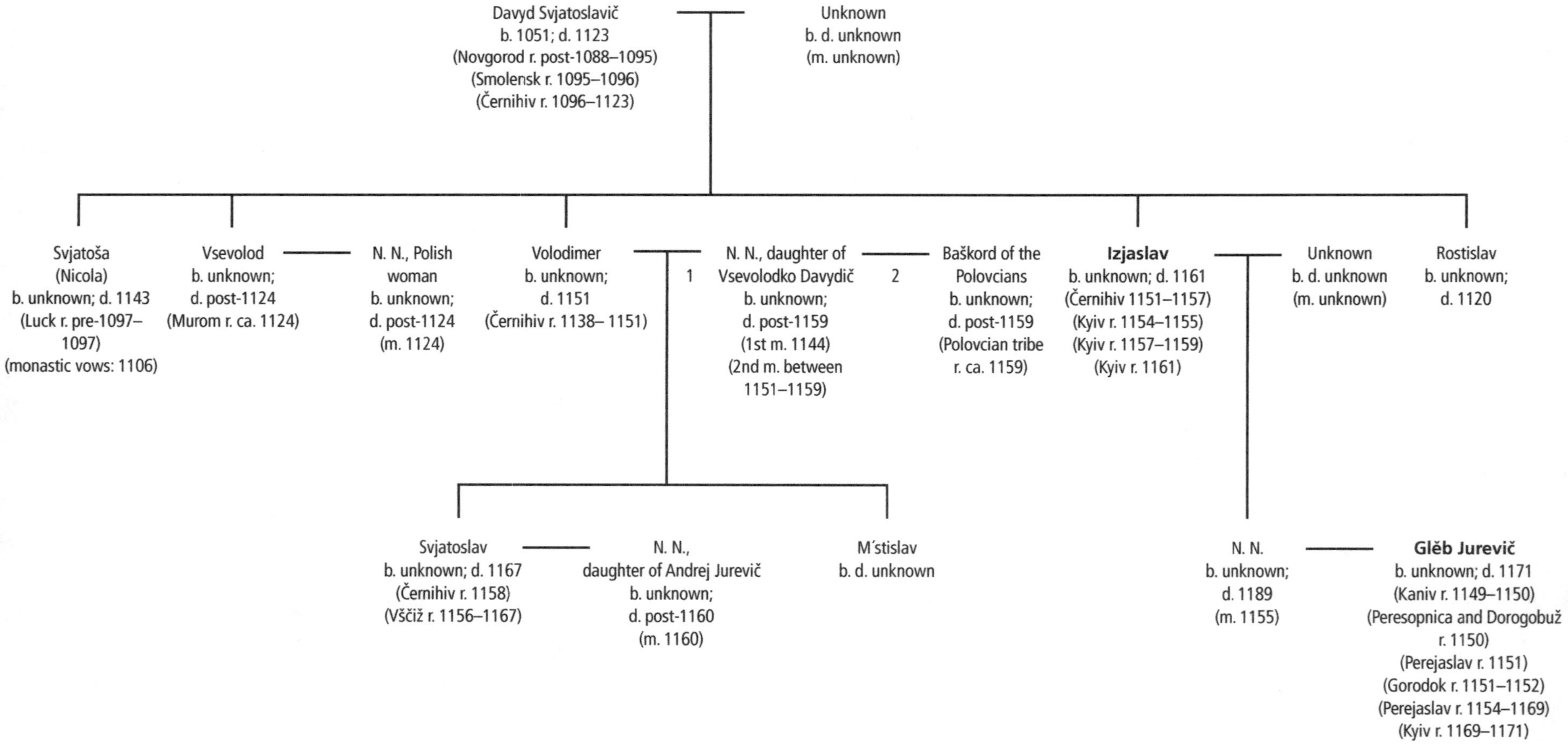

Vsevolod Davydič
Birth date: unknown
Death date: Hypatian Chronicle, s.a. 1124; Voskresenskij Chronicle, s.a. 1124 (last mention of him in the primary sources)
Knjaz′ of Murom: Hypatian Chronicle, s.a. 1124; Voskresenskij Chronicle, s.a. 1124 (listed as receiving a bride there)
Marriage to N. N., Polish woman: Hypatian Chronicle, s.a. 1124; Voskresenskij Chronicle, s.a. 1124. For more information on this marriage see part 1, "Marriages: Generation Four," "Vsevolod Davydič."

N. N., Polish woman
Birth date: unknown
Death date: Her death date can reasonably be assumed to have occurred after her marriage, though when is unknown.
Marriage to Vsevolod Davydič: Hypatian Chronicle, s.a. 1124; Voskresenskij Chronicle, s.a. 1124. For more information on this marriage see part 1, "Marriages: Generation Four," "Vsevolod Davydič."

Volodimer Davydič
Birth date: unknown
Death date: Hypatian Chronicle, s.a. 1151; Laurentian Chronicle, s.a. 1151; Voskresenskij Chronicle, s.a. 1151; Nikon Chronicle, s.a. 1151
Knjaz′ of Černihiv start: Laurentian Chronicle, s.a. 1138; Voskresenskij Chronicle, s.a. 1138; Nikon Chronicle, s.a. 1138; knjaz′ of Černihiv end: Hypatian Chronicle, s.a. 1151; Laurentian Chronicle, s.a. 1151; Voskresenskij Chronicle, s.a. 1151; Nikon Chronicle, s.a. 1151
Marriage to N. N. Vsevolodkovna: Hypatian Chronicle, s.a. 1144. For more information on this marriage see part 1, "Marriages: Generation Four," "Volodimer Davydič."

N. N. Vsevolodkovna
Birth date: unknown
Death date: Her death date can reasonably be assumed to have occurred after her marriage, though when is unknown.
Marriage to Volodimer Davydič: Hypatian Chronicle, s.a. 1144
Marriage to Baškord of the Polovcians: Tver Chronicle, s.a. 1159; Nikon Chronicle, s.a. 1158. For more information on these marriages see part 1, "Marriages: Generation Four," "Volodimer Davydič."

Baškord of the Polovcians
Birth date: unknown
Death date: His death presumably occurred only after he is mentioned

in various sources as a knjaz´ of the Polovcians; see Tver Chronicle, s.a. 1159; Nikon Chronicle, s.a. 1158.

Knjaz´ of Polovcians: Tver Chronicle, s.a. 1159; Nikon Chronicle, s.a. 1158 (only mentions as ruler)

Marriage to N. N. Vsevolodkovna: Tver Chronicle, s.a. 1159; Nikon Chronicle, s.a. 1158. For more on this marriage see part 1, "Marriages: Generation Four," "Volodimer Davydič."

Izjaslav Davydič

Birth date: unknown

Death date: *NPL*, s.a. 1160; Hypatian Chronicle, s.a. 1162; Voskresenskij Chronicle, s.a. 1160; Nikon Chronicle, s.a. 1159

Knjaz´ of Černihiv start: Hypatian Chronicle, s.a. 1151; Laurentian Chronicle, s.a. 1151; Voskresenskij Chronicle, s.a. 1151; Nikon Chronicle, s.a. 1151; knjaz´ of Černihiv end: Tver Chronicle, s.a. 1157

Knjaz´ of Kyiv (1) start: *NPL*, s.a. 1154; Hypatian Chronicle, s.a. 1154; Tver Chronicle, s.a. 1155; Laurentian Chronicle, s.a. 1154; Voskresenskij Chronicle, s.a. 1154; Nikon Chronicle, s.a. 1155; knjaz´ of Kyiv (1) end: *NPL*, s.a. 1155; Hypatian Chronicle, s.a. 1155; Tver Chronicle, s.a. 1155; Laurentian Chronicle, s.a. 1154; Voskresenskij Chronicle, s.a. 1154; Nikon Chronicle, s.a. 1155

Knjaz´ of Kyiv (2) start: *NPL*, s.a. 1157; Hypatian Chronicle, s.a. 1158; Tver Chronicle, s.a. 1157; Voskresenskij Chronicle, s.a. 1157; Nikon Chronicle, s.a. 1157; knjaz´ of Kyiv (2) end: *NPL*, s.a. 1158; Hypatian Chronicle, s.a. 1159; Tver Chronicle, s.a. 1159; Laurentian Chronicle, s.a. 1158; Voskresenskij Chronicle, s.a. 1159; Nikon Chronicle, s.a. 1158

Knjaz´ of Kyiv (3): Hypatian Chronicle, s.a. 1161, 1162; Nikon Chronicle, s.a. 1159; *NPL*, s.a. 1160; Voskresenskij Chronicle, s.a. 1160 (this third reign in Kyiv was brief, and lasted just while Rostislav M´stislavič gathered his forces and then counterattacked)

Relationship with unknown partner: conjectural based upon the citation to a child in Laurentian Chronicle, s.a. 1155, and elsewhere.

Unknown partner of Izjaslav Davydič

Birth date: unknown

Death date: unknown

Relationship with Izjaslav Davydič: conjectural based upon the citation to a child in Laurentian Chronicle, s.a. 1189.

Rostislav Davydič

Birth date: unknown

Death date: Hypatian Chronicle, s.a. 1120.

Svjatoslav Volodimerič
Birth date: unknown
Death date: Hypatian Chronicle, s.a. 1167; Tver Chronicle, s.a. 1166; Voskresenskij Chronicle, s.a. 1166; Nikon Chronicle, s.a. 1166
Knjaz´ of Černihiv start: Hypatian Chronicle, s.a. 1158; Tver Chronicle, s.a. 1157; Voskresenskij Chronicle, s.a. 1157; Nikon Chronicle, s.a. 1157; knjaz´ of Černihiv end: Hypatian Chronicle, s.a. 1158; Tver Chronicle, s.a. 1157; Voskresenskij Chronicle, s.a. 1157; Nikon Chronicle, s.a. 1157
Knjaz´ of Vščiž start: Hypatian Chronicle, s.a. 1156; Tver Chronicle, s.a. 1159; Voskresenskij Chronicle, s.a. 1159 (Tver and Voskresenskij are first mentions as ruler there); knjaz´ of Vščiž end: Hypatian Chronicle, s.a. 1167; Tver Chronicle, s.a. 1166; Voskresenskij Chronicle, s.a. 1166; Nikon Chronicle, s.a. 1166
Marriage to N. N., daughter of Andrej Jurevič: Hypatian Chronicle, s.a. 1160; Tver Chronicle, s.a. 1159; Laurentian Chronicle, s.a. 1159; Voskresenskij Chronicle, s.a. 1159.

N. N., daughter of Andrej Jurevič
Birth date: unknown
Death date: Her death date can reasonably be assumed to have occurred after her marriage, though when is unknown.
Marriage to Svjatoslav Volodimerič: Hypatian Chronicle, s.a. 1160; Tver Chronicle, s.a. 1159; Laurentian Chronicle, s.a. 1159; Voskresenskij Chronicle, s.a. 1159.

M´stislav Volodimerič
Birth date: unknown
Death date: unknown; existence cited in Tver Chronicle, s.a. 1146 (though the chronicler could be mistaken).

N. N. Izjaslavna
Birth date: unknown
Death date: Laurentian Chronicle, s.a. 1189
Marriage to Glěb Jurevič: Hypatian Chronicle, s.a. 1155; Tver Chronicle, s.a. 1155; Laurentian Chronicle, s.a. 1155; Voskresenskij Chronicle, s.a. 1155; Nikon Chronicle, s.a. 1155.

Glěb Jurevič
Birth date: unknown
Death date: *NPL*, s.a. 1170; Hypatian Chronicle, s.a. 1173; Rogožskij Chronicle, s.a. 1172; Tver Chronicle, s.a. 1171; Laurentian Chronicle, s.a. 1172; Voskresenskij Chronicle, s.a. 1172; Nikon Chronicle, s.a. 1172

Knjaz´ of Kaniv start: Hypatian Chronicle, s.a. 1149; knjaz´ of Kaniv end: Hypatian Chroncile, s.a. 1150 (assigned elsewhere)
Knjaz´ of Peresopnica and Dorogobuž: Hypatian Chronicle, s.a. 1150
Knjaz´ of Perejaslav (1): Hypatian Chronicle, s.a. 1151; Tver Chronicle, s.a. 1151; Laurentian Chronicle, s.a. 1151; Voskresenskij Chronicle, s.a. 1151; Nikon Chronicle, s.a. 1151
Knjaz´ of Gorodok start: Hypatian Chronicle, s.a. 1151; Tver Chronicle, s.a. 1151; Laurentian Chronicle, s.a. 1151; Voskresenskij Chronicle, s.a. 1151; Nikon Chronicle, s.a. 1151; knjaz´ of Gorodok end: conjectural based upon his riding with the Polovcians cited in Hypatian Chronicle, s.a. 1152, 1153
Knjaz´ of Perejaslav (2) start: Hypatian Chronicle, s.a. 1154; Tver Chronicle, s.a. 1155; Laurentian Chronicle, s.a. 1154; Voskresenskij Chronicle, s.a. 1154; Nikon Chronicle, s.a. 1155; knjaz´ of Perejaslav (2) end: Hypatian Chronicle, s.a. 1171; Voskresenskij Chronicle, s.a. 1170; placed in 1169 due to his assumption of power in Kyiv and his placement of his son in Perejaslav at that time
Knjaz´ of Kyiv start: Hypatian Chronicle, s.a. 1171; Tver Chronicle, s.a. 1170; Laurentian Chronicle, s.a. 1168 (listed under 1169 as well); Voskresenskij Chronicle, s.a. 1170; Nikon Chronicle, s.a. 1170; I have followed the Laurentian Chronicle's dating here, as I believe it fits the progression of rulers of Kyiv most accurately, though each of the chronicles gives slightly different dates; knjaz´ of Kyiv end: *NPL*, s.a. 1170; Hypatian Chronicle, s.a. 1173; Rogožskij Chronicle, s.a. 1172; Tver Chronicle, s.a. 1171; Laurentian Chronicle, s.a. 1172; Voskresenskij Chronicle, s.a. 1172; Nikon Chronicle, s.a. 1172; here again the dating is difficult and I have accepted the Hypatian's statement that Glěb ruled for two years to be accurate based upon looking at the various gaps in the dating and thus used 1171
Marriage to N. N., wife of Glěb Jurevič: Tver Chronicle, s.a. 1154; Hypatian Chronicle, s.a. 1154; Laurentian Chronicle, s.a. 1154; Voskresenskij Chronicle, s.a. 1154; Nikon Chronicle, s.a. 1154
Marriage to N. N. Izjaslavna: Hypatian Chronicle, s.a. 1155; Tver Chronicle, s.a. 1155; Laurentian Chronicle, s.a. 1155; Voskresenskij Chronicle, s.a. 1155; Nikon Chronicle, s.a. 1155.

Table 12: Volodimer "Monomax" Vsevolodič

Gyða Haroldsdottir
Birth date: unknown
Death date: *PVL*, s.a. 1107
Marriage to Volodimer "Monomax" Vsevolodič: Saxo Grammaticus, bk. 11, ch. 6, 58; Sturluson, *Heimskringla*, 702. For more on this marriage see part 1, "Marriages: Generation Three," "Volodimer 'Monomax' Vsevolodič."

Volodimer "Monomax" Vsevolodič
Birth date: *PVL*, s.a. 1053
Death date: Laurentian Chronicle, s.a. 1125; *NPL*, s.a. 1125; Rogožskij Chronicle, s.a. 1125; Tver Chronicle, s.a. 1125; Nikon Chronicle, s.a. 1125
Knjaz´ of Smolensk start: *PVL*, s.a. 1078; knjaz´ of Smolensk end: *PVL*, s.a. 1095 (based on the assumption that Davyd takes power in Smolensk in that year)
Knjaz´ of Černihiv start: *PVL*, s.a. 1078; knjaz´ of Černihiv end: *PVL*, s.a. 1094
Knjaz´ of Perejaslav start: *PVL*, s.a. 1094; knjaz´ of Perejaslav end: *PVL*, s.a. 1113 (conjectural based upon his assumption of power in Kyiv)
Knjaz´ of Kyiv start: Laurentian Chronicle, s.a. 1114; Hypatian Chronicle, s.a. 1113; *NPL*, s.a. 1113; Rogožskij Chronicle, s.a. 1114; Tver Chronicle, s.a. 1113; Nikon Chronicle, s.a. 1114; knjaz´ of Kyiv end: Laurentian Chronicle, s.a. 1125; *NPL*, s.a. 1125; Rogožskij Chronicle, s.a. 1125; Tver Chronicle, s.a. 1125; Nikon Chronicle, s.a. 1125
Marriage to Gyða Haroldsdottir: Saxo Grammaticus, bk. 11, ch. 6, 58; Sturluson, *Heimskringla*, 702
Marriage to N. N.: Laurentian Chronicle, s.a. 1126; Hypatian Chronicle, s.a. 1127; Voskresenskij Chronicle, s.a. 1126; Nikon Chronicle, s.a.

Table 12: Volodimer "Monomax" Vsevolodič

Gyða Haroldsdottir
b. unknown; d. 1107
(m. ca. 1074)

— 1 —

Volodimer "Monomax" Vsevolodič
b. 1053; d. 1125
(Smolensk r. ca. 1078–ca. 1095)
(Černihiv r. 1078–1094)
(Perejaslav r. 1094–1113)
(Kyiv r. ca. 1113–1125)

— 2 —

N. N.
b. unknown; d. 1126
(m. 1108)

Izjaslav
b. unknown;
d. 1096
(Kursk r. 1095–1096)
(Murom r. 1095–1096)

Svjatoslav
b. unknown; d. 1114
(Smolensk r. ca. 1096–1113)
(Perejaslav r. 1113–1114)

Elena of Ossetia
b. unknown;
d. post-1145
(m. 1116)

—

Jaropolk
b. unknown; d. 1139
(Minsk r. 1115–1116)
(Perejaslav r.1114–1132)
(Kyiv r. 1132–1139)
(Perejaslav r. 1134–1135)

Agafija
b. unknown;
d. post-1116
(m. 1116)

—

Vsevolodko Davydič
b. unknown;
d. 1141
(Hrodna r. pre-1127–1141)

N. N.
b. unknown;
d. post-1144
(m. 1144)

—

Jurij Jaroslavič
b. unknown; d. pre-1170
(Turov r. 1157–1158)
(Turov r. ca. 1160–pre-1170)

Kristín Ingesdottir of Sweden
b. unknown; d. 1122
(m. ca. 1095)

— 1 —

M´stislav "Harald"
b. 1076; d. 1132
(Novgorod r. 1095–1117)
(Bilhorod r. 1117–1125)
(Kyiv r. 1125–1132)

— 2 —

N. N. daughter of Dmitrij Zavidič
b. unknown;
d. post-1169
(m. 1122)

see table 13

Koloman of Hungary
b. unknown; d. 1116
(King of Hungary r. 1095–1116)

—

Evfimija
b. unknown;
d. 1138 (m. 1112)
(repudiated ca. 1112)

Judith, daughter of Bolesław III of Poland
b. unknown;
d. pre-1143
(m. ca. 1132)

— 1 —

Boris
b. 1114; d. 1156

— 2 —

N. N., Comnena of the Byzantine Empire
b. unknown;
d. post-1143
(m. ca. 1143)

Leo Diogenes of Byzantium
b. unknown;
d. 1116

Marija
b. unknown;
d. 1146
(m. 1116)

Vasil′ko
b. ca. 1116;
d. 1136

N. N. daughter of Volodar′ Rostislavič
b. unknown;
d. post-1113
(m. 1113)

Roman
b. unknown;
d. 1119
(Volodymyr r. 1118–1119)

N. N., daughter of Khan Aepa, son of Osen
b. unknown;
d. pre-1162
(m. 1107)

1

Jurij "Dolgorukij"
b. unknown; d. 1157
(Suzdal r. pre-1138–1157)
(Perejaslav r. 1132)
(Perejaslav r. 1135)
(Kyiv r. 1149–1150)
(Perejaslav r. 1151)
(Kyiv r. 1155–1157)
⋮
see table 14

2

N. N.
b. unknown;
d. post-1162
(m. pre-1162)

N. N. granddaughter of Tugorkhan of the Polovcians
b. unknown; d. post-1117
(m.1117)

Andrej
b. unknown; d. 1142
(Volodymyr r. 1119–1135)
(Perejaslav r. 1135–1142)

N. N.
b. d. unknown
(m. pre-1171)

Volodimer
b. unknown; d. 1171
(Peresopnica r. ca. 1152)
(Brest ca. 1153)
(Peresopnica and Dorogobuž r. 1157–1171)

Vjačeslav
b. unknown; d. 1154
(Smolensk r. 1113–pre-1127)
(Turov r. pre-1127–1132)
(Perejaslav r. 1132–1134)
(Turov r. 1134–1146)
(Kyiv r. 1139)
(Perejaslav r. 1142)
(Volodymyr r. 1146–1148)
(Vyšehorod r. 1150–1154)
(Kyiv [w/ Izjaslav M′stislavič] r. 1150–1154)
(Kyiv [w/ Rostislav M′stislavič] r. 1154)

Unknown
b. d. unknown
(m. unknown)

Mixailko
b. unknown; d. 1129
(Rjazan r. unknown–1129)

1126. For more on these marriages see part 1, "Marriages: Generation Three," "Volodimer 'Monomax' Vsevolodič."

N. N., wife of Volodimer "Monomax" Vsevolodič
Birth date: unknown
Death date: Laurentian Chronicle, s.a. 1126; Hypatian Chronicle, s.a. 1127; Voskresenskij Chronicle, s.a. 1126; Nikon Chronicle, s.a. 1126
Marriage to Volodimer "Monomax" Vsevolodič: Laurentian Chronicle, s.a. 1126; Hypatian Chronicle, s.a. 1127; Voskresenskij Chronicle, s.a. 1126; Nikon Chronicle, s.a. 1126. For more on these marriages see part 1, "Marriages: Generation Three," "Volodimer 'Monomax' Vsevolodič."

Kristín Ingesdottir of Sweden
Birth date: unknown
Death date: *NPL*, s.a. 1122; Laurentian Chronicle, s.a. 1122; Hypatian Chronicle, s.a. 1121; Voskresenskij Chronicle, s.a. 1122; Tver Chronicle, s.a. 1122; Nikon Chronicle, s.a. 1122
Marriage to M´stislav "Harald" Volodimerič: Wilhelm, "Wilhelmi abbatis genealogia regum Danorum," in *Scriptores minores historiae danicae medii aevi*, ed. M. C. Gertz (Copenhagen: I Kommission hos G. E. C. Gad, 1917), 182; Sturluson, *Heimskringla*, 702. For more information on this marriage see part 1, "Marriages: Generation Four," "M´stislav Volodimerič."

M´stislav "Harald" Volodimerič
Birth date: *PVL*, s.a. 1076
Death date: *NPL*, s.a. 1132; Laurentian Chronicle, s.a. 1132; Hypatian Chronicle, s.a. 1133; *NČL*, s.a. 1131; Voskresenskij Chronicle, s.a. 1131; Rogožskij Chronicle, s.a. 1132; Tver Chronicle, s.a. 1132; Nikon Chronicle, s.a. 1132
Knjaz´ of Novgorod start: *PVL*, s.a. 1095; knjaz´ of Novgorod end: *NPL*, s.a. 1117; Laurentian Chronicle, s.a. 1117; *NČL*, s.a. 1117; Hypatian Chronicle, s.a. 1117; Voskresenskij Chronicle, s.a. 1117; Tver Chronicle, s.a. 1117; Nikon Chronicle, s.a. 1117
Knjaz´ of Bilhorod start: *NPL*, s.a. 1117; Laurentian Chronicle, s.a. 1117; Hypatian Chronicle, s.a. 1117; *NČL*, s.a. 1117; Voskresenskij Chronicle, s.a. 1117; Tver Chronicle, s.a. 1117; Nikon Chronicle, s.a. 1117 (Hypatian, Voskresenskij, Tver, and Nikon all specifically refer to Bilhorod, while the rest simply assume a move to assist his father in Kyiv); knjaz´ of Bilhorod end: *NPL*, s.a. 1125; Laurentian Chronicle, s.a. 1125; Hypatian Chronicle, s.a. 1126; Voskresenskij Chronicle, s.a. 1125; Tver Chronicle, s.a. 1125

Knjaz´ of Kyiv start: *NPL*, s.a. 1125; Laurentian Chronicle, s.a. 1125; Hypatian Chronicle, s.a. 1126; *NČL*, s.a. 1125; Voskresenskij Chronicle, s.a. 1125; Rogožskij Chronicle, s.a. 1125; Tver Chronicle, s.a. 1125; Nikon Chronicle, s.a. 1125; knjaz´ of Kyiv end: *NPL*, s.a. 1132; Laurentian Chronicle, s.a. 1132; Hypatian Chronicle, s.a. 1133; *NČL*, s.a. 1131; Voskresenskij Chronicle, s.a. 1131; Rogožskij Chronicle, s.a. 1132; Tver Chronicle, s.a. 1132; Nikon Chronicle, s.a. 1132

Marriage to Kristín Ingesdottir: Wilhelm, "Wilhelmi abbatis genealogia regum Danorum," 182; Sturluson, *Heimskringla*, 702

Marriage to N. N., daughter of Dmitrij Zavidič: *NPL*, s.a. 1122; Hypatian Chronicle, s.a. 1122; *NČL*, s.a. 1122; Voskresenskij Chronicle, s.a. 1122. For more information on these marriages see part 1, "Marriages: Generation Four," "M´stislav Volodimerič."

N. N., daughter of Dmitrij Zavidič

Birth date: unknown

Death date: Hypatian Chronicle, s.a. 1169; Voskresenskij Chronicle, s.a. 1169 (both mention her still alive); Dąbrowski has a date of 1167; see Dąbrowski, *Genealogia Mścisławowiczów*, 82

Marriage to M´stislav Volodimerič: *NPL*, s.a. 1122; Hypatian Chronicle, s.a. 1122; *NČL*, s.a. 1122; Voskresenskij Chronicle, s.a. 1122. For more information on this marriage see part 1, "Marriages: Generation Four," "M´stislav Volodimerič."

Izjaslav Volodimerič

Birth date: unknown

Death date: *PVL*, s.a. 1096

Knjaz´ of Kursk start: *PVL*, s.a. 1095; knjaz´ of Kursk end: *PVL*, s.a. 1096

Knjaz´ of Murom start: *PVL*, s.a. 1095; knjaz´ of Murom end: *PVL*, s.a. 1096.

Svjatoslav Volodimerič

Birth date: unknown

Death date: *NPL*, s.a. 1114; Laurentian Chronicle, s.a. 1114; Hypatian Chronicle, s.a. 1114; Voskresenskij Chronicle, s.a. 1114; Tver Chronicle, s.a. 1114; Nikon Chronicle, s.a. 1114

Knjaz´ of Smolensk start: conjectural based upon the end of his father's and then Davyd Svjatoslavič's reigns in Smolensk; knjaz´ of Smolensk end: Voskresenskij Chronicle, s.a. 1114

Knjaz´ of Perejaslav start: Hypatian Chronicle, s.a. 1113; knjaz´ of Perejaslav end: *NPL*, s.a. 1114; Laurentian Chronicle, s.a. 1114; Hypatian Chronicle, s.a. 1114; Voskresenskij Chronicle, s.a. 1114; Tver Chronicle, s.a. 1114; Nikon Chronicle, s.a. 1114.

Elena of Ossetia
Birth date: unknown
Death date: Nikon Chronicle, s.a. 1145; Laurentian Chronicle, s.a. 1145; Hypatian Chronicle, s.a. 1145 (Last mention of her, she is transferring her husband's tomb.)
Marriage to Jaropolk Volodimerič: Laurentian Chronicle, s.a. 1116; Hypatian Chronicle, s.a. 1116; Voskresenskij Chronicle, s.a. 1116; Nikon Chronicle, s.a. 1117. For more information on this marriage see part 1, "Marriages: Generation Four," "Jaropolk Volodimerič."

Jaropolk Volodimerič
Birth date: unknown
Death date: Laurentian Chronicle, s.a. 1138; Hypatian Chronicle, s.a. 1139; *NČL*, s.a. 1138; Voskresenskij Chronicle, s.a. 1138; Rogožskij Chronicle, s.a. 1138; Tver Chronicle, s.a. 1138; Nikon Chronicle, s.a. 1138
Knjaz´ of Minsk start: Voskresenskij Chronicle, s.a. 1115 (places a son of Volodimer here; which son is conjecture, but helped by his identification in Voskresenskij, s.a. 1116); Nikon Chronicle, s.a. 1115 (again, simply a son of Volodimer); knjaz´ of Minsk end: Hypatian Chronicle, s.a. 1116 (Minsk is returned to Glěb Vseslavič)
Knjaz´ of Perejaslav (1) start: Hypatian Chronicle, s.a. 1113 (references his enthronement following his brother Svjatoslav's death. There may be an interregnum here, as the other chronicles do not note his rule here until his father's death); Laurentian Chronicle, s.a 1125; Voskresenskij Chronicle, s.a. 1125; Rogožskij Chronicle, s.a. 1125; Tver Chronicle, s.a. 1125; Nikon Chronicle, s.a. 1125; knjaz´ of Perejaslav (1) end: Laurentian Chronicle, s.a. 1132; Hypatian Chronicle, s.a. 1133
Knjaz´ of Kyiv start: *NPL*, s.a. 1132; Laurentian Chronicle, s.a. 1132; Hypatian Chronicle, s.a. 1133; *NČL*, s.a. 1131; Voskresenskij Chronicle, s.a. 1131; Rogožskij Chronicle, s.a. 1132; Tver Chronicle, s.a. 1132; Nikon Chronicle, s.a. 1132; knjaz´ of Kyiv end: Laurentian Chronicle, s.a. 1138; Hypatian Chronicle, s.a. 1139; *NČL*, s.a. 1138; Voskresenskij Chronicle, s.a. 1138; Rogožskij Chronicle, s.a. 1138; Tver Chronicle, s.a. 1138; Nikon Chronicle, s.a. 1138
Knjaz´ of Perejaslav (2) start: Laurentian Chronicle, s.a. 1133, 1134; knjaz´ of Perejaslav (2) end: Laurentian Chronicle, s.a. 1135; Hypatian Chronicle, s.a. 1135; *NČL*, s.a. 1135
Marriage to Elena of Ossetia: Laurentian Chronicle, s.a. 1116; Hypatian Chronicle, s.a. 1116; Voskresenskij Chronicle, s.a. 1116; Nikon Chronicle, s.a. 1117. For more information on this marriage see part 1, "Marriages: Generation Four," "Jaropolk Volodimerič."

Koloman of Hungary

Birth date: unknown

Death date: Dercsényi, *Chronica de gestis Hungarorum*, 133, lists his death in 1114, and this date is accepted by Wertner in *Az Árpádok családi története*, 217; however, the date is most often corrected to 1116 following Cosmas of Prague, *Chronicle of the Czechs*, bk. 3, ch. 42 (recorded under 1116), including by Dercsényi, *Chronica de gestis Hungarorum*, n455; Pál Engel, *The Realm of St. Stephen: A History of Medieval Hungary, 895–1526* (London and New York: I. B. Tauris, 2005), 49

King of Hungary start: Dercsényi, *Chronica de Gestis Hungarorum*, 130; "Annales Posonienses," ed. Emericus Madszar, in *Scriptores Rerum Hungaricarum*, ed. Imre Szentpétery, 1:119–27 (Budapest: Academia Litter. Hungarica atque Societate Histor. Hungarica, 1937), s.a. 1097, 1098; king of Hungary end: Dercsényi, *Chronica de gestis Hungarorum*, 133, lists his death in 1114, and this date is accepted by Wertner in *Az Árpádok családi története*, 217; however, the date is most often corrected to 1116 following Cosmas of Prague, *Chronicle of the Czechs*, bk. 3, ch. 42 (recorded under 1116), including by Dercsényi, *Chronica de gestis Hungarorum*, n455; Engel, *Realm of St. Stephen*, 49

Marriage to Evfimija Volodimerovna: Hypatian Chronicle, s.a. 1112; Dercsényi, *Chronica de Gestis Hungarorum*, 131; "Cosmae Chronicon Boemorum cum continuatoribus," s.a. 1132 (references repudiation); Otto, Bishop of Freising, *Two Cities*, bk. 7, sec. 21. For more information on this marriage see part 1, "Marriages: Generation Four," "Evfimija Volodimerovna."

Evfimija Volodimerovna

Birth date: unknown

Death date: Laurentian Chronicle, s.a. 1138; Hypatian Chronicle, s.a. 1139; Nikon Chronicle, s.a. 1138

Marriage to Koloman of Hungary: Hypatian Chronicle, s.a. 1112; Dercsényi, *Chronica de Gestis Hungarorum*, 131, 132 (references repudiation); "Cosmae Chronicon Boemorum cum continuatoribus," s.a. 1132 (references repudiation); Otto, Bishop of Freising, *Two Cities*, bk. 7, sec. 21. For more information on this marriage see part 1, "Marriages: Generation Four," "Evfimija Volodimerovna."

Vjačeslav Volodimerič

Birth date: unknown

Death date: *NPL*, s.a. 1154; Hypatian Chronicle, s.a. 1154; Laurentian Chronicle, s.a. 1154; Voskresenskij Chronicle, s.a. 1154; Nikon Chronicle, s.a. 1155

Knjaz´ of Smolensk start: Hypatian Chronicle, s.a. 1113; knjaz´ of Smo-

lensk end: Laurentian Chronicle, s.a. 1127 (has him reassigned to Turov and has Rostislav M′stislavič in Smolensk)
Knjaz′ of Turov (1) start: Laurentian Chronicle, s.a. 1127 (first mention in Turov); knjaz′ of Turov (1) end: Laurentian Chronicle, s.a. 1132; Voskresenskij Chronicle, s.a. 1131
Knjaz′ of Periaslavl′ (1) start: Laurentian Chronicle, s.a. 1132; Voskresenskij Chronicle, s.a. 1131; Tver Chronicle, s.a. 1132; Nikon Chronicle, s.a. 1132; knjaz′ of Perejaslav (1) end: Laurentian Chronicle, s.a. 1134; Hypatian Chronicle, s.a. 1134; Voskresenskij Chronicle, s.a. 1134; Nikon Chronicle, s.a. 1134
Knjaz′ of Turov (2) start: Laurentian Chronicle, s.a. 1134; Hypatian Chronicle, s.a. 1134; Voskresenskij Chronicle, s.a. 1134; Nikon Chronicle, s.a. 1134; knjaz′ of Turov (2) end: Laurentian Chronicle, s.a. 1146; Hypatian Chronicle, s.a. 1146
Knjaz′ of Kyiv (1): *NPL*, s.a. 1138; Laurentian Chronicle, s.a. 1138; Hypatian Chronicle, s.a. 1139; *NČL*, s.a. 1138; Voskresenskij Chronicle, s.a. 1138; Tver Chronicle, s.a. 1138; Nikon Chronicle, s.a. 1138
Knjaz′ of Perejaslav (2): Laurentian Chronicle, s.a. 1142; Hypatian Chronicle, s.a. 1142; Voskresenskij Chronicle, s.a. 1142; Tver Chronicle, s.a. 1142; Nikon Chronicle, s.a. 1142
Knjaz′ of Volodymyr start: Voskresenskij Chronicle, s.a. 1146; Nikon Chronicle, s.a. 1148 (places him already there); knjaz′ of Volodymyr end: *NPL*, s.a. 1148; Tver Chronicle, s.a. 1148; Voskresenskij Chronicle, s.a. 1148; Nikon Chronicle, s.a. 1148 (assigned to Svjatopolk M′stislavič in all of these)
Knjaz′ of Vyšhorod start: Hypatian Chronicle, s.a. 1150; Voskresenskij Chronicle, s.a. 1150; knjaz′ of Vyšhorod end: *NPL*, s.a. 1154; Hypatian Chronicle, s.a. 1154; Laurentian Chronicle, s.a. 1154; Voskresenskij Chronicle, s.a. 1154; Nikon Chronicle, s.a. 1155
Knjaz′ of Kyiv (with Izjaslav M′stislavič) start: Laurentian Chronicle, s.a. 1150; Hypatian Chronicle, s.a. 1150; Tver Chronicle, s.a. 1151; Voskresenskij Chronicle, s.a. 1150; Nikon Chronicle, s.a. 1150; knjaz′ of Kyiv (with Izjaslav M′stislavič) end: *NPL*, s.a. 1154; Hypatian Chronicle, s.a. 1154; Rogožskij Chronicle, s.a. 1155; Tver Chronicle, s.a. 1155; Laurentian Chronicle, s.a. 1154; Voskresenskij Chronicle, s.a. 1154; Nikon Chronicle, s.a. 1155
Knjaz′ of Kyiv (with Rostislav M′stislavič): *NPL*, s.a. 1154; Hypatian Chronicle, s.a. 1154; Tver Chronicle, s.a. 1155; Laurentian Chronicle, s.a. 1154; Voskresenskij Chronicle, s.a. 1154; Nikon Chronicle, s.a. 1155; knjaz′ of Kyiv (with Rostislav M′stislavič) end: *NPL*, s.a. 1154; Hypatian Chronicle, s.a. 1154; Laurentian Chronicle, s.a. 1154; Voskresenskij Chronicle, s.a. 1154; Nikon Chronicle, s.a. 1155
Relationship with unknown partner: conjectural based upon a child cited in Laurentian Chronicle, s.a. 1129; and elsewhere.

Unknown partner of Vjačeslav Volodimerič
Birth date: unknown
Death date: unknown
Relationship with Vjačeslav Volodimerič: conjectural based upon a child cited in Laurentian Chronicle, s.a. 1129; and elsewhere.

Agafija Volodimerovna
Birth date: unknown
Death date: Her death date can reasonably be assumed to have occurred after her marriage, though when is unknown.
Marriage to Vsevolodko Davydič: Hypatian Chronicle, s.a. 1116. For more on this marriage see part 1, "Marriages: Generation Four," "Vsevolodko Davydič."

Vsevolodko Davydič
Birth date: unknown
Death date: Laurentian Chronicle, s.a. 1141; Hypatian Chronicle, s.a. 1141; Voskresenskij Chronicle, s.a. 1141; Nikon Chronicle, s.a. 1141
Knjaz′ of Hrodna start: Laurentian Chronicle, s.a. 1127; Hypatian Chronicle, s.a. 1128 (first mention of his rule there); knjaz′ of Hrodna end: Laurentian Chronicle, s.a. 1141; Hypatian Chronicle, s.a. 1141; Voskresenskij Chronicle, s.a. 1141; Nikon Chronicle, s.a. 1141
Marriage to Agafija Volodimerovna: Hypatian Chronicle, s.a. 1116. For more on this marriage see part 1, "Marriages: Generation Four," "Vsevolodko Davydič."

Leo Diogenes of Byzantium
Birth date: unknown
Death date: Laurentian Chronicle, s.a. 1116; Hypatian Chronicle, s.a. 1116; Nikon Chronicle, s.a. 1117
Marriage to Marija Volodimerovna: Laurentian Chronicle, s.a. 1116; Hypatian Chronicle, s.a. 1116; Každan, "Rus′-Byzantine Princely Marriages in the Eleventh and Twelfth Centuries," 420. For more information on this marriage see part 1, "Marriages: Generation Four," "Marija Volodimerovna."

Marija Volodimerovna
Birth date: unknown
Death date: Laurentian Chronicle, s.a. 1146; Nikon Chronicle, s.a. 1146
Marriage to Leo Diogenes of Byzantium: Laurentian Chronicle, s.a. 1116; Hypatian Chronicle, s.a. 1116; Každan, "Rus′-Byzantine Princely Marriages in the Eleventh and Twelfth Centuries," 420.

For more information on this marriage see part 1, "Marriages: Generation Four," "Marija Volodimerovna."

N. N., daughter of Volodar′ Rostislavič
Birth date: unknown
Death date: her death date can reasonably be assumed to have occurred after her marriage, though when is unknown.
Marriage to Roman Volodimerič: Hypatian Chronicle, s.a. 1113; Voskresenskij Chronicle, s.a. 1113; Tver Chronicle, s.a. 1113. For more on this marriage see part 1, "Marriages: Generation Four," "Roman Volodimerič."

Roman Volodimerič
Birth date: unknown
Death date: Laurentian Chronicle, s.a. 1119; Voskresenskij Chronicle, s.a. 1118; Tver Chronicle, s.a. 1118; Nikon Chronicle, s.a. 1119
Knjaz′ of Volodymyr start: Laurentian Chronicle, s.a. 1119; Hypatian Chronicle, s.a. 1117; Voskresenskij Chronicle, s.a. 1118; Tver Chronicle, s.a. 1118; Nikon Chronicle, s.a. 1119; knjaz′ of Volodymyr end: Laurentian Chronicle, s.a. 1119; Voskresenskij Chronicle, s.a. 1118; Tver Chronicle, s.a. 1118; Nikon Chronicle, s.a. 1119
Marriage to N. N. Volodarovna: Hypatian Chronicle, s.a. 1113; Voskresenskij Chronicle, s.a. 1113; Tver Chronicle, s.a. 1113. For more on this marriage see part 1, "Marriages: Generation Four," "Roman Volodimerič."

N. N., daughter of Khan Aepa, son of Osen
Birth date: unknown
Death date: This is conjectural based upon discussion in the chronicles of an exile to Byzantium in 1162 of Jurij's wife and some of his children. It has been assumed that this was a second wife, and thus N. N., daughter of Khan Aepa, son of Osen, would be dead. For further discussion, see part 1, "Marriages: Generation Four," "Jurij 'Dolgorukij' Volodimerič"; on the exile, see Hypatian Chronicle, s.a 1162; Tver Chronicle, s.a. 1162; Voskresenskij Chronicle, s.a. 1162; Nikon Chronicle, s.a. 1160.
Marriage to Jurij "Dolgorukij" Volodimerič: Laurentian Chronicle, s.a. 1107; Nikon Chronicle, s.a. 1107. For more information on this marriage see part 1, "Marriages: Generation Four," "Jurij 'Dolgorukij' Volodimerič."

Jurij "Dolgorukij" Volodimerič
Birth date: unknown
Death date: Rogožskij Chronicle, s.a. 1157; *NPL*, s.a. 1157; Hypatian

Chronicle, s.a. 1158; Tver Chronicle, s.a. 1157; Laurentian Chronicle, s.a. 1157; Voskresenskij Chronicle, s.a. 1157; Nikon Chronicle, s.a. 1157

Knjaz´ of Suzdal start: *NPL*, s.a. 1138 (first mention of him there); knjaz´ of Suzdal end: Rogožskij Chronicle, s.a. 1157; *NPL*, s.a. 1157; Hypatian Chronicle, s.a. 1158; Tver Chronicle, s.a. 1157; Laurentian Chronicle, s.a. 1157; Voskresenskij Chronicle, s.a. 1157; Nikon Chronicle, s.a. 1157

Knjaz´ of Perejaslav (1): Voskresenskij Chronicle, s.a. 1131 (for eight days); Tver Chronicle, s.a. 1132; Nikon Chronicle, s.a. 1132

Knjaz´ of Perejaslav (2): Laurentian Chronicle, s.a. 1135; Hypatian Chronicle, s.a. 1135; *NČL*, s.a. 1135; Voskresenskij Chronicle, s.a. 1135; Tver Chronicle, s.a. 1135; Nikon Chronicle, s.a. 1135

Knjaz´ of Kyiv (1) start: Laurentian Chronicle, s.a. 1149; *NPL*, s.a. 1149; Hypatian Chronicle, s.a. 1149; Tver Chronicle, s.a. 1149; Voskresenskij Chronicle, s.a. 1149; Nikon Chronicle, s.a. 1149; knjaz´ of Kyiv (1) end: Laurentian Chronicle, s.a. 1150; Hypatian Chronicle, s.a. 1150; Tver Chronicle, s.a. 1151; Voskresenskij Chronicle, s.a. 1150; Nikon Chronicle, s.a. 1150

Knjaz´ of Perejaslav (3): Hypatian Chronicle, s.a. 1151; Tver Chronicle, s.a. 1151

Knjaz´ of Kyiv (2) start: Rogožskij Chronicle, s.a. 1155; *NPL*, s.a. 1155; Hypatian Chronicle, s.a. 1155; Tver Chronicle, s.a. 1155; Laurentian Chronicle, s.a. 1154; Voskresenskij Chronicle, s.a. 1154; Nikon Chronicle, s.a. 1155; knjaz´ of Kyiv (2) end: Rogožskij Chronicle, s.a. 1157; *NPL*, s.a. 1157; Hypatian Chronicle, s.a. 1158; Tver Chronicle, s.a. 1157; Laurentian Chronicle, s.a. 1157; Voskresenskij Chronicle, s.a. 1157; Nikon Chronicle, s.a. 1157

Marriage to N. N., daughter of Khan Aepa, son of Osen: Laurentian Chronicle, s.a. 1107; Nikon Chronicle, s.a. 1107

Marriage to N. N.: conjectural based upon her expulsion to Byzantium, specifically, as discussed in Tver Chronicle, s.a. 1162; Voskresenskij Chronicle, s.a. 1162; Nikon Chronicle, s.a. 1160. For more information on these marriages see part 1, "Marriages: Generation Four," "Jurij 'Dolgorukij' Volodimerič."

N. N.

Birth date: unknown

Death date: conjectural based upon her and her children's expulsion from Rus´ in 1162 cited in Tver Chronicle, s.a. 1162; Voskresenskij Chronicle, s.a. 1162; Nikon Chronicle, s.a. 1160

Marriage to Jurij "Dolgorukij" Volodimerič: conjectural based upon her expulsion to Byzantium, specifically, as discussed in Tver Chronicle, s.a. 1162; Voskresenskij Chronicle, s.a. 1162; Nikon Chronicle, s.a.

1160. For more information on this marriage see part 1, "Marriages: Generation Four," "Jurij 'Dolgorukij' Volodimerič."

N. N., granddaughter of Tugorkhan of the Polovcians
Birth date: unknown
Death date: Her death date can reasonably be assumed to have occurred after her marriage, though when is unknown.
Marriage to Andrej Volodimerič: Hypatian Chronicle, s.a. 1117; Voskresenskij Chronicle, s.a. 1117; Tver Chronicle, s.a. 1117; Nikon Chronicle, s.a. 1118. For more information on this marriage see part 1, "Marriages: Generation Four," "Andrej Volodimerič."

Andrej Volodimerič
Birth date: unknown
Death date: Laurentian Chronicle, s.a. 1141; Hypatian Chronicle, s.a. 1141; *NČL*, s.a. 1141; Voskresenskij Chronicle, s.a. 1141; Tver Chronicle, s.a. 1141; Nikon Chronicle, s.a. 1141
Knjaz´ of Volodymyr start: Hypatian Chronicle, s.a. 1118; Voskresenskij Chronicle, s.a. 1118; Laurentian Chronicle, s.a. 1119; Tver Chronicle, s.a. 1118; Nikon Chronicle, s.a. 1119; knjaz´ of Volodymyr end: Laurentian Chronicle, s.a. 1135; Hypatian Chronicle, s.a. 1135; Voskresenskij Chronicle, s.a. 1135; Nikon Chronicle, s.a. 1135
Knjaz´ of Perejaslav start: Laurentian Chronicle, s.a. 1135; Hypatian Chronicle, s.a. 1135; Voskresenskij Chronicle, s.a. 1135; Nikon Chronicle, s.a. 1135; knjaz´ of Perejaslav end: Laurentian Chronicle, s.a. 1141; Hypatian Chronicle, s.a. 1141; *NČL*, s.a. 1141; Voskresenskij Chronicle, s.a. 1141; Tver Chronicle, s.a. 1141; Nikon Chronicle, s.a. 1141
Marriage to N. N., granddaughter of Tugorkhan: Hypatian Chronicle, s.a. 1117; Voskresenskij Chronicle, s.a. 1117; Tver Chronicle, s.a. 1117; Nikon Chronicle, s.a. 1118. For more information on this marriage see part 1, "Marriages: Generation Four," "Andrej Volodimerič."

Judith, daughter of Bolesław III of Poland
Birth date: unknown
Death date: conjectural based upon Boris's remarriage
Marriage to Boris Kolomanovič: *Chronica Poloniae Maioris*, ch. 27 (listed simply as son of Koloman), "Kronika xiążąt polskich (Chronica principum Poloniae)," ed. Zygmunt Węclewski, in *Monumenta Poloniae Historica*.3:425–578 (Lviv: W Komisie Księgarni Gubrynowicza i Schmidta, 1878), 476; Wiszewski, *Domus Bolezlai*, 110.

Boris Kolomanovič
Birth date: "Cosmae chronicon Boemorum cum continuatoribus,"

215–16; Otto, Bishop of Freising, *Two Cities*, bk. 7, sec. 21; Dercsényi, *Chronica de Gestis Hungarorum*, 131 (all roughly refer to his birth, parentage, and mother's repudiation)

Death date: Otto of Freising, *Deeds of Frederick Barbarossa*, bk. 2, ch. 53

Marriage to Judith, daughter of Bolesław III of Poland: *Chronica Poloniae Maioris*, ch. 27 (listed simply as son of Koloman), "Kronika xiążąt polskich (Chronica principum Poloniae)," 476; Wiszewski, *Domus Bolezlai*, 110

Marriage to N. N., Comnena of the Byzantine Empire: Otto, Bishop of Freising, *Two Cities*, bk. 7, sec. 21; Ioannes Kinnamos, *Deeds of John and Manuel Comnenus*, trans. Charles M. Brand (New York: Columbia University Press, 1976), bk. 3, ch. 11; Odo of Deuil, *De profectione Ludovici VII in Orientem: The Journey of Louis VII to the East*, ed. and trans. Virginia Gingerich Berry (New York: W. W. Norton, 1948), bk. 2, 34–39.

N. N., Comnena of the Byzantine Empire

Birth date: unknown

Death date: Her death date can reasonably be assumed to have occurred after her marriage, though when is unknown.

Marriage to Boris Kolomanovič: Otto, Bishop of Freising, *Two Cities*, bk. 7, sec. 21; Kinnamos, *Deeds of John and Manuel Comnenus*, bk. 3, ch. 11; Odo of Deuil, *Journey of Louis VII to the East*, bk. 2, 34–39.

Mixailko Vjačeslavič

Birth date: unknown

Death date: Laurentian Chronicle, s.a. 1129; Hypatian Chronicle, s.a. 1130; Voskresenskij Chronicle, s.a. 1129; Nikon Chronicle, s.a. 1129

Knjaz´ of Rjazan start: unknown; knjaz´ of Rjazan end: Laurentian Chronicle, s.a. 1129; Hypatian Chronicle, s.a. 1130; Voskresenskij Chronicle, s.a. 1129; Nikon Chronicle, s.a. 1129.

N. N. Vsevolodkovna

Birth date: unknown

Death date: Her death date can reasonably be assumed to have occurred after her marriage, though when is unknown.

Marriage to Jurij Jaroslavič: Hypatian Chronicle, s.a. 1144. For more on this marriage see part 1, "Marriages: Generation Five," "Jurij Jaroslavič."

Jurij Jaroslavič

Birth date: unknown

Death date: Hypatian Chronicle, s.a. 1170 (has his son ruling in Turov)

Knjaz´ of Turov (1) start: Nikon Chronicle, s.a. 1157; knjaz´ of Turov

(1) end: Hypatian Chronicle, s.a. 1158; Voskresenskij Chronicle, s.a. 1157; Nikon Chronicle, s.a. 1157
Knjaz´ of Turov (2) start: Hypatian Chronicle, s.a. 1160; Voskresenskij Chronicle, s.a. 1162 (his son leads forces from Turov); knjaz´ of Turov (2) end: Hypatian Chronicle, s.a. 1170 (has his son ruling in Turov)
Marriage to N. N. Vsevolodkovna: Hypatian Chronicle, s.a. 1144. For more on this marriage see part 1, "Marriages: Generation Five," "Jurij Jaroslavič."

Vasil´ko Maričič
Birth date: conjectural based upon his father's death
Death date: Hypatian Chronicle, s.a. 1136; Laurentian Chronicle, s.a. 1136; *NČL*, s.a. 1136; Voskresenskij Chronicle, s.a. 1136; Nikon Chronicle, s.a. 1136.

N. N., wife of Volodimer Andreevič
Birth date: unknown
Death date: Hypatian Chronicle, s.a. 1171 (last mention in sources)
Marriage to Volodimer Andreevič: Hypatian Chronicle, s.a. 1171.

Volodimer Andreevič
Birth date: unknown
Death date: Hypatian Chronicle, s.a. 1171; Rogožskij Chronicle, s.a. 1170; Tver Chronicle, s.a. 1170; Laurentian Chronicle, s.a. 1170; Voskresenskij Chronicle, s.a. 1170; Nikon Chronicle, s.a. 1171
Knjaz´ of Peresopnica: Hypatian Chronicle, s.a. 1152 (references him as coming from there with an army)
Knjaz´ of Brest: Hypatian Chronicle, s.a. 1153 (references him as coming from there)
Knjaz´ of Peresopnica and Dorogobuž start: Hypatian Chronicle, s.a. 1157; Tver Chronicle, s.a. 1156; Voskresenskij Chronicle, s.a. 1156; Nikon Chronicle, s.a. 1156; knjaz´ of Peresopnica and Dorogobuž end: Hypatian Chronicle, s.a. 1171; Rogožskij Chronicle, s.a. 1170; Tver Chronicle, s.a. 1170; Laurentian Chronicle, s.a. 1170; Voskresenskij Chronicle, s.a. 1170; Nikon Chronicle, s.a. 1171
Marriage to N. N.: Hypatian Chronicle, s.a. 1171.

Table 13: M´stislav "Harald" Volodimerič

Kristín Ingesdottir of Sweden

Birth date: unknown

Death date: *NPL*, s.a. 1122; Laurentian Chronicle, s.a. 1122; Hypatian Chronicle, s.a. 1121; Voskresenskij Chronicle, s.a. 1122; Tver Chronicle, s.a. 1122; Nikon Chronicle, s.a. 1122

Marriage to M´stislav "Harald" Volodimerič: Wilhelm, "Wilhelmi abbatis genealogia regum Danorum," 182; Sturluson, *Heimskringla*, 702; for more information on this marriage see part 1, "Marriages: Generation Four," "M´stislav Volodimerič."

M´stislav "Harald" Volodimerič

Birth date: *PVL*, s.a. 1076

Death date: *NPL*, s.a. 1132; Laurentian Chronicle, s.a. 1132; Hypatian Chronicle, s.a. 1133; *NČL*, s.a. 1131; Voskresenskij Chronicle, s.a. 1131; Rogožskij Chronicle, s.a. 1132; Tver Chronicle, s.a. 1132; Nikon Chronicle, s.a. 1132

Knjaz´ of Novgorod start: *PVL*, s.a. 1095; knjaz´ of Novgorod end: *NPL*, s.a. 1117; Laurentian Chronicle, s.a. 1117; *NČL*, s.a. 1117; Hypatian Chronicle, s.a. 1117; Voskresenskij Chronicle, s.a. 1117; Tver Chronicle, s.a. 1117; Nikon Chronicle, s.a. 1117

Knjaz´ of Bilhorod start: *NPL*, s.a. 1117; Laurentian Chronicle, s.a. 1117; Hypatian Chronicle, s.a. 1117; *NČL*, s.a. 1117; Voskresenskij Chronicle, s.a. 1117; Tver Chronicle, s.a. 1117; Nikon Chronicle, s.a. 1117 (Hypatian, Voskresenskij, Tver, and Nikon all specifically refer to Bilhorod while the rest simply assume a move to assist his father in Kyiv); knjaz´ of Bilhorod end: *NPL*, s.a. 1125; Laurentian Chronicle, s.a. 1125; Hypatian Chronicle, s.a. 1126; Voskresenskij Chronicle, s.a. 1125; Tver Chronicle, s.a. 1125

Knjaz´ of Kyiv start: *NPL*, s.a. 1125; Laurentian Chronicle, s.a. 1125; Hypatian Chronicle, s.a. 1126; *NČL*, s.a. 1125; Voskresenskij Chron-

Table 13: M′stislav "Harald" Volodimerič

Kristín Ingesdottir of Sweden
b. unknown; d. 1122
(m. ca. 1095)

1

M′stislav "Harald" Volodimerič
b. 1076; d. 1132
(Novgorod r. 1095–1117)
(Bilhorod r. 1117–1125)
(Kyiv r. 1125–1132)

Marija
b. unknown;
d. 1178
(m. ca. 1127)

Vsevolod Ol′govič
b. unknown; d. 1146
(Černihiv r. 1127–1138)
(Kyiv r. 1138–1146)

N. N.
b. unknown;
d. post-1118
(m. ca. 1112)
(repudiated 1118)

Jaroslav Svjatopolčič
b. unknown; d. 1123
(Volodymyr r. 1100–1118)

Ingeborg
b. unknown;
d. post-1137
(m. ca. 1115)

Knud "Lavard" Ericsson of Denmark
b. unknown; d. 1131
(Duke of Schleswig r. 1115–1131)
(King of the Abodrite Slavs r. ca. 1128–1131)

Sigurd "the Crusader" Magnusson of Norway
b. unknown; d. 1130
(Norway r. 1103–1130)

1

Malfrid
b. unknown;
d. post-1135
(1st m. 1111)
(2nd m. 1132)

2

Eric "Emune" Ericsson of Denmark
b. unknown; d. 1137
(Denmark r. 1134–1137)

N. N. of the Byzantine Empire
b. unknown;
d. post-1122

N. N.
b. unknown;
d. post-1122
(m. 1122)

Vsevolod
b. unknown; d. 1137
(Novgorod r. 1117–1132)
(Perejaslav r. 1132)
(Novgorod r. 1132–1136)
(Vyšehorod r. 1136–1137)
(Pskov r. 1137)

N. N.
b. unknown;
d. post-1136
(m. 1123)

2 N. N. daughter of Dmitrij Zavidič
b. unknown; d. post-1169
(m. 1122)

N. N.
b. unknown;
d. 1151
(m. pre-1151)

1 **Izjaslav** 2
b. unknown; d. 1154
(Kursk r. 1127–1129)
(Polack r. 1129–1132)
(Perejaslav r. 1132)
(Turov, Pinsk, Minsk r. 1132–1134)
(Volodymyr r. 1135–1142)
(Perejaslav r. 1142–1146)
(Kyiv r. 1146–1149)
(Volodymyr r. 1149–1150)
(Kyiv [w/ Vjačeslav Volodimerič] r. 1150–1154)

N. N. daughter of the ruler of Abkhazia
b. unknown;
d. post-1154
(m. 1154)

Brjačeslav Davydič
b. unknown;
d. post-1128
(Izjaslavl r. ca. 1128)

N. N.
b. unknown;
d. post-1127
(m. pre-1127)

Rogněda
b. unknown;
d. post-1168
(Zarub r. ca. 1168)

N. N., of Moravia
b. unknown;
d. post-1143
(m. 1143)

Svjatopolk
b. unknown; d. 1154
(Polack r. 1132)
(Pskov r. 1137–1140)
(Brest r. 1140–1142)
(Novgorod r.1142–1148)
(Volodymyr r. 1148–1149)
(Luck r. 1149–1150)
(Volodymyr r. 1150–1154)

N. N.
b. unknown;
d. post-1168
(m. unknown)

Rostislav
b. unknown; d. 1168
(Smolensk r. pre-1127–1160)
(Novgorod r. 1154)
(Kyiv [w/ Vjačeslav Volodimerič] r. 1154)
(Novgorod r. 1157–1158)
(Kyiv r. 1160–1168)

Volodimer
b. 1132; d. 1171
(Gorodec r. 1147–1148)
(Volodymyr r. 1154–1156)
(Luck r. ca. 1162)
(Trepole r. 1162–ca. 1170)
(Dorogobuž r. ca. 1170)
(Kyiv r. ca. 1171)

N. N., daughter of Ban of Croatia
b. unknown;
d. post-1169
(m. 1150)

Evfrosinija
b. unknown;
d. ca. 1193
(m. 1144)

Géza II of Hungary
b. 1130; d. 1162
(King of Hungary r. 1141–1162)

Jaropolk
b. unknown;
d. post-1149

icle, s.a. 1125; Rogožskij Chronicle, s.a. 1125; Tver Chronicle, s.a. 1125; Nikon Chronicle, s.a. 1125; knjaz´ of Kyiv end: *NPL*, s.a. 1132; Laurentian Chronicle, s.a. 1132; Hypatian Chronicle, s.a. 1133; *NČL*, s.a. 1131; Voskresenskij Chronicle, s.a. 1131; Rogožskij Chronicle, s.a. 1132; Tver Chronicle, s.a. 1132; Nikon Chronicle, s.a. 1132

Marriage to Kristín Ingesdottir: Wilhelm, "Wilhelmi abbatis genealogia regum Danorum," 182; Sturluson, *Heimskringla*, 702

Marriage to N. N., daughter of Dmitrij Zavidič: *NPL*, s.a. 1122; Hypatian Chronicle, s.a. 1122; *NČL*, s.a. 1122; Voskresenskij Chronicle, s.a. 1122. For more information on these marriages see part 1, "Marriages: Generation Four," "M´stislav Volodimerič."

N. N., daughter of Dmitrij Zavidič

Birth date: unknown

Death date: Hypatian Chronicle, s.a. 1169; Voskresenskij Chronicle, s.a. 1169 (both mention her still alive); Dąbrowski has a date of 1167; see Dąbrowski, *Genealogia Mścisławowiczów*, 82

Marriage to M´stislav Volodimerič: *NPL*, s.a. 1122; Hypatian Chronicle, s.a. 1122; *NČL*, s.a. 1122; Voskresenskij Chronicle, s.a. 1122. For more information on this marriage see part 1, "Marriages: Generation Four," "M´stislav Volodimerič."

Marija M´stislavna

Birth date: unknown

Death date: Hypatian Chronicle, s.a. 1178

Marriage to Vsevolod Ol´govič: Hypatian Chronicle, s.a. 1141 (obliquely); Dimnik, *Dynasty of Chernigov, 1054–1146*, 254–55; date conjectural based upon my analysis. Dąbrowski comes to a similar conclusion; see Dąbrowski, *Genealogia Mścisławowiczów*, 148–55 (for the whole entry on Marija). For more information on this marriage see part 1, "Marriages: Generation Four," "Vsevolod Ol´govič."

Vsevolod Ol´govič

Birth date: unknown

Death date: *NPL*, s.a. 1146; Hypatian Chronicle, s.a. 1146; *NČL*, s.a. 1146; Voskresenskij Chronicle, s.a. 1146; Rogožskij Chronicle, s.a. 1146; Tver Chronicle, s.a. 1146; Nikon Chronicle, s.a. 1146

Knjaz´ of Černihiv start: Hypatian Chronicle, s.a. 1128; Voskresenskij Chronicle, s.a. 1127; Tver Chronicle, s.a. 1127; Nikon Chronicle, s.a. 1127; knjaz´ of Černihiv end: Laurentian Chronicle, s.a. 1138; *NČL*, s.a. 1138; Voskresenskij Chronicle, s.a. 1138; Nikon Chronicle, s.a. 1138

Knjaz´ of Kyiv start: *NPL*, s.a. 1139; Laurentian Chronicle, s.a. 1138;

Hypatian Chronicle, s.a. 1140; *NČL*, s.a. 1138; Voskresenskij Chronicle, s.a. 1138; Rogožskij Chronicle, s.a. 1138; Tver Chronicle, s.a. 1138; Nikon Chronicle, s.a. 1138; knjaz´ of Kyiv end: *NPL*, s.a. 1146; Hypatian Chronicle, s.a. 1146; *NČL*, s.a. 1146; Voskresenskij Chronicle, s.a. 1146; Rogožskij Chronicle, s.a. 1146; Tver Chronicle, s.a. 1146; Nikon Chronicle, s.a. 1146

Marriage to Marija M´stislavna: Hypatian Chronicle, s.a. 1141 (obliquely); Dimnik, *Dynasty of Chernigov, 1054–1146*, 254–55; date conjectural based upon my analysis. For more information on this marriage see part 1, "Marriages: Generation Four," "Vsevolod Ol´govič."

Sigurd "the Crusader" Magnusson

Birth date: unknown

Death date: Sturluson, *Heimskringla*, 714

King of Norway start: Sturluson, *Heimskringla*, 688–89; king of Norway end: Sturluson, *Heimskringla*, 714

Marriage to Malfrid M´stislavna: V. T. Pašuto, *Vnešnjaja politika Drevnej Rusi* (Moscow: Nauka, 1968), 146 (for speculative date); Sturluson, *Heimskringla*, 702; A. F. Litvina and F. B. Uspenskij. *Vybor imeni u russkix knjazej v X–XVI vv.: Dinastičeskaja istorija skvoz´ prizmu antroponimiki* (Moscow: Indrik, 2006), 246n26; Orderic Vitalis, *Ecclesiastical History*, bk. 10, ch. 6. For more information on this marriage see part 1, "Marriages: Generation Five," "Malfrid M´stislavna."

Malfrid M´stislavna

Birth date: unknown

Death date: Dąbrowski, *Genealogia Mścisławowiczów*, 94

Marriage to Sigurd "the Crusader" Magnusson: Pašuto, *Vnešnjaja politika Drevnej Rusi*, 146 (for speculative date), Sturluson, *Heimskringla*, 702; Litvina and Uspenskij, *Vybor imeni u russkix knjazej*, 246n26; Orderic Vitalis, *Ecclesiastical History*, bk. 10, ch. 6

Marriage to Eric "Emune" Ericsson: Saxo Grammaticus, bk. 13, ch. 8, 134; *Knýtlinga Saga: The History of the Kings of Denmark*, trans. Hermann Pálsson and Paul Edwards (Odense: Odense University Press, 1986), 140. For more information on these marriages see part 1, "Marriages: Generation Five," "Malfrid M´stislavna."

Eric "Emune" Ericsson

Birth date: unknown

Death date: *Knýtlinga Saga*, 145 (which dates it eight years after the death of Knud Lavard, thus 1139); I have corrected the date to 1137 following Dąbrowski, *Genealogia Mścisławowiczów*, 97

King of Denmark start: Saxo Grammaticus, bk. 13, ch. 11, 141; king of Denmark end: *Knýtlinga Saga*, 145 (which dates it eight years after the death of Knud Lavard, thus 1139; I have corrected the date to 1137 following Dąbrowski, *Genealogia Mścisławowiczów*, 97)

Marriage to Malfrid M´stislavna: Saxo Grammaticus, bk. 13, ch. 8, 134; *Knýtlinga Saga*, 140. For more information on this marriage see part 1, "Marriages: Generation Five," "Malfrid M´stislavna."

N. N. M´stislavna

Birth date: unknown

Death date: the last reference to her is at her repudiation, or mistreatment and then repudiation; see Nikon Chronicle, s.a. 1119; see also Voskresenskij Chronicle, s.a. 1118; Tver Chronicle, s.a. 1118

Marriage to Jaroslav Svjatopolčič: *NPL*, s.a. 1113; Hypatian Chronicle, s.a. 1112; Voskresenskij Chronicle, s.a. 1112; Tver Chronicle, s.a. 1113; repudiated by Jaroslav Svjatopolčič: Voskresenskij Chronicle, s.a. 1118; Tver Chronicle, s.a. 1118; Nikon Chronicle, s.a. 1119. For more on this marriage see part 1, "Marriages: Generation Four," "Jaroslav Svjatopolčič."

Jaroslav Svjatopolčič

Birth date: unknown

Death date: Laurentian Chronicle, s.a. 1123; Hypatian Chronicle, s.a. 1123; Voskresenskij Chronicle, s.a. 1123; Nikon Chronicle, s.a. 1123

Knjaz´ of Volodymyr start: *PVL*, s.a. 1097; *PVL*, s.a. 1100; knjaz´ of Volodymyr end: Hypatian Chronicle, s.a. 1118; Laurentian Chronicle, s.a. 1119; Voskresenskij Chronicle, s.a. 1118; Tver Chronicle, s.a. 1118; Nikon Chronicle, s.a. 1119

Marriage to N. N. M´stislavna: *NPL*, s.a. 1113; Hypatian Chronicle, s.a. 1112; Voskresenskij Chronicle, s.a. 1112; Tver Chronicle, s.a. 1113; repudiated N. N. M´stislavna: Voskresenskij Chronicle, s.a. 1118; Tver Chronicle, s.a. 1118; Nikon Chronicle, s.a. 1119. For more on these marriages see part 1, "Marriages: Generation Four," "Jaroslav Svjatopolčič."

Vsevolod M´stislavič

Birth date: unknown

Death date: *NPL*, s.a. 1137; Hypatian Chronicle, s.a. 1138; *NČL*, s.a. 1137; Pskov Chronicle, s.a. 1137; Voskresenskij Chronicle, s.a. 1137; Rogožskij Chronicle, s.a. 1137

Knjaz´ of Novgorod (1) start: *NPL*, s.a. 1117; Laurentian Chronicle, s.a. 1117; *NČL*, s.a. 1117; Voskresenskij Chronicle, s.a. 1117; Tver Chronicle, s.a. 1117; Nikon Chronicle, s.a. 1117; knjaz´ of Novgorod (1) end:

NPL, s.a. 1132; Laurentian Chronicle, s.a. 1132; Hypatian Chronicle, s.a. 1133; Tver Chronicle, s.a. 1132; Nikon Chronicle, s.a. 1132

Knjaz´ of Perejaslav: *NPL*, s.a. 1132; Laurentian Chronicle, s.a. 1132; Hypatian Chronicle, s.a. 1133; Voskresenskij Chronicle, s.a. 1131; Tver Chronicle, s.a. 1132; Nikon Chronicle, s.a. 1132

Knjaz´ of Novgorod (2) start: *NPL*, s.a. 1132; Tver Chronicle, s.a. 1132; Nikon Chronicle, s.a. 1132; knjaz´ of Novgorod (2) end: *NPL*, s.a. 1136; Laurentian Chronicle, s.a. 1138; Hypatian Chronicle, s.a. 1138; *NČL*, s.a. 1136; Pskov Chronicle, s.a. 1138; Voskresenskij Chronicle, s.a. 1136; Tver Chronicle, s.a. 1136; Nikon Chronicle, s.a. 1135

Knjaz´ of Vyšhorod start: Laurentian Chronicle, s.a. 1138; Hypatian Chronicle, s.a. 1138; *NČL*, s.a. 1136; Pskov Chronicle, s.a. 1138; Voskresenskij Chronicle, s.a. 1136; Tver Chronicle, s.a. 1136; Nikon Chronicle, s.a. 1135; knjaz´ of Vyšhorod end: Laurentian Chronicle, s.a. 1138; Hypatian Chronicle, s.a. 1138; *NČL*, s.a. 1137; Pskov Chronicle, s.a. 1138; Voskresenskij Chronicle, s.a. 1137; Tver Chronicle, s.a. 1137; Nikon Chronicle, s.a. 1135; Nikon Chronicle, s.a. 1138

Knjaz´ of Pskov: Rogožskij Chronicle, s.a. 1137

Marriage to N. N.: *NPL*, s.a. 1123; *NČL*, s.a. 1123; Nikon Chronicle, s.a. 1123. For more information on this marriage see part 1, "Marriages: Generation Five," "Vsevolod M´stislavič."

N. N., wife of Vsevolod M´stislavič

Birth date: unknown

Death date: The last mention of her is in 1136 when Vsevolod is removed from rule and the family is placed in captivity; see *NPL*, s.a. 1136.

Marriage to Vsevolod M´stislavič: *NPL*, s.a. 1123; *NČL*, s.a. 1123; Nikon Chronicle, s.a. 1123. For more information on this marriage see part 1, "Marriages: Generation Five," "Vsevolod M´stislavič."

Ingeborg M´stislavna

Birth date: unknown

Death date: Her last known appearance is at the election of Eric "Lamb" as king in 1137; see *Knýtlinga Saga*, 145.

Marriage to Knud "Lavard" Ericsson: Sturluson, *Heimskringla*, 702; Wilhelm, "Wilhelmi abbatis genealogia regum Danorum," 180; Saxo Grammaticus, bk. 13, 110. For more information on this marriage see part 1, "Marriages: Generation Five," "Ingeborg M´stislavna."

Knud "Lavard" Ericsson

Birth date: unknown

Death date: Saxo Grammaticus, bk. 13, ch. 6, 126

Duke of Schleswig start: Helmold, *The Chronicle of the Slavs by Helmold,*

Priest of Bosau, trans. Francis J. Tschan (New York: Columbia University Press, 1935), 152; duke of Schleswig end: Saxo Grammaticus, bk. 13, ch. 6, 126

King of the Abodrite Slavs start: Helmold, *Chronicle of the Slavs*, 153; king of the Abodrite Slavs end: Saxo Grammaticus, bk. 13, ch. 6, 126

Marriage to Ingeborg M´stislavna: Sturluson, *Heimskringla*, 702; Wilhelm, "Wilhelmi abbatis genealogia regum Danorum," 180; Saxo Grammaticus, bk. 13, 110. For more information on this marriage see part 1, "Marriages: Generation Five," "Ingeborg M´stislavna."

N. N. of the Byzantine Empire

Birth date: unknown

Death date: His death date can reasonably be assumed to have occurred after his marriage, though when is unknown.

Marriage to N. N. M´stislavna: Hypatian Chronicle, s.a. 1122; Voskresenskij Chronicle, s.a. 1122. For more information on this marriage see part 1, "Marriages: Generation Five," "Irene/Dobrodeja M´stislavna."

N. N. M´stislavna

Birth date: unknown

Death date: Her death date can reasonably be assumed to have occurred after her marriage, though when is unknown

Marriage to N. N. of the Byzantine Empire: Hypatian Chronicle, s.a. 1122; Voskresenskij Chronicle, s.a. 1122. For more information on this marriage see part 1, "Marriages: Generation Five," "Irene/Dobrodeja M´stislavna."

N. N., wife of Izjaslav M´stislavič

Birth date: unknown

Death date: *NPL*, s.a. 1151; Hypatian Chronicle, s.a. 1151; Laurentian Chronicle, s.a. 1151; Voskresenskij Chronicle, s.a. 1151; Nikon Chronicle, s.a. 1151

Marriage to Izjaslav M´stislavič: *NPL*, s.a. 1151; Hypatian Chronicle, s.a. 1151; Laurentian Chronicle, s.a. 1151; Voskresenskij Chronicle, s.a. 1151; Nikon Chronicle, s.a. 1151.

Izjaslav M´stislavič

Birth date: unknown

Death date: Rogožskij Chronicle, s.a. 1155; *NPL*, s.a. 1154; Hypatian Chronicle, s.a. 1154; Tver Chronicle, s.a. 1155; Laurentian Chronicle, s.a. 1154; Voskresenskij Chronicle, s.a. 1154; Nikon Chronicle, s.a. 1155

Knjaz´ of Kursk start: Laurentian Chronicle, s.a. 1127; *NČL*, s.a. 1127;

knjaz´ of Kursk end: conjectural based upon his placement in Polack

Knjaz´ of Polack start: conjectural based upon the displacement of the Polack rulers and his presence there as ruler in 1132; knjaz´ of Polack end: Laurentian Chronicle, s.a. 1132; Voskresenskij Chronicle, s.a. 1131; Tver Chronicle, s.a. 1132

Knjaz´ of Perejaslav (1): Laurentian Chronicle, s.a. 1132; Voskresenskij Chronicle, s.a. 1131; Tver Chronicle, s.a. 1132; Nikon Chronicle, s.a. 1132

Knjaz´ of Turov, Pinsk, and Minsk start: Laurentian Chronicle, s.a. 1132; Voskresenskij Chronicle, s.a. 1131; Tver Chronicle, s.a. 1132; Nikon Chronicle, s.a. 1132; knjaz´ of Turov, Pinsk, and Minsk end: Laurentian Chronicle, s.a. 1134; Hypatian Chronicle, s.a. 1134; *NPL*, s.a. 1134; Nikon Chronicle, s.a. 1135

Knjaz´ of Volodymyr (1) start: Laurentian Chronicle, s.a. 1135; Hypatian Chronicle, s.a. 1135; Voskresenskij Chronicle, s.a. 1135; Nikon Chronicle, s.a. 1135; knjaz´ of Volodymyr (1) end: Laurentian Chronicle, s.a. 1142; Hypatian Chronicle, s.a. 1142; Nikon Chronicle, s.a. 1142

Knjaz´ of Perejaslav (2) start: Laurentian Chronicle, s.a. 1142; Hypatian Chronicle, s.a. 1142; Voskresenskij Chronicle, s.a. 1142; Tver Chronicle, s.a. 1142; Nikon Chronicle, s.a. 1142; knjaz´ of Perejaslav (2) end: Hypatian Chronicle, s.a. 1146

Knjaz´ of Kyiv start: *NPL*, s.a. 1146; Hypatian Chronicle, s.a. 1146; Laurentian Chronicle, s.a. 1146, *NČL*, s.a. 1146; Voskresenskij Chronicle, s.a. 1146; Rogožskij Chronicle, s.a. 1146; Tver Chronicle, s.a. 1146; Nikon Chronicle, s.a. 1146; knjaz´ of Kyiv end: Laurentian Chronicle, s.a. 1149; *NPL*, s.a. 1149; Hypatian Chronicle, s.a. 1149; Tver Chronicle, s.a. 1149; Voskresenskij Chronicle, s.a. 1149; Nikon Chronicle, s.a. 1149

Knjaz´ of Volodymyr (2): Nikon Chronicle, s.a. 1149 (Nikon is the only chronicle that specifically mentions Izjaslav going to Volodymyr and ruling after his expulsion from Kyiv, though others such as Hypatian Chronicle, s.a. 1149, do note that he goes to Volodymyr)

Knjaz´ of Kyiv (with Vjačeslav Volodimerič) start: Laurentian Chronicle, s.a. 1150; Hypatian Chronicle, s.a. 1150; Tver Chronicle, s.a. 1151; Voskresenskij Chronicle, s.a. 1150; Nikon Chronicle, s.a. 1150; knjaz´ of Kyiv (with Vjačeslav Volodimerič) end: Rogožskij Chronicle, s.a. 1155; *NPL*, s.a. 1154; Hypatian Chronicle, s.a. 1154; Tver Chronicle, s.a. 1155; Laurentian Chronicle, s.a. 1154; Voskresenskij Chronicle, s.a. 1154; Nikon Chronicle, s.a. 1155

Marriage to N. N.: *NPL*, s.a. 1151; Hypatian Chronicle, s.a. 1151; Laurentian Chronicle, s.a. 1151; Voskresenskij Chronicle, s.a. 1151; Nikon Chronicle, s.a. 1151

Marriage to N. N., daughter of the ruler of Abkhazia: Hypatian Chronicle, s.a. 1154; Tver Chronicle, s.a. 1154; Laurentian Chronicle, s.a. 1154; Voskresenskij Chronicle, s.a. 1154; Nikon Chronicle, s.a. 1154.

N. N., daughter of ruler of Abkhazia
Birth date: unknown
Death date: Her death date can reasonably be assumed to have occurred after her marriage, though when is unknown; for a fuller identification of N. N., see Dąbrowski, *Genealogia Mścisławowiczów*, 127.
Marriage to Izjaslav M´stislavič: Hypatian Chronicle, s.a. 1154; Tver Chronicle, s.a. 1154; Laurentian Chronicle, s.a. 1154; Voskresenskij Chronicle, s.a. 1154; Nikon Chronicle, s.a. 1154.

Svjatopolk M´stislavič
Birth date: unknown
Death date: Hypatian Chronicle, s.a. 1154; Tver Chronicle, s.a. 1154; Laurentian Chronicle, s.a. 1154; Voskresenskij Chronicle, s.a. 1154; Nikon Chronicle, s.a. 1154
Knjaz´ of Polack: Laurentian Chronicle, s.a. 1132; Tver Chronicle, s.a. 1132; Nikon Chronicle, s.a. 1132
Knjaz´ of Pskov start: *NPL*, s.a. 1137; *NČL*, s.a. 1137; Voskresenskij Chronicle, s.a. 1137; Tver Chronicle, s.a. 1137; Nikon Chronicle, s.a. 1138; knjaz´ of Pskov end: Voskresenskij Chronicle, s.a. 1140; Nikon Chronicle, s.a. 1140 (both referencing his move to Brest, thus conjectural that he is no longer ruler of Pskov)
Knjaz´ of Brest start: Voskresenskij Chronicle, s.a. 1140; Nikon Chronicle, s.a. 1140; knjaz´ of Brest end: conjectural based upon move to Novgorod
Knjaz´ of Novgorod start: *NPL*, s.a. 1142; Laurentian Chronicle, s.a. 1141; Hypatian Chronicle, s.a. 1142; Voskresenskij Chronicle, s.a. 1141; Tver Chronicle, s.a. 1142; knjaz´ of Novgorod end: *NPL*, s.a. 1148; Tver Chronicle, s.a. 1148; Voskresenskij Chronicle, s.a. 1148; Nikon Chronicle, s.a. 1148
Knjaz´ of Volodymyr (1) start: *NPL*, s.a. 1148; Tver Chronicle, s.a. 1148; Voskresenskij Chronicle, s.a. 1148; Nikon Chronicle, s.a. 1148; knjaz´ of Volodymyr (1) end: Tver Chronicle, s.a. 1149; Hypatian Chronicle, s.a. 1149; Nikon Chronicle, s.a. 1149
Knjaz´ of Luck: Hypatian Chronicle, s.a. 1150; Laurentian Chronicle, s.a. 1150 (both place him there and it is likely he went somewhere after leaving Volodymyr and before returning)
Knjaz´ of Volodymyr (2) start: Hypatian Chronicle, s.a. 1150 (obscurely referenced, definitely by s.a. 1153); knjaz´ of Volodymyr (2) end: Hypatian Chronicle, s.a. 1154; Tver Chronicle, s.a. 1154; Laurentian Chronicle, s.a. 1154; Voskresenskij Chronicle, s.a. 1154; Nikon Chronicle, s.a. 1154

Marriage to N. N. of Moravia: *NPL*, s.a. 1143; *NČL*, s.a. 1143 (Svjatopolk is identified as Vsevolodič); Tver Chronicle, s.a. 1143. For more on this marriage see part 1, "Marriages: Generation Five," "Svjatopolk M´stislavič."

N. N. of Moravia
Birth date: unknown
Death date: Her death date can reasonably be assumed to have occurred after her marriage, though when is unknown.
Marriage to Svjatopolk M´stislavič: *NPL*, s.a. 1143; *NČL*, s.a. 1143 (Svjatopolk is identified as Vsevolodič); Tver Chronicle, s.a. 1143. For more on this marriage see part 1, "Marriages: Generation Five," "Svjatopolk M´stislavič."

Brjačeslav Davydič
Birth date: unknown
Death date: The last known date for Brjačeslav is his rule in Izjaslavl; see Hypatian Chronicle, s.a. 1128.
Knjaz´ of Izjaslavl start: Hypatian Chronicle, s.a. 1128 (the people of Izjaslavl refer to him as their knjaz´); knjaz´ of Izjaslavl end: Hypatian Chronicle, s.a. 1128
Marriage to N. N., daughter of M´stislav Volodimerič: Laurentian Chronicle, s.a. 1127; Voskresenskij Chronicle, s.a. 1127 (refer to him as the *zjat´* of M´stislav's son Izjaslav); Hypatian Chronicle, s.a. 1128; Nikon Chronicle, s.a. 1127 (refer to the M´stislaviči as his *zjatja*). For more information on this marriage see part 1, "Marriages: Generation Five," "Brjačeslav Davydič."

N. N., daughter of M´stislav Volodimerič
Birth date: unknown
Death date: The last mention of her is in 1127, in regard to her relationship with Brjačeslav; see Laurentian Chronicle, s.a. 1127; Voskresenskij Chronicle, s.a. 1127, which refer to him as the *zjat´* of M´stislav's son Izjaslav; and Hypatian Chronicle, s.a. 1128; Nikon Chronicle, s.a. 1127, which refer to the M´stislaviči as his *zjatja*.
Marriage to Brjačeslav Davydič: Laurentian Chronicle, s.a. 1127; Voskresenskij Chronicle, s.a. 1127, which refer to him as the *zjat´* of M´stislav's son Izjaslav; and Hypatian Chronicle, s.a. 1128; Nikon Chronicle, s.a. 1127, which refer to the M´stislaviči as his *zjatja*. For more information on this marriage see part 1, "Marriages: Generation Five," "Brjačeslav Davydič."

N. N., wife of Rostislav M´stislavič
Birth date: unknown

Death date: conjectural based upon her being alive at his death; see Hypatian Chronicle, s.a. 1168
Marriage to Rostislav M´stislavič: Hypatian Chronicle, s.a. 1168 (she is cited at his death).

Rostislav M´stislavič
Birth date: unknown
Death date: *NPL*, s.a. 1166; Hypatian Chronicle, s.a. 1168; Tver Chronicle, s.a. 1166; Laurentian Chronicle, s.a. 1167; Voskresenskij Chronicle, s.a. 1167 and 1168; Nikon Chronicle, s.a. 1167; Dąbrowski, *Genealogia Mścisławowiczów*, 128, favors 1167 as the correct death date
Knjaz´ of Smolensk start: Laurentian Chronicle, s.a. 1127 (earliest mention of his rule there); knjaz´ of Smolensk end: Hypatian Chronicle, s.a. 1160;
Knjaz´ of Novgorod (1): *NPL*, s.a. 1154; Tver Chronicle, s.a. 1154
Knjaz´ of Kyiv (with Vjačeslav Volodimerič): *NPL*, s.a. 1154; Hypatian Chronicle, s.a. 1154; Tver Chronicle, s.a. 1155; Laurentian Chronicle, s.a. 1154; Voskresenskij Chronicle, s.a. 1154; Nikon Chronicle, s.a. 1155
Knjaz´ of Novgorod (2) start: *NPL*, s.a. 1157; Tver Chronicle, s.a. 1157; knjaz´ of Novgorod (2) end: *NPL*, s.a. 1158; Tver Chronicle, s.a. 1158
Knjaz´ of Kyiv start: Hypatian Chronicle, s.a. 1160; *NPL*, s.a. 1158; Tver Chronicle, s.a. 1159; Laurentian Chronicle, s.a. 1158; Voskresenskij Chronicle, s.a. 1159; Nikon Chronicle, s.a. 1158; knjaz´ of Kyiv end: *NPL*, s.a. 1166; Hypatian Chronicle, s.a. 1168; Tver Chronicle, s.a. 1166; Laurentian Chronicle, s.a. 1167; Voskresenskij Chronicle, s.a. 1167 and 1168; Nikon Chronicle, s.a. 1167
Marriage to N. N.: Hypatian Chronicle, s.a. 1168 (she is cited at his death).

Rogněda M´stislavna
Birth date: unknown
Death date: After the entries which cite her in 1168; see Hypatian Chronicle, s.a. 1168; existence cited at Rostislav M´stislavič's death in 1168 (Hypatian Chronicle, s.a. 1168, for example)
Knjaginja of Zarub: Hypatian Chronicle, s.a. 1168.

Volodimer M´stislavič
Birth date: Hypatian Chronicle, s.a. 1132
Death date: *NPL*, s.a. 1171; Hypatian Chronicle, s.a. 1174; Tver Chronicle, s.a. 1171
Knjaz´ of Gorodec start: Laurentian Chronicle, s.a. 1147; knjaz´ of Gorodec end: Laurentian Chronicle, s.a. 1148
Knjaz´ of Volodymyr start: conjectural based upon his brother's death;

see Hypatian Chronicle, s.a. 1155 (records him already ruling there); knjaz´ of Volodymyr end: Hypatian Chronicle, s.a. 1156; Voskresenskij Chronicle, s.a. 1156

Knjaz´ of Luck: it is possible that he ruled here from his flight in 1156; see Hypatian Chronicle, s.a. 1156; Hypatian Chronicle, s.a. 1162 (records the end of his rule there)

Knjaz´ of Trepole: Hypatian Chronicle, s.a. 1162; Tver Chronicle, s.a. 1162; Nikon Chronicle, s.a. 1160; did not necessarily give Trepole and associated towns up when he took over Dorogobuž

Knjaz´ of Dorogobuž : Hypatian Chronicle, s.a. 1171; Volodimer assumes control of Dorogobuž after the death of Volodimer Andreevič, which is more reliably dated to 1170; see Laurentian Chronicle, s.a. 1170

Knjaz´ of Kyiv start: *NPL*, s.a. 1170; Hypatian Chronicle, s.a. 1173; Tver Chronicle, s.a. 1171; knjaz´ of Kyiv end: *NPL*, s.a. 1171; Hypatian Chronicle, s.a. 1174; Tver Chronicle, s.a. 1171; the dating of this period in the various chronicles is both confused and confusing, but for elucidation on this particular date choice, in regard to Volodimer's death in particular, see Dąbrowski, *Genealogia Mścisławowiczów*, 176–177

Marriage to N. N., daughter of the Ban of Croatia: Hypatian Chronicle, s.a. 1150. For the suggestion of a second marriage, see Dąbrowski, *Genealogia Mścisławowiczów*, 182–83.

N. N., daughter of the Ban of Croatia

Birth date: unknown

Death date: Hypatian Chronicle, s.a. 1169; Nikon Chronicle, s.a. 1167 (both record her still alive at this time)

Marriage to Volodimer M´stislavič: Hypatian Chronicle, s.a. 1150.

Evfrosinija M´stislavna

Birth date: unknown

Death date: Wertner, *Az Árpádok családi története*, 313, suggests 1175; while Dąbrowski instead suggests in or after 1193 based upon a variety of factors; see Dąbrowski, *Genealogia Mścisławowiczów*, 170–71

Marriage to Géza II of Hungary: Wilhelm, "Wilhelmi abbatis genealogia regum Danorum," 182; for the date of the marriage see Dąbrowski, *Genealogia Mścisławowiczówi*, 174. For more information on this marriage see part 1, "Marriages: Generation Five," "Evfrosinija M´stislavna."

Géza II of Hungary

Birth date: Wertner, *Az Árpádok családi története*, 309

Death date: Kinnamos, *Deeds of John and Manuel Comnenus*, bk. 5, ch. 1; Wertner, *Az Árpádok családi története*, 309 (1161); Dąbrowski, *Genealogia Mścisławowiczówi*, 174 (1162)

King of Hungary start: Wertner, *Az Árpádok családi története*, 309; Kinnamos, *Deeds of John and Manuel Comnenus*, bk. 5, ch. 7 (already ruling ca. 1151); king of Hungary end: Kinnamos, *Deeds of John and Manuel Comnenus*, bk. 5, ch. 1; Wertner, *Az Árpádok családi története*, 309 (1161); Dąbrowski, *Genealogia Mścisławowiczówi*, 174 (1162)

Marriage to Evfrosinija M´stislavna: Wilhelm, "Wilhelmi abbatis genealogia regum Danorum," 182; for the date of the marriage see Dąbrowski, *Genealogia Mścisławowiczówi*, 174. For more information on this marriage see part 1, "Marriages: Generation Five," "Evfrosinija M´stislavna."

Jaropolk M´stislavič

Birth date: unknown

Death date: last appearance in the primary sources is in Hypatian Chronicle, s.a. 1149. For more information about him, including a bibliographic study of why he is not in many genealogical sources, see Dąbrowski, *Genealogia Mścisławowiczów*, 183–87.

Table 14: Jurij "Dolgorukij" Volodimerič

N. N., daughter of Khan Aepa, son of Osen

Birth date: unknown

Death date: This is conjectural based upon discussion in the chronicles of an exile to Byzantium in 1162 of Jurij's wife and some of his children. It has been assumed that this was a second wife, and thus N. N., daughter of Khan Aepa, son of Osen, would be dead. For further discussion, see part 1, "Marriages: Generation Four," "Jurij 'Dolgorukij' Volodimerič"; while for the exile, see Hypatian Chronicle, s.a. 1162; Tver Chronicle, s.a. 1162; Voskresenskij Chronicle, s.a. 1162; Nikon Chronicle, s.a. 1160.

Marriage to Jurij "Dolgorukij" Volodimerič: Laurentian Chronicle, s.a. 1107; Nikon Chronicle, s.a. 1107. For more information on this marriage see part 1, "Marriages: Generation Four," "Jurij 'Dolgorukij' Volodimerič."

Jurij "Dolgorukij" Volodimerič

Birth date: unknown

Death date: Rogožskij Chronicle, s.a. 1157; *NPL*, s.a. 1157; Hypatian Chronicle, s.a. 1158; Tver Chronicle, s.a. 1157; Laurentian Chronicle, s.a. 1157; Voskresenskij Chronicle, s.a. 1157; Nikon Chronicle, s.a. 1157

Knjaz´ of Suzdal start: *NPL*, s.a. 1138 (first mention of him there); knjaz´ of Suzdal end: Rogožskij Chronicle, s.a. 1157; *NPL*, s.a. 1157; Hypatian Chronicle, s.a. 1158; Tver Chronicle, s.a. 1157; Laurentian Chronicle, s.a. 1157; Voskresenskij Chronicle, s.a. 1157; Nikon Chronicle, s.a. 1157

Knjaz´ of Perejaslav (1): Voskresenskij Chronicle, s.a. 1131 (for eight days), Tver Chronicle, s.a. 1132; Nikon Chronicle, s.a. 1132

Knjaz´ of Perejaslav (2): Laurentian Chronicle, s.a. 1135; Hypatian Chronicle, s.a. 1135; *NČL*, s.a. 1135; Voskresenskij Chronicle, s.a. 1135; Tver Chronicle, s.a. 1135; Nikon Chronicle, s.a. 1135

Table 14: Jurij "Dolgorukij" Volodimerič

N. N. daughter of Khan Aepa, son of Osen
b. unknown; d. pre-1162
(m. 1107)

1

Jurij "Dolgorukij" Volodimerič
b. unknown; d. 1157
(Suzdal r. pre-1138–1157)
(Perejaslav r. 1132)
(Perejaslav r. 1135)
(Kyiv r. 1149–1150)
(Perejaslav r. 1151)
(Kyiv r. 1155–1157)

Rostislav
b. unknown; d. 1151
(Novgorod r. 1138–1139)
(Novgorod r. 1141–ca. 1142)
(Busk r. 1148–1149)
(Perejaslav r. 1149–1151)

N. N.
b. unknown;
d. post-1176
(m. unknown)

Andrej "Bogoljubskij"
b. unknown; d. 1174
(Vyšehorod r. 1149–1150)
(Peresopnica r. 1150–1151)
(Vyšehorod r. 1155)
(Vladimir-Suzdal r. 1158–1174)

Unknown
b. d. unknown
(m. unknown)

Jaroslav
b. unknown; d. 1166
(Novgorod r. 1138–1139)

Ivanko
b. unknown;
d. 1147

Oleg Svjatoslavič
b. unknown; d. 1178
(Novhorod-Siverskyj r. 1164–1178)

N. N.
b. unknown;
pre-1165
(m. unknown)

Svjatoslav
b. unknown;
d. 1174

N. N.
b. unknown; d. 1154
(m. unknown)

1

Glěb
b. unknown; d. 1171
(Kaniv r. 1149–1150)
(Peresopnica and Dorogobuž r. 1150)
(Perejaslav r. 1151)
(Gorodok r. 1151–1152)
(Perejaslav r. 1154–1169)
(Kyiv r. 1169–1171)

2

N. N. daughter of Izjaslav Davydič
b. unknown; d. 1189
(m. 1155)

2

N. N.
b. unknown; d. post-1162
(m. pre-1162)

Boris
b. unknown; d. 1159
(Bilhorod r. 1149–1150)
(Turov r. 1155–1159)

Vasil′ko
b. unknown; d. post-1162
(Suzdal r. 1149–1150)
(Novgorod r. 1152)
(Porose r. 1155–pre-1162)
(Danubian lands r. 1162–unknown)

Roman
b. d. unknown

Jaroslav Volodimerič
b. unknown; d. 1187
(Halyč r. 1152–1187)

N. N. "Ol′ga"
b. unknown;
d. 1181
(m. 1150)

N. N.
"Fevronia"
b. unknown; d. 1202
(m. pre-1176)

Mixailko
b. unknown; d. 1176
(Kyiv r. ca. 1172)
(Vladimir-Suzdal r. 1176)

Petrovna
Mixailovica
b. unknown;
d. post-1155
(m. 1155)

M′stislav
b. unknown; d. post-1162
(Peresopnica r. 1150)
(Novgorod r. 1154–1158)
(Oskalana r. 1162–unknown)

Maria of Ossetia
b. unknown; d. 1205
(m. pre-1205)

1

Vsevolod
"Bol′šoe Gnězdo"
b. 1155; d. 1212
(Perejaslav r. 1175–1176)
(Vladimir-Suzdal r. 1176–1212)

2

N. N., daughter of
Vasil′ko Brjačeslavič
b. unknown;
d. post-1209
(m. 1209)

Knjaz´ of Kyiv (1) start: Laurentian Chronicle, s.a. 1149; *NPL*, s.a. 1149; Hypatian Chronicle, s.a. 1149; Tver Chronicle, s.a. 1149; Voskresenskij Chronicle, s.a. 1149; Nikon Chronicle, s.a. 1149; knjaz´ of Kyiv (1) end: Laurentian Chronicle, s.a. 1150; Hypatian Chronicle, s.a. 1150; Tver Chronicle, s.a. 1151; Voskresenskij Chronicle, s.a. 1150; Nikon Chronicle, s.a. 1150

Knjaz´ of Perejaslav (3): Hypatian Chronicle, s.a. 1151; Tver Chronicle, s.a. 1151

Knjaz´ of Kyiv (2) start: Rogožskij Chronicle, s.a. 1155; *NPL*, s.a. 1155; Hypatian Chronicle, s.a. 1155; Tver Chronicle, s.a. 1155; Laurentian Chronicle, s.a. 1154; Voskresenskij Chronicle, s.a. 1154; Nikon Chronicle, s.a. 1155; knjaz´ of Kyiv (2) end: Rogožskij Chronicle, s.a. 1157; *NPL*, s.a. 1157; Hypatian Chronicle, s.a. 1158; Tver Chronicle, s.a. 1157; Laurentian Chronicle, s.a. 1157; Voskresenskij Chronicle, s.a. 1157; Nikon Chronicle, s.a. 1157

Marriage to N. N.: Laurentian Chronicle, s.a. 1107; Nikon Chronicle, s.a. 1107. For more information on this marriage see part 1, "Marriages: Generation Four," "Jurij 'Dolgorukij' Volodimerič."

N. N., wife of Jurij "Dolgorukij" Volodimerič

Birth date: unknown

Death date: conjectural based upon her and her children's expulsion from Rus´ in 1162, cited in Tver Chronicle, s.a. 1162; Voskresenskij Chronicle, s.a. 1162; Nikon Chronicle, s.a. 1160

Marriage to Jurij "Dolgorukij" Volodimerič: conjectural based upon her explusion to Byzantium, specifically, as discussed in Tver Chronicle, s.a. 1162; Voskresenskij Chronicle, s.a. 1162; Nikon Chronicle, s.a. 1160. For more information on this marriage see part 1, "Marriages: Generation Four," "Jurij 'Dolgorukij' Volodimerič."

Rostislav Jurevič

Birth date: unknown

Death date: Hypatian Chronicle, s.a. 1150; Laurentian Chronicle, s.a. 1151; Tver Chronicle, s.a. 1151; Voskresenskij Chronicle, s.a. 1151; Nikon Chronicle, s.a. 1150

Knjaz´ of Novgorod (1) start: Laurentian Chronicle, s.a. 1138; Hypatian Chronicle, s.a. 1139; Voskresenskij Chronicle, s.a. 1138; Tver Chronicle, s.a. 1138; Nikon Chronicle, s.a. 1138; knjaz´ of Novgorod (1) end: Hypatian Chronicle, s.a. 1140; Voskresenskij Chronicle, s.a. 1139; Laurentian Chronicle, s.a. 1139; *NPL*, s.a. 1139; Tver Chronicle, s.a. 1139; Nikon Chronicle, s.a. 1139

Knjaz´ of Novgorod (2) start: *NPL*, s.a. 1141; Laurentian Chronicle, s.a. 1141; Voskresenskij Chronicle, s.a. 1141; Tver Chronicle, s.a. 1141; Nikon Chronicle, s.a. 1141; knjaz´ of Novgorod (2) end: *NPL*, s.a.

1142; Laurentian Chronicle, s.a. 1141; Hypatian Chronicle, s.a. 1141; Voskresenskij Chronicle, s.a. 1141; Tver Chronicle, s.a. 1142

Knjaz´ of Busk start: Hypatian Chronicle, s.a. 1148; Tver Chronicle, s.a. 1148; Voskresenskij Chronicle, s.a. 1148; Nikon Chronicle, s.a. 1148; knjaz´ of Busk end: Hypatian Chronicle, s.a. 1149; Tver Chronicle, s.a. 1149; Voskresenskij Chronicle, s.a. 1149; Nikon Chronicle, s.a. 1149

Knjaz´ of Perejaslav start: Hypatian Chronicle, s.a. 1149; Laurentian Chronicle, s.a. 1149; Tver Chronicle, s.a. 1149; Voskresenskij Chronicle, s.a. 1149; Nikon Chronicle, s.a. 1149; knjaz´ of Perejaslav end: Hypatian Chronicle, s.a. 1150; Laurentian Chronicle, s.a. 1151; Tver Chronicle, s.a. 1151; Voskresenskij Chronicle, s.a. 1151; Nikon Chronicle, s.a. 1150

Marriage with N. N.: conjectural based upon a child cited in *NPL*, s.a. 1160.

N. N., wife of Rostislav Jurevič

Birth date: unknown

Death date: Voskresenskij Chronicle, s.a. 1176 (still alive)

Marriage with Rostislav Jurevič: conjectural based upon a child cited in *NPL*, s.a. 1160.

Ivanko Jurevič

Birth date: unknown

Death date: Hypatian Chronicle, s.a. 1146; Voskresenskij Chronicle, s.a. 1146; Tver Chronicle, s.a. 1147; Nikon Chronicle, s.a. 1146.

Andrej "Bogoljubskij" Jurevič

Birth date: unknown

Death date: *NPL*, s.a. 1174; Hypatian Chronicle, s.a. 1175; Rogožskij Chronicle, s.a. 1175; Tver Chronicle, s.a. 1175; Laurentian Chronicle, s.a. 1175; Voskresenskij Chronicle, s.a. 1175; Nikon Chronicle, s.a. 1175

Knjaz´ of Vyšhorod (1) start: Laurentian Chronicle, s.a. 1150; Hypatian Chronicle, s.a. 1149; knjaz´ of Vyšhorod (1) end: Laurentian Chronicle, s.a. 1150; Hypatian Chronicle, s.a. 1150; Voskresenskij Chronicle, s.a. 1150

Knjaz´ of Peresopnica (and other cities) start: Laurentian Chronicle, s.a. 1150; Hypatian Chronicle, s.a. 1150; Tver Chronicle, s.a. 1151; Voskresenskij Chronicle, s.a. 1150; Nikon Chronicle, s.a. 1150; knjaz´ of Peresopnica (and other cities) end: Laurentian Chronicle, s.a. 1150; Hypatian Chronicle, s.a. 1151 (abandons these possessions to return to Suzdal)

Knjaz´ of Vyšhorod (2) start: Hypatian Chronicle, s.a. 1155; Tver

Chronicle, s.a. 1155; Laurentian Chronicle, s.a. 1154; Voskresenskij Chronicle, s.a. 1154; Nikon Chronicle, s.a. 1155; knjaz´ of Vyšhorod (2) end: Hypatian Chronicle, s.a. 1155; Laurentian Chronicle, s.a. 1155; Voskresenskij Chronicle, s.a. 1155; Nikon Chronicle, s.a. 1155

Knjaz´ of Vladimir-Suzdal start: Rogožskij Chronicle, s.a. 1158; Hypatian Chronicle, s.a. 1158; Tver Chronicle, s.a. 1157; Laurentian Chronicle, s.a. 1157; Nikon Chronicle, s.a. 1157; knjaz´ of Vladimir-Suzdal end: *NPL*, s.a. 1174; Hypatian Chronicle, s.a. 1175; Rogožskij Chronicle, s.a. 1175; Tver Chronicle, s.a. 1175; Laurentian Chronicle, s.a. 1175; Voskresenskij Chronicle, s.a. 1175; Nikon Chronicle, s.a. 1175

Relationship with unknown partner: Baumgarten lists two wives for Andrej "Bogoljubskij," neither of which I was able to confirm in the primary sources, but he definitely had children and thus a partner of some sort.

Unknown partner of Andrej "Bogoljubskij" Jurevič

Birth date: unknown

Death date: unknown

Relationship with Andrej "Bogoljubskij": Baumgarten lists two wives for Andrej "Bogoljubskij," neither of which I was able to confirm in the primary sources, but he definitely had children and thus a partner of some sort.

Oleg Svjatoslavič

Birth date: unknown

Death date: Hypatian Chronicle, s.a. 1178

Knjaz´ of Novhorod-Siverskyj start: Hypatian Chronicle, s.a. 1164; Tver Chronicle, s.a. 1164; Voskresenskij Chronicle, s.a. 1164; Nikon Chronicle, s.a. 1165; knjaz´ of Novhorod-Siverskyj end: Hypatian Chronicle, s.a. 1178

Marriage to N. N., daughter of Jurij Volodimerič: Hypatian Chronicle, s.a. 1150.

N. N. Jurevna

Birth date: unknown

Death date: Voskresenskij Chronicle, s.a. 1166, Hypatian Chronicle, s.a. 1167 (where she is referred to mistakenly as Andreevna)

Marriage to Oleg Svjatoslavič: Hypatian Chronicle, s.a. 1150.

Svjatoslav Jurevič

Birth date: unknown

Death date: Hypatian Chronicle, s.a. 1174; Tver Chronicle, s.a. 1174; Laurentian Chronicle, s.a. 1174; Voskresenskij Chronicle, s.a. 1174; Nikon Chronicle, s.a. 1174.

Jaroslav Jurevič
Birth date: unknown
Death date: Hypatian Chronicle, s.a. 1166; Tver Chronicle, s.a. 1166; Laurentian Chronicle, s.a. 1166; Voskresenskij Chronicle, s.a. 1166; Nikon Chronicle, s.a. 1166
Knjaz′ of Novgorod start: *NPL*, s.a. 1138; *NČL*, s.a. 1138; knjaz′ of Novgorod end: *NPL*, s.a. 1139.

N. N., wife of Glěb Jurevič
Birth date: unknown
Death date: Tver Chronicle, s.a. 1154; Hypatian Chronicle, s.a. 1154; Laurentian Chronicle, s.a. 1154; Voskresenskij Chronicle, s.a. 1154; Nikon Chronicle, s.a. 1154
Marriage to Glěb Jurevič: Tver Chronicle, s.a. 1154; Hypatian Chronicle, s.a. 1154; Laurentian Chronicle, s.a. 1154; Voskresenskij Chronicle, s.a. 1154; Nikon Chronicle, s.a. 1154.

Glěb Jurevič
Birth date: unknown
Death date: *NPL*, s.a. 1170; Hypatian Chronicle, s.a. 1173; Rogožskij Chronicle, s.a. 1172; Tver Chronicle, s.a. 1171; Laurentian Chronicle, s.a. 1172; Voskresenskij Chronicle, s.a. 1172; Nikon Chronicle, s.a. 1172
Knjaz′ of Kaniv start: Hypatian Chronicle, s.a. 1149; knjaz′ of Kaniv end: Hypatian Chronicle, s.a. 1150 (assigned elsewhere)
Knjaz′ of Peresopnica and Dorogobuž: Hypatian Chronicle, s.a. 1150
Knjaz′ of Perejaslav (1): Hypatian Chronicle, s.a. 1151; Tver Chronicle, s.a. 1151; Laurentian Chronicle, s.a. 1151; Voskresenskij Chronicle, s.a. 1151; Nikon Chronicle, s.a. 1151
Knjaz′ of Gorodok start: Hypatian Chronicle, s.a. 1151; Tver Chronicle, s.a. 1151; Laurentian Chronicle, s.a. 1151; Voskresenskij Chronicle, s.a. 1151; Nikon Chronicle, s.a. 1151; knjaz′ of Gorodok end: conjectural based upon his riding with the Polovcians cited in Hypatian Chronicle, s.a. 1152, 1153
Knjaz′ of Perejaslav (2) start: Hypatian Chronicle, s.a. 1154; Tver Chronicle, s.a. 1155; Laurentian Chronicle, s.a. 1154; Voskresenskij Chronicle, s.a. 1154; Nikon Chronicle, s.a. 1155; knjaz′ of Perejaslav (2) end: Hypatian Chronicle, s.a. 1171; Voskresenskij Chronicle, s.a. 1170; placed in 1169 due to his assumption of power in Kyiv and his placement of his son in Perejaslav at that time
Knjaz′ of Kyiv start: Hypatian Chronicle, s.a. 1171; Tver Chronicle, s.a. 1170; Laurentian Chronicle, s.a. 1168 (listed under 1169 as well); Voskresenskij Chronicle, s.a. 1170; Nikon Chronicle, s.a. 1170; I have followed the Laurentian Chronicle's dating here, as I believe

it fits the progression of rulers of Kyiv most accurately, though each of the chronicles gives slightly different dates; knjaz´ of Kyiv end: *NPL*, s.a. 1170; Hypatian Chronicle, s.a. 1173; Rogožskij Chronicle, s.a. 1172; Tver Chronicle, s.a. 1171; Laurentian Chronicle, s.a. 1172; Voskresenskij Chronicle, s.a. 1172; Nikon Chronicle, s.a. 1172; here again the dating is difficult and I have accepted the Hypatian's statement that Glěb ruled for two years to be accurate based upon looking at the various gaps in the dating and thus used 1171

Marriage to N. N., wife of Glěb Jurevič: Tver Chronicle, s.a. 1154; Hypatian Chronicle, s.a. 1154; Laurentian Chronicle, s.a. 1154; Voskresenskij Chronicle, s.a. 1154; Nikon Chronicle, s.a. 1154

Marriage to N. N. Izjaslavna: Hypatian Chronicle, s.a. 1155; Tver Chronicle, s.a. 1155; Laurentian Chronicle, s.a. 1155; Voskresenskij Chronicle, s.a. 1155; Nikon Chronicle, s.a. 1155.

N. N., daughter of Izjaslav Davydič

Birth date: unknown

Death date: Laurentian Chronicle, s.a. 1189

Marriage to Glěb Jurevič: Hypatian Chronicle, s.a. 1155; Tver Chronicle, s.a. 1155; Laurentian Chronicle, s.a. 1155; Voskresenskij Chronicle, s.a. 1155; Nikon Chronicle, s.a. 1155.

Boris Jurevič

Birth date: unknown

Death date: Hypatian Chronicle, s.a. 1159; Tver Chronicle, s.a. 1159; Laurentian Chronicle, s.a. 1159; Voskresenskij Chronicle, s.a. 1159; Nikon Chronicle, s.a. 1158

Knjaz´ of Bilhorod: Laurentian Chronicle, s.a. 1150; Hypatian Chronicle, s.a. 1149

Knjaz´ of Turov start: Hypatian Chronicle, s.a. 1155; Tver Chronicle, s.a. 1155; Laurentian Chronicle, s.a. 1154; Voskresenskij Chronicle, s.a. 1154; Nikon Chronicle, s.a. 1155; knjaz´ of Turov end: Hypatian Chronicle, s.a. 1159; Tver Chronicle, s.a. 1159; Laurentian Chronicle, s.a. 1159; Voskresenskij Chronicle, s.a. 1159; Nikon Chronicle, s.a. 1158.

Jaroslav Volodimerič

Birth date: unknown

Death date: Hypatian Chronicle, s.a. 1187

Knjaz´ of Halyč start: Hypatian Chronicle, s.a. 1152; knjaz´ of Halyč end: Hypatian Chronicle, s.a. 1187

Marriage to N. N., "Ol´ga" Jurevna: Hypatian Chronicle, s.a. 1150.

N. N., "Ol´ga" Jurevna

Birth date: unknown

Death date: Hypatian Chronicle, s.a. 1181; Tver Chronicle, s.a. 1183; Laurentian Chronicle, s.a. 1183; Nikon Chronicle, s.a. 1182
Marriage to Jaroslav Volodimerič: Hypatian Chronicle, s.a. 1150; Baumgarten, "Généalogies," table 6, is responsible for the identification of Jaroslav's wife with Ol´ga Jurevna.

Petrovna Mixailovica
Birth date: unknown
Death date: Her death date can reasonably be assumed to have occurred after her marriage, though when is unknown.
Marriage to M´stislav Jurevič: Hypatian Chronicle, s.a. 1155; Tver Chronicle, s.a. 1155; Laurentian Chronicle, s.a. 1155; Voskresenskij Chronicle, s.a. 1155; Nikon Chronicle, s.a. 1155.

M´stislav Jurevič
Birth date: unknown
Death date: His death can be reasonably presumed to have occurred after his exile, which is dated to 1162; see Hypatian Chronicle, s.a. 1162; Tver Chronicle, s.a. 1162; Voskresenskij Chronicle, s.a. 1162; Nikon Chronicle, s.a. 1160 (all record his exile)
Knjaz´ of Peresopnica: Hypatian Chronicle, s.a. 1150; Voskresenskij Chronicle, s.a. 1150; Nikon Chronicle, s.a. 1150
Knjaz´ of Novgorod start: *NPL*, s.a. 1154; Hypatian Chronicle, s.a. 1154; Tver Chronicle, s.a. 1155; Laurentian Chronicle, s.a. 1154; Voskresenskij Chronicle, s.a. 1154; Nikon Chronicle, s.a. 1155; knjaz´ of Novgorod end: *NPL*, s.a. 1157; Hypatian Chronicle, s.a. 1158; Tver Chronicle, s.a. 1157; Laurentian Chronicle, s.a. 1157; Voskresenskij Chronicle, s.a. 1157; Nikon Chronicle, s.a. 1157
Ruler of Okslana (in exile in Byzantium): Hypatian Chronicle, s.a. 1162; Voskresenskij Chronicle, s.a. 1162
Marriage to Petrovna Mixailovica: Hypatian Chronicle, s.a. 1155; Tver Chronicle, s.a. 1155; Laurentian Chronicle, s.a. 1155; Voskresenskij Chronicle, s.a. 1155; Nikon Chronicle, s.a. 1155.

Vasil´ko Jurevič
Birth date: unknown
Death date: His death can be reasonably presumed to have occurred after his exile, which is dated to 1162; see Hypatian Chronicle, s.a. 1162; Tver Chronicle, s.a. 1162; Voskresenskij Chronicle, s.a. 1162; Nikon Chronicle, s.a. 1160 (all record his exile)
Knjaz´ of Suzdal start: Hypatian Chronicle, s.a. 1149; knjaz´ of Suzdal end: conjectural based upon Jurij's return from Kyiv
Knjaz´ of Novgorod: Laurentian Chronicle, s.a. 1152
Knjaz´ of Porose start: Hypatian Chronicle, s.a. 1155; Tver Chronicle, s.a.

1155; Laurentian Chronicle, s.a. 1154; Voskresenskij Chronicle, s.a. 1154; Nikon Chronicle, s.a. 1155; knjaz´ of Porose end: conjectural based upon exile

Ruler of Danubian lands (in exile in Byzantium): Hypatian Chronicle, s.a. 1162; Tver Chronicle, s.a. 1162; Voskresenskij Chronicle, s.a. 1162; Nikon Chronicle, s.a. 1160; Kinnamos, *Deeds of John and Manuel Comnenus*, bk. 5, ch. 12.

N. N. "Fevronia," wife of Mixailko Jurevič

Birth date: unknown

Death date: Tver Chronicle, s.a. 1202; Laurentian Chronicle, s.a. 1202; Nikon Chronicle, s.a. 1201

Marriage to Mixailko Jurevič: conjectural based on the assumption that she and Mixailko would be married before his death. For their connection, see the chronicle entries at her death: Tver Chronicle, s.a. 1202; Laurentian Chronicle, s.a. 1202; Nikon Chronicle, s.a. 1201.

Mixailko Jurevič

Birth date: unknown

Death date: *NPL*, s.a. 1176; Tver Chronicle, s.a. 1177; Hypatian Chronicle, s.a. 1177 (mentions Vsevolod as ruler, indicating Mixailko is dead); Rogožskij Chronicle, s.a. 1175 (says he ruled one year and died); Laurentian Chronicle, s.a. 1177; Voskresenskij Chronicle, s.a. 1177; Nikon Chronicle, s.a. 1177

Knjaz´ of Kyiv: *NPL*, s.a. 1172, 1173; Tver Chronicle, s.a. 1173; Nikon Chronicle, s.a. 1172. It is interesting to note that these events are not recorded in either the Hypatian or Laurentian Chronicles. Instead, the Hypatian says that after Roman Rostislavič's expulsion from Kyiv, Mixailko was indisposed in the land of the Torks and Vsevolod, his brother, sat in Kyiv for six weeks; see Hypatian Chronicle, s.a. 1174. It is possible that the chronicle traditions confused or conflated the brothers such that a Jurevič ruled in 1172, but not both. I have chosen to include Mixailko for that purpose, while acknowledging that it certainly could have been Vsevolod.

Knjaz´ of Vladimir-Suzdal: Mixailko's reign in Vladimir-Suzdal is a brief one encompassing most of a year. It has generally been accepted that his death occurred in 1176, though the majority of chronicles record it in 1177, and I have followed that trend; see *NPL*, s.a. 1175, 1176; Hypatian Chronicle, s.a. 1176, 1177 (mentions Vsevolod as ruler, indicating Mixailko is dead); Rogožskij Chronicle, s.a. 1175 (says he ruled one year and died); Tver Chronicle, s.a. 1176, 1177; Laurentian Chronicle, s.a. 1176, 1177; Voskresenskij Chronicle, s.a. 1176, 1177; Nikon Chronicle, s.a. 1176, 1177.

Marriage to N. N.: Tver Chronicle, s.a. 1202; Laurentian Chronicle, s.a. 1202; Nikon Chronicle, s.a. 1201.

Roman Jurevič
Birth date: unknown
Death date: unknown; existence cited in *NPL*, s.a. 1176 (though this could be an error, or a reference to another of Jurij's children).

Maria of Ossetia
Birth date: unknown
Death date: *NPL*, s.a. 1205; Tver Chronicle, s.a. 1205; Laurentian Chronicle, s.a. 1206; Voskresenskij Chronicle, s.a. 1205; Nikon Chronicle, s.a. 1205
Marriage to Vsevolod "Bol′šoe Gnězdo" Jurevič: conjectural that their marital date would be before the date of her death. For their relationship, see the chronicle entries at her death: *NPL*, s.a. 1205; Tver Chronicle, s.a. 1205; Laurentian Chronicle, s.a. 1206; Voskresenskij Chronicle, s.a. 1205; Nikon Chronicle, s.a. 1205.

Vsevolod "Bol′šoe Gnězdo" Jurevič
Birth date: Tver Chronicle, s.a. 1155; Voskresenskij Chronicle, s.a. 1154; Nikon Chronicle, s.a. 1155
Death date: Rogožskij Chronicle, s.a. 1212; Tver Chronicle, s.a. 1212; Laurentian Chronicle, s.a. 1212; Voskresenskij Chronicle, s.a. 1212; Nikon Chronicle, s.a. 1213
Knjaz′ of Kyiv: Though the Hypatian Chronicle (s.a. 1174) lists Vsevolod as sitting in Kyiv for six weeks after the expulsion of Roman Rostislavič, which probably occurred in roughly 1172, I have not included that rule here. Instead, the same regnal space was also occupied by his elder brother Mixailko, according to the *NPL*, Tver, and Nikon chronicles (see Mixailko's entry above for specific citations). I believe that one or the other of the brothers occupied Kyiv briefly in that time as a placeholder, but the chronicle tradition is confused as to which. I have privileged Mixailko in this regard, while acknowledging that it could be either.
Knjaz′ of Perejaslav start: *NPL*, s.a. 1175; Tver Chronicle, s.a. 1176; Laurentian Chronicle, s.a. 1176; Voskresenskij Chronicle, s.a. 1176; Nikon Chronicle, s.a. 1176; knjaz′ of Perejaslav end: Tver Chronicle, s.a. 1177; Laurentian Chronicle, s.a. 1177; Voskresenskij Chronicle, s.a. 1177; Nikon Chronicle, s.a. 1177
Knjaz′ of Vladimir-Suzdal start: *NPL*, s.a. 1176; Tver Chronicle, s.a. 1177; Hypatian Chronicle, s.a. 1177; Rogožskij Chronicle, s.a. 1175 (indicating that he began after Mixailko's death in 1176); Laurentian Chronicle, s.a. 1177; Voskresenskij Chronicle, s.a. 1177; Nikon

Chronicle, s.a. 1177; knjaz´ of Vladimir-Suzdal end: Rogožskij Chronicle, s.a. 1212; Tver Chronicle, s.a. 1212; Laurentian Chronicle, s.a. 1212; Voskresenskij Chronicle, s.a. 1212; Nikon Chronicle, s.a. 1213

Marriage to Maria of Ossetia: *NPL*, s.a. 1205; Tver Chronicle, s.a. 1205; Laurentian Chronicle, s.a. 1206; Voskresenskij Chronicle, s.a. 1205; Nikon Chronicle, s.a. 1205

Marriage to N. N., daughter of Vasil´ko Brjačeslavič: Voskresenskij Chronicle, s.a. 1209; Nikon Chronicle, s.a. 1209.

N. N., daughter of Vasil´ko Brjačeslavič

Birth date: unknown

Death date: Her death date can reasonably be assumed to have occurred after her marriage, though when is unknown.

Marriage to Vsevolod "Bol´šoe Gnězdo" Jurevič: Voskresenskij Chronicle, s.a. 1209; Nikon Chronicle, s.a. 1209.

Table 15: Scandinavian Dynastic Marriages

Jaroslav "Mudryj" Volodimerič
Birth date: unknown
Death date: *PVL*, s.a. 1054
Knjaz′ of Rostov: *PVL*, s.a. 988
Knjaz′ of Novgorod start (1): *PVL*, s.a. 988; knjaz′ of Novgorod end (1): *PVL*, s.a. 1015
Knjaz′ of Kyiv (1) start: *PVL*, s.a. 1016; knjaz′ of Kyiv (1) end: *PVL*, s.a. 1018
Knjaz′ of Kyiv (2) start: *PVL*, s.a 1018; knjaz′ of Kyiv (2) end: *PVL*, s.a. 1054
Knjaz′ of Novgorod (2) start: *PVL*, s.a. 1020; knjaz′ of Novgorod (2) end: *PVL*, s.a. 1036
Marriage to Ingigerd: Sturluson, *Heimskringla*, 342–43; *Morkinskinna*, ch. 1. For more on this marriage see part 1, "Marriages: Generation One," "Jaroslav Volodimerič."

Ingigerd of Sweden
Birth date: unknown
Death date: *PVL*, s.a. 1050
Marriage to Jaroslav Volodimerič: Sturluson, *Heimskringla*, 342–43; *Morkinskinna*, ch. 1. For more on this marriage see part 1, "Marriages: Generation One," "Jaroslav Volodimerič."

Harald "Hardrada"
Birth date: unknown
Death date: Sturluson, *Heimskringla*, 655; *Morkinskinna*, ch. 14
King of Norway start: Sturluson, *Heimskringla*, 593; *Morkinskinna*, ch. 14; king of Norway end: Sturluson, *Heimskringla*, 655; *Morkinskinna*, ch. 14
Marriage to Elisabeth Jaroslavna: Sturluson, *Heimskringla*, 590; *Mor-*

Table 15: Scandinavian Dynastic Marriages

Jaroslav "Mudryj" Volodimerič
b. unknown; d. 1054
(Rostov ca. 988)
(Novgorod r. ca. 988–1015)
(Kyiv r. 1016–1018)
(Novgorod r. 1020–1036)

Ingigerd of Sweden
b. unknown; d. 1050
(m. 1019)

Harald "Hardrada" of Norway
b. unknown; d. 1066
(King of Norway r. ca. 1044–1066)

1

Elisabeth
b. unknown;
d. post-1066
(1st m. 1042)
(2nd m. post-1066)

Unknown husband
b. d. unknown

Maria
b. unknown
d. 1066

Olav Sveinsson
b. unknown;
d. 1095
(King of Denmark r. 1088–1095)

1

Ingigerd
b. unknown;
d. post-1096
(1st m. pre-1095)
(2nd m. 1096)

2

Filip
b. unknown;
d. 1118
(Sweden r. 1110–1118)

Gyða Haroldsdottir
b. unknown; d. 1107
(m. ca. 1074)

Volodimer "Monomax" Vsevolodič
b. 1053; d. 1125
(Smolensk r. ca. 1078–ca. 1095)
(Černihiv r. 1078–1094)
(Perejaslav r. 1094–1113)
(Kyiv r. ca. 1113–1125)

M´stislav "Harald"
b. 1076; d. 1132
(Novgorod r. 1095–1117)
(Bilhorod r. 1117–1125)
(Kyiv r. 1125–1132)

Kristín Ingesdottir of Sweden
b. unknown; d. 1122
(m. ca. 1095)

Sigurd "the Crusader" Magnusson of Norway
b. unknown; d. 1130
(Norway r. 1103–1130)

1

Malfrid
b. unknown;
d. post-1135
(1st m. 1111)
(2nd m. 1132)

2

Eric "Emune" Ericsson of Denmark
b. unknown;
d. 1137
(Denmark r. 1134–1137)

Knud "Lavard" Ericsson of Denmark
b. unknown; d. 1131
(Duke of Schleswig r. 1115–1131)
(King of the Abodrite Slavs r. ca. 1128–1131)

Ingeborg
b. unknown;
d. post-1137
(m. ca. 1115)

kinskinna, ch. 13; Adam of Bremen, *History of the Archbishops of Hamburg-Bremen*, bk. 3, xiii.12, schol. 62 (63); *Flateyjarbók*, 290. For more on this marriage see part 1, "Marriages: Generation Two," "Elisabeth Jaroslavna."

Elisabeth Jaroslavna

Birth date: unknown

Death date: Elisabeth's last mention is in 1066 after the death of Harald in England; see Sturluson, *Heimskringla*, 660

Marriage to Harald "Hardrada": Sturluson, *Heimskringla*, 590; *Morkinskinna*, ch. 13; Adam of Bremen, *History of the Archbishops of Hamburg-Bremen*, bk. 3, ch. xiii.12, schol. 62 (63); *Flateyjarbók*, 290

Marriage to unknown husband: see the discussion in part 1 for a full explanation. For more on these marriages see part 1, "Marriages: Generation Two," "Elisabeth Jaroslavna."

Unknown husband

For the details of this unknown husband, see part 1, "Marriages: Generation Two," "Elisabeth Jaroslavna."

Maria Haraldsdottir

Birth date: unknown

Death date: *Morkinskinna*, ch. 51.

Olav Sveinsson

Birth date: unknown

Death date: conjectural based upon the end date of his rule cited in Sturluson, *Heimskringla*, 666

King of Denmark start: Sturluson, *Heimskringla*, 666; king of Denmark end: Sturluson, *Heimskringla*, 666

Marriage to Ingigerd Haraldsdottir: Sturluson, *Heimskringla*, 666; *Morkinskinna*, ch. 53.

Ingigerd Haraldsdottir

Birth date: unknown

Death date: Her death date can reasonably be assumed to have occurred after her second marriage, though when is unknown.

Marriage to Olav Sveinsson: Sturluson, *Heimskringla*, 666; *Morkinskinna*, ch. 53

Marriage to Filip: Lagerqvist, *Sverige och dess regenter under 1000 år*, 45.

Filip

Birth date: unknown

Death date: Lars O. Lagerqvist, *Sverige och dess regenter under 1000 år*, 45

Marriage to Ingigerd Haraldsdottir: Lagerqvist, *Sverige och dess regenter under 1000 år*, 45.

Gyða Haroldsdottir
Birth date: unknown
Death date: *PVL*, s.a. 1107
Marriage to Volodimer "Monomax" Vsevolodič: Saxo Grammaticus, bk. 11, ch. 6, 58; Sturluson, *Heimskringla*, 702. For more on this marriage see part 1, "Marriages: Generation Three," "Volodimer 'Monomax' Vsevolodič."

Volodimer "Monomax" Vsevolodič
Birth date: *PVL*, s.a. 1053
Death date: Laurentian Chronicle, s.a. 1125; *NPL*, s.a. 1125; Rogožskij Chronicle, s.a. 1125; Tver Chronicle, s.a. 1125; Nikon Chronicle, s.a. 1125
Knjaz′ of Smolensk start: *PVL*, s.a. 1078; knjaz′ of Smolensk end: *PVL*, s.a. 1095 (based on the assumption that Davyd takes power in Smolensk in that year)
Knjaz′ of Černihiv start: *PVL*, s.a. 1078; knjaz′ of Černihiv end: *PVL*, s.a. 1094
Knjaz′ of Perejaslav start: *PVL*, s.a. 1094; knjaz′ of Perejaslav end: *PVL*, s.a. 1113 (conjectural based upon his assumption of power in Kyiv)
Knjaz′ of Kyiv start: Laurentian Chronicle, s.a. 1114; Hypatian Chronicle, s.a. 1113; *NPL*, s.a. 1113; Rogožskij Chronicle, s.a. 1114; Tver Chronicle, s.a. 1113; Nikon Chronicle, s.a. 1114; knjaz′ of Kyiv end: Laurentian Chronicle, s.a. 1125; *NPL*, s.a. 1125; Rogožskij Chronicle, s.a. 1125; Tver Chronicle, s.a. 1125; Nikon Chronicle, s.a. 1125
Marriage to Gyða Haroldsdottir: Saxo Grammaticus, bk. 11, ch. 6, 58; Sturluson, *Heimskringla*, 702
Marriage to N. N.: Laurentian Chronicle, s.a. 1126; Hypatian Chronicle, s.a. 1127; Voskresenskij Chronicle, s.a. 1126; Nikon Chronicle, s.a. 1126. For more on these marriages see part 1, "Marriages: Generation Three," "Volodimer 'Monomax' Vsevolodič."

M′stislav "Harald" Volodimerič
Birth date: *PVL*, s.a. 1076
Death date: *NPL*, s.a. 1132; Laurentian Chronicle, s.a. 1132; Hypatian Chronicle, s.a. 1133; *NČL*, s.a. 1131; Voskresenskij Chronicle, s.a. 1131; Rogožskij Chronicle, s.a. 1132; Tver Chronicle, s.a. 1132; Nikon Chronicle, s.a. 1132
Knjaz′ of Novgorod start: *PVL*, s.a. 1095; knjaz′ of Novgorod end: *NPL*, s.a. 1117; Laurentian Chronicle, s.a. 1117; *NČL*, s.a. 1117; Hypatian

Chronicle, s.a. 1117; Voskresenskij Chronicle, s.a. 1117; Tver Chronicle, s.a. 1117; Nikon Chronicle, s.a. 1117

Knjaz′ of Bilhorod start: *NPL*, s.a. 1117; Laurentian Chronicle, s.a. 1117; Hypatian Chronicle, s.a. 1117; *NČL*, s.a. 1117; Voskresenskij Chronicle, s.a. 1117; Tver Chronicle, s.a. 1117; Nikon Chronicle, s.a. 1117 (Hypatian, Voskresenskij, Tver, and Nikon all specifically refer to Bilhorod while the rest simply assume a move to assist his father in Kyiv); knjaz′ of Bilhorod end: *NPL*, s.a. 1125; Laurentian Chronicle, s.a. 1125; Hypatian Chronicle, s.a. 1126; Voskresenskij Chronicle, s.a. 1125; Tver Chronicle, s.a. 1125

Knjaz′ of Kyiv start: *NPL*, s.a. 1125; Laurentian Chronicle, s.a. 1125; Hypatian Chronicle, s.a. 1126; *NČL*, s.a. 1125; Voskresenskij Chronicle, s.a. 1125; Rogožskij Chronicle, s.a. 1125; Tver Chronicle, s.a. 1125; Nikon Chronicle, s.a. 1125; knjaz′ of Kyiv end: *NPL*, s.a. 1132; Laurentian Chronicle, s.a. 1132; Hypatian Chronicle, s.a. 1133; *NČL*, s.a. 1131; Voskresenskij Chronicle, s.a. 1131; Rogožskij Chronicle, s.a. 1132; Tver Chronicle, s.a. 1132; Nikon Chronicle, s.a. 1132

Marriage to Kristín Ingesdottir: Wilhelm, "Wilhelmi abbatis genealogia regum Danorum," 182; Sturluson, *Heimskringla*, 702. For more information on this marriage see part 1, "Marriages: Generation Four," "M′stislav Volodimerič."

Kristín Ingesdottir of Sweden

Birth date: unknown

Death date: *NPL*, s.a. 1122; Laurentian Chronicle, s.a. 1122; Hypatian Chronicle, s.a. 1121; Voskresenskij Chronicle, s.a. 1122; Tver Chronicle, s.a. 1122; Nikon Chronicle, s.a. 1122

Marriage to M′stislav "Harald" Volodimerič: Wilhelm, "Wilhelmi abbatis genealogia regum Danorum," 182; Sturluson, *Heimskringla*, 702. For more information on this marriage see part 1, "Marriages: Generation Four," "M′stislav Volodimerič."

Sigurd "the Crusader" Magnusson

Birth date: unknown

Death date: Sturluson, *Heimskringla*, 714

King of Norway start: Sturluson, *Heimskringla*, 688–89; king of Norway end: Sturluson, *Heimskringla*, 714

Marriage to Malfrid M′stislavna: Pašuto, *Vnešnjaja politika Drevnej Rusi*, 146 (for speculative date); Sturluson, *Heimskringla*, 702; Litvina and Uspenskij, *Vybor imeni u russkix knjazej*, 246n26; Orderic Vitalis, *Ecclesiastical History*, bk. 10, ch. 6. For more information on this marriage see part 1, "Marriages: Generation Five," "Malfrid M′stislavna."

Malfrid M´stislavna

Birth date: unknown

Death date: Dąbrowski, *Genealogia Mścisławowiczów*, 94

Marriage to Sigurd "the Crusader" Magnusson: Pašuto, *Vnešnjaja politika Drevnej Rusi*, 146 (for speculative date), Sturluson, *Heimskringla*, 702; Litvina and Uspenskij *Vybor imeni u russkix knjazej*, 246n26; Orderic Vitalis, *Ecclesiastical History*, bk. 10, ch. 6

Marriage to Eric "Emune" Ericsson: Saxo Grammaticus, bk. 13, ch. 8, 134; *Knýtlinga Saga*, 140. For more information on these marriages see part 1, "Marriages: Generation Five," "Malfrid M´stislavna."

Eric "Emune" Ericsson

Birth date: unknown

Death date: *Knýtlinga Saga*, 145 (which dates it eight years after the death of Knud Lavard, thus 1139); I have corrected the date to 1137 following Dąbrowski, *Genealogia Mścisławowiczów*, 97

King of Denmark start: Saxo Grammaticus, bk. 13, ch. 11, 141; king of Denmark end: *Knýtlinga Saga*, 145 (which dates it eight years after the death of Knud Lavard, thus 1139); I have corrected the date to 1137 following Dąbrowski, *Genealogia Mścisławowiczów*, 97

Marriage to Malfrid M´stislavna: Saxo Grammaticus, bk. 13, ch. 8, 134; *Knýtlinga Saga*, 140. For more information on this marriage see part 1, "Marriages: Generation Five," "Malfrid M´stislavna."

Ingeborg M´stislavna

Birth date: unknown

Death date: Her last known appearance is at the election of Eric "Lamb" as king in 1137; see *Knýtlinga Saga*, 145

Marriage to Knud "Lavard" Ericsson: Sturluson, *Heimskringla*, 702; Wilhelm, "Wilhelmi abbatis genealogia regum Danorum," 180; Saxo Grammaticus, bk. 13, ch. 1, 110. For more information on this marriage see part 1, "Marriages: Generation Five," "Ingeborg M´stislavna."

Knud "Lavard" Ericsson

Birth date: unknown

Death date: Saxo Grammaticus, bk. 13, ch. 6, 126

Duke of Schleswig start: Helmold, *Chronicle of the Slavs*, 152; duke of Schleswig end: Saxo Grammaticus, bk. 13, ch. 6, 126

King of the Abodrite Slavs start: Helmold, *Chronicle of the Slavs*, 153; king of the Abodrite Slavs end: Saxo Grammaticus, bk. 13, ch. 6, 126

Marriage to Ingeborg M´stislavna: Sturluson, *Heimskringla*, 702; Wilhelm, "Wilhelmi abbatis genealogia regum Danorum," 180;

Saxo Grammaticus, bk. 13, ch. 1, 110. For more information on this marriage see part 1, "Marriages: Generation Five," "Ingeborg M´stislavna."

Table 16: Western European Dynastic Marriages

Jaroslav "Mudryj" Volodimerič
Birth date: unknown
Death date: *PVL*, s.a. 1054
Knjaz′ of Rostov: *PVL*, s.a. 988
Knjaz′ of Novgorod start (1): *PVL*, s.a. 988; knjaz′ of Novgorod end (1): *PVL*, s.a. 1015
Knjaz′ of Kyiv (1) start: *PVL*, s.a. 1016; knjaz′ of Kyiv (1) end: *PVL*, s.a. 1018
Knjaz′ of Kyiv (2) start: *PVL*, s.a 1018; knjaz′ of Kyiv (2) end: *PVL*, s.a. 1054
Knjaz′ of Novgorod (2) start: *PVL*, s.a. 1020; knjaz′ of Novgorod (2) end: *PVL*, s.a. 1036
Marriage to Ingigerd: Sturluson, *Heimskringla*, 342–43; *Morkinskinna*, ch. 1. For more on this marriage see part 1, "Marriages: Generation One," "Jaroslav Volodimerič."

Agafija Jaroslavna
Birth date: unknown
Death date: Agafija arrived in England in 1057 with her husband Edward, and died only after that time; see Jetté, "Is the Mystery of the Origin of Agatha, Wife of Edward the Exile, Finally Solved?" 419
Marriage to Edward "the Exile" of England: Ingham, "Has a Missing Daughter of Iaroslav Mudry Been Found?"; Jetté, "Is the Mystery of the Origin of Agatha, Wife of Edward the Exile, Finally Solved?" For more on this marriage see part 1, "Marriages: Generation Two," "Agafija Jaroslavna."

Edward "the Exile"
Birth date: unknown

Table 16: Western European Dynastic Marriages

Jaroslav "Mudryj" Volodimerič
b. unknown; d. 1054
(Rostov r. ca. 988)
(Novgorod r. ca. 988–1015)
(Kyiv r. 1016–1018)
(Novgorod r. 1020–1036)
(Kyiv r. 1018–1054)

Agafija
b. unknown;
d. post-1057
(m. ca. 1028)

Edward "the Exile"
of England
b. unknown; d. 1057

Edgar
"Aetheling"
b. unknown;
d. post-1126

Christina
b. unknown;
d. post-1086

Margaret
b. unknown; d. 1093
(m. 1067)

Malcolm III of
Scotland
b. unknown; d. 1093
(Scotland r.
1058–1093)

Gyða Haroldsdottir
b. unknown; d. 1107
(m. ca. 1074)

Volodimer "Monomax" Vsevolodič
b. 1053; d. 1125
(Smolensk r. ca. 1078–ca. 1095)
(Černihiv r. 1078–1094)
(Perejaslav r. 1094–1113)
(Kyiv r. ca. 1113–1125)

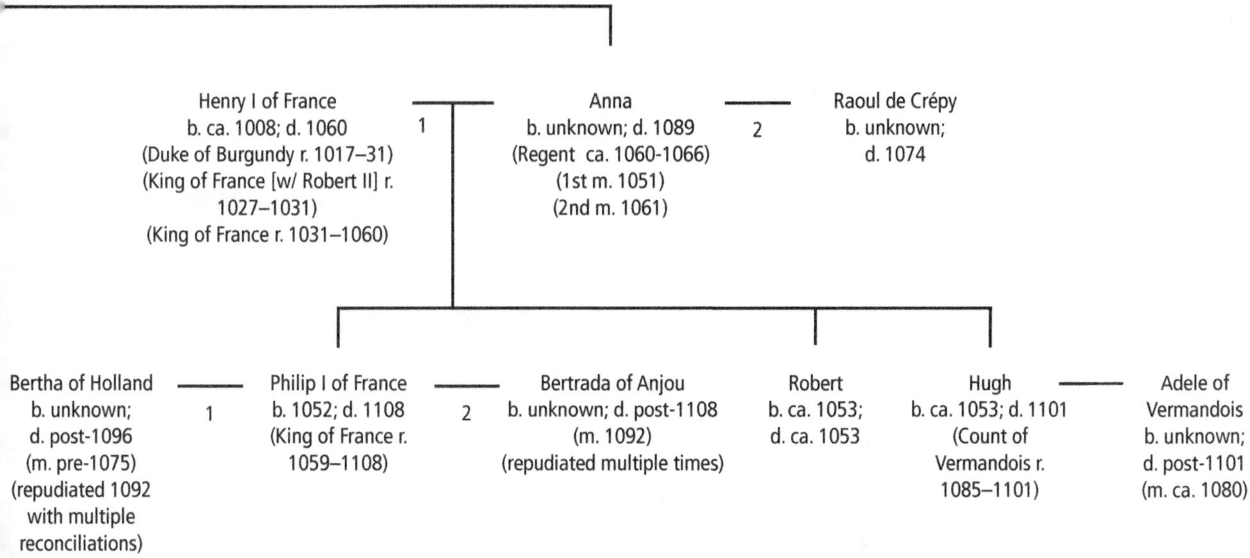
Henry I of France
b. ca. 1008; d. 1060
(Duke of Burgundy r. 1017–31)
(King of France [w/ Robert II] r. 1027–1031)
(King of France r. 1031–1060)
1
Anna
b. unknown; d. 1089
(Regent ca. 1060-1066)
(1st m. 1051)
(2nd m. 1061)
2
Raoul de Crépy
b. unknown;
d. 1074
Bertha of Holland
b. unknown;
d. post-1096
(m. pre-1075)
(repudiated 1092 with multiple reconciliations)
1
Philip I of France
b. 1052; d. 1108
(King of France r. 1059–1108)
2
Bertrada of Anjou
b. unknown; d. post-1108
(m. 1092)
(repudiated multiple times)
Robert
b. ca. 1053;
d. ca. 1053
Hugh
b. ca. 1053; d. 1101
(Count of Vermandois r. 1085–1101)
Adele of Vermandois
b. unknown;
d. post-1101
(m. ca. 1080)

Death date: *Anglo-Saxon Chronicle*, s.a. 1057; John of Fordun, *Chronicle of the Scottish Nation*, bk. 5, chs. 9, 11

Marriage to Agafija Jaroslavna: Ingham, "Has a Missing Daughter of Iaroslav Mudry Been Found?"; Jetté, "Is the Mystery of the Origin of Agatha, Wife of Edward the Exile, Finally Solved?" For more on this marriage see part 1, "Marriages: Generation Two," "Agafija Jaroslavna."

Henry I of France

Birth date: Schwennicke, *Die ausserdeutschen Staaten*, table 187.

Death date: "Chronicon Sancti-Petri-Vivi Senonensis: Auctore Clario," s.a. 1060; Berthold of Reichenau, s.a. 1060

Duke of Burgundy start: Rodulfus Glaber, *Histories*, bk. 3, ch. 34, *Catalogue des Actes d'Henri I–er Roi de France*, #1; Duke of Burgundy end: Rodulfus Glaber, *Five Books of the Histories*, bk. 3, ch. 37

King of France (joint rule with Robert II) start: Rodulfus Glaber, *Five Books of the Histories*, bk. 3, ch. 34; king of France (joint rule with Robert II) end: Rodulfus Glaber, *Five Books of the Histories*, bk. 3, ch. 36

King of France start: Rodulfus Glaber, *Five Books of the Histories*, bk. 3, ch. 36; king of France end: "Chronicon Sancti-Petri-Vivi Senonensis: Auctore Clario," s.a. 1060; Berthold of Reichenau, s.a. 1060; *Anglo-Saxon Chronicle*, s.a. 1060

Marriage to Anna Jaroslavna: "Chronicon: Vindocinense seu de Aquaria," s.a. 1051; Adam of Bremen, *History of the Archbishops of Hamburg-Bremen*, bk. 3, ch. xiii.12, schol. 62 (63); "Chronicon Sancti-Petri-Vivi Senonensis: Auctore Clario," s.a. 1046; *Hugo Floriacensis opera historica*, 388–89; *Psalterium Partitum*, s.a. 1049. For more information on this marriage see part 1, "Marriages: Generation Two," "Anna Jaroslavna."

Anna Jaroslavna

Birth date: unknown

Death date: Dhondt, "Sept femmes et un trio de rois," 60

Regency start: Prou, *Recueil des actes de Philippe Ier*, no. 6; Berthold of Reichenau, s.a. 1060; regency end: Prou, *Recueil des actes de Philippe Ier*, no. 18

Marriage to Henry I of France: "Chronicon: Vindocinense seu de Aquaria," s.a. 1051; Adam of Bremen, *History of the Archbishops of Hamburg-Bremen*, bk. 3, ch. xiii.12, schol. 62 (63); "Chronicon Sancti-Petri-Vivi Senonensis: Auctore Clario," s.a. 1046; *Hugo Floriacensis opera historica*, 388–89; *Psalterium Partitum*, s.a. 1049

Marriage to Raoul de Crépy: "Chronicon Sancti-Petri-Vivi Senonensis: Auctore Clario," s.a. 1060; *Hugo Floriacensis opera historica*, 389;

Soehnée, *Catalogue des Actes d'Henri Ier Roi de France*, no. 102. For more information on these marriages see part 1, "Marriages: Generation Two," "Anna Jaroslavna."

Raoul de Crépy
Birth date: unknown
Death date: Dhondt, "Sept femmes et un trio de rois," 58; Prou, *Recueil des actes de Philippe Ier*, no. 88
Marriage to Anna Jaroslavna: "Chronicon Sancti-Petri-Vivi Senonensis: Auctore Clario," s.a. 1060; *Hugo Floriacensis opera historica*, 389; Soehnée, *Catalogue des Actes d'Henri Ier Roi de France*, no. 102. For more information on this marriage see part 1, "Marriages: Generation Two," "Anna Jaroslavna."

Edgar "Aetheling"
Birth date: unknown
Death date: Jetté, "Is the Mystery of the Origin of Agatha, wife of Edward the Exile, finally solved?" 419.

Christina
Birth date: unknown
Death date: *Anglo-Saxon Chronicle*, s.a. 1086, records that she became a nun in this year; see also John of Fordun, *Chronicle of the Scottish Nation*, bk. 5, chs. 9, 16.

Margaret
Birth date: unknown
Death date: *Anglo-Saxon Chronicle*, s.a. 1093 (referenced obliquely); *Annals of Ulster*, s.a. 1093; John of Fordun, *Chronicle of the Scottish Nation*, bk. 5, ch. 21
Marriage to Malcolm III of Scotland: *Anglo-Saxon Chronicle*, s.a. 1067; John of Fordun, *Chronicle of the Scottish Nation*, bk. 5, chs. 15, 16.

Malcolm III of Scotland
Birth date: unknown
Death date: *Anglo-Saxon Chronicle*, s.a. 1093; *Annals of Ulster*, s.a. 1093; John of Fordun, *Chronicle of the Scottish Nation*, bk. 5, ch. 20
King of Scotland start: *Annals of Ulster*, s.a. 1058; John of Fordun, *Chronicle of the Scottish Nation*, bk. 5, ch. 9; king of Scotland end: *Anglo-Saxon Chronicle*, s.a. 1093; *Annals of Ulster*, s.a. 1093; John of Fordun, *Chronicle of the Scottish Nation*, bk. 5, ch. 20
Marriage to Margaret: *Anglo-Saxon Chronicle*, s.a. 1067; John of Fordun, *Chronicle of the Scottish Nation*, bk. 5, chs. 15, 16.

Bertha of Holland
Birth date: unknown
Death date: conjectural based upon the date of her repudiation
Marriage to Philip I: Dhondt, "Sept femmes et un trio de rois," 61n72; Prou, *Recueil des actes de Philippe Ier*, no. 78, Bernold of St. Blasien, "Chronicle," s.a. 1095, 1096 (mentioned in regard to his excommunication); Orderic Vitalis, *Ecclesiastical History*, bk. 9, ch. 2.

Philip I
Birth date: Prou, *Recueil des actes de Philippe Ier*, xxiii
Death date: *Anglo-Saxon Chronicle*, s.a. 1108; "Chronicon Sancti-Petri-Vivi Senonensis: Auctore Clario," s.a. 1108
King of France start: *Hugo Floriacensis opera historica*, 389; Prou, *Recueil des actes de Philippe Ier*, no. 6; Berthold of Reichenau, s.a. 1060; king of France end: *Anglo-Saxon Chronicle*, s.a. 1108; "Chronicon Sancti-Petri-Vivi Senonensis: Auctore Clario," s.a. 1108
Marriage to Bertha of Holland: Dhondt, "Sept femmes et un trio de rois," 61–69; Prou, *Recueil des actes de Philippe Ier*, no. 78; Bernold of St. Blasien, "Chronicle," s.a. 1095, 1096 (mentioned in regard to his excommunication)
Marriage to Bertrada of Anjou: Dhondt, "Sept femmes et un trio de rois," 61–69; Bernold of St. Blasien, "Chronicle," s.a. 1095, 1096 (mentioned in regard to his excommunication); Orderic Vitalis, *Ecclesiastical History*, bk. 9, ch. 2.

Bertrada of Anjou
Birth date: unknown
Death date: conjectural based upon mentions of her after the death of Philip
Marriage to Philip I: Dhondt, "Sept femmes et un trio de rois," 61–69; Bernold of St. Blasien, "Chronicle," s.a. 1095, 1096 (mentioned in regard to his excommunication); Orderic Vitalis, *Ecclesiastical History*, bk. 9, ch. 2.

Robert
Birth date: conjectural based upon Philip's birth date
Death date: Dhondt, "Sept femmes et un trio de rois," 58.

Hugh
Birth date: conjectural
Death date: Fulcher of Chartres, *Historia Hierosolymitana*, bk. 2, ch. 16
Count of Vermandois start: Dunbabin, *France in the Making*, 218; count of Vermandois end: Fulcher of Chartres, *Historia Hierosolymitana*, bk. 2, ch. 16

Marriage to Adele of Vermandois: Fliche, *Règne de Philippe 1er*, 98; *Albrici Monachi triumfontium chronicon*, s.a. 1061; Guibert of Nogent, *De Vita Sua: De electione domini Bartholomaei episcopi; et nobilitate ejusdem*, in *Patrologia Latina*, edited by J. P. Migne, vol. 156, 837–1016 (Paris: J. P. Migne, 1853), 966–67.

Adele of Vermandois
Birth date: unknown
Death date: Guibert of Nogent, *De Vita Sua*, 966–67
Marriage to Hugh: Fliche, *Règne de Philippe 1er*, 98; *Albrici Monachi triumfontium chronicon*, s.a. 1061; Guibert of Nogent, *De Vita Sua*, 966–67.

Gyða Haroldsdottir
Birth date: unknown
Death date: *PVL*, s.a. 1107
Marriage to Volodimer "Monomax" Vsevolodič: Saxo Grammaticus, bk. 11, ch. 6, 58; Sturluson, *Heimskringla*, 702. For more on this marriage see part 1, "Marriages: Generation Three," "Volodimer 'Monomax' Vsevolodič."

Volodimer "Monomax" Vsevolodič
Birth date: *PVL*, s.a. 1053
Death date: Laurentian Chronicle, s.a. 1125; *NPL*, s.a. 1125; Rogožskij Chronicle, s.a. 1125; Tver Chronicle, s.a. 1125; Nikon Chronicle, s.a. 1125
Knjaz´ of Smolensk start: *PVL*, s.a. 1078; knjaz´ of Smolensk end: *PVL*, s.a. 1095 (based on the assumption that Davyd takes power in Smolensk in that year)
Knjaz´ of Černihiv start: *PVL*, s.a. 1078; knjaz´ of Černihiv end: *PVL*, s.a. 1094
Knjaz´ of Perejaslav start: *PVL*, s.a. 1094; knjaz´ of Perejaslav end: *PVL*, s.a. 1113 (conjectural based upon his assumption of power in Kyiv)
Knjaz´ of Kyiv start: Laurentian Chronicle, s.a. 1114; Hypatian Chronicle, s.a. 1113; *NPL*, s.a. 1113; Rogožskij Chronicle, s.a. 1114; Tver Chronicle, s.a. 1113; Nikon Chronicle, s.a. 1114; knjaz´ of Kyiv end: Laurentian Chronicle, s.a. 1125; *NPL*, s.a. 1125; Rogožskij Chronicle, s.a. 1125; Tver Chronicle, s.a. 1125; Nikon Chronicle, s.a. 1125
Marriage to Gyða Haroldsdottir: Saxo Grammaticus, bk. 11, ch. 6, 58; Sturluson, *Heimskringla*, 702. For more on this marriage see part 1, "Marriages: Generation Three," "Volodimer 'Monomax' Vsevolodič."

Table 17: Polish Dynastic Marriages

Volodimer Svjatoslavič
Birth date: unknown
Death date: *PVL*, s.a. 1015
Knjaz′ of Novgorod start: *PVL*, s.a. 970; knjaz′ of Novgorod end: *PVL*, s.a. 980
Knjaz′ of Kyiv start: *PVL*, s.a. 980; knjaz′ of Kyiv end: *PVL*, s.a. 1015.

Ladislaus of Hungary
Birth date: unknown
Death date: Wertner, *Az Árpádok családi története*, 111
Marriage to "Premislava" Volodimerovna: Dercsényi, *Chronica de Gestis Hungarorum*, 100, 107, 113; the date is conjectural based upon her father's death and the approximate birth dates of the children. For more on this marriage see part 1, "Marriages: Generation One," "Premislava Volodimerovna."

N. N., "Premislava" Volodimerovna
Birth date: unknown
Death date: Her death date can reasonably be assumed to have occurred after her marriage, though when is unknown.
Marriage to Ladislaus of Hungary: Dercsényi, *Chronica de Gestis Hungarorum*, 100, 107, 113; the date is conjectural based upon her father's death, and the approximate birth dates of the children. For more on this marriage see part 1, "Marriages: Generation One," "Premislava Volodimerovna."

Dobronega/Maria Volodimerovna
Birth date: unknown
Death date: "Rocznik Kapitulny Krakowski," s.a. 1087
Marriage to Casimir "the Restorer": *Annalista Saxo*, s.a. 1039; *Lamberti*

Table 17: Polish Dynastic Marriages

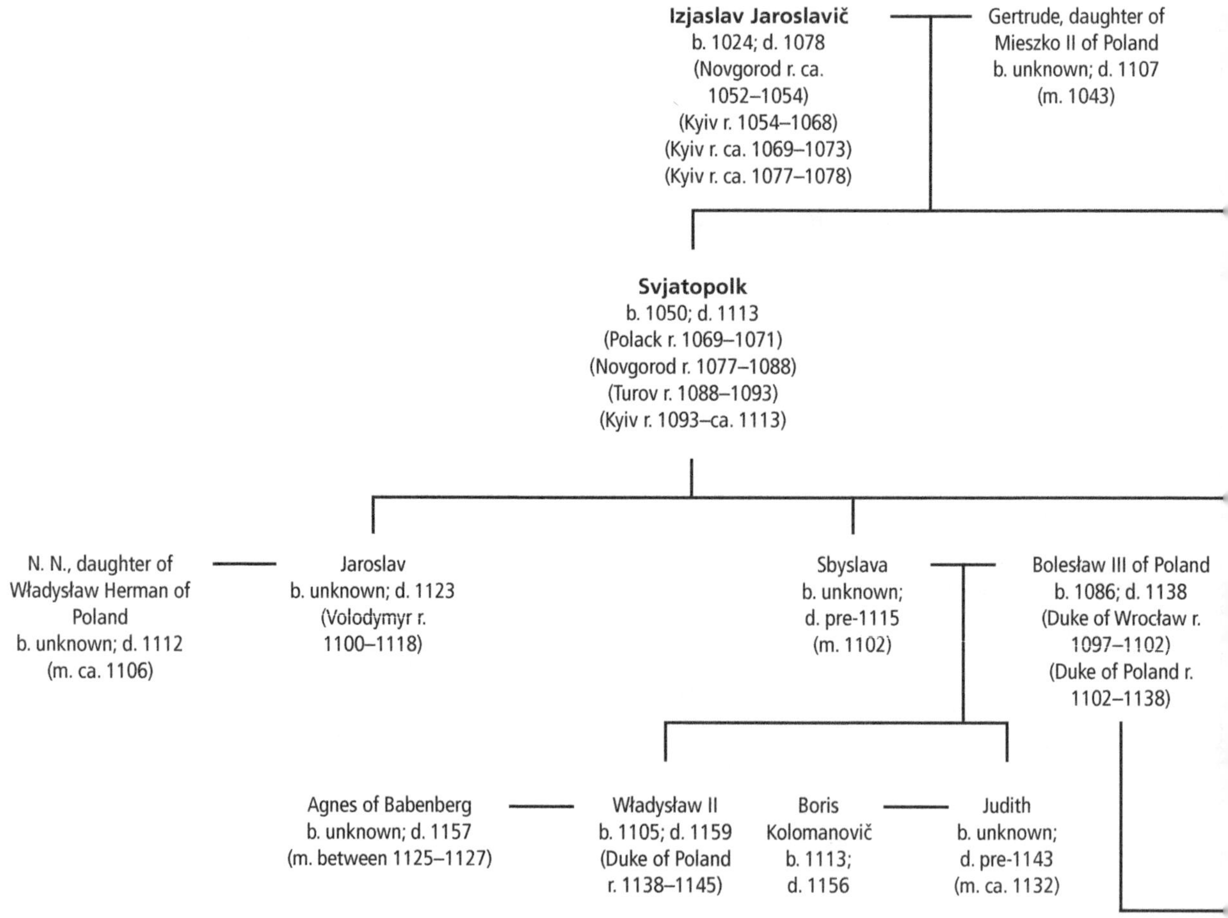

Volodimer Svjatoslavič
b. unknown; d. 1015
(Novgorod r. 970–980)
(Kyiv r. 980–1015)

Ladislaus of Hungary
b. unknown;
d. 1031

N. N., "Premislava"
b. unknown;
d. post-1010
(m. 1010)

Dobronega/Maria
b. unknown; d. 1087
(m. ca. 1039)

Casimir "the Restorer" of Poland
b. 1016; d. 1058
(Poland r. ca. 1039–1058)

N. N., daughter of Mieszko II of Poland
b. d. unknown
(m. unknown)

Béla
b. unknown; d. 1063
(King of Hungary r. 1060–1063)

Vyšeslava Svjatoslavna
b. unknown;
d. post-1067
(m. 1067)

Bolesław II "the Bold"
b. 1039; d. ca. 1081
(Duke of Poland r. 1058–1076)
(King of Poland r. 1076–1079)

N. N. "Eudoxia"
b. unknown;
d. post-1088
(m. 1088)

Mieszko
b. 1069; d. 1089

N. N., of Poland
b. unknown;
d. post-1124
(m. 1124)

Vsevolod Davydič
b. unknown; d. post-1124
(Murom r. ca. 1124)

Marija
b.unknown;
d. pre-1153
(m. 1117)

Piotr Włostowic of Poland
b. unknown; d. 1153
(Count Palatine)

Vsevolod Ol′govič
b. unknown; d. 1146
(Černihiv r. 1127–1138)
(Kyiv r. 1138–1146)

Konstantin
b. d. unknown
(Ruler of Skrzynno)

Svjatoslav
b. d. unknown

Jaksa of Miechów
b. d. unknown
(Prince of Miechów)

N. N.
b. d. unknown
(m. unknown)

Bolesław "the Tall," son of Władysław II
b. unknown; d. 1201

Zvenislava
b. unknown;
d. post-1142
(m. 1142)

Richeza
b. unknown;
d. post-1139
(m. 1135)

Volodimer Vsevolodič
b. unknown; d. ca. 1139

Verxoslava Vsevolodovna
b. unknown;
d. pre-1167
(m. 1137)

Bolesław IV
b. 1125; d. 1173
(Duke of Kujawy and Mazovia r. 1139–1173)

Hersfeldensis Annales, s.a. 1039; *PVL*, s.a. 1043; Gallus Anonymous, *Gesta principum Polonorum*, 80–81; *Chronica Poloniae Maioris*, ch. 12. For more on this marriage see part 1, "Marriages: Generation One," "Dobronega/Maria Volodimerovna."

Casimir "the Restorer," son of Mieszko II of Poland

Birth date: Balzer, *Genealogia Piastów*, table 2

Death date: *Chronica Poloniae Maioris*, ch. 12

King of Poland start: Gallus Anonymous, *Gesta principum Polonorum*, 81; king of Poland end: *Chronica Poloniae Maioris*, ch. 12

Marriage to Dobronega/Maria Volodimerovna: *Annalista Saxo*, s.a. 1039, *Lamberti Hersfeldensis Annales*, s.a. 1039; *PVL*, s.a. 1043; Gallus Anonymous, *Gesta principum Polonorum*, 80–81; *Chronica Poloniae Maioris*, ch. 12. For more on this marriage see part 1, "Marriages: Generation One," "Dobronega/Maria Volodimerovna."

Izjaslav Jaroslavič

Birth date: *PVL*, s.a. 1024

Death date: *PVL*, s.a. 1078; *NPL*, s.a. 1078

Knjaz´ of Novgorod start: conjectural based upon the death of Volodimer Jaroslavič; see *PVL*, s.a. 1052; as well as Izjaslav's place in Novgorod at the death of Jaroslav in 1054; see *PVL*, s.a. 1054. This is buttressed by the *NPL*'s listing of Novgorod along with Kyiv as his possessions after he assumed power in Kyiv; see *NPL*, s.a. 989. Knjaz´ of Novgorod end: Conjectural based upon his assumption of power in Kyiv; see *PVL*, s.a. 1054. This is also the time when his son M´stislav may have been assigned to rule Novgorod, according to the regnal list in *NPL*, s.a. 989.

Knjaz´ of Kyiv (1) start: *PVL*, s.a. 1054; knjaz´ of Kyiv (1) end: *PVL*, s.a. 1068

Knjaz´ of Kyiv (2) start: *PVL*, s.a. 1069; knjaz´ of Kyiv (2) end: *PVL*, s.a. 1073

Knjaz´ of Kyiv (3) start: *PVL*, s.a. 1077; knjaz´ of Kyiv (3) end: *PVL*, s.a. 1078

Marriage to Gertrude: Tver Chronicle, s.a. 1043; Nikon Chronicle, s.a. 1043. For more on this marriage see part 1, "Marriages: Generation Two," "Izjaslav Jaroslavič."

Gertrude of Poland

Birth date: unknown

Death date: Nikon Chronicle, s.a. 1107

Marriage to Izjaslav Jaroslavič: Tver Chronicle, s.a. 1043; Nikon Chronicle, s.a. 1043. For more on this marriage see part 1, "Marriages: Generation Two," "Izjaslav Jaroslavič."

N. N. daughter of Mieszko II of Poland
Birth date: unknown
Death date: unknown
Marriage to Béla I of Hungary: Dercsényi, *Chronica de Gestis Hungarorum*, 110–11, 121.

Béla I of Hungary
Birth date: unknown
Death date: *Lamberti Hersfeldensis Annales*, s.a. 1063
King of Hungary start: *Lamberti Hersfeldensis Annales*, s.a. 1061; king of Hungary end: *Lamberti Hersfeldensis Annales*, s.a. 1063
Marriage to daughter of Mieszko II of Poland: Dercsényi, *Chronica de Gestis Hungarorum*, 110–11, 121.

Vyšeslava Svjatoslavna
Birth date: unknown
Death date: Her death date can reasonably be assumed to have occurred after her marriage, though when is unknown.
Marriage to Bolesław II of Poland: Długosz, *Annales*, 95; Tatiščev, *Istorija Rossijskaja*, 2:123; Baumgarten, "Généalogies," 18–20, table 5; Dimnik, *Dynasty of Chernigov, 1054–1146*, 41. For more on this marriage see part 1, "Marriages: Generation Three," "Vyšeslava Svjatoslavna."

Bolesław II "the Bold"
Birth date: Balzer, *Genealogia Piastów*, table 2
Death date: Balzer, *Genealogia Piastów*, table 2; Gallus Anonymous, *Gesta principum Polonorum*, bk. 1, ch. 28
Duke of Poland start: *Chronica Poloniae Maioris*, ch. 12; Gallus Anonymous, *Gesta principum Polonorum*, bk. 1, ch. 22; duke of Poland end: *Lamberti Hersfeldensis Annales*, s.a. 1077
King of Poland start: *Lamberti Hersfeldensis Annales*, s.a. 1077; Bernold of St. Blasien, "Chronicle," s.a. 1077; king of Poland end: Gallus Anonymous, *Gesta principum Polonorum*, bk. 1, ch. 27
Marriage to Vyšeslava Svjatoslavna: Długosz, *Annales*, 95; Tatiščev, *Istorija Rossijskaja*, 2:123; Baumgarten, "Généalogies," 18–20, table 5; Dimnik, *Dynasty of Chernigov, 1054–1146*, 41. For more on this marriage see part 1, "Marriages: Generation Three," "Vyšeslava Svjatoslavna."

Svjatopolk Izjaslavič
Birth date: *NPL*, s.a. 1050 (though patronymic is not specified and identification is conjectural)
Death date: Laurentian Chronicle, s.a. 1114; Hypatian Chronicle, s.a.

1113; *NPL*, s.a. 1113; *NČL*, s.a. 1114; Rogožskij Chronicle, s.a. 1114; Tver Chronicle, s.a. 1113; Nikon Chronicle, s.a. 1114

Knjaz´ of Polack start: *PVL*, s.a. 1069; knjaz´ of Polack end: *PVL*, s.a. 1071

Knjaz´ of Novgorod start: conjectural based upon surrounding rulers; knjaz´ of Novgorod end: *PVL*, s.a. 1088

Knjaz´ of Turov start: *PVL*, s.a. 1088; knjaz´ of Turov end: *PVL*, s.a. 1093;

Knjaz´ of Kyiv start: *PVL*, s.a. 1093; *NPL*, s.a. 1093; knjaz´ of Kyiv end: Laurentian Chronicle, s.a. 1114; Hypatian Chronicle, s.a. 1113; *NPL*, s.a. 1113; *NČL*, s.a. 1114; Rogožskij Chronicle, s.a. 1114; Tver Chronicle, s.a. 1113; Nikon Chronicle, s.a. 1114.

N. N., "Eudoxia" Izjaslavna

Birth date: unknown

Death date: Her death date can reasonably be assumed to have occurred after her marriage, though when is unknown.

Marriage to Mieszko of Poland: Gallus Anonymous, *Gesta principum Polonorum*, bk. 1, ch. 29; Długosz, *Annales*, 161. For more on this marriage see part 1, "Marriages: Generation Three," "Eudoxia Izjaslavna."

Mieszko of Poland

Birth date: Balzer, *Genealogia Piastów*, table 2

Death date: Gallus Anonymous, *Gesta principum Polonorum*, bk. 1, ch. 29

Marriage to "Eudoxia" Izjaslavna: Gallus Anonymous, *Gesta principum Polonorum*, bk. 1, ch. 29; Długosz, *Annales*, 161. For more on this marriage see part 1, "Marriages: Generation Three," "Eudoxia Izjaslavna."

N. N., Polish woman

Birth date: unknown

Death date: Her death date can reasonably be assumed to have occurred after her marriage, though when is unknown.

Marriage to Vsevolod Davydič: Hypatian Chronicle, s.a. 1124; Voskresenskij Chronicle, s.a. 1124. For more information on this marriage see part 1, "Marriages: Generation Four," "Vsevolod Davydič."

Vsevolod Davydič

Birth date: unknown

Death date: Hypatian Chronicle, s.a. 1124; Voskresenskij Chronicle, s.a. 1124 (last mention of him in the primary sources)

Knjaz´ of Murom: Hypatian Chronicle, s.a. 1124; Voskresenskij Chronicle, s.a. 1124 (listed as receiving a bride there)

Marriage to N. N., Polish woman: Hypatian Chronicle, s.a. 1124;

Voskresenskij Chronicle, s.a. 1124. For more information on this marriage see part 1, "Marriages: Generation Four," "Vsevolod Davydič."

Jaroslav Svjatopolčič
Birth date: unknown
Death date: Laurentian Chronicle, s.a. 1123; Hypatian Chronicle, s.a. 1123; Voskresenskij Chronicle, s.a. 1123; Nikon Chronicle, s.a. 1123
Knjaz′ of Volodymyr start: *PVL*, s.a. 1097; *PVL*, s.a. 1100; knjaz′ of Volodymyr end: Hypatian Chronicle, s.a. 1118; Laurentian Chronicle, s.a. 1119; Voskresenskij Chronicle, s.a. 1118; Tver Chronicle, s.a. 1118; Nikon Chronicle, s.a. 1119
Marriage to unknown daughter of Władysław Herman: Gallus Anonymous, *Gesta principum Polonorum*, 117. For more on this marriage see part 1, "Marriages: Generation Four," "Jaroslav Svjatopolčič."

N. N., daughter of Władysław Herman of Poland
Birth date: unknown
Death date: conjectural based upon the date of Jaroslav's remarriage
Marriage to Jaroslav Svjatopolčič: Gallus Anonymous, *Gesta principum Polonorum*, 117. For more on this marriage see part 1, "Marriages: Generation Four," "Jaroslav Svjatopolčič."

Bolesław III of Poland
Birth date: *Chronica Poloniae Maioris*, ch. 30 (records that he was 56 when he died); Cosmas of Prague, *Chronicle of the Czechs*, bk. 2, ch. 36; Gallus Anonymous, *Gesta principum Polonorum*, bk. 2, ch. 1
Death date: "Chronica Petri comitis Poloniae," 766; *Chronica Poloniae Maioris*, ch. 30
Duke of Wrocław start: Gallus Anonymous, *Gesta principum Polonorum*, bk. 2, chs. 7, 8, 13; duke of Wrocław end: "Chronica Petri comitis Poloniae," 766; *Chronica Poloniae Maioris*, ch. 30
Duke of Poland start: *Chronica Poloniae Maioris*, ch. 16; Cosmas of Prague, *Chronicle of the Czechs*, bk. 3, ch. 16; duke of Poland end: "Chronica Petri comitis Poloniae," 766; *Chronica Poloniae Maioris*, ch. 30
Marriage to Sbyslava Svjatopolkovna: Laurentian Chronicle, s.a. 1102; Długosz, *Annales*, 210–11. For more on this marriage see part 1, "Marriages: Generation Four," "Sbyslava Svjatopolkovna."

Sbyslava Svjatopolkovna
Birth date: unknown
Death date: unknown
Marriage to Bolesław III: Laurentian Chronicle, s.a. 1102; Dlugosz,

Annales, 210–11; for more on this marriage see part 1, "Marriages: Generation Four," "Sbyslava Svjatopolkovna."

Marija Svjatopolkovna
Birth date: unknown
Death date: "Chronica Petri comitis Poloniae," 783 (records Piotr's death, and notes that she predeceased him)
Marriage to Piotr Włostowic: *Chronica Poloniae Maioris*, ch. 27. For more on this marriage see part 1, "Marriages: Generation Four," "Marija Svjatopolkovna."

Piotr Włostowic
Birth date: unknown
Death date: "Chronica Petri comitis Poloniae," 783
Marriage to Marija Svjatopolkovna: *Chronica Poloniae Maioris*, ch. 27. For more on this marriage see part 1, "Marriages: Generation Four," "Marija Svjatopolkovna."

Vsevolod Ol'govič
Birth date: unknown
Death date: *NPL*, s.a. 1146; Hypatian Chronicle, s.a. 1146; *NČL*, s.a. 1146; Voskresenskij Chronicle, s.a. 1146; Rogožskij Chronicle, s.a. 1146; Tver Chronicle, s.a. 1146; Nikon Chronicle, s.a. 1146
Knjaz´ of Černihiv start: Hypatian Chronicle, s.a. 1128; Voskresenskij Chronicle, s.a. 1127; Tver Chronicle, s.a. 1127; Nikon Chronicle, s.a. 1127; knjaz´ of Černihiv end: Laurentian Chronicle, s.a. 1138; *NČL*, s.a. 1138; Voskresenskij Chronicle, s.a. 1138; Nikon Chronicle, s.a. 1138
Knjaz´ of Kyiv start: *NPL*, s.a. 1139; Laurentian Chronicle, s.a. 1138; Hypatian Chronicle, s.a. 1140; *NČL*, s.a. 1138; Voskresenskij Chronicle, s.a. 1138; Rogožskij Chronicle, s.a. 1138; Tver Chronicle, s.a. 1138; Nikon Chronicle, s.a. 1138; knjaz´ of Kyiv end: *NPL*, s.a. 1146; Hypatian Chronicle, s.a. 1146; *NČL*, s.a. 1146; Voskresenskij Chronicle, s.a. 1146; Rogožskij Chronicle, s.a. 1146; Tver Chronicle, s.a. 1146; Nikon Chronicle, s.a. 1146.

Agnes of Babenberg
Birth date: unknown
Death date: Balzer, *Genealogia Piastów*, 131
Marriage to Władysław II: Otto of Friesing, *Deeds of Frederick Barbarossa*, bk. 3, ch. 2 (see n. 16); "Chronica Petri comitis Poloniae," 766; Długosz, *Annales*, 293 (the date given here is 1121; it also says her name was Christina, which the editor corrects to "daughter of Henry V"; however, Agnes was, in fact, the granddaughter of

Henry IV, her mother was Agnes, daughter of Henry IV, and her father was Margrave Leopold III. The date I have used comes from Balzer, who has an analysis of possible dates from the sources); Balzer, *Genealogia Piastów*, 129–30.

Władysław II

Birth date: Balzer, *Genealogia Piastów*, table 3; Długosz, *Annales*, 293

Death date: *Chronica Poloniae Maioris*, ch. 33

Duke of Poland start: "Chronica Petri comitis Poloniae," 766; "Kronika polska (Chronica Polonorum)," 629; *Chronica Poloniae Maioris*, ch. 31; duke of Poland end: *Chronica Poloniae Maioris*, ch. 32

Marriage to Agnes of Babenberg: Otto of Friesing and his continuator, Rahewin, *The Deeds of Frederick Barbarossa*, trans. Charles Christopher Mierow, with Richard Emery (New York: Norton and Co., 1953), bk. 3, ch. 2 (see n. 16); "Chronica Petri comitis Poloniae," 766; Długosz, *Annales*, 293 (the date given here is 1121; it also says her name was Christina, which the editor corrects to "daughter of Henry V"; however, Agnes was, in fact, the granddaughter of Henry IV, her mother was Agnes, daughter of Henry IV, and her father was Margrave Leopold III. The date I have used comes from Balzer, who has an analysis of possible dates from the sources); Balzer, *Genealogia Piastów*, 129–30.

Boris Kolomanovič

Birth date: "Cosmae chronicon Boemorum cum continuatoribus," 215–16; Otto, Bishop of Freising, *Two Cities*, bk. 7, sec. 21; Dercsényi, *Chronica de Gestis Hungarorum*, 131 (all roughly refer to his birth, parentage, and mother's repudiation)

Death date: Otto of Freising, *Deeds of Frederick Barbarossa*, bk. 2, ch. 53

Marriage to Judith, daughter of Bolesław III of Poland: *Chronica Poloniae Maioris*, ch. 27 (listed simply as son of Koloman); Wiszewski, *Domus Bolezlai*, 110.

Judith, daughter of Bolesław III of Poland

Birth date: unknown

Death date: conjectural based upon Boris's remarriage

Marriage to Boris Kolomanovič: *Chronica Poloniae Maioris*, ch. 27 (listed simply as son of Koloman); Wiszewski, *Domus Bolezlai*, 110 (source for the name as well).

Richeza

Birth date: unknown

Death date: Richeza is known to have remarried after Volodimer's death, and as such dies after that time.

Marriage to Volodimer Vsevolodič: *Knýtlinga Saga*, 242; Finnur Jónsson, *Fagrskinna, Nóregs kononga tal* (Copenhagen: S. L. Mollers Bogtrykkeri, 1902–1903), 300. In both instances, her husband's name is listed as Valadar, king of Polinalande. For more on this marriage see part 1, "Marriages: Postscript," "Volodimer Vsevolodič."

Volodimer Vsevolodič
Birth date: unknown, though he was able to assist his father in Novgorod in 1136; *NPL*, s.a. 1136
Death date: conjectural based upon Richeza's remarriage in that year; see *Knýtlinga Saga*, 151
Marriage to Richeza: *Knýtlinga Saga*, 242; Jónsson, *Fagrskinna*, 300. In both sources his name is listed as Valadar, king of Polinalande. For more on this marriage see part 1, "Marriages: Postscript," "Volodimer Vsevolodič."

Verxoslava Vsevolodovna
Birth date: unknown
Death date: conjectural based upon Bolesław IV's remarriage in that year; Balzer, *Genealogia Piastow*, table 3
Marriage to Bolesław IV: Hypatian Chronicle, s.a. 1137. For more information on this marriage see part 1, "Marriages: Postscript," "Verxoslava Vsevolodovna."

Bolesław IV
Birth date: Balzer, *Genealogia Piastów*, table 3
Death date: Balzer, *Genealogia Piastów*, table 3
Duke of Kujawy and Mazovia start: "Chronica Polonorum," 629; duke of Kujawy and Mazovia end: Balzer, *Genealogia Piastów*, table 3
Marriage to Verxoslava Vsevolodovna: Hypatian Chronicle, s.a. 1137. For more information on this marriage see part 1, "Marriages: Postscript," "Verxoslava Vsevolodovna."

Konstantin Petrovič
Birth date: unknown
Death date: unknown
Ruler of Skrzynno: *Chronica Poloniae Maioris*, ch. 32.

Svjatoslav Petrovič
Birth date: unknown
Death date: unknown; existence cited in "Spominki Wrocławskie," 732.

Jaksa of Miechów
Birth date: unknown

Death date: unknown
Prince of Miechów: *Chronica Poloniae Maioris*, ch. 32 (text reads "prince of Sorabia," which the editor corrects to Miechów)
Marriage to N. N. Petrovna: *Chronica Poloniae Maioris*, ch. 32.

N. N. Petrovna
Birth date: unknown
Death date: unknown
Marriage to Jaksa of Miechów: *Chronica Poloniae Maioris*, ch. 32.

Zvenislava Vsevolodovna
Birth date: unknown
Death date: Her death date can reasonably be assumed to have occurred after her marriage, though when is unknown
Marriage to Bolesław "the Tall": Hypatian Chronicle, s.a. 1141, 1142. For more information on this marriage see part 1, "Marriages: Generation Five," "Zvenislava Vsevolodovna."

Bolesław "the Tall"
Birth date: unknown
Death date: Grotefend, *Stammtafeln der schlesischen Fürsten bis zum jahre 1740*, table 1
Marriage to Zvenislava Vsevolodovna: Hypatian Chronicle, s.a. 1141, 1142. For more information on this marriage see part 1, "Marriages: Generation Five," "Zvenislava Vsevolodovna."

Table 18: Hungarian Dynastic Marriages

Volodimer Svjatoslavič
Birth date: unknown
Death date: *PVL*, s.a. 1015
Knjaz′ of Novgorod start: *PVL*, s.a. 970; knjaz′ of Novgorod end: *PVL*, s.a. 980
Knjaz′ of Kyiv start: *PVL*, s.a. 980; knjaz′ of Kyiv end: *PVL*, s.a. 1015.

N. N., "Premislava" Volodimerovna
Birth date: unknown
Death date: Her death date can reasonably be assumed to have occurred after her marriage, though when is unknown
Marriage to Ladislaus of Hungary: Dercsényi, *Chronica de Gestis Hungarorum*, 100, 107, 113; the date is conjectural based upon her father's death, and the approximate birth dates of the children. For more on this marriage see part 1, "Marriages: Generation One," "Premislava Volodimerovna."

Ladislaus of Hungary
Birth date: unknown
Death date: Wertner, *Az Árpádok családi története*, 111
Marriage to "Premislava" Volodimerovna: Dercsényi, *Chronica de Gestis Hungarorum*, 100, 107, 113; the date is conjectural based upon her father's death, and the approximate birth dates of the children. For more on this marriage see part 1, "Marriages: Generation One," "Premislava Volodimerovna."

Jaroslav "Mudryj" Volodimerič
Birth date: unknown
Death date: *PVL*, s.a. 1054
Knjaz′ of Rostov: *PVL*, s.a. 988

Table 18: Hungarian Dynastic Marriages

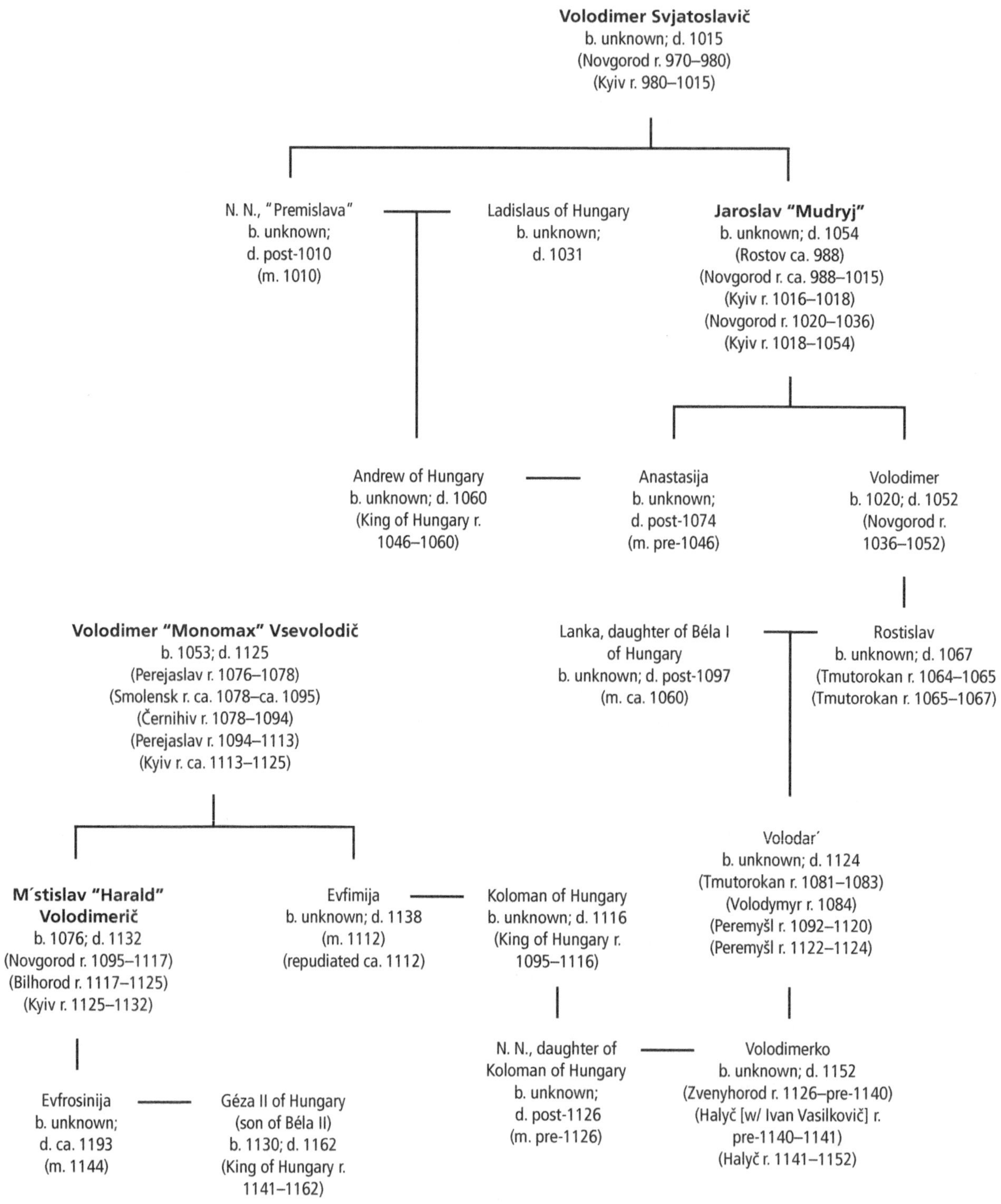

Svjatopolk Izjaslavič
b. 1050; d. 1113
(Polack r. 1069–1071)
(Novgorod r. 1077–1088)
(Turov r. 1088–1093)
(Kyiv r. 1093–ca. 1113)

Almos of Hungary
b. unknown; d. 1129

Peredslava
b. unknown; d. 1116
(m. 1104)

Jaroslav
b. unknown; d. 1123
(Volodymyr r.
1100–1118)

N. N.,
daughter of Ladislaus
of Hungary
b. unknown; d. 1104
(m. ca. 1091)

Béla II
b. 1108; d. 1141
(King of Hungary r.
1131–1141)

Jelena, daughter of
Uroš I of Serbia
b. unknown; d. 1146
(m. 1129)

Knjaz′ of Novgorod start (1): *PVL*, s.a. 988; knjaz′ of Novgorod end (1): *PVL*, s.a. 1015
Knjaz′ of Kyiv (1) start: *PVL*, s.a. 1016; knjaz′ of Kyiv (1) end: *PVL*, s.a. 1018
Knjaz′ of Kyiv (2) start: *PVL*, s.a 1018; knjaz′ of Kyiv (2) end: *PVL*, s.a. 1054
Knjaz′ of Novgorod (2) start: *PVL*, s.a. 1020; knjaz′ of Novgorod (2) end: *PVL*, s.a. 1036.

Andrew of Hungary
Birth date: unknown
Death date: Berthold of Reichenau, s.a. 1060; *Lamberti Hersfeldensis Annales*, s.a. 1061 (referencing his brother's succession)
King of Hungary start: Berthold of Reichenau, s.a. 1046; Wertner, *Az Árpádok családi története*, 114–15; king of Hungary end: *Lamberti Hersfeldensis Annales*, s.a. 1061
Marriage to Anastasija Jaroslavna: Dercsényi, *Chronica de Gestis Hungarorum*, 113; Adam of Bremen, *History of the Archbishops of Hamburg-Bremen*, bk. 3, ch. xiii.12, schol. 62 (63). For more on this marriage see part 1, "Marriages: Generation Two," "Anastasija Jaroslavna."

Anastasija Jaroslavna
Birth date: unknown
Death date: Wertner places her death in 1074; see his *Az Árpádok családi története*, chart. However, this is simply the last year that we have information about her. In that year Salomon left her at Admont Abbey when he was expelled from Hungary and went to fight further with his cousins; see Dercsényi, *Chronica de gestis Hungarorum*, 124
Marriage to Andrew of Hungary: Dercsényi, *Chronica de Gestis Hungarorum*, 113; Adam of Bremen, *History of the Archbishops of Hamburg-Bremen*, bk. 3, ch. xiii.12, schol. 62 (63). For more on this marriage see part 1, "Marriages: Generation Two," "Anastasija Jaroslavna."

Volodimer Jaroslavič
Birth date: *PVL*, s.a. 1020
Death date: *PVL*, s.a. 1052;
Knjaz′ of Novgorod start: *PVL*, s.a. 1036; knjaz′ of Novgorod end: *PVL*, s.a. 1052
Relationship with unknown woman: Conjectural based upon a child cited in *PVL*, s.a. 1064.

Volodimer "Monomax" Vsevolodič

Birth date: *PVL*, s.a. 1053

Death date: Laurentian Chronicle, s.a. 1125; *NPL*, s.a. 1125; Rogožskij Chronicle, s.a. 1125; Tver Chronicle, s.a. 1125; Nikon Chronicle, s.a. 1125

Knjaz′ of Smolensk start: *PVL*, s.a. 1078; knjaz′ of Smolensk end: *PVL*, s.a. 1095 (based on the assumption that Davyd takes power in Smolensk in that year)

Knjaz′ of Černihiv start: *PVL*, s.a. 1078; knjaz′ of Černihiv end: *PVL*, s.a. 1094

Knjaz′ of Perejaslav start: *PVL*, s.a. 1094; knjaz′ of Perejaslav end: *PVL*, s.a. 1113 (conjectural based upon his assumption of power in Kyiv)

Knjaz′ of Kyiv start: Laurentian Chronicle, s.a. 1114; Hypatian Chronicle, s.a. 1113; *NPL*, s.a. 1113; Rogožskij Chronicle, s.a. 1114; Tver Chronicle, s.a. 1113; Nikon Chronicle, s.a. 1114; knjaz′ of Kyiv end: Laurentian Chronicle, s.a. 1125; *NPL*, s.a. 1125; Rogožskij Chronicle, s.a. 1125; Tver Chronicle, s.a. 1125; Nikon Chronicle, s.a. 1125.

Lanka, daughter of Béla I of Hungary

Birth date: unknown

Death date: Her last mention is begging Koloman to spare her children during their conflict at the end of the eleventh century; see *PVL*, s.a. 1097, for the conflict; and Dercsényi, *Chronica de Gestis Hungarorum*, 131, for her supplication

Marriage to Rostislav Volodimerič: Tatiščev, *Istorija Rossijskaja*, 2:83–84; Dercsényi, *Chronica de Gestis Hungarorum*, 131. For more on this marriage see part 1, "Marriages: Generation Three," "Rostislav Volodimerič."

Rostislav Volodimerič

Birth date: unknown

Death date: *PVL*, s.a. 1066

Knjaz′ of Tmutorokan (1) start: *PVL*, s.a. 1064; knjaz′ of Tmutorokan (1) end: *PVL*, s.a. 1065

Knjaz′ of Tmutorokan (2) start: *PVL*, s.a. 1065; knjaz′ of Tmurotokan (2) end: *PVL*, s.a. 1066

Marriage to Lanka, daughter of Béla I of Hungary: Tatiščev, *Istorija Rossijskaja*, 2:83–84; Dercsényi, *Chronica de Gestis Hungarorum*, 131. For more on this marriage see part 1, "Marriages: Generation Three," "Rostislav Volodimerič."

Svjatopolk Izjaslavič

Birth date: *NPL*, s.a. 1050 (though a patronymic is not specified and identification is conjectural)

Death date: Laurentian Chronicle, s.a. 1114; Hypatian Chronicle, s.a. 1113; *NPL*, s.a. 1113; *NČL*, s.a. 1114; Rogožskij Chronicle, s.a. 1114; Tver Chronicle, s.a. 1113; Nikon Chronicle, s.a. 1114

Knjaz′ of Polack start: *PVL*, s.a. 1069; knjaz′ of Polack end: *PVL*, s.a. 1071

Knjaz′ of Novgorod start: conjectural based upon surrounding rulers; knjaz′ of Novgorod end: *PVL*, s.a. 1088

Knjaz′ of Turov start: *PVL*, s.a. 1088; knjaz′ of Turov end: *PVL*, s.a. 1093

Knjaz′ of Kyiv start: *PVL*, s.a. 1093, *NPL*, s.a. 1093; knjaz′ of Kyiv end: Laurentian Chronicle, s.a. 1114; Hypatian Chronicle, s.a. 1113; *NPL*, s.a. 1113; *NČL*, s.a. 1114; Rogožskij Chronicle, s.a. 1114; Tver Chronicle, s.a. 1113; Nikon Chronicle, s.a. 1114.

M′stislav "Harald" Volodimerič

Birth date: *PVL*, s.a. 1076

Death date: *NPL*, s.a. 1132; Laurentian Chronicle, s.a. 1132; Hypatian Chronicle, s.a. 1133; *NČL*, s.a. 1131; Voskresenskij Chronicle, s.a. 1131; Rogožskij Chronicle, s.a. 1132; Tver Chronicle, s.a. 1132; Nikon Chronicle, s.a. 1132

Knjaz′ of Novgorod start: *PVL*, s.a. 1095; knjaz′ of Novgorod end: *NPL*, s.a. 1117; Laurentian Chronicle, s.a. 1117; *NČL*, s.a. 1117; Hypatian Chronicle, s.a. 1117; Voskresenskij Chronicle, s.a. 1117; Tver Chronicle, s.a. 1117; Nikon Chronicle, s.a. 1117

Knjaz′ of Bilhorod start: *NPL*, s.a. 1117; Laurentian Chronicle, s.a. 1117; Hypatian Chronicle, s.a. 1117; *NČL*, s.a. 1117; Voskresenskij Chronicle, s.a. 1117; Tver Chronicle, s.a. 1117; Nikon Chronicle, s.a. 1117 (Hypatian, Voskresenskij, Tver, and Nikon all specifically refer to Bilhorod while the rest simply assume a move to assist his father in Kyiv); knjaz′ of Bilhorod end: *NPL*, s.a. 1125; Laurentian Chronicle, s.a. 1125; Hypatian Chronicle, s.a. 1126; Voskresenskij Chronicle, s.a. 1125; Tver Chronicle, s.a. 1125

Knjaz′ of Kyiv start: *NPL*, s.a. 1125; Laurentian Chronicle, s.a. 1125; Hypatian Chronicle, s.a. 1126; *NČL*, s.a. 1125; Voskresenskij Chronicle, s.a. 1125; Rogožskij Chronicle, s.a. 1125; Tver Chronicle, s.a. 1125; Nikon Chronicle, s.a. 1125; knjaz′ of Kyiv end: *NPL*, s.a. 1132; Laurentian Chronicle, s.a. 1132; Hypatian Chronicle, s.a. 1133; *NČL*, s.a. 1131; Voskresenskij Chronicle, s.a. 1131; Rogožskij Chronicle, s.a. 1132; Tver Chronicle, s.a. 1132; Nikon Chronicle, s.a. 1132.

Evfimija Volodimerovna

Birth date: unknown

Death date: Laurentian Chronicle, s.a. 1138; Hypatian Chronicle, s.a. 1139; Nikon Chronicle, s.a. 1138

Marriage to Koloman of Hungary: Hypatian Chronicle, s.a. 1112;

Dercsényi, *Chronica de Gestis Hungarorum*, 131, 132 (references repudiation); "Cosmae Chronicon Boemorum cum continuatoribus," s.a. 1132 (references repudiation); Otto, Bishop of Freising, *Two Cities*, bk. 7, sec. 21. For more information on this marriage see part 1, "Marriages: Generation Four," "Evfimija Volodimerovna."

Koloman of Hungary

Birth date: unknown

Death date: Dercsényi, *Chronica de gestis Hungarorum*, 133, lists his death in 1114, and this date is accepted by Wertner in his *Az Árpádok családi története*, 217. However, the date is most often corrected to 1116 following Cosmas of Prague, *Chronicle of the Czechs*, bk. 3, ch. 42 (recorded under 1116), including by Dercsényi, *Chronica de gestis Hungarorum*, n455; Engel, *Realm of St. Stephen*, 49.

King of Hungary start: Dercsényi, *Chronica de Gestis Hungarorum*, 130; "Annales Posonienses," s.a. 1097, 1098; king of Hungary end: Dercsényi, *Chronica de gestis Hungarorum*, 133, lists his death in 1114, and this date is accepted by Wertner in his *Az Árpádok családi története*, 217. However, the date is most often corrected to 1116 following Cosmas of Prague, *Chronicle of the Czechs*, bk. 3, ch. 42 (recorded under 1116), including by Dercsényi, *Chronica de gestis Hungarorum*, n455; Engel, *Realm of St. Stephen*, 49.

Marriage to Evfimija Volodimerovna: Hypatian Chronicle, s.a. 1112; Dercsényi, *Chronica de Gestis Hungarorum*, 131; "Cosmae Chronicon Boemorum cum continuatoribus," s.a. 1132 (references repudiation); Otto, Bishop of Freising, *Two Cities*, bk. 7, sec. 21. For more information on this marriage see part 1, "Marriages: Generation Four," "Evfimija Volodimerovna."

Volodar′ Rostislavič

Birth date: unknown

Death date: Laurentian Chronicle, s.a. 1124; Hypatian Chronicle, s.a. 1124

Knjaz′ of Tmutorokan′ start: *PVL*, s.a. 1081; knjaz′ of Tmutorokan′ end: *PVL*, s.a. 1083

Knjaz′ of Volodymyr: *PVL*, s.a. 1084

Knjaz′ of Peremyšl (1) start: *PVL*, s.a. 1097 (records his rule there, but it is conjectural that it began at his brother's death); knjaz′ of Peremyšl (1) end: *Chronica Poloniae Maioris*, ch. 28

Knjaz′ of Peremyšl (2) start: Hypatian Chronicle, s.a. 1122; knjaz′ of Peremyšl′ (2) end: Laurentian Chronicle, s.a. 1124; Hypatian Chronicle, s.a. 1124

Relationship with unknown partner(s): conjectural based upon children cited elsewhere; see Hypatian Chronicle, s.a. 1140, for example.

Almos of Hungary
Birth date: unknown
Death date: Wertner, *Az Árpádok családi története*, table
Marriage to Peredslava Svjatopolkovna: Laurentian Chronicle, s.a. 1104; Hypatian Chronicle, s.a. 1104. For more on this marriage see part 1, "Marriages: Generation Four," "Peredslava Svjatopolkovna."

Peredslava Svjatopolkovna
Birth date: unknown
Death date: Hypatian Chronicle, s.a. 1116, where she is listed as Peredslava Svjatoslavna
Marriage to Almos of Hungary: Laurentian Chronicle, s.a. 1104; Hypatian Chronicle, s.a. 1104. For more on this marriage see part 1, "Marriages: Generation Four," "Peredslava Svjatopolkovna."

Jaroslav Svjatopolčič
Birth date: unknown
Death date: Laurentian Chronicle, s.a. 1123; Hypatian Chronicle, s.a. 1123; Voskresenskij Chronicle, s.a. 1123; Nikon Chronicle, s.a. 1123
Knjaz′ of Volodymyr start: *PVL*, s.a. 1097, 1100; knjaz′ of Volodymyr end: Hypatian Chronicle, s.a. 1118; Laurentian Chronicle, s.a. 1119; Voskresenskij Chronicle, s.a. 1118; Tver Chronicle, s.a. 1118; Nikon Chronicle, s.a. 1119
Marriage to unknown daughter of Ladislaus of Hungary: Fejér, *Codex diplomaticus Hungariae*, 469; Wertner, *Az Árpádok családi története*, 205. For more on this marriage see part 1, "Marriages: Generation Four," "Jaroslav Svjatopolčič."

N. N., daughter of Ladislaus of Hungary
Birth date: unknown
Death date: conjectural based upon the date of Jaroslav's remarriage
Marriage to Jaroslav Svjatopolčič: Fejér, *Codex diplomaticus Hungariae*, 469; Wertner, *Az Árpádok családi története*, 205. For more on this marriage see part 1, "Marriages: Generation Four," "Jaroslav Svjatopolčič."

Evfrosinija M′stislavna
Birth date: unknown
Death date: Wertner, *Az Árpádok családi története*, 313, suggests 1175, while Dąbrowski instead suggests in or after 1193 based upon a variety of factors; see Dąbrowski, *Genealogia Mścisławowiczów*, 170–71
Marriage to Géza II of Hungary: Wilhelm, "Wilhelmi abbatis genealogia regum Danorum," 182; for the date of the marriage see

Dąbrowski, *Genealogia Mścisławowiczówi*, 174. For more information on this marriage see part 1, "Marriages: Generation Five," "Evfrosinija M´stislavna."

Géza II of Hungary

Birth date: Wertner, *Az Árpádok családi története*, 309

Death date: Kinnamos, *Deeds of John and Manuel Comnenus*, bk. 5, ch. 1; Wertner, *Az Árpádok családi története*, 309 (1161); Dąbrowski, *Genealogia Mścisławowiczówi*, 174 (1162)

King of Hungary start: Wertner, *Az Árpádok családi története*, 309; Kinnamos, *Deeds of John and Manuel Comnenus*, bk. 5, ch. 7 (already ruling ca. 1151); king of Hungary end: Kinnamos, *Deeds of John and Manuel Comnenus*, bk. 5, ch. 1; Wertner, *Az Árpádok családi története*, 309 (1161); Dąbrowski, *Genealogia Mścisławowiczówi*, 174 (1162)

Marriage to Evfrosinija M´stislavna: Wilhelm, "Wilhelmi abbatis genealogia regum Danorum," 182; for the date of the marriage see Dąbrowski, *Genealogia Mścisławowiczówi*, 174. For more information on this marriage see part 1, "Marriages: Generation Five," "Evfrosinija M´stislavna."

N. N., daughter of Koloman of Hungary

Birth date: unknown

Death date: Her death date can reasonably be assumed to have occurred after her marriage, though when is unknown.

Marriage to Volodimerko Volodarič: Tatiščev, *Istorija Rossijskaja*, 2:138. For more on this marriage see part 1, "Marriages: Generation Five," "Volodimerko Volodarič."

Volodimerko Volodarič

Birth date: unknown

Death date: Hypatian Chronicle, s.a. 1152; Tver Chronicle, s.a. 1153; Laurentian Chronicle, s.a. 1152; Voskresenskij Chronicle, s.a. 1152; Nikon Chronicle, s.a. 1152

Knjaz´ of Zvenyhorod start: Tatiščev, *Istorija Rossijskaja*, 2:138; knjaz´ of Zvenyhorod end: conjectural based upon presence as co-ruler of Halyč; mentioned in Hypatian Chronicle, s.a. 1140

Knjaz´ of Halyč (with Ivan Vasilkovič) start: Hypatian Chronicle, s.a. 1140 (already in place); knjaz´ of Halyč (with Ivan Vasilkovič) end: Hypatian Chronicle, s.a. 1141

Knjaz´ of Halyč start: Hypatian Chronicle, s.a. 1141; knjaz´ of Halyč end: Hypatian Chronicle, s.a. 1152; Tver Chronicle, s.a. 1153; Laurentian Chronicle, s.a. 1152; Voskresenskij Chronicle, s.a. 1152; Nikon Chronicle, s.a. 1152

Marriage to N. N., daughter of Koloman of Hungary: Tatiščev, *Istorija*

Rossijskaja, 2:138. For more on this marriage see part 1, "Marriages: Generation Five," "Volodimerko Volodarič."

Béla II of Hungary
Birth date: Wertner, *Az Árpádok családi története*, 295
Death date: Wertner, *Az Árpádok családi története*, 296–97
King of Hungary start: Wertner, *Az Árpádok családi története*, 295; king of Hungary end: Wertner, *Az Árpádok családi története*, 296–97
Marriage to Jelena of Serbia: Wertner, *Az Árpádok családi története*, 298.

Jelena of Serbia
Birth date: unknown
Death date: Wertner, *Az Árpádok családi története*, 300–301
Marriage to Béla II of Hungary: Wertner, *Az Árpádok családi története*, 298.

Table 19: German Dynastic Marriages

Jaroslav "Mudryj" Volodimerič
Birth date: unknown
Death date: *PVL*, s.a. 1054
Knjaz′ of Rostov: *PVL*, s.a. 988
Knjaz′ of Novgorod start (1): *PVL*, s.a. 988; knjaz′ of Novgorod end (1): *PVL*, s.a. 1015
Knjaz′ of Kyiv (1) start: *PVL*, s.a. 1016; knjaz′ of Kyiv (1) end: *PVL*, s.a. 1018
Knjaz′ of Kyiv (2) start: *PVL*, s.a 1018; knjaz′ of Kyiv (2) end: *PVL*, s.a. 1054
Knjaz′ of Novgorod (2) start: *PVL*, s.a. 1020; knjaz′ of Novgorod (2) end: *PVL*, s.a. 1036.

Anastasija Jaroslavna
Birth date: unknown
Death date: Wertner places her death in 1074; see his *Az Árpádok családi története*, chart. However, this is simply the last year that we have information about her. In that year Salomon left her at Admont Abbey when he was expelled from Hungary and went to fight further with his cousins; see Dercsényi, *Chronica de gestis Hungarorum*, 124.
Marriage to Andrew of Hungary: Dercsényi, *Chronica de Gestis Hungarorum*, 113; Adam of Bremen, *History of the Archbishops of Hamburg-Bremen*, bk. 3, ch. xiii.12, schol. 62 (63). For more on this marriage see part 1, "Marriages: Generation Two," "Anastasija Jaroslavna."

Andrew of Hungary
Birth date: unknown

Table 19: German Dynastic Marriages

Jaroslav "Mudryj"
b. unknown; d. 1054
(Rostov r. ca. 988)
(Novgorod r. ca. 988–1015)
(Kyiv r. 1016–1018)
(Novgorod r. 1020–1036)
(Kyiv r. 1018–1054)

Anastasija
b. unknown;
d. post-1074
(m. pre-1046)

Andrew of Hungary
b. unknown; d. 1060
(King of Hungary r.
1046–1060)

Svjatoslav
b. 1027; d. 1076
(Volodymyr r.
unknown–1054)
(Černihiv r. 1054–1076)
(Kyiv r. 1073–1076)

2

Oda of Stade
b. unknown;
d. post-1076
(m. ca. 1070)

Vsevolod
b. 1030; d. 1093
(Perejaslav r. 1054–1076)
(Černihiv r. 1077–1078)
(Kyiv r. 1077–1077)
(Kyiv r. 1078–1093)

Judith, daughter of
Henry III of the German
Empire
b. 1047; d. 1092
(m. 1063)

Salomon
b. ca. 1052; d. 1087
(King of Hungary r.
1063–1074)

Cunigunda of the
German Empire
b. unknown;
d. post-1087
(m. ca. 1074)

Jaropolk Izjaslavič
b. unknown; d. 1086
(Vyšhorod r. 1078)
(Volodymyr r. 1078–1084)
(Volodymyr r. 1084–1085)
(Volodymyr r. 1086)

Henry III "the Long"
of Stade
b. unknown; d. 1087
(Margrave of Saxon
Nordmark r. ca.
1082–1087)

1

Evpraksija
b. 1071; d. 1109
(1st m. ca. 1082)
(2nd m. 1089)

2

Henry IV of the German
Empire
b. ca. 1050; d. 1106
(King of the German
Empire r. 1056–1106)
(Emperor 1084–1106)

Death date: Berthold of Reichenau, s.a. 1060; *Lamberti Hersfeldensis Annales*, s.a. 1061 (referencing his brother's succession)
King of Hungary start: Berthold of Reichenau, s.a. 1046; Wertner, *Az Árpádok családi története*, 114–15; king of Hungary end: *Lamberti Hersfeldensis Annales*, s.a. 1061
Marriage to Anastasija Jaroslavna: Dercsényi, *Chronica de Gestis Hungarorum*, 113; Adam of Bremen, *History of the Archbishops of Hamburg-Bremen*, bk. 3, ch. xiii.12, schol. 62 (63). For more on this marriage see part 1, "Marriages: Generation Two," "Anastasija Jaroslavna."

Svjatoslav Jaroslavič
Birth date: *PVL*, s.a. 1027
Death date: *PVL*, s.a. 1076
Knjaz´ of Volodymyr start: unknown; knjaz´ of Volodymyr end: *PVL*, s.a. 1054
Knjaz´ of Černihiv start: *PVL*, s.a. 1054; knjaz´ of Černihiv end: *PVL*, s.a. 1076
Knjaz´ of Kyiv start: *PVL*, s.a. 1073; knjaz´ of Kyiv end: *PVL*, s.a. 1076
Marriage to Oda of Stade: Nazarenko, *Drevnjaja Rus´ na meždunarodnyx putjax*, 515; *Bruno de Bello Saxonico*, 333, ch. 13. For more on this marriage see part 1, "Marriages: Generation Two," "Svjatoslav Jaroslavič."

Oda of Stade
Birth date: unknown
Death date: Oda returned to the German Empire after Svjatoslav's death, and died only after that time. See part 1, "Marriages: Generation Two," "Svjatoslav Jaroslavič," for more information.
Marriage to Svjatoslav Jaroslavič: Nazarenko, *Drevnjaja Rus´ na meždunarodnyx putjax*, 515; *Bruno de Bello Saxonico*, 333, ch. 13. For more on this marriage see part 1, "Marriages: Generation Two," "Svjatoslav Jaroslavič."

Vsevolod Jaroslavič
Birth date: *PVL*, s.a. 1030
Death date: *PVL*, s.a. 1093
Knjaz´ of Perejaslav start: *PVL*, s.a. 1054; knjaz´ of Perejaslav end: *PVL*, s.a. 1093
Knjaz´ of Kyiv (1) start: *PVL*, s.a. 1076; knjaz´ of Kyiv (1) end: *PVL*, s.a. 1077
Knjaz´ of Černihiv start: *PVL*, s.a. 1077; knjaz´ of Černihiv end: *PVL*, s.a. 1078

Knjaz′ of Kyiv (2) start: *PVL*, s.a. 1078; knjaz′ of Kyiv (2) end: *PVL*, s.a. 1093; *NPL*, s.a. 1093.

Judith, daughter of Henry III
Birth date: Balzer, *Genealogia Piastów*, 105; "Annales Altahenses maiores," s.a. 1047 (where the birth of a child to Henry III is recorded); I am following Balzer in his identification of this child as Judith.
Death date: Balzer, *Genealogia Piastów*, 106
Marriage to Salomon: Dercsényi, *Chronica de Gestis Hungarorum*, 115; Gallus Anonymous, *Gesta principum Polonorum*, bk. 2, ch. 1; *Lamberti Hersfeldensis Annales*, s.a. 1063; Berthold of Reichenau, s.a. 1059; Długosz, *Annales*, 161. For Judith's marriage to Władysław Herman see table 1, above.

Salomon
Birth date: conjectural; see Wertner, *Az Árpádok családi története*, 128
Death date: Dercsényi, *Chronica de Gestis Hungarorum*, 129; Bernold of St. Blasien, "Chronicle," s.a. 1087
King of Hungary with Andrew start: Dercsényi, *Chronica de Gestis Hungarorum*, 115; king of Hungary with Andrew end: Berthold of Reichenau, s.a. 1060
King of Hungary start: *Lamberti Hersfeldensis Annales*, s.a. 1063; Dercsényi, *Chronica de Gestis Hungarorum*, 115 (listed under 1058 as co-ruler with father); Bernold of St. Blasien, "Chronicle," s.a. 1063; king of Hungary end: Gallus Anonymous, *Gesta principum Polonorum*, bk. 1, ch. 27; *Lamberti Hersfeldensis Annales*, s.a. 1071; Berthold of Reichenau, s.a. 1074
Marriage to Judith, daughter of Henry III: Dercsényi, *Chronica de Gestis Hungarorum*, 115; Gallus Anonymous, *Gesta principum Polonorum*, bk. 2, ch. 1; *Lamberti Hersfeldensis Annales*, s.a. 1063; Berthold of Reichenau, s.a. 1059; Długosz, *Annales*, 161.

Cunigunda of the German Empire
Birth date: unknown
Death date: Her death date can reasonably be assumed to have occurred after her second marriage, though when is unknown.
Marriage to Jaropolk Izjaslavič: *Annalista Saxo*, s.a. 1062. For more on this marriage see part 1, "Marriages: Generation Three," "Jaropolk Izjaslavič."

Jaropolk Izjaslavič
Birth date: unknown
Death date: *PVL*, s.a. 1086

Knjaz′ of Vyšhorod: *PVL*, s.a. 1078
Knjaz′ of Volodymyr (1) start: *PVL*, s.a. 1078; knjaz′ of Volodymyr (1) end: *PVL*, s.a. 1084
Knjaz′ of Volodymyr (2) start: *PVL*, s.a. 1084; knjaz′ of Volodymyr (2) end: *PVL*, s.a. 1085
Knjaz′ of Volodymyr (3): *PVL*, s.a. 1086
Marriage to Cunigunda: *Annalista Saxo*, s.a. 1062. For more on this marriage see part 1, "Marriages: Generation Three," "Jaropolk Izjaslavič."

Henry III "the Long" of Stade
Birth date: unknown
Death date: *Annales Stadenses*, s.a. 1144, in listing of history of the family dates Henry of Stade's death to 1087.
Margrave of the Saxon Nordmark start: *Annalista Saxo*, s.a. 1082; margrave of the Saxon Nordmark end: *Annales Stadenses*, s.a. 1144, in listing of history of the family dates Henry of Stade's death to 1087
Marriage to Evpraksija Vsevolodovna: *Annalista Saxo*, s.a. 1082; *Annales Stadenses*, s.a. 1144. For more on this marriage see part 1, "Marriages: Generation Three," "Evpraksija Vsevolodovna."

Evpraksija Vsevolodovna
Birth date: conjectural based upon age at date of marriage; see Raffensperger, "Evpraksia Vsevolodovna: Between East and West" for more details
Death date: *PVL*, s.a. 1109
Marriage to Henry III "the Long" of Stade: *Annalista Saxo*, s.a. 1082; *Annales Stadenses*, s.a. 1144
Marriage to Henry IV: Walram, *Liber de unitate ecclesiae conservanda*, bk. 2.26, 100; *Heinrici IV: Diplomata*, 407; *Annalista Saxo*, s.a. 1082, 1089; *Annales Augustani*, s.a. 1089. For more on this marriage see part 1, "Marriages: Generation Three," "Evpraksija Vsevolodovna."

Henry IV of the German Empire
Birth date: Herman of Reichenau, "Chronicle," s.a. 1051 (for baptism); Berthold of Reichenau s.a. 1056 (references Henry's age as seven)
Death date: *Annalista Saxo*, s.a. 1106; Cosmas of Prague, *Chronicle of the Czechs*, bk. 3, ch. 18; Orderic Vitalis, *Ecclesiastical History*, bk. 10, ch. 1
King of the German Empire start: Bernold of St. Blasien, "Chronicle," s.a. 1057; Berthold of Reichneau, s.a. 1056; *Annalista Saxo*, s.a. 1056
Emperor of the German Empire start: Bernold of St. Blasien, "Chronicle," s.a. 1084; *Annalista Saxo*, s.a. 1084; Robinson, *Henry IV of Germany, 1056–1106*, 230–31; king and emperor of the German Empire

end: *Annalista Saxo*, s.a. 1106; Cosmas of Prague, *Chronicle of the Czechs*, bk. 3, ch. 18; Orderic Vitalis, *Ecclesiastical History*, bk. 10, ch. 1

Marriage to Evpraksija Vsevolodovna: Walram, *Liber de unitate ecclesiae conservanda*, bk. 2.26, 100; *Heinrici IV: Diplomata*, 407; *Annalista Saxo*, s.a. 1082, 1089; *Annales Augustani*, s.a. 1089. For more on this marriage see part 1, "Marriages: Generation Three," "Evpraksija Vsevolodovna."

Table 20: Byzantine Dynastic Marriages

Volodimer Svjatoslavič
Birth date: unknown
Death date: *PVL*, s.a. 1015
Knjaz´ of Novgorod start: *PVL*, s.a. 970; knjaz´ of Novgorod end: *PVL*, s.a. 980
Knjaz´ of Kyiv start: *PVL*, s.a. 980; knjaz´ of Kyiv end: *PVL*, s.a. 1015.
Marriage to Anna Porphyrogenita: *PVL*, s.a. 988; Scylitzes, *Ioannis Scylitzae Synopsis historiarum*, 336, 354, 367; Poppe, "Political Background to the Baptism of Rus´" (extensively redates the marriage). For more on this marriage see part 1, "Marriages: Prelude," "Volodimer Svjatoslavič."

Anna Porphyrogenita
Birth date: unknown
Death date: *PVL*, s.a. 1011
Marriage to Volodimer Svjatoslavič: *PVL*, s.a. 988; Scylitzes, *Ioannis Scylitzae Synopsis historiarum*, 336, 354, 367; Poppe, "Political Background to the Baptism of Rus´" (extensively redates the marriage). For more on this marriage see part 1, "Marriages: Prelude," "Volodimer Svjatoslavič."

Vsevolod Jaroslavič
Birth date: *PVL*, s.a. 1030
Death date: *PVL*, s.a. 1093
Knjaz´ of Perejaslav start: *PVL*, s.a. 1054; knjaz´ of Perejaslav end: *PVL*, s.a. 1093
Knjaz´ of Kyiv (1) start: *PVL*, s.a. 1076; knjaz´ of Kyiv (1) end: *PVL*, s.a. 1077
Knjaz´ of Černihiv start: *PVL*, s.a. 1077; knjaz´ of Černihiv end: *PVL*, s.a. 1078

Table 20: Byzantine Dynastic Marriages

Volodimer Svjatoslavič
b. unknown; d. 1015
(Novgorod r. 970–980)
(Kyiv r. 980–1015)

Anna Porphyrogenita
b. unknown; d. 1011
(m. 989)

Vsevolod Jaroslavič
b. 1030; d. 1093
(Perejaslav r. 1054–1055)
(Kyiv r. 1077)
(Černihiv r. 1077–1078)
(Kyiv r. 1078–1093)

"Monomaxina" of Byzantium
b. unknown; d. 1067
(m. ca. 1053)

Volodimer "Monomax" Vsevolodič
b. 1053; d. 1125
(Perejaslav r. 1076–1078)
(Smolensk r. ca. 1078–ca. 1095)
(Černihiv r. 1078–1094)
(Perejaslav r. 1094–1113)
(Kyiv r. ca. 1113–1125)

Volodar′ Rostislavič
b. unknown; d. 1124
(Tmutorokan r. 1081–1083)
(Volodymyr r. 1084)
(Peremyšl r. 1092–1120)
(Peremyšl r. 1122–1124)

Leo Diogenes of Byzantium
b. unknown;
d. 1116

Marija
b. unknown;
d. 1146
(m. 1116)

M′stislav "Harald"
b. 1076; d. 1132
(Novgorod r. 1095–1117)
(Bilhorod r. 1117–1125)
(Kyiv r. 1125–1132)

Jaropolk
b. unknown; d. 1138
(Perejaslav r. 1114–unknown)
(Minsk r. 1115–1116)
(Perejaslav r. 1125–1132)
(Kyiv r. 1132–1138)
(Perejaslav r. 1134–1135)

Elena of Ossetia
b. unknown;
d. post–1145
(m. 1116)

N. N.
b. unknown;
d. post-1104
(m. 1104)

N. N., "Carevič" Comnenus of Byzantium
b. unknown;
d. post-1104

Izjaslav
b. unknown; d. 1154
(Kursk r. 1127–1129)
(Polack r. 1129–1132)
(Perejaslav r. 1132)
(Turov, Pinsk, Minsk r. 1132–1134)
(Volodymyr r. 1135–1142)
(Perejaslav r. 1142–1146)
(Kyiv r. 1146–1149)
(Volodymyr r. 1149–1150)

N. N. daughter of the ruler of Abkhazia
b. unknown;
d. post-1154
(m. 1154)

N. N.
b. unknown;
d. post-1122
(m. 1122)

N. N., of the Byzantine Empire
b. unknown;
d. post-1122

Knjaz´ of Kyiv (2) start: *PVL*, s.a. 1078; knjaz´ of Kyiv (2) end: *PVL*, s.a. 1093; *NPL*, s.a. 1093

Marriage to Monomaxina: *PVL*, s.a. 1053. For more on this marriage see part 1, "Marriages: Generation Two," "Vsevolod Jaroslavič."

Monomaxina

Birth date: unknown

Death date: unknown

Marriage to Vsevolod Jaroslavič: *PVL*, s.a. 1053. For more on this marriage see part 1, "Marriages: Generation Two," "Vsevolod Jaroslavič."

Volodimer "Monomax" Vsevolodič

Birth date: *PVL*, s.a. 1053

Death date: Laurentian Chronicle, s.a. 1125; *NPL*, s.a. 1125; Rogožskij Chronicle, s.a. 1125; Tver Chronicle, s.a. 1125; Nikon Chronicle, s.a. 1125

Knjaz´ of Smolensk start: *PVL*, s.a. 1078; knjaz´ of Smolensk end: *PVL*, s.a. 1095 (based on the assumption that Davyd takes power in Smolensk in that year)

Knjaz´ of Černihiv start: *PVL*, s.a. 1078; knjaz´ of Černihiv end: *PVL*, s.a. 1094

Knjaz´ of Perejaslav start: *PVL*, s.a. 1094; knjaz´ of Perejaslav end: *PVL*, s.a. 1113 (conjectural based upon his assumption of power in Kyiv)

Knjaz´ of Kyiv start: Laurentian Chronicle, s.a. 1114; Hypatian Chronicle, s.a. 1113; *NPL*, s.a. 1113; Rogožskij Chronicle, s.a. 1114; Tver Chronicle, s.a. 1113; Nikon Chronicle, s.a. 1114; knjaz´ of Kyiv end: Laurentian Chronicle, s.a. 1125; *NPL*, s.a. 1125; Rogožskij Chronicle, s.a. 1125; Tver Chronicle, s.a. 1125; Nikon Chronicle, s.a. 1125.

Volodar´ Rostislavič

Birth date: unknown

Death date: Laurentian Chronicle, s.a. 1124; Hypatian Chronicle, s.a. 1124

Knjaz´ of Tmutorokan start: *PVL*, s.a. 1081; knjaz´ of Tmutorokan end: *PVL*, s.a. 1083

Knjaz´ of Volodymyr: *PVL*, s.a. 1084

Knjaz´ of Peremyšl (1) start: *PVL*, s.a. 1097 (records his rule there, but conjectural that it began at his brother's death); knjaz´ of Peremyšl´ (1) end: *Chronica Poloniae Maioris*, ch. 28

Knjaz´ of Peremyšl´ (2) start: Hypatian Chronicle, s.a. 1122; knjaz´ of Peremyšl´ (2) end: Laurentian Chronicle, s.a. 1124; Hypatian Chronicle, s.a. 1124.

Leo Diogenes of Byzantium
Birth date: unknown
Death date: Laurentian Chronicle, s.a. 1116; Hypatian Chronicle, s.a. 1116; Nikon Chronicle, s.a. 1117
Marriage to Marija Volodimerovna:Laurentian Chronicle, s.a. 1116; Hypatian Chronicle, s.a. 1116; Každan, "Rus´-Byzantine Princely Marriages in the Eleventh and Twelfth Centuries," 420. For more information on this marriage see part 1, "Marriages: Generation Four," "Maria Volodimerovna."

Marija Volodimerovna
Birth date: unknown
Death date: Laurentian Chronicle, s.a. 1146; Nikon Chronicle, s.a. 1146
Marriage to Leo Diogenes of Byzantium: Laurentian Chronicle, s.a. 1116; Hypatian Chronicle, s.a. 1116; Každan, "Rus´-Byzantine Princely Marriages in the Eleventh and Twelfth Centuries," 420. For more information on this marriage see part 1, "Marriages: Generation Four," "Marija Volodimerovna."

M´stislav "Harald" Volodimerič
Birth date: *PVL*, s.a. 1076
Death date: *NPL*, s.a. 1132; Laurentian Chronicle, s.a. 1132; Hypatian Chronicle, s.a. 1133; *NČL*, s.a. 1131; Voskresenskij Chronicle, s.a. 1131; Rogožskij Chronicle, s.a. 1132; Tver Chronicle, s.a. 1132; Nikon Chronicle, s.a. 1132
Knjaz´ of Novgorod start: *PVL*, s.a. 1095; knjaz´ of Novgorod end: *NPL*, s.a. 1117; Laurentian Chronicle, s.a. 1117; *NČL*, s.a. 1117; Hypatian Chronicle, s.a. 1117; Voskresenskij Chronicle, s.a. 1117; Tver Chronicle, s.a. 1117; Nikon Chronicle, s.a. 1117
Knjaz´ of Bilhorod start: *NPL*, s.a. 1117; Laurentian Chronicle, s.a. 1117; Hypatian Chronicle, s.a. 1117; *NČL*, s.a. 1117; Voskresenskij Chronicle, s.a. 1117; Tver Chronicle, s.a. 1117; Nikon s.a. 1117 (Hypatian, Voskresenskij, Tver, and Nikon all specifically refer to Bilhorod while the rest simply assume a move to assist his father in Kyiv); knjaz´ of Bilhorod end: *NPL*, s.a. 1125; Laurentian Chronicle, s.a. 1125; Hypatian Chronicle, s.a. 1126; Voskresenskij Chronicle, s.a. 1125; Tver Chronicle, s.a. 1125
Knjaz´ of Kyiv start: *NPL*, s.a. 1125; Laurentian Chronicle, s.a. 1125; Hypatian Chronicle, s.a. 1126; *NČL*, s.a. 1125; Voskresenskij Chronicle, s.a. 1125; Rogožskij Chronicle, s.a. 1125; Tver Chronicle, s.a. 1125; Nikon Chronicle, s.a. 1125; knjaz´ of Kyiv end: *NPL*, s.a. 1132; Laurentian Chronicle, s.a. 1132; Hypatian Chronicle, s.a. 1133; *NČL*, s.a. 1131; Voskresenskij Chronicle, s.a. 1131; Rogožskij Chronicle, s.a. 1132; Tver Chronicle, s.a. 1132; Nikon Chronicle, s.a. 1132.

Jaropolk Volodimerič

Birth date: unknown

Death date: Laurentian Chronicle, s.a. 1138; Hypatian Chronicle, s.a. 1139; *NČL*, s.a. 1138; Voskresenskij Chronicle, s.a. 1138; Rogožskij Chronicle, s.a. 1138; Tver Chronicle, s.a. 1138; Nikon Chronicle, s.a. 1138

Knjaz´ of Minsk start: Voskresenskij Chronicle, s.a. 1115 (places a son of Volodimer here; which son is conjecture, but helped by his identification in the Voskresenskij Chronicle, s.a. 1116); Nikon Chronicle, s.a. 1115 (again, simply a son of Volodimer); knjaz´ of Minsk end: Hypatian Chronicle, s.a. 1116 (Minsk is returned to Glěb Vseslavič)

Knjaz´ of Perejaslav (1) start: Hypatian Chronicle, s.a. 1113 (references his enthronement following his brother Svjatoslav's death. There may be an interregnum here, as the other chronicles do not note his rule here until his father's death); Laurentian Chronicle, s.a 1125; Voskresenskij Chronicle, s.a. 1125; Rogožskij Chronicle, s.a. 1125; Tver Chronicle, s.a. 1125; Nikon Chronicle, s.a. 1125; knjaz´ of Perejaslav (1) end: Laurentian Chronicle, s.a. 1132; Hypatian Chronicle, s.a. 1133

Knjaz´ of Kyiv start: *NPL*, s.a. 1132; Laurentian Chronicle, s.a. 1132; Hypatian Chronicle, s.a. 1133; *NČL*, s.a. 1131; Voskresenskij Chronicle, s.a. 1131; Rogožskij Chronicle, s.a. 1132; Tver Chronicle, s.a. 1132; Nikon Chronicle, s.a. 1132; knjaz´ of Kyiv end: Laurentian Chronicle, s.a. 1138; Hypatian Chronicle, s.a. 1139; *NČL*, s.a. 1138; Voskresenskij Chronicle, s.a. 1138; Rogožskij Chronicle, s.a. 1138; Tver Chronicle, s.a. 1138; Nikon Chronicle, s.a. 1138

Knjaz´ of Perejaslav (2) start: Laurentian Chronicle, s.a. 1133, 1134; knjaz´ of Perejaslav (2) end: Laurentian Chronicle, s.a. 1135; Hypatian Chronicle, s.a. 1135; *NČL*, s.a. 1135

Marriage to Elena of Ossetia: Laurentian Chronicle, s.a. 1116; Hypatian Chronicle, s.a. 1116; Voskresenskij Chronicle, s.a. 1116; Nikon Chronicle, s.a. 1117. For more information on this marriage see part 1, "Marriages: Generation Four," "Jaropolk Volodimerič."

Elena of Ossetia

Birth date: unknown

Death date: Nikon Chronicle, s.a. 1145; Laurentian Chronicle, s.a. 1145; Hypatian Chronicle, s.a. 1145 (last mention of her, she is transferring her husband's tomb.)

Marriage to Jaropolk Volodimerič: Laurentian Chronicle, s.a. 1116; Hypatian Chronicle, s.a. 1116; Voskresenskij Chronicle, s.a. 1116; Nikon Chronicle, s.a. 1117. For more information on this marriage see part 1, "Marriages: Generation Four," "Jaropolk Volodimerič."

N. N. Volodarovna
Birth date: unknown
Death date: Her death date can reasonably be assumed to have occurred after her marriage, though when is unknown
Marriage to N. N., "Carevič" Comnenus: *PVL*, s.a. 1104; for clarification see Každan, "Rus′-Byzantine Princely Marriages in the Eleventh and Twelfth Centuries," 419–20. For more information on this marriage see part 1, "Marriages: Generation Five," "N. N. Volodarovna."

N. N., "Carevič" Comnenus
Birth date: unknown
Death date: His death date can reasonably be assumed to have occurred after his marriage, though when is unknown
Marriage to N. N. Volodarovna: *PVL*, s.a. 1104; for clarification see Každan, "Rus′-Byzantine Princely Marriages in the Eleventh and Twelfth Centuries," 419–20. For more information on this marriage see part 1, "Marriages: Generation Five," "N. N. Volodarovna."

Izjaslav M′stislavič
Birth date: unknown
Death date: Rogožskij Chronicle, s.a. 1155; *NPL*, s.a. 1154; Hypatian Chronicle, s.a. 1154; Tver Chronicle, s.a. 1155; Laurentian Chronicle, s.a. 1154; Voskresenskij Chronicle, s.a. 1154; Nikon Chronicle, s.a. 1155
Knjaz′ of Kursk start: Laurentian Chronicle, s.a. 1127; *NČL*, s.a. 1127; knjaz′ of Kursk end: conjectural based upon his placement in Polack
Knjaz′ of Polack start: conjectural based upon the displacement of the Polack rulers and his presence there as ruler in 1132; knjaz′ of Polack end: Laurentian Chronicle, s.a. 1132; Voskresenskij Chronicle, s.a. 1131; Tver Chronicle, s.a. 1132
Knjaz′ of Perejaslav (1): Laurentian Chronicle, s.a. 1132; Voskresenskij Chronicle, s.a. 1131; Tver Chronicle, s.a. 1132; Nikon Chronicle, s.a. 1132
Knjaz′ of Turov, Pinsk, and Minsk start: Laurentian Chronicle, s.a. 1132; Voskresenskij Chronicle, s.a. 1131; Tver Chronicle, s.a. 1132; Nikon Chronicle, s.a. 1132; knjaz′ of Turov, Pinsk, and Minsk end: Laurentian Chronicle, s.a. 1134; Hypatian Chronicle, s.a. 1134; *NPL*, s.a. 1134; Nikon Chronicle, s.a. 1135
Knjaz′ of Volodymyr (1) start: Laurentian Chronicle, s.a. 1135; Hypatian Chronicle, s.a. 1135; Voskresenskij Chronicle, s.a. 1135; Nikon Chronicle, s.a. 1135; knjaz′ of Volodymyr (1) end: Laurentian Chronicle, s.a. 1142; Hypatian Chronicle, s.a. 1142; Nikon Chronicle, s.a. 1142
Knjaz′ of Perejaslav (2) start: Laurentian Chronicle, s.a. 1142; Hypatian

Chronicle, s.a. 1142; Voskresenskij Chronicle, s.a. 1142; Tver Chronicle, s.a. 1142; Nikon Chronicle, s.a. 1142; knjaz´ of Perejaslav (2) end: Hypatian Chronicle, s.a. 1146

Knjaz´ of Kyiv start: *NPL*, s.a. 1146; Hypatian Chronicle, s.a. 1146; Laurentian Chronicle, s.a. 1146; *NČL*, s.a. 1146; Voskresenskij Chronicle, s.a. 1146; Rogožskij Chronicle, s.a. 1146; Tver Chronicle, s.a. 1146; Nikon Chronicle, s.a. 1146; knjaz´ of Kyiv end: Laurentian Chronicle, s.a. 1149; *NPL*, s.a. 1149; Hypatian Chronicle, s.a. 1149; Tver Chronicle, s.a. 1149; Voskresenskij Chronicle, s.a. 1149; Nikon Chronicle, s.a. 1149

Knjaz´ of Volodymyr (2): Nikon Chronicle, s.a. 1149 (Nikon is the only chronicle that specifically mentions Izjaslav going to Volodymyr and ruling after his expulsion from Kyiv, though others such as Hypatian Chronicle, s.a. 1149, do note that he goes to Volodymyr)

Knjaz´ of Kyiv (with Vjačeslav Volodimerič) start: Laurentian Chronicle, s.a. 1150; Hypatian Chronicle, s.a. 1150; Tver Chronicle, s.a. 1151; Voskresenskij Chronicle, s.a. 1150; Nikon Chronicle, s.a. 1150; knjaz´ of Kyiv (with Vjačeslav Volodimerič) end: Rogožskij Chronicle, s.a. 1155; *NPL*, s.a. 1154; Hypatian Chronicle, s.a. 1154; Tver Chronicle, s.a. 1155; Laurentian Chronicle, s.a. 1154; Voskresenskij Chronicle, s.a. 1154; Nikon Chronicle, s.a. 1155

Marriage to N. N., daughter of the ruler of Abkhazia: Hypatian Chronicle, s.a. 1154; Tver Chronicle, s.a. 1154; Laurentian Chronicle, s.a. 1154; Voskresenskij Chronicle, s.a. 1154; Nikon Chronicle, s.a. 1154.

N. N., daughter of ruler of Abkhazia

Birth date: unknown

Death date: Her death date can reasonably be assumed to have occurred after her marriage, though when is unknown.

Marriage to Izjaslav M´stislavič: Hypatian Chronicle, s.a. 1154; Tver Chronicle, s.a. 1154; Laurentian Chronicle, s.a. 1154; Voskresenskij Chronicle, s.a. 1154; Nikon Chronicle, s.a. 1154.

N. N. M´stislavna

Birth date: unknown

Death date: Her death date can reasonably be assumed to have occurred after her marriage, though when is unknown.

Marriage to N. N., of the Byzantine Empire: Hypatian Chronicle, s.a. 1122; Voskresenskij Chronicle, s.a. 1122. For more information on this marriage see part 1, "Marriages: Generation Five," "N. N. M´stislavna."

N. N., of the Byzantine Empire

Birth date: unknown

Death date: His death date can reasonably be assumed to have occurred after his marriage, though when is unknown.

Marriage to N. N. M´stislavna: Hypatian Chronicle, s.a. 1122; Voskresenskij Chronicle, s.a. 1122. For more information on this marriage see part 1, "Marriages: Generation Five," "N. N. M´stislavna."

Table 21: Polovcian Dynastic Marriages

N. N., daughter of Tugorkhan

Birth date: unknown

Death date: Laurentian Chronicle, s.a. 1124; Hypatian Chronicle, s.a. 1125

Marriage to Svjatopolk Izjaslavič: Hypatian Chronicle, s.a. 1094. For more on this marriage see part 1, "Marriages: Generation Three," "Svjatopolk Izjaslavič."

Svjatopolk Izjaslavič

Birth date: *NPL*, s.a. 1050 (though patronymic is not specified and identification is conjectural)

Death date: Laurentian Chronicle, s.a. 1114; Hypatian Chronicle, s.a. 1113; *NPL*, s.a. 1113; *NČL*, s.a. 1114; Rogožskij Chronicle, s.a. 1114; Tver Chronicle, s.a. 1113; Nikon Chronicle, s.a. 1114

Knjaz´ of Polack start: *PVL*, s.a. 1069; knjaz´ of Polack end: *PVL*, s.a. 1071

Knjaz´ of Novgorod start: conjectural based upon surrounding rulers; knjaz´ of Novgorod end: *PVL*, s.a. 1088

Knjaz´ of Turov start: *PVL*, s.a. 1088; knjaz´ of Turov end: *PVL*, s.a. 1093

Knjaz´ of Kyiv start: *PVL*, s.a. 1093; *NPL*, s.a. 1093; knjaz´ of Kyiv end: Laurentian Chronicle, s.a. 1114; Hypatian Chronicle, s.a. 1113; *NPL*, s.a. 1113; *NČL*, s.a. 1114; Rogožskij Chronicle, s.a. 1114; Tver Chronicle, s.a. 1113; Nikon Chronicle, s.a. 1114

Marriage to daughter of Tugorkhan: Hypatian Chronicle, s.a. 1094. For more on this marriage see part 1, "Marriages: Generation Three," "Svjatopolk Izjaslavič."

Volodimer "Monomax" Vsevolodič

Birth date: *PVL*, s.a. 1053

Death date: Laurentian Chronicle, s.a. 1125; *NPL*, s.a. 1125; Rogožskij

Table 21: Polovcian Dynastic Marriages

N. N. daughter of Tugorkhan of the Polovcians
b. unknown; d. 1125
(m. 1094)

—— **Svjatopolk Izjaslavič**
b. 1050; d. 1113
(Polack r. 1069–1071)
(Novgorod r. 1077–1088)
(Turov r. 1088–1093)
(Kyiv r. 1093–ca. 1113)

Volodimer "Monomax" Vsevolodič
b. 1053; d. 1125
((Smolensk r. ca. 1078–ca. 1095)
(Černihiv r. 1078–1094)
(Perejaslav r. 1094–1113)
(Kyiv r. ca. 1113–1125)

N. N. daughter of Khan Aepa, son of Girgen
b. unknown;
d. pre-1136
(m. 1107)

—— Svjatoslav Ol′govič
b. unknown; d. 1164
(Novgorod r. 1136–1138)
(Kursk r. 1138–1139)
(Novgorod r. 1139–1141)
(Bilhorod r. 1141–ca. 1146)
(Novhorod-Siverskyj r. ca. 1146–1158)
(Černihiv r. 1158–1164)

Jurij "Dolgorukij"
b. unknown; d. 1158
(Suzdal r. pre-1138–1158)
(Perejaslav r. 1132)
(Perejaslav r. 1135)
(Kyiv r. 1149–1150)
(Perejaslav r. 1151)
(Kyiv r. 1155–1157)

—— N. N. daughter of Khan Aepa, son of Osen
b. unknown;
d. pre-1162
(m. 1107)

N. N. granddaughter of Tugorkhan of Polovcians
b. unknown;
d. post-1117
(m. 1117)

—— Andrej
b. unknown; d. 1141
(Volodymyr r. 1119–1135)
(Perejaslav r. 1135–1141)

Vsevolodko Davydič
b. unknown; d. 1141
(Hrodna r. pre-1127–1141)

Baškord of the Polovcians
b. unknown;
d. post-1159
(Polovcian tribe r. ca. 1159)

—— 2 N. N.
b. unknown;
d. post-1159
(2nd m. between 1151–1159)

Chronicle, s.a. 1125; Tver Chronicle, s.a. 1125; Nikon Chronicle, s.a. 1125
Knjaz´ of Smolensk start: *PVL*, s.a. 1078; knjaz´ of Smolensk end: *PVL*, s.a. 1095 (based on the assumption that Davyd takes power in Smolensk in that year)
Knjaz´ of Černihiv start: *PVL*, s.a. 1078; knjaz´ of Černihiv end: *PVL*, s.a. 1094
Knjaz´ of Perejaslav start: *PVL*, s.a. 1094; knjaz´ of Perejaslav end: *PVL*, s.a. 1113 (conjectural based upon his assumption of power in Kyiv)
Knjaz´ of Kyiv start: Laurentian Chronicle, s.a. 1114; Hypatian Chronicle, s.a. 1113; *NPL*, s.a. 1113; Rogožskij Chronicle, s.a. 1114; Tver Chronicle, s.a. 1113; Nikon Chronicle, s.a. 1114; knjaz´ of Kyiv end: Laurentian Chronicle, s.a. 1125; *NPL*, s.a. 1125; Rogožskij Chronicle, s.a. 1125; Tver Chronicle, s.a. 1125; Nikon Chronicle, s.a. 1125.

N. N., daughter of Khan Aepa, son of Girgen
Birth date: unknown
Death date: conjectural based upon Svjatoslav's second marriage
Marriage to Svjatoslav Ol´govič: Laurentian Chronicle, s.a. 1107; Hypatian Chronicle, s.a. 1107; Nikon Chronicle, s.a. 1107. For more on this marriage see part 1, "Marriages: Generation Four," "Svjatoslav Ol´govič."

Svjatoslav Ol´govič
Birth date: unknown
Death date: Hypatian Chronicle, s.a. 1164; Tver Chronicle, s.a. 1164; Voskresenskij Chronicle, s.a. 1164; Nikon Chronicle, s.a. 1165
Knjaz´ of Novgorod (1) start: *NPL*, s.a. 1136; Hypatian Chronicle, s.a. 1138; Laurentian Chronicle, s.a. 1138; *NČL*, s.a. 1136; Pskov Chronicle, s.a. 1138; Voskresenskij Chronicle, s.a. 1136; Tver Chronicle, s.a. 1136; Nikon Chronicle, s.a. 1135; knjaz´ of Novgorod (1) end: *NPL*, s.a. 1138; Laurentian Chronicle, s.a. 1138; Hypatian Chronicle, s.a. 1139; *NČL*, s.a. 1138; Voskresenskij Chronicle, s.a. 1138; Tver Chronicle, s.a. 1138; Nikon Chronicle, s.a. 1138
Knjaz´ of Kursk start: conjectural based upon death of Glěb, and expulsion from Novgorod; knjaz´ of Kursk end: Nikon Chronicle, s.a. 1139 (has him summoned from Kursk)
Knjaz´ of Novgorod (2) start: *NPL*, s.a. 1139; Laurentian Chronicle, s.a. 1139; Hypatian Chronicle, s.a. 1140; *NČL*, s.a. 1139; Voskresenskij Chronicle, s.a. 1139; Tver Chronicle, s.a 1139; Nikon Chronicle, s.a. 1139; knjaz´ of Novgorod (2) end: *NPL*, s.a. 1141; Hypatian Chronicle, s.a. 1140; Voskresenskij Chronicle, s.a. 1140; Tver Chronicle, s.a. 1141; Nikon Chronicle, s.a. 1140
Knjaz´ of Bilhorod start: Hypatian Chronicle, s.a. 1141; knjaz´ of Bil-

horod end: conjectural based upon the death of Vsevolod and the assumption of power in Novhorod-Siverskyj

Knjaz´ of Novhorod-Siverskyj start: Hypatian Chronicle, s.a. 1146 (has him fighting for these lands versus his cousins, the Davydoviči); Hypatian Chronicle, s.a. 1148 (has his daughter sent from here in marriage); Nikon Chronicle, s.a. 1152 (has him ruling here outright); knjaz´ of Novhorod-Siverskyj end: Hypatian Chronicle, s.a. 1158; Nikon Chronicle, s.a. 1157

Knjaz´ of Černihiv start: Hypatian Chronicle, s.a. 1158; Tver Chronicle, s.a. 1157; Voskresenskij Chronicle, s.a. 1157; Nikon Chronicle, s.a. 1157; knjaz´ of Černihiv end: Hypatian Chronicle, s.a. 1164; Tver Chronicle, s.a. 1164; Voskresenskij Chronicle, s.a. 1164; Nikon Chronicle, s.a. 1165

Marriage to N. N., daughter of Khan Aepa, son of Girgen: Laurentian Chronicle, s.a. 1107; Hypatian Chronicle, s.a. 1107; Nikon Chronicle, s.a. 1107; for more information on this marriage, as well as Svjatoslav Ol´govič's other marriage, see part 1, "Marriages: Generation Four," "Svjatoslav Ol´govič."

Jurij "Dolgorukij" Volodimerič

Birth date: unknown

Death date: Rogožskij Chronicle, s.a. 1157; *NPL*, s.a. 1157; Hypatian Chronicle, s.a. 1158; Tver Chronicle, s.a. 1157; Laurentian Chronicle, s.a. 1157; Voskresenskij Chronicle, s.a. 1157; Nikon Chronicle, s.a. 1157

Knjaz´ of Suzdal start: *NPL*, s.a. 1138 (first mention of him there); knjaz´ of Suzdal end: Rogožskij Chronicle, s.a. 1157; *NPL*, s.a. 1157; Hypatian Chronicle, s.a. 1158; Tver Chronicle, s.a. 1157; Laurentian Chronicle, s.a. 1157; Voskresenskij Chronicle, s.a. 1157; Nikon Chronicle, s.a. 1157

Knjaz´ of Perejaslav (1): Voskresenskij Chronicle, s.a. 1131 (for 8 days); Tver Chronicle, s.a. 1132; Nikon Chronicle, s.a. 1132

Knjaz´ of Perejaslav (2): Laurentian Chronicle, s.a. 1135; Hypatian Chronicle, s.a. 1135; *NČL*, s.a. 1135; Voskresenskij Chronicle, s.a. 1135; Tver Chronicle, s.a. 1135; Nikon Chronicle, s.a. 1135

Knjaz´ of Kyiv (1) start: Laurentian Chronicle, s.a. 1149; *NPL*, s.a. 1149; Hypatian Chronicle, s.a. 1149; Tver Chronicle, s.a. 1149; Voskresenskij Chronicle, s.a. 1149; Nikon Chronicle, s.a. 1149; knjaz´ of Kyiv (1) end: Laurentian Chronicle, s.a. 1150; Hypatian Chronicle, s.a. 1150; Tver Chronicle, s.a. 1151; Voskresenskij Chronicle, s.a. 1150; Nikon Chronicle, s.a. 1150

Knjaz´ of Perejaslav (3): Hypatian Chronicle, s.a. 1151; Tver Chronicle, s.a. 1151

Knjaz´ of Kyiv (2) start: Rogožskij Chronicle, s.a. 1155; *NPL*, s.a. 1155; Hypatian Chronicle, s.a. 1155; Tver Chronicle, s.a. 1155; Laurentian Chronicle, s.a. 1154; Voskresenskij Chronicle, s.a. 1154; Nikon Chronicle, s.a. 1155; knjaz´ of Kyiv (2) end: Rogožskij Chronicle, s.a. 1157; *NPL*, s.a. 1157; Hypatian Chronicle, s.a. 1158; Tver Chronicle, s.a. 1157; Laurentian Chronicle, s.a. 1157; Voskresenskij Chronicle, s.a. 1157; Nikon Chronicle, s.a. 1157

Marriage to N. N., daughter of Khan Aepa, son of Osen: Laurentian Chronicle, s.a. 1107; Nikon Chronicle, s.a. 1107. For more information on this marriage see part 1, "Marriages: Generation Four," "Jurij 'Dolgorukij' Volodimerič."

N. N., daughter of Khan Aepa, son of Osen

Birth date: unknown

Death date: This is conjectural based upon discussion in the chronicles of an exile to Byzantium in 1162 of Jurij's wife and some of his children. It has been assumed that this was a second wife, and thus N. N., daughter of Khan Aepa, son of Osen, would be dead. For further discussion see part 1, "Marriages: Generation Four," "Jurij 'Dolgorukij' Volodimerič"; while for the exile, see Hypatian Chronicle, s.a 1162; Tver Chronicle, s.a. 1162; Voskresenskij Chronicle, s.a. 1162; Nikon Chronicle, s.a. 1160.

Marriage to Jurij "Dolgorukij" Volodimerič: Laurentian Chronicle, s.a. 1107; Nikon Chronicle, s.a. 1107. For more information on this marriage see part 1, "Marriages: Generation Four," "Jurij 'Dolgorukij' Volodimerič."

N. N., granddaughter of Tugorkhan of the Polovcians

Birth date: unknown

Death date: Her death date can reasonably be assumed to have occurred after her marriage, though when is unknown.

Marriage to Andrej Volodimerič: Hypatian Chronicle, s.a. 1117; Voskresenskij Chronicle, s.a. 1117; Tver Chronicle, s.a. 1117; Nikon Chronicle, s.a. 1118. For more information on this marriage see part 1, "Marriages: Generation Four," "Andrej Volodimerič."

Andrej Volodimerič

Birth date: unknown

Death date: Laurentian Chronicle, s.a. 1141; Hypatian Chronicle, s.a. 1141; *NČL*, s.a. 1141; Voskresenskij Chronicle, s.a. 1141; Tver Chronicle, s.a. 1141; Nikon Chronicle, s.a. 1141

Knjaz´ of Volodymyr start: Hypatian Chronicle, s.a. 1118; Voskresenskij Chronicle, s.a. 1118; Laurentian Chronicle, s.a. 1119; Tver Chronicle, s.a. 1118; Nikon Chronicle, s.a. 1119; knjaz´ of Volodymyr end: Laurentian Chronicle, s.a. 1135; Hypatian Chronicle, s.a. 1135; Voskresenskij Chronicle, s.a. 1135; Nikon Chronicle, s.a. 1135

Knjaz´ of Perejaslav start: Laurentian Chronicle, s.a. 1135; Hypatian Chronicle, s.a. 1135; Voskresenskij Chronicle, s.a. 1135; Nikon Chronicle, s.a. 1135; knjaz´ of Perejaslav end: Laurentian Chronicle, s.a. 1141; Hypatian Chronicle, s.a. 1141; *NČL*, s.a. 1141; Voskresenskij Chronicle, s.a. 1141; Tver Chronicle, s.a. 1141; Nikon Chronicle, s.a. 1141

Marriage to N. N., granddaughter of Tugorkhan: Hypatian Chronicle, s.a. 1117; Voskresenskij Chronicle, s.a. 1117; Tver Chronicle, s.a. 1117; Nikon Chronicle, s.a. 1118. For more information on this marriage see part 1, "Marriages: Generation Four," "Andrej Volodimerič."

Vsevolodko Davydič

Birth date: unknown

Death date: Laurentian Chronicle, s.a. 1141; Hypatian Chronicle, s.a. 1141; Voskresenskij Chronicle, s.a. 1141; Nikon Chronicle, s.a. 1141

Knjaz´ of Hrodna start: Laurentian Chronicle, s.a. 1127; Hypatian Chronicle, s.a. 1128 (first mention of his rule there); knjaz´ of Hrodna end: Laurentian Chronicle, s.a. 1141; Hypatian Chronicle, s.a. 1141; Voskresenskij Chronicle, s.a. 1141; Nikon Chronicle, s.a. 1141.

Baškord of the Polovcians

Birth date: unknown

Death date: His death presumably occurred only after he is mentioned in various sources as a knjaz´ of the Polovcians; see Tver Chronicle, s.a. 1159; Nikon Chronicle, s.a. 1158

Knjaz´ of Polovcians: Tver Chronicle, s.a. 1159; Nikon Chronicle, s.a. 1158 (only mentions as ruler)

Marriage to N. N. Vsevolodkovna: Tver Chronicle, s.a. 1159; Nikon Chronicle, s.a. 1158. For more on this marriage see part 1, "Marriages: Generation Four," "Volodimer Davydič."

N. N. Vsevolodkovna

Birth date: unknown

Death date: Her death date can reasonably be assumed to have occurred after her second marriage, though when is unknown.

Marriage to Baškord of the Polovcians: Tver Chronicle, s.a. 1159; Nikon Chronicle, s.a. 1158. For more information on this marriage see part 1, "Marriages: Generation Four," "Volodimer Davydič."

Table 22: Bohemian Dynastic Marriages

Anastasija Jaroslavna
Birth date: unknown
Death date: Wertner places her death in 1074; see his *Az Árpádok családi története*, chart. However, this is simply the last year that we have information about her. In that year Salomon left her at Admont Abbey when he was expelled from Hungary and went to fight further with his cousins; see Dercsényi, *Chronica de gestis Hungarorum*, 124.
Marriage to Andrew of Hungary: Dercsényi, *Chronica de Gestis Hungarorum*, 113; Adam of Bremen, *History of the Archbishops of Hamburg-Bremen*, bk. 3, ch. xiii.12, schol. 62 (63). For more on this marriage see part 1, "Marriages: Generation Two," "Anastasija Jaroslavna."

Andrew of Hungary
Birth date: unknown
Death date: Berthold of Reichenau, s.a. 1060; *Lamberti Hersfeldensis Annales*, s.a. 1061 (referencing his brother's succession)
King of Hungary start: Berthold of Reichenau, s.a. 1046; Wertner, *Az Árpádok családi története*, 114–15; king of Hungary end: *Lamberti Hersfeldensis Annales*, s.a. 1061
Marriage to Anastasija Jaroslavna: Dercsényi, *Chronica de Gestis Hungarorum*, 113; Adam of Bremen, *History of the Archbishops of Hamburg-Bremen*, bk. 3, ch. xiii.12, schol. 62 (63). For more on this marriage see part 1, "Marriages: Generation Two," "Anastasija Jaroslavna."

Dobronega/Maria Volodimerovna
Birth date: unknown
Death date: "Rocznik Kapitulny Krakowski," s.a. 1087

Table 22: Bohemian Dynastic Marriages

Dobronega/Maria
b. unknown; d. 1087
(m. ca. 1039)

Casimir "the Restorer" of Poland
b. 1016; d. 1058
(King of Poland r. ca. 1039–1058)

Anastasija Jaroslavna
b. unknown;
d. post-1074
(m. pre-1046)

Andrew of Hungary
b. unknown; d. 1060
(King of Hungary r. 1046–1060)

Adelheid
b. unknown; d. 1062 1
(m. 1055)

Vratislav II of Bohemia
b. unknown; d. 1092
(Duke of Bohemia r. 1061–1086)
(King of Bohemia r. 1086– 1096)

2

Svjatoslava
b. unknown d. 1126
(m. 1062)

Władysław Herman
b. unknown; d. 1102
(King of Poland r. 1081–1102)

Judith, daughter of Vratislav II of Bohemia
b. unknown;
d. 1086
(m. ca. 1081)

Peredslava
b. unknown;
d. 1116
(m. 1104)

Almos of Hungary
b. unknown; d. 1129

Soběslav of Bohemia
b. ca. 1090; d. 1140
(Duke of Bohemia r.1125–1140)

Adelaide
b. unknown; d. 1140
(m. ca. 1122)

Svjatopolk M′stislavič
b. unknown; d. 1154
(Polack r. 1132)
(Pskov r. 1137–1140)
(Brest r. 1140–1142)
(Novgorod r.1142–1148)
(Volodymyr r. 1148–1149)
(Luck r. 1149–1150)
(Volodymyr r. 1150–1154)

N. N., of Moravia
b. unknown;
d. post-1143
(m. 1143)

Marriage to Casimir "the Restorer": *Annalista Saxo*, s.a. 1039; *Lamberti Hersfeldensis Annales*, s.a. 1039; *PVL*, s.a. 1043; Gallus Anonymous, *Gesta principum Polonorum*, 80–81; *Chronica Poloniae Maioris*, ch. 12. For more on this marriage see part 1, "Marriages: Generation One," "Dobronega/Maria Volodimerovna."

Casimir "the Restorer," son of Mieszko II of Poland
Birth date: Balzer, *Genealogia Piastów*, table 2
Death date: *Chronica Poloniae Maioris*, ch. 12
King of Poland start: Gallus Anonymous, *Gesta principum Polonorum*, 81; king of Poland end: *Chronica Poloniae Maioris*, ch. 12
Marriage to Dobronega/Maria Volodimerovna: *Annalista Saxo*, s.a. 1039; *Lamberti Hersfeldensis Annales*, s.a. 1039; *PVL*, s.a. 1043; Gallus Anonymous, *Gesta principum Polonorum*, 80–81; *Chronica Poloniae Maioris*, ch. 12. For more on this marriage see part 1, "Marriages: Generation One," "Dobronega/Maria Volodimerovna."

Adelheid, daughter of Andrew of Hungary
Birth date: unknown
Death date: Cosmas of Prague, *Chronicle of the Czechs*, 2.20
Marriage to Vratislav II of Bohemia: Cosmas of Prague, *Chronicle of the Czechs*, 2.16.

Vratislav II of Bohemia
Birth date: unknown
Death date: Cosmas of Prague, *Chronicle of the Czechs*, 2.50
Duke of Bohemia start: Cosmas of Prague, *Chronicle of the Czechs*, 2.18; duke of Bohemia end: Cosmas of Prague, *Chronicle of the Czechs*, 2.37
King of Bohemia start: Cosmas of Prague, *Chronicle of the Czechs*, 2.37; king of Bohemia end: Cosmas of Prague , *Chronicle of the Czechs*, 2.50
Marriage to Adelheid, daughter of Andrew of Hungary: Cosmas of Prague, *Chronicle of the Czechs*, 2.16
Marriage to Svjatoslava: Cosmas of Prague, *Chronicle of the Czechs*, 2.20.

Svjatoslava
Birth date: unknown
Death date: Balzer, *Genealogia Piastów*, table 2
Marriage to Vratislav II: Cosmas of Prague, *Chronicle of the Czechs*, 2.20.

Judith, daughter of Vratislav II of Bohemia
Birth date: unknown

Death date: Cosmas of Prague, *Chronicle of the Czechs*, 2.36; Gallus Anonymous, *Gesta principum Polonorum*, bk. 2, ch. 1
Marriage to Władysław Herman: Cosmas of Prague, *Chronicle of the Czechs*, 2.36; Gallus Anonymous, *Gesta principum Polonorum*, bk. 1, ch. 30.

Władysław Herman
Birth date: unknown
Death date: *PVL*, s.a. 1102; *Chronica Poloniae Maioris*, ch. 16; Cosmas of Prague, *Chronicle of the Czechs*, 3.16; Gallus Anonymous, *Gesta principum Polonorum*, bk. 2, ch. 21
Duke of Poland start: conjectural based upon Gallus Anonymous, *Gesta principum Polonorum*, bk. 1, chs. 27, 30; duke of Poland end: *PVL*, s.a. 1102; *Chronica Poloniae Maioris*, ch. 16; Cosmas of Prague, *Chronicle of the Czechs*, 3.16; Gallus Anonymous, *Gesta principum Polonorum*, bk. 2, ch. 21
Marriage to Judith, daughter of Vratislav II of Bohemia: Cosmas of Prague, *Chronicle of the Czechs*, 2.36; Gallus Anonymous, *Gesta principum Polonorum*, bk. 1, ch. 30.

Peredslava Svjatopolkovna
Birth date: unknown
Death date: Hypatian Chronicle, s.a. 1116, where she is listed as Peredslava Svjatoslavna
Marriage to Almos of Hungary: Laurentian Chronicle, s.a. 1104; Hypatian Chronicle, s.a. 1104. For more on this marriage see part 1, "Marriages: Generation Four," "Peredslava Svjatopolkovna."

Almos of Hungary
Birth date: unknown
Death date: Wertner, *Az Árpádok családi története*, table
Marriage to Peredslava Svjatopolkovna: Laurentian Chronicle, s.a. 1104; Hypatian Chronicle, s.a. 1104. For more on this marriage see part 1, "Marriages: Generation Four," "Peredslava Svjatopolkovna."

Soběslav
Birth date: *Annalista Saxo*, s.a. 1061 (references his father, mother, and brothers together, but no specifics); Cosmas of Prague, *Chronicle of the Czechs*, 3.20 (records his flight to Poland as a young man), conjectural based upon his father's death in 1192
Death date: Wolverton, *Hastening Toward Prague*, 11–12
Duke of Bohemia start: Cosmas of Prague, *Chronicle of the Czechs*, 3.60; duke of Bohemia end: Wolverton, *Hastening Toward Prague*, 11–12
Marriage to Adelaide: Wertner, *Az Árpádok családi története*, 286–87;

Annalista Saxo, s.a. 1116 (references peace made between Hungary and Bohemia, which may have provided a proximate cause for the marriage); Cosmas of Prague, *Chronicle of the Czechs*, 3.52.

Adelaide
Birth date: unknown
Death date: Wertner, *Az Árpádok családi története*, 286–87
Marriage to Soběslav: Wertner, *Az Árpádok családi története*, 286–87; *Annalista Saxo*, s.a. 1116 (references peace made between Hungary and Bohemia, which may have provided a proximate cause for the marriage); Cosmas of Prague, *Chronicle of the Czechs*, 3.52.

Svjatopolk M´stislavič
Birth date: unknown
Death date: Hypatian Chronicle, s.a. 1154; Tver Chronicle, s.a. 1154; Laurentian Chronicle, s.a. 1154; Voskresenskij Chronicle, s.a. 1154; Nikon Chronicle, s.a. 1154
Knjaz´ of Polack: Laurentian Chronicle, s.a. 1132; Tver Chronicle, s.a. 1132; Nikon Chronicle, s.a. 1132
Knjaz´ of Pskov start: *NPL*, s.a. 1137; *NČL*, s.a. 1137; Voskresenskij Chronicle, s.a. 1137; Tver Chronicle, s.a. 1137; Nikon Chronicle, s.a. 1138; knjaz´ of Pskov end: Voskresenskij Chronicle, s.a. 1140; Nikon Chronicle, s.a. 1140 (both referencing his move to Brest, thus conjectural that he is no longer ruler of Pskov)
Knjaz´ of Brest start: Voskresenskij Chronicle, s.a. 1140; Nikon Chronicle, s.a. 1140; knjaz´ of Brest end:conjectural based upon move to Novgorod
Knjaz´ of Novgorod start: *NPL*, s.a. 1142; Laurentian Chronicle, s.a. 1141; Hypatian Chronicle, s.a. 1142; Voskresenskij Chronicle, s.a. 1141; Tver Chronicle, s.a. 1142; knjaz´ of Novgorod end: *NPL*, s.a. 1148; Tver Chronicle, s.a. 1148; Voskresenskij Chronicle, s.a. 1148; Nikon Chronicle, s.a. 1148
Knjaz´ of Volodymyr (1) start: *NPL*, s.a. 1148; Tver Chronicle, s.a. 1148; Voskresenskij Chronicle, s.a. 1148; Nikon Chronicle, s.a. 1148; knjaz´ of Volodymyr (1) end: Tver Chronicle, s.a. 1149; Hypatian Chronicle, s.a. 1149; Nikon Chronicle, s.a. 1149
Knjaz´ of Luck: Hypatian Chronicle, s.a. 1150; Laurentian Chronicle, s.a. 1150 (both place him there and it is likely he went somewhere after leaving Volodymyr and before returning)
Knjaz´ of Volodymyr (2) start: Hypatian Chronicle, s.a. 1150 (obscurely referenced, definitely by s.a. 1153); knjaz´ of Volodymyr (2) end: Hypatian Chronicle, s.a. 1154; Tver Chronicle, s.a. 1154; Laurentian Chronicle, s.a. 1154; Voskresenskij Chronicle, s.a. 1154; Nikon Chronicle, s.a. 1154

Marriage to N. N. of Moravia: *NPL*, s.a. 1143; *NČL*, s.a. 1143 (Svjatopolk is identified as Vsevolodič); Tver Chronicle, s.a. 1143. For more on this marriage see part 1, "Marriages: Generation Five," "Svjatopolk M´stislavič."

N. N. of Moravia

Birth date: unknown

Death date: Her death date can reasonably be assumed to have occurred after her marriage, though when is unknown.

Marriage to Svjatopolk M´stislavič: *NPL*, s.a. 1143; *NČL*, s.a. 1143 (Svjatopolk is identified as Vsevolodič); Tver Chronicle, s.a. 1143. For more on this marriage see part 1, "Marriages: Generation Five," "Svjatopolk M´stislavič."

Works Cited

Abbreviations and Short Titles

Adam of Bremen	Adam of Bremen. *History of the Archbishops of Hamburg-Bremen*. Translated by Francis J. Tschan. New York: Columbia University Press, 2002.
Berthold of Reichenau	*Bertholdi Annales*. Published by George Pertz. In *Annales et chronica aevi Salici*, 264–326. Monumenta Germaniae Historica: Scriptores 5. Hannover: Impensis Bibliopolii Avlici Hahniani, 1844
Chronica Poloniae Maioris	"Boguphali II episcopi Posnaniensis Chronicon Poloniae, cum continuatione Basconis custodis Posnaniensis." Edited by August Bielowski. In *Monumenta Poloniae Historica*, 2:467–600. Lviv: Nakładem Własnym, 1872.
Sturluson, *Heimskringla*	Snorri Sturluson. *Heimskringla: History of the Kings of Norway*. Translated with an introduction by Lee M. Hollander. Austin, Tx.: University of Texas Press, 1964.
Hypatian Chronicle	*Ipat´evskaja letopis´*. Vol. 2 of *Polnoe sobranie russkix letopisej*. Moscow: Jazyki slavjanskoj kul´tury, 2001.
Laurentian Chronicle	*Lavrent´evskaja letopis´*. Vol. 1 of *Polnoe sobranie russkix letopisej*. Moscow: Jazyki slavjanskoj kul´tury, 2001.

NČL — *Novgorodskaja četvertaja letopis´*. Vol. 4, pt. 1 of *Polnoe sobranie russkix letopisej*. Moscow: Jazyki slavjanskoj kul´tury, 2000.

Nikon Chronicle — *Letopisnyj sbornik, imenuemyj: Patriaršej ili Nikonovskoj letopis´ju*. Vol. 9 of *Polnoe sobranie russkix letopisej*. Moscow: Jazyki russkoj kul´tury, 2000.

NPL — *Novgorodskaja pervaja letopis´ staršego i mladšego izvodov*. Vol. 3 of *Polnoe sobranie russkix letopisej*. Moscow: Jazyki slavjanskoj kul´tury, 2000.

Pskov Chronicle — *Pskovskie letopisi*. Vol. 5 of *Polnoe sobranie russkix letopisej*. Moscow: Jazyki russkoj kul´tury, 2000.

PVL — *The Pověst´ vremennykh lět: An Interlinear Collation and Paradosis*. Compiled and edited by Donald Ostrowski, with David Birnbaum and Horace G. Lunt. Harvard Library of Early Ukrainian Literature: Texts 10. Cambridge, Mass.: Harvard Ukrainian Research Institute, 2003.

Rogožskij Chronicle — *Rogožskij letopisets / Tverskoj sbornik*. Vol. 15 of *Polnoe sobranie russkix letopisej*. Moscow: Jazyki slavjanskoj kul´tury, 2000.

Saxo Grammaticus — Saxo Grammaticus. *Danorum Regum heroumque historia: Books X–XVI*. Translated by Eric Christiansen. 3 vols. Vol. 1, bks. X, XI, XII, and XIII. Oxford: B.A.R., 1980.

Thietmar of Merseburg — *Ottonian Germany: The "Chronicon" of Thietmar of Merseburg*. Translated by David A. Warner. Manchester: Manchester University Press, 2001.

Tver Chronicle — *Rogožskij letopisets / Tverskoj sbornik*. Vol. 15 of *Polnoe sobranie russkix letopisej*. Moscow: Jazyki slavjanskoj kul´tury, 2000.

Voskresenskij Chronicle — *Letopis´ po voskresenskomu spisku*. Vol. 7 of *Polnoe sobranie russkix letopisej*. Moscow: Jazyki slavjanskoj kul´tury, 2001.

Primary Sources

Adam of Bremen. *Adami gesta Hammaburgensis ecclesiae pontificum*. Edited by J. M. Lappenberg. Scriptores rerum germanicarum in usum scholarum ex Monumentis Germaniae historicis recusi. Hannover: Impensis Biblipolii Hahniani, 1876.

Adam of Bremen. *History of the Archbishops of Hamburg-Bremen*. Translated by Francis J. Tschan. New York: Columbia University Press, 2002.

Albrici monachi Triumfontium chronicon. Published by P. Scheffer-Boichorst. In *Chronica aevi Suevici*, 631–950. Monumenta Germaniae Historica: Scriptores 23. Leipzig: Karl W. Hiersemann, 1925.

The Anglo-Saxon Chronicle. Translated by M. J. Swanton. London: J. M. Dent Publishers, 1996. [sec 2 gen 2 n. 30]

"Annales Altahenses maiores." Published by Wilhelm de Giesebrecht and Edmundi L. B. ab Oefele. In *Supplementum Tomi V*, 772–824. Monumenta Germaniae Historica: Scriptores 20. Hannover: Impensis Bibliopolii Avlici Hahniani, 1868.

Annales Augustani. Published by George Pertz. In *Annales, chronica et historiae aevi Saxonici*, 123–36. Monumenta Germaniae Historica: Scriptores 3. Hannover: Impensis Bibliopolii Avlici Hahniani, 1839.

"Annales Posonienses." Edited by Emericus Madszar. In *Scriptores Rerum Hungaricarum*, ed. Imre Szentpétery, 1:119–27. Budapest: Academia Litter. Hungarica atque Societate Histor. Hungarica, 1937.

Annales Sancti Disibodi. Published by G. Waitz. In *Annales aevi Suevici*, 4–30. Monumenta Germaniae Historica: Scriptores 17. Hannover: Impensis Bibliopolii Avlici Hahniani, 1861.

Annales Stadenses auctore M. Alberto. Published by I. M. Lappenberg. In *Annales aevi Suevici*, 271–379. Monumenta Germaniae Historica: Scriptores 16. Hannover: Impensis Bibliopolii Avlici Hahniani, 1859.

Annalista Saxo. Published by D. G. Waitz and P. Killon. In *Chronica et annales aevi Salici*, 542–777. Monumenta Germaniae Historica: Scriptores 6. Hannover: Impensis Bibliopolii Avlici Hahniani, 1844.

Annals of Ulster. Accessed online at http://www.ucc.ie/celt/published/T100001A/index.html.

Antoine, Archevêque de Novgorod. "Description des Lieux-Saints de Constantinople." In *Itinéraires Russes en Orient*, ed. B. de Khitrowo. Geneva: Imprimerie Jules-Guillaume Fick, 1889.

Baronio, Cesare. *Annales ecclesiastici Caesaris Baronii.* Barri-Ducis: Guerin, 1864–83.

Bernold of St. Blasien. "Chronicle." In *Eleventh-Century Germany: The Swabian Chronicles*, ed. and trans. I. S. Robinson, 245–337. Manchester: Manchester University Press, 2008.

Bernoldi Chronicon. Published by George Pertz. In *Annales et chronica aevi Salici*, 385–467. Monumenta Germaniae Historica: Scriptores 5. Hannover: Impensis Bibliopolii Avlici Hahniani, 1844.

Bertholdi Annales. Published by George Pertz. In *Annales et chronica aevi Salici*, 264–326. Monumenta Germaniae Historica: Scriptores 5. Hannover: Impensis Bibliopolii Avlici Hahniani, 1844.

"Boguphali II episcopi Posnaniensis Chronicon Poloniae, cum continuatione Basconis custodis Posnaniensis." Edited by August Bielowski. In *Monumenta Poloniae Historica*, 2:467–600. Lviv: Nakładem Własnym, 1872.

Bruno de Bello Saxonico. Published by George Pertz. In *Annales et chronica aevi Salici*, 327–84. Monumenta Germaniae Historica: Scriptores 5. Hannover: Impensis Bibliopolii Avlici Hahniani, 1844.

"Chronici Hungarici compositio saeculi XIV." Edited by Alexander Domanovszky. In *Scriptores Rerum Hungaricarum*, ed. Imre Szentpétery, 1:217–505. Budapest: Academia Litter. Hungarica atque Societate Histor. Hungarica, 1937.

"Chronica Petri comitis Poloniae" [Kronika o Piotrze Właście]. Edited by Alexander Semkowicz. In *Monumenta Poloniae Historica*, 3:745–84. Lviv: W Komisie księgarni gubrynowicza I schmidta, 1878.

"Chronica Polono-Silesiaci: loci ad Petrum spectantes." In *Monumenta Poloniae Historica, Series Nova*, ed. Marian Plezia, 31–33. Cracow: Subsidio Ministerii Scholarum Superiorum et Studiorum, 1951.

The Chronicle of Novgorod, 1016–1471. Translated by Robert Michell and Nevill Forbes. Camden Third Series 25. London: Offices of the Society, 1914.

"Chronicon: Vindocinense seu de Aquaria." In *Chroniques des églises D'Anjou*, ed. Paul Marchegay and Émile Mabille, 153–78. Paris: Libraire de la société de l'histoire de France, 1869.

"Chronicon Sancti-Petri-Vivi Senonensis: Auctore Clario." In *Bibliothèque Historique de'Lyonne*. Vol. 2. Auxerre: Perriquet et Rouillé, Imprimeurs de la Société, 1863.

Clarius. *Chronique de Sant-Pierre-le-vif de sens, diter de Clarius*. Edited by Robert-Henri Bautier and Monique Gilles. Paris: Centre national de la recherche scientifique, 1979.

Conrad, Klaus, ed. *Pommersches Urkundenbuch*. Vol. 1. Cologne: Böhlau, 1970.

Cosmae Chronica Boemorum. Published by Rudolf Köpke. In *Chronica et annales aevi Salici*, 1–209. Monumenta Germaniae Historica: Scriptores 9. Hannover: Impensis Bibliopolii Avlici Hahniani, 1851.

"Cosmae chronicon Boemorum cum continuatoribus." In *Fontes rerum Bohemicarum*, ed. Jos. Emler. Vol. 2. Prague: Nákladem Musea Království Českého, 1874.

Cosmas of Prague. *The Chronicle of the Czechs by Cosmas of Prague*. Translated by Lisa Wolverton. Washington, D.C.: The Catholic University of America Press, 2009.

Cross, Samuel Hazzard, and Oleg P. Sherbowitz-Wetzor, eds. *The Russian Primary Chronicle: Laurentian Text*. Cambridge, Mass.: The Mediaeval Academy of America, 1953.

Dercsényi, Dezso, ed. *The Hungarian Illuminated Chronicle / Chronica de gestis Hungarorum*. Budapest: Corvina Press, 1969.

Długosz, Jan. *Annales seu cronicae incliti regni Poloniae*. Vols. 1–4. Warsaw: Państwowe Wydawnictwo Naukowe, 1964–70.

Donizonis vita Mathildis. Published by L. Bethmann. In *Historiae aevi Salici*, 348–409. Monumenta Germaniae Historica: Scriptores 12. Hannover: Impensis Bibliopolii Avlici Hahniani, 1861.

Ekkehardi Chronicon. Published by D. G. Waitz and P. Killon. In *Chronica et annales aevi Salici*, 1–267. Monumenta Germaniae Historica: Scriptores 6. Hannover: Impensis Bibliopolii Avlici Hahniani, 1844.

Fejér, Georgii, ed. *Codex diplomaticus Hungariae, ecclesiasticus ac civilis*. Vol. 1. Buda: Regiae Universitatis Ungaricae, 1829.

Flateyjarbók. Edited by C. R. Unger. Vol. 3. Oslo [Christiania]: P. T. Mallings, 1868.

Frutolf of Michelsburg. *Chronica*. Edited by F.-J. Schmale and I. Schmale-Ott. Darmstadt: Ausgewählte Quellen zur deutschen Geschiste des Mittelalters, 1972.

Fulcher of Chartres. *Historia Hierosolymitana*. Edited by Heinrich Hagenmeyer. Heidelberg: Carl Winters Universitätbuchhandlung, 1913.

Gallus Anonymous. *Gesta principum Polonorum / The Deeds of the Princes of the Poles*. Translated by Paul W. Knoll and Frank Schaer. Budapest: Central European University Press, 2003.

Gautier, Paul. "Le typikon de la Théotokos Kécharitôménè." *Revue des études Byzantines* 43 (1985): 5–165.

Gerhoh of Reichersburg. "De investigatione Antichristi liber I." Edited by E. Sackur. In *Gerhohi praepositi Reichersbergensis libelli selecti*, 304–95. Monumenta Germaniae Historica: Libelli de lite imperatorum et pontificum 3. Hannover: Impensis Bibliopolii Avlici Hahniani, 1897.

Glaber, Rodulfus. *The Five Books of the Histories*. Edited and translated by John France. Oxford: Clarendon Press, 1989.

Gregory VII, Pope. *The Register of Pope Gregory VII 1073–1085*. Translated by H. E. J. Cowdrey. Oxford: Oxford University Press, 2002.

Guibert of Nogent. *De Vita Sua: De electione domini Bartholomaei episcopi; et nobilitate ejusdem*. In *Patrologia Latina*, edited by J. P. Migne, vol. 156, 837–1016. Paris: J. P. Migne, 1853.

———. *Gesta Dei per Francos*. In *Patrologia Latina*, edited by J. P. Migne, vol. 156, 675–836. Paris: J. P. Migne, 1853.

Heinrich, Lisa. "The Kievan Chronicle: A Translation and Commentary." PhD dissertation, Vanderbilt University, 1977.

Heinrici IV: Diplomata. Edited by Dietrich von Gladiss and Alfred Gawlik. Monumenta Germaniae Historica: Die Urkunden der deutschen Könige und Kaiser (Diplomatum regum et imperatorum Germaniae) 6. Volume 2 of 3. Weimar: Hermann Bohlaus Nachfolger, 1953.

Helmold. *The Chronicle of the Slavs by Helmold, Priest of Bosau*. Translated by Francis J. Tschan. New York: Columbia University Press, 1935.

Herman of Reichenau. "Chronicle." In *Eleventh-Century Germany: The Swa-*

bian Chronicles. Edited and translated by I. S. Robinson. Manchester: Manchester University Press, 2008.

Hugo Floriacensis opera historica: accedunt aliae Francorum historiae. Edited by Georgio Waitz. In *Chronica et annales aevi Salici*, 337–406. Monumenta Germaniae Historica: Scriptores 9. Hannover: Impensis Bibliopolii Avlici Hahniani, 1851.

Ipat´evskaja letopis´. Vol. 2 of *Polnoe sobranie russkix letopisej*. Moscow: Jazyki slavjanskoj kul´tury, 2001.

John of Fordun. *Chronicle of the Scottish Nation*. Edited by William F. Skene and translated by Feliz J. H. Skene. Edinburgh: Edmonston and Douglas, 1872.

Jónsson, Finnur, ed. *Fagrskinna, Nóregs kononga tal*. Copenhagen: S. L. Møllers Bogtrykkeri, 1902–3.

"Kanoničeskie otvety mitropolita Ioanna II." *Russkaja istoričeskaja biblioteka* 6 (1908): 1–20.

Kinnamos, Ioannes. *Deeds of John and Manuel Comnenus*. Translated by Charles M. Brand. New York: Columbia University Press, 1976.

———. *Ioannis Cinnami Epitome rerum ab Ioanne et Alexio Comnenis gestarum*. Edited by Augustus Meineke. Vol. 26 of *Corpus Scriptorum Historiae Byzantinae*. Bonn: Weberi, 1836.

"Kniga stepennaja tsarskogo rodoslovija." Vol. 21 of *Polnoe sobranie russkix letopisej*, pt. 1. St. Petersburg: Tipografija M. A. Aleksandrova, 1908.

Knýtlinga Saga: The History of the Kings of Denmark. Translated by Hermann Pálsson and Paul Edwards. Odense: Odense University Press, 1986.

"Kronika polska (Chronica Polonorum)." Edited by Ludwik Ćwikliński. In *Monumenta Poloniae Historica*, 3:578–656. Lviv: W Komisie Księgarni Gubrynowicza i Schmidta, 1878.

"Kronika xiążąt polskich (Chronica principum Poloniae)." Edited by Zygmunt Węclewski. In *Monumenta Poloniae Historica*, 3:425–578. Lviv: W Komisie Księgarni Gubrynowicza i Schmidta, 1878.

Lamberti Hersfeldensis Annales. Published by V. Cl. Lud. Frid. Hesse. In *Annales et chronica aevi Salici*, 134–263. Monumenta Germaniae Historica: Scriptores 5. Hanover: Impensis Bibliopolii Hahniani, 1843.

Lavrent´evskaja letopis´. Vol. 1 of *Polnoe sobranie russkix letopisej*. Moscow: Jazyki slavjanskoj kul´tury, 2001.

Letopis´ po voskresenskomu spisku. Vol. 7 of *Polnoe sobranie russkix letopisej*. Moscow: Jazyki slavjanskoj kul´tury, 2001.

Lixačev, D. S., and N. V. Ponyrko, eds. *Epistoljarnoe nasledie Drevnej Rusi XI–XIII: issledovanija, teksty, perevody*. St. Petersburg: Nauka, 1992.

Letopisnyj sbornik, imenuemyj: Patriaršej ili Nikonovskoj letopis´ju. Vol. 9 of *Polnoe sobranie russkix letopisej*. Moscow: Jazyki russkoj kul´tury, 2000.

Medieval Russian Laws. Translated by George Vernadsky. New York: Oxford University Press, 1947.

Morkinskinna: The Earliest Icelandic Chronicle of the Norwegian Kings (1030–

1157). Translated by Theodore M. Andersson and Kari Ellen Gade. Ithaca: Cornell University Press, 2000.

Morozov, T. S., ed. *Izbornik velikago knjazja Svjatoslava Jaroslaviča 1073 goda*. Monumenta Linguae Slavicae Dialecti Veteris 3. Wiesbaden: Otto Harrassowitz, 1965.

The Nikonian Chronicle: From the Beginning to the Year 1132 (Volume One). Translated by Serge A. and Betty Jean Zenkovsky and edited by Serge A. Zenkovsky. Princeton, N.J.: Kingston Press, 1984.

Novgorodskaja četvertaja letopis´. Vol. 4, pt. 1 of *Polnoe sobranie russkix letopisej*. Moscow: Jazyki slavjanskoj kul´tury, 2000.

Novgorodskaja pervaja letopis´ staršego i mladšego izvodov. Vol. 3 of *Polnoe sobranie russkix letopisej*. Moscow: Jazyki slavjanskoj kul´tury, 2000.

Odo of Deuil. *De profectione Ludovici VII in Orientem: The Journey of Louis VII to the East*. Edited and translated by Virginia Gingerich Berry. New York: W. W. Norton, 1948.

The Old Rus´ Kievan and Galician-Volhynian Chronicles: The Ostroz´kyj (Xlebnikov) and Četvertyns´kyj (Pogodin) Codices. Introduction by Omeljan Pritsak. Harvard Library of Early Ukrainian Literature: Texts 8. Cambridge, Mass.: Harvard Ukrainian Research Institute, 1990.

Orderic Vitalis. *The Ecclesiastical History of Orderic Vitalis*. Vol. 5 (bks. 9 and 10). Edited and translated by Marjorie Chibnall. Oxford: Clarendon Press, 1975.

Ortliebi de fundatione monasterii Zwivildensis. Published by Ottone Abel. In *Annales et chronica aevi Salici: Vitae aevi Carolini et Saxonici*, 64–92. Monumenta Germaniae Historica: Scriptores 10. Hannover: Impensis Bibliopolii Avlici Hahniani, 1852.

Otto, Bishop of Freising. *The Two Cities: A Chronicle of Universal History to the Year 1146 A.D.* Translated by Charles Christopher Mierow. New York: Octagon Books, 1966.

Otto of Friesing and his continuator, Rahewin. *The Deeds of Frederick Barbarossa*. Translated by Charles Christopher Mierow, with Richard Emery. New York: Norton and Co., 1953.

Ottonian Germany: The "Chronicon" of Thietmar of Merseburg. Translated by David A. Warner. Manchester: Manchester University Press, 2001.

The Paterik of the Kievan Caves Monastery. Translated by Muriel Heppell. Harvard Library of Early Ukrainian Literature: Translations 1. Cambridge, Mass.: Harvard Ukrainian Research Institute, 1989.

The "Pověst´ vremennykh lět": An Interlinear Collation and Paradosis. Compiled and edited by Donald Ostrowski, with David Birnbaum and Horace G. Lunt. Harvard Library of Early Ukrainian Literature: Texts 10. Cambridge, Mass.: Harvard Ukrainian Research Institute, 2003.

Prou, Maurice, ed. *Recueil des actes de Philippe Ier, roi de France (1059–1108)*. Paris: Imprimerie Nationale, 1908.

Psalterium Partitum. Cited in "Roger II, XLIVe Evéque de Chálons, sa vie et sa mission en Russie (1048)." In *La Chronique de Champagne*, 2:89–100. Reims: Impr. de L. Jacquet, 1837.

Psellus, Michael. *Fourteen Byzantine Rulers: The Chronographia of Michael Psellus*. Translated by E. R. A. Sewter. New York: Penguin Books, 1966.

Pskovskie letopisi. Vol. 5 of *Polnoe sobranie russkix letopisej*. Moscow: Jazyki russkoj kul´tury, 2000.

"Rocznik Kapitulny Krakowski." In *Monumenta Poloniae Historica*, ed. August Bielowski, 2:783–816. Lviv: Nakładem Własnym, 1872.

Rogožskij letopisets / Tverskoj sbornik. Vol. 15 of *Polnoe sobranie russkix letopisej*. Moscow: Jazyki slavjanskoj kul´tury, 2000.

Sächsische Weltchronik. Edited by Ludwig Weiland. In [untitled volume of] Monumenta Germaniae Historica: Deutsche Chroniken und andere Geschichtsbücher des Mittelalters 2. Hannover: Hahnsche Buchhandlung, 1877.

Sauerland, H. U., and A. Haselhoff, eds. *Der Psalter Ezbischof Egberts von Trier: Codex Gertrudianus, in cividale*. Trier: Selbstverlag der Gesellschaft für nützliche Forschungen, 1901.

Saxo Grammaticus. *Danorum Regum heroumque historia: Books X–XVI*. Translated by Eric Christiansen. 3 vols. Vol. 1, bks. 10–13. Oxford: B.A.R., 1980.

———. *Gesta Danorum: The History of the Danes*. Edited by Hilda Ellis Davidson. Translated by Peter Fisher. Totowa, N.J.: Rowman and Littlefield, 1979.

———. *Saxonis Grammatici gesta Danorum*. Strassburg: K. J. Trubner, 1886.

Ščaveleva, N. I. *Drevnjaja Rus´ v "Pol´skoj istorii" Jana Dlugoša, knigi I–VI: Tekst, perevod, kommentarij*. Edited by A. V. Nazarenko. Moscow: Pamjatniki istoričeskoj mysli, 2004.

Ščaveleva, N. I., ed. *"Velikaja xronika" o Pol´še, Rusi i ix sosedjax XI–XIII vv.* Moscow: Izdatel´stvo Moskovskogo universiteta, 1987.

Scylitzes, John, *Ioannis Scylitzae Synopsis historiarum*. Edited by Hans Thurn, Corpus fontium historiae Byzantinae 5. Berlin: De Gruyter, 1973.

Slovo o polku Igoreve: Perevod, predislovie i pojasnenija Ivana Novikova. Edited by N. K. Gudzija. Moscow: Xudožestvennaja literatura, 1938.

Soehnée, Frédéric, ed. and trans. *Catalogue des Actes d'Henri Ier Roi de France (1031–1060)*. Paris: Librairie Honoré Champion, 1907.

"Spominki Wrocławskie." In *Monumenta Poloniae Historica*, ed. Aleksander Semkowicz, 3:732–34. Lwów: W Komisie księgarni gubrynowicza i schmidta, 1878.

Sturluson, Snorre. *Heimskringla, or The Lives of the Norse Kings*. Edited by Erling Monsen and translated by A. H. Smith. New York: Dover Publications, 1990.

Sturluson, Snorri. *Heimskringla: History of the Kings of Norway*. Translated with an introduction by Lee M. Hollander. Austin, Tx.: University of Texas Press, 1964.

Tatiščev, V. N. *Istorija Rossijskaja*. 7 vols. Moscow: Akademija nauk SSSR, 1963.

Theodoricus Monachus. "Theodrici monachi historia de antiquitate regum Norwagiensium." In *Monumenta Historica Norvegiae*, ed. Gustav Storm, 1–68. Oslo [Kristiania]: A. W. Brøgger, 1880.

Thietmar of Merseburg. *Die Chronik des Bischofs Thietmar von Merseburg und ihre Korveier Überarbeitung*. Edited by Robert Holtzmann, 3–533. Monumenta Germaniae Historica: Scriptores rerum Germanicarum. Nova series 9. Berlin: Weidmannsche Buchandlung, 1935.

Tschan, Francis J., ed. *His Works of Art*. Vol. 2 of *Saint Bernward of Hildesheim*. South Bend, Ind.: University of Notre Dame, 1951.

Walram, Bishop of Naumburg. *Liber de unitate ecclesiae conservanda*. Edited by Wilhelm Schwenkenbecher. Monumenta Germaniae Historica: Scriptores rerum Germanicarum in usum scholarum separatim editi 39. Hannover: Impensis Bibliopolii Hahniani, 1883.

Wilhelm. "Wilhelmi abbatis genealogia regum Danorum." In *Scriptores minores historiae Danicae medii aevi*, ed. M. C. Gertz, 145–94. Copenhagen: I Kommission hos G. E. C. Gad, 1917.

"Xoženie Daniila, igumena Russkoj zemli." In *Kniga xoženij: zapiski russkix putešestvennikov XI–XV vv.*, 27–80. Moscow: Sovetskaja Rossija, 1984.

Secondary Sources

Alekseev, M. P. "Anglo-saksonskaja parallel´ k *Poučeniju* Vladimira Monomaxa." *Trudy otdela drevnerusskoj literatury* 2 (1935): 39–80.

Angold, Michael. *The Byzantine Empire, 1025–1204*. New York: Longman, 1997.

Bak, János M. "Roles and Functions of Queens in Árpádian and Angevin Hungary (1000–1386 A.D.)." In *Medieval Queenship*, ed. John Carmi Parsons, 13–24. Gloucestershire: Sutton, 1994.

Baldwin, Stewart. "Agatha." http://sbaldw.home.mindspring.com/hproject/prov/agath000.htm. 20 June 2010. Accessed 24 July 2015.

Balzer, Oswald. *Genealogia Piastów*. Cracow: Nakładem Akademij Umiejętności, 1895.

Bariev, Riza. *Volžskie bulgary: Istorija i kul´tura*. St. Petersburg, 1999. Accessed online at http://www.balkaria.info/library/b/bariev/2/bariev.htm.

Baumgarten, N. de. "Généalogies et mariages Occidentaux des Rurikides Russes du X-e au XIII-e siècle." *Orientalia Christiana* 9, no. 25 (1927): 5–95.

———. "Pervaja vetv´ knjazej Galickix." *Letopis´ istoriko-rodoslovnago obščestva v Moskve* 4 (1907): 1–30.

———. "Pribyslava de Russie." *Orientalia Christiana* 20, no. 3 (1930): 156–61.

———. "Sofija russkaja, koroleva datskaja, a zatem landgrafinja tjuringenskaja." *Seminarium Kondakovianum* 4 (1931): 95–104.

Bautier, Robert-Henri. "Anne de Kiev, reine de France, et la politique royale au XI-e siècle, étude critique de la documentation." *Revue des études Slaves* 57, no. 4 (1985): 539–64.

Berežkov, N. G. *Xronologija russkogo letopisanija*. Moscow: Izdatel′stvo Akademii nauk SSSR, 1963.

Bloch, Raisa. "Verwandtschaftliche Beziehungen des sächsischen Adels zum russischen Fürstenhause im XI. Jahrhundert." In *Festschrift: Albert Brackmann, Dargebracht von Freunden, Kollegen und Schülern*, ed. Leo Santifaller, 194–206. Weimar: Hermann Böhlaus Nachf. G.M.B.H., 1931.

Bouchard, Constance B. "Consanguinity and Noble Marriages in the Tenth and Eleventh Centuries." *Speculum* 56, no. 2 (1981): 268–87.

Cross, Samuel Hazzard. "Yaroslav the Wise in Norse Tradition." *Speculum* 4, no. 2 (1929): 177–97.

Cowdrey, H. E. J. *Pope Gregory VII, 1073–1085*. Oxford: Clarendon Press, 1998.

Dąbrowski, Dariusz. *Genealogia Mścisławowiczów: Pierwsze pokolenia (do początku XIV wieku)*. Cracow: Avalon, 2008.

Davids, Adalbert, ed. *The Empress Theophano: Byzantium and the West at the Turn of the First Millennium*. Cambridge: Cambridge University Press, 1995.

———. "Marriage Negotiations between Byzantium and the West and the Name of Theophano in Byzantium (Eighth to Tenth Centuries)." In *The Empress Theophano: Byzantium and the West at the Turn of the Millennium*, ed. Adalbert Davids, 99–120. Cambridge: Cambridge University Press, 1995.

Davies, Norman. *The Origins to 1795*. Vol. 1 of *God's Playground: A History of Poland in Two Volumes*. Oxford: Oxford University Press, 2005.

Dhondt, Jean. "Sept femmes et un trio de rois." *Contributions à l'histoire économique et sociale* 3 (1964–65): 36–70.

Diers, Carol Jean, and Darrell W. Amundsen. "The Age of Menarche in Medieval Europe." *Human Biology* 45 (1973): 363–69.

Dimnik, Martin. *The Dynasty of Chernigov, 1054–1146*. Toronto: Pontifical Institute of Mediaeval Studies, 1994.

———. *The Dynasty of Chernigov, 1146–1246*. Cambridge: Cambridge University Press, 2003.

———. "The Title 'Grand Prince' in Kievan Rus′." *Mediaeval Studies* 66 (2004): 253–312.

Dubois, Thomas A. and Niels Ingwersen, "St. Knud Lavard: A Saint for Denmark." In *Sanctity in the North: Saints, Lives, and Cults in Medieval Scandinavia*, ed. Thomas A. Dubois, 154–202. Toronto: University of Toronto Press, 2008.

Dunbabin, Jean. *France in the Making, 843–1180*. 2nd ed. Oxford: Oxford University Press, 2000.

———. "What's in a Name? Phillip, King of France." *Speculum* 68, no. 4 (1993): 949–68.

Edwards, Carolyn. "Dynastic Sanctity in Two Early Medieval Women's *Lives*." In *Medieval Family Roles: A Book of Essays*, ed. Cathy Jorgensen Itnyre, 3–20. New York: Garland, 1996.

Engel, Pál. *The Realm of St. Stephen: A History of Medieval Hungary, 895–1526*. London and New York: I. B. Tauris, 2005.

Fliche, Augustin. *Le Règne de Philippe 1er, Roi de France (1060–1108)*. Geneva: Slatkine-Megariotis Reprints, 1975.

Franklin, Simon and Jonathan Shepard. *The Emergence of Rus, 750–1200*. Longman History of Russia. New York: Longman, 1996.

Gallén, J. "Vem var Valdemar den stores drottning Sofia?" *Historisk Tidskrift för Finland* 61 (1976): 273–88.

García de la Puente, Inés. "Anastasia of Minsk: Neglected Evidence on the Rule of a Woman in Rus´ History?" *Russian History* 39 (2012): 347–78.

Grotefend, H. *Stammtafeln der schlesischen Fürsten bis zum jahre 1740*. Breslau: Josef Max and Comp., 1889.

The Hagiography of Kievan Rus´. Translated with an introduction by Paul Hollingsworth. Harvard Library of Early Ukrainian Literature: Translations 2. Cambridge, Mass.: Harvard Ukrainian Research Institute, 1992.

Herrin, Judith. "Theophano: Considerations on the Education of a Byzantine Princess." In *The Empress Theophano: Byzantium and the West at the Turn of the First Millennium*, ed. Adalbert Davids, 64–85. Cambridge: Cambridge University Press, 1995.

Hilsdale, Cecily. "Constructing a Byzantine 'Augusta': A Greek Book for a French Bride." *The Art Bulletin* 87, no. 3 (2005): 458–83.

———. "Diplomacy by Design: Rhetorical Strategies of the Byzantine Gift." PhD dissertation, University of Chicago, 2003.

———. "The Social Life of the Byzantine Gift: The Royal Crown of Hungary Re-Invented." *Art History* 31, no. 5 (2008): 603–31.

Holovko, O. B. [Golovko, A. B.]. *Drevnjaja Rus´ i Pol´ša v političeskix vzaimootnošenijax X–pervoj treti XIII vv.* Kyiv: Naukova dumka, 1988.

Ingham, Norman W. "Has a Missing Daughter of Iaroslav Mudry Been Found?" *Russian History* 25, no. 3 (1998): 231–70.

Janin, V. L., ed. *Aktovye pečati drevnej Rusi X–XV vv.* Moscow: Nauka, 1970.

———. "Pečati Feofano Muzalon." *Numizmatika i sfragistika* 2 (1965): 76–90.

———. "Russkaja knjaginja Olisava-Gertruda i ee syn Jaropolk." *Numizmatika i epigrafika* 4 (1963): 142–64.

Jetté, René. "Is the Mystery of the Origin of Agatha, Wife of Edward the Exile, Finally Solved?" *The New England Historical and Genealogical Register* 150, no. 600 (1996): 417–32.

Karamzin, N. M. *Istorija gosudarstva Rossijskogo*. Vol. 2. Moscow: Kniga, 1988.

Kaštanov, S. M. "Byla li Oda Štadenskaja ženoj velikogo knjazja Svjatoslava Jaroslaviča?" In *Vostočnaja Evropa v drevnosti i srednevekov´e: Drevnjaja Rus´ v sisteme ètnopolitičeskix i kul´turnyx svjazej: čtenija pamjati člena-korrespondenta AN SSSR Vladimira Terent´eviča Pašuto, Moskva, 18–20 aprelja 1994 g.: tezisy dokladov*, ed. V. T. Pašuto, A. P. Novosel´cev, et al., 15–19. Moscow: RAN, 1994.

Každan, A. P. [Kazhdan, Alexander]. "Rus´-Byzantine Princely Marriages in the Eleventh and Twelfth Centuries." *Harvard Ukrainian Studies* 12/13 (1988/89): 414–29.

———. "Vizantijskij podatnoj sborščik na beregax kimmerijskogo bospora v konce XII v." In *Problemy obščestvenno-političeskoj istorii Rossii i slavjanskix stran: sbornik statej k 70-letiju akademika M. N. Tixomirova*, ed. V. I. Šunkov, 93–101. Moscow: Izdatel´stvo vostočnoj literatury, 1963.

Korpela, Jukka. *Beiträge zur Bevölkerungsgeschichte und Prosopographie der Kiever Rus´ bis zum Tode von Vladimir Monomakh.* Jyväskylä: University of Jyväskylä, 1995.

Kosztolynik, Z. J. *Hungary under the Early Árpáds, 890s to 1063.* Boulder, Colo.: East European Monographs, 2002.

Kotljar, M. [N.] F. *Diplomatija južnoj Rusi.* St. Petersburg: Aleteija, 2003.

Labuda, Gerard, and Zdzisław Stieber. *Słownik starożytności słowiańskich: encyklopedyczny zarys kultury słowian od czasów najdawniejszych.* Vol. 4. Wrocław: Zakład Narodowy imienia Ossolińskich, 1970.

Lagerqvist, Lars O. *Sverige och dess regenter under 1000 år.* Stockholm: Alb. Bonniers boktryckeri, 1976.

Leib, Bernard. *Rome, Kiev et Byzance à la fin du XIe siècle.* Paris: Auguste Picard, 1924.

Levin, Eve. *Sex and Society in the World of the Orthodox Slavs, 900–1700.* Ithaca, N.Y.: Cornell University Press, 1989.

Lewis, Andrew W. *Royal Succession in Capetian France: Studies on Familial Order and the State.* Cambridge, Mass.: Harvard University Press, 1981.

Litvina, A. F., and F. B. Uspenskij. "Var´irovanie rodovogo imeni na russkoj počve: Ob odnom iz sposobov imjanarečenija v dinastij Rjurikovičej." *Imenoslov* (2003): 136–83.

———. *Vybor imeni u russkix knjazej v X–XVI vv.* Moscow: Indrik, 2006.

Loparev, X. "Vizantijskaija pečat´ s imenem russkoj knjagini." *Vizantijskij vremennik* 1, no. 1 (1894): 159–66.

Martin, Russell E. *A Bride for the Tsar: Bride-Shows and Marriage Politics in Early Modern Russia.* DeKalb, Ill.: Northern Illinois University Press, 2012.

Meyendorff, John. "From Byzantium to Russia: Religious and Cultural Legacy." In *Studies on the Slavo-Byzantine and West European Middle Ages: In Memoriam Ivan Dujčev*, ed. Petăr Dinekov, Aksinija Džurova, et al., 1:105–14. Sofia: Centr dlja slavjano-vizantijskix issledovanij imeni Ivana Dujčeva, 1988.

Mošin, V. V. "Russkie na Afone i russko-vizantijskie otnošenija v XI–XII vv." *Byzantinoslavica* 9 (1947–48): 55–85.

Nazarenko, A. V. *Drevnjaja Rus´ i slavjane: istoriko-filologičeskie issledovanija.* Moscow: Russkij fond sodejstvija obrazovaniju i nauke, 2009.

———. *Drevnjaja Rus´ na meždunarodnyx putjax: Meždisciplinarnye očerki kul´turnyx, torgovyx, politčeskix svjazej IX–XII vekov*. Moscow: Jazyki russkoj kul´tury, 2001.

———. "Kievskaja knjagina — vnuka papy Lv´a IX (1049–1054): Imperatora Genrixa III (1039–1056): Novye dannye o vnešnej politike Rusi v 70-kh gg. XI v." In *Vostočnaja Evropa v drevnosti i srednevekov´e: Drevnjaja Rus´ v sisteme ètnopolitičeskix i kul´turnyx svjazej: čtenija pamjati člena-korrespondenta AN SSSR Vladimira Terent´eviča Pašuto, Moskva, 18-20 aprelja 1994 g.: tezisy dokladov*, ed. V. T. Pašuto, A. P. Novosel´cev, et al., 26–29. Moscow: RAN, 1994.

———. "Rus´ i germanija v IX–X vv." *Materialy i issledovanija 1991 god*, issue of *Drevnejšie gosudarstva Vostočnoj Evropy*, 1994, 5–138.

Obolensky, Dimitri. *The Byzantine Commonwealth: Eastern Europe 500–1453*. London: Weidenfeld and Nicolson, 1971.

Ostrowski, Donald. *Muscovy and the Mongols: Cross-cultural Influences on the Steppe Frontier, 1304–1589*. Cambridge: Cambridge University Press, 1998.

———. "Pagan Past and Christian Identity in the *Primary Chronicle*." In *Historical Narratives and Christian Identity on a European Periphery: Early History Writing in Northern, East-Central, and Eastern Europe (c. 1070–1200)*, ed. Ildar H. Garipzanov, 229–53. Turnhout: Brepols, 2011.

———. "Systems of Succession in Rus´ and Steppe Societies," *Ruthenica* 11 (2012): 29–58.

Pašuto, V. T. *Vnešnjaja politika Drevnej Rusi*. Moscow: Nauka, 1968.

Pčelov, E. V. *Genealogija drevnerusskix knjazej*. Moscow: Rossijskij gosudarstvennyj gumanitarnyj universitet, 2001.

———. "Pol´skaja knjagina — Marija Dobronega Vladimirovna." In *Vostočnaja Evropa v drevnosti i srednevekov´e: Drevnjaja Rus´ v sisteme ètnopolitičeskix i kul´turnyx svjazej: čtenija pamjati člena-korrespondenta AN SSSR Vladimira Terent´eviča Pašuto, Moskva, 18-20 aprelja 1994 g.: tezisy dokladov*, ed. V. T. Pašuto, A. P. Novosel´cev, et al., 31–33. Moscow: RAN, 1994.

Poppe, Andrzej. "Feofano Novgorodskaja." *Novgorodskij istoričeskij sbornik* 6, no. 16 (1997): 102–20.

———. "The Political Background to the Baptism of Rus´: Byzantine-Russian Relations between 986–989." *Dumbarton Oaks Papers* 30 (1976): 195–244.

———. "Words that Serve the Authority: On the Title of 'Grand Prince' in Kievan Rus´." In *Christian Russia in the Making*, 159–91. Aldershot: Ashgate, 2007.

Poulet, André. "Capetian Women and the Regency: The Genesis of a Vocation." In *Medieval Queenship*, ed. John Carmi Parsons, 93–116. Gloucestershire: Sutton, 1994.

Puškareva, N. L. [Pushkareva]. *Women in Russian History: From the Tenth to the Twentieth Century*. Translated by Eve Levin. Armonk, N.Y.: M. E. Sharpe, 1997.

Raffensperger, Christian. "Dynastic Marriage in Action: How Two Rusian

Princesses Changed Scandinavia." In *Imenoslov: Istorija jazyka, istorija kul′tury*, ed. F. B. Uspenskij, 193–205. Moscow: Aleteja, 2010.

Raffensperger, Christian."Evpraksia Vsevolodovna between East and West." *Russian History/Histoire Russe* 30, no. 1–2 (2003): 23–34.

———. *The Kingdom of Rus′*. Forthcoming.

———. "Identity in Flux: Finding Boris Kolomanovich in the Interstices of Medieval Europe." *Medieval Globe* 2, no. 2 (2015): forthcoming.

———. "Iziaslav Iaroslavich's Excellent Adventure: Constructing Kinship to Gain and Regain Power in Eleventh-Century Europe." *Medieval Prosopography* 30 (2015; forthcoming).

———. "The Missing Rusian Women: The Case of Evpraksia Vsevolodovna." In *Putting Together the Fragments: Writing Medieval Women's Lives*, ed. Amy Livingstone and Charlotte Newman Goldy, 69–84. New York: Palgrave, 2012.

———. *Reimagining Europe: Kievan Rus′ in the Medieval World, 988–1146*. Cambridge, Mass.: Harvard University Press, 2012.

———. "Rusian Influence on European Onomastic Traditions." In *Imenoslov: Istoričeskaja semantika imeni*, ed. F. B. Uspenskij, 116–24. Moscow: Indrik, 2007.

Rapov, O. M. "Vnešnjaja politika Vladimira Velikogo posle oficial′nogo prinjatija Rus′ju xristianstva." In *Vostočnaja Evropa v drevnosti i srednevekov′e: Drevnjaja Rus′ v sisteme ètnopolitičeskix i kul′turnyx svjazej: čtenija pamjati člena-korrespondenta AN SSSR Vladimira Terent′eviča Pašuto, Moskva, 18–20 aprelja 1994 g.: tezisy dokladov*, ed. V. T. Pašuto, A. P. Novosel′cev, et al., 33–36. Moscow: RAN, 1994.

Robinson, I. S. *Henry IV of Germany, 1056–1106*. Cambridge: Cambridge University Press, 1999.

Rozanov, S. P. "Evfimija Vladimirovna i Boris Kolomanovič: iz evropejskoj politiki XII v." *Izvestija Akademii nauk SSSR VII Serija: Otdelenie gumanitarnyx nauk* 8 (1930): 585–99.

———."Evpraksija-Adel′geida Vsevolodovna (1071–1109)." *Izvestija Akademii nauk SSSR VII Serija: Otdelenie gumanitarnyx nauk* 8 (1929): 617–46.

Runciman, Steven. *A History of the Crusades*. Vol. 1. New York: Penguin, 1951.

Rydzevskaja, E. A. "Drevnjaja Rus′ i Skandinavija v IX–XIV vv.: Materialy i issledovanija." *Drevnejšie gosudarstva na territorii SSSR 1978* (1978): 8–236.

Sawyer, Peter. *Kings and Vikings: Scandinavia and Europe, AD 700–1100*. London and New York: Methuen, 1982.

Ščapov, Ja. N. *Gosudarstvo i cerkov′: Drevnej Rusi X–XIII vv*. Moscow: Nauka, 1989.

Ščaveleva, N. I. *Drevnjaja Rus′ v "Pol′skoj istorii" Jana Dlugoša, knigi I–VI: Tekst, perevod, kommentarij*. Edited by A. V. Nazarenko. Moscow: Pamjatniki istoričeskoj mysli, 2004.

———. "Knjaz′ Jaropolk Izjaslavič i xristianskaja cerkov′ XI v." In *Vostočnaja Evropa v drevnosti i srednevekov′e: X čtenija k 80-letiju člena-korrespondenta*

AN SSSR Vladimira Terent´eviča Pašuto, ed. V. T. Pašuto, E. A. Mel´nikova, 132–36. Moscow: RAN, 1994.

———. "Pol´ki—ženy russkix knjazej (XI–seredina XIII v.)." *Drevnejšie gosudarstva na territorii SSSR 1987* (1989): 50–58.

Sheehan, Michael M. "Choice of Marriage Partner in the Middle Ages: Development and Mode of Application of a Theory of Marriage." In *Marriage, Family, and Law in Medieval Europe: Collected Studies*, ed. James K. Farge, 87–117. Toronto: University of Toronto Press, 1997.

Shepard, Jonathan. "Byzantium and Russia in the Eleventh Century: A Study in Political and Ecclesiastical Relations." PhD dissertation, Oxford, 1973.

———. "Why Did the Russians Attack Byzantium in 1043?" *Byzantinisch-neugriechische Jahrbücher* 22 (1985): 147–212.

Smolka, Stanisław. *Mieszko Stary i jego wiek*. Warsaw: Geberthner i Wolff, 1881.

Stafford, Pauline. "The Portrayal of Royal Women in England, Mid-Tenth to Mid-Twelfth Centuries." In *Medieval Queenship*, ed. John Carmi Parsons, 143–68. Gloucestershire: Sutton, 1994.

Toločko, A. P. *Knjaz´ v Drevnej Rusi: Vlast´, sobstvennost´, ideologija*. Kyiv: Naukova dumka, 1992.

Toločko, Oleksij [Aleksej]. *"Istorija Rossijskaja" Vasilija Tatiščeva: istočniki i izvestija*. Kyiv: Kritika, 2005.

Vernadsky, George. *Kievan Russia*. Vol. 2 of *A History of Russia*. New Haven, Conn: Yale University Press, 1948.

Wertner, Mór. *Az Árpádok családi története*. Zrenjanin [Nagybecskerek]: Pleitz Fer. Pál könyvnyomdája, 1892.

Wiszewski, Przemysław. *Domus Bolezlai: Values and Social Identity in Dynastic Traditions of Medieval Poland (c. 966–1138)*. Leiden and Boston: Brill, 2010.

Wolverton, Lisa. *Hastening toward Prague: Power and Society in the Medieval Czech Lands*. Philadelphia: University of Pennsylvania Press, 2001.

Xolodilin, A. N. "Avtografy Anny Jaroslavny – koroleva Francii." *Russkaja reč´*, no. 2 (1985): 109–13.

Zotov, R. V. *O černigovskix knjazjax po Ljubeckomu sinodiku i o Černigovskom knjažestve v tatarskoe vremja*. St. Petersburg: Tipografija brat´ev Panteleevyx, 1892.

Index

The letter *t* following a page number denotes a table.